Children, their World, their Education

- How do children live, think and learn during their early and primary years?
- How well are our primary schools doing?
- What has been the impact of government efforts to raise standards?
- By what values should schools be guided and what curriculum and learning environments should they provide?
- How can primary education best meet the needs of today's children and tomorrow's world?

These were among the many questions that the Cambridge Primary Review set out to answer when it was launched in 2006. Politically independent and grounded in an exhaustive array of national and international evidence, it was the most comprehensive enquiry into English primary education for 40 years. Its 31 interim reports provoked lively headlines and debate.

In this book, the Review presents its findings and recommendations. Compellingly and accessibly written, the book is divided into five parts:

- Part 1 sets the scene and tracks primary education policy since the 1960s
- Part 2 examines children's development and learning; their upbringing and lives in an increasingly diverse society; their needs and aspirations
- Part 3 explores what goes on in schools, from the vital early years to aims, curriculum, pedagogy, assessment, standards and school organisation
- Part 4 deals with the system: ages and stages; teachers, training, leadership and workforce reform; funding, governance and policy
- Part 5 pulls everything together with 78 formal conclusions and 75 recommendations for policy and practice.

Children, their World, their Education is more than a ground-breaking report. It is an unrivalled educational compendium. It assesses two decades of government-led reform. It offers a vision for the future. It goes to the heart of what education in a democracy is about. It deserves to be read by all who care about children, their primary education and the world that they will inherit.

The Cambridge Primary Review is supported by Esmée Fairbairn Foundation: www.primaryreview.org.uk

Children, their World, their Education has a companion volume: *The Cambridge Primary Review Research Surveys*, edited by Robin Alexander with Christine Doddington, John Gray, Linda Hargreaves and Ruth Kershner.

Robin Alexander is Director of the Cambridge Primary Review, Fellow of Wolfson College, University of Cambridge, and Professor of Education Emeritus at the University of Warwick, UK. **Michael Armstrong** is a writer and former head teacher of Harwell Primary School, Oxfordshire, UK. **Julia Flutter** is Research Associate at the Faculty of Education, University of Cambridge, UK. **Linda Hargreaves** is Reader in Education, University of Cambridge, UK. **Wynne Harlen** is Visiting Professor at the Graduate School of Education, University of Bristol, UK. **David Harrison** is a former Research Associate at the Faculty of Education, University of Cambridge, UK. **Elizabeth Hartley-Brewer** is a social policy consultant, parenting adviser, journalist and author. **Ruth Kershner** is Lecturer in Education, University of Cambridge, UK. **John MacBeath** is Professor of Education, University of Cambridge, UK. **Berry Mayall** is Professor of Childhood Studies, Institute of Education, University of London, UK. **Stephanie Northen** is an education journalist and editor. **Gillian Pugh** is Chair of the National Children's Bureau and Visiting Professor, Institute of Education, University of London, UK. **Colin Richards** is Emeritus Professor, University of Cumbria, UK, and a former primary HMI. **David Utting** is a writer, researcher, policy analyst and former Associate Director at the Joseph Rowntree Foundation, UK.

Children, their World, their Education

Final Report and Recommendations of the Cambridge Primary Review

Edited by
Robin Alexander

Contributing authors
Robin Alexander, Michael Armstrong, Julia Flutter,
Linda Hargreaves, David Harrison, Wynne Harlen,
Elizabeth Hartley-Brewer, Ruth Kershner,
John MacBeath, Berry Mayall, Stephanie Northen,
Gillian Pugh, Colin Richards and David Utting

Routledge
Taylor & Francis Group

LONDON AND NEW YORK

Esmée
Fairbairn
FOUNDATION

First published 2010
by Routledge
2 Park Square, Milton Park, Abingdon, Oxon OX14 4RN

Simultaneously published in the USA and Canada
by Routledge
270 Madison Avenue, New York, NY 10016

Reprinted 2010

Routledge is an imprint of the Taylor & Francis Group, an Informa business

Typeset in Times New Roman
by Taylor & Francis Books
Printed and bound in Great Britain
by TJ International, Padstow, Cornwall

British Library Cataloguing in Publication Data
A catalogue record for this book is available from the British Library

Library of Congress Cataloging in Publication Data
Cambridge Primary Review (Organization)
   Children, their world, their education : the final report and recommendations of the
Cambridge Primary Review / edited by Robin Alexander, with contributing authors, Robin
Alexander ... [et al.].
      p. cm.
   Includes bibliographical references and index.
   1. Education, Elementary–Great Britain–Evaluation. 2. Children–Great Britain–Social
conditions. I. Alexander, Robin J. II. Title.
   LA633.C36 2010b
   372'.941–dc22
                                    2009023083

ISBN13: 978-0-415-54870-0 (hbk)
ISBN13: 978-0-415-54871-7 (pbk)

Contents

vi *Contents*

Figures and tables

FIGURES

TABLES

Contributors

EDITOR

Robin Alexander

SUB-EDITORS

Julia Flutter, Stephanie Northen, Colin Richards

AUTHORS

Robin Alexander, Director of the Cambridge Primary Review, Fellow of Wolfson College, University of Cambridge, and Professor of Education Emeritus, University of Warwick, UK.

Michael Armstrong, writer and former head teacher, Harwell Primary School, Oxfordshire, UK.

Julia Flutter, Research Associate, Cambridge Primary Review, Faculty of Education, University of Cambridge, UK.

Linda Hargreaves, Reader in Education, University of Cambridge, UK.

Wynne Harlen, Visiting Professor, Graduate School of Education, University of Bristol, UK.

David Harrison, Research Associate, Cambridge Primary Review, Faculty of Education, University of Cambridge, UK.

Elizabeth Hartley-Brewer, social policy consultant, parenting adviser, journalist and author.

Ruth Kershner, Lecturer in Education, University of Cambridge, UK.

John MacBeath, Professor of Education, University of Cambridge, UK.

Berry Mayall, Professor of Childhood Studies, Institute of Education, University of London, UK.

Stephanie Northen, education journalist and editor.

Gillian Pugh, Chair of the National Children's Bureau and Visiting Professor, Institute of Education, University of London, UK.

Colin Richards, Emeritus Professor, University of Cumbria, UK, and former primary HMI.

David Utting, writer, researcher, policy analyst and former Associate Director at the Joseph Rowntree Foundation, UK.

EDITORIAL ASSISTANT

Catrin Darsley, Administrator, Cambridge Primary Review, Faculty of Education, University of Cambridge, UK.

Abbreviations

AAIA	Association for Achievement and Improvement through Assessment
ADHD	Attention Deficit Hyperactivity Disorder
AERA	American Educational Research Association
AfL	Assessment for Learning
ALI	Adult Learning Inspectorate
ALL	Association for Language Learning
APG	Action Plan for Geography
APU	Assessment of Performance Unit
AREIAC	Association of RE Inspectors, Advisers and Consultants
ASCL	Association of School and College Leaders
ASE	Association for Science Education
ASPE	Association for the Study of Primary Education
AST	Advanced Skills Teacher
ATL	Association of Teachers and Lecturers
ATM	Association of Teachers of Mathematics
ATSE	Association of Tutors in Science Education
BATOD	British Association of Teachers of the Deaf
Becta	British Educational Communications and Technology Agency
BCSE	British Council for School Environments
BESA	British Educational Suppliers Association
BEST	Behaviour and Education Support Team
BHA	British Humanist Association
BSF	Building Schools for the Future
CACE	Central Advisory Council for Education (England)
CAFCASS	Children and Family Court Advisory and Support Service
CATE	Council for the Accreditation of Teacher Education
CATS	Cognitive Abilities Tests
CCP	Community Curriculum Partnership
CILT	Centre for Language Teaching, now National Centre for Languages
CNAA	Council for National Academic Awards
CoE / C of E	Church of England
CPD	Continuing Professional Development
CRE	Commission for Racial Equality
CSCI	Commission for Social Care Inspection
CSPAR	Class Size and Pupil Adult Ratios project
CVA	Contextual Value Added
DCMS	Department for Culture, Media and Sport
DCSF	Department for Children, Schools and Families
DENI	Department of Education, Northern Ireland
DES	Department of Education and Science
DfE	Department for Education

DfEE	Department for Education and Employment
DfES	Department for Education and Skills
DH	Department of Health
DISS	Deployment and Impact of Support Staff in School project
DIUS	Department for Innovation, Universities and Skills
DRC	Disability Rights Commission
DWP	Department for Work and Pensions
EAL	English as an Additional Language
EAZ	Education Action Zone
EBITT	Employment-Based Initial Teacher Training
ECM	Every Child Matters
EEAG	Early Education Advisory Group
EHRC	Equality and Human Rights Commission
EI	Emotional Intelligence
EMAG	Ethnic Minority Achievement Grant
EOC	Equal Opportunities Commission
EPA	Educational Priority Area
EPM	Every Parent Matters
EPPE	Effective Provision of Pre-School Education project
EPPI	Evidence for Policy and Practice Information
ERA	Education Reform Act, 1988
Estyn	Her Majesty's Inspectorate for Education and Training in Wales
EYFS	Early Years Foundation Stage
EYPS	Early Years Professional Status
FSES	Full Service Extended School
FSM	Free School Meals
FSS	Formula Spending Share system
GA	Geographical Association
G&T	Gifted and Talented
GCSE	General Certificate of Secondary Education
GCI	Good Childhood Inquiry
GDP	Gross Domestic Product
GM	Grant Maintained
GEST	Grants for Educational Support and Training
GRIST	Grant Related In-Service Training
GTC(E)	General Teaching Council for England
HBSC	Health Behaviour of School-Aged Children
HEI	Higher Education Institution
HLTA	Higher Level Teaching Assistants
HMCI	Her Majesty's Chief Inspector
HMICA	Her Majesty's Inspectorate of Court Administration
HMI	Her Majesty's Inspector(ate)
HMSCI	Her Majesty's Senior Chief Inspector
HMT	Her Majesty's Treasury
HPA	Health Protection Agency
HSKE	Home–School Knowledge Exchange project
IBG	Institute of British Geographers
ICT	Information and Communication Technology
IDACI	Income Deprivation Affecting Children Index
IDeA	Improvement and Development Agency
IDP	Inclusion Development Programme
IEP	Individual Education Plan
IDZ	Industrial Development Zone

IEA	Institute of Economic Affairs
IEP	Individual Education Plan
INCA	International Review of Curriculum and Assessment
IPPR	Institute for Public Policy Research
ISB	Individual Schools Budget
ITE	Initial Teacher Education
ITT	Initial Teacher Training
KS1 / KS2	Key Stage 1/2
LA	Local Authority
LDD	Learning Difficulties and Disabilities
LEA	Local Education Authority
LGA	Local Government Association
LHTL	Learning How to Learn project
LMS	Local Management of Schools
LSB	Local Schools Budget
MACOS	*Man: A Course of Study*
MEC	Music Education Council
MFL	Modern Foreign Language(s)
MI	Multiple Intelligence(s)
MIT	Monitoring and Intervention Team
MTL	Masters in Teaching and Learning
NAACE	National Association of Advisers for Computers in Education
NACCCE	National Advisory Committee on Creative and Cultural Education
NAHT	National Association of Head Teachers
NAIGS	National Advisers and Inspectors Group for Science
NALDIC	National Association for Language Development in the Curriculum
NAPE	National Association for Primary Education
NASACRE	National Association of Standing Advisory Councils on Religious Education
NASS	National Association for Small Schools
NASUWT	National Association of Schoolmasters Union of Women Teachers
NATE	National Association for the Teaching of English
NATRE	National Association of Teachers of Religious Education
NBPTS	National Board for Professional Teaching Standards
NATT	National Association of Teachers of Travellers
NC	National Curriculum
NCC	National Curriculum Council
NCSL	National College for School Leadership
NDPB	Non-departmental Public Body
NELIG	National Emotional Literacy Interest Group
NERP	National Education Research Panel
NFER	National Foundation for Educational Research
NGA	National Governors' Association
NIESR	National Institute of Economic and Social Research
NLS	National Literacy Strategy
NNS	National Numeracy Strategy
NPH	National Primary Headteachers
NPhA	National Primary Headteachers' Association
NPQH	National Professional Qualification for Headship
NPSA	National Primary Schools' Association
NRwS	New Relationship with Schools
NSPCC	National Society for the Prevention of Cruelty to Children
NQT	Newly Qualified Teacher
NRC	National Resource Centre for Supplementary Education

NUT	National Union of Teachers
OCC	Office of the Children's Commissioner
OECD	Organisation for Economic Co-operation and Development
Ofqual	Office of the Qualifications and Examinations Regulator
Ofsted	Office for Standards in Education, Children's Services and Skills
ONS	Office for National Statistics
P4C	Philosophy for Children
PACE	Parliamentary Assembly of the Council of Europe
PANDA	Performance and Assessment Data
PAT	Pupil Achievement Tracker
PCK	Pedagogical Content Knowledge
PCT	Primary Care Trust
PE	Physical Education
PEAL	Parents, Early Years and Learning
PFI	Private Finance Initiative
PGCE	Post-Graduate Certificate in Education
PIPS	Performance Indicators in Primary Schools
PIRLS	Progress in International Reading and Literacy Study
PISA	Programme for International Student Assessment
PNS	Primary National Strategy
PPA	Planning, Preparation and Assessment time
PSE	Personal and Social Education
PSHE	Personal, Social and Health Education
PSR	Public Service Reform
PTA	Parent-Teacher Association
PTR	Pupil-teacher ratio
PwC	PricewaterhouseCoopers
QCA	Qualifications and Curriculum Authority
QCDA	Qualifications and Curriculum Development Agency
QTS	Qualified Teacher Status
RE	Religious Education
RGS	Royal Geographical Society
ROSLA	Raising of school leaving age
RSA	Royal Society for Arts, Manufacturers and Commerce
RSPCA	Royal Society for the Prevention of Cruelty to Animals
SACRE	Standing Advisory Council on Religious Education
SAPERE	Society for Advancing Philosophical Enquiry and Reflection in Education
SAT(s)	Standard Assessment Task(s) (original definition in the 1988 Education Reform Act)
SAT(s)	Standard Attainment Test(s) (2009 definition on the DCSF Standards Website)
SCAA	School Curriculum and Assessment Authority
SCDC	School Curriculum Development Committee
SCITT	School-Centred Initial Teacher Training
SEAC	School Examinations and Assessment Council
SEBD	Social, Emotional and Behavioural Disorders
SEAL	Social and Emotional Aspects of Learning
SEF	Self Evaluation Form
SEN	Special Educational Needs
SENCO	Special Educational Needs Co-ordinator
SENDA	Special Educational Needs and Disability Act
SES	Socio-Economic Status
SEU	Social Exclusion Unit
SEU	Standards and Effectiveness Unit

SIP	School Improvement Partner
SLC	Science Learning Centre
SLCN	Speech, Language and Communication Needs
SSLP	Sure Start Local Programmes
Project STAR	Steps to Achieving Resilience
STRB	School Teachers' Review Body
TA	Teaching assistant
TCRU	Thomas Coram Research Unit
TDA	Training and Development Agency for Schools
TGAT	Task Group on Assessment and Testing
TIMSS	Trends in International Mathematics and Science Study
TLRP	Teaching and Learning Research Programme
TTA	Teacher Training Agency
TUC	Trades Union Congress
UCET	Universities' Council for the Education of Teachers
UKLA	United Kingdom Literacy Association
UKOWLA	UK One World Linking Organisation
UN	United Nations
UNCRC	United Nations Convention on the Rights of the Child
UNESCO	United Nations Educational, Scientific and Cultural Organization
UNICEF	United Nations Children's Fund (shortened from the original 'United Nations International Children's Emergency Fund)
UNIPCC	United Nations Intergovernmental Panel on Climate Change
VAK	Visual, auditory or kinaesthetic 'learning styles'
WAMG	Workforce Agreement Monitoring Group
WHO	World Health Organisation
WO	Welsh Office
ZPD	Zone of Proximal Development

Preface

ACKNOWLEDGEMENTS

Thanks are due, first and foremost, to the Trustees of Esmée Fairbairn Foundation for their generous support for the Cambridge Primary Review over the four years from October 2006 to September 2010. The Foundation awarded the University of Cambridge three successive grants for the Review. They gave us regular use of their premises for our London meetings. They set up a Review advisory committee, policy group and management group which, in the breadth of their members' experience and the quality of their insight, have been as refreshingly different from the usual project steering group as it is possible to imagine.

In the matter of support, guidance and wisdom sustained through both good times and bad, we owe a particular and incalculable debt to Gillian Pugh, chair of the advisory committee and policy group, and to Hilary Hodgson, chair of the management group. They and their colleagues really have been the best of critical friends.

I would also like to thank those who have shared the day-to-day work of the Review: fellow members of the Cambridge team Catrin Darsley, Christine Doddington, Julia Flutter, Linda Hargreaves, David Harrison and Ruth Kershner; those who gave the team occasional but crucial support – pre-eminently John Gray, Alex James, Catherine Kitsis and Katherine Shaw, but also Qais Almeqdad, Chang Yan-Shing, Calvin Dorion, Boris Jokić, Lin Hsing-Chiung, Sharlene Swartz and Clare Yerbury; and, in a project where the media really mattered, our director of communications Richard Margrave. Thanks are also due to the 70 research consultants whose surveys of published research critically inform this report and appear in full in the companion volume; and to those who provided material which in other ways has been drawn on here, notably Maurice Galton, Karen Gold, Diane Hofkins and Victoria Neumark.

The 'Cambridge Primary Review 100' – those in the interlocking groups of central team, authors, consultants and advisory committee – are listed in Appendix 1. Beyond them are many more who helped shape the Review, provided it with evidence, or reflected on what that evidence might mean. Without them the Review would have had no legitimacy, data or meaning. In June 2004, 40 organisational representatives participated in the initial consultation seminars which led to the decision to press ahead with the detailed planning. Two years later we signed up our 66 consultants and commissioned the research surveys. Between the Review's launch in October 2006 and the completion of this report in April 2009, 1,052 organisations and individuals submitted written evidence to the Review in response to our open invitation, often at considerable length. Meanwhile, 750 parents, teachers, children and local representatives participated in the witness sessions which made up the regional community soundings which we organised between January and March 2007. Willing and enthusiastic primary heads and local authority officers timetabled the 87 sessions, engaged the participants and provided hospitality. The children at the host schools were not only prominent and thoughtful witnesses but in many cases took us on site tours and laid on special assemblies. Later, 70 professional and organisational representatives attended the 2008 national soundings in London and Cambridge at which the emerging evidence was discussed, and helped to refine propositions and proposals from that evidence which eventually led to this report's conclusions and recommendations. On 146 other occasions, organisations sent their representatives to exchange ideas on the Review's remit or provided conference platforms from which I or other team members reported on its progress. Government officials and members of the public bodies concerned with inspection (Ofsted), curriculum and assessment (QCA) and teacher training and development (TDA) gave the Review access to official data and advised on its interpretation. The teaching unions, especially the ATL, NAHT and NUT, were generous in their support for the Review while of course reserving their right to disagree with it when necessary, and they helped to publicise its work. MPs from the three main parties met us from time to time to explore the policy dimensions of our work. The Worshipful Company of Weavers organised a major event at Church House, Westminster, in November 2007 at which, introduced by former Secretary of State Estelle Morris, I was able to present emerging findings from the Review to representatives of national organisations and officials and teachers from across London. Later in the process, in March 2008, the General Teaching Council for England hosted a one-day conference at Central Hall, Westminster, at which the Cambridge Primary Review joined the Children's Society's Good Childhood Inquiry to explore shared findings and insights on children and childhood today with a diverse professional audience. Finally, a vast number of researchers – approaching 3,000 – contributed indirectly to the Review through the 28 studies which fed the research survey strand and hence this report. Together with the additional material cited here, we have drawn on well over 4,000 published sources.

The logistics of multiple authorship of a report which combines evidence from so many sources are far from straightforward. I thank my fellow authors collectively for their collaboration and individually for their contributions. Outside the editorial and authorial group, the following kindly commented on chapter drafts: Patricia Clark, Frank Coffield, Christina Coker, Sheila Dainton, Bernadette Duffy, Kate Frood, John Gray, David Hargreaves, Diane Hofkins, Anna House, Mary James, Fred Jarvis, Pat Jefferson, Gordon Kirk, Hugh Lauder, Roger Luxton, Melody Moran, Tim Oates, Steve Pisano, Andrew Pollard, David Reedy, David Rosenthal, Usha Sahni, Norman Thomas, Sue Tite, Peter Tymms, Isobel Urquhart and John White. David Harrison checked official statistics. Stephanie Northen, Colin Richards and Julia Flutter worked intensively on the chapter drafts checking for accuracy, appropriate use of evidence, continuity and coherence: their editorial support has been truly invaluable. Catrin Darsley sorted out the footnotes and references and hammered the entire text into the typographical shape required by the publisher. Finally, Anna Clarkson and her colleagues at Routledge took on this daunting publishing project and kept faith with it.

THE TEXT: AUTHORSHIP AND ATTRIBUTION

Fourteen writers contributed to this report's 24 chapters. Whereas the companion volume follows the conventional editorial path of attributing authorship chapter by chapter, here this is neither possible nor appropriate. Some chapters had a sole or main author while others were jointly written and most included substantial sections dealing with the Review's evidence which the Cambridge team provided. All chapter drafts were read and commented upon by others than their authors. Chapters were then re-edited, often radically. Versions of the chapters on curriculum (13 and 14) were published as special reports of the Review in February 2009 and before publication were subject to extensive consultation outside the writing team. Chapter 24 was re-drafted several times in light of comments from the authors and members of the Advisory Committee.

So the report, like the Review as a whole, has been a collaborative enterprise. Together we have done our utmost to do justice to the Review's remit and witnesses, to shun the grinding of personal axes, and to balance evidence about what is with a vision of what could be.

However, because we wish to balance the fact of collaboration with the rights of individual contributors, we list here those who led the writing of each chapter on behalf of the team, together with those who provided substantial or significant copy which the lead authors used.

The initials refer to authors' names on the book's title page: 1 (RA), 2 (RA), 3 (CR and RA), 4 (DU), 5 (BM), 6 (EHB), 7 (LH), 8 (RK, with SN), 9 (RK), 10 (JF), 11 (GP, with SN), 12 (RA, with MA and JF), 13 (RA, with JF), 14 (RA), 15 (RA, with JF), 16 (WH), 17 (WH and CR), 18 (JF), 19 (SN, with JF), 20 (SN, with JF), 21 (RA, with JF), 22 (LH and JMcB, with JF and SN), 23 (RA, with JF and DH), 24 (All).

THE CONCLUSIONS AND RECOMMENDATIONS: OWNERSHIP AND AUTHORITY

'What', some may ask, 'is the authority for the conclusions and recommendations with which this report ends? Whose conclusions and recommendations are they?'

These necessary questions should be de-personalised. The conclusions and recommendations, like the Review as a whole, are warranted not by a named individual or group but by a process. We should ask not 'Whose recommendations are they?' but 'Where do they come from?' In the first instance the recommendations come from the evidence: the submissions, research surveys, official documents, other published sources, soundings and other meetings listed above; and the calibre of many of these sources – major national organisations, public bodies, leading professionals, distinguished researchers – should in any event command serious attention. They come next from a collective sifting and sorting of all this evidence by the seven core members and nine temporary members of the Cambridge team. They come then from a translation of these siftings and sortings into the report's central chapters (Parts 2, 3 and 4) by the authorial team, guided by external assessors. They come finally from a distilling of key points from this material into conclusions and recommendations, which in draft form were then worked on intensively by the authors and our advisory committee before being finally confirmed in Chapter 24. Thus:

> The formal conclusions and recommendations of the Cambridge Primary Review have been agreed by the 14 authors of this report. They are fully supported by members of the Review's Advisory Committee other than those whose observer status requires them to remain neutral.

An enquiry commissioned by government carries that government's authority. This does not make its findings and conclusions unimpeachable, nor for that matter does it guarantee a hearing. Readers will recall instances where the conclusions of an official enquiry have seemed to have little to do with the evidence on which they were supposedly based; or where an enquiry's remit was so tightly drawn as to prevent it from investigating what most needed to be investigated; or where an impressive official report sank without trace because it said the right things at the wrong time.

An independent enquiry avoids these problems, in that it can investigate and say what it wishes. But nobody is obliged even to pretend to take notice of it – nobody, that is, who believes that only what government says matters. But we would argue that the Cambridge Primary Review carries a different kind of authority: the authority of financial, political and intellectual independence; of the exhaustive evidential process outlined above; of the thousands of minds and voices, and the wealth of expertise and experience, which that process has brought to bear on the Review's themes and questions; of the high distinction of many of its participants; and of the integrity with which all of them have striven to approach their task. It is on this basis that we commend this report to all who are interested in the education and well-being of the nation's children and the condition of the society and world in which they are growing up.

THE CAMBRIDGE PRIMARY REVIEW TRUST

The Cambridge Primary Review was set up to make a difference, not to make money. Profits from the sale of the final report will be placed in trust to be used to support the education of some of the country's most marginalised and disadvantaged children.

Robin Alexander

1 Introduction

The Cambridge Primary Review is complete. Now is the time to discuss its findings. Whatever readers think about our conclusions and recommendations, we hope that they will treat with due seriousness the matters we explore, the evidence we have assembled, the arguments we present, and the experience and hopes of the thousands who have participated, directly or indirectly, in this enterprise.

When, back in 1998, the idea of an independent enquiry into the condition and future of English primary education was first mooted, New Labour was still basking in the 'new dawn' of its landslide victory in the 1997 general election. Yet the optimism of even that event did not extend to what was going on in primary schools, which since the 1970s had been under intermittent but escalating attack for their supposedly poor standards and suspect ideology.

From the early 1990s, governments announced themselves determined to set matters straight on both counts. Primary education was a problem to be fixed, and the fixers were not to be teachers or local authorities, for they had had their chance and blown it, but central government. 'My belief is a return to basics in education. The progressive theorists have had their say,' proclaimed one prime minister in 1991 (not for the first time, or the last). 'Education, education, education' intoned another in 1997, launching a programme of unprecedented investment and direct government intervention yielding £2 billion initiatives in literacy and numeracy, 35,000 additional teachers, 172,000 teaching assistants, a 27 per cent increase in teachers' pay, a 55 per cent increase in per pupil funding, and a significant transformation of the functions and relationship of local authority services for children. Meanwhile, primary school test results have improved to an extent which has been hotly debated though the trend has been undeniably upwards. Yet in 2009 that sense of malaise still lingers. The difference between then and now is that the government's imposed solution has become, in the eyes of some, the problem[1]; indeed, as we go to press the wider parliamentary process is mired in a scandal about MPs' expenses which is generally viewed as symptomatic of failings in British democracy of a much more fundamental kind.

Putting right what has gone wrong demands not just a viable cure; it also requires an accurate diagnosis. The diagnoses on offer during the late 1990s and early 2000s focused almost exclusively on standards in the so-called 'basics' of literacy and numeracy. Leaving aside until later in this report the question of whether such standards have fallen, risen or stayed the same, there is little doubt that this exclusivity of focus frustrated alternative analyses of what was right in English primary education, what was wrong, and what was needed by way of improvement. We hope that this report will redress the balance.

The standards agenda also left unaddressed some much larger questions about the relationship of education to a wider world about whose condition and prospects many commentators and organisations (and, as we were to discover, ordinary citizens) were deeply worried. Was it education, or education's failure, which had produced a generation of children who, notwithstanding their high material standard of living, were said to be less happy than their peers in other countries?[2] Was it education, or education's failure, which had produced a society described by one leading politician as 'broken'[3] and a world which, in economic, geopolitical and ecological terms, appeared to be spiralling out of control, partly because of the material aspirations of those for whom education supposedly mattered a great deal? What, if anything, could education do to improve children's well-being, repair the social fabric and secure a world which was more just and sustainable? What, since so many were talking about standards in 'the basics', is truly basic to the education of young children growing up in such a world? Are 'standards' as measured by the government's national tests synonymous with educational quality? Have those who repeatedly use such terms ever stopped to think about them? Is it sufficient, as one secretary of state repeatedly told the nation on the BBC's flagship Today programme, for primary schools to teach children 'to read, write and add up' and leave the rest to secondary school, or perhaps merely to chance? Such a diet, after all, is even narrower than that of the Victorian elementary schools whose practices most people claimed the country had outgrown.

If such questions were not going to be asked by government, then conscience and civic duty demanded that they be tackled by others willing and able to do so, for ours is a public system of education which belongs to the people and is not the personal fiefdom of ministers and their unelected advisers. Hence, in part, the Cambridge Primary Review. However, the Review was prompted not just by this sense of inadequate political perspective, but also by a perception that the political perspective had come to matter more than it should, that England's state system of primary education, and the surrounding discourse, had become too centralised, too overtly politicised. Alternative ways of thinking and talking about primary education were needed. They would need to be open as to the analysis of problems and solutions, inclusive as to participants, measured in tone, respectful yet properly critical of evidence, and interested both in thinking about the longer-term future and giving unflinching attention to the lessons of the past.

Following nearly three years of consultation and planning, the Cambridge Primary Review – the Review of Primary Education in England, to give it its full title – was launched in October 2006. It makes fair claim to being the most comprehensive review of primary education for 40 years, that is, since the Plowden Committee published their initially celebrated and later much-criticised report in 1967. Like Plowden, the Cambridge Primary Review seeks to combine retrospective evidence with prospective vision. Like Plowden, it seeks to be wide-ranging. Like Plowden, it hopes to make a difference.

There the similarities cease. Plowden was a publicly funded official commission of the great and good; ours is an independent review funded by a charity and undertaken by academics and professionals. Plowden spoke to an optimistic consensus: a Conservative government commissioned it; a Labour government received its report; and all parties welcomed it before first one and then another turned it into a scapegoat for the country's educational and social ills. The Cambridge Primary Review has been undertaken against a backdrop of political bitterness, public anxiety and – from late 2008 – national recession and global economic chaos, and has itself attracted its fair share of controversy. As to the conduct, methodology and outcomes of the two enquiries, they are vastly different, as we shall see. So though comparisons have been made, we resist any suggestion that the Cambridge Primary Review is a 'new Plowden'.

The October 2006 launch was followed by a period of public reticence while the Review collected evidence. Then, exactly a year later, the Review published the first of its interim reports. This was an account of the 87 regional community soundings which took the public temperature on the Review's 10 themes in locations as far apart as Cornwall and Northumberland, Kent and Lancashire. With the community soundings report[4] the silence surrounding the Review was shattered, for it was the main UK news story of 12 October 2007. 'Children reeling under the pressure of modern life,' shouted the headlines, 'Primary children suffer from stress and anxiety … Study reveals stressed-out 7–11 year olds … Kids face "excessive pressure" … Backlash against testing regime … Primary Review: bleak vision of our world … The pain of a generation forced to grow up before their time … Children robbed of their innocence by guns, gangs and celebrities … Why are our children so unhappy?'

Then on 2 November 2007 the headline writers were at it again, this time in response to our three surveys of published evidence on standards, testing and assessment at the primary stage[5]:

'Primary tests blasted by experts ... Thousands of pupils given wrong grade in 3R tests ... Test regime must change ... Kids lose love of books ... Literacy drive has almost no impact ... £500 million literacy drive is flop, say experts,' and, bizarrely: 'Millions wasted on teaching reading.'

So it continued. Between October 2007 and February 2009, the Cambridge Primary Review published 31 interim reports; 28 of them were the extensively referenced surveys of published research which, in revised form, appear in this report's companion volume. The reports were published in groups on 10 occasions. On six of those occasions they were front-page news and three times they were the top UK news story overall. The media apparently judged that there was something in the national psyche to which such unrelenting accounts of doom, gloom and policy failure would instantly appeal. It goes almost without saying that the inevitably selective coverage was also sometimes inaccurate; that it tended to seek out the negative in the interim reports and ignore the positive, and that it frequently subordinated the educational to the political.

Early on, we learned that although many organisations studied and discussed the interim reports and briefings as we had hoped they would, the media accounts were rather more influential than the reports in precisely those quarters where the true picture particularly needed to be understood, that is to say in Westminster. Consequently, an official view arose of the intentions and stance of the Review which was sharply at odds with its true position, and which progressively frustrated the dialogue to which government and the Review had committed themselves before the 2006 launch. Rattled by what ministers called the 'drip, drip, drip of criticism', the Department for Children, Schools and Families (DCSF) responded in kind. Its counter-measures were, as politicians say, 'robust'. Others described them in less benign terms.

All that, we trust, is behind us. The cycle of interim reports ended in February 2009 and the Cambridge team concentrated on completing the final report. The negative gloss on the Review's interim reports began to be replaced by an awareness of their evidential and political balance, of their richness as a resource for future policy and practice, and their fair assessment of what the government's investment in the improvement of primary education had achieved.

In any event, what happened between October 2006 and February 2009 was no more than the blink of the eye of educational history. Governments and ministers come and go – 'Here today, gone tomorrow' as the late BBC pundit Robin Day taunted one ministerial interviewee, who acted on Day's jibe by leaving the studio immediately and the government shortly afterwards. Initiatives are overtaken by yet more initiatives, often before they have had time to bed down, let alone be properly evaluated. The ever-changing procession of official acronyms on pp ix–xiii bears witness to policy's essential transience.

So we come, after the launch, the collection of evidence and the publication and discussion of the interim reports, to this final report. Whatever our hopes and intentions, we would not be so foolhardy as to predict anything about its impact, for the fate of all such documents seems to depend less on what they say than on the moment and manner of their immediate release and reception. In this matter, not even the most sophisticated communications outfit can do more than hope for the best. Nevertheless, the Cambridge Primary Review is a deeply serious enquiry, and it has assembled evidence and options for the future which we believe repay careful study and to which sensationalising headlines will do nothing like justice. We hope that sufficient numbers of people of goodwill and influence will understand and respect what over the past five years we have tried to accomplish, will acknowledge the breadth, weight and authority of the evidence we have assembled, and will discuss and build on it. We also hope that the report will engage not only politicians and officials, but also parents, teachers, community leaders, teacher trainers, researchers, members of the public and all who have an interest in the needs and capabilities of children and the quality of their education. Primary education belongs to all of them.

For this is our bottom line. The education of young children matters immeasurably – to them both now and in the future, and to our society. It matters to all children, but especially to those who, in our divided society, lack the massively compensating advantages of financial wealth, emotional harmony and a home life which is linguistically, intellectually, culturally and spiritually rich. Such richness is of course not synonymous with financial wealth, and living – as many of our witnesses claimed that we do – in an era obsessed with celebrity and driven by material greed, we know that neither form of wealth guarantees the other.

Yet regardless of the accident of their birth, young children have almost unlimited learning potential: 'learning without limits' was the happy phrase coined by one recent project.[6] Internationally, basic education is defined as a human right and is one of the United Nations Millennium Development Goals, to be achieved in all countries by 2015 (though, tragically, it will probably not be). In Britain, one of the world's richest and politically most stable nations, that right can surely produce primary schooling of a consistently high quality. Provided, that is, we know wherein educational quality resides and understand how it can be assessed and achieved, and that is what we want this report to help people to reconsider and redefine. To couch the debate about quality in terms of test scores alone – though undoubtedly these matter – is to exclude much that education should be about.

We wish, therefore, to stress our common cause with all who share our conviction about the importance of primary education and the rights and potentialities of children: government, opposition, teachers, parents, employers, religious leaders and many others, including children themselves. We can argue about the direction of this or that policy and the efficacy of this or that practice, but let us unite in this belief and in pursuit of fundamental principles such as those which are discussed in this report: equity and empathy, entitlement, engagement and empowerment, expertise and excellence – an alliterative advance, we think, on that tired mantra 'education, education, education'.

STRUCTURE OF THE FINAL REPORT

Structured round the Review's 10 themes, *Children, their World, their Education* discusses the evidence from the various sources described in Chapter 2 and ends with a set of formally framed conclusions and recommendations for future educational policy and practice. The companion volume includes the 28 research surveys which were central to the Review's evidence base, together with editorial commentary. We refer extensively to that research in this report, but because it entailed nearly 3,000 published sources we cannot to do so in detail.

The report has five sections, and to help readers find their way through what has become a weighty publication, we provide some signposts.

Part 1 – Contexts

Part 1 describes the remit, methodology and procedures of the Cambridge Primary Review and the contexts of educational history and policy in which the Review, and English primary education, have been and are situated. These contexts are not mere 'background', for they both shape public education and entail conditions and imperatives which education cannot afford to ignore. Plowden was somewhat parochial in its orientation, concentrating on the child, family, neighbourhood and school and ignoring the wider society (interestingly, though we are sure unconsciously, this is echoed in the renaming of the England's education ministry as the Department of Children, Schools and Families). As a focus for the attention and efforts of those working in schools the Plowden nexus is certainly not to be decried, and in this report, as in recent legislation, the child, the community and relations between parenting, caring and educating loom large. However, as a framework for examining and discussing a national system of public education it is also insufficient. We may need to act locally but we must be prepared to think nationally and indeed globally, especially when there is a diminishing sense of national identity, the interconnectedness of the fates of nations is so dramatically apparent and the sustainability of the world's ecosystem hangs in the balance.

The Review's framework has temporal as well as spatial elements. English primary schools are the direct descendents of Victorian elementary schools, and retain more of the characteristics of those establishments than many people realise or perhaps would care to admit: an unusually early starting age for compulsory schooling; the separation of 'infants' and 'juniors' (now key stages 1 and 2); the generalist class teacher system; a curriculum sharply divided into protected 'basics' and a vulnerable and low-status remainder; and a view of those basics as comprising reading, writing, number and little else. All these are legacies of a wholly different age and as such they cannot be taken as given but must be open to the same degree of questioning as we allow for more recent policies and strategies. Together with the major legislative events and official reports – the 1902 Act, the Hadow Report of 1931, the 1944 Act, the Plowden Report of 1967, the 1988 Education Reform Act, the post-1997 reforms, and other 'policy milestones' shown in Figure 3.3 – all have contributed to that subtle process of sedimentation which creates a culture and an education system. Many are memorials to battles which at the time appeared to have been won, but which turned out to be perennial zones of conflict. All, to some extent, are with us still.

So in Part 1 we explore these resilient historical legacies, concentrating especially on the evolution of policy since 1967 (Chapter three). To these we add (Chapter two) a discussion of the discourses of primary education: discourses, plural, because there are a number of ways of thinking and talking about primary education. In our judgement some are useful; others are ill-conceived and corrosive.

Part 2 – Children and childhood

Childhood has become a hot topic. It is therefore appropriate that we explore the condition of childhood today and ask how far the current anxiety about children's well-being is justified. That said, childhood would have been a central element in this report even without the recent flurry of reports on children's well-being, for it is one of the Review's three overarching perspectives. Full engagement with the nature of childhood, with children's development, their lives and their needs is paramount in an enquiry like ours.

Part 2 considers first the general condition of childhood today (Chapter four), then moves to the more specific matter of children's lives outside school and their impact on what schools do, can do or might do (Chapter five). Chapter six discusses trends in parenting and caring at a time of changing family structures and growing anxiety about the quality of some parenting and the pressures to which many parents are subject (Chapter six). Chapter seven then re-assesses the evidence on how young children develop and learn. For Plowden and the Plowden generation of teachers, this topic mattered almost above all others, and several of our witnesses have insisted that a thorough knowledge of child development is the proper basis for effective primary teaching. While arguing that it is necessary but insufficient, we do not in any sense underrate its fundamental importance, and Chapter seven revisits the developmental process, examines the implications of the shift from a Piagetian to a Vygotskyian view of learning and assesses what recent advances in neuroscience might mean for teachers and children in classrooms.

Developmentally, children have much in common. However, Britain, and especially England, is highly diverse culturally, geographically, ethnically, linguistically and in matters of faith, belief and value. Such diversity is overlaid by variation in individual circumstances and capacities which for some time have been rolled together within the term 'special educational needs'. Britain is also one of the more unequal countries in the developed world, and poverty, disadvantage, marginalisation and risk bear heavily on the lives of millions of the nation's children. Chapters eight and nine examine diversity and inequality, both demographically and qualitatively, and consider the questions of division, equity, inclusion and special provision within a national education system which inevitably follow.

Part 2 ends with children themselves talking (Chapter 10). 'Children's voices' has become a significant strand in educational research and, more recently, in educational policy. The UN Convention on the Rights of the Child (UNCRC), which the British government acknowledges and which features in many of its policies, asserts children's rights not only to the fundamentals of care, protection, survival, development, education and play, but also to express opinions, especially on matters which affect them directly, and to have their opinions taken seriously.[7] Always interested in plurality, we prefer 'children's voices' to 'pupil voice' and here we discuss both what the Primary Review heard in its many direct encounters with children through the regional soundings and the submissions, and what is indicated by other research involving children's voices.

Part 3 – The experience of primary education

Part 3 concentrates on what happens to children when they attend primary school, and on how well their experiences address the concerns raised in Parts 1 and 2.

When we were planning the Review there was much discussion about whether it should cover the primary phase alone or primary and the early years together. That is to say, recognising that what happens to children before they enter primary school has a significant bearing on their subsequent progress, should the enquiry cover the full span from birth to primary/ secondary transition?

In the end, for all kinds of reasons, we decided to concentrate on the statutory primary phase. Nevertheless, we did ask when that phase should start, by what it should be preceded, and how, during the child's vital early years, the transition from pre-primary to primary education might best be managed. In response, one of the most insistent themes in our evidence was the view that children in England are required to do too much, or the wrong things, too young. Chapter 11 brings together our evidence on this and related matters and examines not just the structural question of the starting age for compulsory schooling but also the curricular or experiential challenge of transition from what since 2008 has been called the early years foundation stage (EYFS) to key stage 1 of the national curriculum. Out of our evidence and analysis come proposals for the restructuring of provision for the age range 3–11. The chapter, as is right, is called 'Foundations'.

With the foundations laid we ask, as directly as such a complex and controversial topic allows, 'What is primary education for, and by what values and principles should it be informed?' Chapter 12 takes a careful look at this question, deploying the historical and international lenses referred to earlier. Conventional wisdom about the proper purposes of primary education are deeply entrenched, and it is almost invariably assumed that what is habitually the case must be for ever more. We do not make that assumption. Indeed, in light of what is happening to children, society and the world, it would be reckless to do so. Chapter 12 contrasts the resilience of Victorian values in the political sphere with the more generous views of education's purposes expressed by the Review's witnesses, and leads towards a set of principles by which we believe that the work of education 'providers' – government, local authorities and schools – should be informed, followed by a set of 12 fundamental aims towards which the work of primary schools should be directed.

In Chapter 12 we argue that a curriculum detached from aims makes little sense, yet for much of its history the English primary curriculum has been shaped more by habit than rationale. So in the next four chapters our recommended aims and principles are followed through into the curriculum as specified (Chapters 13 and 14) and then into the teaching and assessment through which curriculum steps off the page and into children's lives (Chapters 15 and 16). One year after the launch of the Review, the government announced its own 'root-and-branch review of the primary curriculum'. The terms of reference for the government's review were precisely set, and its final report was published in April 2009.[8] However, though the timing overlapped ours and though the existence of the government review created obvious pressures, the Cambridge Primary Review's examination of the past development, present condition and future direction of the primary curriculum remains resolutely independent, and is intended for the longer term rather than as a policy quick fix. In any case, we argue that the problems of the contemporary primary curriculum go much further and deeper than what the Rose Review called 'quarts into pint pots' – the challenge of manageability which Sir Jim

Rose identified as the central problem.[9] Chapters 13 and 14 also consider vital contingent questions such as who should determine the content of the curriculum, the balance of elements local, national and international, and the muddled language of 'subjects', 'skills' and 'knowledge' which confounds sensible curriculum debate. The Review proposes a new framework for the primary curriculum which brings together the proposed 12 aims and eight domains of knowledge, skill, enquiry and disposition, in which statutory entitlement determined nationally is combined with a strong local component, the community curriculum. Our analysis and proposals were published in February 2009 to contribute to the debate about Rose.

Chapter 15 is about what goes on in classrooms. It reviews and assesses evidence on what makes for productive teaching, noting that this is an area in which policy-makers were unwilling to intervene until 1997. Part of our brief, therefore, must be to examine the impact of that intervention, as expressed in the post-1997 national strategies for literacy, numeracy and primary education more broadly. But the chapter goes further than this, arguing that we should move from a view of teaching as mere technique to what for centuries continental Europe has called pedagogy: the embedding of the practice of teaching in a body of knowledge about children, their learning, what is to be taught and how, sustained by empirical enquiry and a clear framework of values. In this view, reducing teaching to tips which can be lifted ready-made from 'best practice' websites without regard for the context of their application is no longer adequate. It is the principles by which productive teaching is underpinned which should first command teachers' attention.

For much of the Review's duration, and especially once we started releasing the interim reports, the topics of tests and testing, and their close relations standards and accountability, have swamped most others. Few issues have generated more passionate reactions, or more lurid headlines, or more political statements veering wildly between the rabble-rousing and the timorous, than the tests at the end of key stages 1 and 2, especially the latter. Chapter 16 is about the purposes, nature, methods, uses (and abuses) of assessment, for tests are only one kind of assessment and the first requirement is to understand that. The chapter identifies the conditions which assessment needs to satisfy, and the forms which it should take, to meet the very different purposes of supporting children's learning, judging their progress and meeting proper demands that schools be accountable for what they do.

Chapter 17 takes the matter several stages further. If assessment is, in part at least, about securing and monitoring standards, then it is right to ask what, in a decade dominated by assessment, has happened to standards of primary pupils' learning and attainment. The chapter examines the national and international evidence on this, but it also provokes the question – to which we have already alluded – of what exactly the term 'standards' means and should mean. It then turns to the various procedures, of which inspection by Ofsted is the most prominent and controversial, by which the quality of schools as a whole is judged.

'A school is not just a teaching shop,' said Plowden, memorably but a trifle inelegantly (and maybe disparagingly as far as the profession of teaching was concerned). The drift is right, though, and in Chapter 18 we examine the character of primary schools not just as buildings and resources but as communities of people, ideas and values. Quite apart from what is on offer in the teaching shop, schools convey powerful messages to children of the kind once referred to as the hidden curriculum, until it was understood that these messages are hidden from nobody, least of all the pupils. The chapter also considers other sites for learning, for schools do not have a monopoly of that essential human capacity.

Part 4 – The system of primary education

Part 3 concentrates on primary schools and classrooms. Part 4 shifts our attention to the national system of primary education as a whole.

The structure of English primary schooling – the ages and stages and the ways schools organise children in classes and groups for teaching and learning – has a long pedigree. Chapter 19 explores the parallel and intertwined structures of school type (infant, junior, primary, first, middle, combined), within-school pupil organisation (age-specific/mixed age, setting/streaming/ 'mixed-ability') and key stage. It also discusses problems of transition within each of these and transfer from one to the other.

Schools have their internal structure but are also part of a much larger one. Following Every Child Matters and the 2004 Children's Act, the relatively simple relationship of individual schools and local education authorities gave way to a complex network of agencies, under the aegis of local authority children's services, which was intended to co-ordinate the work of all those responsible for children's care and education, and to ensure protection for the most vulnerable. Chapter 20 examines these changes in the context of wider consideration of the relationship between schools and other agencies.

Chapter 21 is the first of two chapters on the professionals who work in primary schools. It considers the education and training of teachers, asking how and whether teachers are most appropriately deployed in primary schools and what kinds of expertise their roles require. It also questions whether that defining feature of the old elementary schools, the generalist class teacher system, should continue to be treated as sacrosanct, arguing that there is now a widening gulf between the tasks primary schools are required to undertake and the professional resources they have at their disposal. Underpinning the discussion are re-assessments of the nature of professional expertise and the process of professional development, in which assumptions and models enshrined in current policy are compared with those which arise from research.

Chapter 22 examines the relationship between school leadership, workforce reform and school improvement. It tracks the shift in conceptions of headship from absolutism to collegiality, and the supposed flowering of other roles within the new culture of 'distributed leadership'. It examines the impact of recent policies aimed at workforce reform and considers the culture and status of the primary teaching profession as it now stands, after two decades of curricular and professional change.

Finally in this section, we turn in Chapter 23 to the framework within which schools operate: the structure of the system as a whole, its governance and funding, and the way education policy is formulated. Throughout the Review's deliberations, two questions have been raised repeatedly and insistently, and both are a direct consequence of the centralising urge which has characterised public education in England since 1988. Is the balance of national, local and school control and responsibility right? And what has been the impact on the character and quality of primary education, and on those who work in primary schools, of two decades of government-steered reform in education and other public services? The chapter raises serious questions about the policy process and the extent to which the politicisation of all matters educational has enabled or frustrated the changes that needed to be made. Such questions link our evidence and discussion to wider public concern about the condition of Britain's democratic fabric.

Part 5 – Conclusions and recommendations

It is common for the reports of major enquiries to list conclusions and recommendations at the end of each chapter. There are two reasons why, with certain exceptions (for example the chapters on aims and curriculum), we have not followed this course. First, the chapter-by-chapter approach risks fragmentation and duplication and sets up an expectation that for every chapter there must be a corresponding set of recommendations. Second, it deflects attention from the way a report offers, if appropriately structured, a narrative which builds towards outcomes which can be expressed only once the story is told in full.

Our approach, therefore, is to do no more than hint at recommendations within most of the chapters, offering a general summation of issues raised before moving on. In this respect, the report is perhaps more like a book than a conventional report, but this is consistent with the way the Review was conceived – as a single, coherent framework for describing and making sense of a national education system – and it is as a unitary and, we trust, coherent response to that system that we would wish the report to be read.

It follows that our conclusions and recommendations frequently arise not from one paragraph or even one chapter in isolation but from findings which are consolidated across chapters and from arguments which build progressively. It also follows that we are under no obligation to find something to recommend for every chapter and that our final list is somewhat shorter than the catalogue of 197 recommendations with which the Plowden report ended.

We also wish it to be understood, again contrary to convention, that the conclusions and recommendations are not all that matters. The analysis and argument are, in our view, no less important, for without them there can be no recommendations; and when the recommendations have been duly responded to and in some cases have been rejected, the analysis, arguments and ideas remain for discussion and debate into the longer term.

Further, this report is not an official commission and therefore does not stand or fall on how it is received by the government which happens to be in office on the day that it is published; especially as what one government rejects another may well accept. Anyway, as we have now said more than once, this enquiry and its report are for all who are interested in primary education, for practitioners as well as policy-makers, for parents as well as professionals.

Having said all this, we do not expect readers to renounce the pleasure of turning to the end of the book to discover the denouement, and they will find the Cambridge Primary Review's formal conclusions and recommendations in Chapter 24.

NOTES

1 Professor Frank Coffield, Professor Stephen Ball, Professor Richard Taylor and Professor Sir Peter Scott, in a letter to *The Independent*, 2 June 2008: 'We have come independently to the same conclusion, namely that government policy is no longer the solution to the difficulties we face but our greatest problem.' http://www.independent.co.uk/opinion/letters/letters-education-policy-838213.html (accessed April 2009).
2 UNICEF (2007).
3 David Cameron, leader of the Conservative Party, in July 2007.
4 Alexander and Hargreaves (2007).
5 Tymms and Merrell (2010), Whetton, Ruddock and Twist (2010), Harlen (2010) *The Cambridge Primary Review Research Surveys*, Chapters 17, 18 and 19.
6 Hart, Dixon, Drummond and McIntyre (2004).
7 UNCRC, Article 12.
8 Rose (2009).
9 'Update from Sir Jim Rose', http://www.dcsf.gov.uk/primarycurriculumreview/ (accessed April 2009).

Part 1
Contexts

2 The Review and other discourses

If you're going to be a decision-making citizen, you need to know how to make sense and how to recognise when someone else is making sense ... You need to know how to share forms of argumentation. When people don't have methods of argument in common, they can't have intelligent disagreement, they have a fight ... Education is a training in what you can trust and what you can share ... We sometimes over-emphasise the role of education in teaching you to be suspicious; important though that is, to teach people how to be suspicious ought also to be to teach them something of what they can trust; what meaningful action together is like; how arguments and priorities and visions can be communicated; how common languages can be shaped ... Faith and hope are at work, and they're at work in the training of reason ... Faith as the capacity to trust arguments which can be shown to be trustworthy; hope as the conviction that it is possible to act collaboratively in human society, not just with endless rivalry and jostling for position; and I'd like to think that charity comes in somewhere as well – charity in the sense of a generous awareness that there are different ways of making sense, different sorts of questions to ask about the world we're in, and insofar as those questions are pursued with integrity and seriousness they should be heard seriously and charitably.

Rowan Williams, Archbishop of Canterbury, at the
University of Cambridge, 21 February 2008.[1]

Since then [2003], every education secretary and minister has been distinguished by an almost wilful determination to ignore the mass of research that does not suit their agenda. Politically, that is the easiest choice. They are encouraged in this by their senior civil servants, whose careers have been built around delivering a particular agenda, and who have nothing to gain by seeing it change course. What is truly alarming is that ministers rarely even glimpse the reports they dismiss. Last year I mentioned a particularly critical Ofsted report to one minister. 'Oh, my people tell me there's nothing new in that,' he said, breezily. In fact, it had a great deal that was new, and important, and the individuals who put thousands of man-hours into preparing it were probably writing it for an audience of three – of which the minister who never read it was the most important one. It seems that the Cambridge Primary Review is meeting the same fate. This extensive, diligent review of published evidence and new research was dismissed in 10 seconds by another minister in a private conversation: 'My people say it's rehashed.' Publicly, the Department for Children, Schools and Families has written the latest reports off as 'recycled, partial and out-of-date'. It said: 'We do not accept these claims ... We have had a decade of success in raising standards.'

Jenni Russell, journalist, in *The Guardian*, 26 March 2008.

WHY THE CAMBRIDGE PRIMARY REVIEW, AND WHY NOW?

Rowan Williams' advocacy of shared discourse underpinned by intelligence, discrimination and generosity of spirit has two quite distinct applications. It offers a view of what education is all about which is worthy of consideration in its own right; and it serves as a manifesto for the Cambridge Primary Review itself, which has sought to raise and answer questions about primary education and to venture and examine different ways of making sense of it, in the hope that what are currently called education's 'stakeholders' – children, teachers, parents, government, local authorities, employers and so on – might 'seriously and charitably' hear and reflect on what we have to say.

Yet the Review arose not from a sense that English primary schools, or the government, were failing in their duties but from a belief that at any time and as matter of course, but especially during a time of change and uncertainty, we should be asking how well our schools are doing and whether what they are doing is what needs to be done. The questions, then, were open and exploratory rather than inquisitorial or adversarial. Indeed, in 1967 the Plowden Report expressly recommended that such a re-assessment should take place every 10 years.[2] Here, updated, is how we summarised the case when the Review was launched in October 2006:

- There has been no comprehensive investigation of English primary education since the Plowden enquiry of 1963–67. There have been a number of smaller enquiries, reports and initiatives,[3] but none has had the broad scope or visionary aspirations of Plowden, or its independence. Yet, 40 years on, primary education, Britain and the world are very different, and quite apart from the criticism to which earlier enquiries have been properly subject, their analyses, findings and recommendations necessarily have a limited life span. Now, in 2009, traditional demographic and economic assumptions bearing on the presumed purposes and priorities of basic education are being challenged. There is growing debate about the educational implications of ethnic, religious and cultural diversity; about social cohesion and the nation's democratic fabric; about climate change and the environment; and, with increasing urgency since the publication of the 2007 Unicef report, about the condition of childhood itself.[4]
- Since the 1988 Education Reform Act, and particularly since 1997, schools, local authorities and higher education have been required to respond to a large number of government initiatives in areas such as curriculum, assessment, teaching, inspection, performance management, workforce reform, school leadership, governance and finance. It is time to assess the cumulative impact of these initiatives on the quality of educational provision and on the lives of those who learn and teach in primary schools; and to reconsider the balance of national and local in educational decision-making, responsibility and accountability.
- The expansion of pre-school education, the introduction of the foundation stage, the 2004 Children's Act, the Every Child Matters agenda and the 2007 Children's Plan have all placed primary schools in a radically different administrative and indeed philosophical context to that which prevailed until the mid 1990s. This, too, dictates a re-assessment of what primary schools do and how they work that links them to health, welfare and childcare as well as to the secondary and pre-school sectors.
- Primary education suffers more than its fair share of claim, counter claim and mythology. Thus, for example, while government asserts that standards are rising, others insist that they are not, or that the evidence either way is at best unreliable. The Department for Children, Schools and Families (DCSF), Ofsted and the Training and Development Agency (TDA) announce that 'Today's newly qualified teachers (NQTs) are the best trained ever'[5] but others complain that NQTs earn this plaudit merely by doing what they are told, or that the claim is empirically unsustainable. Primary schools are accused of neglecting the 3Rs; yet inspection evidence going back to the 1960s shows that this is the one thing they have never neglected, while more recent evidence suggests that schools are concentrating on the 3Rs to the neglect of much else that is important. Then, while some complain, as adults in every generation do, that children's behaviour is deteriorating, others insist that today's children are better motivated and engaged than ever. Meanwhile, the myth of a 'progressive' or left-wing takeover of the hearts and minds of primary teachers in pursuit of 'dumbed-down' egalitarianism, which was first advanced by the Black Paper authors in 1968, just a year after Plowden, is endlessly recycled,[6] despite clear evidence that progressivism as parodied by these people was never more than a minority pursuit.[7] It is time to cut through all this and establish the true position.

- Our system of primary education was created on the basis of a particular view of society and people's places within it – or rather the place of those children and families who did not want or could not afford private education. But today's Britain is less sure of itself, and the inequalities between rich and poor are no longer assumed to be the way things inevitably are and for ever must be. Some commentators argue the virtues of a pluralist multi-culture. Others deplore the loss of shared identity and social cohesion. It is time to revisit the vital debate about the nature of the 'good society' and the role of education in shaping it.

- This is the era of globalisation, and perhaps of unprecedented opportunity. But there are darker visions. The gap between the world's rich and poor continues to grow. There is political and religious polarisation. Many people are daily denied their basic human rights and suffer violence and oppression. As if that were not enough, escalating climate change may well make this the make-or-break century for humanity as a whole. Such scenarios raise obvious and urgent questions for public education. Should educating children's consciousness and understanding of these global trends, fears and threats be part of the work of schools? If so, what kind of a response should schools seek to foster, given that the issues are moral and political as well as economic, and that schools are properly wary of doing anything which will lay them open to the charge of indoctrination?

- We now have much more evidence about matters relating to primary-aged children and their education – from both official sources and independent research – than was available to the Plowden Committee. It is time to take stock of this material, and to consider how closely it aligns with the much-used claims of 'evidence-based policy' and 'evidence-based practice'.

During 2004–5 we consulted widely on earlier versions of these propositions and on the kinds of questions which a new enquiry into primary education might address. We were heartened to encounter almost unanimous agreement that the enquiry was needed, subject to debate about matters such as whether it should cover statutory primary schooling or the entire period from birth to adolescence. The agreement was almost unanimous, but even the initially sceptical Department for Education and Skills (DfES) moved, by the time we launched, to offers of co-operation and expressions of goodwill.[8]

THE REMIT OF THE REVIEW

The remit negotiated and agreed with Esmée Fairbairn Foundation was as follows:

- With respect to public provision in England, the Review will seek to identify the purposes which the primary phase of education should serve, the values which it should espouse, the curriculum and learning environment which it should provide, and the conditions which are necessary in order to ensure both that these are of the highest and most consistent quality possible, and that they address the needs of children and society over the coming decades.

- The Review will pay close regard to national and international evidence from research, inspection and other sources on the character and adequacy of current provision in respect of the above, on the prospects for recent initiatives, and on other available options. It will seek the advice of expert advisers and witnesses, and it will invite submissions and take soundings from a wide range of interested agencies and individuals, both statutory and non-statutory.

- The Review will publish both interim findings and a final report. The latter will combine evidence, analysis and conclusions together with recommendations for both national policy and the work of schools and other relevant agencies.[9]

This remit focuses in turn on the Review's focus, processes and outcomes and we now provide further detail about each of these.

THE FOCUS OF THE REVIEW: PERSPECTIVES, THEMES AND QUESTIONS

A national system of primary education offers to an enquiry such as this, if that enquiry is properly conceived, a dauntingly vast canvas. It is national, so it raises questions about national values, national identity, the condition of English and indeed British society and the lives and futures of the groups and individuals of which that society is constituted. It is a system, so there are questions about policy, structure, organisation, finance and governance to consider. And being an education system, it raises a distinctively educational array of questions about the children whose needs, along with those of society, the system claims to address, and about schools, what goes on in them, and the contexts within which they operate.

Some enquiries have been restricted to the point where the discussion of even what they treat in detail loses some of its validity. This is because ostensibly practical matters such as curriculum, teaching, assessment, leadership and workforce reform – to take some typical recent instances – raise much larger questions of purpose, value and social context. Thus, a curriculum is much more than a syllabus: it is a response to culture and the future. Teaching is not merely a matter of technique, but reflects ideas about thinking, knowing, learning and relating. Assessment, for better or worse, has become as much a political as a professional activity. In turn, all of these are framed, enabled and/or constrained by policy, structure and finance. And so on.

So breadth of coverage in a national educational review is essential. At the same time, it is impossible to cover everything, and choices must be confronted and made. The Review's coverage was therefore expressed as a hierarchy of 'perspectives', 'themes' and 'questions'. We start with the three broad *perspectives* which are captured in this report's title: children, the world in which they are growing up, and the education which helps mediate that world and prepare them for it. These are the Review's core concerns and recurrent points of reference. Next, 10 themes and 23 *sub-themes* unpack the education perspective in greater detail while remaining permeated by the other two. Finally, for every perspective and theme there is a set of *questions*. These indicate in more direct terms what the Review must investigate if it is to pronounce authoritatively, comprehensively and constructively on the current condition and future character of English primary education.

Being aware of this framework is necessary to an understanding of this report's scope and structure, and the perspectives, themes and questions are listed in full in Appendix 2. It would be a remarkable enquiry which succeeded in addressing all the questions listed, and to claim to have come even close to doing so would smack of more than hubris. Readers of the report will judge for themselves how successful we have been. What is beyond doubt is that the questions are important. Many of them are also urgent.

EVIDENCE – AND VISION

The Cambridge Primary Review is firmly grounded in evidence of different kinds. But not all educational questions – and certainly not all of those listed in Appendix 2 – are empirical. Many are ethical, for education is a fundamentally moral affair, while others move forward from evidence into territory which is more speculative. Frequently, the two kinds of question are deliberately juxtaposed, for example 'What *do* children currently learn during the primary phase?' and 'What *should* they learn?'

This, then, is the age-old distinction between 'is' and 'ought' questions, or questions of fact and value, or of what in the Review we have called matters of *evidence* and *vision*, and we readily understand that knowing what is may provide no guide at all to determining what ought to be. Indeed, philosophers warn us, as a condition of argument at its most elementary level, of the dangers of making this leap. To take two examples, just because primary children's school lives have been dominated since Victorian days by the 3Rs, or during the same period most have been taught by generalist class teachers, this does not mean that such practices should continue indefinitely.

Existing assumptions and practices are there, then, to be questioned for what they are – habits of thought and action which are so deeply ingrained that most people don't pause to think about them. Those who do question such habits are likely to be met with the blank gaze of incomprehension or with the steely dogma of 'There is no alternative'. There is an alternative, of course, as there always was and is, but most who utter this phrase are telling you not that they have weighed the alternatives and found them wanting but that they have not even paused to consider the possibility. Equally – a different slant on the same issue – we can uncover, through the diligent use of evidence, the weaknesses of a particular aspect of our system of primary education, but that evidence of itself may offer no clues to how to put things right. What may be needed is some lateral, not to say visionary, thinking.

What may also be helpful is other kinds of evidence – for example from other countries – though here too there are dangers. During the 1990s, governments were eager to copy the classroom practices of countries located on what was then called the 'Pacific Rim', simply because their pupils did rather better than ours in international surveys of educational achievement and this in turn was presumed to account in part for their economic success. Quite apart from concerns about the validity and reliability of the international achievement surveys (see Chapter 17), the relation between education and economic performance is far too complex to permit such naive attributions of causality.[10] As if to remind us of this, several of the 'tiger' economies concerned collapsed shortly after their classroom practices were held up as the key to their success. In any case, the pedagogical borrowing was done without regard for cultural differences which might be more significant in explaining the national achievement differentials. Nowadays the preferred model is Scandinavia – and especially high-performing Finland – despite the fact that this sparsely populated country of just five million inhabitants, who share a handful of languages and a strong sense of collective identity and purpose, could not be more different from tiny, overcrowded and divided Britain with its 60 million inhabitants who between them speak 240 languages.[11] The true lesson of Finland, if indeed there is one, may come not from its teaching methods but from its sense of what is meant by the 'good society' and how through schooling this is both promoted and enacted.

Such considerations dictated both a balance of evidence of different kinds, and an acute sense of its proper and improper use. Thus we sought to balance empirical data with opinion-seeking; non-interactive expressions of opinion with face-to-face discussion; official data with independent research; and material from England with that from other parts of the UK and from international sources (Figure 2.1). We did so through four distinct procedures or evidential 'strands', and their relationship to the Review's three perspectives and 10 themes can be represented as a matrix (Figure 2.2).

Submissions

Following the convention in enquiries of this kind, submissions were invited from all who wished to contribute. Unlike some official consultations, respondents were not given a prescribed set of essentially leading questions to answer in order to confirm a pre-determined

	Submissions	Soundings	Surveys	Searches
Published empirical data: official			✔	✔
Published empirical data: independent			✔	
Invited opinion: open	✔	✔		
Invited opinion: targeted		✔		
Interactive		✔		
Non-interactive	✔		✔	✔

Figure 2.1 The balance of evidence.

	Evidential strands	Submissions	Soundings	Surveys	Searches
Review foci					
Perspectives					
Children					
Society					
Education					
Themes					
Purposes & values					
Learning & teaching					
Curriculum & assessment					
Quality & standards					
Diversity & inclusion					
Settings & professionals					
Parenting, caring & educating					
Beyond the school					
Structures & phases					
Funding & governance					

Figure 2.2 The evidential matrix.

agenda, but were encouraged to consider the perspectives, themes and questions on the Review website and either address those which spoke to their condition or to press matters which, regardless of the Review's agenda, they regarded as important. The process, then, was as open as we could make it. By April 2009, 1,052 submissions had been received. They ranged from brief single-issue expressions of opinion to substantial documents of up to 300 pages covering several or all of the themes and comprising both detailed evidence and recommendations for the future. The majority of the submissions were from national organisations, but a significant number came from individuals. Many of the organisational submissions were from outside education. Full details appear in Appendix 3.

Soundings

This strand had two parts. The *community soundings* were a series of nine regionally-based one to two-day events, each comprising a sequence of meetings with representatives from schools and the communities they serve. The community soundings took place between January and March 2007, and entailed 87 witness sessions with groups of pupils, parents, governors, teachers, teaching assistants and heads, and with educational and community representatives from the areas in which the soundings took place.

The *national soundings* were more formal meetings with national organisations both inside and outside education. Some of these, with government, statutory agencies, public bodies and unions, took the form of regular consultations throughout the Review's duration. Others, which included three seminars with specially convened groups of teachers and two sessions with representatives of major non-statutory organisations, took place between January and March 2008 and explored issues arising from the Review's by then considerable body of evidence. The national soundings helped the team to clarify matters which were particularly problematic or contested, in preparation for writing this report.

Details of the community and national soundings appear in Appendix 4.

Surveys

Several months before the launch of the Review, 30 surveys of published research relating to the Review's 10 themes were commissioned, on the basis of competitive bidding and peer review, from 66 academic consultants in leading university departments of education and allied fields and from the National Foundation for Educational Research. Of the resulting research reports, 28 were published over several months, starting in autumn 2007 (as shown in Appendix 7). The research surveys, many of them revised, are reprinted in the companion volume to this report.

Searches and policy mapping

With the co-operation of DfES/DCSF, QCA, Ofsted and TDA, the Review tracked recent policy and examined official data bearing on the primary phase (Appendix 6). This provided the necessary legal, demographic, financial and statistical background to the Review and an important resource for its consideration of policy options.

Other consultations

In addition to the formal evidence-gathering procedures, the Review's director and other team members met national and regional bodies for the exchange of information and ideas. At the time of going to press 146 such sessions had taken place, in addition to the 92 community and national soundings, making a total of 238 sessions. For full details, see Appendix 5.

REPORTING

The Cambridge Primary Review was conceived as a formative as well as summative enquiry. That is to say, we believed that to collect evidence and say nothing until we reported on it two years or so later was to miss an important opportunity to engage professionals and the public in the debate. Accordingly, between October 2007 and May 2008 we published a series of interim reports, including the account of the 2007 community soundings and the 28 surveys of published research which were by then available. To these were added the two-volume special report on the primary curriculum (based on Chapters 12, 13 and 14 of this volume) which, as the Cambridge Review's contribution to the government's Rose Review, was published in February 2009. The interim reporting timetable is shown in Figure 2.3.

12 October 2007	*Community soundings: report on the Review's regional witness sessions*
2 November 2007	*How well are we doing? Research on standards, quality and assessment in English primary education* (three reports)
23 November 2007	*Children's lives and voices: research on children at home and school* (four reports)
14 December 2007	*Children in primary schools: research on development, learning, diversity and educational needs* (four reports)
18 January 2008	*Aims and values in primary education: national and international perspectives* (four reports)
8 February 2008	*The structure and content of English primary education: international perspectives* (three reports)
29 February 2008	*Governance, funding, reform and quality assurance: policy frameworks for English primary education* (four reports)
18 April 2008	*Primary teachers: training, development, leadership and workforce reform* (three reports)
16 May 2008	*Learning and teaching in primary schools: processes and contexts* (three reports)
20 February 2009	*Towards a new primary curriculum* (two reports)

Figure 2.3 The interim reports.

The interim reports received extensive media coverage and several of them provoked controversy. More importantly, they began to influence the public debate about policy, and perhaps even policy itself. Thus our reports on standards, testing and assessment exposed ministers to questioning which was taken up by the House of Commons Children, Schools and Families Committee[12] and may have helped to shift the government from the firm line on testing to which it had held since 1997, though the outcome at the time of writing – abandoning key stage 3 testing but continuing to test literacy and numeracy at key stage 2 (and, oddly, using the same argument to justify these opposing decisions) – was not what many in the primary sector would have preferred. Our reports on childhood contributed to the wider discussion of children's well-being and may have influenced aspects of the December 2007 Children's Plan. Our reports on the curriculum generated widespread debate – in other countries as well is in Britain – about the extent to which a narrowly conceived standards agenda may have prevented a genera-tion of children from receiving the curriculum to which they were statutorily entitled.

The fact that curriculum was one of the Review's main themes and that in our interim reports we questioned the current model was almost certainly an important factor in prompt-ing the government's decision to set up its own primary curriculum review under the leadership of Sir Jim Rose. In any event, the timing, nomenclature and aspects of the methodology of Rose were such that several commentators suspected something other than coincidence.

In June 2008, we submitted evidence to the Rose Review in the form of eight of our interim reports together with a brief commentary.[13] Rose's own interim report appeared in December 2008 with a deadline of 28 February 2009 for the receipt of comment.[14] By January the chapters on the primary curriculum for the present report were ready, so they were turned into a special report and forwarded to Rose as a further contribution to his enquiry.[15] They were also sent to the enquiry on the national curriculum which the House of Commons Children, Schools and Families Committee initiated in February 2008, and were discussed with that committee in private session on 19 January 2009. The Select Committee's report includes a detailed comparison of how the Rose and Cambridge reviews approached their tasks.[16] The final report from the Rose Review, published on 30 April 2008, makes frequent mention of the Cambridge analysis and proposals (which is not to say that they have been acted on).[17]

The final report

The final report of the Cambridge Primary Review draws on both first- and second-order evidence. The first-order evidence is what emerged from the submissions, community sound-ings, research surveys and official data searches detailed in appendices 3–7. The second-order evidence arose from the national soundings on this material which were prompted by our publication of the 28 research surveys and which took place early in 2008. Alongside these were the national events organised by the Weavers' Company and the General Teaching Council in November 2007 and March 2008, private meetings with the House of Commons Children, Schools and Families Committee in March 2007, June 2008 and January 2009, and numerous other meetings and conferences at which emerging findings from the Review were aired and discussed. We also received a second wave of submissions which commented directly on the reports.

ADVICE AND ACCOUNTABILITY

The day-to-day work of the Cambridge Primary Review was undertaken by a team based in the Faculty of Education at Cambridge University. The team was assisted by the 70 research consultants whose contributions to the research survey strand are described under 'Surveys' above and whose studies appear in the companion volume. The entire programme was subject to monitoring for accountability purposes by a seven-strong management group set up by the Review's sponsors, Esmée Fairbairn Foundation, and was advised and guided in matters of substance and strategy by an advisory committee whose 20 members came from both inside and outside education. The advisory committee was convened in May 2006, five months before the launch of the Review, and met termly thereafter. By the time this report is published, the committee will have met on nine occasions, and its policy sub-committee on a further five. Membership of these various groups is listed in Appendix 1.

THE CAMBRIDGE PRIMARY REVIEW AND OTHER DISCOURSES

Let us return to that contrast between the ideal and the political reality of contemporary educational discourse with which this chapter began. Discourse is 'situated', so it cannot be presumed that participants in the educational endeavour will readily enter into each other's language and thought on the basis of goodwill alone. Teachers invoke a highly particular world which is bounded for most of the time by the culture, routines and challenges – always immediate, often intense and demanding – of the schools in which they work. This, inevitably and necessarily, is very different from the world of the researcher who is interested in uncovering patterns, similarities and differences, both within and across schools and among populations of teachers and children, and in devising or adapting theories to make sense of what he or she finds. Different again is the perspective of the policy-maker, for it both attends to an entire system of over 17,000 schools, four million pupils and 198,000 teachers and displays an inevitable preoccupation with the political impact of how that perspective is conveyed. What some call 'spin' may be more charitably understood as a wholly reasonable attempt to convey ideas as clearly and unambiguously as possible, mindful that in Britain's pugilistic political culture opponents are waiting for the slip that can be gleefully exploited.

Entrenching these professional, academic and political registers is the discourse of power. The 'primaryspeak' of the 1960s and 1970s was as gently consensual as today's policyspeak – with its 'drivers' and 'levers', its 'tsars', 'task forces' and 'step changes', its 'world-class' strategies and 'tough new' initiatives 'rolled out' to 'hit the ground running' – is adversarial, authoritarian and indeed militaristic.

These are general tendencies in the way education is talked about these days. More corrosive, however, are three patterns of discourse which in recent decades have frustrated the progress of educational thinking, policy and practice, and as we write they continue to do so.

The discourse of dichotomy

Ever since the 1931 Hadow Report on primary education announced that 'the curriculum is to be thought of in terms of activity and experience rather than knowledge to be acquired and facts to be stored',[18] the discourse of primary education has been bedevilled by a tendency to reduce complex questions to a simple choice between standpoints which are presumed to be mutually exclusive. As it happens, the Hadow Committee's first draft of this influential maxim had the inclusive 'and' rather than the oppositional 'rather than', but the committee was dissuaded from its initial formulation by the Froebelians.[19] In its adversarial form it provided a credo for several generations of primary teachers.

Needless to say, this dichotomy, like most dichotomies, is not only unnecessary but also untenable. Coming to know is an activity, and it depends on experience, so knowledge is 'activity and experience', not its antithesis; and factual or propositional knowledge is but one kind of knowledge among many. Thus, at a stroke, the Hadow dichotomy badmouths knowledge in any form, reducing it to a sub-Gradgrindian array of dead subjects. But, again, subjects and knowledge are not the same either. Subjects are a way of organising the school curriculum. They may comprise knowledge, skills, processes of enquiry, activities, experiences and much more, or they may be reduced to something approaching the parody of the dead hand of fact-grubbing. When that happens, it is the fault of the teacher, not of the knowledge which is thereby parodied.

This is just the start (and in Chapter 14 we say much more about the downgrading of knowledge, its opposition to skills and the muddled thinking that surrounds discussion of subjects). Here are some other examples:

- child-centred *versus* subject-centred
- child-centred *versus* teacher-centred
- traditional *versus* progressive
- formal *versus* informal
- quantitative *versus* qualitative
- process *versus* content
- teaching as facilitation *versus* teaching as management
- education as pouring in *versus* education as drawing out
- management *versus* leadership.

And, two that started in the 1960s and somehow retain their popularity:

- we teach children not subjects
- teaching *versus* learning.

Not to mention, from our recent educational past:

- standards not structures
- standards not curriculum.

'We teach children not subjects' is particularly unhelpful, for it elides what we teach with those to whom we teach it, accusative (subjects) and dative (children). So too is 'teaching *versus* learning', for what is teaching if not the bringing about of learning? But the others are no less unsatisfactory. 'Standards not structures' mixes utterly different categories. Content is realised through process, not separate from it. And so it goes on, with perhaps the most pernicious and unwarranted dichotomy of all being that between standards in the 'basics' and breadth, balance and experiential richness in the wider curriculum. Drawing on a long line of evidence from research and inspection, we show in Chapter 14 that the assumption that standards and breadth are incompatible – which has been chiefly fostered by politicians and which many of them still believe – is utterly unfounded. Indeed we show that the reverse is the case, that the basics flourish in the context of a broad and well-managed curriculum. Here, children's statutory educational entitlement has been needlessly sacrificed in pursuit of political dogma.

However:

> One way of slowing if not reversing the downward slide of this debilitating discourse … is to … replace the exclusive 'versus' by an all-embracing 'and'. 'Versus' closes debate; 'and' opens it. The eminent Harvard researcher Courtney Cazden makes the same point in her analysis of the patterns of discourse in 'traditional' and 'non-traditional lessons'. 'Not either/or', she urges, 'but both/and'.[20]

Yet the vein of dichotomous discourse runs deep, as a recent Oxfam analysis shows,[21] and it continues to exert a powerful grip on the professional discourse of primary education. Needless to say, in the chapters which follow we strive for a way of talking about and conceiving of educational questions which is both more nuanced and more inclusive.

The discourse of derision

This telling phrase, popularised by policy analyst Stephen Ball though first coined by Jane Kenway,[22] came to define the political and media alliance of the 1990s, when the two largest political parties moved to the right in order to tap or massage what they took to be the mood of 'middle England':

> 'Doomed by the experts' … 'Happiness but little learning' … 'Back to basics: Clarke[23] shuts the door on 25 years of trendy teaching' … 'Schools chief attacks progressive teachers' …

'Children of nine still counting on fingers' ... 'Trendies produce a lesson in failure' ... 'Uproar over test failures by 11-year-olds' ... 'The Great Betrayal – After affecting our schools for 25 years, the Plowden Report has finally been laid to rest without mourners' ... 'Education's insane bandwagon finally goes into the ditch' ... 'Inspector attacks woolly teachers' ... 'Timewarp teachers' ... 'Sixties dogma is failing youngsters of the nineties' ... 'Progressive teaching gets a caning' ... 'Look on your works, Lady Plowden, and despair' ...[24]

The context was the Leeds report of 1991 and the 'three wise men' report which followed it. It mattered not that the latter warned:

> If things have gone wrong – and the word 'if' is important – then scapegoating is not the answer. All those responsible for administering and delivering our system of primary education need to look carefully at the part they may have played.[25]

Once again, as with the discourse of dichotomy, complex matters are reduced to the lowest common denominator and, where a soft target is available, the abuse becomes personal. Lady Plowden, chair of the committee which produced the 1967 report, was personally and mercilessly hounded by the press, egged on by politicians. None of them was prepared to acknowledge what we remind readers in the next chapter, that in many respects Plowden was a cautious and conservative document, and that the real problem was not Plowden but what some local authority advisers, head teachers and teacher trainers misguidedly advocated in its name. Indeed, Sir Alec Clegg, charismatic director of education in the old West Riding LEA and an important influence on Plowden, had specifically warned:

> What will educational historians say about the transformation of our primary schools since the last war? They will no doubt write about open education, vertical grouping, activity methods, free choice and other clichés which were the verbal shorthand of those who started it all and knew what they were doing, but which more recently have become the jargon of those who have jumped on the bandwagon but cannot play the instruments.[26]

It is even more salutary to note that Plowden itself had issued a similar warning, this time about what had been done a generation earlier in the name of the 1931 Hadow Report:

> For a brief time, 'activity' and child-centred education became dangerously fashionable, and misunderstandings on the part of the camp followers endangered the progress made by the pioneers.[27]

However, in the polarised political climate of 1991, and with a general election approaching, such niceties were swept aside. The idea that Plowden, the champion of child-centredness, might have warned against its own ideas becoming 'dangerously fashionable' among 'camp followers' was far too subtle to be accommodated within the discourse of derision. With most big cities still held by (old) Labour, the opportunity for scapegoating was too good to be missed:

> We will take no lectures from those who led the long march of mediocrity through our schools. What Labour governments did and what all too many Labour councils are still doing is unforgiveable.[28]

For politics was much of the point, and in this sense the discourses of derision and dichotomy are sides of the same coin:

> Such language may be nurtured by politicians and the press long after more discerning educators have abandoned it. In a context where political rhetoric – more than ever since 9/11 – is bounded by the atavism of us and them, the free and the oppressed, the chosen

and the damned, to corral educational ideas and practices into the warring camps of 'traditional' and 'progressive' appeals not just to lazy minds but also to more alert calculations about how the world is best represented for the purposes of selling newspapers and winning elections.[29]

By 2000, the new government's high-profile pursuit of higher educational standards offered less scope for this sort of party-political knockabout; until, that is, the publication of this Review's interim reports in 2007–8:

> 'Primary tests blasted by experts' ... 'Thousands of pupils given wrong grade in 3R tests' ... 'Test regime must change' ... 'Kids lose love of books' ... 'Literacy drive has almost no impact' ... '£500 million literacy drive is flop, say experts' ... 'Millions wasted on teaching reading' ... 'Primary pupils let down by Labour' ... 'Study shows Labour has damaged education' ... 'State control of education under scrutiny' ... 'Government policy has created impersonalised education' ... 'Primary schools have got worse' ... 'Ten years of bold education boasts now look sadly hollow' ... 'Failed! Political interference is damaging our children's education, says report' ... 'A shattering failure for our masters' ...[30]

To which government and its advisers responded:

> 'These reports use tunnel vision to look at education. Primary standards are at their highest ever levels'[31] ... 'A spokeswoman for the DCSF attacked the Primary Review for peddling "a collection of recycled, partial or out of date research"'[32] ... ' "I am not going to apologise for delivering what parents want, even if these researchers – often on the basis of out-of-date research – don't like it," Ed Balls said'[33] ... 'Professor Alexander is entitled to his opinions but once again we fundamentally disagree with his views – as will parents across the country. Parental interest in children's education in the home is vital for their learning. We need parents to make books available, read to their children and take an interest in their homework. Many parents already do this, and unlike Professor Alexander, we think they are right to do so'[34] ... ' "Independent" is certainly not an apt description of today's report from the self-styled 'largest' review of primary education in 40 years. It is another deeply ideological strike against standards and effective teaching of the 3Rs in our primary schools. Many of its contributors oppose the very idea of "standards" ... A return to a situation where the teaching of the basics is subsumed into a process of osmosis would destroy another generation of primary schoolchildren in the same way that the children of the seventies were failed ... The Primary Review is ... about reversing the changes of the last twenty years and returning our schools to a time when there was no public accountability and the basics were largely subsumed into other lessons.'[35]

What happened during this phase of the Review was that government ignored the disclaimer on each of the research surveys which were published as interim reports – 'The views expressed in this report are those of the authors. They do not necessarily reflect the opinions of the Primary Review, Esmée Fairbairn Foundation or the University of Cambridge' – and attacked not the reports' authors but the Review itself, often with scant regard for what the reports in question actually said. Reactions to the publication of the interim report of the Rose Review of the primary curriculum in December 2008, as well as to the reports of the Cambridge Review, indicate that the discourse of derision remains in the rudest of health.[36]

The discourse of myth

In the retaliatory strikes exemplified above something else is at work. Contemplating the horrors of the 20th century and humankind's prospects for learning from them (notably in Britain), Eric Hobsbawm found that:

The destruction of the past, or rather of the social mechanisms that link one's contemporary experience to that of earlier generations, is one of the most characteristic and
eerie phenomena of the late 20th century. Most young men and women at the century's
end grow up in a sort of permanent present lacking any organic relation to the public past
of the times they live in.[37]

One might suggest that this is in part a consequence of affluence, the cult of youth, the loss of
inter-generational contact and respect (all of them recurrent concerns in the Review's evidence,
as it happens) and, no doubt, the decline in history teaching in schools. But while such a
condition may be careless and unthinking, though no less deplorable for all that, 'the destruction
of the past' takes an effort of will.

That destructive process, regrettably, has been a prominent feature of policy discourse during
the past two decades. We refer not so much to the occupational amnesia of politicians who, as
a class, are disinclined to acknowledge the achievements of their opponents and predecessors.
The process we witness seems to be more calculated, and it is illustrated in the discussion of
policy in Chapter 23, where we find government advisers portraying education before 1997 as
'the era of uninformed professional judgement' in which 'standards stayed the same for 50
years', and where the 1970s are parodied as a period of rampant progressivism and professional
anarchy in which all those who dare to question government policy are by definition complicit.
The purpose of advancing claims as false as these, presumably, is to put the achievements of
the government in the best possible light – though their hyperbole or malignity are transparent
enough to undermine that aim. For as long as it is understood that the claims are no more
than this, little harm is done, for we all understand the games that politicians play. The problem
comes when over time such claims are repeated so often, and in contexts where political
gamesmanship is the last thing on an audience's or reader's mind, that they begin to be treated
as a reliable and validated historical account.

The chapter that follows this one initiates an alternative course. The past cannot and must
not be destroyed; nor can it be tidily re-arranged to suit the current political agenda.
The danger – and as the myth making about Plowden and the period before 1997 shows, it is a
real danger – is that with centralisation of educational decision-making comes the centralisation
of history itself. This report is in part about the need for our educational past and present, and
hence our educational future, to be reclaimed.

NOTES

1 R. Williams (2008).
2 CACE (1967): recommendation 42.
3 For example, the 1978 HMI Primary Survey, the first and only of Plowden's recommended decadal reviews
   (DES 1978a), the 1985–86 House of Commons Inquiry (House of Commons 1986), the so-called 'three
   wise men' enquiry of 1991–92 (Alexander, Rose and Woodhead 1992), and the government's Primary
   Strategy manifesto *Excellence and Enjoyment* (DfES 2003b).
4 UNICEF (2007); Alexander and Hargreaves (2007).
5 David Bell, DCSF Permanent Secretary, at the conference of the Cumbria Association of Secondary
   Headteachers in June 2003. The claim was repeated by the DCSF, the TDA and Ofsted.
6 See, for example, Cox and Dyson (1971); Phillips (1996); and numerous newspaper articles documented by
   Alexander (1997).
7 Simon (1981a); Alexander, Rose and Woodhead (1992): paras 19–23.
8 Letters to Robin Alexander from Peter Housden, Permanent Secretary at the Department for Education
   and Skills (DfES), 24 September 2004, and David Bell, Housden's successor, 30 June 2006; email from the
   Secretary of State's office, 20 October 2006.
9 http://www.primaryreview.org.uk/About_us/Whatisitsremit.html.
10 Brown and Lauder (1997); Steedman (1999); Robinson (1999).
11 Recent estimate for the number of languages spoken in England's primary schools: see Chapter 8.
12 House of Commons (2008a).
13 Submission from the Cambridge Primary Review to the Rose Review, 30 June 2008. The interim reports in
    question were the community soundings report (Alexander and Hargreaves 2007) and the research surveys
    by White (2010), Shuyab and O'Donnell (2010), Hall and Øzerk (2010), Wyse, McCreery and Torrance

(2010), Conroy and Menter (2010), Robinson and Fielding (2010), Riggall and Sharp (2010): *The Cambridge Primary Review Research Surveys*, Chapters 11, 12, 14, 28, 15, 2 and 13.

14 Rose (2008).
15 Alexander and Flutter (2009); Alexander (2009).
16 House of Commons (2009).
17 Rose (2009).
18 Board of Education (1931): para 75.
19 The authority for this glimpse into the workings of the Hadow Committee is provided by Brian Simon (1992), who cites his correspondence with a former HM Staff Inspector, Miss A.L. Murton. See also Alexander (2008a): 73.
20 Alexander (2008a): 74; Cazden (2001): 56.
21 Ereaut and Whiting (2008).
22 Kenway in Ball (1990).
23 Kenneth Clarke, Conservative Secretary of State for Education, 1990–92.
24 All these newspaper headlines are quoted and sourced in Alexander (1997). We illustrate this discourse mainly by headlines: it had its counterpart in political speeches.
25 Alexander, Rose and Woodhead (1992): para 22.
26 Quoted in Alexander, Rose and Woodhead (1992): para 21.
27 CACE (1967): para 513.
28 Prime Minister John Major at the Conservative Party conference, 1992.
29 Alexander (2008a): 73.
30 A selection of the newspaper headlines which greeted some of the Primary Review interim reports between October 2007 and May 2008. Many oversimplify and misrepresent the reports in question. For full coverage, see www.primaryreview.org.uk.
31 DCSF spokesperson, quoted in *Times Educational Supplement*, 2 November 2007.
32 DCSF spokesperson, quoted in *Times Educational Supplement*, 29 February 2008.
33 Secretary of State Ed Balls, quoted in The Independent, 29 February 2008.
34 DCSF Press Office briefing, 23.11.07, referring to the research survey commissioned as evidence to the Review from Professor Berry Mayall (2010), Cambridge Primary Review Research Surveys, Chapter 3. Neither she nor Robin Alexander had said what DCSF claimed.
35 Conor Ryan, former special adviser to the Secretary of State and member of the Downing Street Policy Unit, Conor's Commentary, 20.2.09: http://www.conorfryan.blogspot.com/2009/02/lets-not-go-back-to-70s-primary.html (accessed 29 April 2009).
36 See, for example, Phillips (2008) which dismissed Rose's proposals as 'crazy' and – notwithstanding his warnings to the contrary – as encouraging a return to the 'Plowden-style mish-mash of cross-curricular themes that left children ignorant and uneducated.'
37 Hobsbawm (1994): 3.

3 Policies and legacies

'Primary education has been in a state of almost continuous transition throughout its short history'.[1] So commented the late and great education historian Professor Brian Simon in 1980. Primary schooling was first accepted as official government policy in 1928 but it took 40 years to achieve the move away from 'all-age' schools and educate children between the ages of five and 11 in separate 'primary' schools. This chapter continues the story of the evolution of primary education over another 40 years – from 1967 to 2009. For this period too Brian Simon's generalisation holds. Primary education has been in a state of almost continuous change, though his specific point about 'separate' primary education does not quite hold: there has been an emergence, very recently and on a small scale, of 'all-through' ('all-age') schools.

Figures 3.1 and 3.2 provide demographic snapshots of the system and its pupils in 2008. Yet in 2008 English primary education remains a palimpsest, a manuscript on which later writing has not completely effaced or concealed earlier text. Primary education has evolved and altered but still bears traces of its earlier forms.

On the surface level there is not much evidence of far-reaching change. Between 1967 and 2008 the total number of primary schools dropped from 22,831 to 17,205 largely due to amalgamations and small school closures, but primary schools continue to outnumber secondary schools by a factor of at least three. The number of full-time equivalent pupils has dropped from 4,495,259 to 4,087,890,[2] but primary education still constitutes the largest single phase in English education. The average class size has dropped from 32.7 to 26.2 but remains far larger than secondary class sizes. The differentials in primary/secondary funding (to the detriment of the former) were almost as marked in 2008 as they were in 1967.

Scratch the surface a little and the changes appear more pronounced. Forty years on from 1967 a much larger number of under-fives are in primary schools and the ethnic and linguistic composition of those schools has changed beyond recognition. Plowden had one brief chapter entitled 'Children of immigrants', by which it meant those of West Indian, Indian, Pakistani and Cypriot background. The total recorded number in primary and secondary schools together (Plowden did not give separate numbers for primary schools) was 102,000, or just 2.2 per cent of the total school population. By 2008 nearly one-quarter of all *primary* pupils were classified by the Department for Children, Schools and Families (DCSF) as 'other than White British'. And while immigration continued, though from continental Europe now rather than the Commonwealth, most of these pupils were the children or grandchildren of immigrants and were as British as their 'White British' fellows. We examine these demographic and cultural changes, and their educational implications, in Chapter eight.

In 1967 English primary schools devised their own curriculum in accordance with guidelines provided by their local education authorities and, in the case of denominational schools, the churches. The 1944 Act, which still provided the statutory framework (governments in those days were less inclined to legislate at every turn) specified merely that schools must teach a 'religious' and 'secular' curriculum, that the former should be marked by a daily act of (Christian) worship and include religious instruction (with an opt-out clause for both parents and teachers), and that the latter should be the responsibility of LEAs. Since 1989 schools have

Schools	17,205
Pupils	4,087,890
Teachers	198,200
Support staff	172,600
Local authorities	150
Initial training providers	90
Average class size, primary	26.2
Average class size, secondary	20.9
School-based expenditure per pupil: primary (£)	3,360
School-based expenditure per pupil: secondary (£)	4,320

Figure 3.1 English primary schools in 2008[i]

[i] DCSF (2008u) figures. Note that the primary expenditure figure, like that for class sizes, conceals more favourable treatment of pupils in KS1 than KS2.

Aged under 5	826,550
Aged 5-10	3,254,230
Aged over 11	7,050
Pupils whose first language is English	85.5%
Pupils whose first language is other than English	14.4%
By ethnic group: White British	75.9%
By ethnic group: other than White British	23.3%

Figure 3.2 Pupils in English primary schools in 2008[i]

[i] DCSF (2008u) figures. 'Other than White British' includes (i) *White* (Irish, Traveller of Irish Heritage, Gypsy/ Roma, any other White background), (ii) *Mixed* (White and Black Caribbean, African, or Asian and any other mixed background), (iii) *Asian* (Indian, Pakistani, Bangladeshi, any other Asian background), (iv) *Black* (Black Caribbean, Black African, any other Black background), (v) *Chinese*, (vi) *Any other ethnic group*, (vii) *Unclassified* (hence the apparent discrepancy in the White British/other than White British total).

been required to teach a national curriculum which includes what in international terms is an exceptionally high level of detail and prescription, especially in numeracy and literacy.

In 1967, following the Labour government's Circular 10/65, which hastened the end of the 11-plus examination and selective secondary education in most local authorities (though some retain both to this day), primary schools were beginning to unpick the legacy of the 1944 Act's view that, as far as their 'abilities and aptitudes' were concerned, children naturally fell into three groups; that these were a matter of nature rather than nurture; and that they could be precisely measured. Thereafter, testing became less prominent, though it never disappeared: most local authorities, and most schools, continued to test children at the ages of 7 and/or 11 using standardised tests in reading and number from the National Foundation for Educational Research (NFER) and other agencies, and Fred Schonell's famous spelling lists and tests remained a regular if not popular feature of Friday mornings. Now, since 1989, but especially since 1997, primary pupils are subject to one of the most demanding testing regimes in the world, and hugely controversial it is, too (see Chapter 16).

In 1967, teachers in English primary schools – like those in much-admired Finland in 2009 – made their own decisions about how to teach. Sometimes this was within a framework of school or local authority policy. Often it was not. Even in 1991, the Secretary of State insisted that 'questions about how to teach are not for government to determine'.[3] This final professional barrier was unceremoniously breached by his government's New Labour successors in 1998–99, when the national literacy and numeracy strategies were imposed on all primary schools, if not legally (for at that stage they were in the form of 'guidance') then by force of the focus of Ofsted inspections. Now, in 2009, teaching methods in primary schools are subject to a degree of government prescription undreamt of four decades ago, and without parallel in most other countries. Many more examples could be cited of policy-led change in primary education.

Yet scratch still deeper through the educational palimpsest and underlying continuities emerge – continuities long predating Plowden. These include a curriculum dominated by the Victorian 'basics', an updated system of 'payment by results' which poet, essayist and school inspector Matthew Arnold[4] would have criticised; a Victorian pattern of staff deployment involving generalist class teachers; a concern for economy and parsimony which Robert Lowe[5] who introduced payment by results in the 1860s would have applauded, and a devaluing of primary compared with secondary education which Edmund Holmes, who became chief inspector in 1905[6] would have recognised.

This final report of the Cambridge Primary Review addresses issues at all three of these levels but this chapter provides an interpretative overview of developments at the second level – in particular a selection of policy-led changes, but also key events and initiatives that have helped shape contemporary policy and practice. It focuses, particularly but not exclusively, on curriculum, pedagogy and assessment, and it relates developments from 1967 to 2009 in terms of four phases. Each of the phases is given a descriptive title based on the degrees of freedom experienced by those working in primary schools and each ends just before a political/educational landmark. Many of the issues raised will be examined in more detail in later chapters.

1967–76: PRIMARY EDUCATION UNCHALLENGED

With 21st-century hindsight one of the most surprising features of this phase was the almost total absence of government policy directly related to, or of government intervention in, the primary curriculum and teaching methods. This was partly because the Education Act of 1944 left the curriculum as the responsibility of local education authorities and schools with the exception of religious instruction which was made a statutory requirement. The 1944 Act made no reference at all to teaching methods. Very few of the Plowden Report's 197 recommendations led to any central government policy initiatives. Initial steps were taken to introduce positive discrimination to combat social disadvantage through the establishment of educational priority areas but such initiatives had petered out by the mid-1970s. The recommendation to expand nursery education was recognised in the 1972 White Paper *A Framework for Expansion* which also promised to shift more resources towards primary schools. Both this redistribution and the nursery education plans were not realised, in part because of economic recession. Plowden's proposals to change the ages and stages of primary education never became government policy but were implemented by a number of LEAs as part of their secondary reorganisation plans and, in many cases, were later reversed. As recommended by Plowden, Her Majesty's Inspectorate (HMI) began work in 1974 on a survey to assess the quality of primary education 10 years on from Plowden[7] and in the same year the setting up of the Assessment of Performance Unit (APU) was announced.

Despite very real problems – for example, large class sizes by current standards, high teacher turnover and the continuation of the 11-plus in many areas – there was a sense of optimism in the system which was captured in the upbeat style, messages and rhetoric of Plowden itself. Primary education was expanding in terms of numbers of pupils (until 1974), resources and public and professional expectations. There was a sense of freedom (coupled with some anxiety and disorientation) over the removal of the restrictions on teacher initiative following the abolition in many areas of selection at 11. There was a rhetoric too of increased freedom for children to pursue their own needs and interests, though what research there was into primary classrooms[8] revealed in most cases either the continuance of overt teacher direction or the offer of an illusory freedom to do what teachers thought was in the children's best interests. At the same time, Figure 3.3 shows just how forward-looking Plowden was in respect of matters like tackling social disadvantage, increasing parental choice, the provision of universal nursery education and the upgrading of the teaching profession. Contrary to later parodies, this was a thoroughly grounded report, not a lapse into romantic excess.

Yet there arose the myth of a primary school revolution. It was founded to some degree on highly innovative practice in a few schools but was essentially the result of wishful thinking and firm advocacy by educationalists such as Christian Schiller, Alec Clegg, Robin Tanner, Edith Moorhouse, Stewart Mason, Mollie Brearley and John Blackie,[9] who occupied prominent positions in LEAs, the inspectorate and initial teacher education.[10] Though mythical, these ideas added to the sense of interest and anticipation in working in a system where the children, the teachers and the system itself were perceived to be full of unrealised possibilities. Teachers enjoyed (albeit rather anxiously) licensed autonomy; they were subject to only occasional inspection by HMI; and they were trusted by politicians and parents alike to take professional decisions about both the content of the curriculum and the way it should be taught and assessed. However, they did this within a broad implicit consensus concerning the centrality of reading, writing and mathematics.

There were, however, the beginnings of some counter-tendencies. Influential Black Paper writers[11] readily conflated primary education with 'permissive education' and 'the growth of anarchy'. Academics[12] began to question the philosophical foundations of so-called progressive thinking. In 1972 a disquieting report on reading standards was published, though its conclusions were not supported by the subsequent Bullock enquiry into English teaching.[13] By the end of 1975 there were other straws in the wind – including disturbing reports of an almost deliberate lack of order and structure in a London primary school (William Tyndale Junior School) and a remark by the Permanent Secretary at the Department of Education and Science (DES) wondering 'whether the Government could continue to debar itself from what had been termed "the secret garden of the curriculum"'.

The 1960s primary myth, then, had both positive and negative features. To some the period was – and nostalgically remains – a golden age of freedom, creativity, discovery, child-centredness and informality in curriculum, learning and relationships. To others it was a time of educational anarchy, 'trendy teachers' and low standards. However, reflecting on this range of views on the basis of the extensive evidence by then available, the 'three wise men' report of 1992 concluded:

> The commonly held belief that primary schools, after 1967, were swept by a tide of progressivism is untrue. HMI in 1978 for example, reported that only 5 per cent of classrooms exhibited wholeheartedly 'exploratory' characteristics and that didactic teaching was still practised in three quarters of them. The reality, then, was rather more complex. The ideas and practices connoted by words like 'progressive' and 'informal' had a profound impact in certain schools and LEAs. Elsewhere they were either ignored or adopted as so much rhetoric to sustain practice which in visual terms might look attractive and busy but which lacked any serious educational rationale. Here they lost their early intellectual excitement and became little more than a passport to professional approval and advancement. The real problem was not so much radical transformation as mediocrity.[14]

1976–87: PRIMARY EDUCATION CHALLENGED

In 1976 a new phase opened in the evolution of primary (and for that matter secondary) education, characterised by an increasing challenge to licensed autonomy by central government in particular. It saw the beginning of a major political initiative presaging increasing government concern over, and interest in, the school curriculum; it saw the publication of controversial critical research into so-called primary teaching styles; and it saw the end of the Auld public enquiry into the teaching, organisation and management of the William Tyndale Junior and Infant schools, the first of which was held by its critics as emblematic of many more.

The Prime Minister's Ruskin College speech of that year marked the beginning of a protracted yet strangely hesitant attempt by politicians directly to influence what was going on in state schools. James Callaghan argued that a variety of interested parties, not just teachers and parents but also government and industry, 'have an important part to play in formulating and expressing the purpose of education and the standards that we need'. A year on and a so-called but misnamed 'Great Debate' later, Callaghan's speech led to the first of a number of policy statements which stressed the need to establish 'broad agreement ... on a framework for the curriculum and, particularly, on whether ... there should be a "core" or "protected" part.'

Further documents were published by the DES[15] and, separately and in a very different vein, by HMI[16] to aid that process. From a primary perspective, the most important was the publication of HMI's primary survey in 1978.[17] Its evidence helped 'demythologise' the sector by indicating that the 'primary school revolution' (identified in the public's mind with the likes of William Tyndale Junior School) had not been tried and found wanting but had hardly ever been tried at all. Just 5 per cent of the schools surveyed practised 'exploratory' teaching; three-quarters of them remained resolutely 'didactic'; the remaining 20 per cent fell somewhere in between. The report stressed that all primary schools taught English and mathematics, but that beyond these there was considerable variation or inconsistency from school to school. HMI did, however, report a strong association between a broad curriculum and standards as measured by results on standardised tests. Further initiatives followed in pursuit of greater curriculum consistency. For example in DES Circular 14/77, LEAs were required to inquire into schools' curricula and, through their advisory services, to help achieve a professional consensus through the development of curriculum policies. Many ignored the government's request, which did not help their cause when later they complained about the loss of their powers under the 1988 Education Reform Act. In 1984 HMI began publishing a series of Curriculum Matters papers[18] to help further that consensus. These were authoritative, influential and controversial – but only for a brief period before they, too, were overtaken by events. By 1986 the DES claimed that 'wide agreement' had been achieved and that the government had no plans to introduce a statutory curriculum.[19]

Between 1976 and 1987 there were cautious moves by the DES to intervene in matters thought previously to be the professional preserve of teachers, though government was always careful to keep clear of pedagogy. The APU began to monitor the performance of primary pupils in language, mathematics and science. The DES watched with interest the development of school-based financial management in authorities such as Cambridgeshire and Hertfordshire and the introduction of widespread testing in a number of LEAs (for example, Croydon and Redbridge) to see how schools were performing in terms of measurable pupil outcomes. From 1984, the DES required all pre-service programmes of teacher training to be accredited by the new Council for the Accreditation of Teacher Education (CATE), in accordance with statutory criteria. It commissioned the Cockcroft Report into the teaching of mathematics. It took a growing interest in focussing and shaping teachers' professional development through introducing a number of in-service training grant schemes and education support grants to fund government initiatives such as mathematics teaching.

A notable exception to this cautious approach to education policy-making was the 1981 Education Act which followed the 1978 report of the enquiry into the education of handicapped children and young people.[20] The Act dealt with the definition, identification and provision for special educational needs, though still not in ways which infringed on teachers' autonomy in terms of curriculum and pedagogy.

More generally, the period 1976 to 1987 witnessed primary education having to cope with the challenges of falling rolls as pupil numbers dropped by almost a third between 1973 and 1985; of financial contraction consequent on the economic recession of the late 1970s and early 1980s; and of growing public and political concern over the quality of primary education. In 1976, a contentious but flawed study of teaching styles[21] fuelled debate, and concern, over the effects of so-called progressive teaching – a 'moral panic' increased by the publication of the Auld enquiry into the William Tyndale affair.[22] The HMI primary survey of 1978 revealed a substantial gap (inevitable to some degree) between professional rhetoric and practice. Classroom observational research[23] revealed a similar picture but failed to demonstrate a clear relationship between teaching 'style' (a suspect notion, in any event) and pupil attainment, except in so far as cognitively demanding teacher-pupil interaction was shown to be a condition of effective teaching however it was organised.

Nevertheless, factors within and beyond primary education helped consolidate the Black Paper authors' claim of educational decline, especially in literacy and numeracy standards. Though decision-making over curriculum, teaching and assessment remained largely in the hands of schools (and more particularly individual teachers), there was a loss of professional self-confidence in the face of continuing criticism – despite the fact there was no firm evidence from either the HMI primary survey or the APU of either a decline in educational standards or of children being accorded excessive 'degrees of freedom', let alone of Tyndale-style educational anarchy.

Thus, increasingly during this phase teachers were exercising a challenged autonomy as both central and local government began to develop policies for the curriculum and as LEAs tried to monitor and influence practice in individual schools. The publication in 1986 of the House of Commons Select Committee report, *Achievement in Primary Schools*, provides a useful marker for the end of this phase. With minor reservations it commended the view of the curriculum taken by the DES in Better Schools[24] and in the HMI *Curriculum Matters* series. In the words of Norman Thomas, former chief primary inspector and the report's author, its proposals 'would not require a Secretary of State to get into the more difficult issues of levels of children's performance. Nor would they, nor should they, require a definition of methods of teaching or school organisation'.[25] However, all of this was to change, and to change very quickly.

1987–97: PRIMARY EDUCATION REGULATED

The phase beginning in 1987 witnessed a sudden shift in the government's approach to education policy-making. In just two years political caution was replaced by assertion, and guidance by prescription. In 1986, Education Secretary Keith Joseph, in response to professional fears induced by 10 years of curriculum sabre-rattling, had announced that there would be no stat-utory national curriculum. Just one year later, his successor Kenneth Baker published the Education Reform Bill, the centrepiece of which was just that. The Education Reform Act (ERA) of 1988 was, according to Stuart Maclure, then editor of the *Times Educational Supplement*, 'the most important and far-reaching piece of educational law-making for England and Wales since the Education Act of 1944'.[26] It increased enormously the powers of the Secretary of State and thus of central government. It limited the functions of LEAs. It gave schools greater everyday control of their affairs, especially in relation to financial management and opting out of LEA control through acquiring grant-maintained status, but all within the context of a statutory and highly detailed curriculum comprising 10 subjects. Opposition education shadow Jack Straw echoed the views of many critics in arguing that the ERA would 'centralise power and control over schools, colleges and universities in the hands of the Secretary of State in a manner without parallel in the western world'.[27] This centralisation became even more marked with the introduction of mandatory testing at ages 7 and 11 and the publication of test results; and more marked still when Jack Straw's party, by then rebranded as New Labour, took over in 1997.

The context in which primary education operated was dramatically changed by the 1988 Act. For the first time since the abolition of the Elementary Code in 1926, primary schools were required to plan and teach curricula framed by a legal specification. For the first time since the widespread, though not universal, abolition of the 11-plus examination, primary schools had to work to an externally prescribed assessment system requiring the administration of tests to particular year groups, together with continuous assessment in the light of externally set criteria and the publication of the assessment data school-by-school (except for the very smallest schools). The ERA did, however, proscribe the Secretary of State from prescribing teaching methods or forms of curriculum organisation. Thus a form of 'regulated' autonomy was on offer, for the time being at least.

Within a few years of the introduction of the national curriculum (from 1989 onwards), concerns surfaced about the impossibility of covering the required material in the time available and about the overload placed on generalist class teachers attempting to teach across the whole primary curriculum.[28] The original testing arrangements also proved both problematic and burdensome. During the 1990s the range of testing was pared back, written tests were introduced in place of practically based assessment tasks, and assessment arrangements were subtly modified year on year. Anxieties over both curriculum and assessment prompted Sir Ron Dearing's wide-ranging review within just five years of the curriculum's introduction.[29] This led to an apparent scaling down of requirements.

Yet by 1996, on the eve of the transition to New Labour, inspection and research evidence suggested that the national curriculum had brought about real, though in political terms unspectacular, change. All primary schools were complying at least officially with national curriculum requirements as embodied in the statutory orders and programmes of study for its 10 subjects. Ostensibly, curriculum lottery had been replaced by entitlement. There was also growing pedagogical standardisation, more use of whole-class teaching, for example, and the growing prominence of national testing, which by then was fully established. These appeared to be producing a kind of neo-elementary curriculum[30] in which more time than ever was devoted to reading, writing and number (especially those elements found in national tests), with only rudimentary regard given to other subjects and focussing heavily on didactic teaching. Schools were responding in part to government concern over standards in numeracy and literacy occasioned by apparently unfavourable international comparisons and in part to pressure exerted by another major regulatory aspect of the post-1988 educational settlement – the establishment in 1992 of the Office for Standards in Education (Ofsted) headed by Her Majesty's Chief Inspector (HMCI).

This was a deliberate attempt by central government policy-makers to create what was in effect a privatised system of school inspection. Ofsted replaced HMI which had previously offered central government officials independent advice about the effects of government policy on schools on the basis of evidence gathered 'without fear or favour' through full inspections of schools, surveys and routine visits to schools. Although a number of individual HMI inspectors were retained by Ofsted to provide inspection expertise, the latter's remit was very different. Its main operational task was to oversee the introduction and regulation of a new system of school inspection. Inspectors working for private contractors were to ensure that, over a specified period, every maintained school in England had a full inspection based on published criteria. Ofsted's first national cycle of inspections of primary schools began in 1993 and was completed four years later. From its very inception, Ofsted inspection was the subject of considerable controversy in terms of its purposes (school accountability or school development), its relationship with government policy (independent evaluation or compromised validation) and, in particular, its effects on schools and individual teachers (positive or negative). Since 1993, the national cycle of inspections has been, and remains, a very powerful, though indirect, way of regulating the system by 'policing' primary schools' compliance with national directives and severely limiting high- or even medium-risk experimentation with content or process.

Ofsted's second chief inspector was particularly vocal, and controversial, in using his position to make sweeping public criticisms of the quality of teaching and standards in primary schools based on his personal views, rather than on due consideration of the evidence provided by his own inspectors. More than any other single individual, he was responsible for popularising a perception of low standards in the so-called 'basics'. This was epitomised by the statement in his 1996 annual report that standards of pupil achievement needed to be raised in about half of England's primary schools and his statement that 15,000 teachers were incompetent. His comments generated considerable criticism both from professionals and from educational researchers, not just about what one senior politician called the chief inspector's 'intemperate' utterances but also about the reliability of Ofsted's inspection methods and the inappropriate uses to which its findings were being put.[31] With the closure of the Assessment of Performance Unit in 1990 and the demise of HM Inspectorate two years later, there was by 1996 no independent, trusted body of test data or of inspection evidence on which to base this perception of low standards or widespread under-performance in English primary schools. However, that perception, nervousness about Ofsted and unease about what commentators – and we our-selves – have called the 'discourse of derision' (see Chapter 2) contributed to a striking decline in professional self-confidence, a decline not helped by government intervention in the last bastion of teacher autonomy: pedagogy.

Conscious of the ERA's proscription of ministerial involvement in pedagogy, officials moved carefully and indirectly. Exploiting the findings of a five-year study of primary education in Leeds[32] the government commissioned a report on teaching at the upper end of the primary phase from three leading educationists.[33] Whilst critical of poorly conceived practice, the 'three wise men' report re-affirmed the established view that 'questions about how to teach are not for government to determine'.[34] Drawing on evidence from research and inspection, it argued for teaching to be grounded in a broad repertoire of generic strategies and techniques. These would be drawn upon on the basis of 'fitness for purpose' in a way which reflected the unique circumstances of each classroom. The report also stressed that in the light of the now heavy curricular demands being placed on primary schools 'the problem of shortage of subject expertise is an acute one in primary education' and recommended 'the introduction of semi-specialist and specialist teaching to strengthen the existing roles of class teacher and consultant'.

Before long, however, one of the report's co-authors (Ofsted's controversial chief inspector), broke ranks and set off on a personal crusade to promote the particular cause of whole-class teaching, which the report had argued should be balanced by properly conceived group and individual work. The stage was set for much more direct government intervention in classroom life. In this he was helped by the somewhat aggressive tone of some of the report which appeared to many to be unduly critical of prevailing classroom practices. This, it was claimed, had alie-nated teachers and academics. However, Professor Brian Simon argued that beyond what he called the media/professional 'razzmatazz and hullabaloo', the report was firmly grounded in appropriate research and presented a coherent and sustainable position on pedagogy.[35] He applauded the report as the first government-sponsored statement of a position which by 2008 had moved firmly into the pedagogical mainstream:

> The outlook which underlines the whole thrust of this report relates to the emphasis put upon children's cognitive and linguistic competence. This view, based on recent research into children's learning … provides a firm theoretical base … But there is another theo-retical standpoint: the need to start from what children have in common as members of the human species, to establish the general principles of teaching and, in the light of these, to determine what modifications of practice are necessary to meet specific individual needs … The report emphasises the latent educability of the normal child … It stresses that the goals and procedures of teaching need to be founded on characteristics which children share rather than on those which differentiate them one from another … It emphasises the need for children to experience a sustained intellectual challenge within (and outside) the classroom … These ideas are very close to those of Lev Vygotsky.[36]

A largely forgotten but very important symbolic marker for the end of this regulatory phase was the 1996 Education Act's abolition of the requirement for central government to establish from time to time Central Advisory Councils for Education, of which Plowden, 30 years earlier, had been the last. Arguably by 1996 central government no longer felt the need for, or the value of, independent advice on 'primary education in all its aspects' – Plowden's original remit. Government reactions to the present enquiry will provide a useful test of how far that per-ception still prevails.

1997–2009: PRIMARY EDUCATION DOMINATED

1997 saw the election of a New Labour government. Its apologists made much of the sea-change in educational policy and practice that was initiated. They claimed that the previous government's policy of 'high challenge and low support' and 'uninformed prescription' was to be replaced by 'high challenge, high support' and 'informed prescription'.[37] The interpretation to be placed on these initiatives is controversial. Arguably, political intervention in the areas of curriculum, assessment and pedagogy represented an intensification, rather than transformation, of previous policy, though initiatives in relation to workforce reform and to the establishment of a more unified approach to children's services did constitute significant changes. Through this process of intensification, primary schools were dominated, not simply regulated, by central government directives, leaving them notionally with some 'degrees of freedom' but in reality with autonomy which was little more than rhetorical.

New Labour's attitude to primary education was captured in a passage from a pre-election policy statement:

> We do not share the view that primary school standards are adequate. They aren't. Fifty per cent of children are failing to reach appropriate levels in numeracy and literacy tests at age 11. This is unacceptable.[38]

Within a few days of the 1997 general election, the new government set ambitious national targets for 2002: that in literacy 80 per cent and in numeracy 75 per cent of 11 year olds should achieve at least level 4 in the national tests. Most children were now expected to attain a level originally set as an average. In the view of many of the Review's witnesses, these and other targets have come to dominate government policy and have produced an educational culture where measurable outcomes, rather than the quality of learning, have become sole criteria for success in primary education and where policies have been imposed on schools at a rate which has made their meaningful assimilation and implementation well-nigh impossible. By one count, between 1996 and 2004 government and national agencies issued 459 documents on the teaching of literacy alone, or more than one every week for eight years.[39]

In 1998 the government intervened in a review of the national curriculum which was in progress by reducing its requirements in all subjects except English and mathematics, in the conviction that this would greatly facilitate the delivery of the 1997 pledge on targets. The revised primary national curriculum, introduced from 2000 onwards, remained in force as a set of statutory requirements but was pre-empted in operational terms by the virtual imposition of two national strategies – the literacy strategy introduced from September 1998 and the numeracy strategy from September 1999.

Overseen by the Standards and Effectiveness Unit in the Department for Education and Employment (DfEE), these two strategies represented an unprecedented intervention in both the curriculum and pedagogy of primary education. Previous political inhibitions about directly prescribing pedagogy disappeared overnight. Daily literacy 'hours' and numeracy lessons were introduced. Detailed content was prescribed. Specified teaching methods were spelt out. Though in theory schools could opt out if their existing teaching programmes met the strategies' detailed requirements, the combination of government direction, LEA pressure and Ofsted inspection of the extent of schools' compliance meant that in reality the putative autonomy was rhetorical rather than real (and in the case of phonics teaching was withheld altogether in 2007 when mandated programmes were introduced for the very early stages in the teaching of reading).[40]

The speed of implementation of the strategies was swift and, for the most part, uncontested (though often subtly undermined in the privacy of some classrooms), with the numeracy strategy being more favourably received than its literacy counterpart. Ofsted evaluations of the impact of the strategies were almost entirely positive – unsurprising given the close alignment from 1997 onwards of Ofsted's and central government's diagnosis of, and prescription for, primary education's supposed deficiencies. The officially commissioned evaluation of the implementation of the strategies was more nuanced. Teachers were giving yet more emphasis to literacy and numeracy and changing their practice to some degree, but the researchers were much less certain that teachers had internalised the thinking behind the strategies or would be able to develop their practice beyond the surface requirements of official prescription.[41]

Around the same time a clutch of independent research studies[42] were similarly sceptical of the degree of genuine change brought about by adherence to the strategies.

In 2003, mindful of some of the criticisms made of the impact of the strategies on curriculum, pedagogy, professional creativity and autonomy, the Department for Education and Skills (DfES) published the curiously named *Excellence and Enjoyment*. This set out plans for a primary national strategy. It was unclear whether its drafters were genuinely trying to connect with, and re-interpret, educational thinking they associated with the Plowden era, or were cynically attempting to suborn those primary teachers disenchanted with post-1997 rhetoric. At first glance, Excellence and Enjoyment seemed to offer hope of a more flexible and creative approach to the primary curriculum, as it argued that 'teachers have more freedom than they often realise to design the timetable and decide what and how to teach'.[43] Looking at it more closely it was clear from the document and the welter of accompanying material published later that the strategy was less about enshrining 'excellence', 'enjoyment', 'breadth' and 'balance' (whatever these mean) than about embedding the literacy and numeracy strategies through new frameworks, meeting the revised national targets for English and mathematics at the end of key stage 2 and ensuring continuity with the key stage 3 strategy.[44] Unlike with the other strategies, no outside evaluation of the Primary National Strategy was commissioned. The review of the primary curriculum announced by the government in 2007 involved consideration of the impact of all three national strategies, though its terms of reference implied the continuance of a preoccupation with the traditional 'basics' at the expense of the more balanced response and creative curriculum hinted at in *Excellence and Enjoyment*.

Inevitably the focus on literacy and numeracy in these three national initiatives dominated the balance of the primary curriculum as a whole. Longitudinal research and inspection have repeatedly confirmed what teachers claimed – that since 1997 in very many schools there has been an increased concentration of teaching time on English and mathematics and a marked diminution in the time allocated to other foundation subjects.[45] Yet – and it will be a recurrent theme in this report – a commitment to high standards in literacy and numeracy is in no way incompatible with the pursuit of curriculum breadth and diversity. Indeed, echoing the finding of HMI in its major 1978 primary survey, Ofsted reports in 1997 and 2002 found that schools which were most successful in terms of key stage 2 test results in English and mathematics were often the most successful in delivering a curriculum which was broad, balanced and well managed.[46] The basics are meaningless without a context for their acquisition and application, and excellent teaching in primary schools appears to include the capacity to keep the larger goals of education firmly in view. Yet the lessons of these three important reports – also noted in the 1985 White Paper *Better Schools*[47] – have by and large not been heeded and the Cambridge Primary Review's witnesses tend to share the view that children's entitlement to a broad and balanced curriculum, much trumpeted in the aftermath of the 1988 Education Reform Act and again in *Excellence and Enjoyment*, has been compromised by recent policies, especially but not only in schools deemed by Ofsted to be in need of improvement or special measures.

The recent focus has also had repercussions for primary teacher education and training,[48] where at pre-service level intending primary teachers have been subject to a curriculum heavily dominated by preparation to teach literacy and numeracy in accordance with the national strategies, with little attention paid to the other foundation subjects and little time for trainees to reflect on wider professional issues and debates or, for that matter, on the recent history of primary education which could help provide a context for such reflections. This too is a significant theme in evidence to the Cambridge Primary Review. A similarly critical picture could be painted of continuing professional development since 1997 with the decline in the number of courses of advanced independent study, an almost exclusive emphasis on training and consultancy in literacy and numeracy, national leadership programmes constructed so as to advance government policies but little else, and the establishment of set upon set of officially produced professional 'standards' which fail to value critical, evidence-informed professional judgement unconstrained by official orthodoxies. All these trends raise very serious questions about the condition of the primary teaching profession as it now stands, and indeed about how far the usual connotations of the word 'profession' still apply.

However, arguably, it is in the area of testing and assessment that the process of intensification and domination was taken the furthest. Originally introduced to check on the progress of individual pupils, national tests came to be used for several different, some would say contradictory, purposes. Under the 1997 government's standards regime, national testing was used not only for assessing individual pupils' performance but also, through the publication of test data for 11 year olds in so-called performance tables, to evaluate the performance of teachers, school and local authorities.[49] As a result, both compulsory and 'optional' testing and test preparation came to dominate the experience of primary children and teachers, especially in key stage 2. They reinforced a narrowing of the curriculum already dominated by literacy and numeracy, had a detrimental effect on many children's (and teachers') attitudes and self-perceptions,[50] and constrained primary pedagogy. By placing so much emphasis on test data in its 'light-touch' inspections, Ofsted inspectors also reinforced the testing culture. The value and effects of national testing were disputed by both teachers and academics and were the subject of a critical House of Commons Select Committee report.[51] Although some changes were made to assessment at the end of key stage 1 and new tests were piloted for use during, rather than at the end of, key stages, the government re-iterated that 'testing, targets and tables are here to stay'[52] and did not include them in the Rose Review of the primary curriculum announced in 2007. In 2008, children in England remained among the most tested in the world. We consider these matters in detail in Chapter 16.

In its pursuit of test-related targets, the government made great play of the supposed overall improvement in primary pupils' performance since 1997, as measured by the tests. Analysis of test data and independent research revealed some evidence of increases in test performance over time but mainly in the period 1995 to 2000 (followed by a general levelling off of results thereafter).[53] Of particular importance was the Statistics Commission's conclusion in 2005 that 'the improvement in key stage 2 test scores between 1995 and 2000 substantially overstates improvements in English primary schools over that period'.[54] Important too is the fact that no evidence was collected and published about changes in children's performance in any of the other foundation subjects. These were not regarded as important enough to justify investment in their testing. The vexed question as to whether standards are rising or falling in English primary schools comprises in reality a number of different questions, none of which can be answered with precision – certainly not with the precision of a percentage point or a contextual value-added score. These matters are explored more fully in Chapter 17.

Rather than representing an intensification of the previous government's polices, New Labour's workplace reform strategy[55] represented a new departure, though some critics see it as pursuing a myth of modernisation rather than a carefully thought-through policy of preparing schools and teachers for the managerial challenges of the 21st century. Together with *Raising Standards and Tackling Workload* – an agreement signed by most education unions, employers and the government in 2003 – the strategy initiated a major reorganisation of school management and teachers' pay. This resulted in a large expansion in the number and use of support assistants, the allocation of 10 per cent of teachers' time for planning, preparation and assessment (PPA), redesigned patterns of career progression and the introduction of a new performance management system central to which was the criterion of pupil progress – to be 'measured' by test data or level-related assessment.

Probably the most innovative and ambitious of New Labour's later education policy initiatives was heralded in the 2003 green paper, *Every Child Matters*[56] which was followed by the Children Act of 2004. These redefined the relationship between children's well-being (conceived in terms of five broad outcomes) and educational achievement and led to all English local authorities establishing children's services to co-ordinate the work of all agencies concerned with children's well-being and schooling in the hope of creating coherent, responsive provision.

Part of this strategy involved the development of extended primary schooling where a variety of education provision and care would be provided outside the normal school day and where there would be access to, and liaison with, external services (social services, child care, health care). The initiative also led to widespread recognition of the need for the state to intervene to support vulnerable children and their families.[57] From 2003, increasing attention was being paid to the condition of childhood – symbolised by the appointment of the first Children's Commissioner for England in 2005, carried forward by the Children's Society's Good Childhood Inquiry and embodied in the Children's Plan of 2007[58] with its concerns 'to secure the well-being and health of children and young people ... to safeguard the young and vulnerable' and, perhaps predictably (but importantly) given the government's focus on pupil performance, 'to close the gap in educational achievement for disadvantaged children'.

CONCLUSION

Brian Simon, whose words opened this chapter, maintained that 'only historical analysis can throw light on the changing forms of primary education'.[59] Building on that precept this brief historical overview has traced the evolution of English primary education since 1967 in the conviction that an understanding of the recent historical context is crucial to any understanding of current policy and practice, and in the belief that, despite the assumptions of government apologists and writers of official documentation, the history of primary education did not begin in 1997. As we argued in Chapter 2, far too much of the rhetoric surrounding recent policy has been perversely and quite deliberately ahistorical. The real achievements of the period before 1997 have been ignored or denied. Wheels have been pointlessly re-invented. Initiatives have been introduced at such a pace that they have been superseded before being properly evaluated. The lessons of past attempts at reform have not been learned. The lessons of past research and development have been treated as irrelevant not because they are genuinely inapplicable but merely because they are more than a few months old, or maybe because they challenge the preferred political agenda. Yet knowledge, understanding and progress, in policy as in the classroom, grow by cumulation – by understanding, respecting, learning from and building upon past experience – not by the relentless quest for novelty. This is a matter to which, perforce, we return in the closing chapters of this report.

Meanwhile, by way of example, we note that parental choice of schools, a recent flagship policy, was first recommended by Plowden in 1967; the 1998 education action zones were little different from the Plowden-recommended educational priority areas of the 1970s; Plowden argued strongly for the multi-agency collaboration that only began to become an achievable reality with *Every Child Matters* and the 2004 Act;[60] the 2008 Williams Report's proposal to appoint 13,000 mathematics specialists[61] closely resembles the 1986 Commons Select Committee's recommendation that 15,000 extra primary teachers would enable schools' subject strengths to be properly used[62] (and indeed we understand that Peter Williams initially recommended the same number of extra teachers as the 1986 Select Committee, but was asked to reduce it); national testing at 7, 11, 14 and 16 was the invention of neither New Labour nor the Conservatives but of the authors of the 1975 Black Paper;[63] and while successive governments castigate 'progressive' teachers and launch 'back to basics' missions with monotonous regularity, they remain seemingly impervious to the fact that the one thing that primary schools have never in their history neglected is the basics and that progressivism was never more than a minority pursuit.

Of course there are other histories. This chapter has concentrated on policy because during the past 20 years this has become such a powerful force, and the trajectory marked in Figure 3.3 shows very clearly the onward march of centralisation, its acceleration since 1997 and its perhaps surprisingly early roots (for it is certainly quite wrong to treat the 1988 Education Reform Act as a bolt from the blue). But a 'bottom-up' history of primary education in the style of Howard Zinn's 'people's history' of the United States[64] would yield different perspectives, not least in this era of children's voices, while concentrating on the march of educational *ideas*, rather than on policies, would yield yet more.

Thus, another great scholar and advocate of primary education, Professor Alan Blyth, unravelled distinct 'elementary', 'developmental' and 'preparatory' traditions which forged an uneasy alliance in post-1944 English primary education,[65] and there are those who suggest that by 2000 the growing drive to instrumentality and utilitarianism had returned primary education, if not to the Victorian era, then certainly to a kind of neo-elementary condition.[66] One only has to recall the political appeal of the slogan 'back to basics' and the number of political speeches which use the phrase 'Let us return to ...' in order to recognise the lure of the past. But it is a past never properly known or understood, a carelessly-evoked and rose-tinted view of what school and classroom life were like in the 1870s or (more usually) the 1950s. Yet the tension between elementary and developmental (or progressive) in English primary education remains perennial and powerful. We shall return to it in Chapter 13.

It is for all these reasons that we start our consideration of primary education today and tomorrow by reflecting on primary education yesterday. Together with a firm commitment to engaging with contemporary and international realities, this historical sense will pervade much of what follows. To adapt the title of one of the most important curriculum development projects of the 1970s, another brainchild of Alan Blyth, English primary education is embedded in place, time and society and it is only in relation to these that it can be properly understood.[67]

FIGURE 3.3. ENGLISH PRIMARY EDUCATION: POLICY MILESTONES 1944–2009

Explanatory note: by 'milestones' we mean events or publications in the domain of policy which have either affected the provision and conduct of primary education directly through legislation (as in the case of the Acts of 1944, 1988, 1992, 1996, 2004, 2005 and 2006) or – as with influential reports or initiatives like Circular 10/65, Plowden, Warnock, Bullock, Cockcroft and the post-1997 national strategies – have had an impact on the way people think and talk about primary education.

1944–1976

1944	'Butler' Education Act	Establishes primary education in law, sets 'tripartite' framework for selective secondary schooling and gives local education authorities (LEAs) oversight of the 'secular' curriculum. School-leaving age to be raised from 14 to 15.
1948	CACE junior school enquiry	Unpublished report anticipates findings of 1980s research by concluding that there are widespread misunderstandings about the 'activity methods' encouraged by the 1931 Hadow Report.
1959	Primary *Handbook of Suggestions*	Geoffrey Lloyd, the then Minister of Education, commends the new Ministry primary education *Handbook*, the first to focus on primary (as opposed to elementary) education. Strong developmental emphasis and detailed curriculum guidelines. Note respect for professional autonomy: 'Handbook of Suggestions for the consideration of teachers and others ...'[68]
1960	Three year initial training	The majority route into primary teaching, the Teaching Certificate, is extended from two years to three. The training colleges continue to be the main provider.
1964	Schools Council established	Initiates an era of curriculum experimentation involving partnership between LEAs, universities and schools. However, it is criticised as a poodle of the unions and LEAs, and most of its highly innovative curriculum development projects have limited impact on schools. But several stand the test of time and still serve as paradigms of exceptional importance: the secondary Humanities Curriculum Project foreshadows dialogic teaching and philosophy for children in the handling of controversial issues. Science 5-13 heralds a third 'basic', spells the end of mere 'nature study' and influences the treatment of science in the 1988 National Curriculum. Communication Skills in Early

Childhood places classroom talk centre-stage. Meanwhile, though not under the auspices of the Council, Eric Midwinter's educational priority area project, with its emphasis on community schools, local engagement and a locally relevant curriculum anticipates 1998 education action zones.

1965 Circular 10/65	Department of Education and Science invites local authorities 'to reorganise secondary education on comprehensive lines'. Up to this point primary heads have supported streaming. Now, with Plowden coming out against it and 10/65 spelling the gradual demise of the 11-plus, their views change quite quickly. First BEd courses introduced: beginning of drive to make teaching a graduate profession.
1967 Plowden Report	Key document in the development of English primary education. Main recommendations: full parental participation in schooling, and parental choice of schools; educational priority areas to secure 'positive discrimination' in areas of social disadvantage; co-operation between educational, health and social services; 10-yearly surveys of the quality of primary education; nursery education to be available to all three to five year-olds; structure to change from infant/junior to first/middle; end of 11-plus as a basis for secondary selection; regular national surveys of attainment in reading and mathematics; teaching to use a combination of individual, group and whole-class work; elimination of streaming for five- to seven year-olds and its phasing-out for seven to 11 year-olds; full enquiry into 'needs of handicapped children'; introduction of teachers' 'aides'; strengthening of advisory service to meet demands of expanding curriculum; full enquiry into primary teacher training; schools to appoint more men, graduates and mature teachers; expansion of continuing professional development; nursery assistants and teaching assistants to be trained; democratisation of school governance.[69]
1969 Back to basics	Black Papers One and Two initiate anti-progressive backlash. 'Plowden generation', now aged two, is bizarrely blamed for the 1968 student unrest.
1972 The James 'training tricyle'	James Report on teacher training published. Recommends coherent cycle of initial training, induction and in-service.
Raising of school leaving age (ROSLA)	School-leaving age rises from 15 to 16.
1974 Assessment of Performance Unit	Announcement of setting up of an Assessment of Performance Unit (APU) marks first attempt systematically to monitor national standards (in languages, English, maths, science, aesthetic development, personal and social development, and physical development) at ages 11 and 14, in accordance with Plowden recommendation.
1975 Circular 5/75	Massive cuts in teacher-training numbers following post-war slump in the birth rate. Many training colleges (now called 'colleges of education') close or merge following publication of hit list in 1977.
A Language for Life	Bullock Report into the teaching of English published. Further undermines claims that schools are concentrating on 'creativity' at the expense of 'basics'. Argues for an updated concept of literacy in which language is central, and for all schools to have a policy for language across the curriculum. While endorsing the centrality of reading and writing, urges greater attention to talking, listening and drama.[70]

	The William Tyndale affair	Rumours of anarchy at William Tyndale Junior School fuel right-wing claims about rampant progressivism and lead to the Auld inquiry, published in 1976.[71] This and Callaghan's Ruskin speech seen by many as the tipping point: from now on, the shift towards direct government intervention in the work of schools seems inevitable.
1976	Callaghan's Ruskin College speech	In October, Prime Minister James Callaghan launches his 'Great Debate' on education. Its content is foreshadowed in the leaked 'Yellow Book' *School Education in England: problems and initiatives*: standards in the 3Rs, rigour in the teaching of maths and science, adequacy of school examination system, and provision for 16 to 19 year-olds not going on to higher education. Hints at possibility of a national curriculum. Criticism of 'informal' teaching methods, though Callaghan denies Black Paper influence. Teaching unions oppose end of 100 years of government non-interference in the work of schools and the 'attempt to turn teachers into navvies' (Terry Casey of the National Association of Schoolmasters).

1977–1987

1977	Circular 14/77	DES requests details of LEA arrangements for the curriculum, as under the 1944 Act. Many authorities ignore the request: beginning of the end for their curriculum control. Further requests follow: government report eventually issued in 1986.
1978	*Primary Education in England*	Following Plowden recommendation, major HMI survey, 10 years on, identifies serious inconsistencies in curriculum breadth, balance, quality and management across primary schools, but also scotches the myth of a post-1967 progressive takeover.[72] The myth-makers take no notice. Other reports in the same series, on first, combined and middle schools, follow.[73]
	Special Educational Needs	Enquiry chaired by Mary Warnock publishes highly influential report *Special Educational Needs: the education of handicapped children*, which encourages integration of children with SEN, as far as possible, into mainstream schooling and signals move towards a more inclusive pattern of public education.[74] The enquiry was recommended by Plowden.
1980	*A Framework for the Curriculum*	First of long series of contrasting (and competing) government and HMI views of what the school curriculum should contain.[75] HMI responded with *A View of the Curriculum*.[76] In those days the inspectorate was genuinely independent.
	Routes into teaching	The PGCE overtakes the 3/4 year undergraduate course as the majority route into teaching, except for primary.
1982	Cockcroft Report	Major report on mathematics education identifies seven-year gap between highest and lowest attainers by age 11.[77]
1983	*The Content of Initial Training*	Government paper heralds the end of university dominance of teacher training and paves the way for a national teacher-training curriculum, with all courses accredited by the Council for the Accreditation of Teacher Education (CATE), established in 1984. Procedures confirmed in DES Circular 3/84.[78]
	Grant-related in-service training	Beginning of government control of teachers' in-service training: funds to be targeted at government priorities.
1984	Schools Council abolished	

1985	*Better Schools*	White Paper reinforces HMI insistence that standards in literacy and numeracy are not achieved by neglecting the rest of the curriculum, and argues for breadth, balance and progression.[79]
1986	*Achievement in Primary Schools*	Select Committee report identifies problems in schools' ability to teach a broad and consistent curriculum. Proposes 15,000 extra teachers to give schools the flexibility to capitalise on teachers' specialist strengths.[80] Not implemented.
1987	Education Reform Bill	Proposes national curriculum, national testing, local schools budgetary management and reduction in LEA powers.

1988–1997

1988	Education Reform Act	Introduces national curriculum of three core and seven other foundation subjects and 'arrangements for assessing pupils at or near the end of each key stage' which subsequently became national tests at age 7, 11 and 14. Curriculum overseen by National Curriculum Council (NCC) and assessment by School Examinations and Assessment Council (SEAC); these later merged as the School Curriculum and Assessment Authority (SCAA) and then the Qualifications and Curriculum Authority. New arrangements for financing local authority maintained schools (local management of schools) give schools new financial freedoms, including delegated budgets, and are largely welcomed by primary schools. Introduces 'grant-maintained' (GM) schools giving schools the freedom to opt out of local authority control and receive funding directly from central government in the form of a grant. By 1996 there were 1,090 GM schools, of which 40 per cent were primary schools. Under the School Standards and Framework Act 1998, GM was abolished. Former GM schools could choose to become foundation schools or maintained community schools. The 1998 ERA marks shift from local to central government control 'in a manner without parallel in the western world' (Jack Straw, the then Shadow Secretary of State).
1991	National tests	First full run of tests at age 7. Results published in LEA league tables in December.
	Parents' charter	Government introduces raft of accountability measures: written school reports on every child; end of HMI and introduction of regular school inspection by registered independent inspectors; school performance league tables to be published; test results, truancy rates and school-leavers' destinations to be published in governors' reports.
1992	'Three wise men'	Publication of government-commissioned report on primary education at key stage 2 refocusses attention on the character and quality of primary school pedagogy. Also argues for more flexible approach to primary staff deployment, to enable schools to exploit teachers' specialist strengths and children to experience greater consistency in curriculum quality across all subjects. Provokes heated political, media, professional and academic debate.[81] Ofsted follows up with reports on impact in 1993, 1994 and 1995.[82]
	Education (Schools) Act	Office for Standards in Education replaces HMI. School inspectors may now come from any walk of life. Inspection teams must include at least one lay member. Inspections in effect privatised. Small HMI contingent retained for training, regulation and national surveys.

	Back to basics again	Conservative government launches fierce attack on 'progressive' teaching in primary schools in run up to general election, which it goes on to win.
1993	Education Act	Creates Funding Agency for Schools and SCAA, consolidated successor to the separate curriculum and assessment councils established in 1988.
	Circular 14/93	CATE outlines proposals for primary initial teacher training, the first time the distinctiveness of primary teaching has been thus recognised. On pedagogy, it is in line with the 'three wise men' proposals.[83]
	Dearing review	Final report of the Dearing review of the national curriculum proposes ways to make the curriculum more manageable, freeing 20 per cent of time for schools' own curriculum priorities.[84] Given that government has insisted that more than 50 per cent should be devoted to literacy and numeracy, and that eight subjects have to be squeezed into the other 50 per cent, the proposals get nowhere.
	Union boycott	The NUT and NASUWT boycott the National Curriculum tests.
1994	Teacher Training Agency	Under the Education Act 1994, the Teacher Training Agency (TTA) replaces CATE and acquires additional powers: control of teacher-training supply and funding, as well as content. Ushers in contentious era of teacher-training 'standards' and 'competencies' with which providers must comply or be closed down.
	The disparity in funding	Select Committee report deplores continuing wide disparity in funding between primary and secondary schools and recommends monitoring and support time for all primary teachers 'while teaching is in progress'.[85] Not implemented.
	External marking	External markers are introduced for National Curriculum tests at KS2 and KS3.
1996	Education Act	Consolidates recent legislation.
	National Literacy and Numeracy	National literacy and numeracy projects for primary schools are introduced as projects by the Conservatives and later adapted as New Labour's national literacy and numeracy strategies.
1997	National curriculum review	SCAA launches the statutory first full curriculum review. Qualifications and Curriculum Authority Education Act 1997 replaces SCAA by the Qualifications and Curriculum Authority (QCA).
	'Education, education, education'	New Labour general election landslide heralds dramatic increase in pace and penetration and centralisation of educational reform, together with considerable additional investment.
	Excellence in Schools	White Paper sets out New Labour's main education policies, including national literacy and numeracy strategies and test targets for 2002.[86] Secretary of State David Blunkett says he will resign if these are not met.

1998–2009

1998	Back to basics yet again	Ostensibly to secure its national literacy and numeracy strategies, the government removes primary schools' obligation to teach the national curriculum programmes of study in other than the three core and tested subjects.

	School Standards Act	Places limit on infant class sizes; establishes education action zones (EAZs); requires LEAs to prepare education development plans; makes new provision for early years education.
	General Teaching Council	Teaching and Higher Education Act establishes General Teaching Council (GTC) for England and Wales and introduces qualifications for head teachers.
	National Literacy Strategy (NLS)	NLS implemented from September. Spells out the method as well as the detailed content of daily literacy lessons for children aged 5–11. Non-statutory, but treated by Ofsted and most LEAs as obligatory, so schools fall into line.
	Sure Start	First 250, then 520 Sure Start programmes introduced to support parents of children aged under three in areas of high need.
1999	*The Work of Ofsted*	Report of 1998–99 Select Committee enquiry is highly critical of Ofsted, its high stakes inspection (especially of teacher training) and its chief inspector: 'We now need less heat and more light.'[87] Formal government response rejects all criticism of chief inspector, who nevertheless resigns a year later.[88]
	All Our Futures	Report of government-commissioned enquiry, led by Professor Ken Robinson, into creative and cultural education. Important, visionary and timely, and with superstar membership of its committee, including Lenny Henry and Simon Rattle; yet it is the right report at the wrong time and fails to moderate the obsession with the 3Rs.
	National Numeracy Strategy (NNS)	NNS introduced: method as well as content of daily numeracy lessons specified in detail. Like the NLS it is treated as statutory even though it is not. Generally regarded as better founded empirically, less contentious and more successful than the NLS.
	Early Learning Goals	Government published 'early learning goals' to guide early years practitioners.
2000	National curriculum	Following the 1997-8 review and the government's 1998 intervention, a revised national curriculum is introduced in September. Little change from previous version in fundamentals, though much slimmed down. Addition of citizenship, though optional at KS1/2. Creativity, the arts and the humanities continue to cling by their fingertips in the primary phase, especially in Years 5 and 6.
	Foundation stage	Following publication of the 1999 early learning goals, a 'foundation stage' for children aged 3–5 is introduced with a curriculum organised into six areas of learning.[89]
2002	Literacy and numeracy targets	The KS2 test targets set in 1997 are not met.
2003	*Every Child Matters* (ECM)	Key New Labour initiative marks significant change to services to secure the well-being of all children from birth to 19, but especially those at risk of abuse. Local authorities to provide 'joined-up' education and care services with multi-agency co-ordination and extended schools. Every child to have the necessary support to be healthy, stay safe, enjoy and achieve, make a positive contribution, and achieve economic well-being (the five ECM 'outcomes').[90]

	Children's Commissioner	First Children's Commissioner appointed, and Office of the Children's Commissioner established, to promote awareness of the views and interests of children and young people.
	Sure Start extended	1998 scheme expanded to place Sure Start children's centres in the 20 per cent most disadvantaged areas.
	Excellence and Enjoyment	Department for Education and Skills' paper proposes new strategy for primary schools which ostensibly encourages creativity and fun while securing standards.[91] In fact, the Primary National Strategy merely consolidates the literacy and numeracy strategies and maintains the sharp 1998 distinction between standards in the basics (= 'excellence') and children's entitlement to a broad curriculum (= 'enjoyment').
	Social Partnership Agreement	A national agreement signed by all but one of the school workforce unions (the NUT), local government employers and the government. Brought about significant changes to teachers' conditions of service and enhanced roles for school support staff. The agreement also called for workforce 'remodelling'. Signatories work in social partnership through the Workforce Agreement Monitoring Group (WAMG) and the Rewards and Incentives Group (RIG). The NAHT withdrew from the Partnership in 2005 but re-joined in 2007. The NUT remained outside. One generally perceived outcome of the agreement is a reduction in professional criticism of the government and a consolidation of the culture of compliance with non-statutory advice and guidance as well as statutory requirements.
2004	The Children Act	*Every Child Matters* passes into law, commanding widespread support.
	Childcare strategy	Government pre-budget report announces strategy to provide affordable, high-quality and flexible childcare for all families with children up to the age of 14.[92]
2005	Education Act	Aims to raise standards in all schools: more efficient inspection, budgetary reform, profiles of every school's performance.
	Training and Development Agency	Under the 2005 Act the TTA is replaced by the Training and Development Agency for Schools (TDA) which is given additional responsibility for the wider schools workforce and continuing professional development.
	Higher standards, better schools	White Paper radically extends standards agenda. Primary and secondary schools allowed to become independent state schools ('trust schools') backed by private sponsors. Failing schools may be taken over by trusts. Parents may set up new schools, close failing schools and sack head teachers. Good schools encouraged to expand or federate. Local authorities to lose most of their residual powers and become 'parents' champions' rather than 'education providers'. Schools encouraged to 'personalise' education, especially for struggling pupils.[93]
2006	Ofsted reborn	Education and Inspections Act redesignates Ofsted as the Office for Standards in Education, Children's Services and Skills. Chief inspector's title changed to match.
	Strong and Prosperous Communities	White Paper aims to give communities more power to improve local services. Further emphasis on partnership and multi-agency working.[94]
	Childcare Act	New duties for local authorities on childcare, and new regulatory regime for childcare providers.

	Review of the teaching of early reading	Government-commissioned report from Jim Rose seeks to resolve debate about the place of phonics in the teaching of reading, in light of claims that phonics had been neglected despite their prominence in the requirements for the National Curriculum. Report prescribes that 'high quality phonic work should be taught as the prime approach to learning to decode (to read) and to encode (write/spell) print.'[95]
2007	*Every Parent Matters*	Sets out rights and responsibilities of parents. Home-school agreements to be strengthened; parents part of social and emotional aspects of learning (SEAL) programme; all schools to have access to extended services by 2010; local authorities to provide full range of information to all parents about local and national services.[96]
	The Children's Plan	December White Paper announces 10-year strategy 'to make England the best place in the world for children and young people to grow up.' New, higher targets for literacy and numeracy at age 11; for GCSEs; for A-levels and access to higher education; and on child poverty and health. Government softens line on testing, initiating the development of 'stage not age' tests which children take when they are ready. All schools to be zero carbon by 2016.[97]
	Primary curriculum review (i)	Children's Plan announces that the QCA arm's-length secondary review will be followed not by a similarly arm's-length look at primary schools but by a 'root and branch' review led by Sir Jim Rose under the direct control of the DCSF. Interim report in December 2008; final report published April 2009.
	Narrowing the Gap	In its first report, major government-funded project proposes strategies for improving the performance of Children's Trusts in narrowing the gap between vulnerable and excluded children and the rest, against a context of 'improving outcomes for all.' Main focus on children aged 3–13.[98]
2008	Children and Young Persons' Bill	Proposes reforms to statutory framework for the care system to improve quality of care and align this with the work of schools.
	Primary Capital Programme	Start of projected programme to rebuild, remodel or refurbish half of England's primary schools by 2022–23 at an eventual cost of £7 billion. DCSF and LAs each contribute £1.75 billion during the first two years.
	Preparing Britain for the Future	Draft legislative programme maintains focus on standards and equity: every school to become a good school; targets at 11, 16 and 18 confirmed; Children's Trusts to be strengthened.
	Strengthening maths teaching	Final report of government-commissioned Williams review of mathematics teaching in primary schools and early years settings recommends that within 10 years there should be a maths specialist in every primary school,[99] requiring an extra 13,000 teachers. (An old idea recycled: in 1986 15,000 extra teachers were commended by the Commons Select Committee to strengthen curriculum planning and management.)
	Testing, testing	The House of Commons Children, Schools and Families Committee publishes a critical report on the national tests, arguing that they distort the curriculum, expose children and teachers to excessive pressure and invalidly conflate the functions of individual assessment and school accountability.[100] The government rejects the criticisms, then abandons the KS3

tests.[101] The KS2 tests remain, and the DCSF sets up 'expert group' to advise on keeping preparation for the tests 'proportionate and appropriate' and on their use in easing transition to KS3.[102]

Early Years Foundation Stage	The Early Years Foundation Stage (EYFS) brings together *Curriculum Guidance for the Foundation Stage* (2000), the *Birth to Three Matters* (2002) framework and the *National Standards for Under 8s Daycare and Childminding* (2003), aiming to build a coherent and flexible approach to care and learning for all children from birth to the academic year in which they turn five (0–5).
End of QCA	Under draft legislative programme, the government announces that the regulatory system will be modified: qualifications and assessment transferred from the QCA to the Office of the Qualifications and Examinations Regulator (Ofqual); QCA's residual work (on curriculum) to be undertaken by a Qualifications and Curriculum Development Agency (QCDA).
Primary curriculum review (ii)	The government's Rose review of the primary curriculum issues its interim report combining the current national curriculum subjects within six 'areas of learning'.[103]
21ˢᵗ Century Schools	DCSF's *21ˢᵗ Century Schools* prefigures spring 2009 White Paper and invites comments on proposals relating, for example, to new frameworks for personalised learning, children's additional needs, partnership between schools, parents, LAs and other providers and workforce reform.[104]
School Report Cards	Tied in with the above, DCSF consultation starts on new School Report Cards bringing together hitherto separate data on aspects of school performance.[105]
2020 Workforce Strategy	The DCSF opens consultation on the *2020 Children's and Young People's Workforce Strategy* which aims to secure improvements in training, leadership and support for all those working with children and young people. Unusual in the number of government bodies involved: DCSF, DIUS, Home Office, Justice, Health, Culture, Media and Sport.[106]
2009 The national curriculum	The House of Commons Children, Schools and Families Committee publishes report on the national curriculum proposing loosening of government control and prescription, but saying little about aims or content.[107]
Primary curriculum review (iii)	The government's Rose review on the primary curriculum publishes its final report.[108]

NOTES

1 Galton, Simon and Croll (1980): 42.
2 DCSF (2008u). This figure represents the total number of pupils in primary schools, including those unclassified by age, those under five and middle-deemed primary school pupils over 10. The apparent discrepancy between the number of pupils in Figures 3.1 and 3.2 is due to the number of pupils unclassified by age.
3 Conservative Secretary of State for Education and Science Kenneth Clarke, cited in the so-called 'three wise men' report of 1992 (Alexander, Rose and Woodhead, 1992: para 1).
4 Matthew Arnold, poet and essayist, was also an HMI (Her Majesty's Inspector). He was a vocal critic of the deleterious effects of government policy on elementary schools, especially the system of 'payment by results' linking teachers' pay to the results achieved by their pupils when assessed annually by HMIs. He

was also one of the earliest students of comparative primary education, reporting back on the implications of his visits to schools in France, Holland and Switzerland.

5 Robert Lowe was the official responsible for introducing the system of 'payment by results'.

6 Edmund Holmes was chief inspector for elementary education at the turn of the twentieth century and a critic of the limited practice he found in many elementary schools.

7 Published as DES (1978a).

8 For example, Boydell (1974); DES (1978a).

9 Christian Schiller HMI was a staff inspector for junior education who on his retirement ran a very influential one-year course on primary education at the London Institute of Education. Alec Clegg was Chief Education Officer in the old West Riding LEA. Robin Tanner was an HMI and artist based in Oxfordshire, where Edith Moorhouse also worked. Stewart Mason was Director of Education in Leicestershire. Mollie Brearley was head of the Froebel Institute. John Blackie HMI was a chief inspector. The impact of these people is explored by Cunningham (1988) and Alexander (1995: 270–314).

10 Simon (1981a); Alexander (1984); Cunningham (1988).

11 These were academics and other commentators with right-wing views who viewed with dismay what they saw as the baleful effects of 'progressive education' in state schools. See Cox and Dyson (1971), Cox and Boyson (1975).

12 For example Dearden (1968) and Peters (1968).

13 DES (1975).

14 Alexander, Rose and Woodhead (1992): paras 19–20.

15 For example *A Framework for the School Curriculum* (DES 1980a).

16 For example *A View of the Curriculum* (DES 1980b).

17 DES (1978a).

18 In particular *The Curriculum from 5 to 16* (DES 1985b), though the first in the series was *English from 5 to 16*, published in 1984.

19 DES (1986).

20 This is commonly referred to as the Warnock Report (DES 1978b).

21 Bennett (1976).

22 Auld (1976).

23 Galton, Simon and Croll (1980); Galton and Simon (1980); Mortimore *et al.* (1988).

24 DES (1985a).

25 Thomas (1990): 101.

26 MacLure (1988): ix.

27 Quoted in Alexander (2001b): 144.

28 See, for example, Campbell and Neil (1994); Campbell (1994).

29 Dearing Report (Dearing 1993b).

30 Richards (2001a).

31 Richards (1997).

32 Alexander (1991, 1997).

33 Professor Robin Alexander of Leeds University, Chief Primary HMI Jim Rose and Chief Executive of the National Curriculum Council Chris Woodhead. Originally the enquiry was in the hands of Alexander and Rose. Woodhead was added at the last moment, possibly as government 'minder' to the other two. The report of this enquiry was published in Alexander, Rose and Woodhead (1992). For an inside account, see Alexander (1997): 183–287.

34 Alexander, Rose and Woodhead (1992): para 1, quoting the then Secretary of State, Kenneth Clarke.

35 Simon (1992).

36 *Ibid.*

37 See, for example, Barber (2001b).

38 Quoted in Campbell (2001): 38.

39 Moss (2007).

40 Rose (2006).

41 Earl *et al.* (2003a).

42 Wyse, McCreery and Torrance (2010), *The Cambridge Primary Review Research Surveys*, Chapter 29.

43 DfES (2003b).

44 Alexander (2004a).

45 Boyle and Bragg (2008); Webb and Vulliamy (2006); Wyse, McCreery and Torrance (2010), *The Cambridge Primary Review Research Surveys*, Chapter 29.

46 DES (1978a); Ofsted (1997, 2002).

47 DES (1985a).

48 McNamara, Webb and Brundrett (2010), *The Cambridge Primary Review Research Surveys*, Chapter 24.

49 Harlen (2010), *The Cambridge Primary Review Research Surveys*, Chapter 19.

50 See for example Osborn (2000) and Pollard (2000).

51 House of Commons (2008a).

52 DfES (2003b).

53 Tymms and Merrell (2010), *The Cambridge Primary Review Research Surveys*, Chapter 17; Richards (2005).

54 Statistics Commission (2005): 4.

55 Burgess (2010), *The Cambridge Primary Review Research Surveys*, Chapter 25.

56 DfES (2003a).
57 See Burgess (2010) and Daniels and Porter (2010), *The Cambridge Primary Review Research Surveys*, Chapters 25 and 9.
58 DCSF (2007b).
59 Galton, Simon and Croll (1980): 30.
60 CACE (1967): Chapter 7.
61 P. Williams (2008).
62 House of Commons (1986).
63 Cox and Boyson (1975): 4.
64 Zinn (1996).
65 Blyth (1965).
66 Richards (2001a).
67 Blyth *et al.* (1976).
68 Ministry of Education (1959).
69 CACE (1967).
70 DES (1975).
71 Auld (1976).
72 DES (1978a).
73 DES (1982a, 1983, 1985b).
74 DES (1978b).
75 DES (1980a).
76 DES (1980b).
77 DES (1982b).
78 DES (1984).
79 DES (1985a).
80 House of Commons (1986).
81 Alexander, Rose and Woodhead (1992).
82 Ofsted (1993, 1994, 1995).
83 DES (1993).
84 Dearing (1993b).
85 House of Commons (1994).
86 DfEE (1997).
87 House of Commons (1999a).
88 House of Commons (1999b).
89 QCA (2000).
90 DfES (2003a).
91 DfES (2003b).
92 HM Treasury (2004).
93 DfES (2005a).
94 DfES (2006e).
95 Rose (2006).
96 DfES (2007b).
97 DCSF (2007b).
98 Ofsted (2007c).
99 P. Williams (2008).
100 House of Commons (2008a).
101 House of Commons (2008b).
102 DCSF Press release, 14 October: http://www.dcsf.gov.uk/pns/DisplayPN.cgi?pn_id=2008_0229
103 Rose (2008).
104 DCSF (2008b).
105 DSCF (2008v).
106 DCSF (2008a).
107 House of Commons Children, Schools and Families Committee (2009).
108 Rose (2009).

Part 2
Children and childhood

4   Childhood today

Sometimes it must seem to children growing up in Britain today that they cannot win. When their lives and enthusiasms are reported to the adult world in newspapers, on the radio or on television it is all too often in terms of stereotypes. At one extreme they appear as suffering innocents or 'brave little angels' in a dark and menacing world. At the other, they are portrayed as little devils: the 'tiny tearaways' whose anti-social behaviour is supposedly beyond the control of parents, teachers and the police.[1] They find themselves bemoaned as an obese, screen-obsessed generation of couch-potatoes, leading pampered and over-indulged home lives; yet they are also represented as the over-worked and over-stressed victims of a hardened, selfish society where they can no longer be sure of proper physical or emotional nourishment.

Political and media debates about children's education fit all too easily into this polarised framework – not the only example of this tendency, as we noted in Chapter 2. Thus on the one hand, modern teaching is castigated for allegedly failing to give children an adequate grasp of the 3Rs; on the other, the core curriculum of English, mathematics and science is claimed to be so dominant in schools that the love of learning has been lost, and there is no longer time to educate children in the life-skills that they really need. In this context, any indication that children and young people might conceivably be better educated than their parents is treated as anathema. Routinely, they see their scholastic achievements explained away in terms of lower expectations and 'easier' tests and examination papers.

ACCENTUATING THE POSITIVE

This chapter presents an overview of contemporary childhood. It draws on the evidence assembled for the Cambridge Primary Review to provide a context for the more detailed discussions on children and childhood in the following chapters. Like the Review as a whole, it will not shrink from discussing those current circumstances that give rise to genuine concern. But their seriousness is in no sense undermined by starting with some of the good things about children's lives in England today. Although some will view them in a more positive light than others, these are changes that have resulted in a better quality of life than that experienced by their parents and grandparents: Some of the changes were simply unimaginable to previous generations. For example:

- Life expectancy at birth in England has risen to an average of 81.5 years for girls and 77 for boys[2] compared with 49 and 45 a century ago. Girls can now expect to live for an average of 64 years free of limiting, long-standing illness or disability and boys for 62 years. Infant mortality (deaths in the first year of life) fell from 60 per 1,000 live births in 1930 to just 5 per 1,000 in 2006.[3]
- The overwhelming majority of children (94 per cent) described their health as very good or good in 2006,[4] and according to the UK's Children's Commissioners, most children say they are happy.[5] The Good Childhood Inquiry in 2009 provided a more nuanced picture of what makes children more or less happy in the different contexts of family, friendship, health, learning and lifestyle.[6]

- Household disposable incomes per head in the UK tripled in real terms between 1955 and 2005, indicating in 2005 that children were growing up in families that, at least on average, were substantially better off than 50 years earlier.[7] From the mid 1990s until 2007, declining unemployment and a buoyant labour market significantly improved the material quality of life for most children.[8]
- Although one in four properties (6 million) still failed minimum 'decency' standards in 2005,[9] the proportion was well below the 45 per cent (9.1m) identified in 1996.[10]
- Support services for young children and their families have greatly expanded and since 1998 have included Sure Start children's centres in disadvantaged neighbourhoods. Research points to a range of modest, but significant benefits for pre-school children and their parents in Sure Start areas.[11]
- Children enjoy an ever-widening choice of age-appropriate books, as well as 'new media' through computers and the internet, giving them unparalleled access to sources of information, communication, entertainment and leisure. In 2006, nearly half of all eight to 11-year-olds were using the internet at home and a similar proportion had their own mobile phone.[12] Most nine-year-olds and 11-year-olds in 2007 said they enjoyed reading stories, while the proportion who preferred watching TV to reading had declined in the previous four years (from 62 per cent to 55 per cent).[13]
- Growing ethnic diversity at home and the popularity of overseas holidays – alongside access to television and new media – suggests that today's children are far more conscious of other cultures and countries than any previous generation. They are also more environmentally aware and less tolerant of racism and sexism.[14]
- Nearly 60 per cent of 10 to 15 year-olds reported in 2007 that they enjoy school all or most of the time, while 85 per cent said they felt safe going to and from school. Most could also think of occasions when they had raised money for charity or helped other people.[15]
- The abolition of corporal punishment – recommended by the 1967 Plowden Report – became law for state schools in 1986 and independent schools in 1998. What many parents and grandparents vividly recalled as an intimidating and demeaning ritual disappeared.
- There is greater awareness of bullying in schools and greater understanding of how to deal with it. Seventy per cent of 10 to 15-year-olds reported in 2007 that they had never been bullied and nearly 60 per cent believed their schools dealt well with bullying issues.[16]

This list of positives, though far from exhaustive, might at least convince fair-minded observers that current debates about childhood have too often been conducted at a counter-productive level. Like parents who continually criticise their children, while ignoring good behaviour and denying them praise for genuine achievements,[17] popular caricatures of childhood have been in danger of fuelling a deteriorating relationship with the younger generation that makes it more difficult than ever to promote change for the better. For change was what many of the Review's witnesses – parents, teachers, teaching assistants, head teachers, governors, and other community representatives – were eager to see. As detailed in the community soundings report,[18] they identified issues extending from the wider world in which children are growing and learning, to concerns about their day-to-day lives in the classroom and the home. These included:

- A widespread belief, especially among parents, that childhood had become more stressful and troublesome and that children were less happy and carefree than they were when young.
- Anxieties among teachers that some children were under too much pressure from over-zealous parents to achieve at a young age – and among some parents (and governors) that they were under excessive stress from the national tests, especially at key stage 2.
- Negative perceptions of pressures created by consumerism and individualism on children, which some saw as being exacerbated by the cult of celebrity and working against morally-sustainable values and a sense of shared, communal responsibility

- Doubts about the power and negative influence of information technology, consuming children's leisure time disproportionately, damaging their verbal communication skills and potentially exposing them to unsuitable violent or sexual imagery.
- Fears, principally in major cities, that children were unsafe and at risk from aggressive older children, drugs, knives and guns – also that children lacked safe and accessible outdoor recreation opportunities.
- Concerns about parents (or 'other parents') holding low aspirations for their children, and failing to discipline them effectively or accept responsibility for their anti-social behaviour in and out of school.
- Worries, especially among teachers, over the negative effects of conflict and family break-down on children's emotional health and behaviour.
- Regrets concerning a general loss of respect in society, extending from a lack of self-respect to public incivility, aggressive behaviour by some parents as well as children in school, and a lack of respect for the local or global environment.

These perceptions from adults working in primary schools and their wider communities resonated with many of the submissions that the Review received from organisations and from the practitioners in education who subsequently attended the seven national soundings sessions. However, the submissions came from a variety of organisations with contrasting views of childhood (and, indeed, contrasting views of the aims, values and purposes of primary education). While some characterised childhood as a dependent phase where adults should assume responsibility for decision-making, others emphasised children's developing capacity to make their own decisions and express their own views and opinions. Concerns about 'unhealthy' diet, obesity and increasing levels of poor mental health were, nevertheless, common in the submissions and community soundings; as were anxieties about the effects on children of family breakdown and poor parenting.

THE YOUTH OF TODAY ... AND 1500 BCE

It may be noted in passing that the tendency for adults to lament a lack of respect among the younger generation is not peculiar to the 21st century. Tablets from Mesopotamia, dating back some 3,500 years, record a father's concern over his son's alleged truancy and failure to do his homework, not to mention loitering in the street and squandering money on instant grati-fication.[19] It is also worth stating that current concerns about childhood are being voiced by adults in an 'ageing' society where families raising dependent children constitute a declining minority of all households.[20] Nor is the concern confined to England. Even so, the pessimism among the adults consulted during the Review was pervasive. It was also, not surprisingly, reflected in the representative sample surveys of UK residents aged over 18 carried out for the Good Childhood Inquiry conducted by the Children's Society. Just 9 per cent of those inter-viewed believed children were happier than during their own childhood and two-thirds thought computer games, television and other indoor activities were preventing children from being more active. Three out of 10 (29 per cent) thought family breakdown and conflict were having 'the most impact' on children's well-being, followed by peer pressure (23 per cent), bullying (11 per cent), celebrity culture (11 per cent), computer technology (8 per cent) and media reporting of children and young people (8 per cent).[21] Nine out of 10 agreed that today's children were 'more materialistic' than previous generations.[22] The final report[23] also highlighted evidence that the proportion of 15 and 16-year-olds with conduct problems doubled between 1974 and 1999 and that there was a substantial increase in emotional difficulties over the same period[24] (and remained at similar levels after that[25]).

Another influential though contested expression of current anxieties has come from the education writer Sue Palmer, who submitted her book *Toxic Childhood* in evidence to the Review. Her contention was that the clash between technology moving at 'lightning speed' and slower-moving human biology is harming children's ability to think, learn and behave. So much so that, 'to put it bluntly, the next generation may not be bright or balanced enough to keep the show on the road.'[26]

Palmer devoted attention to what she described as a 'special needs explosion' based on growing numbers of children in the United States and Britain diagnosed with attention-deficit/hyperactivity disorders (ADHD), dyslexia, and autistic spectrum disorders. Palmer's statement that 'up to 12 per cent of American children suffer from ADHD' ignored the different diagnostic definitions of hyperactivity used by practitioners in the US and Britain.[27] Nevertheless, she appeared to reflect accurately the concerns of many teachers that children's classroom behaviour has deteriorated in the past 20 years, especially in disadvantaged areas.

LISTENING TO CHILDREN

Often noticeably missing from contrasting discourses (though not the Good Childhood Inquiry or this Review) are the voices of children themselves. Yet research has not only pointed to circumstances and issues where the perspectives of children and their parents tend to diverge, but also to topics where parents are apt to make misplaced assumptions about their children's views, and vice versa.[28] It is, therefore, no great surprise to discover that the most upbeat group of witnesses who contributed to the Review were pupils consulted during the community soundings and who responded to an invitation for submissions. All together 18 of the 87 community soundings involved children and there were 161 submissions from children. As we show throughout this report, and especially in Chapter 9, the Review as a whole has taken children's voices and views very seriously.

Children were certainly anxious about local issues affecting their sense of security, including traffic hazards, a lack of safe play areas or gangs of older children. They also displayed some of their parents' pessimism concerning the future, expressing worries over global issues, including climate change, pollution, world poverty and terrorism. But it was noticeable that where schools had taken account of pupils' concerns and chosen to address them through curricular and non-curricular activities, children had a more positive outlook. For example, a number of the Review's 'sounding-board' schools had involved children in environmental action and energy-saving projects that had given them a strong sense that 'we can do something about it'. Most of all, the Review team's observations of life inside primary schools were far from depressing. As the community soundings report noted, whatever was happening in the wider world, children were seen to be spending their school days 'in communities-within-communities that unfailingly sought to celebrate the positive'.[29] The research survey on what has become known as 'pupil voice' carried out for the Review by Carol Robinson and Michael Fielding, likewise, portrayed primary schools as 'largely happy places'.[30]

From this it will be apparent that the Review's soundings on children's lives produced more nuanced results than some of the garish publicity they attracted when first made public. The headlines that greeted the community soundings report such as

Children being robbed of their innocence by 'guns, gangs and celebrities'[31]

and

The pain of a generation forced to grow up before their time[32]

were, themselves, an example of the tendency for adults to transfer their own anxieties about childhood to children. Indeed, under a headline 'Why are children so unhappy?', *The Independent* newspaper partly attributed claims that England is a nation of unhappy children to the Review: a significant misrepresentation of what the report actually said.[33]

The contrast between heightened adult fears concerning childhood and less negative attitudes among children was also reflected in a report on *Risk and Childhood* published in 2007 by the Royal Society for Arts, Manufactures and Commerce (RSA).[34] It highlighted research evidence[35] that parents often worried most about things like abduction, murder, or even road accidents that were highly unlikely to happen. The report concluded that, with exceptions that include less healthy lifestyles and certain psychological risks, the world was a safer place for children than in the past. Children, it added, needed excitement and challenge and would benefit from more opportunities for calculated risk-taking in settings where they could remain as safe as possible.[36]

CHANGING FAMILIES AND SCHOOLS

The exceptional pace of social and family change in the past 40 years appeared a source of the profound pessimism felt by parents and other adults. A number of Review research surveys highlighted trends that continue to ensure that children's experiences are unlike those of their parents in many important ways. Changes in the structure and formation of families remain striking and include lower birth rates, greater relationship instability and re-partnering among previously separated parents. Yolande Muschamp and her colleagues noted in their research survey on parenting, caring and educating that most dependent children were living with both their birth parents, whether married or co-habiting.[37] But they also had a markedly higher probability of experiencing parental separation, lone parenting, step-families, half-siblings and being an only child than those born in the 1960s. Children were not only more likely to experience care shared between parents who are living apart, but also care provided by other family members or professional childminders while their parents were working. These and other issues raised by the research survey, like the 'long-hours culture' among working fathers, are discussed in greater detail in Chapter 6; but it was clear that family change directly affected how children were parented and how parents engaged with their education.[38] The research evidence here was reinforced by the community soundings and submissions to the Review where teachers and head teachers, especially, expressed anxiety over mismatches between the values and standards of behaviour that children were exposed to at school and the expectations of their parents and carers.[39]

The Review's research survey on demography, culture, diversity and inclusion by Mel Ainscow and colleagues highlighted the growing cultural and social diversity of primary pupils, one fifth of whom were classified as being from a minority ethnic background.[40] One in eight children had a first language other than English, with bilingualism – or even multi-lingualism – forming a normal part of the lives and identities of a growing number of children. Berry Mayall, in her research survey of children's lives outside school, drew further attention to studies suggesting that some teachers have held low expectations for children from minority ethnic groups and failed to respect their linguistic patterns of speech, contributing to institutional racism.[41] Diversity issues are explored further in Chapters 8 and 9 of this report, which also discuss the evidence concerning children's learning needs and difficulties. This latter area, as the research survey by Harry Daniels and Jill Porter made clear, is highly contested.[42] In seeming contradiction of the more alarming claims made about the spread of developmental disorders and learning difficulties, the proportion of children in schools with statements of special educational needs (SEN) has remained relatively stable. Yet this apparent stability may reflect other factors, such as a reluctance among local authorities to incur additional costs by increasing the number of statements. Although teachers were concerned to meet the needs of children with statements, they were particularly anxious about the one in six children who were characterised as having 'special needs, but no statement'. It was acknowledged that the numbers of such children had been steadily increasing.[43]

Berry Mayall's research survey for the Review on children's lives outside school also considered evidence that successive cohorts of children may not only come under pressure to achieve better test results while they are in school, but also increasingly resent the intrusion of school-ordained activities on their lives at home. Research suggested that children tended to think in terms of clear boundaries between school and home, where the latter was a private place affording them 'free time'. As more time was claimed for homework and the school day expanded to include 'extended school' activities, there was a risk that children and their parents might resist further 'scholarisation' of their homes.[44] Children's entitlement under the United Nations Convention on the Rights of the Child (UNCRC)[45] to 'rest and leisure' is reflected in the government's Every Child Matters agenda where parity is given to 'enjoying' as well as 'achieving' (see below).[46] But should schoolwork continue to encroach on children's home time, it will become increasingly necessary to remind policy-makers of that fact.

POVERTY AND EDUCATIONAL DISADVANTAGE

Far from the least of the 'changing childhood' concerns highlighted by the Review's submissions and research surveys is the gap between rich and poor and its impact on learning. Historically, the divide between the poorest households in Britain and those with relatively high incomes widened dramatically during the 1980s. In particular, families with dependent children were disproportionately numbered among a growing minority of households with less than 60 per cent of median net income,[47] placing them below a widely-accepted 'poverty line'.[48] By this definition, the proportion of children living in poverty doubled within a generation. More recently, despite unequivocal government targets and measures for eliminating child poverty over 20 years, the number of low-income families remained stubbornly high. After a decline over six years from 3.4m children in 1998–99, the statistics for 2006–7 showed an upward trend over two years to 2.9m children in poor households.[49] The vast majority of households living below the poverty line could not afford a standard of living considered by most people to be the minimum acceptable, according to a major survey of public expectations about income.[50] Other research and statistics showed that social mobility between generations declined substantially towards the end of the last century and was low in Britain by international standards.[51]

Income inequality and relative disadvantage in the UK and other wealthy nations are in a different league to the absolute poverty of the developing world. But that does not undermine their consequence in relation to social cohesion and, more specifically, educational attainment. Relatively low income has been strongly associated with low attainment in school. Britain – in addition to having one of the least equal distributions of income and wealth – has one of the biggest socio-economic divides in education. In other words, it is more common in the UK than in most other 'western' countries for children from disadvantaged backgrounds to perform poorly in school compared with their peers from more advantaged families.[52] This educational 'gap' can be ascribed to the interaction of many different factors both outside and inside school, of which family income is clearly one and parents' own educational background is another. A Joseph Rowntree Foundation research programme on poverty and educational disadvantage gave a good indication of the contributing forces, including children's own awareness from an early age of the limitations placed on them by low social status and income and perceptions that they were more likely to be criticised and shouted at by teachers. Advantaged children had better experiences of out-of-school activities, were more likely to have their own bedroom at home and to get more help with homework.[53]

The Review's research survey by Stephen Machin and Sandra McNally on the changing national context for the aims of primary education reported further on evidence that social status differences in educational progress start early in children's lives and widen as they grow older.[54] According to one study, which used an index derived from tests of cognitive ability, the gaps between children from high and low socio-economic groups increased slightly from 22 months to five years, but then widened more substantially during the primary school years.[55] In their report for the Review, Mel Ainscow and colleagues noted how poverty tended to be concentrated in urban areas, but also occurred in pockets (and, consequently, was overlooked) in more prosperous rural and suburban areas. They also recorded how children in some ethnic communities were more likely to experience poverty and disadvantage than others, including Traveller families of Irish Heritage, Gypsy/Roma, Bangladeshi, Pakistani and Black groups.[56] However, there was evidence that low family income was even more strongly associated with persistent low achievement among White children.[57] Inequalities in income and educational achievement could, moreover, be expected to reinforce each other as employers placed a growing premium on recruiting workers with good qualifications. The decline of manufacturing, the rise of new technologies, an internationally competitive labour market and other features of a 'globalised' economy meant that the economic prognosis for Britain's 'long tail of under-achievers' was poor unless social inequalities could be reduced.[58]

THE GAP

The evidence of a widening educational gap between advantaged and disadvantaged children goes some way towards reconciling the contrasting perspectives of childhood set out at the start of this chapter. How can it be that growing up in Britain today can be viewed as better in many ways, and yet worse in so many others? The dichotomy can be partly understood in terms of a 'prosperous majority'[59] of children who benefit as never before from factors such as family income, parents' educational background, their neighbourhood and their access to popular schools. Growing up alongside them are a large minority of children experiencing a potentially self-reinforcing cycle of economic and educational disadvantage. This was certainly the picture that emerged from the heavily-publicised Unicef report in 2007 comparing different indicators of children's well-being in rich countries. The lowly position of the UK in comparative tables relating to educational, material and family well-being made a deep, very worrying impression. As the report said in the wider context of all richer nations:

> Many ... feel that it is time to attempt to re-gain a degree of understanding, control and direction over what is happening to our children in their most vital, vulnerable years.[60]

It should, however, be noted that the data reported by Unicef was up to five years old at the time of publication. Results from more recently repeated versions of the surveys used to rate the UK are, in many respects, more positive. In particular, the 2005–6 Health Behaviour of School-Aged Children Study (HSBC), whose 2001–2 predecessor contributed 18 out of 40 indicators in the Unicef report, suggests some remarkable improvements. For example, where only 47 per cent of the British 11, 13 and 15-year olds surveyed in 2001–2 agreed that their peers were 'kind and helpful' – a figure much-highlighted when the Unicef analysis was published – the proportion among their 2005–6 counterparts rose to 72 per cent. The percentage who reported liking school 'a lot' also increased from 20 per cent to an internationally respectable 37 per cent.[61] As analysts at the London School of Economics have observed, there were some important indicators that had showed no change (including inequality in literacy scores and children's experiences of fighting and bullying) or worsened since the Unicef data was collected (including income inequality and some measures of literacy).[62] Even so, they calculated that the latest data, including measures of young people's mathematics and science attainment, would lift the UK 'several places from the bottom' were Unicef to revise its international index.

An investigation by central and local government in England into differences between the social, economic and health experiences of vulnerable children and their luckier peers, meanwhile, concluded that schools, working with other support services, have a critical part to play in 'narrowing the gap'.[63] An analysis by the National Foundation for Educational Research of relevant data suggested that some attainment 'gaps' might be narrowing, notably those of looked-after children and Black Caribbean pupils. The incidence of obesity – although undeniably concentrated among disadvantaged children, appeared to be growing faster among higher socio-economic groups. Nevertheless, the links between relative poverty and low attainment remained incontestable.[64]

EVERY CHILD MATTERS

Given the evidence concerning educational disadvantage and the running tide of public anxiety concerning childhood, is there even a remote possibility that today's children might grow to be more optimistic adults than their parents? Much continues to depend on the public policy agenda. The commitment to tackle poverty is there, but its translation into policy and practice is inconsistent.[65] The same might also be said, in England, of Every Child Matters, the brand name linked to the 2004 Children Act that brought about a far-reaching re-organisation of local children's services. Responsibilities for children's education and social care services were merged into single departments within local authorities. They, in turn, were required to plan and commission children's services in children's trust partnerships with NHS primary care trusts and other local agencies and organisations.[66] Guiding all this activity within and between agencies was a stronger emphasis on judging services according to the results or 'outcomes' they achieve for children, rather than 'outputs' such as the number of children or families who use them.[67]

Submissions to the Review consistently highlighted *Every Child Matters* (ECM) and the subsequent Children's Plan published by the Department for Children, Schools and Families[68] as a strength of the primary-school system and cause for qualified optimism. However, as Ian Barron and colleagues warned in their research survey for the Review on links between primary schools and other agencies, there is still a risk of 'vulnerable' becoming a professional euphemism, couched within a deficit model that views disadvantaged children as a 'nuisance', 'incomplete' or somehow 'insufficient'. Both they and Robinson and Fielding were alive to the dangers that the inclusive approach of ECM and its focus on 'learners for life', was being subverted by contradictory pressures on schools to focus on test results.[69]

Visitors to primary schools will have encountered display boards featuring the five headline 'outcomes' for children that ECM is seeking to achieve:

- being healthy – enjoying good physical and mental health and living a healthy lifestyle
- staying safe – being protected from harm and neglect and growing up able to look after themselves
- enjoying and achieving – getting the most out of life and developing broad skills for adulthood
- making a positive contribution – to the community and to society and not engaging in anti-social or offending behaviour
- achieving economic well-being – not being prevented by economic disadvantage from achieving their full potential in life.

Parents reading this would quickly see the relevance of the first four outcomes, but might still wonder why schools that cater for four to 11-year-olds should highlight such a distant objective as 'economic well-being'. Yet children themselves appear to be in little doubt that the main purpose of their primary schooling is to help them to get a job in the future. As Robinson and Fielding's research survey put it:

> They knew their subsequent careers and employability depended on how well they did in exams and they understood this point fully before they left their primary schools.[70]

Similarly, in the words of a Year 6 boy who made a submission to the Review team:

> We have schools because we need education and to prepare us for secondary school. Secondary school then helps us to get a good job.

Posters advertising the five outcomes might seem to sit uncomfortably with the tendency for the educational gap to widen between economically advantaged and disadvantaged children during the primary years. Yet it has been one of the strengths of the Every Child Matters agenda that it acknowledges the evidence concerning disadvantage and does not pretend that schools (or parents or teachers) can be expected to narrow that gap on their own. It has also been clear that the important contribution that schools and an evolving range of extended services can make towards the fifth outcome is (inter) dependent on the approaches taken to achieving the other four.

CHILDREN'S RIGHTS

Continued progress is also needed in public policy towards acknowledging and enforcing children's fundamental rights. The UN's Convention on the Rights of the Child,[71] which underpinned the ECM outcomes, famously embraced their entitlements to food, shelter, education, health care, leisure and freedom from abuse, neglect and economic exploitation. It also asserted their rights to express their opinions freely, where capable of forming their own views, and to participate in matters affecting them, including their social, economic and cultural lives.[72] Contributors to the national and practitioner soundings for the Review, as well as many of the submissions, supported children's greater participation in decision-making at school, including school councils, and in their wider communities. However, when formally reporting to the UN Committee on the Rights of the Child during 2008, the four UK Children's Commissioners suggested that although Britain had ratified the convention almost 20 years earlier, awareness and knowledge of its provisions remained low. Despite pockets of good practice, there had been limited progress in achieving children's participative rights and there was continued resistance to seeking the views of younger children and enabling children to participate in decisions that affected them at school. Citing the Review's community soundings,[73] the commissioners also expressed concern at the adverse effects of stress on children in relation to school testing. They argued that British children would not fully realise and enjoy their rights under the convention until it has been incorporated into domestic law.[74]

CONCLUSION

Even in the absence of enforceable legislation, there is a powerful case to be made for ensuring that adults, from government ministers to teachers, school governors, parents and the general public, take more careful account of children's views. As Carolyne Willow, a leading UK advocate for children's rights, observed just before the Millennium, children's views are seldom considered when commentators try to synthesise the spirit of the age. An examination of children's changing cultures, pastimes and interests might, she suggested, counter some of the more cynical generalisations given currency in the adult world.[75] A decade later, children's evidence to the Review has done just that; reminding us that while concerns about disadvantage and deprivation are well-founded, more sweeping statements about 'lost' or 'blighted' childhoods should be treated with caution. Aside from a greater sense of perspective, what we also learn from children is a better notion of how schools can help foster a sense of security and optimism for the future. Children's impressive confidence where they had learned about practical strategies for responding to environmental challenges demonstrates the positive part that schools can play in replacing passive anxieties with a hopeful sense of their capacity to act. By empowering the next generation, primary schools may help to ensure that childhood tomorrow is not perceived in quite such dismal terms as childhood today.

NOTES

1 Utting (1998, 2009); Layard and Dunn (2009).
2 National Statistics (2008a).
3 National Statistics (2008b).
4 The NHS Information Centre (2008).
5 UK Children's Commissioners (2008).
6 Layard and Dunn (2009).
7 Piachaud (2007).
8 Bradshaw (2005).
9 A submission to the Cambridge Primary Review from the housing charity Shelter underlined the importance of making improved housing a continuing priority for improving children's lives.
10 National Statistics (2008b).
11 National Evaluation of Sure Start (2008).
12 Ofcom (2006).
13 Sainsbury and Clarkson (2008).

14 Piachaud (2007).
15 Ofsted (2007e).
16 Ofsted (2007e).
17 Kazdin (2005).
18 Alexander and Hargreaves (2007).
19 Kramer (1973).
20 National Statistics (2008b).
21 The Children's Society (2008a).
22 The Children's Society (2008b).
23 Layard and Dunn (2009).
24 Collishaw *et al.* (2004).
25 Green, H. *et al.* (2005).
26 Palmer (2006): 3.
27 Goodman and Scott (2005).
28 Madge and Wilmott (2007).
29 Alexander and Hargreaves (2007).
30 Robinson and Fielding (2010), *The Cambridge Primary Review Research Surveys*, Chapter 2.
31 *Daily Mail* (11 October 2007).
32 *The Independent* (12 October 2007).
33 *The Independent* (11 March 2008).
34 Madge and Barker (2007).
35 Murrin and Martin (2004).
36 Madge and Barker (2007).
37 Muschamp *et al.* (2010), *The Cambridge Primary Review Research Surveys*, Chapter 4.
38 *Ibid.*
39 Alexander and Hargreaves (2007).
40 Ainscow *et al.* (2010), *The Cambridge Primary Review Research Surveys*, Chapter 8.
41 Mayall (2010), *The Cambridge Primary Review Research Surveys*, Chapter 3.
42 Daniels and Porter (2010), *The Cambridge Primary Review Research Surveys*, Chapter 9.
43 *Ibid.*
44 Mayall (2010), *The Cambridge Primary Review Research Surveys*, Chapter 3.
45 UN Convention on the Rights of the Child, adopted into international law (November 1989).
46 DCSF (2008k).
47 Glennerster *et al.* (2004).
48 Measured as net income before housing costs.
49 DWP (Department for Work and Pensions) (2008).
50 Bradshaw *et al.* (2008).
51 Machin and McNally (2010), *The Cambridge Primary Review Research Surveys*, Chapter 10.
52 OECD (2001a); Hirsch (2007a).
53 Hirsch (2007a).
54 Machin and McNally (2010), *The Cambridge Primary Review Research Surveys*, Chapter 10.
55 Feinstein (2003).
56 Ainscow *et al.* (2010), *The Cambridge Primary Review Research Surveys*, Chapter 8.
57 Cassen and Kingdon (2007).
58 Machin and McNally (2010), *The Cambridge Primary Review Research Surveys*, Chapter 10.
59 'Prosperous majority' was the phrase coined more than a decade ago by the Joseph Rowntree Foundation's Inquiry into Income and Wealth (1995), which raised awareness of the widening gap between rich and poor.
60 UNICEF (2007): 39.
61 Currie *et al.* (2008). Averages from aggregated England, Scotland and Wales results in Stewart (2009).
62 Stewart (2009).
63 Local Government Association, DCSF and Improvement and Development Agency (2008).
64 Morris *et al.* (2008).
65 Hirsch (2006); Joseph Rowntree Foundation (2008).
66 Barron *et al.* (2007).
67 DfES (2004a); DCSF (2008k).
68 DCSF (2007b).
69 Barron *et al.* (2010), Robinson and Fielding (2010), *The Cambridge Primary Review Research Surveys*, Chapters 5 and 2.
70 Robinson and Fielding (2010), *The Cambridge Primary Review Research Surveys*, Chapter 2.
71 United Nations (1989).
72 UNICEF UK (2006).
73 Alexander and Hargreaves (2007).
74 UK Children's Commissioners (2008).
75 Willow (1998).

5   Children's lives outside school

There is, of course, more to children's lives than school. Yet there is not as much more as there used to be and what remains is often cribbed and confined by adults. Yet, paradoxically, children's capacity to shape their own lives, to be active agents in learning and in their social worlds is increasingly acknowledged. At least it is acknowledged by many psychologists, sociologists and children's campaigners – and by the majority of people who gave evidence to the Cambridge Primary Review. For all those who credit children with the right to shape their existence, childhood is a time of enabling them, as young citizens, to engage with the world. But there is another view of childhood – that it is a time of dependency and incompetence and that children's innocence and immaturity should be protected in a society laden with risk.

The child as an active agent underpins the children's rights movement, which has become stronger in England since the 1989 UN Convention on the Rights of the Child. Much progress has been made[1] but, as the four UK Children's Commissioners reported in 2008,[2] much remains to be done. With regard to the Review, for example, whilst children did contribute, their voices lacked the power of adult voices. Media coverage of the Review presented adult opinions of childhood experiences as fact – and was overwhelmingly negative and alarmist, consolidating the adult view that childhood in England is in crisis. Yet, as has been noted, children's own submissions to the Review were, in general, positive and optimistic.

Children value a happy home and good relations with parents and other family members. They value love and good open communication, but do not want to be over-protected, for independence and choice are also important to them. Adults who responded to the Good Childhood Inquiry emphasised the importance of encouraging parents to engage with children, to listen to their voices and allow them to choose their own behaviour within reasonable limits.[3]

CHILDREN VERSUS PUPILS

From earners to learners

The history of childhood in industrialised countries reveals the gradual decline in the expectation that children make a contribution to the economic life of the family. Not only was schooling increasingly seen as necessary to equip future adults for social usefulness;[4] but the 'civilising process' also emphasised the need for parents to socialise children, to make them fit to join increasingly complex societies.[5] Longer childhoods, with school and home as key institutions, have resulted.

English children nowadays spend longer in school and school-related settings than they did 10 years ago. Recent policies have promoted an earlier age of starting school and, once there, children can stay for longer thanks to breakfast clubs and after-school clubs. Even when they get home they are not free of school as most primary pupils now do homework. The character of primary schools has also changed since the 1988 Education Reform Act, with the introduction of testing, published league tables and competition between schools. Many adults told the Review of their concerns about the impact of these developments, about their fears that childhood is becoming 'scholarised'. Some felt that children start school too young and are expected to do 'too much too soon'. One parent wrote to question the value of homework. Some submissions welcomed children's centres and the extended school day; others thought that they perhaps encroach too heavily on children's lives. Many voiced anxiety about the negative impact of testing on both their children and the curriculum. These anxieties recur throughout this report.

Homework and work at home

Whilst regarding children as workers is unfamiliar nowadays, evidence from many studies shows that children do work around the home and for the good of the family.[6] They are positive about these jobs, seeing them as responsibilities, sited within concepts of honesty and fairness in family relations. Through their accounts of daily life, children show how they participate in the construction, maintenance and advancement of their family. This includes looking after themselves, maintaining family harmony ('people work') and housework.

For many years, these facts were not recognised in research or policy.[7] Instead, adult commentators stressed, and studied, socialisation at home and school as the main function of childhood and have devalued the agency of children and their contributions both to learning and to the household labour. We think it important to flag up children's work, in complement to other out-of-school activities. In so doing we support the comments made to the Review about the value of children's out-of-school lives. There are dangers, as many commentators noted, for children and families, of schools intruding too much on out-of-school time – children have other worthwhile things to do.

Some witnesses to the Review worried that children at school lack opportunities to develop personal responsibility and self-respect. Community representatives in one area noted that children's skills and abilities were not recognised. The Review endorses this point and again emphasises that children often do take responsibility at home and value themselves as active members of their family.[8]

Learning from experience

Children's learning is largely experiential: through experience at home they learn about relationships, moral codes and how to be healthy. Their engagement with toys, books, computers and television enables them to learn. What children say about the tasks and activities of childhood is based on concepts of both apprenticeship and participation. They talk about learning to be a good enough member of the family, engaging with the project of one's own life, and learning what one needs to know for the future.[9]

These ideas forcibly point to children's understanding that they are active agents, who make a difference through their participation. Their experience of interactive engagement with other people at home was the backdrop for their advocacy, in the Review's community soundings, for interactive learning at school too. Their view was echoed in the practitioner soundings, which proposed that children should take the initiative in learning, that their creativity should be harnessed and fostered, that schools should listen to children. Both practitioners and representatives of organisations argued in favour of schools valuing and building on the knowledge and experience that children have acquired out of school. This argument – especially in relation to children's linguistic development – has a long and honoured history[10] and is supported by recent research on 'home-school knowledge exchange'.[11]

Home-school disagreements

Every society has to determine the respective responsibilities of the state and of parents for the care and education of children, but the English response has been distinctive. Whilst in other European countries, such as France and Finland, there are clear divisions of responsibility, with parents doing the caring and socialising, and schools doing the schooling,[12] these divisions have always been blurred and controversial in England. As with many aspects of English society, this uneasy situation can be traced to social class divides:[13] some parents are thought to be better than others. It seems likely that some children, in seeking to mediate between family and school, are responding to their sense that teachers do not all, or always, look with favour on parents. There were many submissions, especially from teachers, about parental inadequacies, about parental antipathy towards school agendas, and about the many families who do not share the values espoused by the school.

The aim of involving parents in school agendas has a long history[14] and, as the next chapter reveals, efforts to do so have intensified recently. Yet, for children, 'parental involvement' can look like a double dose of control. Research studies have drawn on children's accounts of their negotiations between home and school, between parents and teachers.[15] Children often describe home as a private place, where you have 'free time', where you can act outside the remits of school and where child-adult relations differ from child-teacher relations. So they may try to keep home and school separate, defending their home against teachers' efforts to harness it to their purposes.

Schools and the 'real' world

While many children value the home as a private place, and resist incursions by school into it,[16] they also told the Review that there should be bridges between their family and their academic lives.[17]

They said that school should engage them with real-life issues and not limit itself to inward-looking agendas. They welcomed a broad curriculum including history, geography, science, sports and the arts. They wanted to learn how to manage money and how to manage life, to learn about other societies and other languages; and to engage with macro-problems such as global warming, sustainability and pollution. They also wanted to know about economic and political matters, such as war, terrorism, famine and poverty in other countries. We note here a strong argument in favour of upgrading the status of geography in primary schools,[18] a point endorsed in recent Ofsted reports.

Friends and fun

Children stressed the importance of friends both in and out of school.[19] For them, friends mean fun. They are also confidants and a defence against the adult-ordered environments they live in. As their access to public space is limited, they find important arenas for friendship outside school in organised groups. The significance of children's social relationships, both within school and beyond, was recognised by Save the Children, which aims to help schools celebrate friendship through its 'friendship funday' programme. Children's positive accounts of their friendships act as a counterbalance to the 2007 Unicef report,[20] which found that UK children had the poorest friendships in the developed world, a finding which was taken up by the media, in its enthusiasm for presenting UK children as unhappy.[21] While this finding is now being questioned,[22] some submissions expressed concerns about children's friendships. The Commission for Racial Equality highlighted, in its submission to the Review, research showing that children from varying ethnic groups too often just associated with their own group and that this problem was getting worse in some areas. The commission argued that the encouragement of good cross-ethnic friendships should begin in the early years and continue throughout school.

The not-so great outdoors

In 2007, 300 academics, authors and leaders of children's charities warned that the loss of outdoor play was threatening children's well-being. They blamed the decline in 'unstructured, loosely supervised' play on anxious parents, schools tests and computer games, and said it was adversely affecting children's mental and physical health.[23]

The need for good quality play spaces both in and outside schools was also stressed in the Review's soundings and submissions.[24] Many people worried about inadequate facilities, public spaces made risky by strangers and traffic, and about children's shortage of time to enjoy themselves. One submission pointed out that children with special educational needs were particularly restricted when it came to play. Parents feared for their safety and suitable equipment was lacking. Similarly, disabled children have observed that other children did not always want to play with them.[25]

A small-scale study found that Year 6 children from well-to-do families tended to belong to a rich and varied range of groups outside school, whereas those from poorer homes relied on clubs at school. The researchers also found that group activities enabled children to make new friends, became more responsible and develop the ability to discuss what they had learned.[26] But the social context for these findings was that children live their lives increasingly under adult supervision and their independent activity in public spaces has diminished.[27] The 2007 Children's Plan[28] took up this point; it looked across the arenas where children (up to 18) spend their time and plans to spend £235m providing mainly supervised places for children of all ages to play. It also proposed tackling barriers to children's outdoor play – negative perceptions about young people, bullying in public places, crime on the streets, and road safety. Many strengths in the Children's Plan were identified in the submission from the Early Education Advisory Group which praised its emphasis on children's enjoyment of their childhoods and was firmly behind the proposals to improve play facilities across the country.

Sporting chances

In 2005, four-fifths of children surveyed told the Good Childhood Inquiry that they felt good about their health, and two-thirds exercised on three or more days a week.[29] In 2006, a survey of participation rates looked at PE lessons and other school sport (organised mostly out of school hours).[30] It found that 91 per cent of primary pupils were participating in two or more hours a week of PE and/or school sport – a marked rise over four years. Other research has found that while time spent in sport and play during the academic day has fallen, participation in sports at school, outside school time, has increased.[31] However, experts remain concerned about the amount of exercise children are getting. In 2007, researchers found only one in 40 11-year-olds managed an hour of exercise every day – though they still achieved, on average, twice as much exercise as adults.[32]

Aside from PE and sport, schools have a poor history and current record on child health; yet they are an obvious place for a health service for young people,[33] a point made by some children who wrote to the Review suggesting the need for medical staff, welfare and counselling staff. While adults also expressed interest in schools promoting health, they were more concerned that some aspects of the education agenda were undermining it, particularly in relation to obesity and mental well-being. On obesity, submissions to the Review supported healthy food at school and opportunities for more physical activity, and also legal restrictions, such as banning advertisements for junk food aimed at children.

Creative thinking

Children's right to engagement with the artistic cultures of their society has been recognised in schools, but was not high on late 20th century political agendas.[34] However, change may be afoot. Indicative of this change – and probably influential in it – has been the Creative Partnerships scheme which in 2002 began encouraging 'creative practitioners' to work with children. A report on the scheme, submitted to the Review, described how projects have engaged with children, promoted good social skills and increased creativity.[35] The authors were eager that schools capitalised on these gains and suggested focussing projects on children's out-of-school interests. They also recommended broadening children's experience, by setting projects in theatres, museums and concert venues. Working in and with 'the creative industries' motivated and inspired children, they said, while teachers gained valuable insights from seeing artists, musicians and actors work with their pupils.[36] And they recommended that cultural organisations should seek ways to encourage schools to harness their skills and opportunities.

These points about the central value of creativity were echoed in very many soundings and submissions, and the matter is taken up in our evidence on the curriculum (Chapters 13 and 14). In line with theoretical work on interactive learning, children in the community soundings emphasised their enjoyment of actively engaging with other children when tackling problems. For some practitioners, the desire to raise the profile of creativity tied into their proposals to empower children through shared experiences and collaboration. Others drew on concepts of social and cultural capital, arguing for open discussion at school of what children bring to it and thus increasing their self-knowledge and self-esteem.

The message on the media

Submissions to the Review expressed widespread concerns about children's exposure to commercial pressures, and the impact these have on their attitudes and behaviour, including the sexualisation of childhood. Many worried about children's unsupervised access to the internet and to unsuitable 'adult' material. And while research has shown that use of ICT at home for schoolwork was associated with higher attainment, extensive use of ICT at home for 'fun' had a negative effect on school attainment.[37]

Notably, however, children did not discuss such issues in their submissions or in their contributions to community soundings. Clearly for them, the use of 'new' media such as computers, MP3 players, and games consoles, never mind television and mobile phones, are unquestionably a part of their lives – and it seems schools can benefit from recognising this.

As with other aspects of children's lives touched on in this chapter, research has shown that children's motivation increases when their own cultural knowledge – including that acquired from TV and computers – is acknowledged at school. Work with children using this knowledge can develop critical skills and understanding of how, for example, stories work.[38]

Some witnesses – notably teachers during the practitioner soundings – were positive about computers, perhaps because they have used ICT with children and recognised its potential for school-related work and for children's active engagement. Some teachers argued that computers could be valuable educationally, both in and out of school. They allow children to present their opinions and display their expertise – greater than that of many teachers – thus giving them more control over their learning. Problems with access to inappropriate websites and material were often overstated, they said, though there was a need for openness and discussion with children about where the limits lie and protective measures to ensure that inappropriate material could not be accessed.

However, while these teachers clearly agreed that familiarity with ICT and critical assessment of what was on offer was crucial in today's society,[39] others argued that children should also learn independently of the new technologies. A further point made by teachers was that some families simply could not afford a computer; some suggested computer loans, better facilities at libraries, and measures to increase home ownership of computers (government grants, for instance). The National Association of Teachers of Travellers (NATT), in its submission, pointed not only to poverty as a problem but also to the need for children to have access to computers, alongside distance-learning packs, while travelling.

If more families own computers, it becomes more likely that school-home-community relations can be improved through communication via the internet, as teachers pointed out to the Review. They also talked of bringing parents into school and sharing their knowledge and skill with teachers, while children could be teachers in a 'children's masterclass'.

But media-related work at school is hampered by many factors: demands of the national curriculum, teacher resistance to new technologies and the challenge of keeping up with the pace of media development.[40]

CHILDREN AND THE COMMUNITY

Neglected community assets

Children's lives outside school are clearly shaped by their 'community' and there was widespread concern among Review witnesses that children have a right to spend time out and about, but are too much confined to the home. This is the community's loss, as the Commission for Racial Equality argued in its submission. There are links between children and community, and children play a key role in strengthening local communities, according to research in 2007. They forge connections with neighbours for themselves and for their parents, linking them into local networks.[41]

Research has also suggested serious barriers to children's involvement in community development.[42] They may merely 'take part' rather than influence, barred from effective participation by adult-child power relations and institutional practices.[43] However, government documents have emphasised children's participation in local planning. The Fair Play paper, for example, suggests closely involving children, families and communities in the design of improved play spaces, reporting that having play space gives children a stake in their community.[44] Creative Partnerships saw scope for children's wider learning and enjoyment, in projects based in arts-related settings.[45] As noted earlier, there is potential for ICT to link people up and mobilise them to advance common concerns. The UK Literacy Association's submission insisted that 'culture and pedagogy have to be rooted in the everyday if they are to offer pupils the skills, knowledge and understanding needed for the cultural, social, political and economic milieu in which they are located.'

Schools and communities

Studies during the 1970s considered the extent to which neighbourhoods worked in traditional ways as arenas for reciprocal caring relations, as a bridge between the large-scale services provided by the state and the privacy of family lives, and on the basis of need.[46] Since traditional neighbourhoods have given way in the face of increased mobility and choice consequent on industrialisation and urbanisation, it may be that only networks of parents, mainly mothers and their young children, operate in these time-honoured ways; and that developing community spirit now requires positive creative action to mobilise people.

In this context, the government has made a number of proposals to link formal agencies together. Important among them are the *Every Child Matters* vision of schools as hubs for services; the proposal to improve health and welfare services, by providing clusters of schools with services led by a nurse, and the idea that Sure Start centres and extended schools provide integrated services for children and families.[47] Clearly the government views schools as strong bases for communities to meet people's needs and wishes. This view was shared by the National Association of Head Teachers, which described *Every Child Matters* as a 'pivotal step forward' and identified the universal or holistic character of schools (compared to medical or social services).

Review witnesses also made the point that some families in a very diverse community require specific help in the form of champions or advocates in school. For whilst some submissions saw social diversity as a strength, many others were concerned that, without this extra help, children with disabilities, those with special educational needs, in care, or new to the country cannot lead fulfilling lives. They were keen to endorse collaborative working across agencies and across settings, as set out in *Every Child Matters* and the Children's Plan.[48]

On the other hand, many submissions pointed to the dangers of asking schools 'to do everything' to remedy society's ills. They argued for community responsibility for children's education in the broadest sense and suggested networks for linking up and supporting children and parents (such as 'buddy schemes'). They argued that the community should take responsibility, perhaps shared with schools, for providing a child-friendly environment. These points linked into other proposals: that schools and communities must work together; that families, communities and government must engage with the threat to social cohesion from, for instance, consumerism.

Perhaps it is worth emphasising that for many children the school is their best community resource. It fosters good personal relations among children who may come from different backgrounds but share a locality, and, to some extent, between children and adults. For most children it is the best local resource in that, unlike some other neighbourhood environments, it welcomes them, aims to take account of their interests and is well stocked with stimulating material. These features help to account for children's cheerfulness and positive attitudes in the face of the adult pessimism about childhood which the Review so frequently encountered. Generally, children believe that they have a happy, productive time at school.[49]

Faith in children

Contributions from representatives of religions made up an important strand in the submissions to the Review. Faith groups argued that networks across the triangle of home, school and places of worship have traditionally held neighbourhoods together, as communities – with common purposes and understandings.

For some of these faith groups, family breakdown and 'scholarisation' were identified as undesirable trends, weakening one corner of the cohering triangle. During community soundings, most witnesses from religious faiths said that primary schools were offering a good service to their children; they stressed the common core values of faiths, to which children and schools could subscribe. Although the Christian and Jewish congregations are shrinking, their cohesive traditions and activities may hold families and indeed neighbourhoods together. There are 5,000 supplementary schools run by and for a wide range of minority ethnic groups; these offer help with school work, religious education, opportunities to learn 'mother tongues' and cultural engagement.[50]

In one community soundings session, representatives of various faiths discussed the virtues and problems of faith schools, with some expressing fears of segregation and sectarianism and others claiming that the media had exaggerated these problems. The submission from the British Humanist Association, however, argued that society would be better served by educating all children together, in schools with no religious affiliation or ceremonies, though with teaching of comparative religion and the offer of faith classes out of school hours. Quoting Melissa Benn and Fiona Millar, they said:

> By learning with other children of different backgrounds, faiths and abilities, young people learn how to operate within society, to respect both the strong and the vulnerable, and to understand and work with all elements of a community; this gives each child the strongest moral and intellectual basis for adult citizenship.[51]

CHILDREN AND SOCIETY

Citizens or dependants?

Many contributors to the Review raised the controversial matter of the political status and social positioning of children. If children are defined as different from and inferior to adults, then it is not appropriate for them to work in partnership with adults as citizens; they are *de facto* to be protected by adults. On the other hand, some people argued that we should redefine citizenship within a framework of interdependence between people of whatever age, and thus we can move to understanding children as participating citizens.[52] For, as noted at the start of this chapter, Review witnesses differ as to whether children should be regarded as citizens with rights and responsibilities or as vulnerable dependants on a journey towards citizenship. For instance, one representative in the national soundings proposed that we strengthen the role of children's voices in the system and develop the concept of active citizenship. Another argued: 'The changing social context makes it even more important for children to be active citizens. Even a passive acceptance that there are different people is insufficient. Children must actively embrace and include difference.' And a group session concluded: 'Children need to develop a sense of agency and empowerment with society; and their education. They need to know that their voice is listened to and that they can make a difference.'

On the other hand, for contributors worried about children's vulnerability, the emphasis was on adult teaching and socialisation, to prepare children for their futures as citizens. Their development towards adulthood, under adult guidance and protection, took priority over active citizenship.

A submission from the Citizenship Foundation supported statutory citizenship education in primary schools (in 2009 it remains optional). This would give children the skills, language and confidence to enable them to participate fully in decision-making processes; it would also provide opportunities for broadening cultural, social and political horizons, particularly in respect of developing a sense of identity and appreciation of our diverse society; and it would establish among children social and moral responsibility and a clearer understanding of their legal and moral rights and responsibilities. This submission was therefore concerned with children as citizens now and as citizens for the future. Its points were set within a broad cultural context in a submission from the Jewish school community, which argued that 'education is precisely the process of becoming a citizen, that is, becoming literate and articulate in the laws and narratives that constitute a society in which we are born and for which we carry collective responsibility.' A submission from the International Learning and Research Centre provided a programme of 'personal challenges' for children in KS2 and KS3 to advance their understanding of global citizenship, human rights, values, conflict resolution, diversity, social justice, sustainable development, interdependence and communication. We consider the curriculum implications of views such as these in Chapters 13 and 14.

Other submissions also argued that schools' focus on individual achievement and aspiration deflected attention from the wider role of education: to teach children about their rights and responsibilities as members of their communities and society. More should be done to ensure children learn tolerance, fairness and respect, especially important for life in a diverse society. Some submissions said that the over-arching purpose of primary education lay in developing the 'whole child', fostering each child's personal, social and emotional development, instilling a lifelong love of learning and securing them a bright future.

Many submissions implicitly and in some cases explicitly drew on the UNCRC,[53] in their concern that children's competence, sense of responsibility, and respect for themselves were neither appreciated nor adequately fostered at school. One concern was that children's skills and abilities go unnoticed and are not developed because they are not given responsibility. Others proposed that two-way respect between adults and children, and between children, should be a fundamental principle in education; or they emphasised specifically giving children more choice, autonomy and responsibility. We note a recent change in the law (2008) requires schools to take account of children's participation rights – as advocated by the UN Committee on the Rights of the Child.[54]

CONCLUSION

Media emphasis on bad things happening to childhood in England (mostly without firm foundation) seeped into and even structured many adult submissions and comments to the Review. We agree with those who argued that government and other agencies should promote positive images of childhood, together with evidence, in order to counteract the malign influence of negative representations. The government's own proposals (for instance in the Children's Plan[55]) indicate a commitment not only to improving the quality of childhood, but to engaging with children (as well as other stakeholders) in policy-making and planning, thus promoting the concept of children as valuable citizens in the here-and-now, as well as for the future.

It is important to stress that children are mostly happy at home and at school,[56] as their comments and submissions to the Review testified; and in many but not all schools the power relations are beginning to shift,[57] thus increasing children's well-being. And, very importantly, the government has put children at the centre of its policies. Although this carries some disadvantages, such as a tendency to increase control over childhood, it has many advantages, not least the improvement of local services.

So, yes, English childhoods have changed in the past, say, 25 years. Family forms have changed, formal learning starts at younger ages and other education policy changes impact on children's school experience. Access to a wide range of media has increased, while access to good public space has shrunk, partly as a result of parental fears for children's safety. Some of these changes present children with problems. On the other hand, opportunities for children are greater than they have ever been, both in the present and in the future, in education, health and leisure facilities.[58] What is worrying is the persistence of a long tail of severely disadvantaged children whose early lives are unhappy, whose potential is unrealised and whose future is bleak.

Early years research findings intersect with other research findings[59] which show that working unsocial hours leads a third of mothers and nearly half of fathers to say their job limits the time they can spend reading and playing with children, a concern explored further in Chapter 6. Research suggests strongly that the home learning environment, plus good quality early years experience (see Chapter 10) raises children's school achievement. It seems likely that parents working unsocial hours are among the poorest and most socially disadvantaged, so these findings go some way to explaining why their children's educational chances are in jeopardy.

Interesting points were made in the evidence and submissions on how far children are and can be members of 'the community'. These points reflected, in part, the growing strength of the children's rights movement. The emphasis in recent government documents on children as participants in planning for policy and services is to be welcomed. Children themselves argued for a balance between the security of home and access to the neighbourhood.

Finally we note that a positive and important trend was observable in many Review submissions and soundings: increased respect for children as agents, as valuable people and as citizens. As a discussion at one of the national soundings concluded:

> The real cause of cultural problems is a lack of engagement brought about by a feeling of disempowerment. Education should give children a sense of agency: they can make a difference.

NOTES

1 Franklin (2002); Alderson (2008).
2 UK Children's Commissioners (2008).
3 Children's Society (2007); Layard and Dunn (2009): Chapter 2.
4 Ariès (1962).
5 Elias (1978).
6 Mayall (2010), *The Cambridge Primary Review Research Surveys*, Chapter 3.
7 Pole *et al.* (2001).
8 Mayall (2010).
9 Mayall (2010).
10 Barnes (1969).
11 James and Pollard (2010), *The Cambridge Primary Review Research Surveys*, Chapter 20.
12 Alexander (2001b); Mayall (2002): Chapter 8.
13 For example, Hurt (1979); Muschamp *et al.* (2010), *The Cambridge Primary Review Research Surveys*, Chapter 4.
14 Douglas (1967); Tizard, Mortimore and Burchell (1981).
15 Alldred *et al.* (2002).
16 Edwards and Alldred (2000).
17 Alexander and Hargreaves (2007): 13.
18 Submission from the Royal Geographical Society.
19 Alldred *et al.* (2002); Smith and Barker (2002).

20 UNICEF (2007).
21 Mayall (2010), *The Cambridge Primary Review Research Surveys*, Chapter 3.
22 Ansell *et al.* (2007); Morrow and Mayall (2009).
23 Letter to *The Daily Telegraph* (10 September 2007).
24 See also Layard and Dunn (2009): Chapter 9.
25 Barnes *et al.* (2000); Lewis *et al.* (2007); Mayall (2010).
26 Wikeley *et al.* (2007).
27 Mayall (2010).
28 DCSF (2007b).
29 Children's Society (2008c).
30 TNS Social Research (2007).
31 Blatchford and Baines (2006); Sport England (2003).
32 Mattock *et al.* (2007).
33 Mayall and Storey (1998).
34 Mayall (2010).
35 Ofsted (2006a).
36 See also Turner *et al.* (2004).
37 Valentine *et al.* (2005).
38 Burn and Leach (2004).
39 Buckingham (2003, 2005).
40 Ofsted (2004a).
41 Brugel and Weller (2007).
42 Morrow (2008).
43 Boyden and Ennew (1997).
44 DCSF/DCMS (2008).
45 Ofsted (2006a).
46 Bulmer (1986).
47 Barron *et al.* (2010), *The Cambridge Primary Review Research Surveys*, Chapter 5.
48 DCSF (2007b).
49 Robinson and Fielding (2010), *The Cambridge Primary Review Research Surveys*, Chapter 2; Alexander and Hargeaves (2007).
50 DfES (2006c).
51 Benn and Millar (2006): 8.
52 See Cockburn (1998); Roche (1999); Invernizzi and Williams (2008).
53 United Nations Convention on the Rights of the Child (1989).
54 Children's Rights Alliance for England (2008).
55 DCSF (2007b).
56 Robinson and Fielding (2010), *The Cambridge Primary Review Research Surveys*, Chapter 2.
57 *Ibid.*
58 See Chapter 7.
59 Muschamp *et al.* (2010), *The Cambridge Primary Review Research Surveys*, Chapter 4.

6 Parenting, caring and educating

What happens to children at home affects what happens to them at school. Their family life – particularly its relationship with their school life – can either enhance or erode their chances of fulfilment as primary pupils. While this has been acknowledged for the past 40 years, only since the late 1980s have governments increasingly intervened to prescribe and promote what they define as good practice in home-school relations. In primary schools, parents' and teachers' roles clearly overlap, to a child's advantage: parents are a child's first and continuing educator while teachers, especially in the first years, inevitably combine the vital task of educating with the equally vital task of caring. Beyond this shared role, we know that children thrive educationally and emotionally where parents support their learning and attend school events. We also know that some parents appreciate it when schools show they understand the daily challenges they face.

The relationship of parenting to primary education is profound and multi-faceted, and bears on most of the Cambridge Primary Review's themes. Almost one quarter of the submissions received by the Review concerned parenting and home-school relations. The evidence gathered from these submissions as well as from the research surveys and community and national soundings has helped to frame a range of answers to questions such as how do parents underpin – or undermine – a child's primary education, what can schools do to support parents and carers, and how can schools and families ensure that their goals, if not identical, are not in such conflict as to damage a child's prospects.

CHANGES IN THINKING, POLICY AND PRACTICE

No parents beyond this point

Since Plowden, the relationship between parents and schools has been regularly reassessed and 'involvement' redefined as successive governments have tried ever harder to engage with parents.[1] Each revised approach reflected not only the prevailing political values but also social concerns. For 20 years or more after the end of the Second World War, public and private realms were kept separate, and this was reflected in those notorious warnings on school gates, 'No parents beyond this point.' In the late 1960s and 1970s, however, new ideas emerged about citizenship and participation which recast parental involvement not only as 'good practice' but also as central to education policy. Plowden[2] set out for the first time what would become major concerns in relation to links between home and school. It emphasised the importance of home-school communication, setting expectations of regular meetings, open days and parent-teacher associations (PTAs). Most significantly, it embraced the emerging view that children's success depended as much on family and economic circumstance as on intelligence, willingness to work hard or quality of teaching.[3] However, Plowden's acknowledgement of family influence helped to sustain a 'deficit model' of parenting, and schools were urged to involve parents in order to 'compensate for society'.

In the 1980s, the Conservative government recast parents as consumers and clients of educational services in line with its market ideology.[4] 'Parental choice' became the main driver of excellence. As consumers, parents were encouraged to become more actively involved in running schools. They were given more seats on school governing bodies and expected to report back to all parents once a year via the PTA. This was, in part, a tactic to undermine the influence of left-leaning teaching unions and local authorities with their, in ministerial eyes at least, radical ideas and related low expectations for children. At the family level, the murder of three-year-old James Bulger in 1993 by two boys under the age of 10 refocused public and political attention on parental responsibility. The possibility of teaching 'inadequate' parents how to do the job properly emerged for the first time as a national political issue.

During this period the debate about the relative impact of home and school, such extreme cases apart, veered back and forth, making first the home and then the school pre-eminent. Educational pessimists argued that social inequality remained largely resistant to educational interventions such as the Plowden-inspired educational priority areas, and they found support in Christopher Jencks' landmark study on inequality from the United States.[5] Those committed to the view that intelligence was inherited and immutable, led by psychologists Cyril Burt and Hans Eysenck, argued that humankind is fundamentally unequal, so the task of schools is to sift out the best and do what can be done for the rest.[6] This view, of course, also influenced national policy, up to and well beyond the 1944 Butler Education Act, and it is fair to say that in many people's minds the nature/nurture argument remains not so much unresolved as too firmly resolved in one direction or the other. Meanwhile a scarcity of serious research on school and classroom processes until the 1980s meant that the impact of education was underplayed by evidential default.

In 1992, when the government-commissioned 'three wise men' report on primary teaching was published, it found itself able to summarise the evidence and the emerging consensus thus:

> While there was a time when home circumstances were offered as a convenient explanation for any difficulty which a pupil might experience in the classroom, thus absolving teacher and school of responsibility, there is now a much more balanced and realistic understanding of the relative impact of home and school. Up to a point, the socially advantaged child can compensate for school inadequacy. The disadvantaged child is doubly disadvantaged by a weak school. Schools can and do make a difference, and, given the broad estimate that two thirds of pupils in inner city schools are disadvantaged, it is vitally important that all schools have the highest expectations of all their pupils.[7]

It was also vitally important, the report went on, that they provide children with the best possible teaching.

Parents in partnership

When the New Labour government was elected in 1997, it maintained some of the key beliefs about home-school relations introduced by its predecessors.[8] Parental choice remained a favoured tool for raising standards, readily used by confident and articulate parents comfortable with involvement. However, concern about the long-term costs and consequences of 'social exclusion' and the continuing failure to engage harder-to-reach parents, led to a new family-friendly rhetoric. Avoiding any 'deficit' assumptions, it embraced parity of esteem and equality, using language such as 'alliance', 'agreement' and 'partnership' in order to tempt reluctant parents. The new government declared that family-school partnerships were the route to higher educational standards. Parental support for children's learning was emphasised. Home-school agreements set out 'mutual responsibilities and expectations'. They were to be drafted collaboratively to increase parents' sense of ownership, thereby encouraging greater compliance and commitment.[9] New homework guidelines explained exactly how homework should take place and the number of hours per day children should spend on it.

Sure Start, New Labour's major early-years programme launched in 1999, also focused on parents, particularly in disadvantaged areas. It aimed to close the social and educational gap partly through working with parents to improve their child's health, social and emotional development and readiness to learn on starting school. Then, as further evidence emerged of the impact of family poverty and parental support on children's achievement, partnership was again emphasised in Every Child Matters[10] (ECM) in 2003 and in the White Paper, Higher Standards, Better Schools for All,[11] published two years later. Every Child Matters re-stated the 'building of stronger relationships with parents and the wider community' as a central aim, whilst the White Paper emphasised home-school communication and parents' rights to be kept informed of their child's progress. Indeed, the need to balance parental rights with parental responsibilities has been a consistent theme of New Labour.

At the heart of ECM were extended schools (see Chapter 20) offering various clubs, wrap-around childcare from 8am to 6pm, and parenting support, including adult and family learning. Wrap-around childcare was considered crucial to helping parents back into work, thus pulling themselves and their children out of poverty. An evaluation of 'full-service' extended schools in 2006 found that they 'were able to take individuals and their families through processes of change which re-engaged them with learning and had significant impacts on their life chances'. However, it added that it was not clear that positive outcomes from extended schools' work were sufficiently widespread to transform whole communities, nor did the benefit for schools materialise in every case. More work was also needed to engage the most vulnerable and marginalised people.[12]

In 2006, the Common Assessment Framework for Children and Young People was introduced to provide an integrated and holistic structure for assessing children's development. Early intervention was a key principle with assessment covering how well parents or carers were able to support children's development and respond to their needs as well as the impact of wider family and environmental elements.

In 2007, the government's Every Parent Matters[13] agenda replaced 'involvement' with 'engagement' as the phrase of choice. Local authorities were urged to appoint parenting advisers, and parents were to be given a greater say in shaping services. Once again, parents were put centre stage in recognition of their indelible influence on children's educational achievement despite many measures designed to mitigate this effect. Similarly the 2007 Children's Plan[14] saw parents as central to the task of improving children's lives, saying that 'partnership with parents is a unifying theme' of the plan and that 'parents' support for their child's learning is an essential foundation for educational achievement'. An additional £30 million was to be spent between 2007 and 2010 to 'provide more family learning to help parents and carers develop skills and learn with their children in schools.'

In the 2008 Children and Young Person's Bill, the government, accepting its own role as legal guardian for children in care, set out to improve the education of all looked-after children.

CHANGES IN FAMILY LIFE

Considerable demographic and social changes have occurred over the past 50 years. They have had a profound impact on both patterns of work and the structure of the family, and consequently have affected the daily rhythm and fabric of children's lives at home and school. Parental separation, lone parenting, step-families, half-siblings, and being an only child are all more familiar to today's children than those of 1968.[15] Both parents are more likely to work, and to work long and atypical hours. Overall, more children have to cope with increasingly complex and uncertain lives, inevitably placing extra demands on schools. In Britain, 70 per cent of mothers of 9 to 12-month-old babies now do some paid work, compared with 25 per cent 25 years ago.[16]

Lone parents

Most children still live with their natural parents, either married or cohabiting, though the proportion has fallen gradually from 92 per cent in 1972 to 75 per cent in 2002. Consequently, the proportion of children living with a lone parent rose from 7 per cent in 1972 to 23 per cent in 2007. Until the mid 1980s, divorce accounted for a large part of this rise but more recently the number of single lone mothers has grown at a faster rate. In 1971, only 1 per cent of families were headed by a 'never married' parent; by 2002 this had increased to 12 per cent. This trend is likely to have influenced the rate of re-partnering and child poverty (see below).

Living together – and apart

Cohabiting has significantly increased in Britain. The proportion of (unmarried) women under 60 living with a partner has almost doubled, from 13 per cent in 1986 to 25 per cent in 2006.[17] Cohabitation appears to be more unstable than marriage and more likely to result in separation and lone motherhood – despite the fact that 40 per cent of marriages end in divorce. Although about half of cohabiting couples do get married, the proportion is higher for childless women than for mothers with a dependent child.[18] When cohabiting couples split up they are much more likely to find new partners within a year or two than married couples.[19]

In 2004, 43 per cent of births took place outside marriage, an increase from 9 per cent in 1975. Of those babies,15 per cent were born to women whose average age was 21 and who did not have a live-in partner, while a quarter were born to women who were cohabiting and whose average age was 23.

There are also more step-families today than 40 years ago. It was estimated that in 2004–5 10 per cent of all families with dependent children were step-families, with nearly nine in 10 of these consisting of a couple living with children from the woman's previous relationship.[20] Many children living with a natural parent and a step-parent will also visit an extended step-family headed by the non-resident parent.

Schools shoulder the stress

Increasingly fluid and varied family forms expose more children and parents to distress and difficulty. Many submissions to the Review expressed concern about rising and serial family breakdown, referring to the negative impact on children's education and well-being. For example, representatives from senior management teams in the Review's community soundings highlighted the 'emotional baggage' which children bring into school from broken homes. Senior staff from schools in one region spoke graphically about the latter, which they estimated affected 30 per cent of children in one school and more than half in another. They talked of children being shunted from one care placement to another, and of the growing number forced to take on quasi-adult roles to help their single parents. Several submissions referred to the damage done to children's learning as they struggle to cope with family upheaval, which may also involve moving house and changing school. One local authority commented:

> The connection between health, emotional well-being and learning is huge. If children are unhealthy their ability to concentrate and focus is likely to be reduced. If children feel unhappy they won't be able to concentrate on their learning. If pupils are fearful they are less likely to take risks or try new things.

Family discord, breakdown and change may not only threaten children's sense of security but also undermine their identity. Identity rests in part upon key, close relationships – children know themselves through the feedback of those who care for them. When a care-giver leaves or appears to reject a child, the result can be feelings of bereavement, low self esteem and lack of confidence.

Research shows a strong link between poor mental health and family discord. Children of lone parents are twice as likely as those of married or cohabiting parents to have emotional problems (16 per cent compared to 8 per cent). Problems are also more common in reconstituted families (15 per cent) than in non-step families (9 per cent) and among families headed by a cohabiting couple (11 per cent) than a married couple (7 per cent). The causes of emotional disorder are identified as family changes; parents' mental illness; children's repeated early separations from their parents; harsh or inadequate parenting; exposure to abuse, neglect and domestic violence; and adverse peer influences.[21] Of children with emotional disorders, 44 per cent were behind in their intellectual development, with 23 per cent more than two years behind. The links between mental health problems in children and later adverse outcomes were discussed at length in the Children's Society's Good Childhood Inquiry.

More positively, teachers told the Review that the government-endorsed Social and Emotional Aspects of Learning (SEAL) programme, a comprehensive, whole-school approach to promoting the skills that underpin effective learning, had been a positive step towards helping children to cope with stressful situations. Many called for this approach to be extended further. And parents in a deprived London community were clear that they valued the physical and curriculum space schools provided for stressed children to 'chill out', to learn Tai Chi, and to participate in artistic activities.

Complications of shared care

On an immediate practical level, more broken families mean more 'shared care'. In their research survey for the Review, Yolande Muschamp and her colleagues described shared care as covering arrangements in which children live between two homes in the same area, sometimes with different sets of siblings, both birth and step, in each; or alternatively spending time away visiting the non-resident parent at weekends or during the school holidays often travelling some distance.[22] A 2008 survey by One Parent Families/Gingerbread and Oxford University found that one in 10 children shared their time equally between estranged parents and one quarter visited the non-resident parent once a week. This survey also confirmed that between a half and one third of children rarely, if ever, see their non-resident father after a family breakdown, although 20 per cent of these are likely to have other forms of contact with him.[23] A non-resident father (the usual arrangement) may therefore be a regular presence in homes and schools, or he may appear erratically, or not at all – in which case a longer term stepfather may become involved in a child's school instead. With the increasing practice of same-sex parenting, an identifiable father or mother may not feature, and with more women electing to parent alone, a father may never have been involved in daily care. Shared care is also provided by grandparents in multi-generational 'beanpole' families. As a result of this complexity, many schools find it difficult to know which parent or caring adult to contact, when is the best time to arrange meetings or home visits or what assumptions to make about who might be available to help with homework. For children who live between two homes, many schools provide two sets of books to overcome a common difficulty of not having the right books in the right place when needed.

PATTERNS OF WORK AND POVERTY

In 2007, 2 million children were living in families without a wage earner and the overall number growing up in relative poverty had risen for a second year to reach 3.9 million.[24] This increase paralleled the widening achievement gap between children who do well and those who do not. Married couples with dependent children had the highest gross weekly incomes in 2002 with 71 per cent earning more than £500, compared with 50 per cent of cohabiting couples with children and 16 per cent of lone parents. More than one third of lone-parent families had £150 or less to live on every week, compared with only 5 per cent of married couples and 8 per cent of cohabiting couples with dependent children. Lone mothers who had never married were particularly likely to be poor. Nearly half got by on £150 or less a week, compared with 19 per cent of divorced lone mothers and 30 per cent of separated lone mothers. In OECD countries, larger families were among the poorest.

The subtleties and subtext of poverty

Growing up in poverty is typically thought to hamper children's learning because parents have less money to buy educational toys or books or to pay for out-of-school activities that help children to acquire skills and confidence. In order to level the playing field for advantaged and disadvantaged children, the government has supplied free children's books to families and enabled schools to run more clubs and after-school activities. But the impact of poverty is profound. Quality of parenting suffers and a combination of poor health, cramped housing and the stress of managing on a tight budget in a commercialised world places those who already have to struggle at greater disadvantage. It also often places them at odds with schools. Many impoverished parents left school early with few qualifications and this apparent failure can leave them with feelings of alienation, antagonism or indifference when it comes to education – and many schools reported such attitudes to this Review.

Impact of deprivation on children

Children are likely to be aware from an early age of the limitations placed on them by low social status and low income. A research review conducted for the NSPCC indicated, too, that children who grow up in poverty are more likely to be criticised, punished and shouted at by their parents – perhaps an indicator of the stresses faced by parents at the sharp end.[25] The shame and humiliation often induced by such experiences damage a child's sense of self-worth, perceptions of responsibility and learner identity.[26] The greater prevalence of physical and mental ill-health and substance abuse among such families compared with those of advantaged children may also profoundly unsettle a young child, especially if it is a single parent who is unable to care effectively. Low income, crowded accommodation, delayed language skills and social diffidence combine to make finding and keeping friends harder for disadvantaged children. Those who feel a failure are more likely to team up with the class tearaways to gain at least some affirmation, if, indeed, they are able to make friends at all. Children cite getting help with their class work if they are stuck as an advantage of having friends.[27]

Strategies for helping families on the edge

There was an impressive consensus that educational disadvantage and social disadvantage are closely linked and cannot be addressed effectively with one-off measures. As the report from the large-scale Effective Pre-School and Primary Education 3–11 Project (EPPE), submitted as evidence to the Review, put it: 'We can conclude that no one factor is the key to raising achievement – it is the combination of experiences over time that matters.' Despite the entrenched nature of much social disadvantage, the relevant research surveys indicate that well-conceived school projects and interventions can create better relationships with harder-to-reach parents and improve educational outcomes for disadvantaged children.

Organisations and practitioners at the Review's national soundings acknowledged that policies are in place to help schools support families at the economic margins but that these need time to begin to make a difference. It was argued that schools and teachers need to be trained in how to work with marginalised groups – it is particularly important, they said, that schools reach out to the different groups, instead of waiting for them to come into school. The groups that can benefit from knowing that schools truly understand their circumstances and from having a more detailed, realistic view of what schools expect from them include asylum-seekers and refugees, single mothers – especially teenage and young ones, Travellers of Irish Heritage and Gypsy/Roma groups, families surviving on very low incomes, families living in temporary accommodation and seasonal labourers. Organisations were supportive of measures to reduce the long tail of underachievement, saying these also needed more time 'to actually make a difference'.

HOME-SCHOOL RELATIONS

In a perfect world ...

Mutually supportive, tolerant and respectful relationships between home and school are now regarded as essential if all children, regardless of background, are to achieve their best. Many Review witnesses endorsed this, especially parents themselves. Teachers, head teachers, parents, faith groups and non-denominational organisations all welcomed recent government initiatives to forge more effective links between home, school and local communities. Some children's organisations also mentioned helpful local authority schemes to increase parental involvement in their child's learning.

Regardless of government policies, some parents have always been actively involved in enhancing their children's development and educational progress. This activity has taken a number of forms, described by Professor Charles Desforges and Alberto Abouchaar in 2003 as:

> 'Good parenting' in the home pre-school (which provides a good foundation of skills, values, attitudes and self-concept); visits to school to gather or give relevant information and establish good relationships; discussions with the teacher to keep abreast of the child's progress or to discuss emergent problems; and assisting more broadly in the practical activities and governance of the school.[28]

In addition, parents may supplement formal education after a child starts school by helping with reading and homework, for example; showing interest in and appreciating what a child learns and achieves; and supporting the school's values and rules.

Many schools work hard to improve their working relationship with parents, encouraged by a raft of initiatives. A study of effective school-parent partnerships by the Family and Parenting Institute in 2006 was submitted as evidence to the Review.[29] The project addressed practitioners' concerns about the rapid spread of these initiatives, including school-parent partnerships, parental choice, home-school agreements, parental involvement in learning, family support and extended schools. One anxiety was that parents were expected to become involved in schools without first being enticed or appropriately 'engaged'.

The models of school-parent partnerships the project found were:

- one-to-one work through dedicated workers such as home-school support workers, family liaison officers, parent support advisers, home-school link workers
- starting school information sessions, consultation events with parents, multi-agency working
- lifelong learning, family learning, community development.

Children and young people indicated they were generally happy with their parents' level of involvement and interest in their studies, though they would value more encouragement. That said, submissions to the Review from children described in appreciative terms the help they received at home.

In an imperfect world ...

Establishing good home-school relations is not easy. The challenges include, according to the Family and Parenting Institute's study, parents' lack of time and the need for clarity about the different initiatives. More fundamentally, mutual respect between home and school, though desirable, is not always present, as many Review witnesses reported. A common belief from within schools was that too many parents have strong 'anti-school' attitudes that may stem from their own experiences, and some are apathetic about or openly hostile to educational objectives. Some submissions detailed a rise in incidents that involve 'difficult' and 'disaffected' parents, who seem to target schools and complain constantly, placing an additional burden on school staff. One education consultant referred to the 'increase in disaffected adults who target schools as part of their vendetta against society'.

Many of the rising numbers of parents working long hours in low-paid jobs say they would like to spend more time with their children – reading, playing and helping with homework. Instead, where both parents work long hours, childcare may take place in shifts. Growing numbers of children attend after-school clubs or go to independent carers after school. This plethora of family forms, working patterns and care arrangements was felt by many community soundings witnesses to result in poorer quality parenting.

Many of the 64 teaching assistants (TAs) who participated were strongly critical of parents. Some thought that much parenting, judged by any criteria, was inadequate and recommended remedial classes for parents who lacked the necessary skills. Some believed that many of today's parents fail to socialise their children or even pay them any attention. Some referred to those at the contrasting end of the parenting spectrum who put their children under stress by being too pushy and demanding. Many mentioned the difficulty of working with parents who have low aspirations for themselves and their children. (It may be worth noting here that most of the TAs we met were also parents and that they lived close to their schools, so in effect they were judging their neighbours.)

The teachers in the community soundings expressed similar views. They said they had noticed a marked effect on children of unsettled home life. Some children were badly prepared for school and suffered from a lack of educational stimulus, though others were over-protected and under too much pressure to do well. Governors added a further insightful community perspective to otherwise similar concerns: the pressure on parents of the high cost of housing. Local community representatives highlighted poor parenting as a major problem, though in one area the depressed local economy was acknowledged as a factor. Even the parents present criticised other parents whom, they felt, abdicated their responsibility leading to unruly children with selfish, consumerist attitudes.

Similar concerns are expressed in the submissions to the Review. Many claimed that parents often lack basic parenting skills, citing the perceived increase in levels of behavioural problems as evidence, especially among boys, but also poor socialisation and preparation for school. Some pointed out that parents receive less help now from the extended family, making life particularly hard for those on their own. With almost one in 10 five- to 15-year-olds suffering significant mental health problems,[30] many submissions also referred to the increasingly fluid family structures as a reason for children's disruptive behaviour and emotional problems, though perhaps reflecting children's difficult experiences rather than negligent parenting. The submission from the British Association for Early Childhood Education said:

> There are unresolved tensions between the realisation by government of the key role that parents play in their children's education and development, and the drive to get parents back to work.

Only one parental submission sought to describe what 'adequate' parenting might consist of, and none reflected on the direct and daily hardship that economic, emotional and community impoverishment and family upheaval impose, undermining parents' capacity to nurture happy and successful children. Parenting in stressful circumstances is difficult.

Parents who are deemed antagonistic or apathetic could, perhaps, be understood more sympathetically within this context. Parents, of course, will be antagonistic to school for a number of reasons, but one could be the need to preserve their relationship with the most reliable and important thing in their life – their child. If their child succeeds academically, they may fear loss of their child's respect and love as it moves on and away to lead a life they could find difficult to understand. Unblocking the transmission of low aspiration must include not only valuing parents' 'funds of knowledge' but also ensuring that all parents are given choices and are respected as decision-makers, rather than, yet again, being told what to do.

In all this, without wishing to imply criticism of our witnesses, it is helpful to take a longer perspective. The tendency of education professionals to place parents in the camps of 'poor' and 'pushy' has a long pedigree, as does the equating of 'good' parenting with compliance with the way schools wish things to be. From this alternative perspective, both 'poor' and 'pushy' parents are those who fail to conform to educators' expectations and values, which leaves open the question of whether the expectations are valid and the values command universal acceptance.[31]

Schools' failings

Leading from the opposite corner, some parents and research consultants questioned the role of schools rather than that of families. In the community soundings, several minority ethnic witnesses said that schools should try harder to understand their culture and their children's lives. Other parents, particularly recent arrivals from countries with different work patterns, felt under pressure to get a job rather than to stay at home with their children. They disagreed with the assumption that pre-school childcare was better than their care. These views tend to confirm the concern in the previous paragraph that some professionals may be too ready to assume that their own values are unassailable.

The Review's research survey on primary schools and other agencies considered that:

> The notion of professional partnership with parents … may represent a genuine desire to give parents a greater and more equitable share in decisions about their children's well-being and progress. But it may also be intended to recruit parents to the school's purposes, or to enable the smooth operation of bureaucratic procedures. At times, partnership with parents may even function as a method of passing the child's 'problems' back to the parents.[32]

Parents surveyed by the Family and Parenting Institute said they wanted better communication and consultation. They appreciated being welcomed into school and enjoyed meeting other parents and making friends. They valued family learning as a confidence raiser that improved parent-child relationships, but commented that parent groups, such as PTAs, can be exclusive. They also said that schools often ignore useful skills and knowledge among parents, carers and grandparents.

Schools' tendency to neglect children's and families' home-acquired 'funds of knowledge' and out-of-school interests was also noted in several Review research surveys – and the previous chapter.[33] The research surveys pointed out that when these are drawn upon, classroom learning can be more relevant, lively and effective. By focusing exclusively on formal learning and ignoring what children do know, schools may not only expose cultural differences to the disadvantage of some children but also may devalue what parents contribute from their rich experience. True partnership cannot flourish where respect and power are not equal. As Muschamp and her colleagues identified, the home-school knowledge exchange project (part of a larger research programme exploring influences on teaching and learning) 'highlights the need to understand home-school communication as a complex process in which issues of control and power are present and shape the forms of communication … 'The same project revealed that when effective home-school communication is achieved 'the contribution that parents make to their child's learning was often rich and extensive.'[34]

What is confirmed by these contrasting views is the finding, reported in Chapter 5, that the advances in home-school partnership may still leave the home-school relationship, in the less visible domains of respect for parental values and children's out of school lives, somewhat unequal.

THE ROLE OF PARENTS AND CARERS

Parents as image-makers

'At-home good parenting', viewed as the promotion of attitudes, values and aspirations which are pro-learning, has a major impact on school outcomes 'even after all other forces have been factored out', according to research.[35]

A key research review in 2003 assessed the impact on achievement and behaviour of different forms of parental involvement. It concluded that parents' main influence is exerted indirectly and spontaneously by shaping their child's image of themselves as a learner: setting high aspirations, providing security, stability and plenty of conversation, rather than through working directly with or in schools, helping in class or attending school events.[36] Other research,[37,38] also reported on the importance of parents', and especially mothers', contributions to their children's education, at home and at school, in particular through boosting their self-confidence and learning. The EPPE project, which studied 2,550 children drawn from 950 primary schools, noted that:

> The quality of the home-learning environment and parents' (especially mothers') qualification levels remain the most important background factors relating to a child's attainment in reading and mathematics at Year 5 ...[39]

Expect the best

As we show in the next chapter, children learn with and through others – families, carers, peers and teachers – and have to take frequent risks as they face the prospect of getting something wrong and possibly letting other people down. A child's 'learner identity' is increasingly accepted as a key determinant of performance. Children achieve more if they perceive themselves to be capable and are self-motivated and self-believing. Although friends and teachers also influence identity in school-aged children, for the pre-school child parents and carers have the greatest impact. Several submissions and research surveys pointed to the benefit to children where parents encourage their child and trust in their ability to succeed. According to US research, 'parents' beliefs and expectations have a bigger impact on a child's mathematical and language abilities than do any teachers and school marks, especially in the elementary years.'[40]

Focusing praise on effort has also been shown to benefit children. Again, several Review witnesses mentioned the work of social psychologist Carol Dweck who has demonstrated that receiving praise for effort rather than achievement or performance increases motivation. Dweck's research suggests that a child's beliefs about intelligence can be altered by feedback from teachers and therefore, by implication, parents.[41] Where parents give a child plenty of positive feedback for their efforts rather than results, and do not punish them for mistakes or lapses in behaviour that they cannot yet control, children will have a positive view of what they can achieve and realise that well-directed effort works.

Recent research in neurobiology shows that incremental experience is crucial for learning and knowledge construction.[42] The brain learns from every experience, but cumulative learning is essential to make sense of that experience – to file it away in comprehensible and retrievable categories that help to sequence thoughts and give structure to conceptual understanding. Brain functioning indicates that different levels of exposure to spoken or written language will lead to differential learning. So, for example, children who look at books freely are likely to find reading easier. It is undoubtedly helpful to children if parents reflect on the day's events, answer children's questions in a manner that addresses the root of the query and explain relationships between things and events. The cumulative nature of learning explains why sustained absence from school through illness can be so damaging, and also why emotional distress or family trauma can impede learning. Research in 1997 suggested that as little as two weeks out of school in body or mind can set children back permanently.[43]

The opinions the Review received on the value of educational play at home differed. Although many researchers now believe that pretend play contributes significantly to a young child's cognitive development and imagination[44] (even more so when an adult helps to make it happen or another child is involved), others point out the great value to a child of everyday, simple activities. Researchers in 2002 argued that while many parents do not play obviously educational games or read stories, merely talking about daily domestic life – shopping, helping with babies, looking out of the window – can teach a great deal. They said that 'learning at home occurs in a wide variety of contexts ... and mother-child play [may not be] especially valuable.'[45] Plenty of chat, explanation and review of daily events are, however, widely seen as crucial to:

- develop a child's language skills
- embed the relationship and convey respect and regard
- enable children to gain a better understanding of their world.

HOMEWORK: RIGHT OR WRONG?

Not all parents feel confident about helping their child pre-school or in school, particularly with homework. Many parents at the Review's community soundings questioned the need for primary pupils, especially the younger ones, to have homework, though some welcomed it. One parent submitted a trenchantly-argued case against homework as undermining children's confidence. Travellers of Irish Heritage told the Review that their children were disadvantaged by the rise in homework because they often lacked space, computers, or parents able to help. These limitations might also apply to children from other minority ethnic or disadvantaged families.

Some parent groups welcomed the development of family learning initiatives, saying they had developed parents' confidence and skills. And there was evidence that children do better when schools offer parents specific advice about homework. However, Caroline Sharp, in research on the effectiveness of homework for Ofsted in 2000, said that: 'Evidence at the primary level of a positive relationship between time spent on homework and achievement is inconclusive.'[46]

On parental involvement in homework, she observed:

- In general, parents want schools to set homework although it can be a source of conflict.
- Parents are more involved when their children are younger and the degree of involvement is influenced by cultural and socio-economic factors.
- Research does not indicate a clear relationship between the amount of parental involvement in homework and pupils' achievement in school.
- Parental involvement can be appropriate or inappropriate, leading to different consequences for pupil achievement.
- There is some evidence that lower achievers benefit where parents are both involved and informed.

On evidence of what type of assistance can be effective, research in 2001 concluded:

> Operating largely through modelling, reinforcement and instruction, parents' homework involvement appears to influence student success insofar as it supports student attributes related to achievement.[47]

In other words, where parents are encouraging and not disparaging, and make their children feel successful and capable rather than useless and incompetent, and where they model effort and hard work, a child will be more likely to develop a 'can-do' approach.

Unfair advantages?

Many submissions expressed concern that parental involvement may increase rather than reduce inequality. Reference to research[48] in 2000 summarised the position: 'Parental involvement currently acts as a "lever" maximising the potential of the already advantaged by engaging those parents most likely to reflect the norms and values of the school and ignoring the hard-to-reach parents who are less likely to readily enforce [these] norms .... 'Parental choice in school selection and homework were two areas explored as likely to give unequal advantage to some pupils, serving to widen inequalities rather than drive up standards for all.

In their research survey for the Review, Stephen Machin and Sandra McNally concluded that

> ... choice and competition may exacerbate educational inequalities. Parents are not equal in the extent to which they can exercise choice or use information ... better-off families have the freedom to exercise it whereas poorer families are faced with numerous constraints on their ability to make choices.[49]

They nonetheless consider it important to address educational inequality directly by re-examining factors that discriminate against the poor (such as school admission policies) and targeting disadvantaged schools, families and geographical areas for special assistance.

In relation to homework, obstacles such as limited space, insufficient backup from adults and limited access to computers have led some to query the government's belief that homework can raise attainment and narrow the achievement gap. Some claim that it could have the opposite result, mainly benefiting children whose parents can offer effective help. However, given that the educational benefit of homework itself or of parental involvement in homework has not been proved, the widening achievement gap is unlikely to be significantly reduced or added to by any homework policy.

DIVERSITY, DIFFERENCE AND DIFFICULTIES

Primary pupils represent an increasingly diverse mix of ethnicities, nationalities, languages, cultures, faiths and styles of families (see also Chapter 8). The National Primary Headteachers' Association (NPhA)[50] noted primary schools' great efforts to support all pupils and to engage parents and communities in helping where language and cultural difficulties exist. Speedy contact, induction and support of both child and family are vital, especially in areas of significant population movement. It is also vital that schools strive to make their communications clear and appropriately translated so they can be read and understood by all parents. The Review's research survey by Ian Barron and colleagues references work suggesting that while some minority ethnic families are regarded with approval – for their cohesiveness and close supervision of their children – other parenting styles may not win favour. However, as the authors of the Review's research survey on parenting conclude, home-school relationships should be between individual parents and individual teachers, all of whom have the interests of the child at heart. Parents are not a homogenous group but neither are teachers, and the relationship between these groups needs to acknowledge the strengths and expertise of each.[51]

Communication and socialisation

Many teachers and head teachers worried about the large numbers of children entering school with limited communication skills. It is clear from evidence received by the Review that language is crucial for both development and learning and that there is a huge variation in language skills from an early age, an issue further discussed in Chapter 7. While it is tempting to point the finger at excessive watching of television by young children, at care arrangements that offer little conversation, or at the fragmentation of families and greater numbers of only children, more evidence is needed. The National Literacy Trust found that, while children between the ages of two and five may benefit from good quality educational television, in general children who are heavy television viewers have lower expressive language scores. Viewing by children of general or adult programmes is correlated with poor language development in pre-schoolers, attributable to both the quality and the quantity of exposure to television more generally.[52]

A recent Conservative party enquiry, chaired by John Bercow MP, found that speech and communication problems are associated with disadvantaged areas. He estimated that:

> Approximately 7 per cent of five-year-olds entering school in England – nearly 40,000 children in 2007 – have significant difficulties with speech and language. These children are likely to need specialist and/or targeted intervention at key points in their development.[53]

Overall, it is believed that some 50 per cent of children and young people in some socio-economically disadvantaged populations have speech and language skills significantly lower than their peers. Strong speaking and listening skills are connected with the ability to learn to read and to make friends, which is why untreated problems can lead, according to the Bercow Report, to lower educational attainment, behaviour problems, emotional and psychological difficulties, poorer employment prospects, challenges to mental health and, for some, descent into criminality.[54]

Children who arrive at school poorly socialised were frequently mentioned by witnesses from the caring and teaching professions. In order to learn and fit in at school, children need to be able to sit still, remain in a room, concentrate, see something through, not get angry at every frustration, eat and undertake other tasks when asked, understand the word 'no', share and, of course, give and take while negotiating their way round the classroom and its resources. If a child is chaotic, aggressive and defensive, or does not know how to manage itself in a group setting or form friendships, it will be at a considerable disadvantage. The NPhA recommended parenting classes to those struggling to socialise their children, as did several teaching assistants in the community soundings. It also advocated more consistent outreach work by Sure Start children's centres as well as better co-ordination between Sure Start staff and health visitors. With a clear mandate from *Every Child Matters* to enhance children's well-being, they thought schools would be better able to reach and support all parents.

When the State is the parent

Children looked after by local authorities still fare depressingly badly at school. Government statistics on the 44,200 children who had been in care for 12 months or more in 2007 showed that, on average, 56 per cent reached level 2 at KS1 and 49 per cent reached level 4 at KS2, compared with 85 per cent and 82 per cent respectively for all children.[55] The government has declared its commitment to looked-after children and these figures, though low, were a slight improvement on the previous three years.

Among looked-after five- to 10-year-olds, rates of mental disorder are five times higher than in the general population. Sixty per cent of children in residential care homes have a conduct disorder, as do 30 per cent of foster children – the figure for children growing up in private homes is 5 per cent. Rates for mental health problems were highest for children in a placement for less than one year and lowest for those in a placement for five years or more.

Prisoners' families

More than 150,000 children had a parent in prison in the UK in 2007 and this figure was expected to rise to more than 200,000 by 2012.[56] This is more than double the number of children in care and six times the number on the child protection register. Seven per cent of children will see a parent imprisoned during their school years; 45 per cent of women prisoners had children living with them at the time of imprisonment, 33 per cent had a child under the age of five. A total of 22 per cent of prisoners divorce or separate as a result of their imprisonment and 45 per cent lose contact with their families whilst serving a custodial sentence. Many of their children experience negative consequences which will be affected by such factors as the age of the child, length of sentence, disruption to home life, nature of the crime, witnessing the arrest, poverty and distance from the prison. Children of junior school age may be more conscious of the stigma associated with having a parent in prison, leading to feelings of shame, isolation, confusion and grief. If the family has to split up and move, children can become separated from friends and siblings and have no one to confide in. 'It can be devastating for a child to realise that an outside force can come into their home and split their family up by taking away a parent.'[57]

It is not surprising that children of prisoners have poorer educational outcomes and are at three times the risk of both behaviour and mental health problems compared with their peers. It should be incumbent on schools to strive to provide information that can be passed on to an imprisoned parent to enable them to retain an interest in what their child is learning at school, and this needs to dovetail with greatly improved visiting facilities and opportunities for children and families within prisons.

KEY DILEMMAS AND DYNAMICS

Governments have striven for several decades to close the social and educational divide that exists in the UK. The identified causes have been many, including over-controlling local authorities, community deprivation and social exclusion, poverty and poor parenting. The spotlight has rested upon parents, poverty and educational attainment largely because the more sophisticated data analysis now available finds clear links between them: children's educational achievement substantially determines their future life-chances, and achievement is, in turn, significantly affected by their early experiences at home and in school, including growing up in poverty. The challenge is to understand why the associations are so powerful and what interventions at a family level could counter the downward tug of disadvantage.

Has parenting got worse?

It is hard to determine whether the quality of parenting has deteriorated significantly over the past 20 years. As one witness said, 'there have always been complaints about "feckless" parents'. Although the Review heard complaints from teachers about 'unmanageable' and disruptive behaviour, particularly amongst boys, it should not be forgotten that 'helpful-to-the-child' parenting is located somewhere in between doing nothing and doing too much: parents can over-control as well as under-control, and de-motivate while attempting to motivate. Shortfalls at one end of the spectrum should not always receive more attention than those at the other, disruption excepted. Primary school exclusions are one way of assessing rising rates of disruption, and do not suggest this is a significantly growing problem. Indeed, Sir Alan Steer, in his 2009 report on behaviour in schools concluded: 'While there is legitimate concern in society about standards of behaviour in young people (as in earlier generations), there is strong evidence from a range of sources that the overall standards of behaviour achieved by schools is good and has improved in recent years.'[58]

Following their review of parental involvement, Desforges and Abouchaar concluded, 'there is little or no place for programmes of ad hoc activities, for training which merely makes children biddable, or for any intervention that lacks follow-through.'[59] The cumulative evidence suggests that any family support offered in schools should focus less on managing behaviour, which implies a parenting deficit, and more on encouraging parents to help their child develop a more positive learner identity, an appropriately optimistic view of what they can achieve.

Research has established that parental involvement has a significant positive effect on achievement, more through what happens in the home, through encouragement and enabling conversations, than through direct participation in school activities. Nonetheless, a good relationship between home and school is widely and correctly acknowledged as valuable for children's learning. The Review's evidence makes clear that this relationship is extremely complex and needs to embrace far more factors than are usually addressed, going further than, for example, simply juxtaposing 'home' and 'school' and seeking greater 'partnership' and 'engagement' as if to imply that the problem will be solved if both sides get even closer. But this merely raises questions of how close they should get, according to whose agenda, on what terms and for what purpose. In many areas of the country, schools need to look beyond home visits, meetings in community venues or providing a parents' room in school. Instead they need to help parents overcome any hostility by offering respect and understanding.

In order to frame a comprehensive, balanced, sensitive, respectful and thus more sophisticated and effective programme to improve children and their families' experience of school and learning, we need to explore some of the key dilemmas and dynamics of home-school relationships that the Review's collective investigations have brought into focus.

How close?

There are potential problems with trying to raise school achievement by bringing home and school closer together:

- any appropriate boundaries and differences between home and school could become blurred or even dismantled;
- the 'funds of knowledge' embedded in the cultures of homes and communities may continue to be undervalued or ignored;
- educational inequalities may increase rather than reduce;
- parents may be either treated as a single group, which they are not, or individuals or groups may be ineptly identified as problematic thus perpetuating the notion of 'deficit parenting';
- the existing power imbalance between parents and school could remain;
- the encroachment of school on homes, the 'scholarisation' of home, could continue and could be rejected by parents as intrusive;
- older primary children will miss out on the increasing autonomy and privacy in their school life they say they want.

Hard to reach or hard to change?

Another confusion is the difference between hard to reach and hard to change. A parent can be easy to reach yet hard to change (potentially, a 'pushy' and demanding parent) or hard to reach but, once reached, easy to change. It is at least as important to understand the reasons for any resistance to change as it is to overcome a parent's reluctance to show up at school.

Hard-to-reach parents who have attended parenting programmes are clear about what they want. According to research in 2004, they want support services to treat them like adults, to see them as partners in solving their problems and to receive practical help with finances and housing. Autonomy is a key issue: they need to be able to say yes or no to services, to choose the time or strategies which would work best for them and, above all, to stay in charge of solving any parenting problems. They also want professionals to respect their views and be warm, approving, responsive and ready to listen, not to lecture them.[60] The research concluded that 'the quality of relationship between the giver and receiver of support is a critical element in making some action "supportive"'. It is especially important to enable disadvantaged parents to retain a sense of agency and self-respect during any programme to advance their child's learning.

A parent who wrote to the Review ended her letter: 'I hope your study helps parents and children to feel ownership over the primary-school experience.' Whether a parent is comfortably content or struggling with stress or poverty, no one will lose out if this is the mantra for both policy-makers and teachers.

CONCLUSION

Family breakdown and poverty are huge influences on the growth and development of children. When the two coincide, the effect is potentially dramatic. The impact of poverty is therefore particularly profound when it is associated with unsettling family and social upheaval; and made potentially even worse when experienced during a period of economic expansion and consumerism which accentuates a family's lack of choice about life style and possessions.

Despite the entrenched patterns of transmission of advantage and disadvantage, it remains important to strive to alleviate social and educational inequality – to minimise the waste both of children's talent and of public resources invested in education. Schools can and do make a difference. This is not best achieved by intruding on the privacy of individual families but through modelling the encouragement, trust, respect and optimism that we would wish all parents and carers to convey to their children to give them a positive learner identity. Schools need to move a fair distance to ensure all parents feel respected and empowered, and there is now enough evidence of what works to employ sophisticated, sensitive and multi-layered approaches. Family literacy programmes are valuable. Specific guidance from schools on how to help a child learn seem to work well provided they are not intimidating and do not ask too much. There is no clear evidence that parenting programmes focused on managing behaviour are effective, but there is scope to make sure all parents know about proven ways to motivate and encourage children and help them to feel capable. There are two golden rules for working with parents: it must start from where they are, not where they 'ought' to be; and ethos and style are at least as important as what is being conveyed or 'taught'. Implicit in the second is the need to share power and convey an equal regard for individuals, which does not mean all behaviour is equally acceptable.

A sense of agency is central to emotional health and well-being. Depression, anxiety and a fatalistic approach to life set in when individuals feel they have no control and lose confidence in their ability to decide or influence anything. Work with parents that attempts to value what they know and are good at will help to embed a more positive self-image and identity. Schools need to aim to ensure parents feel respected, capable, involved and empowered. Because then parents will inspire those same feelings in their children.

NOTES

1 Muschamp *et al.* (2010), *The Cambridge Primary Review Research Surveys*, Chapter 4.
2 CACE (1967).
3 CACE (1967).
4 Muschamp *et al.* (2010), *The Cambridge Primary Review Research Surveys*, Chapter 4.
5 Jencks *et al.* (1972).
6 Eysenck (1973).
7 Alexander, Rose and Woodhead (1992): paras 54–55.
8 Cardini (2006).
9 Hartley-Brewer (1999).
10 DfES (2003a).
11 DfES (2005b).
12 Cummings *et al.* (2006).
13 DfES (2007b).
14 DCSF (2007b).
15 Muschamp *et al.* (2010), *The Cambridge Primary Review Research Surveys*, Chapter 4.
16 Layard and Dunn (2009).
17 Office for National Statistics (2008) (*Social Trends* No 38).
18 Office for National Statistics (2006a).
19 Ermisch (2007).
20 Connolly and White (2006).
21 Office for National Statistics (2005).
22 Muschamp *et al.* (2010), *The Cambridge Primary Review Research Surveys*, Chapter 4.
23 Peacey and Hunt (2008).
24 Defined as children living in households with less than 60 per cent of median household income.
25 Dyson (2008).
26 De Zulueta (2006).
27 Hartley-Brewer (2009).
28 Desforges and Abouchaar (2003).
29 Family and Parenting Institute (2006).
30 Maughan, Brock and Ladva (2004).

31 See, for example, Sharp and Green (1975); King (1978).
32 Barron, Holmes, MacLure and Runswick-Cole (2010), *The Cambridge Primary Review Research Surveys*, Chapter 5.
33 For example, James and Pollard (2010), *The Cambridge Primary Review Research Surveys*, Chapter 20.
34 Muschamp *et al.* (2010), *The Cambridge Primary Review Research Surveys*, Chapter 4.
35 Desforges and Abouchaar (2003): 4.
36 Desforges and Abouchaar (2003).
37 Mayall (2010), *The Cambridge Primary Review Research Surveys*, Chapter 3.
38 James and Pollard (2010), *The Cambridge Primary Review Research Surveys*, Chapter 20.
39 Sammons *et al.* (2007a).
40 Eccles (2006).
41 Dweck (1999, 2006).
42 Goswami and Bryant (2010), *The Cambridge Primary Review Research Surveys*, Chapter 6.
43 Kelly (1997).
44 Dunn (2004).
45 Tizard and Hughes (2002): 76.
46 Sharp (2000).
47 Hoover-Dempsey, Battiato, Walker and Reed (2001).
48 Hallgarten (2000).
49 Machin and McNally (2010), *The Cambridge Primary Review Research Surveys*, Chapter 10.
50 The NPhA and NPSA merged in June 2008 to become the NPH, National Primary Headteachers.
51 Muschamp *et al.* (2010), *The Cambridge Primary Review Research Surveys*, Chapter 4.
52 Close (2004).
53 Bercow (2008): 13.
54 Bercow (2008).
55 DCSF (2008z).
56 DCSF / Ministry of Justice (2007).
57 Partners of Prisoners and Families Group (2007).
58 Steer (2009).
59 Desforges and Abouchaar (2003): 90.
60 Quinton (2004).

7   Children's development and learning

How do young children develop, think, feel, act and learn? This question, posed at the outset of the Cambridge Primary Review, is as fundamental to a proper understanding of the task of primary schools and teachers today as it was for the Plowden committee in 1967. The intervening decades have seen considerable progress in research on children's development and learning and in our understanding of the relationship between these and teaching, enabling us now to study childhood from neuroscientific and socio-cultural perspectives.

There is another perspective too of course – that of the witnesses to the Review who questioned whether present policy and practice key into what this research has told us. Parents, teachers and head teachers worried that too many children experience a sense of failure and were anxious about their emotional health. They feared that children do not have enough time to be creative, to play with each other and to converse – that, ironically in an interactive age, they have less opportunity to interact. Yet verbal and social engagement with others is the seed-bed of cognitive development and learning.

One shift in thinking has been towards greater recognition of the inter-relatedness of the biological, social, emotional and intellectual aspects of children's psychological make-up and their dependence on the socio-cultural environment.[1] Keeping this in mind, we shall look in turn at children's physical development, cognitive development and learning, and the debate surrounding the relationship between them. Current knowledge and thinking about children's social, moral and emotional development is summarised in the later part of the chapter.

POST-PLOWDEN INSIGHTS

Here are some examples of ways that thinking on children's development and learning has advanced since Plowden.

- Children, and even babies, are able to think and learn in the same ways as adults, albeit in rudimentary forms. The Review's research survey by Usha Goswami and Peter Bryant reports that infants possess the same neurological structures as adults, and it is experience rather than neurophysiological change that accounts for the greater sophistication of adult thinking.[2] This directly challenges Plowden's perspective, supported by Jean Piaget's cognitive developmental theory, that children's thinking is fundamentally different from that of adults.
- Social interaction plays a vital role in children's development and learning, a point stressed in the Review's research surveys. Plowden has been criticised for underplaying the significance of a child's social environment while emphasising the importance of active manipulation of materials in keeping with Piaget's view that seven to 11-year-olds are in the stage of 'concrete operations'. Together these may have fuelled the characterisation of the child as a 'lone scientist'[3] who interacts with things rather than people – a notion now rejected by Jerome Bruner (whose critical phrase this is) and many others.
- Relatedly, recent studies have demonstrated that the social environment in which children grow up can explain the considerable variation in their achievement in areas such as literacy and numeracy.[4] Plowden did recognise the damage inflicted by 'restricted forms of speech'[5]

on children's learning, and saw the teacher's task as one of 'compensating' for supposed parenting deficits rather than routinely providing cognitively challenging interactions. Today, such simple deficit models are treated as inappropriate and it is understood that cognitive challenge is essential in all teaching, though the understanding is not always reflected in classroom practice (Chapter 15).

- The survey of research on children's social development which the Review commissioned from Christine Howe and Neil Mercer reveals how primary classrooms often fail to exploit opportunities for social interaction and, as has been noted in Chapters 5 and 6, neglect the considerable 'funds of knowledge' that children themselves bring into school.[6] This matter is explored further below and in Chapter 13.

- Advances in psychology and investment in educational research, including the government's £43 million Teaching and Learning Research Programme (TLRP), have challenged and sometimes refuted, but also occasionally upheld some of the claims made by the Plowden committee.[7] For example, Plowden asserted that 'the old nature-versus-nurture controversy' had been laid to rest, and emphasised the interaction between heredity and environment as the determinant of intellectual ability.[8] The committee's views were shaped by Cyril Burt's now discredited work on intelligence and its measurement, but Goswami and Bryant's research survey reminds us that 'the strong heritability of intelligence is now accepted, but the emphasis in research is on the key role of the environment for explaining variability'.[9,10]

- Plowden was influenced strongly by Piaget's constructivist theory, which postulated an unchanging and progressive sequence of stages in children's cognitive development.[11] Furthermore, it rejected B.F. Skinner's behavourist theory that adults' knowledge and skills are entirely the result of learning from encounters with the world around them, and the conditioned reinforcement or punishment of responses to those stimuli.[12] Since then, stage theory has been seriously challenged[13], but Piaget's recognition that children actively construct their knowledge of the world through their physical action upon it has been upheld. As Goswami and Bryant explain, the discovery of 'mirror neurons' (brain cells which fire both when a person performs an action and when they observe someone else performing it) indicates that sensorimotor knowledge is the starting point of cognitive development, but that it is augmented rather than replaced by symbolic representations 'gained through action, language, pretend play and teaching'.

- A final example of developments since 1967 refers to Plowden's insistence that policy and resources must be 'in harmony with the nature of the child, [and] fundamentally acceptable to him' and that 'learning takes place through a continuous process of interaction between the learner and his environment, that results in the building up of consistent and stable patterns of behaviour, physical and mental'.[14,15] The committee perpetuated the by then accepted view that 'the child is the agent in his own learning'.[16,17] An updated version of this view, strengthened by an increasing awareness of the significance of the child's voice and agency, appeared prominently in the Review's research surveys, submissions and soundings.[18] Meanwhile, recent policies aiming to improve connections between schools, children's services, and parents such as Every Child Matters and the Children's Plan have been widely welcomed, as is evident from the reaction of Review witnesses. Whether by design or default, these initiatives are in harmony with contemporary awareness of the importance of social and cultural factors in children's development and learning, and of the complementary rather than comprehensive role of schooling.[19] They may fall short, however, of capitalising on findings from socio-cultural research, fundamental to which is the understanding that learning and development arise from the 'intrinsically social and communicative nature of human life'.[20]

HOW HEALTHY ARE CHILDREN?

Something approaching panic has greeted recent reports of increases in child obesity. For their part, witnesses to the Review voiced more general worries about children's health and physical development, the lack of opportunities for physical recreation discussed in Chapter 5 and, again, the potentially negative impact on learning. Plowden too devoted space to these matters, and, while some concerns about children's health and physical development have receded over time, they have been replaced by others.

Taller, wider, heavier

National statistics on physical development over the last century suggest that children are growing taller, wider and heavier. Plowden charted their physical growth as well as recording maturity rates and growth of the brain. While five-year-old boys were one centimetre taller than five-year-old girls in 1905–12 and 1959, 13-year-old boys were three centimetres shorter than girls of the same age in these years. Plowden reported that in 1966 there was little difference between six-year-old girls and boys in height, weight or other bodily dimensions 'except for the head, which in boys is always larger'.[21] The figures suggest rapid change in the first half of the 20th century, but little change since 1959, with the net result that today's 11-year-olds are on average as tall as London's 13-year-olds of a century earlier.[22]

Childhood obesity

In 1967, with malnutrition in decline, Plowden foresaw a new problem: 'So much has the nutritional state of schoolchildren improved that it is now the fat boy [sic] who is beginning to present more of a problem to school doctors than the under-nourished child.'[23] The government's child measurement programme revealed that, in 2005, 17 per cent of children aged two to 10 were obese, compared with 11 per cent in 1995.[24] The results for 2006–7, based on measurement of 80 per cent of children, show that 13 per cent and 14 per cent of reception and Year 6 children respectively were overweight, and that 10 per cent and 18 per cent were obese. The figures varied with geographical location – obesity was generally more prevalent in towns than in villages. And it was significantly more prevalent among boys than girls, according to the 2006 Health Survey for England. On a positive note, however, the survey noted also an increase in the percentage of children eating at least five portions of fruit and vegetables a day from 10 to 13 per cent between 2001–4 to at least 17 per cent in 2005.

The government announced a £372m 'obesity strategy' in January 2008, aiming to reduce childhood obesity to 2000 levels by 2020. The Department of Health claimed that by February 2008 junk food had been banned from vending machines in schools and '86 per cent of children [were] now doing at least 2 hours sport per week. Food and drink advertising to children had been restricted and there are robust nutritional guidelines in place so all children can benefit from healthy and balanced school meals.'[25] Parents were to be told their child's weight and given information about diet and exercise, cooking was made compulsory in most schools and there was a recognition that school facilities and play areas needed to be improved.[26] While these measures are welcome, researchers have pointed out that establishing relationships between physical activity and health in children is fraught with difficulties of definition, context and measurement.[27] This should be kept in mind when the government's scheme is evaluated.

Are children getting older younger?

Plowden reported that girls in the 1960s entered puberty between 11 and 14 years, about two years earlier than boys, and were typically taller and heavier than boys of the same age. The report showed the steadily decreasing age of the onset of menstruation from about 15 in 1900, to 13 for girls in the south of England (13.2 years in the north) by 1967. They predicted a further reduction to 12.5 in 20 or 30 years. Recent research reviews, however, conclude that 'the evidence supporting a decrease in the age of menarche is still unsubstantiated. There is a greater likelihood that the age of onset of the first stages of puberty may be reducing, but further research is urgently needed'.[28] In 1975, however, English girls were recorded as entering puberty between 10.8 and 14 years, suggesting that observations in the Review's soundings that children were 'getting older younger' may apply to their attitudes, behaviour and appearance perhaps, but not to their physical development.

Plowden noted that little work had been done on children's emotional maturity and stability as they entered puberty, but suggested that this was important in relation both to the age of transfer to secondary school and the 'increasing number of children who begin to enter puberty before they leave primary school'.[29] Recognising that physical and psychological developments might not be in step, and the conflicting evidence as to whether transfer itself was a cause of distress, Plowden concluded: 'What seems most likely is that it brings to the surface psychological difficulties in vulnerable children.'[30] The recent research reviews suggest that Plowden's conclusion remains valid, and that, now as then, claims that ever earlier biological changes might hinder children's adjustment to secondary school at age 11 and adversely affect their academic progress must be treated cautiously. Nevertheless, those parents, teachers and pupils who believe that middle schools offer a more developmentally appropriate environment for children aged nine to 13 should also be heeded, and they were among the witnesses to the Review.[31]

Infectious diseases and immunisation

Overall, there has been a dramatic reduction in infectious diseases since 1967. For example, more than 250,000 children contracted measles in 1963, and 29 died, but, as Plowden noted, the discovery of a vaccine heralded a breakthrough. By 2000, according to Helen Bedford and David Elliman, 'immunisation against infectious diseases has probably saved more lives than any other public health intervention, apart from the provision of clean water'.[32] Compared to the more than 460,000 cases of measles and 99 deaths (all ages) in the UK in 1967, there were only 5,613 cases and no deaths in 1996. However, they continue, 'despite, or perhaps because of, the success of the immunisation programme in the UK, a vocal minority of parents have cast doubt on the wisdom of having their children immunised'. This 'vocal minority' represents two important social developments since Plowden's time: an erosion of trust in medical science, and the rise of the voice of the citizen. Berry Mayall's research survey for the Review focuses on schools' failure to acknowledge, or value, the health-related beliefs and conventions that children have learned at home.[33] In 1967, this was not an issue. Unfortunately, however, late 2008 saw measles figures 'soar' to 1,049, described as 'the highest number of measles cases reported in England and Wales' since 1995.[34] The worst figures were recorded in London (626 cases) and the north west (106). The Health Protection Agency (HPA), attributing the increased incidence to the dip in immunisation take-up since the late 1990s, warns of the 'real risk' of a measles epidemic. While take-up of immunisation has increased recently, the HPA launched a catch-up programme in 2008.

The ailments of affluence

Health concerns which once focused on infectious diseases, malnutrition and inadequate hygiene now revolve around obesity, diet, lack of exercise, and the increased risk of heart disease, diabetes, cancer, and liver disease for children in adulthood. Many children today risk ill-health as a result of affluence and choice, rather than hardship and necessity. As the Department of Health put it, 'eating more healthily and being more active are the solutions to maintaining a healthier weight, decisions that are fundamentally an individual's responsibility'. Education, of course, should help children to make informed and sensible decisions on such matters.

In conclusion, we see that, since 1959, children's heights for their ages appear not to be increasing at the rate observed in the first half of the 20th century (perhaps because present-day measures are based on the population rather than a volunteer sample). Nor is there recent evidence to support the view that the physical onset of puberty is occurring at younger ages, despite some outward appearances. The problem – for that is how many of the Review's witnesses saw it – is the pressure which young children are under from the media and their peers to abandon childhood at the earliest opportunity and affect adolescent dress, habits, attitudes and lifestyles. Such changes are fuelled by increased affluence, and, when combined with the evidence of poor diet and obesity, our witnesses' concern appears justified.

THINKING AND LEARNING

As already mentioned, neuroscientific research is offering new perspectives on our under-standing of neural activity and learning, while social interaction is being revealed as a vital component of cognitive development.[35] We begin, however, with the question of the relation-ship between development and learning, a matter which continues to exercise developmental psychologists and learning theorists.

The relationship between development and learning

A widely used and respected developmental psychology textbook defines development as 'the process by which an organism grows and changes through its life-span' and learning as 'the influence of specific environmental information on behaviour'.[36] It notes that development is typically related to age – the same event, story or problem will elicit different responses from an infant and a teenager. Learning, the textbook explains, is responsible for the variety of different responses to the same event that several infants or several teenagers would produce, within our broader developmentally-based expectations. The relationship between these two concepts is a matter of debate, however.

Plowden, building on Jean Piaget's developmental theory, made plain the view that 'until a child is ready to take a step forward, it is a waste of time to try to teach him to take it'.[37] In short, there was no point in trying to teach a child something for which she or he was not ready, no point in attempting to accelerate development by teaching too many new, complex or advanced ideas. Learning was considered to lag behind development. Since then, Piaget's theory has been challenged – and defended – many times.[38,39] Nevertheless, on the assumption that Lev Vygotsky would have toppled Piaget as favoured theorist in a present-day Plowden report, we turn to the Russian psychologist's discussion of the learning-development relationship. Writing in the 1930s, he reduced contemporary conceptions of the relationship to 'three major theoretical positions' before offering his own interpretation.[40] The three were:

- *Development is independent of learning*
  Vygotsky used Piaget's studies of children's causal reasoning (their responses at different ages to questions such as 'why do the clouds move?') to exemplify the position which divorced development from learning. Thus 'development becomes a pre-requisite for learning' while 'learning trails behind development'. Plowden's conclusion above embodied this view.
- *Learning is development*
  This was one of several such positions exemplified by William James, for whom, according to Vygotsky, 'development is the mastery of conditioned reflexes, that is, the process of learning, is completely and inseparably blended with development'.
- *Learning and development are separate but mutually dependent and interactive*
  Vygotsky cited psychologist Kurt Koffka and the Gestalt school as proponents of this approach in which development was viewed purely as the process of maturation, stimulated and advanced by the process of learning.

Vygotsky then proposed his now well-known concept of the zone of proximal development (ZPD or even ZoPed) as a new way to link development and learning., He defined the zone as 'the distance between the actual developmental level as determined by independent problem-solving and the level of potential development as determined through problem-solving under adult guidance or in collaboration with more capable peers.'[41] Social interaction and cultural conventions are intrinsic to this theory. The width of the zone is determined by how how much the child is able to learn from the teacher (adult or peer). For Vygots developmental process lags behind the learning process' and the difference between them defines the zone. Crucially, however, he also argued that 'the only good teaching is that which outpaces development', a maxim returned to in Chapter 15, and which is diametrically opposed to the Plowden-era belief in the imperative of a child's readiness and the teacher's role of facilitator.

Nevertheless Vygotsky and Piaget should not be seen as incompatible. Vygotsky was a considerable student of Piaget's work, and, while not postulating underlying neurological changes as did Piaget, he proposed that the 'ascent to concept formation [was] made in three basic phases, each divided in turn into several stages.'[42] In other words, the ability to form concepts develops in phases from early childhood to early adolescence. For Vygotsky, this achievement was brought about by social interaction through language.

Develop a child or watch a child develop

Critical to the debate about children's learning is the way in which the word 'development' is used in different cultures. This is implicit to some extent in Vygotsky's analysis above, but Robin Alexander's comparative classroom research in five cultures revealed such differences in practice and everyday educational discourse.[43] Thus, the Anglo-American educational tradition treats 'development' as a natural, almost a passive process: teachers are expected to 'match' new challenges to a child's developmental level, and although Plowden's emphasis on developmental 'readiness' has been repeatedly challenged by British psychologists, there is still an implicit commitment to 'developmental appropriateness'.[44]

It is important to understand just how deeply-rooted the notion of age-related developmental readiness is in English primary education. For example, the National Union of Teachers (NUT) said in response to the 1978 HMI primary survey's concern about the undemanding nature and low expectations of some primary teaching:[45]

> The Union would not agree with [HMI's] analysis of what is suitable in the teaching of history to young children; the passage of time is a very difficult concept for children of this age to grasp ... Advanced reading skills such as skimming need a level of sophistication beyond the reach of most primary children. To suggest that they should be taught at this age betrays a lack of knowledge of children's conceptual development on the part of HMI.[46]

The persistence, or at least the echo of this way of thinking, was apparent in some of the Review's submissions concerning, for example, the age when children should move to a more formal curriculum.

Returning to the comparative perspective, Alexander points out that while in the Anglo-American educational contexts the verb 'develop' is generally used intransitively – the child just develops – in the Russian context the verb is as likely to be used transitively. Both teachers and psychologists see their task as 'developing' the child, sometimes explicitly citing Vygotsky's maxim that 'the only good teaching is that which outpaces development'.[47] As Alexander puts it:

> In Russia, education and development are one, and development is not natural and inevitable but normative and interventive ... In England, development happens; in Russia, schools, parents and the community make it happen.[48]

With this cultural difference in mind, we perhaps need to be wary about some of the claims that schools subject children to excessive pressure, and certainly of the professional stereotype of the 'pushy' parent who elsewhere might merely be regarded as an instinctive Vygotskian.

Domains of the mind

The decades since Plowden have seen an expansion of research within specific domains such as mathematical, spatial, musical and linguistic cognitive development and learning, as well as within psychological constructs such as metacognition and social cognition.[49] Typically, such studies applied and adapted general theories to these specific contexts, but some theories make special reference to particular domains. These include Howard Gardner's multiple intelligence theory, as we shall see below, and neo-Piagetian theories such as the theory of domain specific 'representational redescription'. Researcher Sara Meadows describes this as a 'very general process common to all domains of knowledge, but it may proceed faster or more securely or further in one domain rather than another.' In other words, 'a star dancer may be able to perform a movement beautifully but not describe it verbally'; thus some 'children may have particularly advanced development in some domains, while being considerably impaired in others'.[50]

Neuroscientific perspectives on development and learning

Neuroscientists have investigated the influence of biological and environmental factors on a child's cognitive development. In their research survey for the Review, Goswami and Bryant discuss connectionism, which uses computer modelling to predict the effects of the repeated activation of neural networks, and neuroconstructivism, which studies how neural structures become increasingly specialised in response to a child's (not necessarily deliberate) choice of activities. 'Whereas connectionism offers a biological perspective on learning, neuroconstructivism offers a biological perspective on cognitive development.'[51] These stances do not resolve the debate, however, and there remains a long way to go before this might be achieved.[52] In the meantime, Neil Mercer and Karen Littleton offer a useful way to sum up this section. They remind us that we accept that children often forget things that they have learned, but we become concerned if they show any developmental regression. Their focus is the 'kinds of cognitive intellectual changes' associated with 'the kind of learning [which] is how children make sense of the world, become able to solve problems and ... take on new perspectives'.[53] So, to a large extent, is ours, as we turn to consider how children think and learn.

How do (we think) children think and learn?

Neuroscience suggests that babies have the same learning mechanisms as adults. To some this may be surprising, but Goswami and Bryant's research survey reports experimental studies showing that babies exhibit the unconscious 'statistical' learning of patterns of sensory events, which result in neural networks that enable us to recognise sights (such as faces) and sounds (such as voices), and how these go together.[54] Babies learn by imitation – newborns just one hour old can imitate an adult sticking their tongue out. They also learn by analogy – they can perceive similarities between situations and apply analogous solutions to similar problems.[55] And they appear capable of 'explanation-based' learning – having seen objects falling, babies seem able to work out why they fall and make predictions on the basis of causal rather than associative learning.[56] The difference between children's and adults' learning, according to Goswami and Bryant, is not the structure of their brains but their relative lack of experience, metacognition and self-regulation.

Multisensory learners

Some critical findings for education have emerged from this neuroscientific research. It has shown, for example, that learning is strengthened not only in relation to how many neurons fire in a neural network, but also by how they are distributed across different domains, such as the motor and sensory cortices. This research, therefore, does not support the recent trend to encourage children to find out whether they are left- or right-brain learners or whether they prefer visual (V), auditory (A) or kinaesthetic (K) learning 'styles' and to invest their efforts in these modalities. In other words, multisensory approaches (V, A and K rather than V, A or K) are to be encouraged. Given the popularity of these ideas among teachers, this is an important corrective.[57] A second finding within connectionist psychology, in which computers model neural network activity, has demonstrated, in principle, that learning is strengthened by continuity as well as frequency. Learning without gaps overcomes the need to postulate that there are critical developmental periods during which, for example, children should learn foreign languages, as in Piaget's theory, or that there are innate learning structures, such as Noam Chomsky's language acquisition device.[58] This further undermines the concept of 'readiness to learn' in terms of cognition, although it does not destroy the case for developmentally appropriate methods and resources, nor the case for taking children's attitudes into account.

Home as language laboratory

The Review's research surveys make clear the importance of social interaction for learning and development. Goswami and Bryant, for example, report evidence of stark differences in children's exposure to language. While research in 2003 showed that toddlers heard between 5,000 and 7,000 utterances a day, a US study found that children from wealthy families heard nearly 500 utterances per hour, compared to 180 for children from families on welfare.[59] The researchers extrapolated from these figures to suggest that by age four, these children would have heard 44m and 12m utterances respectively. Such findings help us to appreciate the enormous range – from zero to 500 – in children's word production by age two.[60]

Goswami and Bryant's research survey also reminds us that language development, along with perceptual and spatial development, underpins children's progress in reading and numeracy. In learning to read, a child's phonological awareness (that is, their ability to reflect upon the sound patterns of words – for example by isolating syllables or recognising rhymes) is a critical factor. Children with poor phonological skills are at risk of dyslexia, and their difficulties are compounded by the complexities of written English. The large number of phonemes, inconsistent spelling and complex syllable structure make English a harder language to learn to read than those with more precise and consistent letter-sound correspondences. Research on number acquisition, particularly in cognitive neuroscience, has found evidence for an analogue representation of magnitude in human brains, and those of other animals. This provides an approximate idea of number based on perceptual and spatial representations of quantity. However, accurate manipulation of numbers depends on knowledge of counting, which in turn relies on linguistic rather than spatial coding. Goswami and Bryant point out that Plowden was correct to identify language development as central to learning, but did not sufficiently link this with the crucial role played by social interaction.

Metacognition

Piaget saw social interaction with peers as an essential and powerful element in cognitive development, but this aspect of his work is regularly overlooked.[61] Vygotsky, on the other hand, made social interaction 'the principal element in his account' and his theory initiated the currently prominent socio-cultural approach to explaining children's development.[62] Vygotsky emphasised the role of pretend play, recognising its importance in developing a child's understanding of symbols and social conventions. Contrary to the beliefs of his day, he realised that children's play is highly rule-bound rather than free, and that, typically, it reflects everyday events rather than those of a fantasy world.[63] Goswami and Bryant suggest that the ability to pretend, which appears during a child's second year, is the beginning of the capacity to understand cognition itself, to think about thoughts. Being able to pretend that a stick is a sword is to create a 'meta-representation' which shows, even at this young age, the capacity for three forms of more advanced thought:

- metacognition – the ability to think about one's own knowledge and ideas
- 'theory of mind' – the awareness that other people have minds which may differ in thoughts and feeling from one's own
- self-regulation– the ability to monitor and control thought and action, for example, in setting and abiding by rules in play.

The importance of play as 'the principal means of learning in early childhood,' and the value of play and exploration in new learning in maths and science, were endorsed by Plowden, of course.[64,65] Pretend play, which potentially has so many benefits for social and cognitive development, is less prevalent at key stage 1 and even in reception classes than it was – a decline that our witnesses tended to blame on the national literacy and numeracy strategies and the pressure to start formal learning at an ever-younger age.[66] The Early Education advisory group's submission, in particular, welcomed the recognition of children's right to play-based learning but expressed concern that this entitlement, which it wanted extended through Year 1, may be overridden by the 'letters and sounds' agenda.

No longer fixed: 'intelligence' and 'potential'

Vygotsky's theory of the zone of proximal development provided new ways of thinking about intelligence, first as the ability to learn with help, rather than as a measure of what children can achieve unaided, and second as a characteristic that could itself be changed through learning and teaching. It emphasised the essential role of social interaction in development and learning – teachers share their knowledge with children who then advance intellectually. Previous western concepts of intelligence, notably that of Burt, saw it as a quality that was fixed and predetermined, limiting what could be expected of a child. Today, while heritability is an accepted component of intelligence, as noted earlier, the role of the environment in modifying, over-riding and explaining variability is a key research focus.[67] Indeed, the relative influence of social and cultural environmental factors challenges the validity of referring to or attempting to measure 'intelligence' or 'ability'. Furthermore, the view that in a stimulating environment a child might 'fulfil his or her potential', simply perpetuates outdated notions of fixed intelligence with 'potential' being a euphemism for 'maximum,' as the submission from the authors of the book *Learning without Limits* made clear.[68]

Or, as Alexander argued 25 years ago:

> In an absolute sense, potential is unknowable … Yet what does seem certain is that what children achieve is in part a product of the opportunities with which they are provided and the expectations others have of them: the better the teaching and the higher the expectations the more children may achieve and the greater 'potential' they may thereby demonstrate, thus rendering more and more obsolete the use of terms like 'potential' and 'ability' which are fundamental to current educational thought and practice.[69]

David Berliner and Bruce Biddle provide a striking confirmation of these views, and especially of the susceptibility to environmental factors (which of course include teaching) of intelligence as measured in IQ tests. In their authoritative re-assessment of evidence for the claim that standards of public education in the United States are falling – a familiar complaint here, too – they note, first, an increase rather than a decline in measured IQ (and we stress that IQ and attainment as measured by the available instruments is the issue in the debate about falling/rising standards):

> What, then, can we deduce from these studies of measured intelligence? First, today's children are smarter, not dumber, than their parents. Further, the parents of today's children were also more intelligent than were their own parents, the grandparents of today's youth. Second, intelligence is affected not only by inheritance and early childhood experiences;

schooling also affects IQ test performance. More and better schooling in the US and in other industrialised nations is the most likely reason for those nations' increases in IQ scores. High-quality instructional environments for toddlers, primary school children, teenagers and college students all seem to raise scores on IQ tests ... Access to schooling ... has made people a lot more intelligent, *at least as intelligence is normally measured.*[70]

The message is clear: expect more, teach better, and children will respond, surprising those who still hold to the old Anglo-Saxon belief in the immutability of human intelligence and age-related readiness.

Divided on multiple intelligences

There are of course alternative theories of intelligence. Recent examples include Howard Gardner's theory of multiple intelligences (MI)[71] and the 'triarchic' theory advanced by American psychologist Robert Sternberg.[72] Like the learning styles research, MI theory has proved attractive to teachers, although Gardner himself warned that 'MI theory is in no way an educational prescription'.[73] His original seven intelligences were linguistic, logical-mathematical, spatial, bodily-kinaesthetic, musical, interpersonal, and intrapersonal. By 1987 he had added naturalistic intelligence and was considering an existential intelligence.[74] More cautiously, Goswami and Bryant call MI theory a 'useful metaphor' for recognising that 'intelligence' reflects a range of skills.

Sternberg's triarchic theory identifies three facets or subtheories of intelligence. They are the analytic (academic problem-solving skills), the practical (ability to do everyday tasks) and the creative (ability to synthesise and react to new events and stimuli). Each facet reflects a different aspect of human functioning: analytical intelligence refers to how we relate to our internal worlds, practical intelligence to the external world, and creative intelligence to the relationship between our internal and external worlds. Other theories of intelligence include those based on speed of information processing and the neuroconstructivist approaches mentioned earlier. Neuroconstructivism, which emphasises how neural structures become increasingly specialised in response to a child's activities, endorses and strengthens Plowden's statement that 'the child is the agent in his own learning'.

What happened to creativity?

'Creativity' was frequently mentioned by Review witnesses in the contexts of both teaching and learning. That is to say, witnesses wanted to safeguard 'creative' teaching no less than to give children opportunities to be creative. Yet submissions to the Review united in complaining that children's opportunities to express themselves creatively have been seriously eroded in the past 20 years. Witnesses worried that the current dominant construction of childhood as a preparation for adulthood had stifled enjoyment, creativity and imagination in primary education. Although creativity is in one sense a curricular matter (see Chapter 13), it is also a vital aspect of cognitive and social functioning.[75] Expressions of creativity through pretend play and imagination are important in the development of children's thinking and the development of metacognition and self regulation, as we have seen.

Psychologist Guy Claxton's caricature of creative activity in primary education as '(a) ... specially related to the arts (b) involv[ing] a concentrated episode of colourful, rather manic activity, (c) something that everyone can engage in equally – provided that (d) they are allowed or encouraged' has a ring of truth.[76] His caricature of psychology's take on creativity as the 'sudden moment of abrupt illumination in which the solution to a previously intractable problem leaps into consciousness fully formed' reflects a view identified by Sternberg and Todd Lubart as a 'roadblock' to our understanding of the creative process. Supported by Robert Weisberg's case studies of famous scientists and artists, it appears that the final creative breakthrough, or finished work, arises not from blinding insights and extraordinary thought processes, but from 'the repeated and persistent use of the methods by which ordinary people solve problems, such as reformulations, new interpretations of existing facts, and drawing on inspiration and ideas from other people and situations around them'.[77,78]

In primary education, Claxton calls for an intermediate 'soft creativity' which he suggests might be encouraged by retaining and valuing children's mathematical workings, sketches, discarded paintings or drafts of poems, or by indulging in a process of 'embodied-knowing', or 'thinking at the edge' of what is felt or sensed but not yet articulated. This accords with Sternberg and Lubart's overview, but simultaneously demands time for children to engage wholeheartedly in their projects, and, crucially, the opportunity to do what naturally interests them. Unfortunately, the levels of curricular prescription, the erosion of time for extended engagement in specific tasks, and the shift towards extrinsic rather than intrinsic motivation, render it less likely that children will derive 'flow' or creative satisfaction from the educational process.[79,80]

GENDER DIFFERENCES

Boys – less able or less eager?

Since the late 1990s, media headlines have been expressing alarm that girls were beginning to outperform boys in national exams at 16, and national assessments at 11 and 14. (If it had been the other way round, we wonder, would there have been the same level of concern?) Although apparently a matter of public anxiety, gender differences were not prominent in the Review's soundings or submissions, perhaps because witnesses were more concerned about children and childhood in general. Nevertheless, the ensuing moral panic generated considerable boy-focused activity – research was undertaken, teachers' professional development was adjusted, boy-friendly curricular materials were produced and teaching groups in schools were reorganised.[81] Yet the 2006–7 figures from the government paint a picture of a persistent gap in pupil attainment with key findings indicating girls' superiority across all 13 scales of the foundation stage, at all key stages in English and, to a lesser extent, in mathematics at key stages 1, 3 and 4.[82] Overall the gap was wider in the secondary than primary phase. Between 1997 and 2006 the gender gap in the KS2 English SATs narrowed from 13 and 16 percentage points in favour of girls, to a stable 10 or 11 points. However, not all attainment test studies show such large gender differences. For example Peter Tymms' 1999 analysis of the Performance Indicators in Primary Schools (PIPS) results showed very similar results for boys and girls, although girls performed slightly better than boys, but by at most an average 0.2 (small) effect size.

Boys' and girls' basic abilities were examined by Steve Strand and colleagues in an attempt to explain the gender gap.[83] Their major survey of 320,000 11 to 12-year-olds in 2003 revealed no overall sex differences. Results on the Cognitive Abilities Tests (CATS), for verbal reasoning, quantitative reasoning and non-verbal reasoning, revealed negligible differences between girls' and boys' results.[84] The researchers noted that, given a close correlation between reasoning scores at 11 and attainment at 14 in England and 16 in Scotland, 'the lack of substantial sex differences in reasoning scores suggests there is no *a priori* rationale based on mental ability differences to expect a large gender gap in subsequent test or examination attainment at age 16.' However, their analysis of the variability in boys' and girls' results did indicate that boys were more likely to be among the very high and very low scorers.[85] In 2007, the Department for Children, Schools and Families referred to Strand's findings, admitting that there did not appear to be differences between girls' and boys' cognitive abilities scores.[86] However, it noted that the researchers 'acknowledge that construction of these tests do undergo a procedure that eliminates items that could create gender bias and therefore can reduce overall score differences.'[87] Strand replied that the absence of substantial sex differences in mean CAT scores 'was unlikely to be attributable to test construction'.

In other words, the government played down the discrepancy between Strand's finding of no sex difference in cognitive abilities, and its own finding of a widening gap in school attainment.[88] Both the DCSF and Strand drew attention to the greater influence of social factors and socio-economic circumstances in explaining attainment differences, but the DCSF also recognised the implications for forms of assessment and children's attitudes as contributory factors.

Attitude equals attainment?

Is boys' tendency to see school as 'not cool' therefore the fundamental reason for the gender attainment gap? In pursuit of socio-cultural explanations, boys' socialisation, self-image and constructions of masculinity have been explored.[89] Certainly, research confirms the view that girls hold more positive attitudes to school than boys although, counter-intuitively perhaps, evidence for a positive correlation between attitudes and attainment is equivocal.[90,91] Attempts to recruit more male and more minority ethnic teachers in order to provide same-sex role models for boys may not achieve the desired result. Indeed, some researchers argue that it could be counter-productive, reinforcing laddish behaviour.[92] Analysis of 9,000 pupils' scores on the PIPS test in 1998, after four months with the same teachers, failed to reveal any effects of teacher gender on attainment even after controls were made for vocabulary and non-verbal ability, although boys and girls with women teachers had more positive attitudes to school.[93,94]

In summary, boys' consistently poorer attainment than girls in English appears more likely to be explained by social and environmental factors than by differences in cognitive reasoning abilities. What is needed – as Molly Warrington and Mike Younger, directors of the Raising Boys' Achievement project, have demonstrated – are holistic approaches that go beyond a narrow focus on attainment in literacy and avoid too simplistic a conceptualisation of the issue. Current attempts to understand the gender gap exemplify the need to recognise the inter-relatedness of physical, social, emotional and cognitive aspects of development, and their inextricability from their socio-cultural contexts. As Warrington and Younger put it, progress in ensuring success for all children means 'focussing on girls as well as boys ... espousing an overriding concern for social justice and equity for all pupils, joining with schools in their communities to make a real difference to real pupils' lives.'[95]

SOCIAL DEVELOPMENT AND LEARNING

The importance for children of learning with others in a social context is emphasised in research evidence surveyed by Howe and Mercer for the Review. Much of their report deals with the benefits of collaborative and co-operative activities for cognitive development and learning as well as for social skills. Development and learning are shaped by social and communicative interactions, which 'reflect the historical development, cultural values and social practices of the societies and communities within which schools ... exist, as well as the more local cultures and practices within particular schools and classrooms'.[96] On that basis, they point out, we should look to the quality of the communicative and social processes in the classroom, rather than to the individual child, to understand educational successes and failures. These processes include children's interactions with peers and with teachers in various organisational settings. All this ties in well with the American findings of Berliner and Biddle, referred to above, about the impact of what they call 'high quality instructional environments'.

Piaget postulated that cognitive development takes place through the process of equilibration – children's mental reconciliation of the conflict between their existing beliefs and new, more advanced ones provided by adults or peers. He hypothesised that if peers, rather than adults, expressed the new beliefs the force for cognitive change was enhanced by increasing the cognitive conflict. A child has to grapple with the fact that 'this person is just like me, but thinks differently'.

Two minds are better

Vygotsky's theory, as we have seen, also advocated learning through communication with others by emphasising co-operation, solving problems with more capable others, including adults and children, in a relationship of 'reciprocity, mutuality and the continual (re)negotiation of meaning'. Mercer, whose research has focused mainly on children working co-operatively in classrooms rather than on teacher-pupil interaction, proposes that when 'thinking together' the participants occupy a continually reconstituted 'inter-mental developmental zone' as they solve a problem.[97] Mercer's zone may have been inspired by Vygotsky's ZPD, but whereas a 'teacher' (who in Vygotsky's formulation could be another child) 'scaffolds' the learner within Vygotsky's zone, Mercer's zone extends this idea to emphasise the contributions of both (or all) participants as they 'inter-think'. The scaffolding, then, is mutual. Other psychologists too have identified the value of parent and child jointly focusing on an object, task or event, in promoting the child's learning and cognitive development.[98] They have seen this as antecedent to phenomena such as 'sustained shared thinking', for example, which appears under-used in our nurseries and primary classrooms alike.[99]

These ideas envisage two, three or four adults and children – or just children – concentrating on the same thing. Yet, despite years of encouragement backed up by research, primary teachers still tend to seat children in groups but expect them to work either as individuals or as a whole class.[100] Implementation of the national literacy strategy's framework for teaching doubtless increased the use of what Alexander calls 'collective groups' where a teacher works with a small number of children, as opposed to 'collaborative groups' where the teacher withdraws and children work on a task together.[101] However, whether collective, co-operative or collaborative, such groups, operating intuitively, may not be as effective as they could be. Thus, Alexander argues that learning gains would accrue from teachers developing broader interactional repertoires. He encourages, in particular, forms of talk that he defines as discussion and dialogue.[102] These forms of interaction, which are as yet less common than they should be, involve an exchange of information and ideas in which the teacher genuinely wishes to know what pupils think, and depend to some extent on a changed power relationship between teacher and taught – hence the difficulty, for many teachers, in making the shift.

Conversation not confrontation

As noted above, the use of collaborative peer groups is relatively rare in primary classrooms, although brief episodes of paired talk are now quite common. However, such groups do provide settings and opportunities for effective learning provided that the talk is of high quality or 'productive'. While Howe and Mercer delineate *cognitive* gains in their research survey, it is important not to overlook the *social* learning that is taking place. For Mercer, such gains depend on children engaging in 'exploratory' as opposed to 'disputational' or purely 'narrative' talk. Children trained to work in groups have also learned, for example, to listen to each other, to invite everyone to express their opinions and differing viewpoints, and to reach agreement in the end – all of these highly desirable social and interpersonal skills. These children also replace their basic 'disputational talk', which includes simply being domineering, argumentative, and sometimes aggressive, with being able to express and explain their points of view. Thus cognitive and social learning occur together when effective group discussion is achieved. Furthermore, when children have acquired these skills they are more likely to speak up in whole-class settings.

However, in England the necessary shift in emphasis, according to Alexander's comparative research (which includes teacher-pupil talk as well as the pupil-pupil talk on which Mercer concentrates), is not from the cognitive to social but the other way round. From UK and international classroom studies he shows how teachers in English primary schools have always emphasised the social gains of classroom talk and have tended to attach more importance to the act of participating than to the content of what is said, or 'to developing children's confidence rather than developing their thinking'.[103] This is reflected in the preference for brief exchanges involving many pupils rather than extended exchanges with a smaller number, even though we know that the latter are more likely to probe and advance understanding. In the continental European tradition, which he believes is worth emulating, the cognitive and social are better balanced – for, of course, both are important.

Many parents in the Review's community soundings worried that their children did not have enough opportunity for social interaction at school. Certainly children, as revealed in the community soundings, valued school as a place to make and be with friends. Of course, some children inevitably need more guidance than others in working together and participating in productive talk. Pupils who are rejected by others are at an immediate disadvantage in the classroom and playground because they miss out on the sharing of knowledge and ways in which friends challenge each other's ideas, justify their views and reason about options. In addition to the detriment their cognitive development, this also deprives them of emotional security.

CHILDREN'S MORAL AND EMOTIONAL DEVELOPMENT

Present-day morality and behaviour, and concern that either schools were not doing enough about them or that they were fighting a losing battle against adverse social trends, were common refrains in the Review's community soundings and submissions. Recent policy, however, while for the moment sticking to current curricular and assessment regimes (though at the time of writing both were under review) has begun to place these in a wider social and behavioural context by bringing together services concerned with health, welfare, and education through *Every Child Matters* and the Children's Plan.

Morality in stages

Plowden drew implicitly on Piaget's stage theory of moral development.[104] Piaget had identified moral development as moving from a strict adherence to right and wrong as defined by adults (in judgement if not real life), to an autonomous morality in which 'rules are understood as social constructions formulated in social relations of co-operation with peers', and based on reciprocity and mutual respect.[105] This area of development vividly reveals the importance Piaget attributed to peer social interaction and strongly supports the greater use of peer deliberation in classrooms. American psychologist Lawrence Kohlberg subsequently picked up on Piaget's work, but he attributed young children's adherence to adult rules as motivated principally by the avoidance of punishment. He identified an intervening level of moral judgement determined by a 'law-and-order' perspective, which preceded a third level, achieved by some adults, in which moral judgements are founded on abstract principles of justice and rights.[106]

Right thinking on rules

More recent research, notably that of Elliot Turiel, another American psychologist, shows that young children distinguish between different kinds of social rules and acts.[107] There are those in what is called the moral domain, concerned with doing harm, fairness and rights, and those in the social conventional domain, concerned with rules applicable in and determined by specific social settings, such as etiquette, dress codes, and so on. Children aged between five and 11 years, for example, readily separate the two domains, and even very young children can discriminate not only between social convention and morality in making moral judgements, but can also make decisions on the basis of principle rather than the status of whoever is upholding the convention. Listing studies conducted in the Far East, Africa, South America and India, and including so-called 'collectivist' cultures, Helwig and Turiel conclude that 'although beliefs about reality varied across cultures,' the moral concern 'to avoid inflicting harmful consequences on others appears to be shared', that 'children and adults distinguish morality and social convention'.[108]

Clearly, some primary children take respect for others very seriously while others regard it more as a convention than a moral obligation. Review witnesses believed that disruptive behaviour was on the increase and blamed everything from the family to the media. For some children, as discussed in Chapter 6, altruistic or pro-social behaviour may be precluded by fragmented family lives, lack of skilled parenting, shortage of 'quality time' with parents and the absence of positive role models. However, caution in cause-effect attribution is essential, especially now that anti-social behaviour generally has become so politicised.

Emotional development and learning

Interest in children's emotional development, and their emotional literacy and intelligence, has burgeoned in recent years. The announcement of an extra £13.7m to extend the Social and Emotional Aspects of Learning (SEAL) programme until 2011 showed the government's commitment, though social and emotional aspects of learning may not mean quite the same thing as social and emotional learning.[109] Many submissions, while acknowledging the importance of literacy and numeracy, argued that these have been overemphasised at the expense of children's social and emotional development. This view is paralleled by the findings of two major contemporary studies, namely the Institute for Public Policy Research's 'Thursday's Child' project,[110] which involved international fact-finding and research review, and the vast national consultation constituting the Good Childhood Inquiry.[111] Both identify children's emotional and social well-being as needing much greater attention in schools.

Fathers and mothers matter

In the Good Childhood Inquiry, participating children responded to a seven-point scale ranging from 'completely happy' to 'completely unhappy' with a 'neither happy nor unhappy' midpoint. Eighty-six per cent described themselves as at least 'happy', with 36 per cent saying they were 'completely happy'. Nine per cent were 'neither happy nor unhappy' and 4 per cent were unhappy. This is strong evidence of a nation of happy children. Nevertheless, the report's authors, Richard Layard and Judy Dunn, remind us that this result means 1.5 million children may be unhappy. They attribute at least some of this self-reported unhappiness to social changes, including the breakdown of family life in many cases. While the report implies that the considerable rise in the proportion of mothers who work since the 1970s is a contributing factor, it goes on to stress the importance of fathers' roles in their children's upbringing. Noting a present-day increase in paternal involvement in child-rearing in the pre-school years, the report says that this drops back once school age is reached. It emphasises the positive value of fathers' closeness for their children's later psychological well-being: 'If fathers are more closely involved with their children, other things being equal, children develop better friendships, more empathy, higher self-esteem, better life satisfaction and higher educational achievement'.[112] Layard and Dunn reiterate the importance of children forming positive attachments to parents in infancy, and the benefits of parenting that is '*loving* and yet *firm* – now known in the jargon as *authoritative* – [as] the most effective in terms of children's outcomes and well-being' (original emphases).[113] Citing Dunn's extensive research on children in families,[114] they go on to emphasise the role of positive relationships with and between family members and friends as children grow up, of being able to talk about feelings, and thus increasing children's 'expectations of love from others, and the ease with which they can care for others, and can in turn be cared for themselves'.[115]

Later, the report calls for a 'standard assessment of emotional development at 5 and 11 (primary school) and 14 (secondary school)'.[116] As we shall see next, measurement of children's emotional states, understanding and literacy may be urgently needed, but it remains an under-developed science.

Emotional intelligence and emotional literacy

The present spate of academic interest in children's emotional development seems to date from the 1980s with research by Professor Paul Harris of Harvard on children's understanding of others' emotional and mental states, Howard Gardner's identification of inter- and intra-personal intelligences, and the popular success of Daniel Goleman's book, Emotional Intelligence, which brought the concepts of EI and EQ (as opposed to IQ) to public notice.[117] Psychologists had been studying emotional intelligence for some years, however, and first defined it as 'the subset of social intelligence that involves the ability to monitor one's own and others' feelings and emotions, to discriminate amongst them and to use this information to guide one's thinking and actions'.[118] Researchers continue to debate whether emotional intelligence is actually an 'intelligence' or more akin to a personality trait.[119] Despite the relative immaturity of this field of research and its application, attempts to measure emotional intelligence abound.

Advertisements for commercial programmes designed to boost individual EI, the collective EI of a company, or to transform the emotional awareness of angry and violent youngsters, are common on the internet and have flourished particularly in the US. The idea of developing children's emotional literacy, with a view to boosting their EI, has taken longer to be adopted in England.[120] Emotional literacy has been defined by Claude Steiner, clinical psychologist and author of Achieving Emotional Literacy, as the knowledge of one's own and other's feelings, and the ability to recognise and regulate one's emotional expression. For Steiner, emotional literacy refers not only to the possession of a vocabulary of emotion-related 'feelings, thoughts and behaviours', but also to using certain sentence structures and tones of voice.[121] In England, educational psychologist Peter Sharp has pioneered this field, defining emotional literacy as 'the ability to recognise, understand, handle and appropriately express emotions'.[122]

Feeling the way ahead

Evidence to support attractive hypotheses about relationships between emotional literacy and future success, or between poor emotional literacy and problem behaviour, remain elusive because they are hampered by the lack of reliable ways to measure children's EI or emotional literacy. This makes it difficult to assess the effectiveness of programmes such as SEAL. Nevertheless, the government expected that, by 2007, two-thirds of primary schools would be using SEAL, which includes games and exercises about making wise choices, and dealing peacefully with conflict, which children take home to do with their parents.

Meanwhile, serious psychological research in related areas such as children's understanding of and ability to control emotions is growing. For example, a recent study has shown that five- to eight-year-olds were better at recognising more complex emotional states after listening to an explanation, or attempting to provide their own explanations.[123] Measurement of emotional understanding using pictorial techniques may be more suitable for young children than word-based items, but remains highly problematic.[124]

A star for Sisyphus

Before leaving this section it may be worth noting the relative lack of attention given to children's positive emotions and how to nourish them, despite widespread concern among Review witnesses about the effects of current regimes on children's confidence, self-esteem, ability to empathise, and enjoyment of learning. Several groups, but notably teachers, referred to the importance of learning how to learn, and linked this with their preference for assessment for learning over summative forms of assessment (see Chapter 16). Parents, teaching assistants and teachers all warned that under the present system children could be branded as failures at a very early stage in their school careers. Head teachers, for example, called for an emphasis on 'contexts for success' so that all children, rather than just those who did well in their SATs, could enjoy a sense of achievement.

One way for teachers to improve children's self-esteem and motivation is to acknowledge the effort children put into their work, rather than focusing solely on the results. This follows research on children's personal theories of their own intelligence and whether they can improve through their own efforts.[125] Since many parents and teachers will have grown up in an era of negative contracts ('if you don't finish your work, you can't go out to play'), they too may benefit from practical advice on how to make more positive contracts.[126]

CONCLUSION

So, how do children develop, think, feel, act and learn? Answering that question lies in part in recognising the intricate and intertwined influences of what used to be called nature and nurture: the interdependence of children's development and the social and cultural environment in which it takes place. Among the more significant findings we have noted are these:

- Though children seem to be 'growing older younger', they are neither growing taller, nor maturing physically earlier, at the rapid rate implied by pre-Plowden statistics. What we see instead is young children under pressure to appear and act older than they are.
- Neuroscientific research suggests that children can learn in as many different ways as adults and multisensory approaches are more likely to achieve understanding.
- The relationship between cognitive development and learning is now understood as an interactive process in which development is brought about by appropriately tuned teaching by teachers or more capable peers.
- Research evidence confirms the importance for a child's cognitive development of social interaction with teachers and other children. The quality of classroom talk is critical, whether between teacher and pupil or among pupils themselves.
- The gender gap in attainment cannot be attributed to basic reasoning abilities, and must therefore be a consequence of socio-cultural factors in and out of school. Holistic and infrastructural remedies involving boys, girls, teachers, parents and wider curricular interventions which value learning outside the core skills, are needed to redress imbalances while promoting higher achievement.
- In the same vein, repeated calls for more opportunities for children to develop their creativity in school are supported by research which recognises the quality of the thinking, as well as the perseverance, which the creative process entails. Children need more time to engage with their projects, and the creative process as well as the product should be valued.
- Strong concerns were voiced in the soundings and submissions about the effects of various sources of emotional stress, and the case for schools to accommodate children's needs for space and time to 'chill out' and, crucially, to be listened to. Extension of the SEAL programme and more opportunities for the development of children's social skills and emotional understanding are welcomed and are likely to have a positive impact on learning outcomes.

While *Every Child Matters* and the Children's Plan offer a way forward with respect to some of these points, others will be frustrated by the pressures of time, testing and targets of which many Review witnesses complained. Our understanding of how children develop and learn has been greatly enhanced by neuroscientific evidence and by the refinement of socio-cultural theory and research. Clearly, there is a strong case for schools to make better use of the unique social, linguistic and cognitive environment that the classroom provides. Respecting children's voices and acknowledging that they have a role in what and how they learn require appreciation of their lives beyond school, and acceptance of what they bring into school; all of which underscores arguments presented in earlier chapters. Responding to what we now know about children's development and learning requires attention to evidence on a broad and diverse front. What links the evidence is the need to square the circle of the cognitive and the social. Where this is achieved, self-esteem, motivation, capability and attainment go hand in hand.

NOTES

1 For example Cole (1996); Cole and Cole (1996).
2 Goswami and Bryant (2010), *The Cambridge Primary Review Research Surveys*, Chapter 6.
3 Bruner and Haste (1987).
4 See Goswami and Bryant (2010), *The Cambridge Primary Review Research Surveys*, Chapter 6.
5 CACE (1967): para 55.

6 Howe and Mercer (2010, *The Cambridge Primary Review Research Surveys*, Chapter 7.

7 James and Pollard (2010), Blatchford *et al.* (2010), *The Cambridge Primary Review Research Surveys*, Chapters 20–21.

8 CACE (1967): para 11.

9 Kamin (1982).

10 Goswami and Bryant (2010) *The Cambridge Primary Review Research Surveys*, Chapter 6, citing, for example, Plomin and Spinath (2002).

11 As was the 1931 Hadow report on the primary school (Gillard 2007).

12 Saying in paragraph 520, for example, as a 'warning to schools run on traditional lines', that 'prolonged periods of routine practice in … computation or handwriting, reduce rather than improve accuracy.'

13 Notably by Bryant (1974), and McGarrigle and Donaldson's (1974) 'naughty teddy'.

14 CACE (1967): para 9.

15 *Ibid.*: para 521.

16 Board of Education (1905), Edmond Holmes (1911), and the Hadow report of 1931. See Gillard (2007).

17 CACE (1967): para 529.

18 Mayall (2010) *The Cambridge Primary Review Research Surveys*, Chapter 3; and Chapter 9 of this volume.

19 Alexander and Hargreaves (2007).

20 Mercer and Littleton (2007).

21 CACE (1967): para 13.

22 The 1959 and 1905–12 figures may over-estimate average heights due to the samples employed, whereas the NHS 2006–7 figures are based on measurement of 80 per cent of the population.

23 CACE (1967): para 96.

24 Percentages rounded to nearest whole number.

25 DH and DCSF (2008).

26 Department of Health (2008).

27 Fox and Riddoch (2000).

28 Coleman and Coleman (2002): 548.

29 CACE (1967): para 74.

30 CACE (1967): para 74.

31 Alexander and Hargreaves (2007).

32 Bedford and Elliman (2000): 240.

33 Mayall (2010), *The Cambridge Primary Review Research Surveys*, Chapter 3.

34 Health Protection Agency (2008).

35 Goswami and Bryant (2010), Howe and Mercer (2010), *The Cambridge Primary Review Research Surveys*, Chapters 6–7.

36 Smith *et al.* (2003).

37 CACE (1967): para 75.

38 For example Brown and Desforges (1977).

39 Lourenco and Machado (1996).

40 Vygotsky (Translated by Cole *et al.* 1978).

41 Vygotsky (1978): 86.

42 Vygotsky (1936/1986): 110.

43 Alexander (2001b).

44 Goswami (2001); Donaldson (1978).

45 DES (1978a).

46 NUT (1979), quoted in Alexander (1984): 24.

47 Vygotsky (1978): 89.

48 Alexander (2001b): 216.

49 See, for example, Wood (1997); Meadows (2006); Howe and Mercer (2010), *The Cambridge Primary Review Research Surveys*, Chapter 7; North and Hargreaves (2008).

50 Meadows (2006): 294–95.

51 Goswami and Bryant (2010), *The Cambridge Primary Review Research Surveys*, Chapter 6.

52 TLRP (2006).

53 Mercer and Littleton (2007): 3.

54 Goswami and Bryant (2010), *The Cambridge Primary Review Research Surveys*, Chapter 6.

55 Meltzoff and Moore (1983).

56 Baillargeon *et al.* (2008).

57 The measurement of 'learning styles', notably in secondary and further education using psychometric measures and inventories, has been called into question also by the work of Frank Coffield and colleagues, whose major evaluation of learning styles inventories found most of them to be unreliable or invalid. (Coffield 2005).

58 Goswami and Bryant (2010), *The Cambridge Primary Review Research Surveys*, Chapter 6.

59 Hart and Risley (1995).

60 Fenson *et al.* (1994).

61 Smith (1996).

62 Smith (1996): 110.

63 Vygotsky (1933) in Cole *et al.* (1978): 94ff.

64 CACE (1967): para 523.
65 CACE (1967): para 528.
66 See also Sodha and Margo (2008).
67 Plomin and Spinath (2002), in Goswami and Bryant (2010), *The Cambridge Primary Review Research Surveys*, Chapter 6.
68 Hart *et al.* (2004).
69 Alexander (1984): 42–43.
70 Berliner and Biddle (1995): 50–51. The final italics are ours.
71 Gardner (1983).
72 Sternberg (1985).
73 Gardner (1995, 2006).
74 Gardner (1987): 49–50.
75 Sternberg and Lubart (1999).
76 Claxton (2006).
77 Weisberg (1993). Case studies of scientists and artists including Darwin, Crick and Watson, Picasso, Blake, Coleridge.
78 North and Hargreaves (2008): 16.
79 Amabile's (1996) intrinsic motivation hypothesis of creativity states that 'the intrinsically motivated state is conducive to creativity, whereas the extrinsically motivated state is detrimental' (p.107).
80 Pell *et al.* (2007); Csikszentmihalyi (1996); Galton and MacBeath (2008).
81 See, for example, Epstein *et al.* (1998); Warrington and Younger (2006).
82 DCSF (2007d).
83 Strand *et al.* (2006).
84 Effect sizes of 0.2 or less are considered small and would not be noticeable in the population as a whole (Cohen 1977). Strand *et al.* cite Feingold's view that the smallest meaningful effect size is 1.10.
85 For example, Deary *et al.* (2003) analysed scores of over 87,000 people born in 1921, on the Moray House Verbal Reasoning test taken in 1932, and found no overall sex differences in the mean scores but greater variability among boys, that is more boys at the extremes.
86 DCSF (2007d).
87 DCSF (2007d): 82.
88 See Connolly and White (2006) for discussion of the measurement of such differences in percentage points, proportions or effect sizes.
89 For example, Skelton and Francis (2003).
90 Galton *et al.* (2003); Gray and McLellan (2006); Carrington *et al.* (2008).
91 Galton *et al.* (1999); Galton *et al.* (2003).
92 For example, Skelton (2001).
93 113 men, 300 women, as identified by their first names, and therefore acknowledging a margin of error. Data on teacher ethnicity were not collected.
94 Carrington *et al.* (2008).
95 Warrington and Younger (2005).
96 Howe and Mercer (2010), *The Cambridge Primary Review Research Surveys*, Chapter 7.
97 Mercer (2000): 140–41.
98 See Anning and Edwards (1999): 69ff for a summary.
99 Sylva *et al.* (2004).
100 Galton *et al.* (1999); Blatchford and Kutnick (2003).
101 Alexander (2001b): 407–8.
102 Alexander (2008a): 39. Briefly defined, discussion, between teacher and class, teacher and group, teacher and individual, or among pupils themselves, is 'the exchange of ideas with a view to sharing information and solving problems'. Dialogue, in the same organisational contexts, seeks to 'achieve common understanding through structured and cumulative questioning and discussion which guide and prompt, reduce choices, minimise risk and error, and expedite 'handover' of concepts and principles'. Alexander acknowledges Bruner's contribution to this definition of dialogue.
103 Alexander (2008b): 19.
104 CACE (1967): para 73.
105 Helwig and Turiel (2002): 476.
106 Kohlberg (1981).
107 Reviewed by Helwig and Turiel (2002).
108 Helwig and Turiel (2002): 483.
109 http://www.teachernet.gov.uk/teachingandlearning/socialandpastoral/sebs1/seal/
110 Sodha and Margo (2008).
111 Layard and Dunn (2009).
112 Layard and Dunn (2009): 18.
113 Layard and Dunn (2009): 20.
114 See, for example, Dunn *et al.* (1991).
115 Layard and Dunn (2009): 17.
116 Layard and Dunn (2009): 111.
117 The concept dates back to Guilford's model of intelligence (1912).

118 Salovey and Mayer (1990): 189.
119 See Petrides *et al.* (2004) for a brief overview.
120 See, for example, materials produced by Sharp (2001) for the Southampton Psychological Services.
121 'Emotional literacy' defined at http://www.emotional-literacy.com/aelbook.htm; Learning emotional literacy at http://emotionalliteracyeducation.com/emotional-literacy-language-vocabulary.shtml.
122 The National Emotional Literacy Interest Group (NELIG) set up by Peter Sharp in 2000 (www.nelig.com)
123 Tenenbaum *et al.* (2008).
124 Pons *et al.* (2004).
125 Dweck (1999, 2006), cited in Goswami and Bryant (2010), *The Cambridge Primary Review Research Surveys*, Chapter 6.
126 For example, Hartley-Brewer (2006).

8 Children, diversity and equity

So far in Part 2 we have looked at how children learn and develop, their lives outside school, and the influence of family and home. But all these aspects of childhood are shaped by culture, and England today is a country of exceptional cultural diversity. Acknowledging this diversity means accepting that primary schools will be called on to serve not just the traditional centre of society, but its boundaries and margins as well. Clearly people at these margins – conventionally defined by poverty, prejudice, or lifestyle – are sometimes at odds with the centre. In any case, the centre is undoubtedly more diverse than political appeals to 'middle England' imply; and throughout recent history the experiences of migration, economic division, religion, gender and social class have challenged the notion of a definable national centre or character, other than as related to power, wealth and social status.

The need to achieve an equitable balance between personal or sectional interests and wider social concerns is a challenge both for the system as a whole and for each school. Considerations of equity in education do not apply only to those children and communities in need of different or preferential treatment, whether permanently or temporarily. There are implications for all children in any attempt to respond fairly and effectively to a group singled out for particular support. Similarly, all children are implicated in attempts to categorise and selectively target need. While such categories change over time, the tendency is always to view them in a negative light, thus risking accentuating perceptions of difference and constructing barriers to learning. As the previous chapter showed, concerns about boys' attainment led to many boy-centred strategies when greater success lay in holistic strategies that benefited both boys and girls.

Of course, diversity has implications that reach beyond the classroom. Differences in culture, gender, language and wealth shape the totality of young lives. Sometimes these differences appear closely connected with educational success, but not all of them and not for every child. Teachers need to be able to identify and understand the educationally relevant aspects of pupil diversity – not easy in an education system where 'fairness', 'inclusion' and 'effectiveness' are often regarded as incompatible.

Considering this point, as the Cambridge Primary Review did, also focused attention on the purposes of education for all children and the desirability of a plurality of educational experiences and outcomes in a highly plural culture. This in turn raised the question of how education for a diversity of pupils can best be planned, accommodated, funded, governed and evaluated.

INTERLINKED INEQUALITIES

The old 'early-to-bed' adage linked health, wealth and wisdom. A more threatening version might have linked sickness, poverty and failure. Crucially, differences in educational achievement, at least as defined by SAT scores at age 11, conform closely with other inequalities in wealth, health, social mobility, risk and opportunity. Among low-attaining children, certain groups are disproportionately represented: children from poor families, White working-class boys, looked-after children, children with disabilities, children from particular minority ethnic backgrounds, and children of refugees and Gypsy/Roma or Travellers. Success in education terms is very unevenly distributed in England. The country's 'long tail of underachievement' and the gap between the children who do well and those who do not were of acute concern to the Review's witnesses.

The government recognised this 'fundamental weakness in equality of opportunity' in its 2004 Five Year Strategy for Children and Learners:

> Those from higher socio-economic groups do significantly better at each stage of our system than those from lower ones ... socio-economic group is a stronger predictor of attainment than early ability. In general ... those that do well early do even better later in life, while those that do not perform well fall further behind; and the chances of breaking out of this cycle of underachievement reduce with age ... We also fail our most disadvantaged children and young people – those in public care, those with complex family lives, and those most at risk of drug abuse, teenage pregnancy, and involvement in criminal activity. Internationally, our rate of child poverty is still high, as are the rates of worklessness in one-parent families, the rate of teenage pregnancy, and the level of poor diet among children. The links between poor health, disadvantage and low educational outcomes are stark.[1]

The influences of poverty

No chapter that deals with issues of equity can ignore England's unequal distribution of wealth. The Joseph Rowntree Foundation reported that levels of inequality in the UK grew rapidly in the 1980s and 1990s, until in 2005 they were as high as they had been for 40 years.[2] The gap between rich and poor was greater than in three-quarters of the world's 30 most developed countries, according to the Organisation for Economic Co-operation and Development. In 2006, the richest 1 per cent held 21 per cent of the country's wealth, while 50 per cent of the population shared a mere 7 per cent of the wealth. Nearly a fifth of households were classified as low income.[3] Free school meals – a common measure of social deprivation – were offered to 641,510 (15.5 per cent) of primary pupils.

The proportion of impoverished children – as opposed to households – fell from 14 per cent to 10 per cent between the mid-1990s and 2005, the second largest fall (behind Italy) among OECD countries over this period.[4] Even so, poverty still afflicted a higher percentage of children than in the mid-1980s (7–8 per cent) or mid-1970s (5 per cent). And it is rising again. According to the Child Poverty Action Group, 3.9 million children were living in relative poverty in 2006–7, compared to 3.6 million in 2004–5.[5] (Comparable government figures are 2.9 million and 2.7 million.) Most at risk were the children of unemployed, lone or disabled parents, those growing up in large families and members of some minority ethnic groups. Two-fifths of minority ethnic people in the UK live in low-income households, twice the rate for White people.[6] In 2007, the Joseph Rowntree Foundation reported that 65 per cent of Bangladeshi people were poor, as were 55 per cent of Pakistanis, 45 per cent of Black Africans and 30 per cent of Indians and Black Caribbeans. More than half of Pakistani and Black African children in the UK were deprived, with what the foundation described as a 'staggering' 70 per cent of Bangladeshi children growing up in poverty.[7]

The wealth gap is mirrored by the health gap. To put it crudely, poor people do not, on average, live as long as rich people and their children are more likely to die in infancy – and in 2006 the gaps were widening. While the overall health of the nation has improved dramatically in the past 100 years, the difference in life expectancy between the poorest fifth of people and the population as a whole actually widened by 2 per cent for men and 11 per cent for women between 1997–99 and 2004–6.[8,9] People living in England's wealthiest areas could expect to live seven to eight years longer than those in the poorest areas. Similarly, the inequality gap in the infant mortality rate was 4 points higher in 2004–6 than in 1997. Babies born to manual workers had a 17 per cent higher than average chance of dying, compared to a 13 per cent higher than average chance in 1997. Poverty increases a child's risk of becoming obese, suffering from a chronic illness or mental ill health – even of dying in an accident.[10]

Poverty can also exert a negative influence on a child's cognitive development. Back in 1999, researchers using data from the National Child Development Study studied the tested cognitive development of young children from the 1958 cohort. Where the parents had themselves grown up in socially disadvantaged situations, the average cognitive development of children was lower. The researchers concluded that: 'This suggests a potentially important cross-generational link that may well spill over to affect the subsequent economic fortunes of the children of disadvantaged individuals.'[11] Some studies suggest that an impoverished childhood can directly affect brain development. In 2008, American scientists measured brain activity in 26 nine- and 10-year-olds. The pre-frontal cortex, an area associated with problem solving, was found to be less responsive to visual stimuli in deprived children.[12] One of the researchers remarked that: 'This is a wake-up call – it's not just that these kids are poor and more likely to have health problems, but they might actually not be getting full brain development from the stressful and relatively impoverished environment associated with low socioeconomic status. Fewer books, less reading, fewer games, fewer visits to museums.' Plus, as discussed in Chapter 7, fewer opportunities for the conversation and social interaction vital to healthy development, although many poor homes can be rich in experience.

The Review's research survey on parenting, caring and educating concluded that child poverty is one of the education system's biggest challenges.[13] Other evidence supports this view. A Rowntree Foundation enquiry reported that 'children from poor homes are nearly a year behind when they start school, and two years behind by age 14. Most never catch up.'[14] The charity Barnardo's warned that deprived children were a third less likely to get five A*-C grade GCSEs than their richer peers. The strong negative correlation between deprivation and attainment was further confirmed by the 2007 Progress in International Reading and Literacy Study (PIRLS) report on reading standards among 10-year-olds, with due caution about the narrowly focused attainment measures in this area.[15]

In the same year, the Child Poverty Action Group warned of a 'chicken-and-egg' cycle of deprivation.[16] The charity told MPs:

> Children in poverty fall further behind their peers at every stage of schooling. By age three, poverty makes a difference equivalent to nine months' development in school readiness. And at each stage of compulsory schooling the poverty gap grows. Moreover, the association between growing up in poverty and being poor in adulthood has become stronger since the 1970s. CPAG believes that without targeted educational investment the government's long-term goal of eradicating child poverty by 2020 will not be reached.[17]

The diminishing chances of a child escaping a life of poverty was confirmed by the OECD's finding that there was less social mobility in the UK than in Australia, Canada or Denmark. The UK, the OECD found, was similar to the United States and Italy in that parental income was a much stronger indicator of a child's future earnings than in more mobile countries.[18] In recognition of this problem, the government's 2009 New Opportunities White Paper on social mobility proposed imposing an 'over-arching requirement on public authorities to address the inequalities people face associated with where they live, their family background or the job they do'. It commented that: 'Inequality does not just come from your gender or ethnicity, your sexual orientation or your disability. Co-existing and interwoven with these specific inequalities lies the persistent inequality of social class.' The persistence of class divides in education is revealed by concerns about the under-achievement of many White working-class boys. (It is perhaps worth noting, however, that 'low' social class is not synonymous with low income: the 2007 British Social Attitudes survey found that 57 per cent of Britons considered themselves working class even though only 31 per cent were employed in traditional 'blue collar' jobs.)

In addition, the Review's soundings and submissions commented on how inequality of income was exacerbated by broad social, cultural and educational pressures. These included: materialistic values; the effects of globalisation on people's economic and social standing; the loss of local jobs, and of educational routes to employment, for 'less academic' children.

The influences of gender

Gender is not as strong a predictor of attainment as socio-economic status, according to research which found that the social class attainment gap at key stage 4 (as measured by percentage point difference in attainment between those eligible and not eligible for free school meals) is three times as wide as the gender gap.[19] Nevertheless it is an important one given that boys appear over-represented in special needs categories, in school exclusions and are lagging behind girls at all stages of education from the early years onwards. Raising boys' attainment, particularly that of White working-class boys, has become a government priority. One government minister has explained the reasons for boys' underachievement as 'complex but mainly related to biological differences, differences in maturation, and differences in attitudes to learning and reading at different ages'.[20] He added that gender gaps can be minimised by good teaching practice. While this is undoubtedly true, some evidence suggests that less-than-good teaching practice is actually exacerbating gender gaps – a factor discussed later in the chapter.

The influences of ethnicity

At the time of the Cambridge Primary Review, England's mobile, changing and multicultural population of 50.8 million was increasing and ageing, and was predicted to grow by 8 per cent by 2016. Its primary schools catered for just over 4 million children, including nearly 827,000 under the age of five.[21] Boys marginally outnumbered girls – 1.95 million to 1.87 million – among full-time pupils over the age of five.

Ethnically the population was growing more varied. 'White British' people comprised 87 per cent of the population in 2006, but only 75.9 per cent of primary pupils in 2008 (see Table 8.1).[22] A similar picture emerged with regard to some other ethnic groups, for example, Indian and Pakistani (both 2 per cent of the general population, and 2.4 and 3.7 per cent respectively of primary pupils), Bangladeshi (1 per cent and 1.5 per cent) 'other Asian' (1 per cent and 1.2 per cent), Black Caribbean (1 per cent and 1.4 per cent) and Black African (1 per cent and 2.8 per cent).

Of the 3.26 million pupils aged over five, 758,700 (23.3 per cent), were from minority ethnic groups. This was an increase from 21.9 per cent in 2007, and more than the 19.5 per cent in secondary schools. Pakistani children comprised the largest minority ethnic group at 3.7 per cent. Other groups were much smaller, with only 0.1 per cent of primary pupils identified as Travellers of Irish Heritage.

Of course, ethnic diversity brings linguistic diversity and in 2008 an estimated 240 languages were spoken in England's primary and secondary schools. The most common were Punjabi, Urdu, Bengali, Gujarati, Somali, Polish and Arabic. English was not the first language of one in seven (470,080) primary pupils, compared with one in 10 in 2004.[23] Many of these children were concentrated in certain areas – for example 53.4 per cent of pupils in inner London had English as a second language.

Such concentrations have prompted concern. In 2005, Trevor Phillips, then chair of the Commission for Racial Equality, discussed what he saw as the challenges facing policy-makers and others in building an integrated society in Britain. He received much media coverage for his warning that Britain was 'sleepwalking to segregation'. Both residential and educational segregation concerned him, as well as the growing tendency for different groups of people to inhabit separate cultural and social worlds:

> The fact is that we are a society which, almost without noticing it, is becoming more divided by race and religion. We are becoming more unequal by ethnicity. If we allow this to continue, we could end up ... living in a Britain of passively co-existing ethnic and religious communities, eyeing each other uneasily over the fences of our differences.[24]

Phillips' remarks sparked extensive public debate, and not all agreed with his final analysis. Some focussed on what they saw as more fundamental problems and divisions in 'a society

Table 8.1 English primary pupils of compulsory school age and above: number and percentage by ethnic group January 2008 (provisional)

	Number	Percentage
White	*2,609,120*	*80.0*
White British	2,474,960	75.9
Irish	11,250	0.3
Traveller of Irish Heritage	2,840	0.1
Gypsy/ Roma	5,690	0.2
Any other White background	114,390	3.5
Mixed	*127,320*	*3.9*
White and Black Caribbean	41,280	1.3
White and Black African	14,070	0.4
White and Asian	26,760	0.8
Any other mixed background	45,200	1.4
Asian	*288,620*	*8.9*
Indian	79,430	2.4
Pakistani	120,740	3.7
Bangladeshi	50,290	1.5
Any other Asian background	38,170	1.2
Black	*155,320*	*4.8*
Black Caribbean	46,390	1.4
Black African	91,620	2.8
Any other Black background	17,310	0.5
Chinese	*10,930*	*0.3*
Any other ethnic group	*42,350*	*1.3*
Minority ethnic pupils	*758,710*	*23.3*
All pupils	*3,261,280*	*100.0*

Source: DCSFu.

fractured by poverty, wealth disparity, wars abroad, terror attacks, religious bigotry from all faiths, and competition for schools and employment'.[25] Others questioned the inevitability of increased social division rather than compatibility or community cohesion. Yet recent research in one London borough's primary schools showed that children of Bangladeshi origin made up 90 per cent of the pupils at 17 schools, but fewer than 10 per cent in nine other schools. Another report showed that 59 per cent of primary pupils in Bradford attended schools where more than 90 per cent of the children were of one 'single cultural or ethnic identity'.[26]

The wide range of attainment between different ethnic groups has long been a political and educational concern. Nevertheless the problem persists and in 2007 the Commission for Racial Equality reported that:

> Children of Indian, Chinese and Irish origin have attainment levels which exceed the national average, while Black children, White working-class boys, Gypsies and Irish Travellers and those of Bangladeshi and Pakistani origin consistently fall below the average at all key stages. At key stage 1, 28 per cent of Irish Travellers and 42 per cent of Gypsy or Roma pupils achieved level 2 or above in reading, compared with 84 per cent of all pupils. At key stage 4, 42 per cent of Irish Travellers and 23 per cent of Gypsy or Roma pupils achieved five or more A*-C GCSE/GNVQs, compared with 51 per cent of all pupils.[27]

Poverty and ethnicity combined

Of course, the influences of poverty cannot be ignored in any discussion of the attainment of minority ethnic children as many of them are among the poorest in England. However, research published in 2008 attempted to untangle the complex relationship between ethnicity, socio-economic status and gender among secondary pupils.[28] It found that Indian pupils fared better in their GCSEs than White British pupils, while, on average, Black African, Bangladeshi and mixed-race pupils did as well as White British pupils. Pakistani students did slightly worse and Black Caribbean students did substantially worse. Socio-economic status was found to have the greatest impact on pupils' achievement. The attainment gap between children of high and low socio-economic status was roughly three times as large as the gap between ethnic groups.

Once socio-economic status was factored out, the gap between many of the ethnic groups narrowed – but clear differences remained. Pakistani and Bangladeshi pupils joined Indian pupils in doing better than their White counterparts. Black Caribbean children were the only group to underachieve. Researchers concluded that the two groups that should be cause for greatest concern were middle-class Black Caribbean children and White working-class pupils. They suggested that White working-class pupils may do badly as a result of low aspirations, and that low teacher expectations may be holding back middle-class Black Caribbean children and Black African boys.

Some confirmation of these low expectations comes in relation to key stage 2 English test and teacher assessment results. While all pupils, on average, do less well in the teacher assessment than in the test – a difference of 4 percentage points in 2005 – the discrepancy between teacher assessment and test results for Asian and Black pupils and for pupils with English as an additional language is larger.[29] For Bangladeshi pupils in 2005 the difference was 7 points, while for Black African pupils it was 8 points. Clearly, attitudes to poverty, class and ethnicity influence children's experience of education and their likelihood of success.

Low attainment and social exclusion relate closely to geographical differences in funding, as well as to prejudice and power differentials in England, with its divisions of class, wealth, race and religion. Half of all children entitled to free school meals are concentrated in a fifth of schools[30] which face a particular challenge in relation to values and expectations – as Mel Ainscow and colleagues conclude in their research survey for the Review:

> ... differences are never neutral. Belonging to a particular ethnic group, or coming from a particular social background, or even having a particular gender, has a value insofar as it inhibits or facilitates the achievement of particular outcomes. Characteristics with a negative value are cast as obstacles to be overcome through policy and practice interventions. Given the tendency ... for poor outcomes to be associated with particular clusters of characteristics, and for these clusters to be distributed unevenly in geographical terms, this means that particular groups of learners in particular places are likely to be seen as overwhelmed by negative characteristics – as are the schools that serve them.[31]

HOW THE EDUCATION SYSTEM EXACERBATES INEQUALITIES

Construction of difference

While the quantity of statistical data about children's lives has mushroomed in recent years, it is important to remember that focusing on single dimensions of difference such as ethnicity or gender cannot take into account the complex experiences and interactions which are the reality of children's lives.[32] Certainly evidence has been increasingly highlighting the tremendous differences in the circumstances, aspirations and progress of individual pupils from particular social groups. As the Briefing for the Review's research survey by Ainscow and colleagues warned:

Statistical constructions of this kind reveal important aspects of diversity, though they can also conceal the extent to which children with similar characteristics – particular ethnic backgrounds, special educational needs status, or entitlement to free school meals, for instance – tend to cluster together in particular schools and areas. Moreover, the procedures are constrained by the need to support large databases. They focus on data that are easily quantifiable and easy to collect on a large scale. In so doing, they are highly selective, and reduce subtle and complex characteristics among individuals and groups to whatever the most readily-available measures make of them. So, for instance, the complexities of children's social background are often reduced to whether or not they are entitled to free school meals; and the complexities of children's language competence and usage tend to be reduced to whether or not they have English as an additional language.

With government education policy focused on standards, there is a danger that 'diversity as constructed in national statistics is understood primarily in its relation to attainment'. These 'somewhat uni-dimensional constructions' feed into policy, prompting interventions targeted at, for example, boys or some low-attaining minority groups. They also offer 'an impoverished understanding of difference' and risk perpetuating stereotypes and 'deficit thinking' among teachers.[33]

Special needs

Some evidence of deficit thinking can be gleaned from a study of children identified with special needs (discussed in detail in Chapter 9) and those nominated as gifted and talented. The question must be asked as to whether the education system is failing to accommodate difference and, in doing so, widening gaps it should be helping to narrow. Disproportionately represented in special needs categories in 2008 were:

- *Boys*
  Many more boys than girls are identified as having special needs. Government statistics for 2008 indicated that 92,000 primary and secondary boys had statements (around 1 in 40), compared with 34,400 girls (less than 1 in 100). For those without statements, about 20 per cent of boys were considered to have special needs compared to about 14 per cent of girls.
- *Deprived children*
  While pupils entitled to free school meals make up 13 per cent of all pupils, they comprise 28 per cent of children identified with special needs (with and without statements).
- *Black children*
  A higher proportion of Black primary pupils (1.9 per cent) had statements of special needs than White pupils (1.7 per cent). Traveller children of Irish Heritage had the highest proportion at around 2.9 per cent but the comparatively small numbers (just 80 pupils) can be statistically misleading here.[34] In total, 26.3 per cent of Black pupils were identified as having special needs without statements, compared to 20.1 per cent of Asian pupils, 20.7 per cent of White pupils and 11.8 per cent of Chinese pupils.

A similar pattern can also be seen in the identification of 'gifted and talented' (G and T) pupils. In 2008, the following were under-represented in G and T selections:

- *Deprived children*
  Pupils eligible for free school meals comprised 15.5 per cent of all nursery and primary pupils but only 11 per cent of G and T pupils (although the numbers were not directly comparable due to lack of separate nursery and primary free school meals figures).
- *Children with special needs*
  Children with special needs (with and without statements) comprised 8.4 per cent of G and T pupils compared to around 20 per cent of all pupils.

- *Minority ethnic children*
  Children whose first language was not English comprised 14.4 per cent of all primary pupils but only 12.5 per cent of G and T pupils. A total of 80 per cent of G and T pupils were White, compared to 75.9 per cent of all primary pupils.[35] The picture is complex though. Chinese children, at both primary and secondary level, were over-represented by 8 per cent in 2007, while Pakistani pupils were under-represented by 3.6 per cent and Travellers and Gypsy/ Roma children under-represented by about 8 per cent (though, as before, the numbers are small).

One researcher commented after analysing the G and T minority ethnic figures that: 'It is difficult to look at these figures and not see evidence of institutional racism. It is tempting to see G and T as a mirror held up to society providing a reflection of and on our level of inclusiveness.'[36]

Ethnicity

There is no doubt that issues of diversity, pluralism and national identity remain central to public, political and professional thinking in England. To take the example of minority ethnic groups and immigration, Professor Sally Tomlinson remarked in her wide and detailed survey of policy from the 1960s to 2007:

> While minority groups historically have often been blamed for their failure to 'integrate', minorities in a majority culture need some sense of solidarity, to defend themselves in an often hostile society, and such solidarity can provide a base from which to lay claim to equal rights. Minority community organisations, especially in education, over the years have pressed for an acknowledgement of the legitimacy of their presence as minorities but also as equal citizens.[37]

This multi-faceted position needs expression in educational policy. Certainly governments have, over this time, touched on many aspects of social diversity and division, including race, language, religion, disability and so on. Yet their policies have been characterised by alternative, overlapping and sometimes contradictory responses. One example, noted by Tomlinson, was the realisation in the early 1980s that minority groups could not and should not be pigeon-holed as 'disadvantaged'. It was the racism and ignorance in society that needed to be tackled.[38]

Some witnesses to the Review raised doubts about a long-standing pedagogical tradition, asking whether the tendency to celebrate individuality and respect difference might have actually widened rather than reduced the gap in attainment. Such doubts are of particular significance to minority ethnic groups. From the 1980s onwards, attention was increasingly paid to the concerns and preferences of local communities, including those with minority home languages and religions. This added to the culturally diverse feel of many primary schools: displays, books, assemblies and so on reflected the 'celebration' of multiculturalism and, in a smaller number, a drive against racism. These were active forces for primary-school development in many parts of England through the 1990s (particularly, but not solely, in the inner cities), although both approaches were controversial and criticised for their limited aims and achievements.[39]

The awareness that some ethnic groups were being disproportionately suspended and expelled from school and were over-represented in units for pupils with emotional and behavioural difficulties and in special schools has been growing for decades. With this awareness came an understanding that the reasons lay, at least in part, in classroom processes and pedagogical biases. Sometimes, teachers misunderstood cultural norms – such as minority ethnic pupils using eye contact in 'challenging' or 'disrespectful' ways. Sometimes, they tended to channel certain pupils, particularly Black boys, towards sports rather than academic subjects.[40] The relatively high achievement of Indian pupils compared to their Pakistani and Bangladeshi peers, now less pronounced, revealed the complex interaction of attitudes to social class and ethnicity.

Attitudes to children with English as an additional language (EAL) were examined in the Review's research survey by Ainscow and colleagues. This pointed to the need to challenge negative thinking in relation to these pupils. Even the title EAL – now slowly being replaced with the more positive 'bilingual' – suggests these children have a problem and are in need of extra help in school. The 2000 statement on the national curriculum spelt out the view that EAL could constitute a 'barrier to learning'. Yet the discrepancies in the key stage 2 test results, mentioned above, suggest that it is this negative view that is the real barrier.

> Such a deficit model seems to be embedded in teachers' expectations of their pupils with EAL, as suggested by the disparities between teacher assessment and test results at KS2 for EAL learners, particularly in English. Indeed, the proportionality of these disparities by ethnicity matches the socio-economic status of the different groups, with Bangladeshi and Black African pupils showing higher percentage point differences than Indian and Pakistani.[41]

The researchers suggest that current conceptions of ethnic and language diversity are simplistic and unhelpful in understanding the complex nature of English society. Bilingualism, indeed multilingualism, is a natural and normal part of the lives and identities of many second and third generation minority ethnic primary pupils. There is evidence that children growing up in multilingual environments become confident users of a range of literacies, but that this advantage remains little understood by mainstream teachers. Indeed, the researchers add, it is another manifestation of the 'deficit discourses' that children who are becoming multiliterate are sometimes categorised by their teachers as in need of extra support and even as having special needs.[42] Furthermore, a greater understanding of the reality of bilingualism or even multilingualism might help those immigrant families in the Review's community soundings who feared that their children will lose their first language as they learn to speak English and with it their cultural identity and heritage.

Boys

Aside from forming the majority of children identified with special needs, boys are also far more likely to be permanently excluded from primary schools – 1,510 boys compared to 130 girls in 2006–7.[43] In 2008, a small-scale piece of research picked up on a theme that has been gaining increasing prominence – that in some ways primary schools are not adequately responding to boys. The research showed that boys were five times more likely than girls to be told off and far less likely to be praised or picked to answer a question.[44] But, just as research has shown that boys are no less able than girls, so this study indicates they are actually no more likely to misbehave than girls. The researcher concludes that: 'Teachers assume that boys are more badly behaved, possibly because the sort of bad behaviour they engage in is likely to be louder.' Girls' misbehaviour – reading under the desk or passing notes to friends – is less likely to be spotted. Also, when girls are bored they tend to 'switch off' whereas boys tend to start being disruptive. The study speculates that this unequal treatment could partly explain boys' lagging attainment. 'Perhaps some boys get disenchanted with lessons because they are being told off too much.' Certainly, the National Union of Teachers' submission to the Review considered that more work was needed to counter gender stereotypes and inequalities in the classroom.

The findings chimed with views expressed by children in the Review's community soundings. They said there were differences in the ways that boys and girls were treated at school. Girls were seen as being brighter and more likely to be picked to answer questions – though they were not chosen for football.

Similar theories have been advanced in relation to special needs. In 2002, the Audit Commission reported that:

> Although some conditions are known to occur more commonly among the male population – for example, speech and language difficulties – data from Wales show that boys are

more likely to have a statement than girls, across every type of need. Data from Scotland show the same pattern. Academic research also indicates that referrals by teachers and other professionals are biased towards boys. This could mean that:

- girls may be disadvantaged by not having their needs identified and appropriate action taken; and/or
- boys may be disadvantaged by having their needs emphasised and being 'labelled' unnecessarily.

The commission also commented on the high proportion of boys in special schools. 'This may reflect the fact that boys are over-represented among those with statements and in particular, among those with behavioural difficulties. However, it also raises questions about how effectively schools are responding to boys' needs.'[45]

Structural inequalities

The education system was considered by some Review witnesses to exacerbate inequalities through, for example, aspects of curriculum and assessment, school and classroom structures, and funding and governance. Elements of teacher training and professional development were also mentioned by some Review witnesses as needing improvement. Another concern was the failure of a largely urban education system to address the distinctive needs of small rural schools and communities (in contexts where schools are driven more to compete than to collaborate). The community soundings in particular highlighted the difficulties of quickly and effectively catering for dispersed, rapidly changing communities, such as immigrant bilingual children in rural areas.

In addition to this, primary schools were perceived, valued and used differently in affluent and less affluent areas. In the southeast, as the community soundings revealed, some schools were supplemented by parallel systems of coaching and out-of-school support. In less wealthy areas, parents tended to see the school itself as the best available social and educational resource. Admissions policies were a concern as witnesses considered they favoured affluent and mobile families. Parents on low incomes were further disadvantaged by the retention of selective secondary and special school systems, as well as the admissions policies of some faith schools. Such factors skew the intake of neighbouring schools and, as Mel Ainscow and colleagues point out in their research survey,[46] magnify community divisions.

Then there is the culture of primary schools themselves. Several Review witnesses expressed concern about the narrowness and apparent cultural bias of the primary curriculum and the distortion of children's educational chances by national tests. They also worried about school and classroom structures. The organisation of primary schools by age, and the educational system by phase, were both seen to provide too limited an environment for such a variety of pupils. Particular difficulties emerged in relation to the standard starting age and to stressful age-related transitions – especially from the foundation stage to key stage 1 (see Chapter 11).

PROMOTING EQUALITY AND UNDERSTANDING DIVERSITY

Early intervention

Some Review witnesses suggested that inequality is born at home, in the culture and attitudes of parents who lack interest in and ambition for their children at school (a matter in which England is said to compare unfavourably with countries in continental Europe and southeast Asia). Many witnesses stressed the compensatory need to tackle educationally significant differences, particularly in relation to language and communication, in the early years of primary education. As the government acknowledged in 2004, the chance of breaking out of cycles of underachievement reduces with age. The NUT's submission commented that:

Controlling for prior attainment, a key message from the DfES data is that Travellers of Irish heritage, Gypsy/Roma, Black Caribbean boys, White working-class boys, Black Other and Pakistani pupils make less progress at primary school than White British pupils with the same prior attainment. There is a strong need, therefore, for early intervention to ensure that all pupils have equal access to the curriculum, which is reflected in corresponding levels of educational attainment.

The union added that early intervention should also be a 'top priority at national, local and school level' to support children with challenging behaviour.

Concerns about the importance of attending to early experience and home life could be interpreted as criticisms of identifiable social groups. However some witnesses made a clear case against this, advocating respectful acknowledgement of and constructive responses to social and cultural differences in lifestyles and attitudes. For instance, as the submission from the National Association of Teachers of Travellers (NATT) proposed:

> Without positive reflection of their culture and values, and respect for the Gypsy, Roma, Traveller and other diverse communities represented in our schools, there is likely to be disaffection ... It is essential that differences are respected, but at the same time it is important that similarities are also acknowledged within the school system. In order to achieve equality of outcomes, different communities will need a variety of approaches to meet their aspirations for their children's education.

The Review's national soundings highlighted the need for schools to reach out to marginalised families and groups rather than waiting for them to come to school, together with a need for groups to have advocates in the system (see Chapter 20). The submission from 4 Children, a charity that 'aims to place children at the centre of policy development and service delivery', recognised that:

> ... it is engagement with and outreach to the 'hardest to reach' which is proving to be one of the biggest challenges in the new children's services agenda. While many initiatives and policies which aim to target the most disadvantaged families and children in our communities are making some headway, evaluations show that there is still a long way to go to reach the hardest to reach, and that more emphasis needs to focus on drawing in these groups who are traditionally wary or suspicious of engaging with services ... Some schools and local authorities are succeeding, but they need the buy-in of all staff and partners to enable this. Also, they need funding to provide the dedicated 'outreach' teams who can engage families, by home visiting or direct consultation and providing information ... a key concern is that by reaching some of the hardest to reach groups, schools and social work teams are also likely to uncover more problems that need to be addressed by more specialist teams.

There are signs that the government's Sure Start early years programme is beginning to have an impact on families in disadvantaged areas. An evaluation in 2008 indicated more positive benefits for parents and children than had been suggested in an earlier 2005 evaluation. Researchers cautiously concluded that such improvements may result from the 'greater exposure of children and families to better organised and more effective services, as Sure Start local programmes have matured over time, though it remains possible that differences in research design across the two studies could also be responsible'.[47]

In general, the Review's evidence revealed a need for better communication with parents and, where appropriate, 'catch-up' opportunities for children who miss large amounts of school. Co-ordinated support for hard-to-reach families needed to improve, witnesses said, as did support for England's 60,000 looked-after children. Also recommended was reliable, centrally co-ordinated tracking of groups such as migrants and Gypsy/Roma and Traveller communities with a central structure for supporting these children's education – similarly useful in the case of children with long absences. One submission urged the government to establish a grant for refugees' education to allow local authorities to target help at refugee and asylum-seeking families.

Community links

Much evidence was given about the need to understand children's varying experiences out of school, a recurrent theme of the Review. Crucially, schools were considered to need a better understanding of children's lives in local communities and faith groups. Analysis of submissions to the Review showed some support for enhancing the role of local authorities in bridging national-school perspectives regarding local needs, including establishing links with local community and faith groups.

Some witnesses also argued that there was a need for both local and national perspectives in curriculum planning and content, discussed in detail in Chapter 14. This should involve personally relevant topics and out-of-school learning, as well as assuming that learning requires investigating many different sources. The NATT referred to the need for 'family-based learning', as did some groups in the Review's community soundings. Views expressed in the submissions and the national soundings also emphasised the importance of curriculum flexibility for understanding and 'celebrating' community diversity. According to the NUT's submission:

> The question of whether our primary schools attend fairly and effectively to the cultural backgrounds of all pupils fundamentally relates to the nature and contents of the national curriculum and the scope, active encouragement and support teachers are given, in this context, to explore, value and celebrate different cultural identities. A key concern here is the mainstreaming of equality issues so that the emphasis on cultural diversity does not become an add-on to the existing curriculum, but that the curriculum is revised accordingly to incorporate knowledge and understanding of different cultural heritages and contributions. There is evidence that, at present, there is insufficient clarity about the flexibility within the curriculum and how links to education for diversity can be made. Moreover, links with the community, which is a rich resource for education for diversity, are often tenuous or non-existent.

The National Association of Head Teachers' (NAHT) submission remarked:

> … while central curriculum guidance is useful to schools, there must be scope for the school to develop aspects of the curriculum specifically relevant to the area in which the pupils live. Responsibility for this must remain with the school, taking account of the views of parents, governing body and the local community.

Communities were seen to need a voice. If, as many witnesses argued, there is a need for more to be done, nationally and locally, to address social inequalities, this is likely to require a more explicit consensus on values and priorities, which could be developed through dialogue. The point that schools cannot and should not 'do everything themselves' was made at several stages of the Review, including at the national soundings. Complex, holistic issues about community require parents, communities and governments to engage in review and change – just as children's own development takes place in these wider contexts. The Review's proposals for a community curriculum focusing on local needs and opportunities could provide the appropriate forum.

Integration

One submission to the Review urged the government to monitor the composition of school populations, provide an annual report on trends and develop techniques to encourage parents to send their children to mixed intake schools. Issues of integration are tricky, potentially pitting the dangers of 'sleepwalking to segregation' against parental choice. For example, community representatives from a religiously diverse Lancashire town told the Review that they wanted separate faith schools though children should also have opportunities to come together to avoid separatism and segregation.

However, research in 2008 indicates the benefits of mixed intake schools – and, by implication, the risks of encouraging single faith schools. In a year-long study carried out in 20 schools in Sussex and Kent, researchers from the Economic and Social Research Council interviewed children from minority ethnic groups about their attitudes towards themselves, their heritage, culture and their relationships with their peers.[48]

> The interviews revealed that the vast majority of children from immigrant backgrounds wanted to keep their ethnic identity including their language and religious customs but, at the same time, they were keen to adopt as many of the practices and values of the host society as possible. This preference, known as an integrationist orientation, was already clear in children as young as five years old but was even more marked in the older age groups.

While some 'integrationists' found balancing the demands of English society with that of their own cultural heritage somewhat stressful, their approach was shown to benefit them both emotionally and socially. Significantly, adverse effects were less pronounced in ethnically diverse schools. The researchers commented that:

> When the proportion of ethnic minority children in a school is at least 20 per cent, both ethnic minority children and the majority children tended to have higher self-esteem, children had more friendships with children from other ethnic groups, and there were fewer problems with peer relationships such as bullying.

Beyond constructions of difference

The original Review framework included fundamental questions about the construction of personal and social identity in a highly plural culture, and the role of primary education in fostering this. In 21st-century England primary education is seen as a right for all children but is not the same for all children. One submission to the Review urged that qualitative information about the learning environment be regarded as important as data on attainment in terms of deciding whether schools meet the different learning needs of all their pupils. For, as mentioned earlier, there is a risk in any categorisation of difference, be it in terms of gender, ethnicity or attainment. Categorisation, as the Review's research survey by Ainscow and colleagues warns, ignores the complexities of children's lives, overlooking the resources to which those differences give children access and neglecting the role of the child as agent, making sense of and acting within their worlds.[49] Again, the importance of acknowledging children's experiences outside school is relevant here, as is the issue of giving them a voice within school (see Chapter 10). Similar points were made in the Review's national soundings of organisations – already quoted in Chapter 5, but worth repeating:

> The changing social context makes it even more important for children to be active citizens. Even a passive acceptance that there are different people is insufficient. Children must actively embrace and include difference. The real cause of cultural problems is a lack of engagement in young people brought about by a feeling of disempowerment. Education should give children a sense of agency (they can make a difference) which means that they are engaged with society.

Ainscow and colleagues point to the benefits of

... very different constructions of difference – not in terms of fixed and evaluative categories, but of much more fluid constructions that are negotiated in particular contexts. So, what children 'are' and how they are 'different' from each other cannot be read off from a list of characteristics. Instead, it emerges from the interactions amongst children, and between them and their teachers, as they work together in particular educational contexts, on particular tasks and priorities. Moreover, each child plays a part in shaping the way that their distinctive and shared characteristics come to be understood.

Schools are required to work with fixed categories but are nonetheless capable of moving beyond them. Those that succeed can 'come to understand their pupils in terms other than those proposed by official discourse, and in this way are enabled to invent alternative forms of practice to respond to difference constructed in these ways'.

CONCLUSION

The issues raised in this chapter clearly represent complex national challenges with few immediately obvious solutions or ways forward. Nevertheless, three broad principles for decision-making and action can be identified here, while more specific recommendations for change are made in Chapter 24.

Acknowledging dilemmas and opposing views

First, it is essential to acknowledge openly that there are different and sometimes opposing views about how diversity should be handled in society, and about how teachers should respond to diversity in the classroom. There are many conflicts and quandaries. How best to support the girl whose Urdu is fluent but whose English is not, without stigmatising or stereotyping her? How best to raise the aspirations of a White working-class boy without undermining his identity? How best to reconcile the parents who want single faith schools and the evidence that children benefit from going to schools with a diverse intake? If such sensitive issues are not discussed openly then those people most closely involved with children's education may feel that they are personally to blame for difficulties and frustrations which children who are on the margins of mainstream education experience.

To help teachers cope with this we might argue for a stronger historical and cultural content in teachers' initial training and continuing professional development, so that teachers can be better informed about the dilemmas they will face in this aspect of their work.

Educationists could do more to promote their equivalent of the 'public understanding of science' through activities which would aim to raise public awareness and understanding of key issues in primary education, especially those which are inherently problematic or controversial. In a society as complex culturally as ours, where diversity is compounded by inequality, this could both inform policy development and help to move away from the often ill-informed public debates which are prompted by tragic events or controversial pronouncements.

Accommodating diversity

Classroom activities have the potential to connect with all children's developmental progress and immediate interests in the way argued in Chapters 5 and 7. Yet classroom life is not always as appreciative of the needs or talents of particular children and communities as it might be. Strengthening children's 'voice', acknowledging their lives outside school and giving them a greater sense that they have a role to play in embracing difference may all help here. Schools and teachers are clearly not immune to the influence of negative stereotypes of, particularly, boys and some ethnic minorities and may need help to ensure that they reduce inequality rather than unwittingly perpetuate divisions. More widely, the trajectory of educational planning, review meetings, budget decisions and so on is unlikely to be in step with the needs of particular children at particular times, or with rapid community changes. This is inevitable in a national system, but it is undeniably frustrating for children, teachers and parents. It can also be the point at which divisions among children start to increase.

As with the first principle, action might focus initially on improving professional and public understanding. This should start at the local level for particular schools and pupils, where there still remains a need to improve communication between all those involved with children's lives, inside and outside school, and to make it genuinely reciprocal. This was a strong theme in the Review's soundings and submissions, which also insisted that successful communication is about considerably more than formal procedures. It requires that teachers and others, including parents, understand the changing patterns of diversity, migration and community development in England, and the cultural and familial contexts from which pupils come. Most important here could be a more critically informed professional and public understanding of the uses of statistical data about social diversity, disadvantage and educational attainment, including in particular the evidence about the interacting and cumulative factors and experiences which influence children's progress (such as ethnicity, gender, familial stability, poverty, risk and special educational needs).

Defining and rewarding equity in education

Notwithstanding the dilemmas and differences of opinion about diversity, there is one matter on which all parties agree: the close relationship between social inequity and children's educational attainment. The phrase 'narrowing the gap', which was coined for a government-sponsored initiative, strikes a chord across a wide range of groups.[50] Although most Review witnesses believe that *Every Child Matters* and the Children's Plan are useful steps in addressing the gap (or gaps, for they are multiple), many argue that further action must be taken. Some make specific calls for more resources, teacher time and long-term funding. Others argue that until British society itself becomes vastly more equitable, educational initiatives will have at best a modest impact.

It would nevertheless be helpful to acknowledge that apparently equitable outcomes (such as high national test scores) may mask inequitable procedures in admission, teaching and learning. One obvious example from our evidence is the high incidence of coaching for the key stage 2 SATs in affluent areas, and of course its absence in poorer areas. Broad notions of 'value-added' have been found to be helpful as a way of contextualising the differential achievement of individual schools and local authorities, but they have their limits. Where high test scores are associated with coaching, is it the school or the parents who add the value? The rewards to schools and teachers for test results alone could be fundamentally inequitable without associated rewards for equity in admissions and classroom activity.

With these three broad principles in mind, and considering the range of evidence presented elsewhere in this chapter, we believe that action is merited to:

- foster a deeper professional understanding of social diversity and children's individual differences
- promote equality of treatment and perception of all children at school, especially with regard to boys and ethnic minorities
- improve understanding between primary schools, local communities and multi-professional teams
- advance the understanding of young children's learning and the importance of early intervention to help counteract the negative influences of poverty and prejudice
- extend the scope of initial teacher education and continuing professional development
- improve systems and procedures for tracking, monitoring and communicating with marginalised groups
- remove rewards for school effectiveness which take insufficient account of equity issues such as those raised here.

Achieving the above would go some considerable way to ensuring that the many children in England who are in some way 'different' are not also disadvantaged.

NOTES

1 DfES (2004c): para 20.
2 Joseph Rowntree Foundation (2007c).
3 ONS (2006a, 2006b).
4 OECD (2008c).
5 CPAG (2008).
6 The Poverty site, www.poverty.org.uk/summary/ethnic
7 Joseph Rowntree Foundation (2007b).
8 Professor Sir Michael Marmot, chair Scientific Reference Group of Health Inequalities, speaking on Radio 4 Today programme, August 11, 2005.
9 Department of Health (2008a).
10 CPAG (Feb 2000) 'Health and poverty', online briefing (www.cpag.org.uk/info/sp_briefings/0200healthpov.htm).
11 Gregg (1999).
12 Kishiyama *et al.* (2008).
13 Muschamp *et al.* (2010), *The Cambridge Primary Review Research Surveys*, Chapter 4.
14 Joseph Rowntree Foundation (2007a).
15 Twist *et al.* (2007).
16 Hirsch (2007b).
17 CPAG (2007), written evidence to Commons Select Committee on Work and Pensions (September).
18 OECD (2008c).
19 DfES (2007c).
20 Letter from schools minister Jim Knight to Dennis Laws, MP, July 2007 (www.literacytrust.org.uk).
21 DCSF (2008u).
22 DCSF (2008u).
23 DCSF (2008u).
24 CRE (2006).
25 Tomlinson (2008): 162.
26 CRE (2007).
27 CRE (2007).
28 Strand (2008b).
29 DfES (2006a).
30 The Poverty Site, www.poverty.org.uk/summary/children
31 Ainscow *et al.* (2010), *The Cambridge Primary Review Research Surveys,* Chapter 8.
32 Ainscow *et al.* (2010), Daniels and Porter (2010), *The Cambridge Primary Review Research Surveys*, Chapter 8.
33 Ainscow *et al.* (2010), *The Cambridge Primary Review Research Surveys*, Chapter 8.
34 DCSF (2008y).
35 DCSF (2008u).
36 Monaghan (2007).
37 Tomlinson (2008): 6–7.
38 Tomlinson (2008): 82.
39 Cole and Blair (2006): 79–80, argue that both approaches had their limitations. Multicultural education suffered from its tokenistic focus on the exotic otherness of different cultures rather than radical reform of curriculum or pedagogy or pervading societal inequalities. Anti-racism shifted the focus to a greater awareness of personal and institutional inequalities and the manifestations of racism, but its promotion in schools was seen to be counterproductive when based on the assumption that all White people were simplistically racist.
40 Cole and Blair (2006).
41 Ainscow *et al.* (2010), *The Cambridge Primary Review Research Surveys*, Chapter 8.
42 Ainscow *et al.* (2010), *The Cambridge Primary Review Research Surveys*, Chapter 8.
43 DCSF (2008u).
44 Swinson and Harrop (in press).
45 Audit Commission (2002).
46 Ainscow *et al.* (2010), *The Cambridge Primary Review Research Surveys*, Chapter 8.
47 National Evaluation of Sure Start (2008).
48 Brown, Rutland and Watters. (2008).
49 Ainscow *et al.* (2010), *The Cambridge Primary Review Research Surveys*, Chapter 8.
50 DCSF (2007e).

9 Children with special needs

As previous chapters have shown, England remains a country in which poverty, inequity and prejudice impede the progress of many children. Teachers, local authority children's services and government initiatives have all worked hard to counteract these and other negative influences, overtly so in the case of children who, for whatever reason, struggle to learn, do not behave appropriately or seem to need particular attention, adjustment and resources if they are to make progress. In 2008, nearly a fifth of all primary-aged pupils – 800,000 children – had been identified as having special educational needs, 1.4 per cent severe enough to merit an official statement of these needs and how they should be met.[1] This chapter examines the serious concerns brought to the Review's attention about how effectively the education system is catering for such a large and diverse group and reflects on possible alternative approaches.

In 1997, the government gave public support to the UN statement on special needs education which said 'the integration of children and youth with special educational needs is best achieved within inclusive schools that serve all children within a community. It is within this context that those with SEN can achieve the fullest educational progress and social integration'.[2] It added, significantly, that inclusive schools require 'a concerted effort, not only by teachers and school staff, but also by peers, parents, families and volunteers'. In England, acceptance of the basic rights and principles of inclusion has not always been matched by knowledge, attitudes, skills and practical support among all those involved. Educational funding, provision and achievement vary widely, even for children with apparently similar learning needs, in different local authorities and in different schools, both mainstream and special.

Moves towards inclusion have also highlighted the long-standing tension between the desire to respond more effectively to particular identified needs and a reluctance to pigeonhole children with these needs as 'special' in all respects. For instance, a hearing impairment requires appropriate communication systems; it does not mean that every aspect of a child's educational experience has to be adjusted. Differences between children are not easily defined or necessarily relevant to decisions about their education. As many minority ethnic groups and disabled people know, over-simplifying social and personal differences can result in stereotyping and discrimination. The Cambridge Primary Review revealed concerns about children being labelled and segregated unnecessarily by the type of school they attend and the education they are offered. As MPs concluded in 2006:

> Children exist on a broad continuum of needs and learning styles but do not fit into neat categories of different sorts of children – those with and those without SEN. The category of 'SEN' is an arbitrary distinction that leads to false classifications and, it can be argued, that this is what is causing the high levels of conflict and frustration with all those involved.[3]

Faced with a diversity of children, provision and outcomes, it is not sufficient to consider teaching in isolation or to focus only on particular groups of children. Any recommendations for improving the prospects of all children, including those with special educational needs, are inevitably linked with and dependent on each other. This applies particularly to the limits set by funding systems, curriculum aims, professional relationships, accountability and other broad aspects of primary education, as discussed in other chapters. What was strongly evident in the Review, however, was the anxiety and frustration caused by the varied and limited support for children identified with special needs, with deep concern about the lack of appropriate help being expressed by parents, teachers and local authorities. According to a former secretary of state, seeking an enquiry into SEN in 2009, there is 'probably a higher level of parental dissatisfaction with this aspect of our education system than with any other'.[4]

SPECIAL NEEDS: NUMBERS

In 2008, 59,130 primary pupils (1.4 per cent) had an official statement of special needs with nearly 740,000 (18 per cent)[5] identified as having special needs but no statement.[6] On average, three-quarters of schools reported between 5 per cent and 25 per cent of their pupils had special needs (with and without statements), peaking at 80.7 per cent in the east of England. However, a few (0.5 per cent) reported that at least half of their pupils had special needs (with and without statements), ranging from 0.1 per cent in the southwest to 1.1 per cent in the northeast and 1.2 per cent in the southeast.

There has been a decline in the number of statements given to primary pupils – from 69,610 (1.6 per cent of the total) in 2004 to 59,130 (1.4 per cent of the total) in 2008. Statements, which have cost implications, are awarded by local authorities to greatly varying degrees. The Review research survey by Harry Daniels and Jill Porter found some local authorities were making formal statements of support to only 0.3 per cent of pupils, compared to 3.1 per cent of pupils in others.[7] Such variations were criticised by the Audit Commission in 2002 and again by MPs in 2006.

'Moderate learning difficulties' was the most common non-statemented special need (30.4 per cent), followed by 'speech, language and communication needs' (23.9 per cent), 'behaviour, emotional and social difficulties' (20.1 per cent) and 'specific learning difficulties' (12.1 per cent). Among statemented needs, the most common concerned speech, language and communication difficulties (23.8 per cent). Just over 60 per cent of the 23,000 children given statements in 2007 attended mainstream primary schools, with a quarter going to special schools.[8] The fastest growing categories of special need relate to emotional, social and behavioural difficulties and autistic spectrum disorders. As discussed in the previous chapter, a disproportionate number of boys and children from deprived backgrounds are identified with special needs.

SPECIAL NEEDS AND DIVERSITY: CHANGING VIEWS

Despite an espoused commitment to respecting children as individuals, primary education in England has long appeared to reflect the belief that there are common patterns and trends in young children's development, particularly regarding what, and how, they need to learn at certain ages. The familiar organisation of compulsory education into early years, primary and secondary phases, and within the primary phase into infants, juniors, KS1, KS2 and seven year groups, emphasises the progress expected of children of roughly the same age as they move together through the school system. In 2009, this age-related approach is firmly embedded in English education policy and school structures, dictating the beginning and end of formal education and its many staging posts. Yet it goes without saying that children of the same age are not the same – and those who do not fit the average profile present a challenge for a large-scale education system.

The standard response to diversity in pupils, families and local communities has been to identify particular needs and interests and make alternative, 'special' and sometimes separate educational arrangements for them. This applies not only to children exhibiting educational difficulties, but also to 'at-risk' groups such as pupils from deprived backgrounds, bilingual children and Gypsy/ Roma pupils and Travellers of Irish Heritage. In a rather inflexible and pressured educational system largely designed for the 'average' child, this has been generally seen as the fair and appropriate response. As the Review research survey by Mel Ainscow and colleagues points out, however, the act of making such arrangements results in the 'construction' of difference among primary pupils, involving different explanations and responses in policy and practice at different times.[9]

Thus from the 1980s onwards, some children were designated as having special educational needs.[10] Those seen as struggling socially, educationally or developmentally were assumed to require additional support, resources or some other special arrangement. More recently, 'gifted and talented' children have also been seen as needing – or meriting – special arrangements, such as curriculum enrichment and summer schools.[11] Both of these approaches focus primarily on the strengths and weaknesses of children, rather than on the opportunities and constraints found in schools.

Over the past 20 years, some teachers have become interested in alternative ways of understanding individual differences in children's learning and have applied ideas about 'multiple intelligences', 'learning styles' and so on.[12] Such approaches, even those of dubious scientific validity, appear to offer a way to focus directly on learning and teaching, cutting across fixed categories of learning difficulty, giftedness, gender or cultural difference. Some schools began to identify children's learning differences in this way and extended the curriculum accordingly, often giving greater value to alternative modes of learning and communication in different areas.[13] This could be seen as an attempt to respond to every pupil's 'specialness' without targeting or marginalising anyone. Other approaches, such as Learning without Limits, focused on the collective nature of learning in school. They attempted to identify the types of classroom practice and relationships that emerged when teachers emphasised the potential transformability of all children and radically rejected the idea that their progress should be constrained by notions of fixed abilities.[14] Essentially, this approach denies the very concept of 'special educational needs'.

Simple theories of fixed intelligence and developmental stages are less prominent in primary professional training and discourse than they were 30 or 40 years ago, but they retain a residual influence with recent research suggesting concerns remain about 'fixed-ability labelling'.[15] Yet the Plowden Report proposed that children's educational needs and progress are the result of developmental differences interacting with family and social backgrounds.[16] More recently, the obvious differences in 'learning paths' between children of the same age have tended to confirm the significant influence of school experience on children's development and educational progress.

As discussed in Chapter 7, researchers from different disciplines have moved towards a 'bio-psycho-social' model of development, acknowledging the interplay of different aspects of children's lives from birth. This has been particularly influential in relation to the identification of children with special educational needs, including complex syndromes such as attention deficit/hyperactivity disorder.[17] It has provided a way of tracing educational success and failure without reverting to simplistic allocations of deficit and blame (whether within-child, within-family, within-social class, within-school and so on). The implications are that a full picture of a child's life is gained only by examining how the processes of biology, psychology, society and culture interact over time.[18]

Studies of children's resilience in the face of adversity have demonstrated the interacting 'spheres of influence shaping individual adjustment', including children's responses to the family, neighbourhood, institutions and the broad socio-historical context.[19] The implications are that differences in educational progress are not just the result of individual accidents of biology, psychology or family circumstances, although each will clearly play a part. The submission from the Association for the Study of Primary Education (ASPE) drew out implications for education:

> Acculturation happens differently to different learners, sufficiently to recommend matching provision to need in ways respecting school pupils as unique individuals. This requirement takes us beyond 'personalised learning' strategies bent on bringing learners to common standards – i.e. reinforcing acculturation in a fairly straightforward manner – to diverse curricula and pedagogy ... There is a need for broad curricula feeding into diverse banks of skills and talents implicit in learners' inherited repertoires.

Current theories of learning, together with classroom evidence, suggest that effective responses to pupil diversity rely as much on teachers' expertise as they do on educational structures and resourcing.[20] Teachers' knowledge of how children develop and learn allows them to make sound judgements and successfully deploy their repertoire of teaching strategies, assuming that they have a repertoire of sufficient range and the requisite knowledge of what is to be taught. When teachers are able to combine their generalised knowledge of the multifaceted nature of young children's development with their specific knowledge of an individual child, and can also bring to bear knowledge of curriculum and pedagogy, they have the potential to help all pupils to learn – but only, as the submission from the Learning without Limits team insisted, if there is no more 'fixed-ability labelling'.[21] These researchers and teachers argued that when teachers' thinking is no longer hampered by such labelling, they are able to focus on interlinked pedagogical aims relevant to all children in relation to their emotional, social and intellectual development. These aims, when combined with an atmosphere of support, participation and trust, generate the potential to transform all children's capacity to learn.

POLICY RESPONSES TO DIVERSITY

Legislation and official guidance with regard to children with special needs have attempted to keep pace with changing views of child development and learning. Some of the main initiatives are outlined in Figure 9.1.

The Warnock Report in 1978[22] marked a move away from the 1944 Education Act's rigid categories of 'handicap' – 'defective of speech, blind, partially sighted, deaf, partially deaf, delicate, diabetic, educationally subnormal, maladjusted and physically handicapped'. Instead, children's needs were to be assessed by a multidisciplinary team who would prepare a profile of learning difficulties and low attainments. Special educational provision would then be made, mainly in mainstream schools, taking into account available resources. Within this new thinking and legislation, it was assumed that learning difficulties were susceptible to change. Low attainment was no longer regarded in terms of a fixed learning capacity or potential, caused by ingrained personal or family difficulties. Children with special needs were seen to have strengths as well as weaknesses, as was the environment in which they learned.[23]

Ten years later, the 1988 Education Reform Act (ERA) established the notion that all children were entitled to a national curriculum. This entitlement appeared to be in line with Warnock principles, offering a benefit to children with special needs, especially when we remember that, before 1970, some severely handicapped children had been judged 'ineducable'.[24] Yet other aspects of the new standards agenda worked against the new approaches.[25] For instance, the national testing system largely failed to acknowledge or value other forms of achievement – a departure from the post-Warnock focus on children's strengths as well as weaknesses.

The 1988 Act undermined the 1981 Education Act's promotion of 'integration' as a strategy for educating all children together in mainstream schools rather than relying on special schools.[26] Some influential research programmes had supported this approach, including work in the 1980s on integrating children with Down's syndrome in mainstream primary schools in London which confirmed equal if not better educational outcomes.[27]

The post-1997 standards agenda may also have worked against integration, especially as a school's success or even survival may hinge on the test results of a relatively small proportion of children.[28] Thus, all parents' rights to choose a 'high-performing' school were pitted against some parents' rights to choose a school for their children with special needs who might, in some way, appear to disrupt or disadvantage other pupils.

More recently, some primary schools and local authorities have become more confident and diverse in their responses to special needs, despite the perceived constraints of central direction and league tables. The importance of whole-school development was emphasised in the late 1990s and early 2000s and the focus was on inclusion rather than integration. 'Inclusion' has tended to be interpreted as requiring fundamental changes to schools, education systems and society in order to welcome and accommodate pupils in all their diversity, while 'integration' has in simple

Legislation and policy documents	Implications for provision for children with SEN
The Education Act (1944)	'Local educational authorities should secure that provision is made for pupils who suffer from any disability of mind or body, by providing either in special schools or otherwise, special educational treatment, that is to say education by special methods for persons suffering from that disability'.
The Education Act (1981)	The 1981 Act replaced the term 'pupils with disabilities' with the phrase 'pupils with special educational needs'. Clear guidelines were given on assessment and issuing statements of special educational need in which pupils' learning difficulties are summarised and appropriate provision is outlined. Following the Warnock Report's recommendations, parental involvement in decision-making was emphasised.
The Education Reform Act (1988) (ERA)	The ERA stated that all children have a right to a 'broad, balanced, relevant and differentiated curriculum'. However, several aspects of the Act were regarded as having a negative impact on SEN provision, particularly with regard to the standards and performance agenda.
The Children Act (1989)	This Act was not specifically related to education or schools but was influential in establishing the principles of the UNCRC regarding children's rights. This Act influenced the thinking behind the 1994 Code of Practice (see below) which highlighted the importance of children's rights and participation in decision-making.
The Education Act (1993) and Code of Practice (1994)[a]	The Education Act (1993) (Part 3) set up the SEN tribunal and led to the publication of the *Code of Practice on the Identification and Assessment of Special Educational Needs*. Schools and parents were granted greater say in decisions regarding statements and provision, although local education authorities still had the final say and control of funding.
Disability Discrimination Act (1995) (DDA)	Part 4 of the DDA related to schools, requiring them to widen access to the curriculum, the school environment and information. The DDA also introduced some employment rights for school staff with disabilities.
The Special Education Needs and Disability Act (2001) (SENDA)	This Act required schools to produce an 'accessibility plan' to demonstrate how access to the curriculum, school environment and information would be improved over a three-year period. Schools were not allowed to discriminate against pupils with disabilities or SEN, or to treat them less favourably than other pupils.

Figure 9.1 Legislation and policies relating to children with special educational needs in England.

[a]DfEE (1994)

The SEN Code of Practice (2001)[b]	This revised Code of Practice included new sections on working with parents as partners and listening to pupils' views. It also re-introduced a system of SEN categories as part of its guidance on identification and assessment. The staged assessment procedure was simplified with a graduated system of response.
Every Child Matters: Change for Children (2003)[c]	The government's flagship policy for re-structuring all services for children (including education) has sought to develop a more holistic approach to ensuring positive outcomes for all children, including those with learning difficulties and disabilities. Multi-agency working, information-sharing and early intervention strategies are promoted as key areas for developing more effective support for children with SEN and their families.
The Children Act (2004)	Closely aligned with the Every Child Matters guidance, the Act provides the legal framework for the radical re-structuring of children's services. Although it applies to all children it is focused on those in greatest need such as looked-after children and children with mental health difficulties, disabilities or complex needs.
Removing Barriers to Achievement (2004) [d]	Following the rationale of the ECM agenda, this policy document focuses on securing positive outcomes for children with SEN and disabilities. The strategy addresses four key aspects: early intervention; removing barriers to learning; raising expectations and achievement; delivering improvements in partnership.
Disability Discrimination Act (2005)	This Act gave public authorities a duty to promote disability equality; to eliminate discrimination and harassment and to publish a Disability Equality Scheme.
The Children's Plan (2007)[e]	This ambitious 10-year plan sets a series of targets for improving outcomes for children and young people. In relation to children with SEN and disabilities, the plan sets out improvements in teacher training, an enhanced role for SENCOs and better monitoring and assessment procedures to evaluate children's progress. The plan also announced a full review of the quality of SEN provision in 2009 to be carried out by Ofsted.
Aiming High for Disabled Children: Better Support for Families (2007)[f]	This document draws on conclusions from the Disabled Children Review to recommend the establishment of a 'core offer'. This offer, which will encompass minimum standards on information, transparency, participation, assessment and feedback, is intended to make clear what entitlements and services disabled children, young people and their families can expect.

Figure 9.1 (continued)

[b]DfES (2001c)
[c]DfES (2004a)
[d]DfES (2004e)
[e]DCSF (2007b)
[f]HM Treasury/DfES (2007)

terms implied that children are attached and assimilated, to different degrees, into schools as they are.[29] Certain inclusion principles and strategies were incorporated into the national curriculum[30] and policies on removing barriers to achievement[31] were initiated, as were research programmes on school improvement, effectiveness and inclusion.[32] While many of these initiatives remained cautious about achieving inclusive education for all, they did question the existence of separate mainstream and special schools. In support of this, the Review's research survey by Daniels and Porter found little evidence of the need for entirely separate teaching strategies for children with special needs.[33]

The past few years have seen the growth of a more differentiated and nuanced understanding of appropriate responses to child minorities, within a longer-term discussion of how education ought to develop for all children, bearing in mind principles of inclusion as well as 'excellence', 'enjoyment', 'personalisation', and so on.[34] Yet the 2001 revised SEN Code of Practice continued to guide school and local authorities towards categorising individual children's special needs in the areas of communication and interaction, cognition and learning, behaviour, emotional and social development, sensory and/or physical development. Formal statements were still heavily influenced by funding criteria and limited educational budgets. This did not easily sit with the fundamental changes in thinking and practice required to uphold inclusion as an intrinsic principle applying to all children, not just a strategy or process to cater for those identified with special needs.

In 2006, MPs on the Education and Skills Select Committee condemned the special needs system as 'unfit for purpose' and in need of serious overhaul. The closure of special schools, inconsistency of provision and teacher training were all criticised while the statementing process was described as a 'postcode lottery'. The MPs also commented that: 'The evidence clearly demonstrates that SEN and the raising attainment agenda sit very uncomfortably together at present.'[35]

Three years later, former secretary of state Estelle Morris, reiterated the need for change. Calling for an urgent government enquiry into special needs, she said:[36]

> There hasn't been a comprehensive look at SEN since the Warnock Report over 30 years ago. We now have more evidence of what patterns of schooling work and what parents want; there's been a revolution in our knowledge about learning difficulties. Yet government policies on inclusion and special schools are often misinterpreted by the public and there is probably a higher level of parental dissatisfaction with this aspect of our education system than with any other.

Towards personalisation

The 2007 Children's Plan continued to embed identifiable special needs as a concept within education, promising £18 million over three years to cover improvements in teacher training and continuing professional development,[37] data on children's progress, a pilot scheme for teaching pupils with dyslexia, and a 2009 review of special needs by the chief inspector 'in the light of the greater impact of personalised learning'.[38] This latter point is an indication of the recent growth of 'personalisation' as a possible replacement for 'inclusion'. Personalised learning, as described by the Department for Children, Schools and Families, has five 'components':

- assessment for learning
- effective teaching and learning
- curriculum entitlement and choice
- organising the school
- beyond the classroom.[39]

These components – arenas for change in school decision-making and practice – have struck a chord with many supporters of inclusive education,[40] and certain tools, such as the Pupil

Achievement Tracker (PAT), are presented by the government as useful for inclusion as well for personalisation.[41] Yet uncertainties about precisely what personalised learning is and what it entails make it hard to assess the significance of its potential convergence with inclusion. For some, it could be that personalisation helpfully removes the persistent 'special educational needs' element which implies that inclusion applies to some but not all children. However, personalised learning tends to be perceived as a largely individual process, addressing individual interests and needs, as remarked in the submission from the Association of Teachers and Lecturers. The ATL's interpretation was drawn from the Excellence and Enjoyment White Paper and quoted a 2004 speech by the then education minister David Miliband:

> In Excellence and Enjoyment personalised learning is based on assessment knowledge about individual children's progress and pupil self-assessment according to individual improvement targets. It underpins the inclusion agenda as 'it will be the single most important force in mainstreaming (without diluting) the support that is given to pupils with special educational needs' to try to tackle the resistant lengthy tail of underachievement, especially of pupils from areas of disadvantage. It is also intended to inform provision for gifted and talented children and those from ethnic minorities.[42]

Principles of personalisation and choice do not sit easily with beliefs about the value of collective learning and equity. Wider public concerns about social exclusion and social justice also cannot easily be separated from personalisation in education, especially if contradictions emerge in practice. For the National Union of Teachers, personalisation may represent a way forward, particularly for children with challenging behaviour, but there are caveats. Its submission to the Review commented:

> The NUT believes that the constraints of a narrow, prescriptive curriculum generate inappropriate pupil behaviour. The Government's desire to increase personalisation of pupil learning at the primary stage is welcomed by the NUT but it must be conceived in such a way as to widen children's opportunities within the curriculum and not to narrow them further. A child requiring additional support in reading, for example, should not focus on reading to the detriment of other areas of the curriculum.

In addition, as Daniels and Porter point out in their research survey, there are challenging questions about how the most vulnerable children can be helped to express their views and make decisions within the personalisation framework, particularly those with difficulties in learning and communication who may lack self-esteem and confidence.

PRESENT CHALLENGES

The broad, and perhaps obvious, conclusion from this discussion of policy responses to pupils' diversity in learning is that coherence is desirable. Conflicts and competing pressures create many difficulties for schools, teachers, parents and children. Identifying special groups for special treatment presents problems of both principle and practice – and carries with it serious implications for funding, as well as for teacher training, skills and workload. Families can be disappointed and frustrated by inadequate responses to their child's special needs, a problem often exacerbated by disagreements between teachers, parents and children about the actual nature and urgency of these needs. Nationally, there is evidence of inequity. Some individuals, groups and even communities have suffered discrimination while others have been over-represented. Boys, as mentioned earlier, have long been disproportionately represented in most forms of special education. Socio-economic class is also a factor, with children from professional families more likely to receive help than those from working-class families with apparently similar educational difficulties.[43]

The submission to the Review from the National Association of Head Teachers expressed some of the concerns and dilemmas thus:

> Mainstream primary schools are admitting pupils with increasingly serious special educational needs and disabilities. When a pupil can learn effectively in a mainstream school, with additional support, that is where the child should be. However, NAHT is very concerned to note that the required support is too often not available, so that the pupil is not genuinely included in the school. Provision depends on local authority funding arrangements, leading to disparities in provision. A child who may be supported effectively in one authority would not necessarily receive the same support elsewhere ... Co-operation between mainstream and special schools has increased in recent years. Early intervention is essential to the effective education of children with special educational needs or disability.

One local authority's submission expressed similar concerns and identified many consequences of inconsistent educational policy, particularly in the light of increasing numbers of children identified with communication disorders and with complex needs. These were:

- the lack of funding and suitable support for children with special needs within mainstream schools
- the lack of additional funding and appropriate support for children sent to mainstream schools following the closure of special schools
- the lack of resources and poor response/delay from outside agencies including social services resulting in an inability to meet the needs of the most vulnerable pupils
- the process of identifying special needs failing to promote trust between professionals
- physical and learning environments which were often not able to meet a range of diverse needs.

Instead, the local authority called for:

- schools to be genuine holistic and inclusive communities where every child has the right to the support they need funded by the government
- appropriate staff with the skills, knowledge and understanding to support individual children where necessary
- improved staff:pupil ratios to minimise disruption of learning
- social services to be adequately funded to ensure that high quality staff are recruited and retained.

Many submissions echoed these fundamental anxieties about school and local authority funding inequities and anomalies. Local authorities were thought to delay support until a child's problems became very serious and to decide the future of special schools on financial, rather than educational, grounds. Whilst accepting the principle of inclusion, there was concern among teachers, heads and governors that providing mainstream places for children with special needs required more teaching staff, teaching assistants and other resources. Many witnesses believed that inclusion was under-resourced and therefore an added burden on primary schools which then felt under pressure to attract additional resources. As one submission commented:

> Much of what we currently do in SEN is driven by the need to attract and retain resources. The emphasis is often on paperwork, on proving to others what the school has done for a particular child, and demonstrating that a child is still failing to make sufficient progress – so that the case for extra funding can be made. Paradoxically, if the child's progress is poor, we conclude that this demonstrates the severity or complexity of the child's needs; relatively rarely do schools use the information on rate of progress to review the type and nature of the provision they are offering.

Several submissions argued strongly in favour of specialist teaching for certain groups with special needs, for example, for children with dyslexia. Some submissions called for parents of children with special needs to have better access to 'diagnostic services', implying specialist expertise beyond that which primary teachers would normally be expected to have. One submission commented: 'School leaders, including governors, are not confident in the leadership of inclusion. They tend to see special needs as a litigious secret garden of arcane processes, best left to the Senco (special educational needs coordinator) rather than tackled through normal school improvement mechanisms.'

There was broad agreement that home-school-community relations were important in responding to pupil diversity and promoting inclusion. However, witnesses, particularly in the community soundings, disagreed about the best forms of home-school relations for children with special needs and other often marginalised groups, such as 'hard-to-reach' families with low or unconventional aspirations. Similarly, with regard to other aspects of diversity, agreement about the principle of inclusion did not extend to agreement about what should be done.

The classroom disruption caused by children with behavioural difficulties was another prominent concern that featured widely in the Review's evidence. Research carried out by the NASUWT union highlighted the challenges that teachers face in supporting children with social, emotional and behavioural disorders (SEBD). The NASUWT report noted: 'Though teachers generally endorse the principles of inclusion they express concern about the inclusion of children with SEBD ... There is continued tension between the needs of the one and the needs of the many within debates on inclusion. The debate is probably nowhere more sharply focused than in the area of the inclusion of children with SEBD'.[44] However, the nature of behavioural difficulties differs widely, as the revised Code of Practice suggests:

> Children and young people who demonstrate features of emotional and behavioural difficulties, who are withdrawn or isolated, disruptive or disturbing, hyperactive or lack concentration; those with immature social skills; and those presenting challenging behaviours arising from other complex special needs.[45]

Teachers clearly need appropriate training, support and guidance to enable them to respond to this wide range of needs effectively. We return to consider this issue further in Chapter 15 on teaching, and in Chapter 21 in relation to professional organisation and teacher training.

AREAS FOR IMPROVEMENT

Across the Review's submissions and soundings, witnesses broadly agreed on the need for improvements in nine areas.

1. National assessment and testing

Many comments were made by Review witnesses about the perceived disadvantages for children and schools of current prescriptive national testing arrangements, which over-simplify expected measures of attainment for different age groups. The Review's national soundings emphasised the need to deal with tensions between notions of inclusive education and the market values behind league tables of SATs results. Concerns expressed of particular relevance to children with special needs included: the unhelpful stress of SATs; the pressures on small schools to achieve percentage targets in pursuit of which one child can make a large difference; and the need, in general, to measure and value children's learning outcomes and achievements more widely. The NUT's submission to the Review commented:

> The continuing focus on measuring, testing and categorising all pupils is too rigid to account for the diversity of needs. Recognising the achievements and progress of children with SEN requires a move away from narrow measures of attainment to look at all-round

achievement. A national assessment system should aim to recognise and celebrate the wider achievements of all children with SEN.

The practitioner soundings identified a need to value collective, as well as individual, classroom achievement, drawing on the work of Michael Armstrong.[46] This related to calls from several sources about the need for 'relationships' to become the fourth 'R' in the curriculum, highlighting the importance of curricular opportunities for productive collaborative learning.[47] Also considered desirable, to relieve narrow, age-focussed assessment procedures, was flexibility in class size and staffing for particular groups, including children learning English as an additional language. Some of these ideas came together in approaches advocated for children with particular social, emotional and learning needs. One such approach, the nurture group, takes a small group of troubled children off the timetable for all or part of the school day to build their confidence, enhance their well-being and improve their behaviour in a safe and encouraging environment. According to the Hampshire Nurture Group Project's submission:

> Experience in Hampshire has shown that nurture group approaches enable schools to work positively with the most challenging and needy children facilitating their inclusion and promoting the achievement of the five outcomes of Every Child Matters.

2. Identifying educationally significant differences

Evidence clearly pointed to the need for a sophisticated understanding of pupil diversity, rather than simple labelling (in terms of assessment levels, special needs categories, and so on). While this labelling was often seen as necessary for administrative reasons, it nevertheless was seen both to reflect and affect perceptions of difference. There was a call to make better use of classroom-based assessment for learning (in its fullest and original sense) to understand and respond to individual learners. This would apply to children's learning and participation, to curriculum planning and teaching.[48] The Review's practitioner soundings emphasised that teachers need to be better at analysing what they see, with clear implications for teachers' initial training and professional development. The point, again, is the need to go beyond simple categorisations of special need. As the British Association of Teachers of the Deaf (BATOD) remarked in its submission:

> For deaf children, specialist qualified teachers of the deaf are essential to provide support to learning as are appropriately qualified learning support professionals. Similar support is needed for other children with SEN. However, it must be underlined that not all children with SEN and disability have the same needs and indeed not all deaf children have the same needs – they do not represent a homogenous group.

A submission from a teacher training institution similarly pointed out that labels may be administratively necessary but were educationally limiting:

> In practice it is often necessary to label children's needs … to achieve the necessary support for the child. Therefore the teacher tries to match the child's needs to one of the broad areas of SEN which do not fit complex learning difficulties – e.g. a child with 'dyslexia' may have communication difficulties and may also have cognitive and learning difficulties. Their frustration level may contribute towards behavioural issues and they may have visual disturbance e.g. scotopic dyslexia.

There was a determined call for a more sensitive and sophisticated approach to disaffected children and families. The Review's national and practitioner soundings indicated a need for a broader understanding of children's achievements and their differences in out-of-school experiences, home life and culture as well as curriculum-related attainments and aptitudes. The point was made in the national soundings that we need 'expanded, extended and new definitions' of marginalised groups of pupils, who themselves need a greater voice in the system. There was some support in the submissions for individual learning mentors for vulnerable pupils.

3. Early intervention

Many Review witnesses supported the principle of early intervention and, in general, early years education was regarded as having a key role. Some advocated targeting specific groups, particularly in relation to the early diagnosis of speech and language difficulties, with guidance for parents and teachers. Political concern was demonstrated in the government's 2008 Bercow Report (see Chapter 6) and the 2007 Inclusion Development Programme which included communication needs as a priority. The Bercow Report identified the following key points:

- communication is crucial
- early identification and intervention are essential
- a continuum of services designed around the family is needed
- joint working is critical
- the current system is characterised by high variability and a lack of equity.

The submission from the charity I CAN represented a number of similar views in the Review evidence:

> Because of their poor conversational skills, limited non-verbal skills and often poorly developed social understanding, children with a communication disability are more likely than their peers to find peer interaction and forming real friendships difficult. This puts them at risk of rejection and isolation – evidenced in studies of both school-aged children and adults. Social isolation has been identified as a risk factor for bullying in children with special educational needs. Not surprisingly children with a communication disability rate the risk of being bullied higher than their peers.

We should note, however, that these calls for early intervention should be balanced with concerns about the risk of labelling children's 'potential' at an early age. There was strong support for using ongoing teacher assessment in the classroom as the route to understanding children's learning needs. In the national soundings the point was made that 'early intervention' should not just apply to pre-school children, but to newly arrived migrants and others in similar circumstances. Further, as the I CAN submission commented, learning problems may not end in the early years:

> Children who thrive in the more nurturing atmosphere of a nursery or primary school may find that transition to the next phase of education causes problems. Good practice, in the form of nurture groups, good liaison between staff and carefully planned transition programmes can help to overcome these. Effective support or intervention in the early years to ameliorate persistent language disorders or speed up the resolution of transient language difficulties is crucial and can ensure that children have the communication and social skills to cope more confidently with the demands of secondary school.

4. Improvements to curriculum content

Curriculum and pedagogy received much attention in the Review evidence on diversity and inclusion. Several witnesses spoke of the benefits of extending foundation stage curriculum principles into key stage 1, allowing more flexible learning and play for young children at different stages of development, and easing the problems of transition to formal schooling. This matter is taken further in Chapter 11 and in the Review's formal recommendations.

Some Review witnesses supported an expanded model of 'literacy', embracing oracy and multi-modal literacy and integrated across the curriculum. The UK Literacy Association argued that teachers need to understand the interaction of multiple modes of communication, and emphasised the need to employ a range of reading and learning strategies, placing relevance and creativity at the heart of the curriculum.

Several similar arguments were made in respect of acknowledging children's experiences of cultural, ethnic and religious differences to help them form 'respectful relationships', and for the use of cross-curricular approaches like personal, social and health education to teach about diversity and inclusion. Research has demonstrated the potential power of using innovative approaches here, such as projects harnessing the internet to teach anti-racism.[49]

5. Teachers' knowledge, strategies and skills

With regard to children experiencing learning difficulties, research suggests that teachers need different types of knowledge about children, about learning and teaching, and about their own values, beliefs and skills, together with a willingness to take an investigative and problem-solving approach to teaching strategies.[50] In their research survey for the Review, Daniels and Porter conclude that this applies to the majority of children with special needs, for whom no simple pedagogical recipes or specialist 'toolkits' exist.[51] Some researchers and teachers support specialised programmes for children with certain sensory impairments, complex, profound and multiple learning difficulties, autistic spectrum disorders and attention deficit/hyperactivity disorder. However in many cases teaching strategies may differ more in intensity than in type.[52]

Some witnesses commented that teachers need more help in how to counter ill-informed stereotypes. The submission from the Changing Faces organisation remarked, in relation to disfigurement, that:

> ... measures commonly taken by well-intentioned but inadequately trained staff tend further to isolate children who are vulnerable to being seen as 'different' ... Inclusion has for a long time focused on the (very important) areas of curriculum and physical access. For most children with disfigurements, there are few or no 'access' concerns. And yet, for a long time, these children have been experiencing great difficulties at school – initiated by their social difficulties. The problem is that teacher training and professional development fail to equip professionals in education with the knowledge and skills they need to address the social dimension of inclusion.

Improved access to ICT and better support in its use for communication and networking as well as learning was an issue noted in the national soundings and other evidence. A submission from Coventry City Council highlighted its potential contribution to inclusion:

> High quality and relevant ICT are essential classroom tools which, when used appropriately, make learning more effective and efficient. They harness the power to make learning relevant and accessible to all learners and are key to supporting the inclusion agenda. ICT can extend children's boundaries of experience in a unique way, empowering them to be independent learners.

6. Raising attainment

Some submissions to the Review gave examples of cross-curricular approaches that schools have found to be of value. For example, in an inner-city primary school with high levels of deprivation there were concerns about many children across the ability spectrum experiencing similar 'barriers' to learning:

... lack of concentration, low self esteem, poor organisational skills, lack of visual accuracy, reluctance to record work, immature dexterity and movement difficulties. They observed that many of these children had not reached milestones in their physical development necessary for success i.e. the shoulder strength and agility to support the skill of handwriting, eyes moving smoothly to track print on a page, posture to sit on a chair, hand/eye coordination skills to receive and pass a ball. Balance and coordination for these children was almost always poor. They began to work with small groups of 'special needs' Year 6 children using postural activities, and found that this had a significant impact on children's focus, self-esteem and attitudes to work.

7. Teamwork and professional roles in school

Teamwork across the school workforce provided an essential structure for effective support for children identified with special educational needs within schools. Working with outside agencies as part of multi-disciplinary teams was also crucial but teachers, heads and governors recognised that these arrangements placed an additional burden on teachers' time and expertise. The Senco has a pivotal role in co-ordinating support, practice and monitoring of all children with SEN within a school: reservations were expressed, however, that where Sencos were not part of the senior management team, their influence on planning and decision-making was sometimes limited. In response to these concerns, recognised in the 2006 Select Committee report,[53] new regulations for Sencos were introduced in 2008 requiring that a member of a school's senior management team must be appointed as a 'champion' of SEN and disability matters, liaising closely with the Senco.[54]

Meeting with teaching assistants in the community soundings provided strong evidence of their specialised knowledge and skills in working with pupils. Review witnesses supported further acknowledgement, help and training for TAs, especially with regard to children with special needs. However this did not simply mean putting more adults into classrooms.

Witnesses also called for more professionals, such as speech therapists and social workers, to be based in schools. Generally, there was strong support for the integrated approach of Every Child Matters, consistently seen as a positive development compared to the potential constraints and disempowerment of certain other recent initiatives. However, the Review's national soundings emphasised that multi-agency working needs to be evaluated and extended; roles need to be clear and agreed; and knowledge shared. Several witnesses called for the better integration of housing departments and other services such as school transport to support homeless and other disadvantaged families.

8. Procedures, funding and the law

Witnesses saw streamlined funding and consistent and unified priorities as essential to SEN provision. They sought an urgent review of the statementing process to make it less bureaucratic, slow, divisive, competitive and easily manipulated. According to witnesses at the national and practitioner soundings, the statementing process also diverted resources and attention away from the task of ensuring a fair deal for all children. Witnesses wanted equity across the regions (with increased funding for areas with changing populations). A specific point was made about the potential value and uses of the Disability Discrimination Act in supporting change in school.

9. Empowerment, agency and voice

The ninth agreed area for improvement touched on all of the above. It was seen as vital that teachers, parents and children gain genuine power to respond to outside pressures or changes. Children need to be 'authentic agents' rather than tokenistic participants in educational change, while teachers need to be free to innovate. Research by Ann Lewis on giving children and young people with SEN opportunities to talk about their lives in school illustrates the importance of having a 'voice' and a right to active participation.[55]

CONCLUSION

We end by building on the three broad principles for action proposed in Chapter 8.

Dilemmas and opposing views: are some children clearly 'special'?

The main dilemmas relating to inclusion and special educational needs reflect problems of conceptualising and categorising pupil differences. Individual differences between young children are readily observable from infancy, but there is strong evidence that these differences are not entirely located within the child's personal or family experience: schools, friendships and wider social influences also influence the way children develop. So to what extent is special educational provision needed for certain children and how could this work without compromising alternative principles of equity in educational opportunity, learning and outcomes?

In considering how to capitalise on the evidence that education can and does have a substantial impact on children's progress, we might give much more weight to the importance of the early years of learning, as discussed in Chapters 7 and 11. There might also be implications for assessing children's individual differences over time, as they develop and learn in the context of the classroom and school. This is likely to apply not just to children who fall behind their peers without obvious reason, but also to those who have a particular need (such as a specific difficulty in phonological processing) but whose day-to-day learning needs are not dictated by that one factor.

There is evidence that the current curriculum – in terms of balance, content and progression – does not suit all children equally well, even though it is presented as an entitlement for all. The absence or marginalisation of some activities and subjects raises the likelihood that some children will fall behind, misunderstand or opt out completely. This is particularly likely if teaching is not sufficiently sustained, co-ordinated and flexible to help them to make progress. Such children might also benefit from flexibility in the timetable and classroom organisation, allowing them to engage in extended project work and independent or collaborative study, and to receive individual tuition. This has implications for teacher expertise, training and development as well as for school and classroom organisation.

Understanding and responding to change in school: pressures and coping strategies

Children's day-to-day experience of school can too easily be amplified into division and disadvantage for those who do not have the necessary coping strategies and social support systems. This might be seen as both the beginning and the essence of the marginalisation and labelling which are sometimes associated with identifications of special needs.

So we might argue, pressing still further the arrangements encouraged by Every Child Matters and the Children's Plan, for more flexible use of primary school buildings and staff to create opportunities for children to take time out of the classroom for independent study, emotional support, relaxation, play and other activities which allow the extension of their learning in school. This could usefully involve parents, mentors and older children, and might entail locating other professionals, at least part-time, in primary schools.

Then, following our discussion of home-school relations in Chapter 6 we would argue for improved communication between home and school and between teachers and other professionals in and out of school. This applies not only to the availability and management of telephones, email, written diaries, office space, and so on, but also to the identification of convenient office hours and drop-in centres for meetings which it may not be possible to plan in advance but which are none the less urgent for that.

With a similar eye on the need for flexibility in the way we respond to children's needs, it would be sensible for schools to hold contingency funds so that teachers can respond immediately and creatively to the problems and opportunities arising from pupil diversity, such as the provision of transport, employment of temporary staff, curriculum enrichment, and ICT resources.

Cutting through the complexity of educational decision-making

There should be explicit planning for individual children identified with special needs, with regular reviews applying both to the short-term achievement of specific goals and to longer-term views on future learning needs and preferences (including transitions to new classes and schools). Short-term planning should identify any immediate constraints or dilemmas requiring further discussion. Long-term planning for individuals should be explicitly linked with other areas of school development applying to all pupils. This could be the basis for developing the 'package' of connected strategies likely to be required for children with special needs, bearing in mind the need for co-ordinated action at different levels of school, home and community for any one child.

These broad principles, together with the chapter's earlier discussion, indicate the need for action in the following areas:

- understanding and assessing children's individual differences
- clarifying the appropriate use of labels such as SEN, and replacing the relatively fixed SEN categories by diagnostic procedures which are more open and subject to regular re-assessment
- curriculum development and timetabling
- training teachers in investigative and problem-solving techniques
- developing teachers' communication skills
- developing comprehensive intervention packages.

It is clear that decisions for children identified with special educational needs cannot be separated from decisions that are made for all children. It is also evident that decisions about teaching these children are closely linked to funding, school structures, curriculum, assessment, professional relationships, home-school relationships and community location. It is essential to differentiate decisions made for short-term management and long-term improvement, and to attempt to connect these where possible. There is an urgency about providing educational and social support for particular children in difficulty which cannot wait for primary education – or society as a whole – to become more equitable and inclusive.

NOTES

1 DCSF (2008y).
2 UNESCO (1994).
3 House of Commons (2006).
4 Morris, E., *The Guardian*, 27 January 2009.
5 DCSF (2008y).
6 According to DCSF figures, 12,590 pupils with statements were being educated in independent schools or non-maintained special schools and 52,870 pupils without statements were in the independent sector, but it should be noted that these figures include both primary and secondary phases.
7 Daniels and Porter (2010), *The Cambridge Primary Review Research Surveys*, Chapter 9.
8 DCSF (2008y).
9 Ainscow *et al.* (2010), *The Cambridge Primary Review Research Surveys*, Chapter 8.
10 Following the Warnock Report (DES 1978b) and the subsequent 1981 Education Act.
11 The term 'Gifted and Talented' was brought in as one of the seven strands of the Government's Excellence in Cities programme in 1999 and remained as a priority in the 2000s, incorporated into the national strategies under the umbrella of personalised learning.
12 Smith and Call (1999).
13 As discussed in Chapter 7, even this approach resulted in the inappropriate perception and fixing of some children as certain types of learner requiring certain types of teaching. Yet, as seen in the application of this

approach to understanding boys' learning in school (for example Warrington and Younger 2006), it proved to have some educational value in encouraging children and teachers to talk about learning even without any solid psychological evidence to back this up at a cognitive level.

14 Hart *et al.* (2004).
15 Hart *et al.* (2004).
16 CACE (1967).
17 Norwich (1990); Cooper (2005).
18 Morton (2004).
19 Schoon (2006): 25.
20 Lewis and Norwich (2005); Davis and Florian (2004).
21 Hart *et al.* (2004).
22 DES (1978b).
23 Wedell (2003/1981).
24 The 1970 Education Act was noted for introducing education rights for all children, remembered for the slogan 'no child is ineducable'.
25 Wedell (1988).
26 Although with certain conditions attached to integration, including the requirement to attend to the needs of the child, the needs of other children, the parents' wishes, and the 'efficient use of resources'.
27 Tizard *et al.* (1982).
28 Particularly for small schools when target percentages can be significantly lowered by even one child's results.
29 See, for instance, Ainscow *et al.* (2006) and Black-Hawkins *et al.* (2007).
30 DfEE/QCA (1999a).
31 DfES (2004e).
32 Ainscow *et al.* (2010), *The Cambridge Primary Review Research Surveys*, Chapter 8.
33 Daniels and Porter (2010), *The Cambridge Primary Review Research Surveys*, Chapter 9.
34 DfES (2003b).
35 House of Commons (2006).
36 Morris, E., *The Guardian*, 27 January 2009.
37 As seen in the July 2008 press release on training for SENCOs, found at http://www.tda.gov.uk/teachers/sen/senco_consultation.aspx and regarding developments in initial teacher education (www.tda.gov.uk). The Inclusion Development Programme of continuing professional development has a clear 'SEN' focus in identifying particular categories of need: 'In 2008, the IDP will focus on dyslexia and speech, language and communication needs (SLCN). In 2009, the focus will be on autistic spectrum disorders (ASD), and after that, on behavioural, emotional and social difficulties (BESD)'. (See website: http://www.standards.dcsf.gov.uk/primary/features/inclusion/sen/idp, accessed November 2008).
38 http://www.everychildmatters.gov.uk/strategy/childrensplan/, accessed November 2008.
39 http://nationalstrategies.standards.dcsf.gov.uk/node/41687?uc=force_uj, accessed January 2009.
40 http://www.standards.dfes.gov.uk/personalisedlearning/, accessed November 2008.
41 http://www.standards.dfes.gov.uk/performance/pat/, accessed November 2008.
42 Miliband (2004b).
43 Daniels and Porter (2010), *The Cambridge Primary Review Research Surveys*, Chapter 9.
44 Ellis *et al.* (2008): 14–15.
45 DfES (2001c): 87.
46 Armstrong (1980).
47 Howe and Mercer (2010), *The Cambridge Primary Review Research Surveys*, Chapter 7.
48 This can also be viewed as promoting more equal 'opportunity to learn' as promoted in the USA; see Moss *et al.* (2008).
49 Gaine and Weiner (2005) (see also http://www.britkid.org/). Cole and Blair (2006: 84) argue for curriculum development, including the amendment of the National Curriculum to promote both antiracism and anti-racist multiculturalism, including ' ... the promotion of respect and non-exploitative difference in a multi-cultural world ... (and) ... an honest and critical analysis of imperialism, past and present'.
50 Davis and Florian (2004); Lewis and Norwich (2005).
51 Daniels and Porter (2010), *The Cambridge Primary Review Research Surveys*, Chapter 9.
52 Lewis and Norwich (2005).
53 House of Commons (2006).
54 DCSF (2008x).
55 Lewis (2006).

10 Children's voices

Forty years ago, for all that the public face of primary education emphasised choice, flexibility and respect for children's interests, the idea that children's views should influence school or national policy would have been considered unusual and, by some, subversive. In practice, with certain well-known exceptions, choice was carefully constrained and channelled, even in that part of the school day which in some schools was called 'choosing.' But, paradoxically, during the two decades when teachers' freedom of professional action has been reduced, policy-makers and practitioners have begun to accept not only that children's opinions matter but that children should participate in educational decision-making. Of course, not everyone is convinced. Sociologist Bren Neale finds adult views polarised between children as 'welfare dependants' and 'young citizens'. 'Welfare dependants' are viewed as incompetent, vulnerable, and in need of care, protection and guidance; and their lives are determined by adults. 'Young citizens' have strengths and capabilities, need recognition, respect and opportunities to participate; and they are able to shape their own lives.[1]

The Cambridge Primary Review sought to include children's voices because, in a unique way, children are expert witnesses on many of the issues with which the Review is most fundamentally concerned. It would have been indefensible to ignore the voices of those whose lives, education and futures are what primary education is all about, and who have to live with the consequences of decisions made by those whose power in such matters is so much greater than theirs. This focus also reflected the wider momentum of the children's voice movement and its potentially significant influence on policy-making and practice. Yet, in spite of this apparent growth, the four Children's Commissioners for the United Kingdom recently reported that evidence of genuine change is hard to find. They point out that education is:

> ... a key part of children's lives and is one of the most frequent topics of discussion between the Commissioners and children and young people. [Yet] children are ... still not viewed as key participants in education: discussions around improving education are often adult-based and fail to include children and their views.[2]

This chapter takes to its logical conclusion a theme which has run through several of the preceding chapters in this part of our report: young children bring to their schooling experiences and capabilities of real value and substance, and the old doctrine of age-capped developmental 'readiness', with its fixation on what children cannot do, has given way to an understanding that given opportunity and the best of teaching, learning has few limits. The chapter starts with what children say about their learning, their schools and their futures. It considers the children's voice movement and examines strategies for consultation and participation in primary schools and classrooms. Finally, it looks at the potential benefits, drawbacks and tensions in developing these approaches and considers how the principles of children's rights and children's voices could shape the future of primary education.

CHILDREN'S VOICES AND CHILDREN'S RIGHTS

All talk, little action

Children's rights and the children's voice movement are often traced back to the United Nations Convention on the Rights of the Child (UNCRC) of 1989 which stipulated:

> 1. States Parties shall assure to the child who is capable of forming his or her own views the right to express those views freely in all matters affecting the child, the views of the child being given due weight in accordance with the age and maturity of the child.[3]

Although the UNCRC has not been incorporated into English law, it has influenced policy in social welfare, family law[4] and health. Education has been slower to respond, as Lynn Davies and Gordon Kirkpatrick point out, 'England and Wales seem out of line with the rest of Europe in the way that young people have no legislated and government-supported ways to participate in decisions about their education'.[5]

While UNCRC gave some impetus to the children's voice movement, the principles underpinning the movement have a longer history. The development of the 'pupil voice' principles owes much to the efforts of researchers like Peter Woods[6] and Roland Meighan,[7] whose studies in the 1970s demonstrated the value in looking at teaching and learning from the learner's viewpoint. In the early 1990s, the publication of 'School Improvement: What can pupils tell us?' by Jean Rudduck, Gwen Wallace and Roland Chaplain, introduced schools to the notion that consulting children and young people could offer a useful tool for school improvement.[8] Ideas like evidence-based practice, school self-review and teacher-led research lent the children's voice approach a new legitimacy and placed it on the policy-makers' radar. However, as Jean Rudduck and Donald McIntyre suggest, government support for the children's voice approach tended to be 'strong on rhetoric but less forthcoming in terms of practical support' and its future, they argued, may be uncertain as these commitments became submerged under a tide of politically-driven, short-term initiatives.[9]

The principles of 'children's voices' and children's participation

The notion of 'voice' is complex and is used in various ways, reflecting different contexts, aims and beliefs. The word 'voice' itself can be defined as the capacity to make an utterance (as a noun) and to express oneself through speech (as a verb) but generally the attachment of 'voice' to a particular group (for example, consumers) implies a collective set of interests. However, it is in this idea of collectiveness that we meet the first of many controversies surrounding the children's voice approach, as Diane Reay points out, 'One of the main difficulties in consulting pupils is that instead of a common pupil voice there is often a cacophony of competing voices'.[10] A further difficulty is that what the 'children's voice' or 'pupil voice' approach entails is often unclear. Rudduck offered a definition that encompassed two 'wings' – consultation and participation:

> (1) Consultation is about talking with pupils about things that matter in school. It may involve pupils in:
>
> - offering advice about policy and other initiatives
> - commenting on their experiences of teaching and learning and offering suggestions for improvement
> - reviewing recent major initiatives at school or year-group level or of changes in classroom practice.
>
> Ideally, consultations are conversations that build a habit of easy discussion between teachers and pupils, and among pupils, about learning in school.

(2) Participation is about involving pupils in the school's work and development

- through a wider range of roles and responsibilities
- through membership of committees and working parties, and focusing on real issues, events, problems and opportunities.

At classroom level, participation is about

- opportunities for decision-making
- understanding and managing your own learning priorities.[11]

In a similar vein, researcher and government adviser David Hargreaves, describes the 'pupil voice' approach as:

> ... how students come to play a more active role in their education and schooling as a direct result of teachers becoming more attentive, in sustained or routine ways, to what students want say about their experience of learning and of school life.[12]

While both Rudduck and Hargreaves regard the children's voices approach largely in terms of its potential for the conditions of learning in schools, others emphasise that it is integral to a democratic educational system that respects children's rights.[13] Geoff Whitty and Emma Wisby describe four different 'drivers' of the approach:

- a children's rights driver, which recognises that children have rights, including the right to have their opinions taken into account in decisions that concern them – something recently reinforced by the Every Child Matters agenda;
- an 'active citizenship' driver which highlights the way in which pupil voice can contribute to preparation for citizenship by improving pupils' knowledge and their 'transferable' and 'social' skills and, in doing so, enhance the quality of democracy;
- a 'school improvement' driver which recognises that consultation with pupils can lead to better school performance, whether in terms of behaviour, engagement or attainment;
- a 'personalisation' driver, which utilises pupil voice to ensure that schools are meeting the specific needs of their pupils as consumers of education.[14]

In this chapter and throughout this report, we prefer to use the term 'children's voices' rather than 'pupil voice' although we recognise that the latter has been more widely adopted. We do so for two reasons: first, the word 'children' denotes that we are talking about people rather than the roles conferred upon them in the context of school. Second, the plural 'voices' removes the temptation to assume that children's views are homogeneous.

Impact on policy

After 1997 a series of government policies drew, to varying degrees, on the principles of children's rights and children's voices. Three of the most significant policy developments to embrace these principles were the Children's Fund (2000), *Every Child Matters* and the 2004 Children Act. Each reflected a fundamental change in government thinking about the state's role in children's lives and collectively they have blurred the traditional lines between education and other children's services.

The Children's Fund came into being in November 2000 and focused on addressing social disadvantage. The Fund promoted the development of partnerships, bringing together voluntary organisations, community and faith groups, local statutory agencies, and children and families to work on strategies for reducing the risk of social exclusion. The Fund's stated aims made it clear that children and young people were to be seen as key partners in these efforts:

- Prevention
  To address the gap in preventative services for children and young people at risk of social exclusion, by providing increased and better coordinated preventative services for 5–13-year-olds and their families
- Partnership
  To take responsibility at local level for the delivery of the Children's Fund plan, involving partners from the statutory and voluntary sectors, community and faith groups, and ensuring that the views of children and young people are represented
- Participation
  The voices of children and young people are at the heart of the Children's Fund, with children and young people being involved in the design, operation and evaluation of the programme.[15]

The national evaluation of the Children's Fund highlighted the impact of its approach with respect to children's participation:

> Engaging children and young people in services development was often associated with building a sense of self-efficacy through involving them in making both small and relatively large decisions about provision, ranging from the choice of a particular activity to involvement in staff recruitment. These opportunities and the respect for children they demonstrated were highly valued by the children concerned.[16]

Interestingly, the outcomes for children and young people originally proposed in the Children's Fund – being healthy, being emotionally secure and confident, succeeding at school, staying out of trouble, living in a safe place and having the opportunity to achieve their dreams – later reappeared in modified form in *Every Child Matters* and the subsequent 2004 Children Act. This legislation was premised on the principles of children's rights and resulted in the appointment of the four UK Children's Commissioners. In the same year, regulations from the Commission for Social Care Inspection,[17] saw the first Children's Rights Director appointed with the remit to advise Ofsted's chief inspector: to safeguard and promote children's rights and welfare, and to listen to children and young people's views on services provided for them. The Office of the Children's Rights Director was responsible for consulting children and young people in relation to the UK's response to the UNCRC during 2008.

Gaps between policy and practice

Acceptance of the principles of children's voices and children's participation is evident in a number of recent educational policies: for example, Ofsted's 2005 inspection framework[18] not only required that schools take account of children's views but also said that they must be consulted during an inspection and informed in writing about its results. The Special Education Needs Code of Practice[19] stipulated that children contribute to their statements of special needs and individual education plans (IEPs). Citizenship education, introduced in 2002 though not at the time of writing compulsory in primary schools, aimed to equip children with skills for active participation in a democratic society.

The wider implications of these policies are considered elsewhere in this report but, for the moment, it is important to note that, in spite of the high profile status of children's voices, many commentators question the sincerity and credibility of policies claiming adherence to its principles. For example, the UK Children's Commissioners commented in 2008:

> While children and young people in Wales and Scotland have the right to appeal their exclusion, children in England and Northern Ireland do not. During the exclusion process, there is a lack of access to representation and a lack of information shared with both the child and the family.[20]

WHAT DO THE CHILDREN SAY?

The Review explored children's opinions of their schools and their learning through the community soundings and submissions. At the same time, the Review commissioned Carol Robinson and Michael Fielding to undertake a broad survey of published research in the field.[21] The community soundings included 19 sessions with 197 children in nine regions: some were school council representatives while others included children from different schools and different year groups. While at these sessions we can confirm the children spoke for themselves, many of the child submissions were school-initiated and in some cases obviously adult-led.

Balancing employment with enjoyment

The children in our community soundings generally felt that one of the most important purposes of education was to teach them the skills needed for getting a good job. Other studies[22] had also noted that children of all ages place a strong emphasis on the link between education and employability. This Year 6 boy's submission expressed a view shared by many others:

> We have school because we will be able to learn things for later on in life and to get a job we will enjoy! Most activities can be fun to learn. Also, you never know when learning things will come in handy. You need education to do things later in life. It is important.

Being able to read, to write and 'do sums' were most frequently mentioned as key skills. However, our evidence showed that children felt learning serves many purposes and it was often enjoyable. One 10-year-old boy explained his view of the balance of obligation and pleasure in learning, 'I think schools are important because you learn what you need to learn and sometimes what you want to learn as well'. Children also talked about the value of education in helping them to become 'good people'. Schools, they said, help you learn to get along with other people and to be a respectful, responsible member of your community.

A haven of positive feeling

Robinson and Fielding's Review research survey noted that primary pupils were acutely aware of the structure of authority within their schools. Research in 2000 found that, for some children, compliance with this authority diminished as they moved from reception through to Year 6.[23] The Review's evidence indicated that children generally accepted the need for authority so long as it was just, consistent and fair. Children generally liked being in school and appreciated the opportunities it offered. This observation was supported in other studies: the New Economics Foundation,[24] for example, reported that 65 per cent of the children in their study felt positive about being at school. Children told the Review they particularly valued the opportunity to make friends: as Chapter 5 explains, their socialising was increasingly constrained outside school as a result of fears about their safety. Children also suggested that in an often-confusing world, their schools represented a haven of stability. However, some children commented on differences between the culture of home and school. They described the ways in which teachers' and parents' expectations could sharply differ and said that they found it hard to navigate between these conflicting demands.

Organised – and aware of it

Children frequently commented on grouping arrangements within classes. They were often astute in their observations about how teachers decided on groupings and how sometimes setting could have a negative impact on their confidence and self-esteem, although some children saw ability grouping as helpful because it allowed work to be set at the right level. Their comments illustrate how sensitive they are to the social conditions of learning and, although friendships were highly important to them, they preferred to sit next to children with whom they worked well.[25]

Time was another aspect of primary-school organisation that concerned children. They were aware that teachers were in charge of time management but evidence from the Primary, Assessment, Curriculum and Experience (PACE) project and other studies suggested that they often wanted more time to complete their work, or to look at something in more depth. Research also showed that children sometimes felt that the pace of learning was too fast or, conversely, that they were working too slowly or waiting for others to catch up.[26]

Menu for teaching and learning

Children were clear about what helped them to learn. They relished a challenge and being given opportunities for active, 'hands-on' kinds of learning. They wanted to feel able to succeed and to experience success. Praise from adults was important but so too was having a sense of personal satisfaction, and feeling that getting something wrong was part of learning. In their submissions to the Review, children said they found it easier to learn when lessons were exciting or involved a variety of activities. On the other hand, they could switch off when learning was mundane and repetitive: copying from the whiteboard and 'drill and practice' tasks were among the 'consolidating' tasks that children disliked. However, while accepting that learning could not always be fun, they noted that if lessons persistently failed to engage their interest some pupils could become disruptive or, in some cases, truant.[27]

Opportunities for choice and having a sense of ownership of their work were also key ingredients of a good learning experience. Some children said that although they needed help at certain times, in general they preferred to work autonomously, finding things out for themselves and exploring topics. As one Year 6 child said: 'When we find things out for ourselves we learn more.'

Wanted: an even-tempered, even-handed, enthusiastic expert

The Review's submissions and community soundings also painted a clear picture of what children looked for in a good teacher. They liked consistency rather than moodiness; fair but firm discipline, not shouting or nagging; individual help with their work and patient support when they struggled with something hard. Children described the best teachers as being those who listened, were kind and 'understood how you feel'. A good teacher, they suggested, should:

- 'really know their stuff'
- be able to make learning fun
- know everyone's names
- tell you things in advance so that you know what a lesson is about
- give you a permanent record of what you learn
- be able to explain things clearly so that you understand
- have lots of energy and enthusiasm.

Teachers who shouted, or who were perceived as unfair or unpredictable, made children anxious. Some teachers were seen as biased towards particular children or groups and, whether or not these perceptions were justified, children could become resentful of the attention given to others. Children felt particularly vulnerable when they changed classes or school and encountered new teachers, a situation which meant having to adjust to new ways of working as well as new expectations and routines.

The curriculum

Children recognised that learning was divided into discrete 'areas' such as literacy, art, music, mathematics (or numeracy) and so on. They tended to see these subjects as important and interesting but, as we noted earlier, the 3Rs were seen as vital for future job prospects. Children also felt that particular subjects and topics should be studied for their own sake because they were engaging and enjoyable. Two Year 6 boys, in their joint submission, described what they thought schools should teach:

> We should learn maths, for everyday life; science for how things work in the world. English to learn Standard English so we can talk properly; RE [religious education] to learn about other cultures and countries, ICT [information and communication technology] to learn the world of technology, history to learn the global history and geography to learn where places are and how our world is.

Children also talked about changes they would like to see in the curriculum: for example, there were requests to learn modern foreign languages, such as Mandarin Chinese and Portuguese. More unusual suggestions included looking after animals, growing fruit and vegetables and learning how to be a good friend. Children were also keen on creative projects in design and technology, art, music and drama. Interestingly, the experience of success did not guarantee liking a subject or activity as some children felt little enthusiasm for the core curriculum subjects in spite of achieving good results in the key stage 2 tests.[28]

Ambivalent about assessment

Research in 2000 suggested that younger children tended to be positive about assessment. However, as children progressed through primary school they appeared to become more wary and, by the end of key stage 2, they were using words like 'worried', 'nervous', 'scared', 'upset', 'guilty', 'ashamed', 'embarrassed', 'shaky' and 'doubtful' to describe their feelings about assessment, especially national tests.[29] Children often applied criteria of quality that differed from those of their teachers'. For example, children considered neatness or quantity and their own perception of effort when evaluating their work: if they received negative feedback on work they perceived to be good, they were disappointed and discouraged. Some children said in their submissions that they would like learning objectives to be more explicit so that they knew exactly what they were trying to achieve. Some also thought that it would helpful to talk through their work on a one-to-one basis with the teacher. One Year 6 boy wanted 'more individual help from teachers. Once a week, have an appointment with the teacher to discuss different things'.

On the question of testing, children's views varied. While a few were confident and thought of tests as interesting challenges, others worried that they might do badly. One study[30] noted that children became stressed when they didn't know what tests were for, or when they thought the tests were being used to 'catch them out'. The way in which testing was presented could make a significant difference to children's reactions, however: in schools where tests were carefully explained, children were more positive and relaxed about them. Our submissions evidence indicates that formal assessment weighed heavily on many children's minds: when asked what schools should teach, one 11-year-old replied, 'Respect, responsibility and things that will help us pass our SATs'. Children were also acutely aware that SAT results were important for their schools and their teachers, a point emphasised through Ofsted's policy of writing to children about their school's test performance. (These and other aspects of assessment are considered in Chapter 16).

Transfer to secondary school

Research has suggested that children approach transfer to secondary school with mixed feelings and this was confirmed in their submissions to the Review. Children feared losing their primary school friends and worried about making new ones. There were anxieties about getting used to new surroundings, routines and expectations and having different teachers for each lesson.

Similar findings were reported for those transferring from primary to middle schools.[31] However, trepidation was mixed with excitement: children's submissions talked about looking forward to new facilities, subjects and resources. Nevertheless, some children suggested having 'all-through' schools, from reception to Year 11, to avoid the uncomfortable experience of transfer.

It was not only children who were concerned about the impact of transfer, however. Since the early 1990s Ofsted has drawn attention to a 'dip' in children's performance as they cross the institutional, curricular and pedagogical boundaries between key stages 2 and 3 and this has led schools and local authorities to strive to improve primary/secondary transfer arrangements. One aspect of transfer which is often overlooked is the impact of secondary school choice: those who fail to secure a place at their preferred school can feel disappointed and anxious and this in turn may affect their motivation.[32] Given the media preoccupation with league tables and the naming and shaming of failing schools, it is not surprising that school placement decisions make children as well as parents anxious. (For further discussion of transfer and transition see Chapter 19).

Ofsted also noted a similar 'dip' in children's performance between key stages 1 and 2 and this was the focus for Christine Doddington's study of children's experiences of transfer and transition from Year 2 to Year 3[33] which concluded that one of the most important factors affecting children's progress at this point was their difficulty in coping with the different demands of key stage 1 and 2 teaching and learning.

Children's global perspective

In looking forward to adulthood most children talked about jobs; but employment was not the only future that concerned them. They worried about global problems like climate change, pollution and the depletion of natural resources. Some were concerned about those countries whose peoples faced poverty and war, and they wanted to help. Others had more personal ambitions, like going to university or travelling to other countries. While children generally expected to carry on learning after leaving school, some said that learning for adults is harder.

CHILDREN'S VOICES AND PARTICIPATION: EXAMPLES

Passive resistance

The children's voices approach has a key role to play in developing more effective teaching and learning because it offers a model of learning premised on active engagement and dialogue. Children contributing to the Review's community soundings expressed particular dislike of passive forms of learning which they described as 'just looking at books or screens'.

Actively improving learning

As we saw in Chapter 7, research now strongly supports the proposition that learning is an essentially active and social process which requires that children are given opportunities to think and talk about their developing understanding in order to enhance it; and, even more fundamentally perhaps, neuroscientific evidence demonstrates the power of language, especially spoken language, in the building of the brain's neural connections, especially during the early and primary years, but also throughout life. As we shall also see in Chapter 15, classroom research confirms the dividends, in terms of both attainment as conventionally measured and children's metacognitive capacities and their ability to 'learn how to learn', of talk which is probing, challenging and reciprocal, whether on an individual child-teacher basis, or in small groups of children or whole-class, teacher-led discussions. As Robin Alexander suggests, a dialogic approach in the classroom enables children to develop various kinds of 'learning talk' which they will need both as learners and as future citizens. These include:

… the ability to narrate, explain, question, answer, analyse, explain, question, justify, negotiate; and the dispositions with which these are necessarily associated: the preparedness to listen, to be receptive to new ideas, to think and to give others time to do so.[34]

Linking the pedagogical and civic justifications he argues:

Process and process-product research shows that cognitively-enriching talk engages pupils' attention and motivation, increases time on task and produces measurable learning gains. … Democracies need citizens who can argue, reason, challenge, question, present cases and evaluate them. Democracies decline when citizens listen rather than talk, and when they comply rather than debate.[35]

This link was also pursued by the major EPPI review on citizenship education. This showed that dialogic pedagogy – as much as information about political institutions – generated the true understanding of what citizenship in a democracy entails and of the capacities to translate that understanding into effective democratic action.[36]

Thus, consultation with children takes the link between language and learning several steps further than the descriptive analysis of classroom discourse. Engaging in a learning-focused dialogue effectively changes the child's role from one of being an 'object' of research attention to one involving active agency and empowerment. The benefits of such an approach are multifaceted: 'Fostering dialogue at the classroom level, enabling the child's voice to be heard and valued, has the potential not only to improve relationships but to enhance the learning and achievement which policy-makers seek.'[37]

Evaluating teaching – and children's impact upon it

Perhaps one of the most common uses for the children's voices approach is as a means for teachers to obtain feedback on their teaching. Teachers have generally found that children's commentary is constructive and useful and children usually appreciate being asked for their opinions. Sometimes teachers have consulted groups of children they are concerned about and the approach not only offers insights into why these children are experiencing problems but also helps to create more positive child-teacher relationships. John MacBeath and colleagues worked in primary and secondary schools to explore techniques for consulting children about teaching and learning. They compiled a toolbox of strategies for consulting children, using four basic approaches: talking, writing, drawing and role play. However, they pointed out that it was important that teachers tailor the techniques to the children, in particular taking their ages into account. The researchers argued that these kinds of techniques yield useful information about children's responses to teaching and may help to establish a more positive culture for learning within schools.[38]

In another project, Years 5/6 pupils diverted a video-recording strategy initially intended to support teacher self-evaluation to the cause of evaluating their own activities. The focus was classroom talk, and the videotapes prepared for teachers' use were viewed and commented on, at their request, by the pupils. The experience so sensitised them to the dynamics of talk and to body language, turn-taking and the equitable handling of discussion – as well as to some of the teacher's own dilemmas – that some of the teachers concerned mainstreamed the procedure.[39]

School councils – tokens or beacons?

Although originally a feature of secondary schools, the school council became common in the primary sector towards the end of the 20th century. Usually comprising representatives elected from different year groups, school councils were widely seen as a useful means of teaching democratic principles. Head teachers were encouraged to set them up, but while in England there was no official requirement to do so, the Welsh Assembly introduced a statutory requirement in 2006. Gerison Lansdown, a leading proponent of children's rights, pointed to the importance of children experiencing democracy at firsthand:

> Participation can be defined as the process of sharing in decisions which affect one's life and the life of the community in which one lives ... In the field of education in this country there is a great deal of discussion about the need to teach children responsibility, citizenship and respect for others, but these skills and attitudes are not ones which can be acquired merely through the taught curriculum. The understanding, competence and commitment to democratic participation can only be achieved through practice and experience.[40]

The European Commission expressed a similar view, urging schools to become more participatory:

> Participation requires young people to acquire skills or improve existing skills. It involves a gradual learning process. The first stage, generally in their own environment (school, local district, town, youth centre, association, etc.) is crucial. It gives them the opportunity to gain the self-confidence and experience needed to reach the subsequent stages.[41]

The functions of school councils varied, with some being largely adult-led and focused on a narrow agenda of charity fundraising and school rules. A few primary schools broadened the scope of their school councils to include discussion of teaching and learning. However, some schools recognised the potential of the school council as a vehicle for citizenship education and there were some innovative examples of school councils playing active roles in school decision-making, including staff recruitment.

In a report for DfES, Judy Sebba and colleagues observed that having a school council does not necessarily offer children real participation Many councils have very limited scope for discussion and children's ideas and suggestions are often not acted upon.[42] Schools Council UK, a support and training organisation, has recommended that the council's role should be extended to include strategies such as child-led behaviour management panels; sub-groups with specific tasks and peer mediation schemes. Save the Children UK's submission to the Review described the benefits of involving children in school governance:

> Through our participation work we have encountered primary schools that involve pupils as governors and evidence suggests that not only do children take the role very seriously but they also become more confident young people.

Under 2003 school governance statutory guidance, those under the age of 18 may be appointed as associate members of school governing bodies though they may not vote on admissions, discipline, the appointment of governors or budgets. They may be members of a governing body committee but not of the body itself. Rita Cheminais describes the 'pupil associate member' role:

> Pupil associate members work with the governing body to support and develop all areas of the school, and are considered to be at the heart of school decision making. However, they are not allowed to vote on decisions relating to admissions; the appointment of governors; pupil discipline; or the budget and financial commitments of the governing body. Associate members of the governing body can hold office for up to four years.[43]

However, governing body membership is not necessarily the ultimate prize for advocates of children's voices. It is more important that children speak and are heard on a day-to-day basis in school and classroom than at set-piece formal events. And at the far end of the spectrum from the tokenism reported by Sebba, the Review team visited primary schools where school councils did not confine their discussions to uniforms and school meals, and where their members met shortlisted candidates for teaching appointments and passed their comments to the interview panel.

CHILDREN'S VOICES AND PARTICIPATION: POSSIBILITIES

There is ample evidence that children's voices can make a positive difference in schools but it must be recognised that its potential is shaped by the aims envisaged for it. For those who see the approach as tool for improving school performance, its potential lies in improving the conditions of learning in schools, as an Ofsted-commissioned review concludes:

> A common finding of effective schools research is that there can be quite substantial gains in effectiveness when the self-esteem of pupils is raised, when they have an active role in the life of the school, and when they are given a share of responsibility for their own learning.[44]

Participating in culture change

The Review's evidence included broader notions of children's voices as a means of establishing a more democratic and participatory culture for learning.

Some submissions warned that children's voices should not be regarded as a short-term initiative but as a sustained principle informing a school's ethos, culture and practice. Future-lab, the government-funded technology think-tank, argued:

> Learner voice should not be a tokenistic or add-on exercise. It should represent a deeper culture change towards genuine ongoing participation and engagement with learners. Much still needs to be done to improve the quality and level of engagement with learners about their education.[45]

David Hargreaves describes student voice as one of nine 'gateways' through which

- school is designed and organised to provide personalised education for all students;
- roles are blurred and overlapping: teachers learn as well as teach, students mentor other students as well as learn for themselves, and new professional roles emerge to complement that of the teacher;
- education is user-led (though at what point students rather than their parents are the users is an open question).[46]

Since the school context for Hargreaves' advocacy is secondary rather than primary, his parenthesised 'open question' might seem to be even more open in the present context. Yet, mindful of both our evidence-based emphasis on young children's capability, and Jerome Bruner's maxim that 'any subject can be taught effectively in some intellectually honest form to any child at any stage of development',[47] we would argue there must be an effective and intellectually honest way to encourage and attend to children's voices at any age.

Linked to the personalised learning agenda, Hargreaves' ideas offer a framework that enculcates the transformative potential of the approach, acknowledging the need to empower both children and teachers in reforming the conditions of learning in schools. An Ofsted research report[48] on schools which have turned themselves around also concluded that the children's voices approach was a vital element in their transformation:

> Increasing levels of participation had measurable benefits in all the schools. It created a more collaborative ethos. It improved attitudes, the working environment and the enjoyment of learning. There were specific gains, such as reducing the number of pupils and students who were excluded.[49]

The Rights Respecting Schools programme of UNICEF presents an alternative approach, based on the UN Convention on the Rights of the Child. Schools are required to weave the principles and values of the convention into key aspects of school life, working via a detailed action plan and carefully-constructed benchmarks. Schools receive externally-validated awards for achieving different levels, with each level requiring a set of benchmarks to be met. To achieve level 1, for example, schools must show that 'there are effective and inclusive arrangements for pupils actively to participate in decision-making'. Around 150 primary schools have taken part in the programme and early evaluation reports indicate that both children and adults found it 'empowering'.[50]

CHILDREN'S VOICES AND PARTICIPATION: CONSTRAINTS

Politics of power sharing

In 1993 researchers Barrie Wade and Maggie Moore surveyed 115 primary and secondary teachers and found that less than a third reported taking any account of children's views.[51] Similarly, in 1996, Ronald Davie and David Galloway pointed out that 'in education especially – perhaps because it inevitably mirrors society – there is a long way to go before teachers as a whole accept either the probity or the value of seeking pupils' opinions or perspectives'.[52]

Even now, the Review's evidence suggests that there are still doubts and fears among practitioners about the implications of children's voices. The submission from Association of Teachers and Lecturers (ATL) warned:

> Schools that embrace citizenship tend to treat it not only as a 'subject' but also as a value that runs across school life. It must be admitted that this kind of political skill is dangerous for schools; in developing pupils' skills to challenge power, schools are laying themselves open to challenge.

With this in mind, it is perhaps unsurprising that while teachers welcomed children's comments on school life outside the classroom, some were sometimes reluctant to hear what their children thought about teaching. Others, in line with ATL's warning, were concerned that allowing children to have a say in school matters might radically alter the traditional power relationships: a concern backed, to some extent, in evidence from the Effective Provision of Pre-school Education project (EPPE) which warned that if children's voices strategies extended too far they could undermine school discipline. Schools where school council members were involved in staff recruitment found that some applicants refused to be interviewed by children's panels. In their research survey for the Review, Robinson and Fielding warn: 'Pupil voice will never be seriously supported by other than a small proportion of teachers and other staff unless there are clear messages that this new approach is not a covert way of trying to control, "discipline", or reform teachers.'[53]

Graham Sutherland notes that teachers who were establishing children's voices approaches in their schools were sometimes, '… under fire from colleagues who feel that teacher voice may be marginalised in the drive to listen to, and involve, pupils'.[54] This view was echoed in a TES article by primary head teacher, Mike Kent, 'Everybody seems entitled to a "voice" apart from the teachers. Who are the professionals supposed to be, I wonder?'[55] In response to these anxieties, it should be pointed out that when teachers worked on children's voices initiatives which they themselves had instigated, they found the experience rewarding and their enthusiasm served to reassure and inspire other teachers. Suggesting that children should have a voice does not negate the importance of teacher voice, and the value of these strategies lies, in part, on the mutual benefits they can bestow on teachers and children alike.

No incentive to innovate

Even where teachers were keen to introduce children's voices strategies, they often encountered obstacles and restrictions. The prevailing climate of 'performativity', with its narrowly-defined quality standards and public accountability, was perhaps the greatest constraint: teachers were often too pressured, and sometimes fearful, to risk trying something new:

> Teachers need to be able to use their professional expertise and judgement in working more creatively with their pupils; at present, however, as they start to develop consultation and participation practices in their classrooms they are constantly looking over their shoulders, aware of the negative power of central surveillance mechanisms ...[56]

Rudduck and McIntyre also argued that teachers' enthusiasm for children's voices strategies had been dampened by initiative overload, ' ... there might, at any one time, be a diversity of initiatives in a school, each reflecting rather different concerns and values. In these circumstances it is difficult for the senior management team to offer adequate encouragement to every initiative'.

CONCLUSION

Clearly, there is a steadily widening recognition that children's voices are worth listening to and that the benefits of doing so are many. Some argue that exploring children's experiences of teaching and learning provide valuable insights into the difficulties and challenges children experience in their learning. From a psychological and pedagogical perspective, there is persuasive evidence that voice and dialogue support both learning and metacognition, enabling children to become independent and reflective learners. Others emphasise the moral or civic imperative that children have a right to be heard and to have their views taken seriously. However, although 'student voice' has moved beyond the confines of the school council and its agenda has broadened to encompass many aspects of children's lives both inside and outside schools, it is unclear whether these developments yet represent a real and fundamental change in how we see children and how we respond to what they have to say.

Children's voices currently have a modish appeal, and 'student voice' occurs with increasing frequency in policy statements and documents. But this apparent recognition presents dangers as well as opportunities, for in recent years some notable ideas originating outside the arena of policy have been cherry-picked for political advantage and so prominently plagiarised that they cannot be recovered in their original form. The late Jean Rudduck, one of the leading advocates of children's voices in education, warned that the movement will be short-lived if it fails to be properly understood and embedded in practice; and as Colin Richards suggests, the picture so far has been mixed:

> Through the primary national strategy schools are being encouraged to be more innovative and creative and to use the increased 'freedom' to provide a more flexible curriculum (though the possible role of pupils in influencing that curriculum is unclear). Assessment for learning, including pupil self-assessment, is in favour (though not at the expense of national assessment of learning) ... Extended schools offer exciting possibilities (but are children being consulted, or even making decisions, as to the activities made available?). Two enquiries – one into the nature of childhood[57] and one reviewing the state of primary education[58] – have just been launched, though not by the government; in both, children's views are being sought. School councils are gaining ground; work with children as researchers is beginning to develop; children as decision-makers is on the research agenda but is it on schools' or the government's agenda?[59]

If, as we shall argue in this report's next section, the vision is of schools as communities that respect and empower those within them – teachers as well as children – then efforts must be made to address, with due sensitivity, the constraints and challenges described in this chapter.

NOTES

1 Neale (2004): 7.
2 UK Children's Commissioners (2008): 27.
3 United Nations (1989).
4 Most notably, for example, in the provisions of the Children Act 1988.
5 Davies and Kirkpatrick (2000).
6 For example, Woods (1976).
7 For example, Meighan (1977).
8 Rudduck *et al.* (1996).
9 Rudduck and McIntyre (2007): 7.
10 Reay (2006).
11 Rudduck (2006): 10.
12 Hargreaves (2004c): 7.
13 Alderson (2003).
14 Whitty and Wisby (2007): 5.
15 http://www.everychildmatters.gov.uk/strategy/childrensfund/ (accessed 18 June 2008).
16 Edwards, Barnes *et al.* (2006): 5.
17 Commission for Social Care Inspection (2004).
18 Ofsted (2005a).
19 DfES (2001c): 29.
20 UK Children's Commissioners (2008): 27.
21 Robinson and Fielding (2010), *The Cambridge Primary Review Research Surveys*, Chapter 2.
22 For example, see studies such as Cullingford (1986); Silcock and Wyness (2000).
23 Pollard *et al.* (2000).
24 Marks *et al.* (2004).
25 Bearne (2002).
26 Doddington *et al.* (2001).
27 Kinder *et al.* (1996).
28 Pollard *et al.* (2000).
29 Pollard *et al.* (2000).
30 Doddington *et al.* (2001).
31 Measor and Woods (1984).
32 Urquhart (2001).
33 Doddington *et al.* (2002).
34 Alexander (2008a): 135.
35 Alexander (2008a): 184.
36 Deakin Crick *et al.* (2005).
37 Nixon *et al.* (1996): 272.
38 MacBeath *et al.* (2001).
39 Alexander (2004b): 17.
40 Lansdown (1995): 17.
41 European Commission (2001): 18.
42 Sebba *et al.* (2007).
43 Cheminais (2008): 21.
44 Sammons *et al.* (1995).
45 Futurelab (2006).
46 Hargreaves, D. (2004c): 4–5.
47 Bruner (1963): 33.
48 Ofsted (2008g): 13.
49 Ofsted (2008g): 11.
50 Waller (2008).
51 Wade and Moore (1993).
52 Davie and Galloway (1996).
53 Robinson and Fielding (2010) *The Cambridge Primary Review Research Surveys*, Chapter 2.
54 Sutherland (2006): 9.
55 Kent (2008): 29.
56 Rudduck and McIntyre (2007): 200.
57 The Good Childhood Inquiry.
58 The Cambridge Primary Review.
59 Richards (2006).

Part 3
The experience of primary education

11 Foundations

The early years

Although the remit of the Cambridge Primary Review covered the years of compulsory schooling from age 4/5 to 11 and did not therefore include the pre-school years, a report that did not acknowledge the critical importance of early childhood and of laying secure foundations for later learning would not enable us fully to reflect upon the broad aims of this review or to make viable proposals for the rest of the primary phase.

Before we go further, we need to be clear about what we mean by 'early years'. It can mean either a phase of children's development or a kind of provision. But to equate early years as *development* with what a particular country or local authority offers by way of early years *provision* is clearly wrong. By way of illustrating the absurdity of conflating the two definitions, it would mean that in England children's early years end at age 4/5 while in Finland or Denmark they continue until age 7.

Having said that, there are three further reasons for presenting a chapter on the early years in general and on the related structures of education and care. The first is that many of the Review themes and the questions that we asked reflect directly on policy, research and practice in relation to the education and care of our youngest children. The changing nature of childhood and of children's lives both in and out of school or pre-school, for example, are as fundamental to very young children as they are to children approaching the end of primary education; and the importance of parents and carers as their children's first and most enduring educators, and of the need for a close partnership between home and school, are both at their most poignant as a child first experiences the education system. Some themes have a specific bearing on the early years – for example managing the transition from pre-school to school and questioning the age at which formal – or statutory – schooling should begin. Others have their foundations in the earliest years: for example what we know about how children develop and learn and the implications of this for how they are taught; and how far primary schools attend fairly and effectively to the different learning needs and cultural backgrounds of their pupils.

The second reason is the wealth of evidence on the importance of the early years presented to the Review in the research surveys, the written submissions and the community and national soundings. The Early Childhood Forum, which represents over 50 professional associations and national voluntary organisations and interest groups, sums up the conviction behind much of this evidence:

> Primary schooling can only build on what has gone before. Children will have experienced 3–4 years of development and learning before entering primary school ... It is a crucial time in children's development, and their pre-school experience provides many of the building blocks for the rest of their lives.

Thirdly, since 1997, and even more so in the two years since the Review was launched, the early years have become a significant focus of national policy and public debate and the government has extended the brief of its own review of the primary curriculum to include aspects of the early years curriculum.

For these reasons we are including this chapter on the early years, which in structural terms is interpreted as the years up to and including the start of statutory schooling (that is, the end of the academic year in which a child becomes five), though – as we have noted – developmentally it may last for longer. After a brief review of the current policy context, including developments in early years services, we consider the research evidence on what young children need from early years settings if they are to gain maximum benefit from their primary education; then draw on evidence from the Review to look at both the strengths and any concerns in the current provision; and finally ask whether the current structures for the early years foundation stage (EYFS) and the statutory school starting age of five are appropriate in the light of evidence from this country and overseas.

At issue, in light of this introduction, are four questions:

1. What kinds of provision does our knowledge of children's early years dictate, regardless of context – what, in other words, are the developmental needs of early childhood?
2. How far does existing provision, both in pre-school and primary school settings, meet those needs?
3. What changes are required in order to secure experiences during the early years which are developmentally appropriate?
4. What are the implications for the early years curriculum and for the structures of pre-school and primary education?

THE CURRENT POLICY CONTEXT

Eleven years of expansion

The years since 1997 have seen a dramatic increase in services for young children, albeit starting from a very low base. Although the first nursery school was established in Scotland by Robert Owen in 1816, the development of early childhood care and education in the UK was remarkably slow by comparison to much of mainland Europe. In 1870, publicly-funded education became compulsory at the age of five, but from the earliest days two-year-olds were admitted to primary schools. During the course of the 20th century, successive governments supported the principle of free nursery education but seldom found the resources to fund it. Even with the gradual establishment of nursery schools, and, during the First World War, some public day-care centres, the predominant form of early education in the UK has always involved the primary school. This lack of appropriate provision led to two parallel developments during the second half of the 20th century: on the one hand, the emergence of voluntary-sector playgroups during the 1960s; on the other, the growth of full day-care to meet the needs of working parents, initially through childminding and, since the 1990s, through private-sector nurseries.

But the past 11 years have witnessed rapid change. From lagging well behind our continental neighbours in the early 1990s, the UK has become the highest spender on early years services in Europe, according to the Organisation for Economic Co-operation and Development.[1] Figures from the National Audit Office[2] showed that the government's 10-year childcare strategy[3] was on course to quadruple expenditure between 1997 and 2008 from £1.1 billion to £4.4bn. Nursery education, provided through the private and voluntary sectors as well as through nursery and primary schools, is currently available for 12.5 hours a week in term time. This will increase to 15 hours a week by 2010 and 20 hours in due course. It is already being accessed by 92 per cent of three-year-olds and 97 per cent of four-year-olds.[4] A pilot to extend this offer to 20,000 two-year-olds in disadvantaged communities is currently underway and is likely to be expanded.

Much of the expansion has been in the private and voluntary sector, where public funding is available provided that nationally approved standards are met. Only one third of childcare and early years places are in maintained schools: in 2007 there were 450 nursery schools, 6,800 primary schools with nursery and reception classes, and 8,900 primary schools with reception classes but no nursery.[5] This has led to very variable quality, both within the private and voluntary sector where practitioners are less well trained and qualified, but also in reception classes of schools which are often not well suited to the needs of such young children. The growth of services has been fuelled both by research on the benefits to children of high quality early education, and by an explicit government policy to reduce, and in time eliminate, child poverty, largely through providing childcare to help parents return to work.

In search of 'educare'

However, despite this level of investment and the bringing together of childcare and education within one government department, the aim of achieving a fully integrated early childhood care and education system has not yet been realised, and there are still considerable funding challenges, with the costs of providing care before and after school and during the holidays largely being borne by parents.[6]

The national childcare strategy (not, as one might have expected, the national early childhood strategy, or early education strategy) not only led to the expansion of free nursery places. It also included the establishment in 1998 of 250 local Sure Start programmes providing support for parents with children under the age of three in areas of high need, an initiative that was expanded to 520 communities even before the ink was dry on the contract for a substantial evaluation programme. The goalposts were moved again in 2003 with the creation of a national programme of Sure Start children's centres in the 20 per cent most disadvantaged areas. These brought together the concept of 'early excellence centres' (originally launched in 1998) with Sure Start local programmes, though with the jam spread considerably more thinly.[7] Central to the much broader *Every Child Matters* initiative, also launched in 2003, children's centres were to provide integrated care and education but with a much stronger link with health services, as well as adult education and access to employment and other advice. In 2008, three-year-olds in Sure Start areas were showing better social development than those in other similar areas and parents were providing a better learning environment at home using more of the services offered. However, a more recent emphasis has been on reaching out to the most vulnerable families, following the early evaluation of Sure Start which showed that the most disadvantaged families did not always use the services.[8]

This level of investment in services has been matched by developments in other areas such as:

- a programme of workforce reform and a national qualifications and training framework, intended to improve the skills of a poorly trained early years workforce[9]
- an integrated inspection service for all early years services within Ofsted
- much greater support for parents, and a commitment, reinforced in the 2007 Children's Plan,[10] to involve parents more fully in their children's learning
- the establishment of the foundation stage of early education, first through two documents – *Curriculum Guidance for the Foundation Stage*[11] for three- to five-year-olds and *Birth to Three Matters*[12] – and more recently through the early years foundation stage (EYFS) framework[13] for children from birth to five, which became statutory in September 2008.

The Early Years Foundation Stage

The early years foundation stage (EYFS) enshrines a statutory commitment to play-based developmentally-appropriate care and education for children up to five years of age. By building on the two earlier documents, both developed by experienced early years academics and practitioners and enthusiastically implemented across the country, the EYFS provides a regulatory framework aimed at raising quality in all settings. It recognises the central contribution that parents make to their children's development, and specifies the integration of childcare, education and – where possible – health services. Perhaps most importantly it is based on four key principles:

- every child is a competent learner from birth, who can be resilient, capable, confident and self-assured
- children learn to be strong and independent from a base of loving and secure relationships with parents and/or a key person
- the environment plays a key role in supporting and extending children's development and learning
- children develop and learn in different ways and at different rates and all areas of learning and development are equally important and inter-connected.[14]

The 2006 Childcare Act provided for the three EYFS elements – the knowledge, skills and understanding which young children should have acquired by the end of the academic year in which they turn five (the early learning goals), the educational programmes, and the assessment arrangements. The six areas of learning are broad based and inter-dependent:

- personal, social and emotional development
- communication, language and literacy
- problem solving, reasoning and numeracy
- knowledge and understanding of the world
- physical development
- creative development

and are to be delivered through 'planned, purposeful play, with a balance of adult-led and child-initiated activities'.[15]

The 2006 Act also put the provision of early years services on a legal footing for the first time, requiring local authorities to 'secure sufficient childcare to enable parents to work' as well as requiring them, through the early years services in their area, to improve outcomes for young children and reduce the gap between those who do well and those who do not.

EARLY YEARS RESEARCH EVIDENCE

The research evidence on children's development and learning presented in Chapter 7, drawing on Usha Goswami and Peter Bryant's research survey for the Review,[16] pointed to the extent to which our understanding of how young children develop, think, feel and learn has developed since the Plowden Report. Two lines of research in particular have emphasised the importance of early learning: the many neuroscientific studies suggesting that early learning contributes to the brain's developing architecture;[17] and the evidence from developmental psychology that the earliest interactions between child and carers provide the cultural structure that underpins the development of intellectual schema.[18] As Kathy Sylva and Gillian Pugh have argued, neurological research has confirmed the importance of learning in the early years, while the psychological studies have suggested what kind of learning is best.[19]

Scaffolding and learning

Children learn from interactions and conversations with adults and older peers, and it is through these conversations that they acquire the cultural 'tools' to aid them in setting and achieving goals and in becoming members of communities. Lev Vygotsky's work, discussed in Chapter 7, on the adult's role in supporting and extending children's learning (through the 'zone of proximal development') has been influential in early years thinking, as has his stress on pretend play and imagination in relation to cognitive development.[20] And Carol Dweck's contribution, discussed in Chapter 6, has also been important, pointing to the extent to which early-learning experiences shape children towards either a 'mastery' orientation in learning or a 'performance' one. Children who believe that their intelligence is fixed are less likely to make the effort to learn, whereas those who believe that their intelligence can grow, will try harder when faced with a learning challenge.[21] Two themes are clear here – the important role that a skilled adult can play in 'scaffolding' children's learning, and that young children have learned dispositions as well as key cognitive skills well before entering school.

These themes were picked up in the many studies, initially from the United States, which demonstrated the powerful effects of early education on children's readiness for school and for their attainment throughout education and even employment. The most influential of these were the Perry Pre-school Study[22] and the Abercedarian study[23] which both used randomised control designs and both demonstrated the lasting effects of early education and care, especially for children from disadvantaged backgrounds. The UK government's response was to commission its own large-scale longitudinal research study on effective early education in 1997, the Effective Provision of Pre-School Education 3–11 (EPPE) project. Studying some 3,000 children from 141 settings drawn from a range of providers (statutory, voluntary and private) plus some children who had no or minimal pre-school experience, the EPPE study has been very influential on both policy and practice.

Shaped by mother, home and pre-school

The most recent EPPE report presented findings on the relationships between child, family, home, pre-school and primary-school characteristics and children's cognitive and social/behavioural outcomes at age 11 in Year 6 of primary school.[24] The results confirmed earlier findings on the importance of mothers' qualifications and of the home learning environment. They also showed that the quality and effectiveness of the pre-school remained significant predictors of attainment and social/behavioural outcomes right through primary school. Children gained most from attending high quality settings, employing trained teachers, but the influence of home continued to be stronger. Interestingly, in view of the still-notorious long tail of under-achievement in this country, having attended a high quality pre-school was found to be of particular benefit to boys, to children with special educational needs and to disadvantaged children. While higher quality pre-school benefits all children, the benefits are greater for these groups.

EARLY YEARS: WHAT WITNESSES SAID

Although the Review's remit did not include the early years, a large number of witnesses made a point of stressing both their developmental importance and the need for high quality provision as preparation for the primary phase and all that follows. The Early Years Curriculum Group, for example, said:

> We believe that this country has made successive errors in its education policy by designing a curriculum and assessments for older children which then press, top-down, upon the experiences of the youngest children. The Cambridge Primary Review has a great opportunity to start from the earliest years and build upwards, to make the foundations strong and, thereby, the whole educational edifice more robust.

Many of the submissions were both encouraged about recent developments in early years services and concerned about some of the direction of travel. The Early Education Advisory Group (EEAG),[25] for example, praised government initiatives including: the expansion of nursery education, day-care and Sure Start local programmes and children's centres; the integration of services within the government's education department and the integrative principles of the foundation stage, which apply to all early years services. They also welcomed government support for parents and the priority given to workforce training. However, they were concerned about unresolved tensions between the drive to get parents to work and the recognition of parenting as key to children's development. They worried too that the current market approach to providing early years services, and conceptual differences between the foundation stage and key stage 1, were leading to fragmentation, rather than continuity. Too early exposure to some of the literacy goals put unnecessary stress on children; and they proposed, rather, that a curriculum based on the EYFS be extended into key stage 1. They also wanted higher investment aimed at securing a well-trained and well-paid workforce, quality improvements and greater coherence between early years and school.

These themes – curriculum and assessment, workforce quality, parents, and continuity between pre-school and school – were echoed in many other submissions and will be examined further in turn.

Learning, teaching and communicating

Submissions once again pointed to the importance of thinking and talking – and of the relationship between them – during the early years. The communications charity I CAN believes that 'communication skills' are a key foundation for education, learning, literacy and building relationships, and yet 10 per cent of children have a communication disability, a disproportionate number of them boys, and often with associated behavioural, emotional and social difficulties. Teachers in the Review's community soundings also spoke of the growing numbers of children entering primary schools with impoverished speech and language.

There was also emphasis on specific activities which encourage children to think – for example by reference to the EPPE findings on the importance of 'sustained shared thinking' between adults and children in promoting children's cognitive, linguistic and social-behavioural progress.[26]

The importance of good mental health in order to be able to sustain mutually satisfying personal relationships was also stressed, as was the negative impact on children's confidence and self-esteem of a system which introduces too formal a curriculum too soon.

Early childhood education: not a blank slate

Several submissions, as well as the Review's national soundings, stressed the need to recognise and appreciate the learning children bring with them into the early years setting and the importance of rooting early education in children's prior knowledge and experiences. As the British Association for Early Childhood Education pointed out, babies and young children are social beings, and are competent learners from birth. Learning is a shared process and children learn most effectively when, with the support of a knowledgeable and trusted adult, they are actively involved and interested. Children learn when they are given appropriate responsibility, allowed to make errors, decisions and choices, and respected as autonomous and competent learners; and children learn by doing as well as by being told. Young children are vulnerable, but they learn to be independent by having someone they can depend upon. There is now a strong tradition in the early years of listening to young children and ensuring that their voices are heard in all aspects of their daily life. This has been strongly supported by the emphasis within the sector on young children's rights and entitlements.[27]

A recurring theme in the submissions was the need for flexibility and for a curriculum appropriate to individual children's stage of development. Development at this age is rapid but uneven, and children need time to play, to reflect, to repeat and to talk to peers and adults.

Literacy goals and the foundation stage

The EYFS was broadly welcomed and its underpinning principles were warmly endorsed. In settings where staff are well trained, it was viewed as offering an appropriate framework for young children's learning. There was, however, criticism of the impact of the literacy and numeracy strategies, which the Early Childhood Forum felt were inconsistent with current understanding about early learning. The Early Education Advisory Group was concerned that synthetic phonics would be used indiscriminately and inappropriately within the foundation stage rather than as part of a balanced and integrated approach to language development and reading. It argued that children needed until age six to meet two of the literacy goals as attempting to meet them by age five risked creating 'a culture of deficiency' in young children by showing them what they could not do. The United Kingdom Literacy Association (UKLA) also felt that the government's emphasis on phonics in the teaching of reading was too narrow. In June 2008, the government responded to these concerns by extending the remit of its Rose review of the primary curriculum. Sir Jim Rose was asked:

> ... to review two of the milestones set out in the early years foundation stage as part of his review of the primary curriculum. The review will now consider whether two statements on developing literacy strike the right balance between giving children a good start in literacy skills and supporting a smooth transition from the early years into key stage 1 of primary school.[28]

Passions in this matter ran high. On 24 July 2008, in an open letter to The Times, members of the Open EYE campaign, including some eminent educationists, psychologists and children's authors, wrote:

> We continue to campaign for the compulsory learning requirements being changed to voluntary guidance; for EYFS to be extended until the end of the school year when children turn six; and for no achievement targets to be imposed on local authorities before then. Parents should have the right to choose how their pre-school children are cared for and educated. Young children should also have the right to be protected from an imposed system which harnesses their development to prescribed targets, and which may well force them into inappropriate early learning.[29]

Some submissions outlined a different approach to the curriculum. One local authority, for example, reported on an 'improving the foundation stage' project, influenced by the Swiss model of early learning. With a strong emphasis on developing oral language, improving concentration and social and behavioural skills, this project claimed considerable success, through an enhanced nursery and reception curriculum with the stress on structured talk, story, rhyme and song.

Under pressure from the profile

A number of commentators felt that, in assessing whether children were doing better and gaps were being narrowed, the foundation stage profile was being put to a use beyond that for which it was originally intended. Reception teachers told the Review that they were under considerable pressure to ensure that outcomes were improving, and this tended to skew the curriculum in the same way that SATs did in later years. This was particularly true in relation to the literacy goals noted above. There were concerns that, in the hands of inexperienced staff, the EYFS profile could become burdensome and ineffectual.

The problem of quality

For many years, there has been considerable concern about the variable quality of early years provision. Current difficulties within the expanded day-care system include problems faced by some childminders in using the EYFS, in particular its complex and time-consuming assessments, and the challenges for the many private and voluntary-sector nurseries in improving the quality of their service and their staff. Both the EPPE study[30] and the Millennium cohort study[31] found that quality was significantly higher in maintained settings than in the private or voluntary sector, and in settings with a trained teacher. This was confirmed in Ofsted inspections[32] where 98 per cent of early education settings were found to be satisfactory or better (with 65 per cent good or outstanding) compared to only 65 per cent of day-care settings. The Ofsted report also found poorer standards of care in poorer areas.

Evidence indicates that staff are the main determinant of quality of early years settings. The British Association for Early Childhood Education pointed out that

> ... for young children to be effectively supported in all aspects of their development they need knowledgeable, interested and responsive adults who know how best to challenge and extend their thinking and their understandings and can model positive dispositions and approaches to learning. These adults need to have the ability to 'tune into' the children they are with. They should respond to and not restrict or limit their potential. To do this they need a thorough understanding of how children learn and develop and how to put this into practice.

The need for properly-trained early years teachers was also noted in the EPPE research, but in 2008 the workforce included only a relatively small number of teachers, working mainly in schools, even though legislation required children's centres to have access to teachers. While early years practitioners were becoming better qualified, only 65 per cent of childcare staff and 79 per cent of early years staff in maintained schools had at least a level 3 qualification, and only 11 per cent of the workforce were qualified at level 6 (graduate level) or above.[33] The new graduate-level 'early years professional' (EYP) status was welcomed, although concern was expressed that funding was only available for EYPs to work in the private and voluntary sectors. Submissions pointed to the lack of clarity over how EYPs related to qualified teachers, both in terms of role and salary. Different pay and conditions within the early years workforce have long been of concern, and when seen in relation to primary education they take on an added dimension. The Thomas Coram Research Unit suggested that lessons could be learnt from the emergence of 'pedagogues' in Sweden and Denmark and some other European countries, a role that has a more holistic and developmental orientation than teachers.[34] Some early years settings were now employing pedagogues, but the practice had not yet spread very widely.

Review witnesses also commented on how early years practitioners were trained, and expressed the view that student teachers were not taught enough about either child development or how to work with parents and other practitioners. The first phase of teacher training covers three- to seven-year-olds, and the EEAG recommended that this should be reformed to encompass teaching children from birth to age six or seven in line with the earlier start of the early years foundation stage.

Parents: carers or earners?

The key role of parents in their children's care, development and learning was acknowledged in many submissions and was central to the findings of EPPE and many other research studies. Parenting and caring are considered in depth in Chapter 6, but it is worth noting here the considerable potential there is during the early years for creating sound partnerships between parents and the practitioners who care for and educate their children. Respectful relationships, that recognise the complementary roles of both partners, have been supported by innovative training courses such as Parents Early Years and Learning (PEAL)[35] and other initiatives within the Early Learning Partnership Project[36] which have enabled practitioners to engage effectively with parents in supporting their children's learning. However, there are unresolved tensions reflected in some submissions between, on the one hand, the realisation by government and most practitioners of the importance of parents' relationships with their children and, on the other, the drive to get as many parents as possible into employment as a key element in the policy to reduce child poverty.

Smooth the way to primary school

The final theme from the Review's evidence was the continuity – or lack of it – between early years settings and primary education. The submission from the Thomas Coram Research Unit, in line with the OECD Starting Strong reviews,[37] argued for a unified approach to learning at pre-primary and primary levels and the facilitation of transfer for children from one stage to the next:

> We profoundly agree with the principle in Starting Strong that 'a strong and equal partnership' between early childhood care and education and the primary education system is fundamental to the optimal cognitive, socio-emotional and physical development of children in their early years and of primary-school age.

The submission continued by noting, as did others, the downward pressures on the pre-primary curriculum, citing research which showed how formal learning, notably through the literacy and numeracy strategies, appeared to conflict with the approaches to learning adopted in the foundation stage.[38] Thomas Coram's submission also noted that the foundation stage, with its detailed monitoring and assessment of children's progress, may increase the 'scholarisation' of children's early years experience, a theme discussed in Chapter 5.

STARTING SCHOOL: 1870–2009

Victorian values

The debate surrounding the age at which children in England start school began 140 years ago. The Elementary Education Act of 1870, which laid down the principle that all children should go to school until they were at least 10, proposed that they should start 'when they were not less than five'. Five was picked not for educational or child-development reasons,[39] but in an attempt to service the demands of industry.

The mill and factory owners needed their workers educated, but they needed it done quickly. MPs pondered how 'to obtain time for an education without trenching on time for gaining a living,' according to a verbatim report of the parliamentary debates.[40] Clearly, the earlier children started, the sooner they would finish. Another reason for picking five – the Swedes had already resolved on seven – still resonates in 2009. Children, it was felt, were better off at school. Some MPs argued that 'it was never too early to inculcate the habits of decency, cleanliness and order. Besides children thus brought up learned more rapidly than those who had passed their time in the gutter.'[41] Other MPs demurred, protesting that 'five was too tender an age for compulsory attendance.' Despite their qualms, many three- and four-year-olds were also enrolled. By 1900, 43 per cent of children aged three to five were in school.

The under-fives were to be extricated from the monotonous repetition and rote learning that characterised many elementary lessons by inspectors from the Board of Education in 1905. Such young children needed separate schools they said, essentially giving birth to the nursery-school movement. Sixty years later, the Plowden Committee attempted to raise the school starting age slightly,[42] on condition that parents could request a nursery-style education for their children (in either a nursery or infant school) up to the age of six. Plowden's reluctance to propose a later starting age arose from a desire to protect infant and nursery schools from the pressures of more formal teaching, allowing them to continue their 'learning through play and creative work'.[43]

Plowden suggested children start school in the September term following their fifth birthday, in effect raising the median starting age to five years, six months, though the recommendation was made conditional upon the availability of part-time nursery education for all children whose parents wanted it.[44] By 1986, however, the demand for childcare from working parents persuaded MPs on the House of Commons Education, Science and Arts Committee to call for entry 'at the beginning of the school year in which the child becomes five'.[45] For a child born in July this entailed starting school aged four years and two months.

Welcome to reception

Three years later government backtracked, principally because schools were unable to afford the staff, equipment and space associated with high quality nursery education. But it was too late. The 1988 Education Reform Act had given schools control over their budgets and head teachers a financial incentive to recruit four-year-olds into 'reception' classes, though not enough of one to fund nursery-style education.

By 2007, 97 per cent of five-year-olds in England were in primary school (compared with a European Union average of 16 per cent), as were 61 per cent of four-year-olds.[46] Six was the starting age in 20 out of 34 European countries, with a further eight, including Sweden, waiting until seven.[47] Only England, Wales, Scotland and the Netherlands set a starting age of five. Since then, Northern Ireland, with Europe's earliest starting age of four, has announced a review. In England the government said in 2008 that it had no plans to change the starting age, though it would explore offering the parents of summer-born children greater flexibility. However, the interim report of the DCSF's Rose review, published in December 2008, proposed that 'entry into reception class in the September immediately following a child's fourth birthday should become the norm,[48] a proposal which provoked considerable opposition, not least from the House of Commons Children, Schools and Families Committee:

> We recommend that the Rose Review does not pursue its interim recommendation that entry into reception class in the September immediately following a child's fourth birthday should become the norm.[49]

The Welsh Assembly, on the other hand, went ahead with the development of a foundation phase for three-to seven-year-olds. The thematically-structured, outdoor-focussed and play-based curriculum represented an attempt to import best European practice into the UK and was one supported by several submissions to the Review. Despite disputes about funding and concerns about consistency across the settings, practitioners in Wales remain committed to the phase and reported that boys in particular were benefiting. With 84 per cent of three to four-year-olds in schools aiming to offer a seamless curriculum until age seven, the statutory starting date becomes almost irrelevant.

STARTING SCHOOL: THE REVIEW'S EVIDENCE

Four is too young

In light of the Rose Review's recommendation (above) we have to record that this Review's soundings and submissions reveal a strong and widespread conviction that children are ill-served by starting school at four and embarking on formal, subject-based, learning almost immediately. Parents in the community soundings said children should not start until they were ready and 'interested'. Teachers, parents and consultants were concerned that for children (especially those with special needs) transition between the early years foundation stage and KS1 is difficult; and some proposed that KS1 as a whole should be based on play, especially for children with learning difficulties and for those who were among the youngest in their year/cohort.

Many submissions called for a starting age of six or seven, arguing that formal schooling any earlier dents children's confidence and risks long-term damage to their learning. One local authority claimed that the combination of an early start, testing and pressure to reach government standards was creating a generation with mental health problems. Another proposed a start to formal school at age seven following an orally rich, exploratory, experiential, but structured curriculum. A submission from the Steiner schools commented: 'Developmentally, children are more ready for literacy after six and the benefits of concentrating on social skills and oracy are often understated.' In the meetings with parents which formed part of the Review's community soundings, the voices of recent arrivals in England from other European countries were sometimes influential in this matter, for they could commend alternatives on the basis of experience. With few exceptions they found England's relatively early starting age unacceptable, and one French parent called it 'cruel'.

Against this general trend the submission from Jolly Learning sounded a warning note:

> Children in independent schools also start at age four and often three. International studies show a wide variation between UK children's literacy achievement. It suggests that one reason why Scandinavian children are able to catch up is because of failings in parts of the UK education system (which a later start would not address).

To attribute one country's educational successes to another's educational failings is, however, somewhat suspect. As this report notes elsewhere, the unusually wide gap between high and low attainers in English schools relates to social, and indeed economic, as well as educational factors. Scandinavian children do not 'catch up' and indeed overtake their English peers so much as pursue their education in countries which are less densely populated, economically less unequal and culturally more homogeneous than England.

In any event, submissions from consultants and teachers pressed the case for play-based active learning led by well-qualified staff until at least the age of six. Similar proposals arose from the Review's national soundings with practitioners and organisations. In addition, they urged more help for parents in determining when children were ready to start, a precise definition of formal schooling, and greater coherence and consistency across all nursery and infant settings. The word 'formal' tends to be used loosely to indicate statutory schooling, with a subject-based curriculum. But statutory schooling does not, of course, have to be formal any more than non-statutory schooling is always play-based.

No gain from early start?

Pressure to start school young stems in large part from the assumption that this will help children's later attainment. The Review's research survey by Anna Riggall and Caroline Sharp does not support this assumption.[50] Nor, they argue, is there evidence indicating that children from deprived backgrounds – who are presumed to be the main beneficiaries – gain from an early start to formal school. Nor, similarly, do summer-born children profit from simply spending more time in school, as the government acknowledged in its decision to consider offering greater flexibility. In 14 of the 15 countries that scored higher than England in the 2006 Progress in International Reading and Literacy Study (PIRLS),[51] children do not start formal school until six or seven. In Bulgaria, for example, most three-to six-year-olds attend optional nursery schools before moving on to primary school at six or, if their parents prefer, at seven. Similarly, in high-performing Finland, children do not start formal school until seven. Prior to that, their pre-schools and kindergartens focus on social, physical and moral development and, in the final compulsory year, on preparing them for school. An Ofsted study conducted in 2002–3, comparing the achievements of Danish, Finnish and English children, revealed that, while English children had the edge in literacy at age six, by age 15 Finnish children outperformed them in reading, and in mathematical and scientific literacy.[52] The range of measured attainment among the Finnish children – the gap – was also much narrower, a finding of relevance to England where in 2007 three-year-olds from supportive homes were a year ahead of their more deprived peers in terms of social and educational development.[53]

Just as at the start of this chapter we argued the need to distinguish early years as development from early years as provision, so we need to be clear that the debate about an early start centres not on early access to provision as such – which in fact nearly all witnesses welcome – but to the provision typically provided in the first year or two of primary school. On this matter, weaknesses in the curriculum and pedagogy four-year-olds experience in reception classes have been highlighted for many years. A recent study concluded (our italics):

> If the purpose of the foundation stage was to extend to four and five-year-olds in primary/ infant schools the best practice in the education of three and four-year-olds, then it has not succeeded. *There is a demonstrable gap between the quality of children's experiences in the reception classes and the quality of their experiences earlier in the foundation stage.*[54]

Many reception classes still appear caught between early years developmental principles and key-stage pressures, now exacerbated by the requirements to show that outcomes are improving and gaps are being narrowed at the end of the EYFS. Research has indicated a lack of opportunities for active play, lack of space and equipment, and lack of suitably qualified staff. And in 2008 many reception teachers were, reluctantly, still giving way to pressure to prioritise literacy and numeracy and to drill children in school routines such as lining up and sitting still and listening. Recently, medical research found that levels of the stress hormone cortisol were raised in children six months before they were due to start school, a factor which researchers put down to parents' anxieties affecting their children. However, in the more extrovert children, levels were still high six months after starting school.[55] Similarly, Ofsted claimed that reception-class pupils, boys in particular, lacked the confidence to speak or the ability to listen.[56]

Professor Lilian Katz, the highly respected American early years expert, warned that Britain risked putting children off reading for life if they were forced to learn before they were ready:

> The evidence we have so far is that if you start formal teaching of reading very early the children do well in tests, but when you follow them up to the age of 11 or 12 they don't do better than those who have had a more informal approach. The evidence also suggests starting formal instruction early is more damaging for boys than girls. Boys are expected to be active and assertive but during formal instruction they are being passive not active.[57]

Confirming the need for a more balanced approach, the Review's survey of international research and test data on pupil attainment in England and other countries reported that English pupils' relatively high attainment in reading appeared to be at the expense of their enjoyment of reading. Drawing on the 2001 PIRLS data, the research survey expressed concern 'that England had the highest proportion of children who expressed clearly negative views about reading.'[58]

Arguing against extending the foundation stage upwards are those Review witnesses who believe that children from deprived homes or with unsupportive parents need an early start to literacy if they are to make sufficient progress by age 11. Relatedly, they suggest that the later start may disadvantage the very children who most need help: those in the long tail of under-achievement which is so conspicuous in international comparison and which represents such a waste of individual potential. But this, again, is to equate provision with schooling and mis-interprets how an effective early years curriculum delivered by well-trained practitioners can, as EPPE showed, create sure foundations for the development of language and literacy.

These matters were once again thrown into sharp relief by the recommendation of the Rose Review's interim report that 'entry into reception class in the September immediately following the child's fourth birthday should become the norm.'[59] Anxieties about an excessively early start and the often inappropriate environment of reception classes were widely voiced, as were fears that the change would exacerbate rather than diminish the 'birthdate effect'. The effect is confirmed in international evidence reviewed by Cambridge Assessment:

> The youngest children in their year group perform at a lower level than their older classmates ... In the UK, where the school year starts on September 1st, the disadvantage

is greatest for children born during the summer months (June, July, August) ... The birthdate effect is most pronounced during infant and primary school but the magnitude ... gradually and continually decreases through key stage 3 and 4 ... The disadvantage for August-born children over September-born children in expected attainment dropped from 25% at KS 1 to 12% at KS2 ... and 1% at A level ... The effect remains significant at GCSE.[60]

The review from Cambridge Assessment also reminds us of the two competing explanations for the birthdate effect: length of schooling and relative cognitive, social and emotional levels of maturation. The evidence on the birthdate effect confirms the importance of getting the provision for young children right, whether they are in pre-school settings or school, and of paying close attention to those three identified areas of their development so that any birthdate effect is minimised. But it also underlines the need to pay the closest possible attention to the nature and quality of their experiences during the reception year,

CONCLUSION

The Cambridge Primary Review found widespread appreciation of the huge investment that government has made in early childhood services over the past 11 years, based on an understanding of the importance of their earliest years for children in the here-and-now, and in laying the foundations for all later learning. Many developments have been applauded and have already made a considerable difference to the lives of thousands of children and their parents. They include:

- the expansion of nursery education
- substantial increase in day-care places to meet the needs of working parents
- introduction of local Sure Start schemes and the ambitious programme of developing children's centres in the country's most deprived wards
- emphasis on integrating education, care and health with support and advice for parents
- the introduction of the early years foundation stage
- recognition that parents are their children's first educators and that bringing up children can be challenging and may require support
- priority given to improving the skills of the early years workforce
- introduction of the early years professional status, comparable to qualified teacher status.

There are, however, some challenges in ensuring that early years services are of a sufficiently high quality to be to be effective. The evidence in this chapter shows that quality is still very variable, with much expansion in the private and voluntary sectors where low levels of funding can lead to poorly qualified and poorly paid staff.

Sustainability is an issue across all sectors. As the number of hours to be offered to children increases to 15 a week, and as parents become entitled to a 'flexible offer' to reflect their work commitments, there is concern that not only will it become harder to achieve the improved outcomes because of a lack of continuity, but that the funding will not cover all the costs as the jam is spread ever more thinly.

While research evidence points to the key role that qualified teachers can play in early years settings, particularly with regard to the most vulnerable children, many settings do not employ teachers. Although children's centres are required by law to do so – initially part time then full time within 18 months – it is difficult to prove that this is actually happening and there is some anecdotal evidence that often it is not. The Children's Workforce Development Council is working to increase the number of graduate leaders (the new EYP status) and ensure that all those employed in early years settings are qualified to at least level 3, but there is still a long way to go before this becomes a reality.

The ideal of a children's centre in every community is to be applauded, and could help unify a system still divided between nursery education on the one hand and day-care on the other.

The Neighbourhood Nursery Initiative also showed that such nurseries, many now becoming children's centres, can successfully reach some of the most disadvantaged families.[61] But funding remains an issue, and many centres and nurseries are struggling. As a recent government report said: 'The financial situation of full day care providers within children's centres appeared to have worsened since 2006 with the proportion having made a loss increasing from 37 per cent to 52 per cent in 2007.'[62] In the current financial climate this situation can only get worse.

The EYFS has been broadly welcomed, particularly for its underpinning principles and its curriculum framework of six areas of learning. But there is already evidence, particularly in reception classes, that the well-intentioned requirement to narrow the gap in outcomes for the most vulnerable children is leading to pressure on some early years practitioners to skew the otherwise holistic and balanced curriculum to meet goals that are not all appropriate for all children.

With regard to the length of the foundation phase, the overwhelming consensus from both research and the Review's other evidence is that a high quality pre-school experience benefits all children, particularly those who are disadvantaged or from less supportive homes. And many practitioners believe, again backed by considerable research evidence and the positive examples of many other countries, that the principles that shape effective pre-school education should govern children's experiences in primary school at least until age six, and possibly until age seven. Some primary schools are already extending the foundation stage into the later years and finding that this pays dividends in terms of children's confidence and attainment. Ofsted also reported on the value of extending play into Year 1, while the government acknowledged the strength of these arguments when it commissioned the Rose Review to look at ways of creating a smoother transition between the foundation stage and key stage 1.

With almost all three- to four-year-olds already receiving at least 12.5 hours of early years education a week, the crucial issue becomes not when children 'start school', but when they move from play-based to subject-based or area-based learning. Extending the early years phase to age six or seven would give schools up to three years to work with children to establish positive attitudes to learning and the necessary language and study skills which are crucial to raising standards in the long term. Curiosity and confidence, social and oral skills would be more likely to flourish in what the British Association for Early Childhood Education described as 'play-based developmentally appropriate education and care'. Such a move would also signal an acceptance of the oft-repeated warnings that too-formal-too-soon may be dangerously counterproductive.

Underlying all that we have said on this matter are three important principles. First, the early years of children's development matter enormously, and that is why we have called this chapter 'Foundations'. Second, the early years should not be assumed to be synonymous with provision, statutory or voluntary, which also bears the 'early years' label. Third, what matters is that the country provides for children's early years, both in pre-school/early years settings and during the first part of the primary phase, in a way which fully meets children's needs during those years. That is why arguments about the quality of early years education and care transcend the narrower question of when children should enter compulsory education. If there is a case for an early start, then what matters is that the nature and quality of the provision are right. At the moment, according to our evidence, they are not, and it is not evident that this was fully grasped by the Rose Review when it recommended entry to reception at age four as the norm. One way of addressing the problem is to extend upwards the EYFS, as many of the Review's witnesses argued. Another is to align more exactly the early years as developmental stage and the stages of provision, for example by raising both the EYFS and the school starting age to 6.

We hope that this chapter will provoke a proper debate on these important questions, and in Chapter 24 we translate them into specific proposals for (i) re-aligning the relationship between what we wish to call simply 'the foundation phase' (the current EYFS) and the primary phase, (ii) extending children's entitlement to high quality early years provision, (iii) raising the age at which compulsory primary schooling starts, and (iv) restructuring the current two 'key stages' of primary education into a single, coherent primary phase.

NOTES

1 OECD (2008a).
2 National Audit Office (2004).
3 HM Treasury (2004).
4 DCSF (2008t).
5 DCSF (2008t).
6 Sylva and Pugh (2005).
7 HM Treasury (2004).
8 National Evaluation of Sure Start (2005) National Evaluation of Sure Start (2008).
9 DfES (2005a).
10 DCSF (2007b).
11 Qualifications and Curriculum Authority (2000).
12 David, Goouch, Powell and Abbott (2002).
13 DfES (2007e).
14 DfES (2007e): 9.
15 DfES (2007e): 9.
16 Goswami and Bryant (2010), *The Cambridge Primary Review Research Surveys*, Chapter 6.
17 See Blakemore and Frith (2005).
18 See Gopnik *et al.* (1999).
19 Sylva and Pugh *op cit*: 13.
20 Vygotsky (1978, 1986).
21 Dweck (2006).
22 Schweinhart *et al.* (1993).
23 Ramey and Ramey (1998).
24 Sammons *et al.* (2008).
25 A small informal group of early years experts who advise ministers and DCSF officials.
26 Sylva *et al.* (2004).
27 See Early Childhood Forum (2007).
28 DCFS (2008) Press notice, June 30.
29 R. House *et al.* (July 24, 2008), in an open letter to *The Times*.
30 Sylva *et al.* (2008) *op cit.*
31 Mathers *et al.* (2007).
32 Ofsted (2008d).
33 DCSF (2008t).
34 See Boddy *et al.* (2005).
35 Wheeler and Connor (2006).
36 Evangelou *et al.* (2008).
37 OECD (2001b); OECD (2006).
38 Sanders *et al.* (2005).
39 Woodhead (1989).
40 National Education Union (1870) Verbatim report of the debate in Parliament during the progress of the Elementary Education Bill, quoted in Whitbread (1972).
41 *Ibid.*
42 CACE (1967): para 358.
43 *Ibid.*: para 357.
44 *Ibid.*: paras 385–87.
45 House of Commons (1986).
46 DCSF (2007b).
47 Riggall and Sharp (2010), *The Cambridge Primary Review Research Surveys*, Chapter 14.
48 Rose (2008): recommendation 10.
49 House of Commons Children, Schools and Families Committee (2009).
50 Riggall and Sharp (2010), *The Cambridge Primary Review Research Surveys*, Chapter 14.
51 See the PIRLS website (http://timss.bc.edu/pirls2006/index.html).
52 Ofsted (2003a).
53 Millennium Cohort Study, Centre for Longitudinal Studies, Institute of Education, London (http://www.cls.ioe.ac.uk/mcs/).
54 Adams *et al.* (2004).
55 Turner-Cobb (2007).
56 Ofsted (2007b).
57 L. Katz, from a speech to an Early Years Foundation Stage conference, Oxford University, November 22. Quoted by BBC News Online (22 November 2007) (Available: http://news.bbc.co.uk/1/hi/education/7107798.stm).
58 Whetton *et al.* (2010), *The Cambridge Primary Review Research Surveys*, Chapter 18.
59 Rose (2008): recommendation 10.
60 Sykes *et al.* (2009): 3–4.
61 Smith *et al.* (2007).
62 Nicholson, Jordan, Cooper and Mason (2008): 6.

12 What is primary education for?

Prominent among the questions which the Cambridge Primary Review posed for itself and its witnesses in 2006 were these:

> What is primary education for? To what needs and purposes should it be chiefly directed over the coming decades? What core values and principles should it uphold and advance? Taking account of the country and the world in which our children are growing up, to what individual, social, cultural, economic and other circumstances and needs should it principally attend?

Hinting that the task of defining the aims of primary education was not entirely straightforward, we also asked:

> How far can a national system reflect and respect the values and aspirations of the many different communities – cultural, ethnic, religious, political, economic, regional, local – for which it purportedly caters? In envisaging the future purposes and shape of this phase of education how far ahead is it possible or sensible to look?

This chapter attempts to address these questions. In doing so, it acknowledges four important provisos:

- Educational aims, however self-evident or instrumental they may seem, reside by their nature in the domains of values and even speculation. To define the purposes of primary education, children's future as well as present needs must be considered, and though the future may be predicted it is also in a strict sense unknowable. Even if we can predict future trends with a reasonable degree of certainty, we may not wish simply to accept them as they stand. Some trends we may regard as undesirable and to be discouraged rather than passively accepted as inevitable, while schools will almost certainly wish to advance some values and principles above others. The exercise of defining aims for a national education system, then, is ethical and political, and all such aims are by their nature contestable. Far from being a matter of 'mere common sense' as generations of politicians would have us believe, education is fundamentally a moral pursuit.
- The historical evidence, which we briefly review below, shows that attempts to define official aims for the education system as a whole have a poor track record. The result, all too often, has been a succession of statements so brief or anodyne as to be pointless, and these, more often than not, have been added to policy to give it a cloak of consensus when the true purposes are already pretty apparent in the policies themselves and may be much more partisan politically than is desirable.
- The problem of *post hoc* aims, or of aims as rationalisation rather than rationale, is not unique to government policy. Local authorities and schools have also tended to devise grand statements of aims which have been grafted onto existing policies and practices without regard for their compatibility.

- Yet there is little point in prescribing educational aims unless they shape what schools and teachers do, and what children encounter and experience. In defining aims, values and principles, therefore, there are two challenges: first, to produce a meaningful and viable statement which can command reasonable support in a plural society; second, to ensure that the statement's function is more than rhetorical and that it really does shape what children experience at school.

In this chapter we consider first the aims of primary education as they have been defined in policy over the years, showing how a particular view of the purposes of this phase of education has been sustained, pretty well unchanged, ever since the 1860s and is long overdue for re-assessment; but also showing how that view began to be challenged from the outset. We then contrast these official statements with views received from a wide range of organisations and individuals via the Review's submissions and soundings. Next, we identify problems inherent in existing and earlier specifications of aims, and in current approaches to the task, and suggest ways that they might be overcome. Finally, we propose the Review's own set of aims and principles which, we believe, attend to what matters most at this stage of education. These are then carried forward to provide the basis for our proposals on the curriculum in Chapter 14.

AIMS PAST AND PRESENT

The elementary legacy

As Chapter 3 showed, primary education today is something of a palimpsest and retains the influence of every stage of its earlier development, and it is impossible to overestimate the particular and powerful resonance of those primordial values which shaped the work of the elementary schools of the late nineteenth and early twentieth centuries. There are the obvious structural continuities to which we referred in Chapter 3 – the early starting age, the split between 5–7 and 7–11 (infant/junior, KS1/KS2), the generalist class teacher system, the primary/secondary funding disparity, a curriculum sharply divided between 'the basics' and 'the rest', and the mandatory component of religious education[1] – and it is clear that many of these continue to define the central purposes of primary education.

Thus the Newcastle Commission Report of 1861:

> The duty of a state in public education ... is to obtain the greatest possible quantity of reading, writing and arithmetic for the greatest number.[2]

The Dearing Report of 1993:

> The principal task of the teacher ... is to ensure that pupils master the basics skills of reading, writing and number.[3]

And the 1997 White Paper *Excellence in Schools*:

> The first task of the education service is to ensure that every child is taught to read, write and add up.[4]

Merely to question the continuing hegemony of this view is to court ridicule, for what blocks further discussion is the double whammy of those discourses of dichotomy and derision against which Chapter 2 warned. Thus 'the basics' and the wider curriculum are set in a state of permanent opposition. If teachers do a proper job on one, we are told that they cannot do justice to the other. That, as successive HMI and Ofsted reports have shown, is not only untrue; it is the exact opposite of the conditions which have been shown to be essential for successful learning of 'the basics.'[5]

Literacy and numeracy are fundamental to primary education. There can never be any argument about that. But that does not mean that we may not ask whether, 150 years on from the Newcastle Commission, literacy should still be defined as reading and writing but not talking; or whether mathematics should be reduced to the four rules (or, in the 1997 White Paper's case, to addition alone); or whether literacy and numeracy, however defined, should have absolute parity of time and attention in our primary schools; or whether, in 2009, the question of what is truly 'basic' to young children's education might be re-assessed.

Signs of change: Hadow

The first hint of a change in official thinking about the purposes of primary education came in the 1931 Hadow Report. Prefiguring the Plowden Report of 36 years later, Hadow was intensely pre-occupied with children's growth and development, and with the more liberal thinking on curriculum and pedagogy associated with the American philosopher and educationist John Dewey, whose ideas were directly echoed in Hadow's 'activity and experience rather than knowledge' dichotomy referred to in Chapter 2. For a while, indeed, Dewey and democratic pedagogy turned up in surprising places: during the 1920s, at the time when Sidney and Beatrice Webb visited Russian schools and commended their 'luxuriant experiments', Nadezdha Krupskaya, Lenin's wife, was a strong advocate of American educational progressivism in general and of Dewey in particular.[6]

Thus, and in the sharpest possible contrast to the Newcastle Commission, Hadow's admittedly brief statement on aims said:

> The primary school should not ... be regarded merely as a preparatory department for the subsequent stage, and the courses should be planned and conditioned, not mainly by the supposed requirements of the secondary stage, nor by the exigencies of an examination at the age of eleven, but by the needs of the child at that particular stage in his physical and mental development. The primary school should ... arouse in the pupil a keen interest in the things of the mind and in general culture, fix certain habits, and develop a reasonable degree of self-confidence.[7]

The reference to 'things of the mind and ... general culture' also closely echoes the primacy given in contemporary French educational aims to *la culture générale*.[8] A long way indeed from 'read, write and add up.'

Plowden

For a document picking up Hadow's mantle and widely viewed as visionary, the Plowden Report had surprisingly little to say about aims. Its mere four pages on 'The aims of primary education'[9] offered no coherent steer and, as John White points out in the study of aims commissioned by the Review,[10] it 'swings this way and that'.

Plowden begins by speaking of the need to equip children for their adult lives, in a society facing rapid economic and social change, by highlighting adaptability, tolerance, empathy, respect, being emotionally 'well-balanced' and understanding the responsibilities of citizenship. To these is added what we now call lifelong learning: '[Children] will need throughout their adult life to be capable of being taught, and of learning, the new skills called for by the changing economic scene'.[11] This, however, is a somewhat restricted view of what lifelong learning might entail and overall the Plowden vision, such as it is, appears tacitly to reinforce the old elementary school order of fitting children for a society whose character is determined by others and over whose development they can expect to have little influence.

In any case, Plowden then appeared to throw in the towel, suggesting that 'general statements of aims [are] of limited value ... It is difficult to reach agreement if anything but the broadest terms are used, but formulations of that kind are little more than platitudes ... a pragmatic approach to the purposes of education [is] more likely to be fruitful.'[12] Schools and teachers were therefore to be encouraged to decide their own aims, and to consider the aims implicit in what they were doing, and Plowden believed – or hoped – that the aims thus identified would 'correspond to a recognisable philosophy of education, and to a view of society'.[13]

Then, in a further *volte-face* which instantly doubts the wisdom of this free-for-all, Plowden abandons equivocation and launches its famous credo whose every sentence is redolent of values which are both contestable and largely unexamined:

> A school is not merely a teaching shop. It is a community in which children learn to live first and foremost as children and not as future adults ... The school sets out deliberately to devise the right environment for children, to allow them to be themselves and to develop in the way and at the pace appropriate to them. It tries to equalise opportunities and to compensate for handicaps. It lays special stress on individual discovery, on first hand experience and on opportunities for creative work. It insists that knowledge does not fall into neatly separate compartments and that work and play are not opposite but complementary. A child brought up in such an atmosphere at all stages of his education has some hope of becoming a balanced and mature adult and of being able to live in, to contribute to, and to look critically at the society of which he forms a part.[14]

Yet, hedging its bets, Plowden also commends the traditional virtues of 'neatness, accuracy, care and perseverance, and the sheer knowledge which is an essential of being educated'.[15]

On all this John White comments:

> On the one hand, it reflects the fact that aims no longer emanated from the political community but were the province of professionals in the schools. On the other, it reveals how difficult it is in a national system to avoid national aims altogether. The result is its curious notion that national aims can be abstracted from what schools say they aim at, and its half-hearted attempt at spelling out such national aims, lazily dependent on an amalgam of traditional virtues and progressive nostrums rather than on a more considered and thorough investigation.[16]

However, as Robert Dearden argued in 1968, aims and values thread the entire report, including its well known advocacy of child centredness: 'No advances in policy, no acquisitions of new equipment have their desired effect unless they are in harmony with the nature of the child, unless they are fundamentally acceptable to him.'[17] Even this brief assertion is problematic: it appears to deny the possibility of education as acculturation, and it confuses wants with needs.

Yet, buried in Plowden's somewhat confused discussion of aims is a warning which – knowing what we know about the condition of Britain 40 years on   seems to display a certain prescience:

> About such a society we can be both hopeful and fearful. We can hope that it will care for all its members, for the old as well as the young, for the handicapped as well as the gifted, for the deviant as well as the conformer, and that it will create an environment which is stimulating, honest and tolerant. We can fear that it will be much engrossed with the pursuit of material wealth, too hostile to minorities, too dominated by mass opinion, and too uncertain of its values.[18]

There, in a nutshell, are some of the most prominent anxieties revealed in the Primary Review's 2007–8 soundings and submissions: the loss of intergenerational contact and respect, the canker of greed and consumerism, the cult of shallowness and celebrity, the growing intolerance of ethnic and religious minorities, the contempt for the life of the mind, and the pervasive decline in our sense of who, individually and collectively, we are. It is to these declining social conditions, Plowden and the Cambridge Review witnesses seem to be saying, that primary education must somehow respond.

From Plowden's child to government's pupil

In the ten years following Plowden, its message that schools should determine the aims of primary education continued to hold sway; so much so that the Schools Council commissioned a major project to explicate and codify what teachers had to say on this matter. Patricia Ashton and her colleagues identified the top six teacher-defined aims, in order of priority as:

- Children should be happy, cheerful and well-balanced.
- They should enjoy school work and find satisfaction in their achievements.
- Individuals should be encouraged to develop in their own ways.
- Moral values should be taught as a basis of behaviour.
- Children should be taught to respect property.
- They should be taught courtesy and good manners.[19]

This being the heyday of 'We teach children not subjects' and 'Child not curriculum', teachers in the Ashton survey did not mention the more traditional academic goals that even Plowden had included, concentrating on aims which were behavioural and attitudinal rather than educational. Eight years later, the Schools Council's working paper *Primary Practice* took a similar line in arguing that aims were the teacher's territory and nobody else's, and in the language through which such professionally-distilled aims were expressed.[20] Notwithstanding its somewhat superficial treatment of these matters, *Primary Practice* was endlessly and approvingly cited in local authority and school curriculum policies.

There were other reasons why, by the mid-1970s, the notion that schools should autonomously decide their aims was being challenged, and indeed the catalogue of aims in the Ashton study had come in for a fair amount of criticism on substantive grounds.[21] In 1975 the regime at William Tyndale Primary School in Islington caused a public furore, and a year later Prime Minister James Callaghan's speech at Ruskin College caught this less tolerant mood and mooted the idea of a national 'core curriculum'.

In 1981 the Department of Education and Science proposed a set of aims that would apply nationally and, as a sharp riposte to both Plowden and the teacher-dominated Schools Council, asserted that 'What each school teaches cannot be determined in isolation.'[22] The 1981 aims could not have been more different from those in Ashton's teacher survey:

- To help pupils to develop lively, enquiring minds, the ability to question and argue rationally and to apply themselves to tasks, and physical skills.
- To help pupils to acquire knowledge and skills relevant to adult life and employment in a fast-changing world.
- To help pupils to use language and number effectively.
- To instil respect for religious and moral values, and tolerance of other races, religions, and ways of life.
- To help pupils to understand the world in which they live, and the interdependence of individuals, groups and nations.
- To help pupils to appreciate human achievements and aspirations.[23]

Here knowledge, understanding and intellectual attributes are placed centred-stage, although the rationale for doing so is left unstated and little attention is paid to the development of personal qualities. Meanwhile, Plowden's 'child', with whose unique nature all policies were to be 'in harmony', becomes 'the pupil' whose nature and role it is for the school and the system to define.

ERA and after

Although the 1988 Education Reform Act established a national curriculum which was specified in immense detail, the aims of this monumental structure were brief, anodyne and zeugmatic. 'A balanced and broadly based curriculum', the Act announced:

- promotes the spiritual, moral, cultural, mental and physical development of pupils at the school and of society; and
- prepares pupils at the school for the opportunities, responsibilities and experiences of adult life.[24]

Nobody explained just how, in this formulation, an entire society might develop physically, mentally or morally or for what kinds of 'opportunities, responsibilities and experiences' pupils should be prepared, for it read less as a ringing statement of intent than an afterthought. What mattered, from this point forward, was not the aims of education but the content, and the 10 subjects of the national curriculum provided a framework whose purpose was deemed self-evident. Yet to determine a curriculum and then add educational aims was hardly a logical way to proceed, and primary schools felt particularly constrained by a curriculum which, while lacking a rationale, included extensive and detailed prescriptions of what should be taught at every stage in a child's school career. Indeed, by the late 1990s aims were driven not just by content but also and increasingly by those aspects of the curriculum upon which the national tests at age seven and 11 happened to focus.

However, it should not be supposed that until ERA the logic of aims determining content had been impeccably pursued. Far from it. Many or most of the local authority curriculum statements which eventually emerged in response to the government's Circular 14/77 showed precisely the same disjunction,[25] and it is only fair to acknowledge that the gulf between aims and curriculum, then and now, is but an extension of the general human failing to match practice with aspiration. In human affairs, justification is all too often retrospective.

By the 1990s, teachers were increasingly questioning the purposes of the national curriculum, asking the government to tell them what it was for. In response to these pressures, the Department for Education and Employment and the Qualifications and Curriculum Authority published a statement of aims and values at the beginning of the two national curriculum handbooks,[26] drawing loosely on a consultation for the 1997–98 curriculum review carried out by the National Forum for Values in Education and the Community.[27] This two-page outline of aims and values was structured under two headings: 'values and purposes underpinning the school curriculum' and 'aims for the school curriculum',[28] with the latter largely re-stating the threadbare aims of 1988:

Aim 1:   The school curriculum should provide opportunities for all pupils to learn and to achieve.

Aim 2:   The school curriculum should aim to promote pupils' spiritual, moral, social and cultural development and prepare for the opportunities, responsibilities and experiences of life.[29]

(Note, in Aim 2, that the word 'adult' was dropped from this version of the second 1988 aim). What rendered this statement just as unhelpful as its 1988 predecessor was the small print, which offered a mix of values which in its specifics was generous and sometimes far-sighted, but collectively was confused and occasionally contradictory. Whereas the National Forum for Values had worked hard to secure coherence under the headings of 'the self', 'relationships', 'society' and 'the environment', the QCA's separate consultation of national organisations had yielded a less satisfactory outcome. Faced with a large number of competing submissions on the purposes of education from a variety of special interests, the QCA seems to have tossed them all into the pot, grouping them roughly under the two statutory headings above, regardless of whether in combination they produced a coherent statement. Meanwhile, the much more convincing set of values from the National Forum was consigned to an appendix.

In any event, the 1999 aims were not translated into guiding principles for the revised curriculum. Although they appeared in the national curriculum handbooks, the remainder of each handbook concerned itself with the business of explaining the importance of each subject, its programmes of study, attainment targets and level descriptions, with little attempt to connect these to the general aims presented elsewhere. This was not wholly the case, for three subjects – personal, social and health education, design and technology and citizenship – aligned reasonably well with the National Forum's values. The main emphasis, nevertheless, was on 'laying the foundations of specialist knowledge in their subject so that learners can go more deeply into the field at a later stage'.[30]

The position in 2009

In 2005 the QCA began developing a set of aims for English maintained schools which followed the precedent of earlier schemes in regarding aims as something that could be overlaid onto curriculum content. Under the revisions proposed for secondary schools, the national curriculum's programmes of study were scaled down and schools were to be given greater flexibility in working out their own curricular arrangements. The three overarching aims of the curriculum were to enable young people to become:

- successful learners, who enjoy learning, make progress and achieve
- confident individuals, who are able to live safe, healthy and fulfilling lives
- responsible citizens, who make a positive contribution to society.[31]

Linked to each of these aims were sets of sub-aims (below) and these became statutory for key stages 3 and 4. It was anticipated that they would also become statutory for key stages 1 and 2 but by 2008 this had not happened, partly because the government took control of the primary curriculum review which was to have followed the secondary review. Unlike the 1999 aims outlined in the handbooks, the QCA's aims were logically structured and coherent, and both aims and sub-aims were more closely integrated with the curriculum itself. The curriculum, said the QCA, should enable all young people to become:

successful learners who:
- have the essential learning skills of literacy, numeracy and information and communication technology
- are creative, resourceful and able to identify and solve problems
- have enquiring minds and think for themselves to process information, reason, question and evaluate
- communicate well in a range of ways
- understand how they learn and learn from their mistakes
- are able to learn independently and with others
- know about big ideas and events that shape our world
- enjoy learning and are motivated to achieve the best they can, now and in the future;

confident individuals who:
- have a sense of self-worth and personal identity
- relate well to others and form good relationships
- are self-aware and deal well with their emotions
- have secure values and beliefs and have principles to distinguish right from wrong
- become increasingly independent, are able to take the initiative and organise themselves
- make healthy lifestyle choices
- are physically competent and confident

- take managed risks and stay safe
- recognise their talents and have ambitions
- are willing to try new things and make the most of opportunities
- are able to take the initiative and organise themselves
- are open to the excitement and inspiration offered by the natural world and human achievements;

responsible citizens who:
- are well prepared for life and work
- are enterprising
- are able to work co-operatively with others
- respect others and act with integrity
- understand their own and others' cultures and traditions, within the context of British heritage, and have a strong sense of their own place in the world
- appreciate the benefits of diversity
- challenge injustice, are committed to human rights and strive to live peaceably with others
- sustain and improve the environment, locally and globally
- take account of the needs of present and future generations in the choices they make
- can change things for the better.[32]

The QCA aims were the first statutory aims for education and, potentially, their impact on schools would be profound. The emphasis on the development of personal qualities might serve to counterbalance, or perhaps outweigh, the long-standing focus on test and examination results as a measure of schools' and pupils' performances. In 2009, the aims were too recently introduced – and in primary schools still non-statutory – for their influence to be fully determined. In any case, they were subject to change.

By 2007 the QCA had published a 'big picture of the curriculum' to inform its secondary curriculum review and much was made of this at subsequent QCA events and in its publications, to the extent that it was clearly expected to serve as a template for the Rose primary curriculum review as well. The 'big picture' started with the three headline aims above, tied them to the five outcomes of *Every Child Matters* (be healthy, stay safe, enjoy and achieve, make a positive contribution, achieve economic well-being) and posited a developmental cycle comprising three questions.

- *What* are we trying to achieve?
- *How* do we organise learning?
- *How well* are we achieving our aims?[33]

The other question raised by QCA's 'big picture' is substantive. Is it sufficient for the aims of a national system of education to be reduced to three such generalised outcomes as 'successful learners', 'confident individuals' and 'responsible citizens'? After all, it might be suggested that these are not so much challenging aspirations as minimal expectations. Schools should certainly help their pupils to become successful and confident learners; otherwise they might as well close down. But 'successful' in relation to what, and displaying what kind of 'confidence'? The only one of the three that offers any kind of signpost for the curriculum – for a direct link between aims and curriculum is essential – is 'responsible citizens', which would appear to indicate a place for citizenship and aspects of 'personal, social and health education' (PSHE). It is true that the first aim makes the usual mention of the 3Rs, now expanded for the information age – 'the essential learning skills of literacy, numeracy and information and communication technology' – but a curriculum is, or ought to be, a lot more than that, and in any case we would contest the reduction of such important and complex areas of human endeavour as literacy, numeracy and ICT to 'skill' alone. This is a typical example of that curriculum reductionism on which we shall comment later.

For the rest, there is no sense of what kinds of knowledge, understanding and skill are deemed worthwhile; and in this there is an echo of the list of process-heavy but content-free teachers' aims from the Ashton survey of 1975. One can be a 'successful learner' of matters which are trivial or undesirable, and 'confident individuals' are not immune from arrogance or insensitivity, so as they stand these aims don't take us very far. In other words, apart from the nudge towards citizenship, the remaining two QCA aims leave open the substantive matters with which education should deal, and thus allow the same detachment of curriculum from aims of which John White and others have been so critical.

We might add that Scotland's much-praised *Curriculum for Excellence* has a variant on the QCA aims:

> The purposes of the curriculum 3–18 are to provide the structure and support in learning which will enable [all children and young people] to develop these four capacities:
> - successful learners
> - confident individuals
> - responsible citizens
> - effective contributors[34]

The outcomes listed under each aim are similar but not identical to those in the QCA statement, and the additional aim *effective contributors* highlights attributes like communication, collaboration, initiative, critical thinking and problem solving. Generally, Scotland's list of attributes or 'capacities' are more coherent than those provided by QCA, and under each aim are listed general qualities together with specific behaviours. Under *responsible citizens*, for example, they list the two qualities 'respect for others' and 'commitment to participate in political, economic, social and cultural life' and five behaviours such as 'make informed choices and decisions' and 'develop informed, ethical views of complex issues.'

Matthew Arnold has become an unfashionable figure, and cultural relativists and post-modernists alike tend to be scornful of his high-minded appeal to 'the best that has been thought and said',[35] but it makes little sense to define educational aims without explicit reference to the culture, society and world that children inhabit – the way these currently are, the way they may become, the way they ought to be, and what they offer which is most worthy of exploration in schools and classrooms. Denis Lawton was surely right when he argued that however the curriculum is conceptualised and structured a curriculum remains in the end a 'selection from culture',[36] and culture is conspicuous by its absence from both the QCA and Scottish Government formulations. This applies even – or especially – to the many models of education which claim to look to the future, for no vision of the future, however radical it may seem or claim to be, is more than an extrapolation from past or current trends. We note once again Eric Hobsbawm's warning about today's 'young men and women' living 'in a sort of permanent present lacking any organic relation to the public past of the times they live in', and suggest that far from being outdated, Arnold offers a real challenge to us to define afresh just what it is in our inherited and increasingly complex culture – what knowledge and under-standing, what achievements, what ways of thinking, exploring and acting – which is of most worth and should form the centrepiece of a future curriculum.

At the time of going to press, the latest hints on policy in relation to aims for primary education come from the reports of the Rose Review on the primary curriculum. As anticipated, Rose has accepted existing statements as they stand. Thus the interim Rose report says, somewhat tautologously: 'The Children's Plan is the platform on which this Review is based. This is because the aims and values for primary education must be seen in the light of the Children's Plan.'[37]

There are several rather unsatisfactory features of the Rose Review's treatment of aims. The interim report recommends that 'The revised primary curriculum should be underpinned by a statement of aims and values which is fit for all stages of education',[38] which encourages readers of what is supposedly a consultation document to see the debate as open; but the report then not only insists on the primacy of the Children's Plan but adds: 'Although this Review will continue to test views upon it and comment in the final report, the statement of aims for secondary education compares well with its international counterparts and holds good for the primary phase and indeed the EYFS.'[39] Then, as further and final discouragement to readers to entertain the possibility of alternatives, Rose builds the DCFS/QCA secondary aims firmly into its structure for the revised primary curriculum[40] and adds (our italics) that 'each programme [for Rose's six "areas of learning"] *must show, explicitly*, how the area of learning helps all children to become ...' Then follow the three main secondary aims.

In his final report, Rose mentions the arguments here (which were included in our special report on the curriculum, published in February 2009 as a contribution to the debate about the interim Rose report), and then diagrammatically compares the QCA and Cambridge aims and finds a 'considerable match'.[41] We find this astonishing, and can only conclude that the Rose Review's QCA advisers contented themselves with the headings of our 12 aims and did not read the detail. In truth, there are important differences. Unsurprisingly, Rose goes on to confirm his view that the QCA secondary aims should be adopted for both phases.[42]

So the government's curriculum review allows no room for debate here, either about the aims as such or whether an identical set is appropriate for early years, primary and secondary. Yet so much is taken for granted – about the efficacy of a well-received but untried Children's Plan, about the wisdom of validating one country's aims by reference to another's, about making aims uniform across educational stages, about the usefulness of the existing QCA secondary aims in any context – that to proceed without proper debate in this vital area is wholly wrong. Above all, bringing together educational aims conceived for one context and a view of the curriculum conceived for another, in the hope that they will more or less fit, is the antithesis of the proper approach. Aims, values and priorities for primary education should be sorted out first; the curriculum should then be devised to enact and implement them. With the Rose Review, as on all previous occasions, the curriculum was devised first and aims were added.

The Cambridge Primary Review is not so constrained. In this chapter we reach our recommended twelve aims for primary education after considering evidence received from a wide variety of sources, not only on aims as such but also on the on the contingent questions listed at the start of this chapter. It must be said, too, that on the condition of childhood, Britain and the world today, many of our witnesses expressed hopes and concerns which translated readily into values and aims which bear little relation to the QCA secondary school aims which the Rose Review suggests should be accepted as a basis for the primary and EYFS curriculum. The issue here is partly the secondary backwash problem – later stages of education determining rather than building on earlier stages – for although aims should be consistent from one stage to the next there is no reason why they should be identical; but there is also the matter, considered above, of the validity of the QCA aims themselves. Were they to be completely satisfactory, they could indeed serve as a uniting framework for the whole of compulsory education, and could be combined with separate sets of aims highlighting the distinctive developmental and educational needs and tasks of each phase.

For example, while the independent Nuffield review of 14–19 education shares Rose's opinion that there should be a single set of aims for the whole education system, it does so more convincingly than QCA. Rather than identifying minimal learning outcomes it addresses the larger question of what might be the characteristics of an educated person, identifying first a number of *individual* characteristics (intellectual development, practical capability, community participation, moral seriousness, pursuit of excellence, self-awareness) and balancing these with the *communal* goals of social justice and citizenship.[43]

WHAT THE REVIEW'S WITNESSES SAID

The Review's submissions and soundings gave a detailed picture of the beliefs, principles, aims and values held by a wide spectrum of people and organisations, both within and outside education. In analysing this opinion-based evidence, it was apparent that though views varied widely the following recurrent themes could be identified:

- the 3Rs and beyond
- the 'whole child'
- faith and spirituality
- balancing individual and societal needs
- community and citizenship
- addressing disadvantage
- global awareness and concern about the future

The 3Rs and beyond

Some submissions described the acquisition of basic skills (principally, literacy and numeracy) as the main purpose of primary education. In particular, children's submissions linked learning to read, write and be numerate to their future adult lives and work. However, in the community soundings sessions, children said that they wanted more than 'the basics' alone. They wanted breadth in the curriculum, enabling them to learn about the wider world. Whilst most submissions from adult individuals and organisations also acknowledged the value of the 3Rs in their own right, they suggested that the development of these skills should open the door to wider opportunities. One head teacher suggested:

> The purpose of primary education should be to give children the skills to be able to access higher, more specialised education. This means literate and numerate children, in whom the innate thirst for learning is developed and encouraged.

Unsurprisingly, the link between basic skills and the workplace was emphasised in submissions from employment organisations and the Trades Union Congress (TUC). However, many practitioners and organisations argued that basic skills encompassed a wider range of capabilities than the 3Rs: in particular, knowing 'how to learn' and how to communicate effectively were seen as essential foundations for later learning. Teaching assistants taking part in the community soundings wanted schools to concentrate on the 'basics' of literacy, numeracy and ICT, but not to confine their priorities to these skills. No less important, they argued, were the 'life skills' of communication, successful relationships with others, and independent thinking, and they were particularly concerned that schools should arrest a perceived decline in the quality of children's spoken language.

The 'whole child'

For many, the 3Rs, though vital, were not enough. Submissions frequently argued that the main purpose of primary education was to develop the 'whole child'. Teacher submissions often spoke of the importance of fostering each child's personal, social and emotional development and well-being, and of the need to secure a positive future. Submissions from some national organisations stressed that primary education should enhance children's enthusiasm, joy, curiosity, skills, self-confidence, interpersonal skills, empowerment and understanding of the world. All of these were perceived to provide children with a secure foundation for the future, establishing the skills and knowledge necessary for achieving their aspirations. Parents, too, were concerned that schools should help children to become 'well-rounded' human beings rather than focusing too heavily on performance standards. One parent's submission warned:

> I do not relish being looked after in my older years by a generation, all of whom have level 5 in their SATs, 5A* GCSEs, but who will not be nice to me or each other and who will

not value or seek to invest in relationships which hold communities and ultimately society in place.

During several of the community soundings adults deplored contemporary children's lack of independence. Some proposed that an important aim for education was developing children's 'autonomous thinking', 'the capacity to make reasoned choices', 'personal responsibility' and 'respect for themselves'. Community representatives at one sounding suggested that children's existing skills and abilities often went unrecognised and therefore they were not afforded the chance to develop them (a similar point was made in the research survey commissioned from Professor Berry Mayall[44]). The idea that children should have a greater say in decision-making in schools was put forward in several submissions. Several referred specifically to the United Nations Convention on the Rights of the Child and one suggested that the convention itself offers a suitable framework for education. Some submissions drew attention to particular articles in the Convention. Article 3 stipulates that the interests of the child must come first in decision-making; Article 12 states that children have a right to express their views on matters that concern their lives; Article 23 says that children with disabilities must be given access to suitable educational provision; while Article 29.1 states:

The education of the child shall be directed to:

(a) The development of the child's personality, talents and mental and physical abilities to their fullest potential;
(b) The development of respect for human rights and fundamental freedoms, and for the principles enshrined in the Charter of the United Nations;
(c) The development of respect for the child's parents, his or her own cultural identity, language and values, for the national values of the country in which the child is living, the country from which he or she may originate, and for civilisations different from his or her own;
(d) The preparation of the child for responsible life in a free society, in the spirit of understanding, peace, tolerance, equality of sexes, and friendship among all peoples, ethnic, national and religious groups and persons of indigenous origin;
(e) The development of respect for the natural environment.[45]

Several submissions also pointed to the importance of listening closely to pupils: for example, the National Union of Teachers said that the pupils' voice is integral to enhancing their education (for further discussion of pupil voice see Chapter 10).

Faith and spirituality

As would be expected, faith organisations advanced specific views on the role of religion in education and placed spiritual development at the heart of the curriculum. Community representatives at one sounding were concerned that schools too slavishly adopted society's predominantly secular aims and material aspirations and looked for success 'at all costs', relegating faith and spiritual development to the margins. In a similar vein, the submission from the Sri Sathya Sai World Foundation called for education to be, 'expanded from its emphasis on the secular to encompass the spiritual'. While some groups called for more faith schools, arguing that they would provide the most appropriate setting for teaching about the tenets and heritage of particular faiths, others argued that all schools should give greater attention to the fact of religious faith, the form that it takes, and alongside these to humanism and non-religious world views in order to develop children's awareness, understanding and tolerance of different beliefs. The submission from the Association of RE Inspectors, Advisors and Consultants, for example, pointed out: 'We live in a multi-faith society and children need to be prepared to live in this plural context'. In a similar vein, the submission from the

Churches Together in England and Free Church Education Unit said that children needed to be taught:

> Respect for others (not just tolerance), a positive attitude to learning, a sense of self worth, a sense of their own place within the world and an appreciation of cultural, religious and social identity.

Arguments for education developing children's sense of spirituality came from some non-religious organisations, including the British Humanist Association:

> We believe that the notion of 'spiritual development' (though perhaps an unhelpful phrase, carrying as it does, religious baggage) as promoted by the national curriculum and by Ofsted is a helpful one in capturing the wider development of the child that we want to see in primary schools. As a BHA leaflet of 1993 put it: ' … the spiritual dimension comes from our deepest humanity. It finds expression in aspirations, moral sensibility, creativity, love and friendship, response to natural and human beauty, scientific and artistic endeavour, appreciation and wonder at the natural world, intellectual achievement and physical activity, surmounting suffering and persecution, selfless love, the quest for meaning and purpose by which to live.' We would be happy if we thought that primary school education was contributing to pupils' development in these areas.

Balancing individual and societal needs

While the focus on individual needs is a prominent theme in contemporary educational debate, and was evidenced in a wide range of current policy (from *Every Child Matters* through to the promotion of 'personalised learning'), some submissions argued that it was important to recognise that education serves both the individual and society. Some parents, for example, suggested that while education should aim to help children to become 'good people', it should also ensure that they are able to make positive contributions to society. The need to balance individual and societal objectives appeared in many submissions, although there were differences in how this balance was envisaged. Some head teachers felt that education starts with children learning about themselves, both as learners and as people, and that this allows them to 'appreciate their own humanity and that of others'. No less concerned about the societal dimension of education, children themselves suggested that it was about learning how to behave and they stressed the importance of having respect for other people, for authority and the law.

Parents at the community soundings believed that children no longer respected authority and they argued that schools needed to have stricter disciplinary procedures for pupils who were disruptive or disobedient. In fact, the word 'respect' was used more frequently by parents than by any other community soundings group. In meeting after meeting parents deplored the loss of respect in society, especially among the young, and therefore commended, as guiding values for schools:

- respect for oneself;
- respect for peers and adults;
- respect for other generations;
- respect for difference;
- respect in the use of language;
- respect for courtesy and good manners;
- respect for the environment, both globally and locally.

In contrast, senior teachers who took part in the community soundings said that the values at home and at school were often markedly different and that schools faced a dilemma when parents did not support their attempts to discipline children. The buck, they argued, was being passed from parents to schools.

Community and citizenship

The submission on behalf of the United Synagogue Agency for Jewish Education also cited respect as a fundamental purpose of education and this was described in terms of developing children's collective, social and moral responsibility, community involvement and political literacy.

Appropriately adopting a local perspective, local authorities' submissions suggested that the focus of primary education should be on children as future members of their communities, a point that was reiterated in the submission from the National Association of Head Teachers, echoing Plowden, 'At the heart of the education process lies the child ... (and) a good primary school is the heart of its local community'. Members of one higher education institution took this argument further in proposing that education should provide 'the skills to build strong communities in which optimism is able to flourish, relationships are strengthened and regeneration can take place'.

Meanwhile, witnesses at the community soundings suggested that primary schools provided constancy and stability in a world where values often seem fluid and uncertain. Community representatives said that primary schools were often the only places where children and adults could eat and talk together and children themselves valued their schools as 'communities-within-communities'. One senior management team expressed the countervailing values of school and the wider world precisely and starkly: selfishness, retaliation and survival outside the school; caring, mutual respect, negotiation and arbitration within it. Governors and parents also argued for schools to celebrate and model community.

Alongside community, the notion of citizenship also featured prominently, as fleshed out here in the submission from the Commission for Racial Equality:

> Citizenship education should aim to not only provide skills for children and young people for life as a citizen, but also the opportunities to exercise citizenship, which should also be evident throughout the wider curriculum. By this, we mean skills for engagement in public debate, which offer opportunities to participate in debates on school, local, national and international issues.

Addressing disadvantage

There was extensive concern about the widening gap in children's attainment and its alignment with poverty and social disadvantage. Many submissions argued strongly that one of the foremost aims of a national system of education must be to redress social inequality, ensuring that all children achieve their full potential. There was agreement that educational disadvantage and social disadvantage are linked and some broached the question of whether and how education can tackle these inequalities. Some felt that the best response was for the state to take greater responsibility for children's lives and there were calls for intervention as early as possible to ameliorate the effects of poverty, poor housing, homelessness, parental neglect and ill-health. One local authority submission noted:

> Not all children are in a position to access education easily when they are living in social deprivation (poor diet, family break up). However good the provision, if the children are not ready to learn this is a real barrier.

Some organisations voiced their belief that education could redress inequality, although there was also a recognition that schools could not 'do everything on their own'. An education consultant proposed that though tackling inequalities was an important aim for primary schools it must be part of a wider strategy for combating the impact of disadvantage:

Research shows ... that if gains made in the pre-school years are not to fade, there is a need for investment in primary settings, using targeted, evidence-based approaches aimed at tackling inequalities in language, literacy, numeracy and social and emotional skills. Evidence suggests that what works are approaches which simultaneously target home, schools and community – working at the level of the child's family relationships, social relationships and success in school.

Material desires and global needs

Some witnesses moved beyond community and nation to argue for a global perspective in which education's two most fundamental aims should be integrating humanity and protecting the environment. Some organisations believed that schools should balance responsiveness to rapid change in a competitive society with the need to provide children with a stable and positive learning environment.

Commercialism and materialism were prominent themes, and they provoked strong views. Head teachers at more than one community sounding felt that consumerism, materialism and the cult of celebrity were having a negative influence on children's attitudes, beliefs and behaviour and that schools must consciously challenge such transient values and their consequences. School governors suggested that schools need to teach children how to handle the pressures of commercialism and the media, and do more to counter materialism and the urge for immediate gratification. One local authority submission expressed this vividly: 'Society is too much *me, me* and *I want it now!*'

Uncertainty about the future led some to argue that education needs to prepare children to cope with the challenges and changes ahead. Many were concerned that the employment market that children would eventually enter is highly unpredictable and that no one can say what skills and knowledge it will require. As one teacher said:

> It has been fairly identified that at present we do not know what 80 per cent of the jobs will be in 20 years time. In this case ... it is important that we make sure that children learn the necessary skills that will provide them with the ability successfully to transfer these skills in a range of situations.

In response to these uncertainties, many submissions felt that schools should equip children with a set of skills that would enable them to adapt. One individual argued:

> The speed of change means that children should be helped to develop problem-solving skills, flexibility and creativity in order to prepare them for the world they will face and the knowledge economy that the UK depends on.

Others, such as this education consultant, felt that preparing for the future held too many unknowns:

> We don't know exactly what our students will need for the world into which they will go. There will be paradox; there will be situations when the answers are not known requiring new and previously unknown solutions; and there will be a need for lifelong learning. Unfortunately we don't know what the paradoxes will be, we do not know what the situations are for which the answers will be not known, and we don't know what it is that we will have to learn, unlearn or relearn.

While the economy and job market were predominant concerns, some also suggested that encouraging children to be optimistic was essential. The community soundings with children, and their written submissions, showed that many young people are worried about the future, although there was also a readiness to tackle the challenges ahead. One submission from an educational researcher argued that schools should aim to support children's positive outlook:

> I believe that it is imperative that, as educators, we strive to help our children to maintain optimism without naivety, to help them to develop knowledge and a willingness to act appropriately while maintaining their sense of personal security and their hopes for the future. This is no easy task when we, and they, are bombarded by apocalyptic visions of what that future might hold.

However, there were also calls for children to be made aware of the dangers, as well as the opportunities, that new technologies bring. Head teachers at one community sounding said that it was important to recognise that new technologies gave children greater and more immediate access to the world than was available to previous generations, and schools therefore have a vital role in helping children to make critical judgements on how these media are used.

A finding in the Review's community soundings report which attracted considerable attention when published in October 2007 was the way schools could counter the sense of hopelessness and pessimism which children's awareness of the condition of British society and the wider world might too readily provoke. On the one hand, we recorded:

> What is ... striking is the pessimistic and critical tenor of much that we heard ... Thus, we were frequently told children are under intense and perhaps excessive pressure from the policy-driven demands of their schools and the commercially-driven values of the wider society; that family life and community are breaking down; that there is a pervasive loss of respect and empathy both within and between generations; that life outside the school gates is increasingly insecure and dangerous; that the wider world is changing, rapidly and in ways which it is not always easy to comprehend, though on balance they give cause for alarm, especially in respect of climate change and environmental sustainability; that the primary school curriculum is too narrow and rigid; that the curriculum and children's educational careers are being compromised by the national tests, especially the Key Stage 2 SATs; that while some government initiatives, notably *Every Child Matters*, are to be warmly welcomed, others may constrain and disempower rather than enable; and that the task facing teachers and other professionals who work with children is, for these and other reasons, much more difficult now than it was a generation ago.[46]

But, the report continued:

> [Yet] pessimism turned to hope when witnesses felt they had the power to act. Thus, the children who were most confident that climate change need not overwhelm them were those whose schools had decided to replace unfocussed fear by factual information and practical strategies for energy reduction and sustainability. Similarly, the teachers who were least worried by national initiatives were those who responded to them with robust and knowledgeable criticism rather than resentful compliance, and asserted their professional right to go their own way. There is an important lesson from such empowerment for governments with centralising tendencies, as well as for primary schools themselves. Given that some witnesses complained that primary teacher training courses train for compliance with the national strategies and little more, there is also food for thought here for teacher education institutions and the Training and Development Agency for Schools (TDA). Of course, not even the most enterprising school can reverse some of the social trends which worried many of our witnesses. That being so, these community soundings have implications for social and economic policy more generally, and for public attitudes and values, not merely for DCSF and the schools.[47]

THE AIMS GAME: PROBLEMS AND POSSIBLE SOLUTIONS

Government, parents and teachers: contrasting visions

The contrast between official and public views of the purposes of primary education, as illustrated above, is striking. Where official specifications – at least until recently – have remained fixated on the narrowly instrumental, teachers, parents and the wider public are ready to entertain a much more generous vision. This does not mean that they deny the importance of securing literacy and numeracy – far from it – but they seem much more closely attuned than government to wider aspects of children's development and education, and to the social and global conditions which need to be addressed if children are to have a future worth looking forward to. This, perhaps, is inevitable, for in contrast to the notorious short-termism of governments, many of today's parents – to take just one prominent theme in our evidence – are painfully aware of what their children may face by the middle of this century, when they are only in their forties. By then, according to authoritative estimates, unchecked global warming may have tipped the world beyond the point of no return, plunging humanity into a crisis at once ecological, economic, political and social, and on a scale that can be barely imagined.[48] It is today's children, on this pessimistic but respected projection, who will have to cope with what past generations have created and failed to deal with. In a very real sense, they are the sons and daughters on whom the sins of the figurative father will be visited. That is why, in ways which our evidence so readily and clearly demonstrates, for others than government the neo-elementary vision of primary education is simply not good enough.

What is also notable about the Review's submissions and soundings is their strong commitment to human rights and social justice, and to values through which these might be pursued. The UN Rights of the Child were widely endorsed as an educational template. Many witnesses were exercised by the extent of material and social disadvantage in England and believed that education must somehow work to reduce it. Others believed that the prevailing values of consumerism and celebrity actively worked against a more just society. If there is an official view that the aims of primary education are a matter of mere 'common sense', those who contributed to the soundings and submissions did not share it. For them, education was pre-eminently a moral matter.

Having said all this, the 2008 QCA aims reviewed earlier do appear to mark a departure from the neo-elementary formula. This must be acknowledged and warmly welcomed. However, on past form there may remain a gulf between the relative breadth and generosity of the QCA statement and government intentions. After all, during most of the period when the September 2000 version of the national curriculum applied – and it included the broad statement of values from the National Forum for Values in Education and the Community referred to earlier – ministers lost no opportunity to tell the nation on prime time radio and television that the sole task of primary schools was to teach children 'to read, write and add up.' Equally, the statutory commitment to a broad and balanced curriculum was flouted in 1998 when the government suspended the KS1/2 programmes of study in the non-core subjects, and the witnesses generally agreed that this commitment has been compromised since then by the combination of the national strategies and the pressure of the KS2 tests. This strongly suggests that for government a written statement of national aims may be no more than window dressing and that it may be overruled by the policy preoccupation of the moment. Governments, at least as they have latterly operated, do not seem to be up to the task of defining educational aims.

Not just adults in the making

Official statements of aims tend tacitly to conceive of education as preparation – 'to prepare for the opportunities, responsibilities and experiences of life' in the words of the 1988 and 1996 Acts. Again, the importance of ensuring that primary education gives children the knowledge and skills to gain full benefit from subsequent education, and to gain a worthwhile and rewarding job, cannot be underestimated. However, in looking only to the future we are in danger of failing to understand that young children have needs here and now, while they are growing up, and that if these are not addressed their prospects are likely to be diminished.

For example, Chapter 5 argued that schools should take greater account of children's lives outside school and build on what they come to know, understand and accomplish at home with parents, siblings and friends, or in the community. Chapter 7 revisited research on how children develop and learn, revealing a number of clear and pressing educational imperatives: the primacy in successful learning of social interaction and of teacher-pupil and pupil-pupil talk which is linguistically rich and cognitively challenging; the importance of creativity not in the popular (and misguidedly narrow) sense of art lessons but as a cognitively demanding process which supports perseverance and problem-solving, and enhances children's emotional, moral and – by some definitions – spiritual development; the need to understand young children's emotional vulnerability and for schools, classrooms, teaching and the curriculum to provide experiences which deliberately pattern and encourage sound relationships, emotional strength and a sense of security; the importance of reflecting in every aspect of schooling what we now know about the power of pupil voice to secure real engagement in learning and the basis for active citizenship.

All this dictates that a statement of aims for primary education should balance children's future educational and employment needs with their developmental and educational needs during the primary phase itself. As shown above, that imperative of balance was well conveyed in many of the Primary Review's submissions and soundings.

LEVELS OF AIMS

One size does not fit all

Official approaches to the specification of aims display confusion about what it is appropriate for governments to prescribe and how far such inevitably generalised statements are able to shape what happens at local and school levels. What is needed is a more careful delineation of the respective and proper contributions to the process of those who operate at different levels in the education system.

National

Though this report has commented on a tendency to excessive instrumentality in government thinking, we readily recognise the weight of evidence which demonstrates the economic returns of a good education. The Review's research survey by Stephen Machin and Sandra McNally of LSE noted that:

- The acquisition even of very basic skills in numeracy and literacy has an important effect on the probability of employment and on wages.
- There is good evidence of larger than average wage returns for additional years of schooling.
- There are higher wage returns to academic than to vocational qualifications, and low-level vocational qualifications yield little return.
- There is evidence of important effects of education on individual outcomes beyond the labour market, for example in health, crime and civic engagement.[49]

However, while this appears to underline the current emphasis on the 3Rs, the fourth point hints at the impact of wider aspects of education.

It is appropriate and right for government to provide a general statement on the aims of the education system as a whole, though not to seek to determine the aims of individual schools. The focus of such a statement, backed by appropriate infrastructure and resources, would be what the country needs from its primary schools for future economic and social progress. In return, government should spell out the principles by which its own work is underpinned.

One existing example of principles along the latter lines is provided in the 2000 national curriculum's statement of 'values, aims and purposes'. This said:

> The Secretary of State meets his responsibilities ... by providing a national framework which incorporates the national curriculum, religious education and other statutory requirements ... [in order] to enable all schools to respond effectively to national and local priorities, to meet the individual learning needs of all pupils and to develop a distinctive character and ethos rooted in their local communities.[50]

The statement went on to list 'the four main purposes of the national curriculum: 'to establish an entitlement, to establish standards, to promote continuity and coherence, to promote public understanding'.[51]

The parenthesised words indicate what we take to be the intended thrust of this statement – balancing the national and the local. On the basis of what we have discussed, and given the weight of evidence about the impact of the post-1988 drive to centralisation, the government should concentrate on the national framework, for it is neither appropriate nor feasible for government to tell schools precisely how 'to respond to national and local priorities; still less how 'to meet individual learning needs and to develop a distinctive [local] character and ethos'.

Having said that, if national aims have no impact on the education and lives of individuals then they serve a limited purpose. If we take the parallel examples of the National Health Service and local authority children's services, the goals and targets set by central government, and the resources provided, are all there, clearly, for the benefit of individuals. And it is essential that if local provision fails in some way government should be able to step in, for there is no other court of appeal and the problem may well be systemic. In the domain of child protection, tragic cases ranging from Maria Colwell in 1973 to 'Baby P' in 2008 illustrate that government must have the right, and the responsibility, to intervene. With schools, too, it is no less essential that professional autonomy should not mean condoning mediocrity, for, again, the victims are individual children. After visiting a failing school in 1997, chief inspector Mike Tomlinson said, 'I don't give a monkey's toss for the teachers. All I care about is the children'.[52] He was roundly criticised by the unions, and his words, albeit colourful, were ill-chosen; but we know what he meant, and the priorities he was signalling for the education system. Ours is a public system of education, and public accountability – to parents, communities and government, and by government as well as schools – is essential.

Local

Since 1988, much of the power granted to local authorities by the 1944 Act has been transferred to central government or – in the case of budgetary management – to schools. On the strength of research and inspection evidence about the conduct of some LEAs (as they then were), and of their collective attitude to government's legitimate need to know how they were fulfilling their statutory responsibilities in respects of the curriculum (the Circular 14/77 episode noted in Chapter 3), some might argue that they brought this reversal on themselves. Nevertheless, Britain does have a system of local government, with local democratic procedures and local authority children's services. At best, local authority elected representatives and officials know their communities and schools and are deeply committed to them. Outstanding and outstandingly-led local authorities – ranging from the old West Riding under Alec Clegg in the 1960s to Birmingham under Tim Brighouse during the 1990s – can galvanise schools and secure impressive advances in the quality of their work, as well as in educational standards as more narrowly defined. These examples, and there are others, are there to be studied and emulated.

On this basis, national government might specify the aims for the national system, and the principles by which its work might be guided. A local authority might specify what the local community, in all its diversity, needs from its local network of primary schools in order to advance communal vitality and cohesion, and it should also propose principles which make visible the way it intends to support schools in their part of the enterprise. But, again, it is neither right nor feasible for either government or local authorities to tell schools exactly what to do.

The Review's approach to the curriculum in Chapter 14 will show how, through the combination of a 'national' and a 'community' curriculum, national and local can be more appropriately balanced and effectively represented.

School

Following this argument, it is for schools to translate national and local aims and principles into meaningful specific statements to guide everyday practice, and which secure that vital balance, outlined above, between the needs of society and the needs of the individual, and between the future needs of the adult and the present needs of the child. Only at the level of the school can such judgements be made, for the school knows the children and families who are its raison d'être and can judge – in partnership with them – what each child needs in other than the generalised sense of what all children have in common (which is a great deal) and what the aims of primary education as a whole should be. This kind of detail is not for central government, the QCA, or the national strategies – the very name of the latter eschews the local, communal and individual – nor even for local authorities. The focus for aims at the school level, then, should be the needs of the children in each school – these particular children, in this particular community. However, localism must never be blinkered, and school aims should be consciously framed by those specified locally and nationally; and schools should not forget that there are many ways in which parents and carers know their children far better than teachers ever can. The principles may be clear but the balance is less easily struck.

Global

This is the additional element, and to some acclimatised to the traditional and comforting primary nexus of child, home and school it may seem inappropriate and perhaps even threatening. Yet government repeatedly and rightly reminds us of the need for education to address the imperatives of economic and informational globalisation, while many of the Review's witnesses issued darker warnings about global inequality and the fragility of that proper and selfless sense of global interdependence on which the survival of everyone seems likely to depend. From whichever point one starts, and however one defines it, a global dimension in 21st century education is essential.

The Review's research survey on changing global contexts for primary education by Rita Chawla-Duggan and John Lowe reminded us that since the 1990 Jomtien Declaration, the 2000 Dakar Framework and the publication of the United Nations Millennium Development Goals, the universalisation of primary education by 2015 has become a global objective.[53] Universalisation is pursued because education is deemed a basic human right and is one of the most potent means available for addressing so many other international challenges: gender equality and female empowerment, childhood mortality; the scourges of HIV/Aids and malaria; environmental sustainability.

But there is another side to this. For many, especially those who operate daily in the political and business arenas, the true face of globalisation is not benign interdependence but cut-throat competition:

> ... the use of education to enable one national economy to outsmart another ... Globalisation may lead to tensions and even contradictions in national education policy as 'social

justice' competes with 'social cohesion for the sake of stability' and 'individualism, the market and meritocracy.'[54]

Such competition is regularly manifested not so much in the rhetoric of 'world class schools' as in the breast-beating which follows the publication of England's ranking in the latest survey of educational achievement, as measured by TIMSS, PISA, PIRLS or their heavily-acronymed successors. In turn, and again as one of the Review's research surveys warned:

> The goal of national global competitiveness has … led to standards being defined largely and relatively unquestioningly in terms of what is most marketable, even though what constitute standards and quality in education ought to be a matter for debate … The consequent narrowing of the entire discourse of education is recognised only in some quarters as a risk.[55]

There would thus seem to be a choice:

> There are two broad senses in which the architects of a national education system can think internationally. They can view the world as an essentially competitive arena of trade and influence and use education in order to maximise national advantage – economic, scientific, technological, ideological, military – over other countries. Alternatively, they can apply a more genuinely international outlook (international rather than contra-national), acknowledging that global interdependence carries moral obligations from which no country is immune; and that education can serve to unite rather than divide.[56]

Lest this be taken as lapsing into one of those dichotomies deplored in Chapter 2, it should be noted that an increasing number of experts and commentators believe we must and can outgrow the kind of thinking that leads some national leaders to oppose action on global warming because it is not in their country's short-term economic interests, and that we need urgently to understand that tackling climate change and working towards sustainability make sound economic sense. That, certainly, is the central thesis of the Stern Report[57] and it is why government advisers like Jonathon Porritt argue that sustainable development can and should stand as an absolute and inalienable principle for the full range of government policy, including education.[58]

Yet a debate is needed on exactly what, in the context of primary education, the 'global dimension' should mean. In this matter England might look north. Scotland, with its rather different education system, has pioneered global awareness in its *Curriculum for Excellence*. Interestingly, it sees global awareness not as free-floating, but as an essential feature of citizenship. The Scottish citizen is also a world citizen:

> The global dimension recognises that we now live in an interdependent global society. It incorporates key concepts of human rights, diversity, conflict resolution, social justice, interdependence and sustainable development in an international context. It is an essential component of developing responsible global citizens. It contributes to young people's awareness of the role of values in public life, and supports the development of young people as effective contributors, successful learners and confident individuals.[59]

The idea that global awareness is an essential aspect of a modern definition of citizenship is relatively new. It did not feature at all in the 2000 national curriculum's specification for citizenship at key stages 1 and 2, which had a slant which today looks somewhat parochial. Now, as they say, the global is local, and in the approach fostered by Oxfam for teachers in England, 'the focus is what links us to other peoples, places and cultures' and the 'global citizen' is one who not only knows about the world but is morally committed to making it 'a more equitable and sustainable place.'[60]

Aims, objectives, targets, values and principles

At this point, and before embarking on the Review's own tentative statement of aims, it is as well to clarify the terminology of this part of the educational landscape. An *aim* we take to be a broad statement of purpose, a road to travel rather than the terminal point represented by those *objectives* which translate aims into specific actions. Both are underpinned by *values* which represent essentially moral standpoints on human behaviour, whether individual or collective. A *target* is something rather different: targets are what governments are fond of setting for others to achieve, and they are typically formulated numerically and temporally: for example, the percentage of children nationally and/or in each LEA who must achieve a given score in a national test by a specified date.

Meanwhile, *principles* speak to a rather different approach and to an earlier and more considered discourse. Amid the heated debate of the 1960s about behavioural objectives, and at a time when no self-respecting school or LEA was without its list of 'aimsandobjectives' (the two were rarely differentiated and so might just as well have been a single word), Richard Peters and Lawrence Stenhouse argued for 'principles of procedure': that is, rules or standards of individual or collective conduct.[61] These focused attention not on some vague point in the distant future but on the ethical basis on which schools, teachers and pupils (and, for that matter, governments) act *now*. Instead of encouraging, as long-term aims all too readily may, the separation of action from intention, of deed from word and of reality from what, because of this, is termed mere 'rhetoric', principles of procedure say: 'Rather than confine ourselves to grand statements of intent, we are going to spell out, clearly and simply, the values and principles by which our everyday conduct will be guided and against which it may be judged. If we succeed in acting in accordance with these principles, the aims are more likely to be achieved than if we merely state them and hope for the best. The principles, then, light our path to the achievement of the aims.' The idea is well worth re-consideration. There is some overlap between principles and aims, in that both are informed by values, but the distinction, though slightly untidy, remains useful.

We now draw together the threads by proposing for discussion an alternative framework to those with which we are more familiar, including the 2007 QCA secondary aims which the Rose Review – unwisely in our view – recommends should apply to primary education also.[62] In doing so, we separate educational aims from the principles which guide the work of those who in different ways are responsible for ensuring that the aims are achieved. We start with the latter.

PRINCIPLES

- *Entitlement.* Government should specify in broad terms the character of the education and scope of the curriculum to which all children in England are entitled, and should ensure that it does all in its power to guarantee such entitlement and that it does not introduce policies or strategies which might compromise it.

- *Equity.* Government, local authorities and schools should work to ensure that every family and child, regardless of circumstance or income, has *equality of access* to a primary education of the best possible quality. They should give no less urgent attention – as indeed at the time of writing the government is doing – to achieving *equity of outcome*: that is to reducing the still considerable extent of pupil underachievement and, within that larger group of underachievers, to 'narrowing the gap in outcomes between vulnerable and excluded children and the rest.'[63] Children who are falling behind require sustained support in what are called 'the basics' but – as noted elsewhere – to deny them access at the same time to a broad and rich curriculum is counter-productive in terms of both well-being and attainment.

- *Quality, standards and accountability.* It is also right that government should define in broad terms, both as guidance for local authorities and schools and in the interests of accountability, the quality of the primary education which local authorities and schools should provide and the standards which should be achieved. However 'quality' and 'standards' should no longer be treated as synonymous, for standards in key stage 2 tests (for instance) are but one aspect of what quality in education ought to entail, and it should never be presumed that what is tested is all that matters.

- *Responsiveness to national need.* Government is in a position to identify and predict the national needs which the education system as a whole should seek to address and it is right that these should feature in the priorities which are agreed for a national system of education. However, government does not have a monopoly in such matters and should be careful to balance its proper concern for economic and workplace needs with attention to broader social and cultural imperatives.

- *Balancing national, local and individual.* The needs of communities and individuals are not merely scaled-down versions of national needs, and many needs in this sense are outside the knowledge and competence of a national government and require a genuinely local response. Local authorities and schools are well placed to understand the character of the communities they serve, and to identify not just distinctive local needs but also local educational opportunities. Yet, just as national public bodies should offer guidance and support without an overbearing degree of prescription, so local authorities should not presume to define local needs without proper consultation with those who collectively constitute the local community. The same principle applies at the level of the school. Teachers have special knowledge of individual children, but not the only knowledge which is available: in the matter of children's needs and capabilities, parents, carers and children themselves are also highly knowledgeable.

- *Balancing preparation and development.* Official statements of aims tend to see primary education solely as preparation for what follows – secondary education, employment, adult life – and to neglect the fact that children have needs and powers now, as children rather than merely as future adults. These arise from their development, their lives outside school, their home circumstances, their cultural and social backgrounds, and from their unique natures and experiences. Apart from those developmental patterns which are common to all or most children, such immediate needs and capacities are apparent only at the levels of community, school and home, and they are therefore an essential component of a school's interpretation of any principles and aims which are determined nationally.

- *Guidance, not prescription.* In keeping with the above, national and local bodies should move away from prescription towards guidance, and in some cases they should not presume to offer even that, unless schools request their assistance.

- *Continuity and consistency.* Mindful that England has separate pre-school, primary and secondary sectors rather than the all-age schools common in some other countries, national and local government should ensure that its policies for each sector are in harmony, so that the child's transition from one to the other is as seamless as possible, while schools and other providers should collaborate to achieve this in practice.

- *Respect for human rights.* Government, local authorities and schools should respect the rights of teachers and pupils and should not produce statements or policies which so closely or inappropriately prescribe what they do that these rights are infringed. Government commitment to the UN Convention on the Rights of the Child should be maintained.

- *Sustainability.* The goal of global sustainability, for humanity as a whole, is widely perceived to be both urgent and of supreme importance. It is therefore right that government, together with local authorities and schools, should strive to pursue policies and follow courses of action which are ecologically sustainable.

- *Democratic engagement.* The way a government acts in the realm of education is a good indicator of the seriousness of its commitment to democratic principles. Mindful of evidence of widespread disengagement from formal political processes,[64] national and local government should seek to engender a climate and discourse for education which is genuinely open and responsive, and schools should reflect this in their own professional and pedagogical practices.

- *Respect for evidence.* Government should counter cynicism about its commitment to 'evidence based' policy by ensuring that its approach to evidence is entirely open and responsive, rather than politically selective, and that it attends to and acts on evidence from independent as well as official or approved sources.

- *Resources and support.* No education policy should be introduced which does not have the level of resourcing necessary to secure its implementation.

TWELVE AIMS FOR PRIMARY EDUCATION

So we proceed from principles by which the work of government, public bodies, local authorities and schools might be guided, to the twelve core educational aims which schools might pursue through the way they organise themselves, through the curriculum, through pedagogy, and through the relationships they daily seek to foster and enact.

The first group identifies those individual qualities and capacities which schools should strive to foster and build upon in each child, in whatever they do, and the individual needs to which they should attend. The second group includes four critically important orientations to people and the wider world. The third group focuses on the content, processes and outcomes of learning, or the central experiences and encounters which primary schools should provide.

The individual

- *Well-being.* To attend to children's capabilities, needs, hopes and anxieties here and now, and promote their mental, emotional and physical well-being and welfare. Happiness, a strong sense of self and a positive outlook on life are not only desirable in themselves: they are also conducive to engagement and learning. But well-being goes much further than this, and 'happiness' on its own looks merely self-indulgent. Caring for children's well-being is about attending to their physical and emotional welfare. It is about inducting them into a life where they will be wholeheartedly engaged in all kinds of worthwhile activities and relationships, defined generously rather than narrowly. It is about maximising children's learning potential through good teaching and the proper application of evidence about how children develop and learn and how teachers most effectively teach. Fostering children's well-being requires us to attend to their future fulfilment as well as their present needs and capabilities. Well-being thus defined is both a precondition and an outcome of successful primary education.

- *Engagement.* To secure children's active, willing and enthusiastic engagement in their learning.

- *Empowerment.* To excite, promote and sustain children's agency, empowering them through knowledge, understanding, skill and personal qualities to profit from their present and later learning, to discover and lead rewarding lives, and to manage life and find new meaning in a changing world.

- *Autonomy.* To foster children's autonomy and sense of self through a growing understanding of the world present and past, and through productive relationships with others. Autonomy enables individuals to establish who they are and to what they might aspire; it enables the child to translate knowledge into meaning; it encourages that critical independence of thought which is essential both to the growth of knowledge and to citizenship; it enables children to discriminate in their choice of activities and relationships; and it helps them to see beyond the surface appeal of appearance, fashion and celebrity to what is of abiding value.

Self, others and the wider world

- *Encouraging respect and reciprocity.* To promote respect for self, for peers and adults, for other generations, for diversity and difference, for language, culture and custom, for ideas and values, and for those habits of willing courtesy between persons on which civilised relations depend. To ensure that respect is mutual: between adult and child as well as between child and adult. To understand the essential reciprocity of learning and human relations.

- *Promoting interdependence and sustainability.* To develop children's understanding of humanity's dependence for well-being and survival on equitable relationships between individuals, groups, communities and nations, and on a sustainable relationship with the natural world, and help children to move from understanding to positive action in order that they can make a difference and know that they have the power to do so.

- *Empowering local, national and global citizenship.* To help children to become active citizens by encouraging their full participation in decision-making within the classroom and school, especially where their own learning is concerned, and to advance their understanding of human rights, democratic engagement, diversity, conflict resolution and social justice. To develop a sense that human interdependence and the fragility of the world order require a concept of citizenship which is global is well as local and national.

- *Celebrating culture and community.* To establish the school as a cultural site, a focal point of community life and thought. To enact within the school the behaviours and relationships on which community most directly depends, and in so doing to counter the loss of community outside the school. To appreciate that 'education is a major embodiment of a culture's way of life, not just as a preparation for it;'[65] and 'School is a place of culture – that is, a place where a personal and collective culture is developed that influences the social political and values context and, in turn, is influenced by this context in a relationship of deep and authentic reciprocity.'[66] Policy has paid little attention to the cultural and communal significance of primary schools and their pupils, except perhaps in the context of decisions about rural school closures, and then only after the event, as it were. This is a grave omission. To establish itself as a thriving cultural and communal site should be a principal aim of every school.

Learning, knowing and doing

- *Exploring, knowing, understanding and making sense.* To enable children to encounter and begin to explore the wealth of human experience through induction into, and active engagement in, the different ways through which humans make sense of their world and act upon it: intellectual, moral, spiritual, aesthetic, social, emotional and physical; through language, mathematics, science, the humanities, the arts, religion and other ways of knowing and understanding. *Induction* acknowledges and respects our membership of a culture with its own deeply-embedded ways of thinking and acting which can make sense of complexity and through which human understanding constantly changes and advances. Education is necessarily a process of acculturation. *Exploration* is grounded in that distinctive mixture of amazement, perplexity and curiosity which constitutes childhood wonder; a commitment to discovery, invention, experiment, speculation, fantasy, play and growing linguistic agility which are the essence of childhood.

- *Fostering skill.* To foster children's skills in those domains on which learning, employment and a rewarding life most critically depend: in oracy and literacy, in mathematics, science, information technology, the creative and performing arts and financial management; but also and no less in practical activities, communication, creativity, invention, problem-solving, critical practice and human relations. To ally skills to knowledge and a sense of purpose in order that they do not become empty formulae devoid of significance.

- *Exciting the imagination.* To excite children's imagination in order that they can advance beyond present understanding, extend the boundaries of their lives, contemplate worlds possible as well as actual, understand cause and consequence, develop the capacity for empathy, and reflect on and regulate their behaviour; to explore and test language, ideas and arguments in every activity and form of thought. In these severely utilitarian and philistine times it has become necessary to argue the case for creativity and the imagination on the grounds of their contribution to the economy alone. Creative thinking is certainly an asset in any circumstance, and the economic case, as many arts organisations have found, can readily be made. At the same time, we assert the need to emphasise the intrinsic value of exciting children's imagination. To experience the delights – and pains – of imagining, and of entering into the imaginative worlds of others, is to become 'a more rounded person.

- *Enacting dialogue.* To help children grasp that learning is an interactive process and that understanding builds through joint activity between teacher and pupil and among pupils in collaboration, and thereby to develop pupils' increasing sense of responsibility for what and how they learn. To help children recognise that knowledge is not only transmitted but also negotiated and re-created; and that each of us in the end makes our own sense out of the meeting of knowledge both personal and collective. To advance a pedagogy in which dialogue is central: between self and others, between personal and collective knowledge, between present and past, between different ways of making sense.[67]

The aims are interdependent. Thus, for example, empowerment and autonomy are achieved in part through exploring, knowing, understanding and making sense, through the development of skill, through the liberation of the imagination, and through the power of dialogue; and well-being comes not only from having one's immediate needs met in the way rightly emphasised in *Every Child Matters*, but also from deep engagement in culture and the life of the community, from the development of meaningful relationships with others, and from engagement in those domains of collective action on which the larger well-being of civil society and the global community depend. In other words, our twelve aims are not a pick-and-mix checklist but the necessary elements in a coherent view of what it takes to become an educated person.

Note that welfare is subsumed in well-being. In law they are defined separately, and 'welfare' tends to focus on maltreatment, abuse and neglect. It is right that these have received attention in recent years and the emphasis on welfare in Every Child Matters and the Children's Plan is applauded by the Review's witnesses. However, in defining aims for primary education we must attend to the needs of all children, not only those who are at risk and for whom welfare in the more focused sense is a priority. We believe that the necessary balance is secured by making well-being a central aim of primary education but incorporating welfare into its definition.

Finally, we warn against reductionism. The Rose Review interim report tells us:

> No matter how they are configured, educational aims and values generally recognise two mutually beneficial sets of outcomes: those for the benefit of the individual and those for the benefit of society (personal fulfilment and utilitarian benefits).[68]

On that basis, some may see our first group of aims as 'individual' and the second as 'societal' in Rose's sense. However, 'the individual' and 'society' in the quoted definition imply mutual exclusivity, even though Rose allows aims which lean one way or the other to be 'mutually beneficial'. Thus, individuals who are engaged, empowered and capable of autonomous thought and decision are likely to act for the greater 'benefit of society' than those who are not; conversely, the 'societal' aims of respect, reciprocity, interdependence and cultural engagement clearly benefit the individual no less than others. We would particularly wish to distance ourselves from the equating of 'for the benefit of society' with 'utilitarian benefits'. This seems utterly to debase the exceptionally high aspirations of citizenship, mutual respect, sustainability, community and cultural engagement.

CONCLUSION

These, then, are the overall principles and aims which the Cambridge Primary Review proposes for primary education. They unashamedly reflect values and moral purposes, for that is what education is about, and they are designed to empower children to manage life and find new meaning in the 21st century.

We need to ask whether the aims should be statutory or centrally determined. The opinion of those whom we consulted was divided. Some questioned whether in a complex, pluralist and fast-changing society the determination of educational aims should be politicised to this extent, and in any case the precedent is not good, for when governments and national agencies have turned their hand to educational aims the results have usually been disappointing. We have also argued that government should stick to the national, leaving local authorities and schools to deal with the local.

On the other hand, as John White argues in the study he undertook for the Review,

> The broad outlines of the curriculum and the aims on which they should rest should be inextricable from the kind of society which is thought desirable and which school education can help to bring about. What kind of society this should be is a political matter, something to be determined by all of us through the ballot box as democratic citizens.[69]

We leave that matter open, not just because it needs to be discussed but because it perhaps presupposes that ours is a properly functioning democracy and there is evidence that at the moment it is not.[70] There are also those who have concluded that, in what one-time Minister of Education Quintin Hogg called an 'elective dictatorship', the ballot box is the least promising route to the good society and that other kinds of engagement are both needed and embarked upon. In any case, we have made much of the distinctive concerns of national government, local authority and school in the matter of determining aims, while the value of local voice and initiative has been a constant theme in the evidence which we have collected. We have also argued strongly for the fundamental importance of children's agency so it would be inconsistent for us to ignore the importance of agency on the part of parents, teachers and school governors. Indeed the commitment of all those directly involved in the life and work of schools is closely related to their collective sense of agency. It is this that gives rise to the conviction, so evident in the Review's evidence, that a good primary school is at the heart of its local community, and that – a point which rural local authorities might note – a community without a primary school is in a fundamental sense bereft.

The conclusion, therefore, is that within a broad statutory framework of aims and principles such as we have discussed, detailed aims, along with the fleshing out of curricula and decisions about pedagogy, are best determined at the level of the community and school or group of schools. Local initiative implies considerable variation in the culture of individual schools, in accordance with the diverse aspirations and experiences of the many different communities which public education serves. Such variation has its problems in a society in which the movement of families from place to place and region to region is commonplace but in general it is a source of strength within a broad statutory framework. It encourages innovation, strengthens commitment, and empowers the schools themselves. And few things are more important than to restore to schools and their members a sense of empowerment and self-respect.

Yet we would be delighted if, after due discussion, the principles and aims proposed here could command sufficiently widespread support at school and local levels to be commended by government too.

NOTES

1 Alexander (1984): 75–79.
2 Quoted, scathingly, by Matthew Arnold (1862) in 'The twice-revised code' (Arnold 1973). Even then there were those who believed that the 3Rs, while essential, were not enough. Other eminent critics of the excessively narrow instrumentalism of the Revised Code included Edmond Holmes, author of *What is and What Might Be* (Holmes 1912). Like Arnold, Holmes had been a senior HMI.
3 Dearing (1993b).
4 DfEE (1997): 9.
5 DES (1978a); Ofsted (1997b, 2002).
6 Alexander (2001b): 73; Webb and Webb (1936): 897.
7 Board of Education (1931): 57.
8 Ministère de l'Education Nationale (2002).
9 CACE (1967): Chapter 15.
10 White (2010), *The Cambridge Primary Review Research Surveys*, Chapter 12.
11 CACE (1967): para 496.
12 CACE (1967): para 501.
13 CACE (1967): para 504.
14 CACE (1967): para 505.
15 CACE (1967): para 506.
16 White (2010), *The Cambridge Primary Review Research Surveys*, Chapter 12.
17 CACE (1967): para 9.
18 CACE (1967): para 495.
19 Ashton *et al.* (1975).
20 Schools Council (1983).
21 Most prominently by contributors to the Black Papers (Cox and Dyson 1971) but also by academics (Dearden 1976; White 1982; Alexander 1984).
22 DES (1981): 3.
23 DES (1981): 3.
24 Great Britain (1988): 1.
25 DES (1977a, 1986).
26 DfEE/QCA (1999a, 1999b).
27 National Forum for Values in Education and the Community (1999).
28 DfEE/QCA (1999a): 10–12.
29 DfEE/QCA (1999a): 10–12.
30 White (2010), *The Cambridge Primary Review Research Surveys*, Chapter 12.
31 QCA (2007b).
32 QCA (2007b).
33 QCA (2007b) (QCA's emphasis).
34 Government of Scotland (2008) online (Available: http://www.ltscotland.org.uk/curriculumforexcellence/whatiscfe/purposes.asp).
35 Arnold (1993): Preface.
36 Lawton (1983).
37 Rose (2008): para 1.1.
38 Rose (2008): recommendation 3.
39 Rose (2008): para 1.34.
40 Rose (2008): 39.
41 Rose (2009): para 1.22.
42 *Ibid.*: para 1.26.
43 Pring *et al.* (2009), 18–22.
44 Mayall (2010), *The Cambridge Primary Review Research Surveys*, Chapter 3.
45 United Nations (1990): Article 29.1.
46 Alexander and Hargreaves (2007): 1–2.
47 Alexander and Hargreaves (2007): 44.
48 United Nations Intergovernmental Panel on Climate Change (UNIPCC) (2007); Stern (2007).
49 Machin and McNally (2010), *The Cambridge Primary Review Research Surveys*, Chapter 10.
50 DfEE/QCA (1999a): 12–13.
51 *Ibid.*
52 BBC News Online: http://news.bbc.co.uk/1/hi/education/1049417.stm
53 Chawla-Duggan and Lowe (2010), *The Cambridge Primary Review Research Surveys*, Chapter 11; UNESCO (2000); United Nations (2005).
54 Chawla-Duggan and Lowe (2010), *The Cambridge Primary Review Research Surveys*, Chapter 11.

55 *Ibid.*
56 Alexander (2008a): 123.
57 Stern (2007).
58 Sustainable Development Commission (2007).
59 Learning and Teaching Scotland (2007): 13.
60 Oxfam (2008).
61 Peters (1978); Stenhouse (1975).
62 Rose (2008): paras 1.33–1.34.
63 DCSF (2007b).
64 The independent enquiry into the condition of democracy in Britain sponsored by the Joseph Rowntree Trust (Power 2006).
65 Bruner (1996): 13.
66 Rinaldi (2001): 38.
67 On engagement, co-construction and the importance of student voice in securing both, see Hargreaves (2004, 2006) and the series of booklets prepared under his direction for the Specialist Schools and Academies Trust. On pedagogic and educational dialogue see Alexander (2008a, Chapters 5 and 6).
68 Rose (2008): para 1.32.
69 White (2010), *The Cambridge Primary Review Research Surveys*, Chapter 12.
70 As documented by the Joseph Rowntree Trust's enquiry into the condition of British democracy (Power 2006). See Chapter 23.

13 Curriculum past and present

We turn now from the purposes of primary education to its content. Here and in Chapter 14 we consider the curriculum. The present chapter identifies the curriculum questions which need to be addressed. It then describes England's national primary curriculum as this stands in 2009, tracing its origins and comparing it with its equivalent in other countries. The rest of the chapter is taken up with considering what the Review's witnesses, through the submissions, soundings and research surveys, told us about the strengths and weaknesses of existing arrangements and how they would like the curriculum to change. The account of this evidence is lengthy, for the curriculum attracted more comment than any other Review theme. The chapter which follows summarises this evidence, highlights other problems and moves on to consider what a new primary curriculum should look like, linking its proposed framework with the principles and aims which we outlined earlier.

Some readers may be impatient with the history, the accounts of witnesses' concerns and our preoccupation with the problematic, preferring practical solutions. They are of course welcome to turn straight to Chapter 14. Yet we believe that it is only by understanding the history, recognising the deeply-rooted and often cyclic nature of the problems, and by exposing the inadequacy of some of the surrounding discourse, that we can make progress. Otherwise, we shall simply repeat past mistakes.

The Cambridge Primary Review does not pluck a curriculum out of the air. Nor does it tinker with existing arrangements while ignoring the fundamentals. Nor does it treat some parts of the curriculum as sacrosanct or beyond debate. Instead, it strives to arrive at a framework for a future primary curriculum which is grounded in aims, evidence and argument. Yet it provides a framework only. The detail is for others to supply, mindful that one of the most consistent themes to emerge from our evidence is that that there must be less national prescription and more scope for local variation and flexibility. We go further, and argue for an explicit and protected local component to the curriculum.

CURRICULUM QUESTIONS

An opportunity dashed

'At the heart of the educational process lies the child,' announced the Plowden Report in 1967.[1] 'The school curriculum is at the heart of education,' retorted the government in 1981, during the countdown to England's national curriculum.[2]

Both were right of course, and indeed there are other contenders for the seemingly coveted place at or near the 'heart' of primary education – pedagogy, for instance. But whether one harks back to this 1960s opposition of child and curriculum, or registers current polarisations – no less untenable – such as skills/knowledge or standards/breadth, we need to warn readers that the curriculum is not just a political and professional battleground; it is also a conceptual minefield.

Treading a path through the obstacles, and – with any luck – removing some of them, is one of the tasks of these two chapters. The curriculum, and the debate it stimulates, are of the most profound importance to children and to the country in which the fruits of their learning are applied. Yet in recent years curriculum debate has gone largely by default. There was no real debate about the 1987 proposals for a national curriculum, in the sense of an open and mutually-respectful conversation in which the different points of view were heard and heeded. Instead, in the teeth of strong professional opposition the version of the national curriculum which in its essentials remains in force in 2009 was imposed by the Education Reform Act. Similarly, there was no significant debate when the national curriculum came up for formal review in 1997–98, at least as far as the primary curriculum was concerned, because the newly-established QCA was instructed by another government to make minor adjustments at the margins, if it wished, but to do nothing which might compromise the newly-introduced national literacy and numeracy strategies.

So we came to 2008–9, and a third official bite at the curriculum cherry. Following the QCA's secondary curriculum review,[3] the government invited Sir Jim Rose to undertake 'an independent review of the primary curriculum' with a view to making 'final recommendations to the Secretary of State by March 2009 so that the new primary curriculum can be introduced from September 2011.'[4]

This, then, looked like a moment of rare opportunity, for in 2009 we had not one primary curriculum review but two, and discussing what they separately proposed offered an unprecedented chance to right the consultative wrongs of 1987–88 and 1997–98. However, the Rose Review interim report soon qualified such optimism. Published on 8 December 2008 for 'consultation', it announced that the QCA would produce draft programmes of study for the six specified 'areas of learning' and have them ready by 31 December 2008, just two working weeks after the consultation opened[5] (thus making it clear that work on them was already well advanced) and two months before the end of the consultation period.[6] QCA would then consult 'informally' on these in order to have final versions ready for the final report. Thus, there might well be consultation on the detail, but the basic Rose framework of three imported secondary curriculum aims, four 'skills for learning and life' and six 'areas of learning' – arguably what the consultation needed first to consider – all appeared to be non-negotiable.

Later stages of the Rose Review confirmed that its consultations were to be both restricted and brief. In late March 2009, DCSF circulated the proposed programmes of study to the subject associations for comment, though not to other bodies having a legitimate interest in them. The subject associations were given just three working days to respond. Meanwhile, teaching unions and members of Parliament requested copies of the draft programmes of study but their requests were rejected. Those excluded from the process could only conclude that the consultations were cosmetic and that DCSF had already made up its mind on the future of the primary curriculum. As its own contribution, the Cambridge Review brought forward the analysis and proposals contained here and in Chapter 14 and published them in a special report within the Rose consultation period. The government dismissed them out of hand. The final report of the Rose Review did mention the Cambridge Review's curriculum proposals, but only where these were judged, correctly or otherwise, to support Rose. Points of divergence – the stuff of real debate – were largely ignored, and in the matter of aims more agreement was claimed than existed.[7]

Curriculum questions: the Cambridge Primary Review and the government's Rose Review

So it remains the case that there are

> ... different ways of making sense, different sorts of questions to ask about the world we're in, and insofar as those questions are pursued with integrity and seriousness they should be heard seriously and charitably.[8]

What, in the domain of curriculum, are the 'different sorts of questions' which should be asked? Although we wish to concentrate in this chapter on the Cambridge Review's own line of enquiry, it is instructive to address this meta-question by comparing the remits of the two reviews.

The Review's third theme (curriculum and assessment) invited us to start with just six questions. They remain here as posed in 2005–6, though their order has been changed so as to convey their logic more clearly (Figure 13.1).

The remit for the government's Rose Review provided a rather different list (Figure 13.2).[9] To the 'core aspects' in Figure 13.2 were later added:

- consideration of two of the more controversial 'milestones' in the early years foundation stage (children's use, by the age of five, of the phonic knowledge to write simple words, and their ability to write their names and labels, captions and the beginning of simple sentences).
- provision for children with dyslexia.

- What do children currently learn during the primary phase?
- Do the current national curriculum and attendant foundation, literacy, numeracy and primary strategies provide the range and approach which children of this age really need?
- What should children learn during the primary phase?
- What kinds of curriculum experience will best serve children's varying needs during the next few decades?
- Do notions like 'basics' and 'core curriculum' have continuing validity, and if so of what should 21st century basics and cores for the primary phase be constituted?
- What constitutes a meaningful, balanced and relevant primary curriculum?

Figure 13.1 Curriculum questions 1: The Cambridge Review (core questions).

---

1. *Curriculum design and content*
   a. In relation to the curriculum what is it reasonable to expect schools to provide and manage within the statutory requirements of the primary school day?
   b. Should primary pupils continue to be introduced to all the subjects of the National Curriculum from Year 1?
   c. What should be the position of science and ICT within the primary curriculum?
   d. Should some of the Early Years Foundation Stage areas of learning and development, and pedagogy, be extended into the primary curriculum?
   e. What is case [sic] and scope for reducing prescription and content in the programmes of study?

2. *Reading, writing and numeracy*
   a. How might schools be enabled to strengthen their focus on raising attainment in reading, writing and numeracy?
   b. What can be done to ensure that these vital subjects are taught thoroughly and systematically, and fully integrated within all areas of the curriculum?

3. *Modern foreign languages*
   a. What are the best ways of introducing a modern foreign language as a compulsory requirement at Key Stage 2 as recommended by Lord Dearing's Languages review?

4. *Personal development*
   a. What are the personal, social and emotional capabilities that children need to develop through their schooling?
   b. What is the most appropriate framework for achieving greater integration of these capabilities throughout the curriculum?

5. *Transition and progression*
   a. How might schools make best use of the information available about prior learning, and information from parents and other professionals working with children, to secure optimum continuity and progression for all children from the Early Years Foundation Stage onwards, paying particular attention to the key transition points?
   b. What are the options for providing more choice and flexibility in start dates for children entering primary school, especially summer-born children?

6. *Other*
   a. Do you have any other comments or contributions to make?

Figure 13.2 Curriculum questions 2: The Rose Review.

The two sets of questions were so strikingly different that they lent support to the hope of many, including two of the largest teaching unions,[10] that the resulting curriculum proposals might be seen as complementary rather than in opposition. Unfortunately, the very focused remit of Rose, and the number of problems which were specifically excluded from that enquiry (most notably, testing), suggested otherwise.

Let us persist with our questions, though. The six in Figure 13.1, from the Review's third designated theme, are not the only questions within its remit which bear directly on this matter. Under the other nine Review thematic headings there are others (Figure 13.3).

The contingent questions are, in their way, no less fundamental than the six with which we started.

- What aims, values and principles should the primary curriculum pursue and enact? (Theme 1)
- What are the implications of recent research on children's development and learning on what, as well as how, they should be taught? (Theme 2)
- What is the place of ICT and other new technologies in learning, teaching and the curriculum? (Theme 2)
- How can children's engagement in their learning best be secured? (Theme 2)
- How should children's learning and curricular needs be diagnosed? (Theme 3)
- How should their progress and attainment be assessed? (Theme 3)
- How should standards and quality in education be defined and assessed? (Theme 4)
- How should the curriculum reflect and/or respond to children's different learning needs and different cultural backgrounds? (Theme 5)
- How should the curriculum and teaching address children's special educational needs and the circumstances of the nation's most disadvantaged and marginalised children (Theme 5)
- What kinds of professional expertise does a modern primary curriculum require? (Theme 6)
- How can it best be acquired and refined through initial training and continuing professional development? (Theme 6)
- How should schools deploy staff so as to meet their curriculum obligations? (Theme 6)
- What is the role of parents and carers in shaping the curriculum and supporting children's learning? (Theme 7)
- How can the school curriculum respect and build on what children learn and do outside school? (Theme 8)
- How can coherence and progression in children's educational experiences be secured as they move from pre-school to primary, through the primary phase and on to secondary school? (Theme 9)
- What is the proper balance of control and responsibility in curriculum and related matters between national government, the relevant public bodies (QCA, TDA, Ofsted), local authorities and schools? (Theme 10)
- What has been the impact of two decades of curriculum reform and what can be learned from the experience? (Theme 10)

Figure 13.3 Curriculum questions 3: The Cambridge Review (contingent questions).

THE PRESENT PRIMARY CURRICULUM

The national curriculum in 2009

What at the time of Plowden was a variable curriculum ostensibly determined by LEAs and schools is now a national curriculum which applies to all pupils of compulsory school age in community and foundation schools, including special schools, and in schools which are voluntary aided or controlled. At key stages 1 and 2 it consists of 10 'foundation subjects', three of which carried the additional designation of 'core subjects'. (The tendency to use the word 'foundation' only for the non-core subjects is in fact incorrect, as all the specified subjects have 'foundation' status. Those outside the core are 'other foundation' subjects).

In addition – a legacy of the 1944 Act, which differentiated the 'secular' and 'religious' curriculum – religious education (RE) is handled separately. Under current legislation (the 1996 Education Act):

Schools must provide RE for all pupils, though parents can choose to withdraw their children. Schools, other than voluntary-aided schools and those of a religious character, must teach religious education according to the locally agreed syllabus. Each agreed syllabus should reflect the fact that the religious traditions in Great Britain are in the main Christian, while taking account of the teachings and practices of the other principal religions represented in Great Britain.[11]

Not all subjects are statutory. At key stages 1 and 2, personal, social and health education (PSHE) and citizenship are encouraged but not required by law, as is the case for a modern foreign language at key stage 2, at least until 2010. Further, schools are required to have a policy on sex education, from which, like religious education, parents have the right to withdraw their children. Thus, the complete specification, which, according to the remit for the Rose Review, remains in force until autumn 2011, is shown in Figure 13.4.

Figure 13.4 shows the bare bones of England's national curriculum in 2009. For each key stage, 'programmes of study' specify in detail what pupils should be taught for the foundation subjects, while 'attainment targets' set out 'the knowledge, skills and understanding which pupils of different abilities and maturities are expected to have by the end of each key stage.'[12] Except for those subjects whose programmes of study are non-statutory, attainment targets 'consist of eight level descriptions of increasing difficulty, plus a description for exceptional performance above level 8.'[13]

Providing a vertical axis to what is in effect a conceptual grid, schools are also encouraged to 'promote learning across the national curriculum' (Figure 13.5).

The approach illustrated by combining figures 13.4 and 13.5 – subjects on one axis, cross-curricular elements on the other – has a long pedigree, was commended by HMI in their *Curriculum from 5 to 16* paper of 1985,[14] and is in common use in other countries. In France, for example, the current equivalent of the list above is a set of *domaines transversaux*.[15] Sometimes there is even a third axis: principles to guide curriculum planning. Thus *Curriculum from 5 to 16* nominated breadth, balance, relevance, differentiation, progression and continuity, while Scotland's *Curriculum for Excellence*, clearly influenced by this earlier work, has challenge and enjoyment, breadth, progression, depth, personalisation and choice, coherence,

---

Core subjects
- English
- Mathematics
- Science

Other foundation subjects
- Art and design
- Citizenship (non-statutory at KS1 and 2)
- Design and technology
- Geography
- History
- Information and communications technology (ICT)
- Modern foreign languages (non-statutory in 2009, statutory at KS2 from 2010)
- Music
- Physical education
- Personal, social and health education (PSHE) (non-statutory at KS1 and 2)

Also statutory
- Religious education (statutory at KS1 and 2, but with non-statutory programme of study)

Also required
- Sex education

Figure 13.4 England's primary national curriculum in 2009: subjects.

- Spiritual, moral, social and cultural development
- Key skills
  - o communication (defined as 'skills in speaking, listening, reading and writing')
  - o application of number
  - o information technology
  - o working with others
  - o improving own learning and performance
  - o problem solving
- Thinking skills
  - o information-processing
  - o reasoning
  - o enquiry
  - o creative thinking
  - o evaluation
- Financial capability
- Enterprise education
- Education for sustainable development

Figure 13.5 England's primary national curriculum in 2009: learning across the curriculum.

and relevance.[16] The drawback of the more complex frameworks is that the laudable desire to ensure that they cover every eventuality makes them difficult to implement.

The Rose Review's remit explicitly excluded any consideration of assessment, but the levels and level descriptions are the point at which the national curriculum and the statutory arrangements for assessing children at the end of each key stage become inseparable. The majority of pupils are expected to work within the range of levels 1–3 at KS1 and levels 2–5 at KS2. The expected level to be attained by the majority of pupils by the end of each key stage is level 2 at KS1 and level 4 at KS2. These 'expected' levels changed from what, in the 1989 version of the national curriculum, were defined as averages into national targets which, from 1997, 'the majority' of pupils were expected to achieve. Further, over the past decade the precise proportion of the nation's pupils defined as 'the majority' has changed: the initial targets were 80 per cent of 11-year-olds at level 4 in literacy and 75 per cent in numeracy by 2002; the 2007 Children's Plan revised that to at least 90 per cent in both English and mathematics by 2020.[17] The target-setting procedure has changed too and now involves greater participation by schools and local authorities. Schools set their own targets for the proportion of their pupils expected to reach the national targets. The latter, however, remain paramount.[18]

Given that, for the primary phase as a whole, what it is proper for pupils to learn is defined by what they are expected to know and understand by the time they take the KS2 tests in Year 6, and that the content of the curriculum is calibrated back from that point through the five levels applicable to the phase, it is not an overstatement to suggest, as many do, that in England the assessment tail wags the curriculum dog, quite apart from the extent to which this Review's evidence shows that the KS2 tests distort the curriculum in Years 5 and 6.

Non-statutory but obligatory: the national strategies

Since 1997, the arrangements summarised above have no longer started and ended with the subjects, programmes of study, attainment targets and level descriptions specified in the framework which came into force in September 2000. With the government's introduction of national strategies for literacy and numeracy in 1998 and 1999, England's already cumbersome primary curriculum became an even more complex affair.

The 1998 national literacy strategy (NLS) specified the content, structure and teaching processes of a daily 'literacy hour' which was expected to be taught in every primary school in England. The 1999 national numeracy strategy (NNS) did the same for numeracy, except that the daily lesson was not one hour for all pupils but 45 minutes in KS1 rising to 50–60 minutes in KS2.[19] Both were then incorporated into the government's primary framework for literacy and mathematics, part of the 2003 primary national strategy. The strategies have been developed separately from the rest of the curriculum and are directly controlled by the DCSF as part of its 'standards' drive. The rest of the curriculum is overseen by the QCA/QCDA. This separation of power and purpose, as we shall see, has created difficulties.

The strategies and framework have been non-statutory, but from the outset it has been expected that all schools would abide by them, and this quasi-statutory requirement has been reinforced through ministerial rhetoric, Ofsted inspections, initial teacher-training requirements, professional development and, at local authority level, by the appointment of primary strategy managers. The message has been clear, and has been confirmed as such by our witnesses: though the strategies were not statutory, they were almost universally viewed as obligatory.

With the arrival of the EYFS (below), statutory and non-statutory have been intertwined in a way which makes the exercise of professional autonomy even more difficult. In its FAQ (frequently asked questions) for teachers, the DCSF website says:

> *What about the primary framework for literacy and mathematics? Will reception teachers have to teach to that as well as getting their heads around the EYFS?* The EYFS is statutory from September 2008; the framework remains guidance. The early learning goals remain the outcomes that children in reception classes are working towards. In order to minimise confusion and help reception teachers make links between the EYFS and the frameworks, the early learning goals are highlighted in the literacy and mathematics frameworks. For guidance on effective practice, practitioners are referred to the EYFS.[20]

Completing the jigsaw: the EYFS

We discussed the early years foundation stage in some detail in Chapter 11. Here we need to register merely that our description of the 2009 primary national curriculum is incomplete without reference to the requirements for pre-fives. The revised national curriculum introduced in 2000 replaced the earlier 'desirable learning outcomes' by 69 early learning goals, and from September 2008 the EYFS became statutory for all children under five, whether in schools or other settings. The EYFS curriculum includes six 'areas of learning and development', three of them subdivided as shown:

- personal, social and emotional development (dispositions and attitudes, social development, emotional development)
- communication, language and literacy (language for communication and thinking, linking sounds and letters, reading, writing)
- problem solving, reasoning and numeracy (numbers as labels and for counting, calculating, shape, space and measures) [formerly 'mathematical development']
- knowledge and understanding of the world
- physical development
- creative development

It is on these six 'areas of learning and development' that the primary curriculum must now build. How it might do so is a matter of some controversy: advocates of play-based learning and a developmentally-appropriate curriculum seek to protect the hard-won distinctiveness of the EYFS, ideally extending it to age six or even seven, while others urge the earliest possible start on formal learning, especially in literacy.

Unmanageability guaranteed?

In 2009, then, England has a statutory national curriculum for the primary phase with non-statutory or quasi non-statutory elements, which combines the following:

- three core subjects, two of which (literacy and mathematics) are subject to separate arrangements in pursuit of the 'standards' agenda and between them are expected to take half of the available teaching time in specifically structured and focused lessons
- seven other statutory foundation subjects
- three non-statutory foundation subjects, one of which (a modern foreign language) becomes statutory in 2010
- two subjects (religious education and sex education) which are, respectively, statutory and required, but which fall outside the national curriculum framework
- six areas of learning across the curriculum, some of which are identical to named foundation subjects.

Thus, once literacy and mathematics are attended to, the remaining half of the available teaching time must accommodate a further core subject (science) and no fewer than 12 statutory or recommended subjects. This complex and logistically challenging curriculum is expected to build in a coherent way on an early years curriculum comprising just six areas of learning, inevitably making reception and Year 1 hugely challenging for teachers. It is thus hardly surprising that the manageability of the national curriculum has been a major cause for professional complaint since its inception, or that for the children in our primary schools – as our evidence shows – entitlement has been so seriously eroded.

What is perhaps more than merely surprising is that throughout this period the national curriculum has been co-ordinated by well-resourced public bodies – NCC, SCAA, QCA – whose responsibility, by any reasonable or even barely minimal definition of that word, should have been to ensure that what they were imposing on schools could be put into practice. However, we shall see that until 1997 it was possible to show, by reference to successful schools, that the primary national curriculum was not inherently unmanageable. With the introduction of the national strategies in 1998 and 1999 matters became much more difficult.

At the same time it is important, in the interests of both fact and equity, to recognise the extent of variation which occurs even under such a tightly-prescribed regime. Schools implement the requirements of the national curriculum in different ways, and manageability is more of a challenge for some than for others. Their own agency in such matters cannot be ignored.

Historical and international continuities

In Chapter 11 we showed the striking similarities, in the matter of official views of what primary education is centrally about, between the vision and language of the Newcastle Commission report of 1861, the Dearing report of 1993, and the 1997 White Paper *Excellence in Schools*. It is no less striking to pursue this historical continuity into formal requirements for the curriculum. Historian Richard Aldrich has shown how at one level – that of subjects specified – the 1988 national curriculum was little different from its 1904 Board of Education predecessor.[21] In Figure 13.6, to underline his point, we include the 1904 regulations, the curriculum as specified in the 1967 Plowden report – which in these and other matters was not nearly as revolutionary as it was later portrayed – and the national curriculum as it stands in 2009.

We stress that we are not arguing that such remarkable similarity between the three specifications makes the current curriculum redundant. We do not agree with those who believe that a changing world makes everything inherited from the past irrelevant, or that a curriculum justifies its claim to modernity by bearing no resemblance to anything that has gone before. The comparison is made, instead, to prompt the contrasting claims of continuity and change:

1904	1967	2009
English	English	English
Mathematics	Mathematics	Mathematics
Science	Science	Science
History	History	History
Geography	Geography	Geography
Foreign language	Modern languages	Modern foreign language (from 2010)
Drawing	Art and Craft	Art
Physical exercise	Physical education	Physical education
Music	Music	Music
Manual work / Housewifery	(Craft, from Art and Craft)	Design and technology
	Religious education	Religious education (SNS)
		ICT
		PSHE (NS)
		Citizenship (NS)
	Sex education	Sex education (P)

Figure 13.6 The 1904 Board of Education Regulations, the 1967 Plowden Report and the 2009 National Curriculum.

NS: non-statutory programme of study
P: school policy required, no centrally-determined programme of study
SNS: statutory subject, non-statutory programme of study

- If the current curriculum is a variant of a framework which has served for over a century, is this not an argument for retaining it in its essentials? Yet –
- If the framework has survived for so long, might this demonstrate not that it is right but that we are incapable of thinking of alternatives, regardless of its relevance to a changing world?

By and large, people are either for continuity or they are for radical change, and they see these as mutually exclusive. This is yet another unhelpful dichotomy to add to our growing list: we commend continuity, cumulation – learning from and building on past thinking and practice – and change.

In fact, the continuities reach across space as well as time. UNESCO policy analyst Aaron Benavot and his colleagues have shown how, worldwide, national primary curricula exhibit remarkable similarity at the level of subject labels and priorities,[22] and this is confirmed in the comparative analysis of arrangements in England and 21 other countries which the Review commissioned from Kathy Hall and Kamil Øzerk. Their survey concludes:

> There is strong convergence in officially-stated curriculum provision across all the countries surveyed. England is in line with international trends in its provision of the following: first language, mathematics, science, information technology, history, geography, art and craft, music, physical education and sport and religious education. All of these areas of study are now standard in the primary curriculum of the vast majority of the countries in the survey.[23]

But, Hall and Øzerk add:

> England differs from many other countries in not (as yet) making PSHE, citizenship and a modern foreign language compulsory at the primary stage. There is also a grey area where matters like global awareness are concerned. They are increasingly encouraged though not obligatory.[24]

The Rose Review commissioned its own comparative studies from the INCA database at the National Foundation for Educational Research (on which the Cambridge Primary Review has also drawn).[25] Their conclusions were in line with ours. One of the studies, involving just 10 countries, noted a move away from 'subjects' towards 'learning areas'.[26] We comment below on nomenclature and ponder whether this adjustment means anything. We are not sure that it does.

Another and more interesting extrapolation from the INCA database looked for similarities and differences in the way that what England defines as literacy, mathematics and science are conceived in 19 countries.[27] Actually, the number was smaller, because the NFER study defined as 'countries' two Canadian provinces and one Chinese special administrative region, and overall it gave disproportionate emphasis to small countries and city states. The NFER study found general similarities in the structure of the mathematics curriculum, with data handling broader and more demanding in England than elsewhere *but the curriculum for number narrower and less demanding*. Given the scale of the government's investment in its national numeracy strategy since 1997, and the claims that have been made for it, such a finding might well merit the epithet 'astonishing'. That is why we place it in italics: the finding should not be ignored.

There was much greater variation in primary science curricula, while for literacy the structures were more variable still. However, what we judge to be particularly significant about the findings for literacy was this statement:

> The literacy curricula in the comparator countries are much more likely to include an elaboration of their underlying philosophy and rationale than England, where this is extremely brief.[28]

This, we suggest, takes us back to the apparent inviolability of that mantra 'read, write and add up'. There was a relatively limited rationale for England's literacy curriculum because nothing more was believed to be necessary. Indeed, the truths of the national literacy strategy were assumed to be self-evident; and though the strategy claimed to be grounded in national and international evidence, it was only after the NLS was finalised that the government decided to commission a study to discover what that evidence might be.[29]

No less serious methodologically and conceptually, the NFER comparative study looked at literacy in isolation. Had it investigated the nature of the first language curriculum as a whole, it would have found, as have other international studies, that a very clear feature emerges. England is strikingly different from many other countries in the way it treats the relationship between literacy and oracy, and hence in the way literacy is conceived.[30] In England, leading researchers, including several members of the 'Cambridge Primary Review 100',[31] have combined with professional organisations like the National Association for the Teaching of English (NATE) and the United Kingdom Literacy Association (UKLA) to press for a proper reconceptualisation of this critically important domain of learning and classroom activity. That reconceptualisation, most of these individuals and organisations argue, must go a lot further than increasing the number of mentions in official documents of what the current national curriculum rather weakly calls 'speaking and listening'.

As a result of such efforts, which reach back many years via the National Oracy Project and the Bullock Report[32] to pioneers like Douglas Barnes[33] and tap into a substantial international research literature, the balance in this matter has slowly begun to shift. Yet there remains a historically-rooted tendency in England to detach talk from reading and writing and indeed make it subservient – so much so, that the 2003 launch document of the primary national strategy mentioned talk just once in 79 pages[34] – and we are not convinced that some of those who nowadays tell teachers to give greater attention to 'speaking and listening' fully understand the fundamental nature of what is required. In many other countries, in contrast, oracy and literacy are not just inseparable but are also integrated within a more generous conception of language education. Bearing in mind what we have noted in Chapter 7 about the importance of talk in the development of the brain and the child's cognitive powers, and the evidence to which we refer in Chapter 15 about the character of talk in English primary classrooms, this is a matter of considerable importance, and it is something of a leitmotif in our report as a whole.

What is now increasingly clear is that international comparison of subject labels takes us only so far: it is what the labels denote which matters. That reservation applies as much to our historical comparisons. Though the mantra 'read, write and add up' has survived unscathed, what is indicated by most of the various subject labels in Figure 13.6 is without doubt different in 2009 from 1904. That is another reason to resist the claim that subjects are no longer relevant or that there should now be a wholesale shift to 'areas of learning' or 'skills', for subjects change of themselves.

PRESENT AND FUTURE: WHAT THE REVIEW'S WITNESSES SAID

The national curriculum: a vote of confidence, up to a point?

When it was first introduced the national curriculum was viewed with both scepticism and alarm in the teaching profession but, 20 years on, criticism is moderated by recognition of its advantages. Our submissions and soundings evidence indicated that the principle of having a national curriculum is now generally accepted as beneficial, particularly if it succeeds in establishing a clear, basic entitlement for children's learning across the country's 17,000 or so primary schools.

In their evidence to the Review, several local authorities confirmed that the national curriculum had brought essential consistency to their schools. Some educational organisations felt that the curriculum had now reached an appropriate balance of breadth and depth to ensure that children have a wide range of learning experiences. New developments were welcomed: the Training and Development Agency for Schools (TDA) felt that the introduction of foreign languages would enliven the curriculum and generate a more positive mood in schools: the Commission for Racial Equality was among several organisations which applauded what it saw as the increased emphasis on values; the Wellcome Trust, among many others, was pleased that science now has a secure place in primary education (though other witnesses were less sanguine on this score).

Children's submissions were also largely positive, with science, geography, history, sports and the arts singled out for particular mention because they were enjoyable and offered children opportunities to be active and involved in what they are learning. Many children said that they liked subjects where they could use their imagination – art, music, creative writing and drama were all mentioned – and they also valued those subjects that sparked their curiosity and encouraged them to explore. (It is perhaps worth noting that children themselves seem to be confirming, notwithstanding the claimed intentions of the primary national strategy, that the 'enjoyment' in *Excellence and Enjoyment*' is confined to subjects other than literacy and numeracy).

Beyond this initial consensus, views of what has happened since 1988 became more critical and divided.

The overcrowded curriculum

The most frequent of all charges laid by our witnesses against the current National Curriculum was that it is overcrowded, leaving teachers with insufficient time to enable children to engage adequately with every subject required by law. The NUT position paper *Bringing Down the Barriers*, which was submitted as part of that union's evidence, noted in a way which is representative of a large number of submissions on this matter:

> In primary schools, children's access to a broad and balanced curriculum is still limited. The introduction of the government's Creative Partnerships scheme ... is a positive step but there remains too little curriculum time for creative subjects ... National Curriculum testing and associated targets at Key Stage 2 distort the curriculum ... Despite the

inclusion statements in the National Curriculum, equality is still not at its heart. The National Curriculum does not facilitate easily the preparation of pupils for adult life in a diverse society and in a global context. Neither does it encourage the meeting of specific needs such as those of ethnic minority pupils and those from socially and economically deprived backgrounds.[35]

Another submission wryly observed: 'The curriculum that has evolved over the past twenty years needs thinning in order to remove the eccentricities of a long line of secretaries of state and prime ministers'. One local authority commented simply: 'We need to do less, but better'. Many teachers called for the curriculum to be slimmed down. The report on the Review's national soundings notes that teachers attending them concluded:

> The current national curriculum is overcrowded and subject to considerable pressures from testing and inspection and from a series of 'bolted-on' additions which have made it logistically non-viable. It has also been diminished by the pressure of testing and the requirements of the national strategies. The 1988 ERA vision of 'entitlement to a broad and balanced curriculum' is no longer a reality.

The 'bolt-on' problem, which has been a significant theme in the curriculum literature of the past two decades, is clearly illustrated in Figure 13.6. The list of subjects has simply become longer and longer, and nothing has been removed to accommodate the newcomers. In practice, 'the basics' have been protected but aspects of the wider curriculum have been squeezed almost out of existence. Many organisations expressed deep concern about the plight of the arts, and called for music and drama to be rescued before they disappeared altogether. The submission from the National Association of Head Teachers (NAHT) showed how Ofsted's inspection procedures have exacerbated the problem:

> The publication of *Excellence and Enjoyment* in 2004 stressed the importance of the broad curriculum that was once the defining quality of most English primary schools. Despite this, and government statements on flexibility, primary schools still feel pressured; they recognise the value to children's learning of music, drama, poetry and creative subjects, while the inspection system still focuses on standards in maths and English.

With so much ground to cover, the curriculum was also seen as placing a strain on resources. The Music Education Council, for example, condemned the government for 'telling us that creativity should be at the heart of the curriculum' whilst not providing enough resources for instrumental and vocal tuition. The council complained that many schools were still 'shackled' by league tables and performance statistics and were therefore reluctant to divert resources into music. The constant, yet again, is the distortion of the child's entitlement to breadth and balance by a powerful combination of high stakes testing, national strategies and selective inspection. Together these make it not only difficult or impossible to timetable the low stakes subjects with any seriousness, but also – as the council's submission suggested – risky in terms of schools' decisions about resources. There was much support in our evidence for the post-1988 budgetary delegation to schools, but the council's submission hints that there are other and subtler ways that government can control the distribution of resources at school level than by holding the purse strings.

　　The matter of resources also exercised those who otherwise welcomed the introduction of a modern foreign language in the primary phase. Many observed that there was an acute shortage of teachers trained to teach other languages, and the Parker Association for Language Learning argued that 'robust systems must be put in place to ensure confidence and competence on the part of [those] primary teachers' who would be undertaking this work.

　　While witnesses generally deplored the way recent policies and initiatives had compromised the 1988 Act's welcome insistence on breadth and balance as a statutory entitlement, few mentioned the HMI and Ofsted evidence on this matter, to which we referred earlier in this report, that far from being a threat to achieved standards in 'the basics' a broad, rich, balanced and well-managed curriculum is actually the prerequisite for those standards, and this has been demonstrated consistently in school inspection. It is perhaps worth recalling this finding, confirmed in 1978, 1985, 1997 and 2002,[36] in case there be any who wish to defuse the chorus of complaint from our witnesses by arguing that the loss of curriculum breadth and balance since 1997 has been a necessary sacrifice in the cause of improved standards in literacy and numeracy. The evidence could not be clearer. If breadth is attained, so are standards. If breadth is sacrificed, so are standards.

Overcrowding drastically reduces the room for manoeuvre. This, according to our witnesses, affects not just teachers but, more fundamentally, the quality of children's learning. The heavy emphasis on coverage and pace reduces curriculum to content to be checked off, and curtails exploration. It places a premium on the retention and recall of facts, and downgrades other than superficial understanding. It denies children opportunities to plan for themselves how to approach their learning tasks – a vital ingredient in engagement, cognitive advance and the development of the capacity to learn how to learn. It forces teachers into transmission mode even though they would like, and children need, opportunities for ideas to be properly discussed and explored. It reduces, for both teachers and children, time for reflection and evaluation.

Having said all this, we are left with a paradox: the primary curriculum is believed to be overcrowded; but everybody wants most that it currently contains to be retained, and many wish to extend it.

The micro-managed curriculum

Many witnesses, in both the submissions and soundings, told us that the curriculum as specified by the DCSF and QCA was excessively prescriptive and needlessly detailed, and that it had undermined teachers' professionalism. Moreover, many added, it had failed to improve the quality of teaching and learning. Those schools wishing to adopt a more adventurous approach felt unable to do so, despite the opportunities which were supposedly available.

The submission from the NUT contrasted the legal position with the perceived reality:

> Disapplication under Section 90 of the Education Act 2002 allows a school or a local authority to submit to the Secretary of State an application to disapply all or part of the national curriculum in order to meet their aims through innovative curriculum development. It is a power unused since the passing of the 1988 Education and Reform Act. It allows schools to develop their curricula beyond that which is facilitated by the general flexibility available within the national curriculum. Unless the disapplication direction includes statutory assessment arrangements, Key stage 2 statutory tests and teacher assessments in all subjects except those disapplied must continue and school performance continues to be included in the annual national performance tables. To date, this has proved to be a powerful influence on the willingness of schools to experiment with curriculum provision which might better meet pupils' needs.

The NUT continued:

> Although the national agencies such as QCA exhort schools to become more creative in their curriculum provision, unless schools feel able to undertake some level of experimentation without punitive high stakes consequences if the experiment fails, there will be little development from the current curriculum offer.

With anxieties like these in mind, some submissions argued that the curriculum should not be in the hands of politicians and policy-makers at all, especially as it was felt that they displayed little understanding of primary education, teaching or learning.

Criticism was also levelled at specific aspects of the curriculum and the national strategies which were felt to be ill-conceived. For example, the Association of Teachers of Mathematics (ATM) roundly condemned both the revised early years foundation strategy and national numeracy strategy as being hastily conceived, oversimplified and over-reliant on a limited range of teaching methods. The ATM provided a detailed critique of the strategies and listed several serious weaknesses. In similar vein, the Geographical Association (GA) believed that the curriculum offered an essentially secondary-orientated view of geography which could profitably be revised in line with its Action Plan for Geography[37] which offered a more appropriate primary-level approach. These are just two examples: we report further on specific subjects below.

National and local: who should decide?

We have seen that the degree and intensity of the control of the curriculum exercised by national agencies, notably the DCSF, QCA/QCDA and the national strategies, were widely seen as excessive. Teachers attending our national soundings went further: they believed that successive governments since 1988 had proved themselves incompetent to manage the curriculum and that henceforth the role of the DCSF and the national agencies should be confined to providing a loose curriculum framework, leaving local authorities and schools to work out the detail.

The idea that schools should be able to adapt the curriculum in response to the local community's needs and circumstances was proposed in submissions from a wide range of individuals and organisations, and we anticipated it in the previous chapter through the key principle of 'responsiveness to local need and circumstance'. One local authority's submission to the Review summed up the views of many thus:

> A national system cannot accurately reflect the wide diversity of values and aspirations in society but should give scope for schools to develop an understanding and appreciation of their local community and its relationship to others, including tolerance and respect. This enables pupils to understand their place within their society and the inter-relationships it brings, as well as fostering opportunities for them to make a positive contribution.

We came across interesting examples of local curriculum adaptations in our community soundings: in one area, the local authority's new religious education syllabus was warmly welcomed by representatives from the highly diverse community. In law, the content of the religious education curriculum is, uniquely, a local matter. Beyond RE, however, teachers attending the community soundings felt that the national curriculum was markedly unresponsive to the interests and needs of local communities, and to the considerable opportunities for learning which the community and its environment present.

The Association of Teachers and Lecturers (ATL), quoting from its 2007 publication *Subject to Change*,[38] said:

> According to a recent survey under 4 per cent of teachers believe that the national curriculum meets the needs of all their pupils. Almost 90 per cent of them wanted the school to have greater freedom to develop the curriculum.

However, it is important to note that local decision-making does not necessarily result in local responsiveness. It may merely produce an off-the-peg national curriculum from the websites of the QCA or DCSF. Local responsiveness needs to be established as a principle, and indeed as a conscious strategy, rather than merely a hope. By the same token, though giving schools 'greater freedom to develop the curriculum' might seem the best way to ensure that 'the national curriculum meets the needs of all … pupils', this does not necessarily follow. We know as much from inspection evidence during the long era of curriculum localism before 1988. We know it also from several decades of classroom research (see Chapter 15). The critical issue here is how, and with what competence, freedom at local, school and classroom levels is exercised. The same of course goes for government and its agencies, who currently hold the prerogative of freedom in curriculum matters, and about whose exercise of that freedom the Review's witnesses were so deeply concerned. It is a matter of capacity and expertise as well as right.

Children themselves should have their say in curriculum design and planning, according to some witnesses. Lambeth Children and Young People's Services, for example, suggested that 'the curriculum needs to move from mere coverage to a deeper, more meaningful and relevant curriculum, incorporating our understanding of how children learn, and seeking out their perspective and input on its design'. (Again, we have to say, there is an apparent connection between the two parts of this sentence, but not a necessary one.)

Optimum Education, in its submission to the Review, argued the case for involving children thus:

> The methodological expectation is that teachers find ways to transfer curriculum under-standings to children. Therefore, the fundamental element which generates learning in almost all areas of life outside of school – identifying for oneself what needs to be learned – is denied to children ... The school curriculum is highly selective and narrow, presenting carefully identified aspects of a world that children might eventually enter ... and derives from experts and legislators, not from the consumers or parents. It therefore seems to imply a lack of confidence as if to democratise the curriculum would be to devalue it in some way. The curriculum offers up strange knowledge, not knowledge that would extend or interact with children's everyday experience. Indeed, if school knowledge drifts towards children's everyday understandings then children's power is increased, [which is] not something organisations interested in control and induction are looking for ... The school curriculum in effect paints a picture of a supposed reality but it is abstract painting. Selecting (sometimes tasty) morsels for children's consumption cannot overcome their general feelings of puzzlement – why this, now?

Another local authority argued that both teachers and children need to be empowered: 'We should be designing a curriculum that makes sense to children and frees teachers to think about learning rather than delivering chunks of work'.

Subjects, skills, themes, areas of learning?

We turn now from witnesses' preoccupation with the downside of a centralised national curri-culum to the response to the Review's very open question 'What should children learn?' Pro-posals ranged from small amendments to the existing national curriculum framework to fundamental re-structuring. Some argued that primary education needs new aims and that these should either specify desirable skills and dispositions or use broader conceptualisations of knowledge than at present to guide the specification of content. However, many witnesses responded to this question not in its own terms but by repeating the pleas for greater flexibility, less prescription and more local control.

In our national and community soundings, and in the submissions, there was extensive debate about the way the curriculum should be structured. It was at this point that subjects, notwithstanding our earlier warning, became immediately contentious. Some submissions challenged the subject-based curriculum and argued for a shift to skills and dispositions. The National Union of Teachers (NUT), for example, argued that

> There is increasing agreement amongst politicians, economists and the business and academic communities that current approaches to learning are not equipping children and young people with the skills and dispositions necessary for Great Britain to compete in a global society.

Some submissions did attempt to define the kinds of skills and aptitudes that the curriculum should seek to develop. One local authority, for example, spoke of the need for children to learn how to 'find, sort, assimilate, manipulate, synthesise and interpret information'. The importance for the workplace and the country's economic future of both generic skills like these and those more familiarly packaged as literacy, numeracy and ICT was emphasised in submissions from employers and the Trades Union Congress (TUC).

'Skills' were not the only mooted alternatives to subjects. During our community soundings, some teachers and head teachers suggested replacing the current national curriculum subjects by the six foundation stage 'areas of learning and development'. Local authorities, teacher trainers and some children's organisations also welcomed the foundation stage's more open approach and saw it as a model which could be applied to the primary phase, and especially to key stage 1. 'Areas of learning' were commended in the 2008 Rose Review interim report as providing the best means of securing continuity from the EYFS to primary and from primary to secondary.[39]

For many practitioners and organisations the restructuring issue was less about subjects vs skills vs areas of learning than restoring the balance which had been lost following the intro-duction of the national literacy and numeracy strategies, and in particular the need to give greater emphasis to the humanities, the arts and PSHE. The Citizenship Foundation's submis-sion, for example, observed:

> We believe that primary education should try to achieve *Excellence and Enjoyment* across all subjects. Currently there is a tendency to focus on 'excellence' in the core subjects while restricting 'enjoyment' to the foundation subjects in the wider curriculum.

With similar concern for mood and dynamics rather than structure, others argued that the standards drive had turned children off school learning and that 'fun', 'challenge' and 'excite-ment' should be injected into the curriculum to ward off disengagement. It was important, they argued, that the curriculum allowed for 'hands-on' learning experiences, opportunities for speaking and listening and using exciting texts. On the other hand, many submissions welcomed the predominant concern with literacy and numeracy. In its assessment of what should be retained in a slimmed-down curriculum, Lambeth Children and Young People's Service said:

> Well worth preserving is the developmental process undertaken by schools and institutions that has brought the primary curriculum to where it is today. The core skills of literacy, mathematics and information technology need to remain high profile, as these are the skills that are essential for day-to-day life (and indeed for further study). Also to be pre-served and developed are the principles and key elements of *Excellence and Enjoyment* in the primary years.

When the Humanities Education Centre invited children to answer the question, 'What kinds of things should children learn in school?', the responses were almost universally given in terms of subjects, although children often qualified their responses with reasons why these subjects were important. Two Year 6 children, for example, wrote in their submission:

> Maths for our everyday life, science for how things work in the world, English to learn standard English so we can talk properly, RE to learn about other cultures and countries, ICT to learn the world's technology, history to learn the world's history and geography to learn where places are and how our world is.

This succinct set of justifications is perhaps more utilitarian than those who value education for its own sake would prefer, though its internationalism is notable: 'the world … other cultures and countries … global … the world.'

Specific aspects of the curriculum

English

The central place of English in the curriculum was underlined by the English Association's submission:

> In an English-speaking country a wide and exciting curriculum must have English at its heart – whatever the subject matter, children must listen to learn; must speak to articulate their understanding; must read to find out more; must write to consolidate what they've learned and thoughtfully consider the best ways of expressing it.

We record in a later section how the standards drive initiated in 1997 detached literacy from national curriculum English and confirmed that detachment politically and structurally by transferring control of literacy from QCA to the DfES/DCSF. However, for UKLA neither 'English' nor 'literacy' is adequate. In its submission it recommended 'the use of the label *communication, language and literacy* in line with the EYFS and to signal that literacy in a new media age is multimodal in nature'.

Also concerned with labels and categories but making a rather different point about the historic neglect of oracy to which we referred earlier, the National Association for Teachers of English (NATE) asked:

> Why do we divide English into *reading*, *writing* and, almost as an afterthought, *speaking and listening*? Would it not make more sense to think in terms of *reading and listening* and *writing and speaking*?

Submissions from many teachers and head teachers argued that the status of 'speaking and listening' should be elevated and/or that oracy should be given a much more prominent place in the curriculum. In this matter it is important to note that the scope of oracy, at least as explored by the National Oracy Project[40] and by those working in the fields of language and classroom interaction, is considerably broader than 'speaking and listening' as defined in the current national curriculum. 'Speaking and listening' is a component of national curriculum English. Oracy encompasses talk in all areas and contexts of learning. Even at level 5 of the attainment target for speaking and listening, what is expected of the highest-attaining 11-year-old seems relatively basic:

> Pupils talk and listen confidently in a wide range of contexts, including some which are of a formal nature. Their talk engages the interest of the learner as they begin to vary their expression and vocabulary. In discussion, they pay close attention to what others say, ask questions to develop ideas and make contributions that take account of others' views. They begin to use standard English in formal situations.[41]

This is some way from the view of oracy and classroom interaction being advanced by those in the current Anglo-American talk reform movement to which we shall refer in Chapter 15, and it is behind it in terms of aspiration. We mention this now by way of warning that the problem of curriculum labels raised by UKLA and NATE is but the tip of a curricular and pedagogical iceberg.

Beginning to probe this problem, the Society for Advancing Philosophical Enquiry and Reflection in Education (SAPERE) called for a daily oracy session which would aim not just to develop fluency and confidence in speaking and listening but also help children advance their thinking and understanding and evolve their own thinking. In this the society pointed to the success of programmes like Philosophy for Children (P4C).

UKLA drew attention to the impact of modern communication technologies on literacy and was among the organisations which recommended that media studies should be included in the primary curriculum. Developing this line, the Association for the Study of Primary Education (ASPE) proposed that

> ... much more scope and account needs to be given to ways in which children could be encouraged to be more critical and analytical of film and DVD adaptations of book texts in order to learn and understand how they differ from and compare with [the actual] texts.

Also attempting to extend the received view of literacy, NATE's submission argued:

> As Margaret Meek memorably remarked, 'confident literates know what they need not read'. What is important is the ability to select, prioritise and comprehend – regardless of the manner (or medium) in which data is presented.

English, for those children whose first language it is not, has added challenges and dimensions. UKLA was critical of the way in which bi- and multi-lingualism are regarded as 'a minor or background consideration, often resulting in tokenistic or ill-informed attitudes in school'. It pointed out that the different learning needs of all children, including those with other languages, disabilities, and of different social class and gender, meant that a single model of the curriculum for English will not cover all children and eventualities and that the government should encourage teachers to 'respond creatively, plan holistically and make good use of talk, drama and film in their literacy curriculum provision'.

The National Literacy Strategy (NLS)

The Hamilton Trust's submission characterised the first version of the NLS thus:

> In 1997, with the National Literacy Strategy (1998) teachers were effectively told:
> * to teach to given objectives, 1,024 of them, with not a single one prioritised
> * not to do individual reading since only 'shared' or 'guided' reading was advised
> * to eschew structured phonics and to adopt the half-way house approach of 'rime and analogy' and to teach blends such as /tr/ rather than individual phonemes
> * to believe that 'speaking and listening' were no longer considered important as not one of those 1,024 objectives prioritised them.

ASPE concurred with this line of criticism:

> Since the introduction of the National Literacy Strategy in 1998 teachers have been directed to teach a literacy curriculum with an overriding emphasis on reading, writing and grammatical awareness. Not only has the content been centrally managed and directed but so too have the methods and teaching strategies.

The ATL's submission remarked:

> Although the structure of the literacy hour has helped some teachers to improve their practice and has given more pace to lessons, for others the structure has been applied too rigidly and has hampered development and innovation.

ASPE pointed to a slackening of this pressure with the arrival of the primary strategy and *Excellence and Enjoyment* but the ATL called the twin aims of excellence and enjoyment an 'irresolvable contradiction'.

Updating its critical comments on the 1998 version of the NLS in light of the 2007 primary framework,[42] the Hamilton Trust remained sceptical:

Now, in 2007, we are informed that:

- structured phonics is now obligatory
- speaking and listening is flavour of the month (implied question: why have we irresponsible teachers not been doing enough of it?)
- most of the 1,024 objectives were not important and we often prioritised the wrong ones
- it is bad to mix text types and therefore teaching some poetry about dogs which then leads on to discussing how to look after a dog is now considered bad teaching.

UKLA regarded the NLS as excessively reductive, especially in its neglect of oracy and dialogue. The association criticised the Rose Report on early literacy[43] (whose recommendations on phonics have now become mandatory) for being unbalanced in its advocacy of synthetic phonics, pointing out that while phonics may develop the skills of reading, children may be disinclined to use them unless their reading experiences encourage autonomy, enthusiasm, achievement and a sense of enjoyment. UKLA identified a 'simple' view of reading in official discourse that appears to decouple decoding from comprehension.

The submission from ASPE was scathing about 'the extracts' culture which it said characterised the NLS/PNS, and continued:

> How can we continue to design an English curriculum which marginalises the role that reading and telling stories has to play in children's cognitive, social and emotional development? Whilst this will clearly not be the experience for all children or for all teachers, the fact that it occurs in any primary school in the 21st century is a scandal and needs to be a priority for review.

One witness, citing her experience as an English teacher, primary head and English examiner, condemned the 'abject state of affairs' where reading for pleasure has disappeared under the pressure to pass tests.

This is strong stuff, but we confirm that it is a fair sample of the many comments on the NLS which the Review received. We might also note that if the literacy requirements of the 2007 primary framework contradict those of the 1998 NLS as dramatically as the Hamilton Trust claimed, it is hard to see how teachers can have confidence in them.

The Review commissioned a survey of research, evaluation and inspection evidence on the impact of recent curriculum and assessment reforms, including the NLS, which we consider elsewhere.[44] That survey also summarises changes to the NLS since its incorporation into the primary national strategy framework from 2007. Drawing on the work of Dominic Wyse and Russell Jones,[45] our survey authors comment:

> The number of objectives in the new framework was drastically reduced in comparison with the old framework. The tendency to encourage one-off lessons was replaced with longer units of work. The division of objectives into word-level, sentence-level and text-level was abolished. In spite of the overall reduction in objectives, the framework as a whole, which includes many guidance documents and hyperlinks to other government resources, may prove to be unwieldy and prescriptive. The types of books children will study is prescribed, the types of writing they will carry out is prescribed. The way this is to be taught has been specified in greater detail than the NLS. It appears that a dominant teaching model, rather than encouragement to use a range of approaches, is still being applied ... The emphasis on grammar through reference to the old objectives is still encouraged ... The method of teaching reading has been subject to increased control by government ... Teachers are required to adopt the 'synthetic phonics' approach to the teaching of reading, a recommendation which continues to be contentious and some argue is not supported by sufficient research evidence.[46]

There is much more that could be said about the NLS and its current manifestation within the PNS framework, both from our evidence and from research and inspection. For the moment we confine ourselves to this selection of witness views on the NLS as a somewhat semi-detached aspect of the curriculum for English. In this chapter, it is the concept of literacy which matters, not the strategy's impact on literacy standards, teachers and teaching. The latter aspect is discussed in Chapters 15, 17 and 23.

Equally, we must stress that the NLS has its supporters too, and not just in the arena of policy.[47] Many younger teachers involved in the community soundings welcomed the provision of a clear conceptual and organisational framework to support their work in an aspect of teaching which they knew was both important and contentious. By and large, it was their elders in the schools, and the national organisations which represent the professional communities of teachers, advisers and researchers, who were most sceptical. This tendency for reactions to be age-related has been noted in other studies, though the 2006 teacher survey of Rosemary Webb and Graham Vulliamy found it less marked than in the early years of the NLS.[48] Perhaps more significant is the sharp difference in reactions to the literacy and numeracy strategies, with the latter generating a markedly more favourable professional response.

Mathematics

Mathematics was a subject that children identified as particularly important for their adult lives and with this in mind some suggested that it should attend more to financial understanding and skill. Submissions from practitioners and curriculum organisations focused more on how maths should be taught. The Association of Teachers of Mathematics (ATM) pressed for 'a consistent focus on children understanding the mathematics they are doing rather than just regurgitating rote-learnt rules' and applauded the spiral model where modules of learning build from one to the next. The submission from the ATM objected to the prescribing of particular calculation procedures without checking on the understanding – or misunderstanding – they produce:

> Teach a child a procedure without understanding and they may remember it for a day. Teach a child to think mathematically and understand what they are doing and they can apply it for life.

On the whole, less concern was expressed about mathematics than about English, and the main reason for this appeared to be that the national numeracy strategy (NNS) was considerably more popular among teachers than its literacy counterpart. In the Webb and Vulliamy study referred to above, 50 per cent of experienced teachers 'strongly liked' the NNS, but only 17 per cent said the same of the NLS. The sample sizes, though, were small: 82 teachers (NLS) and 78 (NNS).[49]

The Hamilton Trust's submission went further, claiming that the NNS was greeted with almost universal enthusiasm amongst classroom teachers and head teachers alike:

> It is rare to hear sustained critiques of it – certainly from those 'at the chalk face'. As a consequence, we have enjoyed a period in which:
> - maths teaching in primary schools has generally improved
> - the focus on mental methods of calculation has been accepted as useful and is generally being applied to an increasing degree each year
> - mental-oral practice as a short daily activity has without doubt improved children's numerical fluency by keeping previously taught strategies as well as number facts 'simmering' as children progress through primary education
> - a structured spiral curriculum has enabled both effective teaching, with 'revisiting' a mathematical idea or topic built in, and active learning as children come back to things to reinforce their conceptual understanding.

The ATM was less convinced, identifying a list of fundamental flaws in the way the NNS had been conceived and was expected, through the tripartite daily maths lesson, to be taught. Its submission was particularly concerned that the same basic pedagogical model had been applied to the youngest primary pupils as to the oldest:

> It has never been the case that foundation stage maths teaching has been based in learning through practice ... We are aware of no evidence that under-7s learn best by having whole class objective-led maths lessons, led by adults, every day ... The message that mathematics is a linear process of lots of small objectives is not one that ATM supports.

The association also took issue – at a level of detail which we cannot repeat here – with the way the NNS/PNS conceived the teaching of particular aspects of mathematics. For example:

> The notion of multiplication as repeated addition, and division as repeated subtraction, doesn't tell the whole story and needs further consideration ... The whole issue of ratio and proportion and the definitions needs to be considered. At present it is a bit like saying 'you always take the smaller number from the larger' – the definitions are setting up later problems in understanding the structure. The notion that fractions are always part to whole does not sit comfortably with the type comparisons that children frequently make ... Consideration needs to be given to teaching the division aspect of fractions. Perhaps this should be left until KS3 and the notion of counting and multiplying ... could be used in KS2. This might well prevent later misconceptions when adding fractions.

Several submissions warned that the government's preoccupation with numeracy risked a similar kind of reductionism in mathematics as has happened to English. As one witness reminded us:

> A joint Royal Society and Joint Mathematical Council reported in July 2000 that the teaching of mathematics was increasingly being reduced to nothing but numbers, and that the death of geometry and the study of shape and space in mathematics teaching could only be to the detriment of visual and spatial intelligence. It takes little to see in this entirely quantitative approach a verification of René Guénon's vision of 'The Reign of Quantity.'

However, the ATM did celebrate the rise, since 1999, of

> the number of pupils achieving level 4 and above. These gains have been achieved using a consistent focus on children understanding the mathematics they are doing rather than just regurgitating rote-learnt rules.

There is one much more controversial perspective on primary mathematics. Such is the historical dominance of the '3Rs' in first elementary and then primary education that it has become almost heretical to ask whether that dominance continues to be justified. A few witnesses were prepared to do so. One questioned the assumption implicit in the national strategies (though not in the national curriculum as originally specified in 1988) that literacy and numeracy, or English and mathematics, should have parity of esteem, arguing that literacy and the wider study of language are considerably more 'basic' to the child's education than mathematics, in that the former enable and underpin everything else and remain critical to the individual's future education, employment and life to an extent which cannot be argued for mathematics. A second believed that the 3Rs was a Victorian throwback and in 2009 science could make a much stronger claim than mathematics to the status of 'basic'; in any event it needed to be reinstated in the curriculum core. A third witness saw the matter in somewhat more political terms, as a dominance secured less by argument than by effective lobbying. The witness was happy to be provocative:

> The delusional grandeur of the maths lobby needs challenging – it's held unthinking sway for far too long!

A more measured challenge came from Professor Guy Claxton:

> Beyond the obvious usefulness of basic arithmetic, mathematics has the status it has, not because it is intrinsically important but because it seems to fit the methods and assumptions of Zumbac's school so well. Mathematical knowledge is timeless. It can be easily segmented into topics. It can be clearly explained. Graded exercise can be constructed to guide practice. The steps of reasoning can be set out so errors are easily spotted. There are unambiguously right answers, which make for rigorous and objective assessment.[50]

'Zumbac's school', Caxton explains, perpetuates the classical and mediaeval primacy of logical or quasi-logical systems of thought, and values above all knowledge which is reliable, timeless and readily parcelled up and transmitted, regardless of its relevance. Mathematics, he believes, fits this bill perfectly and thereby escapes challenge on the grounds of relevance to which other subjects must submit. Claxton adds, though, that 'the real way mathematicians actually solve problems and make discoveries is ... a million miles away from this clinical kind of learning.'

Clearly, there is scope for debate here: to date there has been a somewhat deferential silence. If we are to have a proper review of the curriculum no element should be exempt.

Science

Science was generally recognised as an important aspect of the curriculum. Children viewed it as one of the keys to their understanding of the world around them. Some adults, however, expressed concern about the handling of science in the national curriculum, arguing that it valued content over scientific understanding and investigation. The submission from the National Inspectors and Advisers Group for Science (NAIGS) felt that science teaching had been skewed by the demands of formal assessment:

> The science education community faces a dilemma. The status of science as a core subject is key for the country in terms of future economic development and it needs to be maintained ... There is a wide perception that [this status] is reinforced ... by having an external national SAT at the end of KS2 ... [Yet] the KS2 science SAT has changed the way that science is taught in KS2 classrooms (and viewed by senior managers), to the detriment of the children's learning experience and love of science.

The National Network of Science Learning Centres shared this concern and its submission claimed that:

> Children and teachers are increasingly turned off science as it becomes a content-led, vocabulary-heavy subject where personal curiosity is thwarted and opportunities for children to develop investigative, questioning and thinking skills are limited ... Primary science should offer children the opportunity to engage with big ideas about how the world works through first-hand practical activity. It is the fundamental right of every individual child to explore, to investigate, and to gain scientific skills and knowledge.

Prominent among the submissions dealing with primary science was a substantial and detailed document from the Association for Science Education (ASE), which also drew on contributions from NAIGS (see above) and the Association of Tutors in Science Education (ATSE). Space does not allow us to do it full justice to the ASE submission here, but we believe that the following key points should be noted:

- Science is currently a core subject but does not have parity with literacy and numeracy in terms of status, time, support, CD and funding; it should have.
- Science teaching at the primary stage must involve enquiry and 'hands-on' activity.
- Teaching to the KS2 test has reduced both the extent and quality of primary science at the top end of the primary school.
- Primary science requires a constructivist pedagogy in which pupils' existing ideas and understandings are respected, elicited, explored and built upon.
- Science teaching should be relevant to pupils' lives in order to provide the basis for that public understanding of science which in a scientific and technological age is essential to a functioning democracy. This also means engaging with major global issues such as sustainability.

The emphasis on public understanding for an active and informed citizenry was taken up by the Wellcome Trust, which also called for a full review of the content of the primary science curriculum:

> Primary science education should not just be concerned with knowledge but also with the acquisition of scientific concepts and the development of scientific and thinking skills. It should aim ... to develop ... perseverance, independence, co-operation and curiosity.

Also from the Wellcome Trust came a persuasive statement on the importance of primary science in education and life which is worth quoting in full:

- Primary school science enables children to develop ideas about the world around, laying a foundation for scientific literacy, the general grasp of key ideas of and about science that are necessary for effective operation in the modern world.
- Children's experience of undertaking scientific inquiry can develop appreciation of how science works, of the power and the limitations of science, as well as the enjoyment of finding out through scientific activity.
- Science can help children's understanding of scientific aspects of their daily lives that affect their health and safety during the primary years and have wider implications for their and others' future through longer-term effects on the environment.
- Scientific activity and learning about the people and history of science support appreciation of science as an important human endeavour in which reliable knowledge is built up through the systematic collection and use of evidence.
- Involvement in scientific activity leads to the recognition of the importance of reasoning about evidence, which is needed for future learning in science and beyond.[51]

The extent to which the post-1997 literacy and numeracy strategies had marginalised what, in the late 1980s and early 1990s was regarded as one of the national curriculum's success stories, was quantified in the NAIGS submission. In contrast to daily literacy and mathematics lessons taking half of the available teaching time or more, NAIGS reckoned that time devoted to discernibly scientific study now equated to 'around 1.5 hours [a week] at KS1 and 2 hours at KS2 ... frequently limited to afternoon slots with little if any teaching assistant (TA) support.' (For those unfamiliar with the professional folk-wisdom of primary education we should point out that there is a long-held belief that mornings should be reserved for the most important subjects 'when the children are fresh', that afternoons are for the 'soft' subjects, and Friday afternoon is the curriculum graveyard. Independent-minded heads sometimes invert the timetabling in order to subvert the belief.)

ICT

Few witnesses doubted the importance of ICT in the lives of today's children and tomorrow's adults. ASPE and the TDA were among those arguing for ICT on the basis of future need: 'Primary education, particularly the latter stages, should offer pupils the support they may need for them to live successfully in an age dominated by rapidly expanding technology' (ASPE). 'Emerging technologies will continue to develop and will be a central, integrative and interactive part of the learning cycle' (TDA).

Similar arguments were frequently presented at the community soundings. There, however, they were often tempered by anxiety about the downside of children's unlimited access to an unmonitored web, by the adverse consequences to children's physical health and social development of spending long solitary hours at the computer screen and by the addictive nature of computer games. The National Association for Advisers for Computers in Education (NAACE), inevitably a staunch advocate of ICT in schools, also warned in its submission that:

> ICT is critical to developing more complex thought and creative thinking. To do this its use must be taught systematically and intelligently, with sufficient recognition of its limitations. It is a principal task of teachers to educate children to be critical readers and users of all information material, especially the world wide web.

Despite its ubiquity in the lives of children inside and outside school, there was some concern about whether its importance was properly reflected in the curriculum. Several submissions argued that the 'C' in ICT (communications) was neglected and that its prominence in our lives now demanded that it should take its place within an expanded concept of literacy. In any event, they argued, to restrict 'communication skills' to speaking and listening was no longer adequate.

NAACE argued that ICT was of sufficient importance and complexity to be handled as a stand-alone subject, like mathematics. Many teachers and teacher trainers, on the other hand, viewed it more as a resource, for example for children's writing. NAACE was unhappy about this, and believed that it represented a sidelining of ICT which would have damaging longer-term consequences. The division between those who regarded ICT as a cross-curricular tool or skill and those who believed it should be timetabled as a subject in its own right was marked.

Creativity and the arts

The words 'creative' and 'creativity' appeared in the submissions more frequently than almost any others. They were applied both to children's learning and the conditions for teaching, and invariably were regarded positively. The words were also used somewhat loosely, and it was therefore helpful to receive this warning in the submission from Professor Anna Craft:

> The very nature of creativity in education remains ambiguous. To what extent creativity in primary education is conceived of as involving creative partnerships, as opposed simply to valuing and nourishing children's ideas in multiple contexts, is not clear. To what extent collective or collaborative creativity is valued as against individualised models, is also unclear; similarly there are still slippages in language between 'creative teaching', 'teaching for creativity' and 'creative learning'.

In the submissions, creativity referred variously to the child's creativity, teacher creativity, and 'creative' subjects like art, music or drama. It was also used to refer to individual qualities, aims, processes or outcomes. Sometimes 'creative' appeared to mean taking risks or just doing things differently. Like 'skills', 'creativity' has become something of a cliché, and an important idea has thereby been devalued.

Many submissions argued that teachers' and children's opportunities for creative activities had been undermined by curriculum prescription and high stakes assessment. The case for creativity was often made with reference to the skills needed by tomorrow's adults, as in this individual submission to the Review:

> Since the introduction of the national curriculum in England, central policy in education has restricted learning by focusing too much on prescribed knowledge and the assessment of this. Schooling has primarily focused in recent years on the transmission of knowledge and skills. There is a growing concern that this has been accompanied by a narrowing of the curriculum, with the result that many of our young people are launching into adult life lacking the flexible creative thinking required for negotiating a complex world.

Here, 'creativity' is defined as a way of thinking. Some submissions, however, argued that recent initiatives were moving in the right direction. One curriculum organisation commented:

> We are now coming almost full circle with *Every Child Matters* and personalised learning at the centre of the debate and with government telling us that creativity should be at the heart of the curriculum. It would indeed be a transformation of the curriculum if these agendas were followed through and we could achieve a really creative environment for all our children's learning.[52]

Both children and teachers said that they would welcome more time for the visual and performing arts. One local authority suggested that the creative arts should be integrated with other areas of the curriculum to support 'key aspects of learning'. Teachers at our national soundings also highlighted the important role of the arts in increasing children's engagement with learning. One head teacher described how her school's links with local theatres and artists had helped to create a more positive learning culture within the school, inspiring children, parents and teachers alike.

The extensive and fully-documented submission from Creative Partnerships included case studies of schools where the creative arts had been used as a focus for re-structuring schools' approaches to the curriculum. One school worked with Creative Partnerships to rationalise both the structure of the curriculum and the timetable to create the much needed space and time for creativity and the arts. Mornings were devoted to the national curriculum core subjects (mathematics, English/literacy and science) while in the afternoons remaining subjects were taught through the themes stimulated by works of art and in collaboration with professional actors, dancers and a local artist. According to Creative Partnerships, the impact of this initiative was 'profound': teachers felt that children had gained in confidence and 'children now approach their work with greater attention to detail and a more sustained interest'.[53] Interestingly, though, the approach did not challenge the long-held assumption that the 'basics' belong to the morning prime time and the arts to the afternoon. The comment from the NUT, cited earlier, that the work of Creative Partnerships was prevented by national testing and other requirements from achieving its deserved impact should also be noted. Creative Partnerships is DCSF-sponsored, but the NUT appear to be arguing that in this matter government has restricted the prospects for success of one of its most promising initiatives.

It is not just a matter of time. Some felt that, generally speaking, art was not well handled in the primary curriculum. The submission from the National Association for Primary Education (NAPE) included an article by Peter Dixon, who voiced concern that children's imaginative and expressive artwork was being constrained:

> Sadly in recent years the unique and precious quality of children's drawing and painting has been lost in many schools where the focus has been on the work of adult artists. Visits to galleries and school visits by practising artists are to be encouraged. But rows of six-year-olds copying rather obscure paintings by Kandinsky, for no other reason than they have been told to do so, defeats me.[54]

Deep concern was also expressed about the state of music in primary schools. Teachers believed that its foundation status guaranteed nothing. Teacher trainers argued that music had become so marginalised that it could disappear from the curriculum altogether. Yet children themselves said that they wanted more opportunities to learn about and to enjoy music in school. The Music Education Council (MEC) reminded us of the benefits of music, from reflecting and embracing cultural, ethnic, religious, regional and local aspirations to the 'sense of social awareness, linguistic development, level of concentration, self discipline and sense of both individual and corporate pride' to be found in the members of young choirs.

Curiously, that list says nothing about the unique and irreplaceable aural, imaginative, emotional, intellectual and kinaesthetic power of music as music, and over the past decade there has been an increasing tendency to seek to justify the arts by reference to outcome measures of social or economic utility which have little to do with how the arts are experienced. Even arts organisations have felt obliged to accede to creeping utilitarianism. This has been unhelpful to the cause of the arts in schools, and we might suggest that the preference for labels like 'creativity' or 'visual skills' also reflects this unseemly capitulation. We return to this matter later.

Support for the arts was not universal. One parental submission, for example, objected that school plays took away time from the 3Rs. And in an important reminder that educational values may be problematic, the Muslim Council of Britain asked us to note that certain kinds of music and dance are unacceptable under the tenets of Islam and urged schools to be sensitive to the beliefs and practices of Muslim families:

> Some Muslims may hold a very conservative attitude towards music and may seek to avoid it altogether, not wishing their children to participate in school music lessons. In such cases the school can show great understanding by providing alternative musical learning opportunities.

The humanities

Geography and history were widely regarded as being undervalued in primary education and under-represented in the curriculum. Many submissions called for a greater emphasis on the humanities. Some, possibly following the same line of reasoning which reduced art to 'visual skills', suggested that the humanities were a good way to teach 'key skills'.

A slightly different take was provided by the submission from a teacher training institution which argued that

> literacy and numeracy skills should be taught in the context of learning through other subjects, especially the humanities, retaining the focus on using the learning process and thinking skills, but through these methods allowing children to gain some knowledge of the past, the world today and an understanding of their own and other cultures.

It is not wholly clear what is being argued for here: possibly the familiar contention that unless literacy and numeracy are applied they are meaningless; or perhaps that if the content of literacy and numeracy can somehow be made 'historical' or 'geographical', then that satisfies those who are worried about the decline in school humanities. There is a worryingly reductionist trend here, quite marked in submissions about the arts and humanities, on which we shall need to comment later.

The same cannot be said about the submissions from the Royal Geographical Society (RGS) and the Geographical Association (GA). The RGS deplored the way the restriction of testing to literacy, numeracy and science had created a hierarchy of subjects in which the contribution of the humanities has been devalued. It too commended geography as a relevant and easily understandable context within which to teach both literacy and numeracy, but also underscored the necessity of geographical understanding in its own right, and on its own ground. With high-quality geography lessons, and real-world experiences in the field, geography, said the RGS, can help prepare primary pupils to understand their neighbourhoods, their nation and the world. Their world can span their locality, their nation and connections beyond.

The GA wanted the primary geography curriculum to be re-designed to ensure that children, 'develop a sound understanding of the world from the local perspective to the global context'. Starting geography in the child's locality has long been a popular approach, and it chimed with the more general concern for localism in the curriculum which we raised in our discussion of aims and principles in Chapter 12.

Submissions on the place and teaching of history also criticised the growing marginalisation at the primary stage of a perspective on the world which witnesses believed was of central importance in both education and life. But there were other concerns: the controversial question of the relationship between history teaching and identity, for one. Here, parents at one community sounding, in common with some politicians, argued that 'Britishness' arises from a knowledge of British history. Others took a very different view, believing that a condition of cultural plurality may demand if not as many histories as there are cultures, then certainly an approach to history which highlights diversity and the very different tales that can be told about the past, depending on where in the cultural mix one happens to find oneself. The ATL's submission warned:

> Some ... argue that the national curriculum must transmit the British heritage, but this cannot be done by national prescription because the concept of Britishness becomes ever more problematic in an age of mass migration and global communication.

Focusing on the link between the humanities and values, ASPE said:

> Primary education is also about the eventual growth of pupils into full human society with an understanding of values. The [non-core] foundation subjects are needed to secure this. Why is this? Historical and social thinking are not the same as other kinds of thinking.

Roy Hughes, quoting his own work on behalf of NAPE, added:

> History can help our children to make meaning. Conceptual thinking is a vital part of children's developing work in history. Children's classroom activities would be framed by cause, consequence, interpretation and evidence.[55]

Citizenship: local, national and global

Citizenship education, a recent and currently non-statutory addition to the national curriculum, was highlighted in our submissions and soundings evidence. Some organisations argued that England lags behind other countries in the seriousness with which it treats citizenship education and called for it to be made mandatory at the primary stage. However, some questioned whether it was necessary to introduce primary-aged children to citizenship education.

Opinion was similarly divided on the matter of cultural identity. Some witnesses felt that schools should place a clear emphasis on celebrating diversity and plurality, whilst others wanted schools to promote a common set of values. Organisations which took part in our national soundings cautioned that terms like 'Britishness' were unhelpful and may accentuate division. The Citizenship Foundation called for a more holistic, coherent approach to citizenship education, with children's personal experiences as a key focus. As well as classroom debate on social and environmental issues, the foundation recommended classroom approaches based on dialogue, active learning and emotional literacy as tools which future citizens would need.

It wanted citizenship to become statutory, with a clear pathway of progression through key stages. The foundation was concerned that bullying, theft, respect for law, and community cohesion issues are commonly addressed in primary schools but not always from a citizenship perspective or in a consistent manner. AREIAC also felt that citizenship education required further support and suggested that a cross-curricular approach should be developed to establish links with other areas, such as religious education and PHSE.

Concerns stretched beyond national boundaries. The curriculum, many argued, should embrace an international perspective, developing children's awareness and understanding of climate change, sustainability and global economics. It was widely acknowledged that Britain and the wider world were changing rapidly and it was imperative that the curriculum should have a clear global and international orientation. While educating children for economic understanding, schools should make them aware of the dilemmas of balancing prosperity and sustainability, competitiveness and interdependence. The submission from the UK One World Linking Organisation (UKOWLA) drew attention to the potential of communication technology in supporting the development of global education:

> With the growing emphasis on global interdependence, internationalism and the IT revolution enabling easier access to all kinds of communication and distance learning and with the movement of people across the globe, there has recently been an increasing interest in global education allowing young people to put their lives in the context of the world in which they are being brought up and enabling them to become active global citizens. IT has made this joint curriculum work much more accessible to all.

Many witnesses insisted that sustainability was no abstract aspiration but required teachers to involve children directly in projects to protect the environment, conserve wildlife and reduce carbon emissions. The RSPCA said that children should be taught to have 'respect for all animals and the environments within which they live'. During the community soundings we saw some of these projects in action, including a Forest School in Devon and a community sustainability project in Northumberland, and impressive and heartening they were too, especially in the way they combined enthusiasm, hard knowledge and practical action.

Health and physical education

As we noted earlier in this report (Chapters 4 and 7), concern has been growing in recent years about children's physical health and the rise in childhood obesity, and this concern is reflected in the Review's own evidence as well as in government policy. Many organisations and practitioners urged that more time, resources and emphasis should be given to physical education and outdoor play. Several parent submissions lamented the loss of competitive sports in many primary schools, one commenting that 'Our school has particular problems with a lack of playing space which the governors are trying to address, but competitive sport and matches between schools seem to have all but disappeared'. One submission felt that the 2012 Olympic Games in London could be used to help raise the profile of sports in schools.

Many believed that PE is inadequately resourced. The ATL said that, '… a comprehensive curriculum recognises humanity as physical beings'. It called for greater recognition of the importance of physical skills such as co-ordination, control, manipulation and movement, and for schools to provide more opportunities for pupils to develop these skills. Some groups at our community soundings wanted more time to be allocated to physical education.

Children often talked or wrote to us about (and some drew) their favourite school sports. In thinking about what resources they would like to see in their schools, children prioritised pitches, gymnasia and indoor swimming pools. The submission from Swim 2000 called for the introduction of its method to teach children how to swim using efficient strokes, enabling them to swim greater distances.

From financial to emotional literacy

Children were concerned that they should enter the adult world properly prepared, not just by the well-trodden routes of literacy and numeracy but also with a grasp of financial and life skills. This was a strong theme in the witness sessions with children which formed part of each set of community soundings:

> Children's views of educational priorities highlighted the development of generic capacities for managing life in a changing world: learning how to learn, preparing for life, developing relationships, handling responsibility, citizenship, life skills, financial management and generally 'thinking about the future'.[56]

Some adult submissions also commented on the importance of teaching children about financial management, though generally children's priorities for their learning differed quite markedly from those of adults. Children valued a curriculum which combined relevance with enjoyment; adults wished to foster the development of the rounded personality.

Teaching children how to manage their emotions and cope with the stresses of everyday life was also regarded as extremely important. Many organisations commended the Social and Emotional Aspects of Learning (SEAL) curriculum and suggested that it should be more widely adopted in schools. The Child Bereavement Network's submission called for discussion of death and bereavement with children:

> Given the numbers of children who will experience bereavement during childhood, there is a strong case for them to learn ways of managing feelings associated with loss. The general provision of education about loss and bereavement can help to dispel myths and taboos. ... By including death and loss in the wider curriculum (for example, in science, English and geography), schools can help to normalise these topics.

The British Humanist Association argued that sex and relationship education should become statutory at primary level, a view that was endorsed by several children's organisations and faith groups. However, some of the latter were concerned that teaching about relationships should not run counter to the tenets of their religion.

Some readers may find it odd that we have bracketed together goals as disparate as 'financial literacy' and 'emotional literacy'. We do so partly because this is how these matters were often presented to the Review and partly to make a point. It does perhaps overstretch the concept of 'literacy' when it is used, as in many submissions it was, to define the ability to read and write, the ability to operate with confidence and discrimination in the ever-changing world of ICT, the capacity to manage money and make sound financial decisions, and the complex combination of attributes which make up the way a person expresses and handles emotions and responds affectively to people and experiences.

In any event, as we showed in Chapter 7, 'emotional literacy' may be a popular concept but among psychologists it is also a contested one and should therefore be used with caution. What is beyond dispute is that children's emotional development matters and that many of the Review's witnesses were deeply concerned both about the impact of current patterns of life on children's emotional condition and the need to see education of the emotions as no less fundamental to primary education than the historical 'basics.'

In their survey of curriculum alternatives commissioned by the Review, Jim Conroy, Moira Hulme and Ian Menter of Glasgow University note that many ideas in this area have been imported into mainstream schooling from outside the state system, for example, from Steiner-Waldorf schools, pre-schools in Britain and other countries influenced by the Reggio Emilia approach from Italy, and the home-school movement. But with reference to the emotional literacy movement more generally, they warn:

There are significant questions … about the efficacy and purposes of what has come to be regarded as 'therapeutic pedagogy'; that is, a pedagogy which aims to 'empower' less confident learners to overcome (self-imposed) barriers to the achievement of learning goals. Some commentators warn of the commodification of 'emotional intelligence' (EI) as a newly constructed 'competence' to be traded by trainers and teachers. Moreover, it is not always clear that the positive relationship that is often assumed between self-esteem and academic attainment is always or inevitably justified. Indeed, others suggest that therapeutic approaches to tackle the self-esteem deficit are little more than 'snake oil' remedies.[57]

Modern foreign languages

Although modern foreign languages at key stage 2 will become statutory from 2010, there were many who wished to remind us of their importance – perhaps aware that having foundation subject status guarantees little, as the recent fate of primary arts and humanities shows. The Association for Language Learning (ALL) made an important case for the relationship between foreign language learning and mother tongue literacy (though others argued that for children experiencing difficulties in literacy the addition of a second language is a hindrance rather than a help. CILT (Centre for Language Teaching) made the broader case that teaching a foreign language at primary level can help produce not only literate and numerate children but also those with

> a sense of their own self-worth and a joy in knowing and getting to know, an appreciation of the contributions they can make in the economic, social and emotional development of their own communities and beyond and the desire to contribute to these; children who are tolerant, interested in and with some understanding of the commonalities and differences between people both next door and on the other side of the world.

The TDA was an enthusiastic supporter of foreign language teaching. It reported that its research shows that language teaching helps to create a more creative curriculum and a more positive mood in schools. No less enthusiastic were many witnesses at the community soundings, including children.

ALL admitted that much of the evidence for the benefits of teaching languages was anecdotal but highlighted the usefulness of languages in linking curricular areas and promoting diversity. CILT claimed that, '… all primary schools are "language schools" since all of their activity is concerned with language and how to use it appropriately'. ALL wanted schools to develop a more inclusive approach to language teaching, saying that pupils of all abilities can be included in primary language lessons, given appropriate extension activities.

Religious education

In the 1944 Education Act religious education (RE) was the only named compulsory subject. 65 years later, opinion is sharply and sometimes bitterly divided about whether it should be in the curriculum at all.

We received submissions from organisations representing some of Britain's prominent faiths: nationally from the Catholic Education Service, the Church of England Education Division, the United Synagogue Agency for Jewish Education, the office of the Chief Rabbi and the Muslim Council of Britain; locally from several Standing Advisory Councils on Religious Education (SACREs), the organisations which are responsible in law for advising local authorities on religious education and acts of worship in schools, and from individual diocesan boards of education. All of them argued eloquently that religion is as essential to education as it is to life well-lived, though their perspectives on how it might be fostered in schools were not identical. We also received submissions from professional organisations concerned with RE – the

National Association of Teachers of Religious Education (NATRE), and the Association of RE Inspectors, Advisors and Consultants (AREIAC).

The case for religious education within faith schools was clearly put by the Church of England Education Division, quoting the words of its former Chief Education Officer, the Very Reverend John Hall:

> Religious education in any faith-based school is not simply a subject making up a proportion of the taught curriculum. It pervades the whole life of the school. The religious character of the school and the belief on which it is founded will be discernible in the attitudes and values of the school, the priorities the school sets and what it prizes most highly, the quality of relationships throughout and beyond the school community, the place and nature of worship in the school, the whole taught curriculum and curriculum enrichment, the use of and attitude towards the school premises and what surrounds the school day.

In the context of non-denominational schools, Bradford SACRE's submission pressed a wider argument:

> Religious education is often seen only in relation to its contribution to community cohesion. While the value of this should not be underestimated, it is also important to note that RE contributes significantly to pupils' cognitive and conceptual development. It deals with some of the world's most significant and ancient teachings and literatures and is, at its best, a very challenging subject area.

In contrast, we received submissions from individuals and organisations which were strongly opposed to the teaching of religion and religious education in schools. They argued that England should follow the route taken by some other countries and make the curriculum of non-denominational schools explicitly secular, pursuing instead a framework of common values and emphasising by other means the importance of moral and spiritual development. Several pointed out that the words 'spiritual' and 'religious' are wrongly treated as synonymous, and that the visual and performing arts can make as powerful a claim as organised religion to provide the sense of transcendence to which religious believers attest.

It is also worth recalling that even the United States, in which faith and indeed God are invoked in public and political life with a frequency and zeal which would be unthinkable in England, insist that schools should be secular institutions, and in France the principle of *laïcité* is strongly defended. In both cases, secularism is bound up with republican ideals, and the examples remind us that the mandatory status of RE within the English state school curriculum arises ultimately from those events over 450 years ago which made Anglicanism the state religion and the monarch its head.

But, as one parent wrote:

> The UK is *de facto* a secular state. I would suggest that now is the time for the education system to reflect this and change [school] assemblies to give less time to outmoded and divisive constructs which are threatening the cohesiveness of our society. RE should be re-named and re-focused as a subject to look critically at philosophies (including, but not limited to, religious ones), their history, contribution and relevance. Above all, children should be given the tools to question and challenge, in order to equip them to reach their own conclusions.

Another wrote:

> Knowledge of religious beliefs, specifically Christian, is necessary of course for an understanding of history, in the same way that knowledge of Greek, Roman and Norse gods is a useful aid for an understanding of their people's history and behaviour. However, no one

now teaches the ancient pantheons as if they are still valid beliefs and in the same way 'modern' religion should not be taught as fact, although I am not arguing that it shouldn't be mentioned that some people choose to believe in a god. At such a young age children are willing and encouraged to believe whatever an adult tells them but school should be where they are taught facts and ideas, not beliefs misrepresented as facts.

AREIAC emphasised its support for the system of SACREs, as locally accountable and responsive. It was vital, they argued, that children should understand the nature of a multi-faith society and learn how to live within it. The Muslim Council of Britain also welcomed efforts to increase inter-faith understanding but called for a balanced approach:

> Most Muslims have no objection to learning about other religions and their beliefs and practices. A serious study of the Qur'an, for example, leads us naturally to a study of the 'People of the Book' (Jews and Christians). A balance needs to be kept between giving Muslims a good grounding in and detailed study of their own faith and learning about other major faiths practised within society.

In several of the community soundings it was noted that many Muslim children are attending both regular schools and madrasahs. The issue here was felt to be not so much the possibility of diverging values as excessive demands on children's time and energies, especially when they also have to do homework.

We cannot report the content of all the many submissions we received on these matters. They covered a broad spectrum: RE as the inculcation of a particular faith; RE as an exercise in multi-faith awareness; RE as teaching about religion as an inescapable historical and cultural phenomenon; religion as a value system to be placed alongside others, both religious and non-religious; secularism on the grounds that except for denominational schools faith is for indivi-duals and their families, not for schools. But from not one single organisation or individual did we receive any suggestion of the kind which has polarised discussion of this matter in several American states, that schools should teach 'creationism' or 'intelligent design' as a no less valid alternative to science. RE may be contentious, but the discussion remains, in comparison with some countries, moderate.

If there is a middle ground it is probably best represented by the submission from the British Humanist Association, which accepted the cultural case for teaching about religion but within a framework of even-handed and sympathetic exploration of belief, morality and worldview from both religious and non-religious perspectives.

The Cambridge Primary Review, clearly, has to take a defensible position on this matter, and we attempt to do so in our proposals on the future primary curriculum in Chapter 14. But it is as well to accept that the extreme positions, even in relatively moderate England, cannot readily be reconciled. Meanwhile, we record that at a particularly illuminating community sounding session attended by an imam, a rabbi, a representative of one of the local Christian churches and several non-believers, the parties agreed on the following:

- Faith can and should be respected from the outside, regardless of personal belief. The issue is not religious education but a recognition that faith of one kind or another is intrinsic to culture and that it needs to be respected, whatever form it takes.
- The major faiths, and certainly the monotheistic ones, have a great deal in common, and this common ground should be emphasised as core values to which schools and children can subscribe.
- Yet faith is not just about theistic belief. With faith goes a world-view which can encompass everything from custom to morality, from how relationships should be conducted to how knowledge should be conceived.
- The common bonds of faith tend to make parents happier to send their children, in the absence of their own faith school, to a school of another religious denomination.

• Sex education is problematic for some faiths because (a) it places in the public arena what they prefer to treat as private, and (b) it may run counter to their moral codes.

CONCLUSION

The sheer extent and diversity of the witness views we have reported makes them difficult to summarise, and since much of what we have reported has already been extracted or reduced from longer statements we cannot really justify further compression. Yet there are recurrent concerns of a general kind, and our next chapter reviews these before moving on to propose, on the basis of all that has gone before, the framework for a new primary curriculum.

NOTES

1 CACE (1967): para 9.
2 DES (1981).
3 QCA (2007b).
4 DCSF (2008a).
5 That is, discounting the period between Christmas and the new year when schools and offices are closed.
6 Rose (2008), para 2.130: 'The QCA will continue to develop the new areas of learning in order to produce draft programmes of learning by 31 December. QCA will carry out informal consultations on the draft programmes of learning early in 2009 in order that final versions for statutory consultation can be included as part of the final report and recommendations next spring.'
7 Rose (2009), para 1.22. On the approach to aims taken by each review, see Chapter 12.
8 R. Williams (2008). The passage from which this is taken is quoted more fully at the beginning of Chapter 2.
9 Taken from the questionnaire issued to schools and others by DCSF in February 2008 (DCSF 2008q).
10 The NUT and NAHT, in press statements issued on 20 February 2009.
11 QCA (2008a).
12 Education Act 1996: section 353a.
13 QCA (1999): 17.
14 DES (1985b).
15 Ministère de l'Éducation Nationale (2008).
16 Scottish Government (2008a): http://www.ltscotland.org.uk/curriculumforexcellence/whatiscfe/principles.asp
17 DCSF (2007g): para 3.11.
18 DCSF (2008l).
19 DfEE (1998a, 1999a).
20 DCSF website: http://www.standards.dfes.gov.uk/eyfs/site/help/about.htm#faq18
21 Aldrich, cited in Chitty (2008).
22 Benavot and Braslavsky (2007); Meyer, Kamens and Benavot (1992).
23 Hall and Øzerk (2010), *The Cambridge Primary Review Research Surveys*, Chapter 15.
24 *Ibid.*
25 INCA: International Review of Curriculum and Assessment Frameworks (www.nfer.ac.uk).
26 QCA (2008b).
27 Ruddock and Sainsbury (2008).
28 Ruddock and Sainsbury (2008): 2.
29 Beard (1998).
30 Alexander (2001b, 2008a).
31 For example, from the 'Cambridge Primary Review 100', Robin Alexander, Harry Daniels, Maurice Galton, Usha Goswami, Linda Hargreaves, Christine Howe and Neil Mercer.
32 DES (1975).
33 Norman (1992); DES (1975); Barnes, Britton and Rosen (1969).
34 DfES (2003b): 28.
35 NUT (2004): paras 38–42.
36 DES (1978a, 1985b); Ofsted (1997b, 2002).
37 The Action Plan for Geography (APG) is a two year programme funded by DCSF and led by the GA, the Royal Geographical Society (RGS) and the Institute of British Geographers (IBG).
38 Association of Teachers and Lecturers (2007).
39 Rose (2008): para 2.13.
40 Norman (1992).
41 QCA/DfEE (1999): 45. 2009 online: http://curriculum.qca.org.uk/key-stages-1-and-2/subjects/english/attainmenttargets/index.aspx
42 DCSF (2007g).
43 Rose (2006).
44 Wyse, McCreery and Torrance (2010), *The Cambridge Primary Review Research Surveys*, Chapter 29.
45 Wyse and Jones (2008).

46 Wyse, McCreery and Torrance (2010), *The Cambridge Primary Review Research Surveys*, Chapter 29; Wyse and Styles (2007).
47 For an extended justification of the NLS, see Stannard and Huxford (2007). John Stannard was director of the NLS from 1997 to 2000 and Laura Huxford was training director from 1997 to 2004.
48 Day (2002); Osborn *et al.* (2000); Webb and Vulliamy (2006).
49 Webb and Vulliamy (2006): 19.
50 Claxton (2008): 83, submitted as evidence to the Review.
51 Harlen (2008): 15.
52 All organisations submitting evidence were asked if they could be named if quoted in this report. This organisation did not reply, and therefore needs to remain anonymous.
53 Creative Partnerships (2007): 13.
54 Dixon (2007): 15.
55 Hughes (2007): 17.
56 Alexander and Hargreaves (2007): 13.
57 Conroy, Hulme and Menter (2010), *The Cambridge Primary Review Research Surveys*, Chapter 16.

14 Towards a new curriculum

Not only did the condition of the primary curriculum attract more attention from our witnesses than any other Primary Review theme; the responses were also much more diverse. This was in sharp contrast, for example, to assessment and testing, on which there was general agreement.

Nevertheless, from the evidence reviewed in Chapter 13 there is broad agreement on the following propositions:

- The need for a national curriculum is accepted in principle, but its current form is viewed as overcrowded, unmanageable and in certain respects inappropriately conceived.
- There have been significant gains from the national curriculum, notably in science, citizenship and the handling of values, though the place of science now seems less secure than it did before the arrival of the literacy and numeracy strategies in 1998–99.
- The initial promise – and achievement – of entitlement to a broad, balanced and rich curriculum has been sacrificed in pursuit of a well-intentioned but narrowly-conceived 'standards' agenda. The most conspicuous casualties have been the arts, the humanities and those generic kinds of learning, across the entire curriculum, which require time for thinking, talking, problem-solving and that depth of exploration which engages children and makes their learning meaningful and rewarding. The case for art, music, drama, history and geography needs to be vigorously re-asserted; so too does the case for that reflective and interactive pedagogy on which the advancement of children's understanding in large part depends, in 'the basics' no less than other subjects.
- The curriculum is subject to excessive prescription and micro-management from the DCSF, the national strategies and the QCA, and this level of control from the centre has been, on balance, counter-productive.
- The national strategies – literacy, numeracy, primary – have their supporters, and younger teachers in particular welcome the structure and guidance which they have provided, but it is these strategies which, together with the national tests, are seen to have contributed most to perceptions of curriculum overcrowding, distortion and micro-management. The national literacy strategy (now part of the primary framework) is viewed by many as unsatisfactory in both conception and implementation, and is believed to have adversely affected the teaching of English more generally. The national numeracy strategy provoked a much more favourable response.
- The problem of the curriculum is inseparable from the problem of assessment and testing. Unless the national assessment system is reformed, especially at KS2, changes to the curriculum will have limited impact and the curriculum outside the favoured zone of tested subjects will continue to be compromised.
- Some subject associations are deeply concerned about the loss of the conceptual and heuristic integrity of the disciplines whose cause they seek to advance. Many teachers are happier to advocate thematic approaches to which, usually in an unspecified way, subjects will 'contribute'. In turn, some in the subject associations see this as capitulation to the view that a discipline is not important enough to justify stand-alone status. A rather different defence comes from those witnesses who warn that the continuity and security of a subject/

discipline-based curriculum is one of the attractions, for those who can afford them, of private schools. The position of subjects remains contentious, so we have agreement that there is a problem about subjects but disagreement about its nature and solution.

Even if we can identify consensus on the successes and problems of the primary national curriculum, there is no obvious agreement on the way forward, other than by extrapolating from the negatives above: less prescription, less micro-management, less testing, and so on. Otherwise, witnesses argued variously that the curriculum should:

- stay more or less as it is, but be amended and tidied up
- be radically redesigned
- be less prescriptive and more open and flexible
- concentrate on those areas of knowledge and understanding which schools have always taught
- be re-designed around skills, capabilities and attributes
- be structured through areas of experience, as in the early years foundation stage
- have a revised core
- have a national core but reserve substantial time for local variation
- take a new approach to language and literacy.

There is considerable food for thought in what our many witnesses said about the curriculum. However, we cannot arrive at a new model of the primary curriculum merely by following the majority witness line. Witnesses concentrated on the national curriculum, but some of the most intractable problems reach back to well before its birth in 1988. Combining what our witnesses told us about the curriculum with the Review's wider evidence and analysis, we believe that the following most urgently need to be addressed.

Where are the aims and values?

Such was witnesses' preoccupation with the logistics and politics of the national curriculum that many did not ask what it was all for. Yet one can hardly argue about a curriculum's scope, balance and priorities without a clear view of the educational aims which it should pursue and the values by which it, and the work of schools more widely, should be underpinned. Of course, values are pervasive, so in making a case for or against a particular approach to the curriculum witnesses to the Review are voicing their values in another way. But these frequently remain tacit.

In a research survey commissioned by the Review, Professor John White shows how England's national curriculum has tended to be detached from such statements of aims as have been provided,[1] which in any case have been too brief or generalised to be useful. Regardless of these, however, the curriculum as structured has always embodied aims and reflected values, and these can be readily inferred from the hierarchy of subjects and the way each of these is conceived. What is unsatisfactory about the inherited approach, however, is that the stated aims may tend to head grandly in one direction while the curriculum slinks pragmatically in another. For aims to be other than cosmetic, not only should they be in harmony with the curriculum but they should also shape it.

The Cambridge Primary Review has devoted considerable attention to this matter, for one of its principal 10 themes is 'purposes and values'. In this report we have argued not only a new set of aims for primary education but also procedural principles to guide the respective contributions of government, local authorities and schools, for how these bodies act is no less critical for the achievement of the aims than what and how teachers teach. These aims and principles are built in an explicit way into the curriculum framework we propose. This approach contrasts with that taken by the Rose Review, which is to accept as given the existing statements of aims and hope that they will somehow fit the proposed primary curriculum. Yet one can hardly have what has been billed as a 'root-and-branch' review of the curriculum without a root-and-branch review of the aims which it supposedly advances.

Progression or backwash?

The national curriculum sought to achieve much needed continuity from primary to secondary education by devising a single framework for the age-range five to 16, divided into four key stages and defined in terms of a single set of subjects. However, although entitlement was welcomed, many in the primary world saw this as the imposition of a secondary view of the curriculum on primary schools and believed that in the process something distinctively and properly 'primary' had been lost.

As we noted in Chapter 11, the recent expansion of early years provision has generated similar anxiety, this time about the downward thrust of a mainstream primary curriculum into the lives of three to five-year-olds, with the reception class becoming the point at which the two worlds collide. The pressure is always in the same direction, downwards.

The early years foundation stage has been broadly welcomed, as have its six areas of learning and development. But the fear of inappropriate downward pressure has persisted, especially in relation to expectations in literacy, and the recommendation of the Rose Review that children should enter reception classes in the September immediately following their fourth birthday has generated considerable opposition from early years experts, mainly on the grounds that in terms of staffing, training, space, resources and/or provision many reception classes as currently organised do not provide an appropriate environment for such young children.[2] Chapter 11 pointed out that policy in England appears to be premised on the questionable principle that the younger children start formal schooling the better they will eventually do. The experience of those countries whose children start formal schooling up to two years later than in England yet manage to outperform their English peers by age 11 is usually cited here, but it is also important to be clear that in a world where pre-school education and care are increasingly the norm, the argument is less about starting ages than about the nature and appropriateness of provision on either side of the line, wherever it is drawn. In any case, research surveyed for the Review, and reported in Chapter 11, does not support claims made for an early start to *schooling* though the case for appropriate early years *provision* is evidentially very strong.

This chapter is not the place to discuss structures and starting ages. Elsewhere we make proposals on the length and structure of primary education and its relationship to both what precedes and follows it. For the moment, we wish to make clear that the Review's evidence supports the EYFS and the character of its six 'areas of learning and experience'. The task of the primary curriculum is to build in a meaningful way upon these and respect their appropriateness and integrity.

'A dream at conception, a nightmare at delivery'?

Back, however, to logistics. The above phrase is Professor Jim Campbell's;[3] the sentiment is that of thousands of teachers who, since 1989, have struggled to contain a large and expanding national curriculum within a finite school day, week or year: three core subjects, two of which between them are expected to take half of the available time, seven other statutory foundation subjects, three non-statutory foundation subjects, two subjects (RE and sex education) which are, respectively, statutory and required, but which fall outside the foundation subject framework, and six areas of learning across the curriculum.

The problem arose not so much from the original 10-subject specification as from the way each programme of study was independently devised for the National Curriculum Council (NCC) by a group of specialists eager to take advantage of the opportunity to secure the strongest possible foothold for their subject by spelling out content in irrefutable detail. Whether in combination the 10 programmes of study would be logistically feasible appeared not to matter. The subject-by-subject ring binders of the first national curriculum rapidly acquired totemic status as the physical face of curriculum overload. Without the slightest consciousness of irony, the NCC and its successors, SCAA and QCA, added to the mountain of material by supplying document after document telling teachers how to reduce it, sometimes reverting to the 1960s/1970s models of thematic topics in order to show that this was possible. Some schools achieved the necessary miracle of planning. Many others did not.

The experience is salutary and the warning is clear. The national curriculum risked overload from the start. More elements were subsequently added but none was removed, for what subject lobby would be happy to relinquish the claims of a subject in whose educational importance it so passionately believes? Meanwhile, the school day, week and year remained the same length. Something had to give, and it did (see next section).

The warning has two parts. First, the logistical 'nightmare at delivery' remains today's problem, not yesterday's. It has yet to be solved. Second, reducing between 10 and 15 subjects to a smaller number of, say, 'areas of learning' (as in the Rose Review's report) may look promising as a way out of the nightmare but will solve nothing if the programmes of study remain as densely packed as they have been, or if time for some subjects is ring-fenced while other subjects – the majority – must fight for what little time remains.

'Standards, not curriculum'? The anomaly of the national strategies

We consider the pedagogical implications of these two initiatives in Chapter 15, and their educational and professional impact in Chapters 17 and 23. For the moment we note three ways in which they have over-complicated the curriculum and have exacerbated the problem of overload.

First, though they were technically non-statutory, the strategies were treated by government and the national agencies, and hence by schools, as obligatory. Being so, they immediately corralled half of the teaching time available. Indeed, it was expected that literacy and numeracy would take half the available teaching time and the rest would be shared among the other national curriculum subjects *together with the rest of English and mathematics*. On that basis, the time available for the remaining eight subjects would be substantially less than 50 per cent.

Second, the strategies focused in a wholly different way from that established in 1989 on parts of the English and mathematics national curriculum, but not the whole. The NLS was about literacy, not English; the NNS was about numeracy, not mathematics. In turn, though initially defined as 'reading and writing', literacy within the NLS increasingly concentrated on the teaching of reading, with the inevitable result that the quality of children's writing suffered,[4] not to mention speaking and listening, which, though an important part of English in the national curriculum, was not seen as having a significant part to play in the acquisition of literacy. The NNS placed particular emphasis on developing pupils' speed and agility in mental calculation. Somehow, the rest of the national curriculum for English and mathematics had to articulate with these new requirements. The problems of this disarticulation, especially between literacy and English, were voiced by many of our witnesses, as we have reported.

The third complicating factor was political. In 1998–99, when the NLS and NNS were introduced, the national curriculum was the responsibility of the newly-established QCA, which by then had published, after consultation, programmes of study for literacy and numeracy as part of English and mathematics. But the literacy and numeracy strategies themselves were to be run directly by what was then the Department for Education and Employment (now the DCSF). This caused tension between the two bodies and confusion in schools and local authorities.

The response of the government to this situation was highly significant for our examination of the nature of the primary curriculum. In January 1998, a delegation from the board of the QCA met the Minister of State to discuss the new arrangements and to express concern about the department's sudden decision to suspend the programmes of study for the non-core subjects in order to allow schools to concentrate on the new literacy and numeracy strategies and the achievement of the 2002 test targets for 11-year-olds. In the course of the meeting the delegation asked why, having only just set up the QCA, the government had immediately deprived it of responsibility for literacy and numeracy, which, by any definition, are pivotal to a successful primary curriculum. The Secretary of State's standards and effectiveness adviser was present and speedily forestalled the Minister's reply: 'Literacy and numeracy,' he said, 'are standards, not curriculum, and standards are the government's responsibility, not QCA's.'

Clearly, whatever might be claimed for the government's post-1997 standards drive, it was unfortunate, to say the least, that it defined literacy and numeracy not as fundamental and fully integrated aspects of a broad and rich entitlement curriculum – as they had been defined under the 1988 Education Reform Act – but merely as measures of educational standards annexed to a party-political agenda. But if the overt politicisation of literacy and numeracy was damaging, the impact on the curriculum as a whole of this separation of powers was even more so. That apart, the opposition of 'standards' and 'curriculum' is yet another unproductive instance of that discourse of dichotomy which we noted in Chapter 2. In this case there was a clear implication that standards outside literacy and numeracy did not really matter.

However, from 2003 the government sought to reconcile 'standards' and 'curriculum'. The primary national strategy (PNS) was principally concerned with building on the literacy and numeracy strategies but also sought to re-integrate them into the wider curriculum, while at the same time encouraging schools to aim for 'enjoyment' as well as 'excellence'.[5] The PNS was given responsibility for the literacy and numeracy strategies and in October 2006 a combined primary framework for literacy and mathematics was launched.[6] Quietly, 'numeracy' had been replaced by 'mathematics' though the talismanic 'literacy' was retained.

Yet it hardly needs pointing out that the opposition of 'enjoyment' and 'excellence' (for the latter was defined only by reference to literacy and numeracy) is little different from the opposition of 'curriculum' and 'standards.' This, then, would seem to be a persistent problem with the way the primary curriculum has been conceived. We see below that it goes back much further than 1997.

One curriculum or two?

Building on their 1978 primary survey, HM Inspectors advanced, as necessary criteria for planning a coherent whole curriculum, breadth, balance, relevance, differentiation, and progression and continuity.[7] In 2009, Scotland's Curriculum for Excellence retains three of these as stated. A fourth ('coherence') is defined in similar terms to HMI's 'balance', while HMI's 'differentiation' is updated to 'personalisation and choice'.

HMI applied the criterion of breadth at two levels. It is not sufficient, they said, to ensure that a wide range of what they called 'areas of learning and experience' are listed in the paper curriculum or even included in the timetable. Each must be pursued in sufficient breadth and depth to ensure that justice is done to its significance and distinctiveness, for a subject compressed to the bare minimum ceases to be meaningful as an 'area of learning and experience' and thereby reduces the breadth of the whole. Similarly, balance has to be achieved both across the curriculum as a whole and within each area, so as to ensure, for example, that mathematics is not reduced to computation or English to the 'basic skills' of reading and writing alone (a prescient warning, as it turned out). Relevance is about tailoring curriculum experiences to meet children's present and future needs, however these are defined.

The criterion of differentiation grew out of HMI's preoccupation in the 1978 and subsequent surveys with what they called 'match', or 'the relationship between the standard of work children in the groups were doing and what they were considered to be capable of doing'.[8] Generally, then as subsequently, HMI/Ofsted have found that a significant proportion of primary teachers expect too little of their pupils rather than too much. Progression and continuity, again, had both micro and macro aspects: building, minute by minute and day by day, on the child's existing understandings; and ensuring continuity between classes and schools.

The criteria of breadth, balance and relevance beg questions of value and purpose and immediately remind us that a curriculum which is not rooted in an explicit statement of aims and principles makes little sense. Differentiation, progression and continuity focus more on developmental, pedagogical and organisational considerations, though they too are about the curriculum as conceived as well as enacted.

It will be apparent from our witnesses' evidence that in recent years and in many primary schools the eminently worthwhile criteria of breadth and balance have not been met, except by the narrowest definition – that is, including a named subject in the paper curriculum regardless of its quality at 'delivery'. Schools, clearly, blame the government and the national agencies. Are they right to do so?

However, this is a much older problem than many may realise. The primary curriculum has always been a divided curriculum. The Victorian split between the 'basics' or 3Rs and 'the rest' was as sharp as it was sacrosanct. Indeed, striving during the 1970s to develop a curriculum relevant to disadvantaged children living in the shadow of Liverpool's two cathedrals, Eric Midwinter spoke – with an irreverence that only he could get away with – of 'the ritualistic celebration of Holy Maths'.[9] The split was sustained until 1988, when it morphed into 'core' and 'other foundation subjects', with science at last finding its place as the new 'basic' though only temporarily, as our witnesses have noted. By 2008, the Rose Review's interim report confirmed that science had been supplanted as the third 'basic' by ICT, within a new core named 'skills for learning and life'.[10] This new core also included 'personal development', and objections to the dropping of science were anticipated by broadening the concept of literacy to include 'scientific, technological, mathematical and economic "literacy"'.[11]

The division between the two primary curricula starts with a perceived sense of the relative importance of 'the basics'. Were the matter one of relative significance alone there would be no problem, for clearly at every stage of education there must be priorities. But the gap between what in 1984 were called 'curriculum 1' and 'curriculum 2'[12] widens dramatically because it is reinforced in so many other ways. Thus, updating the curriculum 1 and 2 thesis, we now find the situation summarised in Figure 14.1.

It will be seen, then, that for curriculum 2 low valuation or priority is compounded by deprivations in time, resourcing and expertise. Taken together, these almost certainly mean that, for many pupils, minimal time is exacerbated by activities which are trivial, poorly conceived and lacking in cognitive or imaginative challenge. In the 1978 HMI primary survey, the subjects in curriculum 2 were the most heavily criticised for superficial teaching which lacked

CURRICULUM 1: 'THE BASICS' *Assumptions*	CURRICULUM 2: THE REST *Assumptions*
High priority	Low priority
Seen as key indicator of educational 'standards'	The notion of 'standards' does not apply
Provides a curriculum for 'excellence'	Provides a curriculum for 'enjoyment'
Prepares children for life and work	Prepares children for relevant aspects of the secondary curriculum
Preserves separate subject identity	Likely to be merged within 'themes' or 'areas of learning', or taught through other subjects
Has substantial and protected time allocation	Is allocated little time, and this is not protected
Pupil attainment is tested	Pupil attainment is not tested, and sometimes not even assessed
High time/priority in initial training	Low time/priority in initial training, or omitted
High priority in Ofsted inspections	Low priority in inspections, or ignored
Substantial CPD provision	Minimal CPD provision
Specialist expertise welcomed: this teaching is demanding.	Specialist expertise not required: anyone can do it.[i]

Figure 14.1 One curriculum or two?

[i]Music is generally the exception to the 'anyone can do it' assumption (but not art).

structure and progression and for inadequate professional training and understanding. The 1982 Gulbenkian Report on the arts in schools found primary-school art widely perceived as pleasurable, occasionally cathartic but in the end frivolous and inessential – a far cry from what the arts at best can offer.[13] Since these studies, whose findings have been reinforced by classroom research and the comments of our witnesses, little has happened to halt the down-ward spiral of low valuation, inadequate training, limited expertise and undemanding practice which, all too often, is the fate of curriculum 2. On the contrary, the raising of the stakes for literacy or numeracy since 1997 has been at the expense of much or most else, and this is confirmed annually in Ofsted inspections. The problem is readily and frequently identified, but for curriculum 2 there is no billion-pound national strategy waiting in the wings.

It is inevitable that some aspects of primary education will receive more time than others. What is neither inevitable nor educationally defensible is that priority should be negatively tied to quality. The point is so important, yet so open to misunderstanding, that it is italicised: *a truly 'whole' curriculum is one where the quality and seriousness of the teaching are consistently high across all its aspects, regardless of how much time is allocated to them.* Breadth and balance are about the quality of provision no less than the allocation of time. This means that tackling the incomplete, divided and unbalanced curriculum takes us into pedagogy, teacher deploy-ment, expertise and training, and the future of the generalist class teacher system, all of them matters which are considered in later chapters. A curriculum is only as good as those who teach it.

Meanwhile, we are glad to note that Ofsted shares our concern. In 2004, chief inspector David Bell (later Permanent Secretary at DCSF) said in his annual report: 'We cannot afford, and our children do not deserve, a two-tier curriculum.'[14]

Basics and breadth: the pernicious dichotomy

The curriculum 1 and 2 problem is exacerbated by a long-held official assumption that standards in the basics are best secured by concentrating upon them to the exclusion of all or most else. As we noted in earlier chapters, this assumption has been challenged in a succession of official reports going back to 1931, and their findings are succinctly expressed in the 1985 White Paper *Better Schools*:

> The mistaken belief, once widely held, that a concentration on basic skills is by itself enough to improve achievement in literacy and numeracy has left its mark; many children are still given too little opportunity for work in the practical, scientific and aesthetic areas of the curriculum which increases not only their understanding in these areas but also their literacy and numeracy ... Over-concentration on the practice of basic skills in lit-eracy and numeracy unrelated to a context in which they are needed means that those skills are insufficiently extended and applied.[15]

Thus, for some, the continuing curriculum 1 and 2 divide is an obstacle to progress towards a genuinely broad and balanced whole primary curriculum. But we can also see that it may also be an obstacle to progress in curriculum 1 itself, for, as Hadow, Plowden, HMI and Ofsted have all said (though of course not in precisely these terms), attention to curriculum 2 can help to raise standards in curriculum 1.[16] The difficulty for some, and they tend to be politicians, is that the breadth/basics connection seems counter-intuitive. Their common sense dictates that the 'mistaken belief' referred to by the authors of the 1985 White Paper should be sustained. Again, this is a battle which is far from won.

The non-core subjects: capitulation and courage

The threat to curriculum breadth, balance and coherence has in recent years been given a new twist. Aware that in today's educational and economic climate the criterion of 'relevance' to 'the world of work' has become paramount, and regardless of the fact that paid employment is only one kind of work and that both kinds of work constitute but a part of adults' lives, those seeking to defend the place of the non-core subjects against marginalisation cite 'relevance' as their pre-eminent justification. They do so by invoking the claim and language of economic utility. The old claim, that some subjects justify their place in the curriculum because they are intrinsically worthwhile, or because they are what help to hold the line between civilisation and philistinism, no longer cuts much ice. What matters now is marketable skill.

Marketable skill certainly does matter, but it is not all that matters, and this response is as timorous as it is transparent. To each such subject is dutifully appended the word 'skills'. Art becomes 'artistic skills' and for good measure adds the eminently marketable 'design'. The arts generally are repackaged as generic 'creative skills', servants to 'the creative industries'. Other subjects follow suit, the complexities of feeling, empathising, responding and relating are designated 'personal, social and emotional skills'. Even language, unassailably established within curriculum 1 as it is, is repackaged as 'communication skills'. Meanwhile, the entire field of cognition – thinking, knowing, understanding, exploring, imagining, speculating, reasoning and pushing at the boundaries of what is intellectually possible, in all its astonishing aspects – is reduced to 'thinking skills'.

As the Leitch Report shows, there is a case, and a powerful one socially and economically, for paying much more attention than hitherto to the development of skill in public education, and we refer to it below.[17] But merely relabelling everything as a skill is not the answer. Worse, it diminishes the case that can and should be made for the centrality in young children's education of, say, learning in a consciously historical or geographical way about the past or the world around us; or of the educational importance of those irreplaceable pinnacles of human endeavour, imagination and insight represented by science, literature, art, music and drama. In the face of what some call 'the skills revolution' those who really believe in these things should exhibit greater courage.

A historical perspective, as always, exposes the trend for what it is. During the 1970s, primary education took a strongly developmental turn. Being at one with the way children 'naturally' develop was the touchstone for what was called 'good primary practice'. As a result, and at a stroke, 'development' became a required curriculum suffix in LEA and school curriculum plans and schemes of work. English, maths, science, arts, history and geography were out; language development, mathematical development, scientific development, creative development, historical development and geographical development were in. Physical education, which had already supplanted physical training, became physical development. Clearly, some of these can be conceived as genuinely developmental, but like the later over-use of 'skill', this all-purpose application of 'development' was a pronounced case of *reductio ad absurdum*. For children develop anyway, without the intervention of schools. In part, the use of 'development' acknowledged this, but it also implied – and often explicitly endorsed – a view of teaching as no more than developmental facilitation. Words like 'development' and – now – 'skill' have ideological overtones of which we should be keenly aware.

Curriculum manageability or curriculum expertise?

In all the talk of a divided and unmanageable curriculum one possibility is rarely mentioned: that the problems may relate to expertise as well as logistics. After all, if the time and attention given to curriculum 2 in initial teaching training, CPD and inspection are markedly and consistently less than for curriculum 1, this cannot but diminish knowledge of what the curriculum 2 subjects are about and understanding of what they should contribute both to children's education and to the wider culture.

We shall recommend in Chapter 24 that reform of curriculum must be accompanied by reform in teacher training and CPD, and by a re-examination of the curriculum-related roles which primary teachers undertake and the way they are deployed. For the moment we venture the argument that the primary curriculum has become unmanageable not only because the national agencies planned it in overfacing detail without regard for the logistics of the whole, and then added more and more subjects without taking anything away; but also because there has been insufficient conceptual grasp of what exactly needed to be managed. Such a grasp would have enabled professionals to cut straight to the essentials of each subject, recognising what must at all costs be advanced, and what could be jettisoned. Having done so, they could surely have worked out ways to contain even a 12-subject curriculum within the required weekly lesson times of 21 hours for five to seven-year-olds and 23.5 hours for eight to 11-year-olds; or, since there is no reason why the week should be taken as the inevitable or only way of dividing curriculum time, within a school year of 798 hours at KS1 and 893 hours at KS2.[18]

Here it is salutary to note two findings from our enquiries on this matter. First, we have spoken to primary heads who have managed to fit the entire national curriculum into the time available. Second, many independent preparatory schools have voluntarily adopted the national curriculum and from that sector the complaint about overload is never heard. This would seem to suggest, contrary to the received wisdom and contrary even to our own earlier line, that the national curriculum may have been overloaded content-wise but it was not inherently unmanageable – at least, not until the arrival of what one writer has called 'the elephant in the curriculum', high stakes testing,[19] and the national strategies.

According to the primary heads in question, a manageable national curriculum requires that three conditions should be met:

- an intelligent and flexible approach to curriculum planning and timetabling
- a refusal to be bound by the government's expectation that literacy and mathematics should be allocated at least half of the available daily teaching time
- high quality teaching in *all* subjects.

Given the immense pressure to which schools have been subjected, or to which they feel themselves subject, in order to ensure that literacy and numeracy dominate the school day, it is a brave head who asserts his or her independence in this matter. As for our hypothesis about expertise, it is confirmed not only by the evidence from teacher training and inspection, but also by the prevailing discourse of subjects, knowledge and skills, to which we turn next.

THE PRIMARY CURRICULUM: VICTIM OF A MUDDLED DISCOURSE

It is essential to get the structure, balance and content of the primary curriculum right. It is no less essential to ensure that schools have the time and expertise to ensure that it is coherently planned and well taught. Neither of these things will happen until we sort out three essential terms in curriculum discourse. These terms are *subjects, knowledge* and *skill*. To these, at the end of this section, we add the contingent terms *discipline, curriculum* and *timetable*.

Subjects

The furore which greeted the interim report of the Rose Review,[20] in December 2008, illustrated the problem. Opinion split sharply into two camps: those who cheered the departure of subjects and those who condemned it. One side piled up the anti-subject insults – 'traditional', 'old-fashioned', 'artificial', 'irrelevant' and, for good measure, 'Victorian'. The other defended subjects in the name of culture, continuity and standards and deplored alternatives such as Rose's 'areas of learning' as recipes for ignorance or a return to the bad old days of the ubiquitous topic or project (even though Rose emphasised the place of subjects, however the curriculum was organised).

Older readers will recall that during the 1960s and 1970s subjects were similarly demonised and defended. At that time they were seen by many primary teachers, teacher trainers and LEA advisers as the antithesis of that seamless curriculum which children's nature and development required. Subjects, it was claimed, fragmented and compartmentalised learning into 'little boxes'. 'It is important,' said a memorandum in one school at this time, 'that the natural flow of activity, language and thought be uninterrupted by artificial breaks such as subject matter', and to reinforce the message that subjects were outmoded there were frequent references to the 'rigid timetables, clanging bells, silent cloakrooms, cramping desks and absurd rules' of the dark days of elementary schools,[21] though it was never clear what silent cloakrooms had to do with the curriculum. The contributors to the Black Papers responded in no less baleful terms. The folk memory of this discourse remains powerful, even though a large and growing proportion of primary teachers have known no educational world – their own or their pupils' – other than the national curriculum.

Apart from its residual 1970s colouring, what has happened here is that discussion of subjects has become entangled with a distinctly ill-informed discourse about the nature of knowledge. A subject is merely a named conceptual or organisational component of the curriculum. It can mean anything we want it to mean. It is, or ought to be, a wholly neutral term, available to support the efforts of those who strive to work out how, in terms of organisation, timetabling and professional expertise, the goals of a curriculum – any curriculum, ancient, modern or post-modern – can be achieved. Time may be seamless but children's attention is not; nor is their teacher's expertise. The different aspects of the curriculum need to be named, otherwise how else can we talk about them to children, parents or each other? The day and week need to be divided into periods of time which sensibly and appropriately enable these different aspects to be taught.

A subject's relevance, or lack of relevance, resides not in its name but, under whatever name is chosen, in exactly what is taught and how. A subject is not of itself 'old-fashioned' just because subjects have been used as an organising device for over a century. If, as enacted in the classroom, a subject is irrelevant, it is the teacher who makes it so.

This problem, we have to note, is very much a primary school one. Universities woo applicants with long and expanding lists of subjects, and no academic would countenance the accusation that his or her subject remains static or moribund in the way presumed by those who label subjects, *ipso facto*, 'old-fashioned'. For pushing at the boundaries of knowledge, understanding and enquiry is what academics do. For them, though many of the labels have a kind of permanence, the subjects themselves are constantly on the move. Indeed – and this perhaps is the ultimate irony – knowledge does not become outdated because it is framed by subjects; it does so because of the efforts of the very people who work within the boundaries of those subjects. In this sense, knowledge obsolescence and change are marks not of a subject's decline but of its vitality.

Throughout this chapter we use the word 'subject'. We would not wish any readers to assume that the usage is other than neutral. Because some people object to 'subjects' we could talk of 'components', 'elements' or 'parts' of the curriculum, but this would be an exercise in mere political correctness.

So when critics of the Rose Review's interim report complained of the 'death of subjects' there is a sense in which they were quite wrong, for one set of names, or subjects, was merely replaced by another, and what matters above all else is what, in terms of knowledge, understanding and skill, such new names denote. What the critics were really worried about was the exclusion from primary education of disciplinary-based knowledge and enquiry, and this exclusion in no way automatically follows from the renaming of subjects as 'areas of learning'. It is possible that within Rose's 'areas of learning' what critics of his model associate with subjects (that is, disciplines) is not only alive and well but may even be strengthened. Equally, it is possible that the new labels reflect that very dilution or exclusion of discipline-based knowledge and enquiry which critics most fear and deplore. At the time of writing, that remains to be seen.

In any case, subjects, disciplines and knowledge, still less subjects and a particular view of knowledge, are not synonymous. A subject, as we have said, is an organisational segment of the curriculum. It may or may not be coterminous with a particular discipline such as mathematics, science, art or geography. Knowledge is central to every discipline, but its precise place and character in school subjects as diverse as mathematics and PSHE are highly variable. The three terms should be used much more discriminatingly, and the word 'subjects', in particular, should be divested of its inherited ideological charge.

A different though related point was made by Norman Thomas, former chief inspector of primary education, in a post-Rose comment to the Cambridge Review. He was pleased that the Rose Review interim report acknowledged that there is a place on the timetable for both specific subject lessons and for thematic work. He argued, however, 'that it should be made very clear that the sub-headings used in describing the curriculum do not prescribe the headings for the periods into which the timetable is divided. Indeed, whatever the title of the lesson, whether a subject or a theme, it is bound to include aspects of learning referred to within a number of different sections of the curriculum definition.' Thus, while subjects divide the curriculum conceptually or organisationally, the timetable divides it temporally into lessons, and the two forms of division are not necessarily synonymous.

Knowledge

> Children do not need to know lots of dates. They can look up information on Google and store it on their mobile phones … The days of teachers barking out facts are long gone. Our job is to prepare children so that they can access information and knowledge in the modern world.[22]

Lest readers imagine that we quote with approval this testimonial to Rose's 'areas of learning', we say immediately that it puts in a nutshell much that is wrong with the way knowledge is talked about in primary education. Consider the assumptions here:

• knowledge is mere facts or information
• such facts and information are there to be 'looked up' and 'stored', but never engaged with or questioned
• knowledge is ineradicably associated with old-fashioned quasi-Gradgrindian teaching ('Teach these boys and girls nothing but Facts. Facts alone are wanted in life …'[23])
• children may 'access' knowledge but it is no longer necessary for them, or their teachers, to know anything.

and, as a gratuitous swipe at one subject among several:

• history is about the learning of dates.

The most serious problem here is the equating of knowledge with facts or information. Propositional knowledge is but one kind of knowledge, and it is the essence of the mature disciplines that propositions must be tested, whether through the assembling and examination of evidence which marks out the methodology of the physical and human sciences, or by tests of authenticity and artistry which may be applied in the arts, or simply in relation to honestly-assessed experience. In any case, propositional knowledge need not be as sterile as 'the learning of dates' portrays it, and for many people the acquisition of information both excites and liberates. To tell children, at the start of lives in which they will be assailed by information which they fail to evaluate at their peril, and in which they will need and want to know and discover a great deal, that Google and a mobile phone will do the trick, is a travesty of what knowing and understanding ought to be about. Educationally, it is also highly irresponsible.

What is doubly disturbing about the point of view illustrated above is that England's national curriculum was initially credited with breaking away from such perceptions and encouraging greater attention to modes of enquiry and the assessing of evidence. But then, our witnesses have reported that one consequence of curriculum overcrowding in the past decade has been to force teachers more and more into transmission mode.

If the various domains of knowledge are viewed not as collections of inert or obsolete information but as distinct ways of knowing, understanding, enquiring and making sense which include processes of enquiry, modes of explanation and criteria for verification which are generic to all content in the domain, then, far from being redundant or irrelevant, knowledge provides the means to tackle future problems and needs as well as offering windows of unparalleled richness on past and present. Knowledge in this sense also provides the pupil with essential tools for testing the truth and value of all that information which pours from the internet, television, radio and newspapers, and the teacher's task becomes one of initiation into this critically-armed frame of mind rather than the mere transmission that is the stock-in-trade of the teacher 'barking out facts'. We cannot at the same time hope that science will enable us to cure the hitherto incurable disease, or offer the world a route to sustainability and survival, while asserting that subjects – including of course science – are educational old hat and need to be replaced by skills or themes. If teachers confine themselves to 'barking out facts', then they understand neither knowledge nor pedagogy.

Rejection of a knowledge-based curriculum, therefore, reflects in part a simple mis-apprehension about the nature of knowledge itself, and the partisan bodies of information with which mere transmission pedagogy and its totalitarian variant, indoctrination, are associated. But in the processual sense advocated above, mathematics, the sciences, arts and humanities will be no less relevant and useful in the 21st century than they were in the 20th. For they develop rather than stand still, proceeding on the basis of cumulation, verification and/or falsification. Thus, Matthew Arnold's view of culture as 'the best that has been known and said in the world' needs to submit neither to relativist sneers nor to post-modernist nihilism. For by its sheer intellectual and imaginative power, and by its dogged integrity in the face of ignor-ance, scepticism or autocracy, the best of past thinking always tells us something new about ourselves and our world. Knowledge may be cumulative, but certain knowledge transforma-tions and acts of artistic creation or scientific discovery are so fundamental that they never lose their power and should be visited afresh by each generation.

No less fundamentally, knowledge looks forward as well as back. Scientific research is per-manently on the move and its truths are no sooner accepted than superseded, the arts are constantly pushing at the boundaries of form and expression, and for every conventional history there is a radical alternative. As for that traditional core of all curricula, literacy, it is right to ask whether what counted as literacy for the pen-pushing Victorian clerks of the British Empire can serve also as literacy for the global information age, even though some would continue to confine the debate to endless arguments about phonics. As Luke and Carrington argue, we may now need a pluralist vocabulary of 'literacies' which can accommodate, in a convincing and coherent way, text both print and virtual, literature both canonical and popular, and narratives both local and international.[24] The Rose Review's interim report commends the broadening of the concept of literacy to include 'scientific, technological, mathematical and economic "literacy"'.[25] On the other hand, we may also need to be alert to the possibility that the proliferation of 'literacies' carries the same danger as the proliferation of 'skills': the force and discipline of the word as originally used, and of the practice undertaken in its name, is weakened or lost.

All this is before we have begun to talk about public and private knowledge; about the way, within and outside the public forms of knowing and understanding, individuals make their own sense of knowledge 'out there' and accommodate it to their personal worlds. This, too, is an important area for debate in primary education, especially in the context of the movement towards constructivist pedagogy to which we refer in our next chapter. So too is an under-standing of the relationship between knowledge, social structure and power, for without that understanding we may not perceive how the elevation of certain kinds of knowledge represses others, and how a curriculum's 'selection from culture' may be interested only in the culture of a society's upper layers, thereby fuelling the sense of marginalisation or exclusion among those whose culture appears not to be valued. In our culturally plural, divided and unequal society, this apparently theoretical issue has very direct relevance to the work of teachers in some of the country's most challenging educational environments.

All these matters should be the stock in trade of the teachers who select, mediate and pronounce upon the knowledge which children encounter. The one thing needful here, apart from a very different discourse about knowledge from the one with which we are all too familiar, is that the study of knowledge itself should secure a central place in the training of teachers. At the moment, it is rarely seen.

Skills

A rather different kind of reductionism attends discussion of skills, currently the fashionable educational antidote to knowledge. At the same time as knowledge is downgraded to obsolescent information, everything else is elevated to a skill. So, for example, the Association of Teachers and Lecturers' submission to the Review claimed that today's children need

> a skills based curriculum, focused on the physical skills, the communication, interpersonal and intrapersonal skills and the thinking and learning skills as well as the academic skills which will be essential components of the educated person who is able to think and act effectively in the 21st century.

The belief here is that skills combine contemporary relevance, future flexibility and hands-on experience: that is, those attributes which knowledge is presumed to lack. The modes of knowing, understanding and enquiring embodied in the established disciplines are themselves reduced to 'academic skills' from which, presumably, knowledge is excluded. Skills, it is believed, transcend both knowledge and time.

In similar vein, the Rose Review's interim report proposes replacing the knowledge-rich core of the current national curriculum – English, mathematics and science – by a new core of four 'skills for learning and life' – literacy, numeracy, ICT and personal development;[26] while the QCA's 'big picture of the curriculum' highlights 'literacy, numeracy, ICT, personal, learning and thinking skills' but defines 'knowledge and understanding' merely as 'big ideas that shape the world'.[27]

In all such cases, the concomitant to the elevation of skill – in itself, as we see below, a necessary development – is the downgrading of knowledge, understanding, enquiry and exploration. But to set them in opposition is foolish, unnecessary and epistemologically unsound, for all but the most elemental skills – and certainly those that in educational circles are defined as 'basic skills' – require knowledge, and knowledge itself is far more than 'big ideas that have shaped the world'. Or indeed, far less, for is it proposed that ideas that have not 'shaped the world' should be excluded from the curriculum, that eminence matters more than destiny obscure? Whose world are we talking about anyway? Is there an applied judgement here that to 'shape' is to shape for the better? Does the definition encompass the casualties of world-shaping ambition as well as the usual list of heroes? And who decides on all these matters? QCA?

Further, in terms of our argument (Chapter 12) that primary education should balance preparation for future needs and circumstances with attention to the needs and capabilities of children here and now, this shift is clearly driven by the former. Thus the Royal Society of Arts, Manufacture and Commerce (RSA) reworks the entire curriculum in terms of five areas of 'competence': for learning, citizenship, relating to people, managing situations, and managing information,[28] and the government identifies three broad domains of 'skill': vocational skills which are specific to particular work settings; job-specific skills distinctive to particular positions within a given occupation; and generic skills, transferable across different work and life settings.[29]

Clearly, the first two groups – vocational and job-specific skills – may provoke the same objection on the grounds of built-in obsolescence as knowledge-as-information. For this reason many advocates of this approach prefer to transfer them to the category of training/retraining in the more specific domain of vocational education, and place greatest emphasis during general schooling on the lifelong learning potential of the third group, generic skills. Here is a typical list:

- managing one's own learning
- problem-solving
- thinking
- research, enquiry and investigation
- invention, enterprise and entrepreneurship
- communication
- social and interpersonal skills
- teamwork
- leadership[30]

We note immediately that David Hargreaves' list is no mere exercise in curriculum re-naming in pursuit of a spurious notion of 'relevance'. Everything here can make a strong claim to the status of skill as properly defined: the 'ability to do something (especially manual or physical) well; proficiency, expertness, dexterity … acquired through practice or learning'.[31] During the last few decades, 'skill' has lost its embedding in 'manual or physical' activity, possibly as these have lost their dominance in the world of work. What has not been lost is the sense of skill as the capacity to do something: a capacity which is in the broadest sense practical and which is honed through concentration and practice. This is why skill is so important in education, why it must complement knowing and understanding rather than supplant them, and why as a concept it must not be debased through inappropriate use.

It is therefore useful to note that Hargreaves' list includes capacities which are needed to advance knowledge and understanding (problem-solving, research, enquiry and investigation) and those which do not necessarily lie within the boundaries of a knowledge-based curriculum (invention, enterprise and entrepreneurship, social and interpersonal skills, teamwork, leadership). In this formulation, and unlike the re-naming instances we have given, skills extend the scope of the curriculum in a convincing and wholly necessary way.

Even so, if skills are all that a curriculum offers, as some of our witnesses have advocated, then we have a problem. Even when one hives off the explicitly vocational skills, most such models tend to be more strongly influenced by the needs of the workplace than by other contexts for life after school, let alone the needs of children here and now. And though the generic skills approach purports to address the claims of lifelong learning, it actually sells such learning short, for it elevates being able to do something over knowing, understanding, reflecting, speculating, analysing and evaluating, which arguably are no less essential to the fulfilled, successful and useful life. Indeed, without these capacities the exercise of skill becomes in a very real sense meaningless.

Skills are vital. We cannot survive without them. But, once again, educators should use the term more discriminatingly, otherwise we shall carelessly lose not only knowledge and understanding, but also skill itself.

Definitional footnote

We end up, then, with six basic curriculum terms in need of differentiation:

- *Curriculum:* what is intended to be taught and learned overall (the planned curriculum); what is taught (the curriculum as enacted); what is learned (the curriculum as experienced).
- *Subject:* an organisational or conceptual segment of the planned curriculum; may be disciplinary, cross-disciplinary or thematic.
- *Timetable:* the way the planned curriculum is divided temporally into lessons or sessions as opposed to being divided conceptually into subjects.
- *Knowledge:* the process and outcome of coming to know, or the combination of what is known and how such knowledge is acquired. It encompasses knowledge both propositional

and procedural, and both public and personal, and it allows for reservation and scepticism as well as certainty. It is neither synonymous with subjects nor all that a curriculum contains, though it is nevertheless a central goal of all education.

- *Discipline:* a branch of knowledge as systematised into distinct ways of enquiring, knowing, exploring, creating, explaining and making sense, each with their own key foci, preoccupations, concepts, procedures and products.
- *Skill:* the ability to make or do something, especially of a practical kind; requires knowledge but is distinct from it.

TOWARDS A NEW PRIMARY CURRICULUM

Our approach

We have described present curriculum arrangements and traced their roots. We have summarised the considerable quantity of evidence on curriculum matters received by the Review. On some of this evidence we have felt obliged to comment, and combining it with our own analysis we have identified what appear to be the central problems in contemporary primary curriculum policy and practice and in the thinking which informs them.

We are now ready to move forward. The Review's position is that a future primary curriculum must:

- confront and attempt to address the problems and challenges in current arrangements
- be grounded in explicit principles of design and implementation
- pursue and remain faithful to a clear and defensible statement of educational aims and values.

These criteria structure what follows.

Tackling the problems

The main problems in existing national curriculum arrangements which must be addressed are these:

- The detachment of curriculum from aims.
- The supplanting of long-term educational goals by short-term targets of attainment.
- The real or perceived problem of curriculum overload, in the sense that many teachers believe that far too much is prescribed for the time available.
- The loss, for whatever reason, of the principle of children's entitlement to a broad, balanced and rich curriculum, and the marginalisation, in particular, of the arts, the humanities and – latterly – science.
- The test-induced regression to a valuing of memorisation and recall over understanding and enquiry, and to a pedagogy which rates transmission more important than the pursuit of knowledge in its wider sense.
- The dislocation and politicisation of both the whole curriculum and two major elements within it – English and mathematics – by the national strategies and the accompanying rhetoric of 'standards'.
- The use of a narrow spectrum of the curriculum as a proxy for the quality of the whole, and the loss of breadth and balance across and within subjects as a result of the pressures of testing, especially at the upper end of the primary school.
- The parallel pressure at the start of the primary phase, this time of formal learning on the developmental curriculum of the EYFS.
- The excess of prescription and micro-management by the DCSF and the QCA, their reinforcement through the focus of Ofsted inspection and TDA requirements for initial teacher training, and the resulting loss of professional flexibility and autonomy.

- The historical split between 'the basics' and the rest of the curriculum, in which differential time allocations legitimately set in pursuit of curriculum priorities are compounded by unacceptable differences in the quality of provision as between these two segments.
- The continuing and demonstrably mistaken assumption that high standards in 'the basics' can be achieved only by marginalising much of the rest of the curriculum.
- A muddled discourse about subjects, knowledge and skills which infects the entire debate about curriculum, needlessly polarises discussion of how it might be organised, parodies knowledge and undervalues its place in education and inflates the undeniably important notion of skill to a point where it, too, becomes meaningless.

Curriculum overload, real or perceived

On the face of it, the solution is to prescribe less and leave more to the judgement of individual schools. However, because we know that some schools manage the same curriculum much more successfully than others, the answer must also lie in improved planning at school level, a better match of professional expertise to curriculum task, and more effective ways of deploying that expertise. In these matters local authorities have an essential role, quite apart from the part they can play in the realisation of our aims of local citizenship and the celebration of local culture and community.

Marginalisation of the arts and humanities

This is not, or not only, about reducing prescription overall. In the first instance, it requires a much more confident – perhaps even aggressive – assertion of the educational importance of the arts and humanities in human development, culture and education, and a refusal to capitulate to narrowly-conceived criteria of 'relevance'. Ministerial support for the arts in education tends to sound tokenistic and insincere, whether or not it is. Authoritative official enquiries on the arts, creativity and culture are warmly applauded and then disappear without trace.[32] At school level, the persistence of the 'two curricula' problem suggests that the marginalisation relates also to teacher expertise and the neglect of the non-core subjects in initial teacher training (ITT) and continuing professional development (CPD). Those primary schools which do not allow vulnerable subjects to be marginalised are those which are confident and knowledgeable about their value and which have the expertise to teach them well. Reinstating the arts and humanities in primary education requires a campaign on several fronts simultaneously.

The distortion of the curriculum as a whole by the national strategies

Leaving aside the question of the impact of the strategies on standards, their non-statutory status should be insisted upon, and should not be countermanded by inspection procedures or teacher training requirements which treat them as obligatory. In any event, it is for individual schools to ensure, through sound planning and good teaching, that the strategies support rather than deny children's entitlement to a broad and balanced curriculum.

The strategies' dislocation of English and mathematics

Eliminating this problem would seem to require that the PNS and primary framework, successors to the NLS and NNS, be abandoned as separate initiatives, that literacy be reunited with English and numeracy with mathematics, and that they once again become the responsibility of the QCA or whatever agency is responsible for the rest of the curriculum (though on the powers of the latter, see below). It is of course acknowledged that the strategies have generated a large body of useful professional support material, but this need not be lost in the re-integration of English and mathematics. The professional networking latterly encouraged by the PNS should also be built upon, and indeed is essential to what we propose below.

The adverse impact of the national KS2 tests on the curriculum

This requires wholesale reform of the testing regime, as discussed in Chapters 16 and 17. A reduced obsession with targets might also re-invigorate discussion of aims more broadly conceived.

Pressure on the EYFS

Some see a contradiction in the Rose Review's approach. On the one hand it supports 'play-based' learning in the EYFS and teaching in Y1 which is more aligned to the six EYFS areas of learning and development. On the other it proposes a single entry point into the reception class – the September immediately following a child's fourth birthday – on the grounds that this will secure more positive learning outcomes for all children, including the summer born and those from disadvantaged backgrounds.[33] As we noted earlier, the real issue here is the nature of the provision. However, early years experts are concerned that too many reception classes reflect downward pressure from KS1 rather than the integrity of the EYFS as conceived, and for that reason resist such a move and view it as incompatible with the Rose Review's support for the principles embodied in the EYFS.

Unease about the reception year started as soon as the national curriculum was introduced in 1989. Whatever they have separately achieved, the expansion of pre-school provision and the KS1/2 standards agenda have made this vital point of transition increasingly fraught, for it has been squeezed by two very different views of what primary education should be about.

In this report we take the view that the integrity of the EYFS must be preserved but also that the curriculum we propose can build readily onto the EYFS areas of learning and experience, provided that – and it is an important proviso – schools are able to make their own decisions about how this is done. But, as we showed in Chapter 11, there is a structural issue here too. In our final chapter we shall make proposals for rationalising the phasing of primary education as a whole, in respect of both organisation and curriculum, which we believe will help to resolve the problem.

The 'two curricula' problem

This goes right back to the beginning of mass basic education and it cannot be solved overnight. It entails attention to all those tendencies which exacerbate differential time allocation by unacceptable qualitative variation in what children encounter and experience in different subjects, and it requires:

- re-educating the public about what the 'curriculum 2' subjects offer and about children's developmental and educational need for a broad and balanced curriculum at the primary stage;
- re-instating 'curriculum 2' in ITT and CPD at a properly demanding level so that teachers understand the true worth and potential of the subjects in question;
- ensuring that every school has the professional expertise to teach all subjects well, regardless of how much time is allocated to them;
- re-assessing the balance of generalist, semi-specialist and specialist teaching and of the staffing which schools require in order to deploy such teaching as needed.

The loss of breadth and balance within subjects

This is partly about reducing the scope of what is prescribed, partly about re-balancing the programmes of study, and partly about pedagogy. If it is the case, as it is, that many teachers succeed in making individual subjects lively and challenging without capitulating to mere transmission, then at stake is not just what is prescribed but also teachers' understanding of the subjects in question and the scope of their pedagogic repertoire. This takes us back, yet again, to ITT and CPD.

Excessive micro-management

This is a systemic problem which affects many aspects of English primary education. In the specific context of curriculum, there would appear to be three solutions:

- reduce the scope of the prescribed curriculum to a broad framework which encourages and indeed requires schools to provide the detail
- change the QC(D)A's role to a purely advisory one
- replace professional dependence by autonomy through training which deepens teachers' curriculum knowledge and understanding, including both their specialist knowledge of particular subjects and their capacity to use the language and concepts of curriculum more expertly. Changes are also dictated in inspection and teacher training (see Chapters 17 and 21).

The opposing of standards and breadth

We have to be blunt: it is time that ministers and officials started taking notice of the evidence on the necessary relationship between standards and breadth. The evidence may be politically counter-intuitive but it is also well-established, consistent and unequivocal.

Subjects, disciplines, knowledge, skills and the discourse of curriculum

In the long term, the pervasive failure to speak with proper understanding and discrimination about subjects, disciplines, knowledge and skills can only be addressed through ITT and CPD. While supposedly training teachers to advance children's knowledge and skill in specific subjects, ITT has (a) neglected many of those subjects and (b) failed to educate teachers in even the basics of epistemology. Learning, knowing, understanding, acquiring skill and developing personal qualities are the essence of education. Disciplines provide a significant resource and focus for that endeavour, though not the only one. Subjects offer one way, though again not the only way, of translating what is to be learned and taught into a curriculum which is manageable on a day-to-day basis.

The ability to move with ease around this conceptual and organisational territory is particularly important for primary teachers because the generalist tradition requires them to think about, plan and teach the curriculum as a whole. Unless it is prepared to be radical about the curriculum, a secondary school may be able to confine its thinking about the whole curriculum to the admittedly complex task of timetabling, knowing that the boundaries of what is to be timetabled are set and agreed. It seems almost inconceivable that this complex field has been neglected in primary teachers' training; but it has, and the matter should be addressed without delay.

However, the pressure is on to devise a new primary curriculum to start in 2011 and that is too soon for changes in ITT and CPD to make the necessary impact, and in any event the changes will not touch those who make the decisions. All we can do is insist that there is a problem, and urge those concerned to recognise it as such and attend to it with due seriousness. It cannot be the task of the Cambridge Primary Review to plan the curriculum in detail; but to those charged with this task we would urge very careful attention to the business of differentiating the different kinds of knowledge and understanding, the skills and the personal qualities and attributes which the new curriculum seeks to advance and foster.

In particular, the fundamental place in primary education of both knowledge and skill needs to be asserted, and the skills which children need for today's learning and tomorrow's world need to be identified with precision.

Warning: the blame game

To this brief summation we add that although there is a clear case for less central prescription and micro-management, in a centralised system it is all too easy for professionals to blame government and national agencies for problems which, partly or even wholly, may have their roots in professional understanding, expertise and resourcefulness, not to mention school leadership. This is clearly demonstrated by the fact that some schools and teachers transcend what appear to be systemic problems, and are led with the dynamism and independence of spirit which give their staff the necessary confidence to break free of the culture of dependence and compliance. Yet there is no doubt that there is considerable pressure from the top to conform to particular views of 'best practice' and that asserting such independence requires both real courage and a record of success as conventionally defined. All this demonstrates the importance for a sound curriculum of matters discussed not only here but also in other chapters, notably aims, values and principles (Chapter 12), pedagogy (Chapter 15), teacher expertise, training and deployment (Chapter 21), and school leadership (Chapter 22).

Forward from principles

The principles upon which the Review has concluded that primary education should be based are set out and elaborated in Chapter 12 and therefore do not need to be repeated here. What is important about the analysis is not just the principles themselves but the notion that each level has its part to play in implementing them, in contrast to both what some see as the full-blown centralism of recent years and the countervailing rhetoric of 'partnership' between government and schools, which underplays the contribution of local authorities and communities. Instead, the principles re-assert the need for a genuine and vibrant localism in which partnership between school and community, school and school, and school and local authority are essential to a curriculum which can respond to children's needs and circumstances, and which is able to realise the aim of 'celebrating culture and community', one of our new aims for primary education. It is pertinent, however, to add further notes about four of the principles.

Universal entitlement. Entitlement – of all children, to a curriculum in which aims are universally pursued, through content which is reasonably consistent, in pursuit of outcomes, standards and quality which apply regardless of which school the child attends – can only be guaranteed by a national curriculum framework. However, we must bear in mind our evidence that in recent years government appears to have been at the same time the official guarantor of children's entitlement to a broad and balanced curriculum and a threat to it through some of its other policies. Therefore those bodies which are in a position to scrutinise the impact of such policies, notably Parliament, Ofsted and the House of Commons Children, Schools and Families Committee, will need to be vigilant and vocal in upholding both the principle and the law in this regard. Further, the sheer diversity of local circumstances means that national bodies can safeguard entitlement only up to a point: local authorities and schools must play their part too.

Quality, standards and accountability. We have asserted that those involved in a public system of education should be accountable for what they do, and this requires standards against which such accountability can be demonstrated. But we have also noted that educational 'quality' and 'standards', still less 'standards' as defined solely by reference to selected aspects of literacy and numeracy, must not be treated as synonymous, and that what is meant by quality in primary education needs urgently to be re-assessed and re-defined.

It is also important to note that in centralised regimes accountability tends to be one-directional. That is to say, those with most power habitually call to account those with least, despite the fact that culpability for what goes wrong may well lie with those who determine policy rather than with those who implement it. Under the old HMI system, an independent inspectorate was able to balance comment on schools with critique, where necessary, of government policy.

Under the current Ofsted system this is less likely, and there is a tendency to treat policy as beyond reproach and to concentrate on how far schools comply with it. In the interests of both efficiency and justice there now needs to be greater mutuality in the mechanisms for educational accountability.

Guidance, not prescription. This principle has two direct practical consequences: first, reduction in the amount of curriculum detail emanating from government and the national agencies, so that local flexibility and freedom become a realistic prospect; second, a clear statement to the effect that, subject to the broad curriculum framework proposed below, the role of the national agencies becomes advisory. We have argued separately that the national strategies should cease to operate in their present form and that guidance on literacy and numeracy should be re-integrated into the national curriculum framework.

Responsiveness to local need and circumstance. Local circumstances and needs, by their nature, cannot be made subject to national prescription. Responsiveness to local need and circumstance requires three changes: first, a re-balancing of responsibility between national and local government; second, a preparedness by local government to generate a culture of genuine partnership with and between schools rather than regress to that lower-tier centralisation and paternalism for which some local authorities were notable during the 1970s and 1980s; third, the reservation of time and space for local elements in the national curriculum framework. At present, curriculum localism applies only, through the SACREs, to religious education. There may be a need for a whole-curriculum equivalent to the SACREs – for example a 'Community Curriculum Partnership' – which would identify the local needs and circumstances which the curriculum should or might address. However, on the principle of 'guidance, not prescription', schools would determine their own response to the outcome. Some might argue, indeed, that true localism leaves such matters entirely to individual schools. Past evidence should discourage that.

There are two main ways of creating conceptual and planning space for the local element. The national curriculum can be specified in such a way that it can be accommodated in its entirety within a given proportion of the week or year – say 80 per cent – and the local authorities and schools would then determine what is done with the remainder. This was the recommendation of the 1993 Dearing Report[34] but the weight of national curriculum detail, augmented later by the national strategies, ensured that it could never work. Or each element in the national curriculum can have both a national and a local component. That would be particularly apposite, within a conventionally subject-based curriculum, for history and geography, which lend themselves readily to a combination of national and local, though not to the same degree for other subjects. To complicate matters, one of the proposed 12 aims for primary education in Chapter 12 ('empowering local, national and global citizenship') pursues not just a balance of the national and local but also global purposes. In contrast, another aim ('celebrating culture and community') is more obviously local in orientation. These examples suggest that a composite model is needed, and this is attempted in the framework below.

Forward from aims

Implementing the aims proposed in Chapter 12 requires a similar sense of the different opportunities of the various contexts of education, but here the legal and administrative contexts of government, local authority and school are less important than the various aspects of the school itself. Some aims apply in an obvious fashion to the curriculum as formally specified. Some relate more to the generic features of pedagogy and the relationships and culture of the classroom. Some are pursued equally or even more appropriately through the ethos and collective practices of the school as a whole. Some are engaged with all of these contexts simultaneously. For example:

Well-being (aim 1) is on the face of it fostered in school mainly through relationships. However, to say – as frequently used to be said of primary education as a whole – 'it's all about relationships' is to miss the point that well-being follows no less from securing children's engagement in learning, giving them access to stimulating and worthwhile activities, exciting their interest and imagination and helping them to achieve high standards. In this sense, *Every Child Matters* is right that an enhanced concept of childhood well-being requires that children should not only 'be healthy' and 'stay safe' – the minimal definition of well-being – but also 'enjoy and achieve' and 'make a positive contribution'. ECM is right, too, in balancing well-being now and in the future ('make a positive contribution' and 'achieve economic well-being'), though on the latter it might be argued that 'not being prevented by economic disadvantage' is one vital precondition for 'achieving their full potential in life' but not the only one.

Exploring, knowing, understanding and making sense (aim 9) reasserts the fundamental importance to the child's education of encountering and being inducted into 'the different ways that humans make sense or their world and act upon it', principally through what we call the disciplines – language, mathematics, science, the arts, the humanities and so on – but also through other ways of knowing and understanding, both collective and personal. However, 'exploring' in this aim ensures that this induction does not stop short at the transmission and recall which have given subject teaching its arid reputation and reminds us that to enliven the child's 'amazement, perplexity, curiosity, discovery, invention, speculation, fantasy, play and linguistic agility' requires a special and heightened form of pedagogy.

Celebrating culture and community (aim 8) is as much about what happens in the school – and indeed outside it – as in the classroom. Celebration, it must be noted, is not merely unfocused merriment but is as rooted in knowledge and understanding as are mathematics and science.

These three examples show how, although the proposed curriculum domains may seem familiar enough, a new primary curriculum as proposed in this report uses every resource at the school's disposal to pursue the specified educational aims. These are aims for primary education in all its aspects. This chapter has insisted that if for pupils or former pupils a subject is identified with only transmission, memorisation and recall, this reflects not the intrinsic character of the subject but the way their teachers have chosen to define and teach it. In the same way, if our 12 aims for primary education are presumed to start and end with the various domains of the formal or paper curriculum, then a large part of their potential, and certainly of their impact on children, will be lost.

During the 1960s and 1970s much was made, of the counterpoint between the 'formal' curriculum of specified subjects and a 'hidden' curriculum of values and expectations which were less explicit but no less important to a pupil's successful progress. Then David Hargreaves suggested that the 'hidden' curriculum was in fact hidden from nobody, least of all from pupils, and proposed instead the term 'paracurriculum'.[35] Nowadays we are less squeamish about values in education. We understand that values are central and we make them explicit through statements like that devised by the National Forum and discussed in the previous chapter, and much of what used to be connoted by the 'hidden' curriculum is now dignified by the acronym PSE (or even, with health, moral education and citizenship added, PSHMCE).

Educational aims, then, are pursued, in different ways and to varying degrees, through the structure and content of specific curriculum domains, through the generic character of pedagogy, and through the life of the school as a whole. Taking the proposed 12 aims for primary education, Figure 14.2 invites consideration of this idea.

What should children learn?

It is a conventional truth, but a useful one, that *how* children learn is as important as *what* they learn, in as far as a curriculum, however relevant or inspiring it is on paper, will make little headway unless the teacher succeeds (aim 2) in igniting 'children's active, willing and enthusiastic engagement in their learning.' The aims we have proposed contain other such reminders: the importance of the imagination (aim 11); of dialogue and joint activity which both motivate pupils and capitalise on what is now known about how brain, mind and understanding develop during the early and primary years (aim 12); and of generating that

	Through specific curriculum domains	Through generic pedagogy	Through the life of the school and community
The individual			
Well-being			
Engagement			
Empowerment			
Autonomy			
Self, others and the wider world			
Encouraging respect and reciprocity			
Promoting interdependence & sustainability			
Empowering local, national & global citizenship			
Celebrating culture and community			
Learning, knowing and doing			
Exploring, knowing, understanding, making sense			
Fostering skill			
Exciting the imagination			
Enacting dialogue			

Figure 14.2 Aims into practice: contexts for implementation.

sense of empowerment allied to skill through which learning becomes inner-directed and autonomous rather than dependent on pressure from others (aims 3 and 4).

Yet we cannot accept the claims in some of the Review submissions that 'process' is all that matters, that the content of the curriculum is no longer significant, and that in a fast-changing world knowledge is merely an ephemeral commodity to be downloaded, accepted without question or summarily discarded. Indeed, this is a view which we have deemed it necessary to contest with some vigour, for we believe it to be based on a fundamental misunderstanding about the nature and possibilities of knowledge and on a caricature of teaching as telling and of learning as factual memorisation and recall. We have also suggested that if the caricature has substance, it is a comment not on knowledge but on teachers.

That is why the aims, for all their apparent emphasis on process, include the unambiguous statement (aim 9) that primary education should enable children

> to encounter and begin to explore the wealth of human experience through induction into, and active engagement in, the different ways through which humans make sense of their world and act upon it: intellectual, moral, spiritual, aesthetic, social, emotional and physical; through language, mathematics, science, the humanities, the arts, religion and other ways of knowing and understanding.

The statement goes on to remind us that knowledge matters because culture matters. Indeed, culture is what defines us:

> Induction acknowledges and respects our membership of a culture with its own deeply-embedded ways of thinking and acting which can make sense of complexity and through which human understanding constantly changes and advances. Education is necessarily a process of acculturation.

That, too, is why the same statement couples knowing and understanding with exploring, discovering, experimenting, speculating and playing, for 'content' and 'process' are not mutually exclusive as in yet another of primary education's dichotomies they are held to be, but are equally essential aspects of knowing and understanding.

All this has now been rehearsed, but it leaves unanswered the question of what knowledge and understanding matter most at the primary stage. Since, as Denis Lawton notes, curriculum is necessarily a selection from culture, and Britain is anything but a monoculture, there are two questions:

- What knowledge?
- Which culture?

As the demography of Britain has changed, so discussion of the second question has shifted from the collision of 'high' and 'mass' or 'popular' culture which once preoccupied T.S. Eliot, F.R. Leavis and Richard Hoggart, to a keener awareness of the need somehow to balance the collective culture and identity of the nation, if there is such a thing, with the often very different cultures of Britain's many minorities and majorities, whether these are defined by race, faith, gender, age, class, income, politics or geography (see Chapter 8). Set against this many-layered complexity, the old debates about the 'canon' of English literature, art and music, or about cultural elitism and dumbing-down, seem almost straightforward. Now there is no longer one 'high' culture and another 'popular' culture, but many. In any case, culture in the artistic sense is not synonymous with culture in its wider sense of the values, beliefs and ways of life of particular societies or groups.

This Review and its witnesses have added a further twist which was barely discussed by educators until very recently, the idea of culture as global. Initially this arose from a recognition of the extent to which economic and information globalisation have internationalised the way people and nations operate and have made them increasingly competitive in their dealings. Now there is a sharper and more urgent moral understanding of the inequity of international relationships, of the collision of cultures, and of the other collision of expanding consumer demand and diminishing natural resource. The earlier single-minded pursuit of the economic advantages of globalisation is now offset by a concern for interdependence and sustainability (aim 6), the idea that citizenship is global and local as well as national (aim 7), and that the necessary sense of community begins not with abstract tests of 'Britishness' but with how people relate to each locally (aims 5, 7 and 8).

It is both impossible and inappropriate for the Review to seek to arbitrate on these matters. However, the last point above supports the principle of local involvement in curriculum decision-making, and hence of a protected local element in the curriculum. Beyond that, we extrapolate, from the Review's evidence and the foregoing discussion, a broad consensus that a properly-conceived primary education should include appropriate knowledge, understanding, skills and dispositions in the following 14 areas (there is a perceptible logic to the sequence, though not a watertight one):

- spoken language
- reading and writing
- wider aspects of language and communication, including literature and a modern foreign language
- the electronic handling of communication and information through ICT
- numeracy, wider aspects of mathematics and their applications
- science, the workings of the physical world, human action on that world through science and technology, and its consequences
- artistic, imaginative, creative and cultural endeavour, with particular reference to art, music, drama and dance, but also in other contexts
- history, its impact on culture, consciousness and identity, and the lessons it offers for the present and future
- geographical location, other people and other places – locally, nationally and globally – and their interdependence

- the values, ethics, civil customs and procedures by which individuals, groups and nations act, co-exist and regulate their affairs
- religious and other kinds of belief through which people make sense of their condition and guide their lives
- the financial and other capacities needed for everyday transactions
- the handling of emotions and relationships
- the human body, its development and health.

It is not difficult to attach labels to most of these, whether they are the subjects of the current national curriculum, the six 'areas of learning' proposed in the Rose Review interim report, or the eight 'curriculum areas' in Scotland's *Curriculum for Excellence*:

- sciences
- languages
- mathematics
- expressive arts
- social studies
- technologies
- health and well-being
- religious and moral education.[36]

Having said that, it is important to be alert to another kind of reductionism, the wrapping up of distinct and not necessarily compatible pursuits in larger parcels headed 'personal and social education' or 'human, social and environmental understanding'. The motivation is to make an unmanageable curriculum of 10 or 12 subjects (or, as in our list, 14 areas of knowledge, understanding, skill and disposition) more manageable by collapsing it to half a dozen. This may not solve the problem, and in the process much that is important is almost certain to be lost.

A rather different kind of grouping comes from Howard Gardner's 'multiple intelligences', or what he posits as the distinct ways and domains of the operation of the human brain:

- linguistic
- logico-mathematical
- spatial
- musical
- bodily-kinaesthetic
- interpersonal (relating to other people)
- intrapersonal (understanding oneself)
- naturalist (understanding the observable world)
- existential (understanding one's existence and place in the universe).[37]

It will be observed that Gardner's model is not that far removed from a typical generic approach to a knowledge-based curriculum. But then, it must be asked, which came first, a human mind which has linguistic, mathematical and musical intelligences, or a curriculum which contains the language, mathematics and music that such intelligences have created? It would be stranger still if the culturally-evolved forms of knowledge and understanding and the posited multiple intelligences bore no relation to each other. The fact that there is overlap between the two kinds of framework, from utterly different starting points, actually strengthens the argument for a curriculum grounded in the different ways of knowing and understanding through which humans make sense of themselves and the world.

Yet for the moment none of the categories above is much more than a heading. What matters no less than defining the educationally essential domains of human knowledge, understanding and skill is what each of them subsumes. That is where the principles and aims proposed by this Review come in.

PULLING IT ALL TOGETHER: A NEW CURRICULUM FRAMEWORK

The essentials of the proposed framework are as follows.

Aims

The framework has just two axes: aims and domains. Such is the importance that we attach to the aims and of ensuring that aims and practice are consistent, that we place the aims firmly within the framework rather than leave them outside it to be referred to only if the will or opportunity exists.

Domains

The term 'domains' has been chosen in preference to a number of alternatives. 'Subjects' carry too much historical and political baggage to be helpful, and we have no wish to see discussion of our proposals splinter into pro-subject/anti-subject factionalism. 'Disciplines' strongly inform most of the domains but are not synonymous with them, and in any case they do not encompass the full range of knowledge, skill, disposition and modes of enquiry to which primary schools need to attend. 'Areas of learning' remind us that learning is what the curriculum is about, though it is somewhat vague, and in any case as the preferred term of the Rose Review it is best avoided to prevent confusion. Scotland's 'curriculum areas' is a no-nonsense descriptive term which, unlike 'subjects', is helpfully neutral in its connotations. However, 'areas' is ragged at the edges and we believe that 'domain' better captures the sense that each of the components has its own internal coherence. We are tempted to attach 'cultural' as in 'cultural domains' – since aspects of the wider culture rather than school subjects more narrowly defined is what these are – but the phrase will be rejected as cumbersome or pretentious.

The old core …

In a departure from established practice, but in line with the evidence about the historic and continuing split between 'the basics' and 'the rest' and the educational damage that this has caused, the framework does not include a core in the familiar sense of a small number of subjects which, as recommended in Prime Minister Callaghan's 1976 Ruskin speech, are 'protected' (see Chapter 3), while the others are not.

Self-evidently, language and literacy (though re-defined as below) remain the undisputed priority for primary education, both as a coherent domain and as capacities which can and must be developed and applied across the entire curriculum. Self-evidently, too, the domains will be allocated different amounts of time. However, experience over the past 150 years has shown that creating a two-tier curriculum is an invitation to treat the second tier with far less seriousness than the first. Indeed, since 1997 primary schools have had in effect a *three*-tier primary curriculum: (i) literacy and numeracy, (ii) other aspects of English and mathematics, (iii) the rest of the curriculum, with the added anomaly, according to the Review's evidence, that science has hovered between the essential core in name and the dispensable non-core in practice.

It is possible that the Rose Review's new core of 'skills for learning and life'[38] will, if implemented, perpetuate the problem. For although Rose says that '"core" and "foundation subjects would no longer apply in the same way,' he adds 'but the essential knowledge, skills and understanding that characterise these subjects will still be prioritised.'[39] This is capable of only one interpretation: the name 'core' has been abandoned but the concept of core subjects, and all that follows from it, has been retained.

In contrast, the approach commended by the Cambridge Primary Review presumes that every domain, if it is significant enough to be included, is essential and belongs in a properly-conceived primary curriculum. Thus, every domain, however much time is allocated to it, should be treated with the same degree of seriousness and be accorded teaching of the highest possible quality. That being so, the term 'core' – which has meaning only if there is a non-core – becomes redundant.

... and the new curriculum

This report, and much of the evidence it cites, has argued that a 'one-size-fits-all' national curriculum is appropriate neither to the diversity of British culture nor to the very different circumstances of England's 17,000 or so primary schools and the communities they serve, and 'responsiveness to local need and circumstance' is one of the listed guiding principles for primary education as a whole.

This requirement arises for cultural and social as well as educational reasons, for one of the defining themes of our community soundings, and many of the submissions, is the loss of community itself, a trend which is also deplored by politicians and religious leaders. The Review's proposed aims, with their emphasis on interdependence, respect, reciprocity and citizenship, respond to this, and one of them – 'celebrating culture and community' – gives an explicit steer towards both the regeneration of communal life and an education in which mutuality in learning as well as relationships is axiomatic.

Articulating such aims takes us only so far: unless they are enacted in the curriculum we shall be left with the current dissonance of high ideals and expedient practice – which, we suggest, is risked by the Rose Review's quest for educational aims after the curriculum has been determined. And if the local and communal are so important and distinctive, they can neither be defined by national agencies nor left to chance in a curriculum in which nationally-defined requirements take all the time available. They must have an explicit and protected allocation of time, and local mechanisms for defining and validating them.

It is therefore proposed that each domain should have national and local components, with the time available for the local component across all domains set at 30 per cent of the yearly total.

This needs further explanation. A local element in the curriculum is appropriate, essential and therefore required, but making it mandatory in each domain would make little sense since a domain like mathematics has relatively limited scope for local variation while others – for example through local history or ecology, the exploration of local culture and faith, the arts in the local community and the work of local writers – offer considerable scope. Setting the expected allocation at 30 per cent overall allows schools to make some domains more local than others. It also allows schools to compensate for over or under-representation in the national component. But if local planners cannot conceive of anything distinctly local in a particular domain this should not mean that it disappears from that level; rather that what is proposed nationally becomes local as well.

The local component is valuable, and indeed essential, in three further senses:

- This enquiry has reviewed research which confirms, in reaction against earlier deficit or 'blank slate' views of childhood, just how much young children know, understand and do outside school and how competent and capable many of them are from an early age.[40] On the basis of this research we argue that primary schools can and should respect and build on children's non-school learning, experience and capability. The local component encourages this.
- The government-initiated *Narrowing the Gap* programme, which focuses on what can be done to narrow the gap in outcomes between vulnerable and excluded children and the rest, makes success in this vital area heavily dependent on the work and collaboration of local agencies, including local authorities. Significantly, curriculum initiatives are prominent in the 115 case studies provided in the programme's November 2008 report.[41] By their nature, these are local. Our proposed local component to the curriculum provides a framework for embedding such responses. It also invites schools, LAs and other agencies to make the local

in curriculum matters habitual rather than exceptional, for although *Narrowing the Gap* concentrates on the specific groups identified as most vulnerable, the 'gap' is more correctly seen as a continuum, with children's educational engagement shading gradually from full through many stages of partial to minimal, and their educational attainment likewise. And it is not only the vulnerable who under-achieve.

- The capacity to innovate is not restricted to national government and its agencies. Schools, local authorities and the communities they serve have massive potential in this regard. Some of the most interesting and powerful educational ideas and practices of recent years have come from the educational grass roots, but their later adoption by national agencies has been marred by an unwillingness to acknowledge their source, and even by plagiarism, for centralisation justifies itself by contrasting government omniscience with local ignorance. Noting how much is made of the importance of speaking and listening in the Rose Review's report after it was barely mentioned in the primary national strategy's *Excellence and Enjoyment*, and the way that this shift reflects not the inspiration of national agencies but the combined efforts of researchers, schools and local authorities, one eminent director of children's services commented:

> It is a commonplace that, historically, many system-wide innovations have originated in specific localities and local authorities ... For over two decades this has not been recognised. I believe that in a climate where the local potential for nationally-relevant innovation was acknowledged, [the work on talk reform] would have spread faster and further. It is absurd that the system has to wait so long for the Rose seal of approval for the centrality of the spoken word.

In sum, then, the core curriculum at the primary stage is redefined as requirements for all the specified domains, not just some of them, so 'core' disappears. Each domain has both national and local components which, below, we term the *national curriculum* and the *community curriculum*.

The use of time

The national/local division is proposed as 70/30 for the school year as a whole. The failure of Dearing's 80/20 recommendation in 1993 to come to anything shows that the local component must have a sufficient proportion of the whole to be viable and to resist erosion by national requirements. But because the domains pervade both national and local components, this does not mean that any domain loses out, whereas with Dearing all the national curriculum subjects were to be contained within the recommended 80 per cent, which would have made the non-core subjects unviable once the core had taken its 50–60 per cent. Our approach is different. There is no core/non-core distinction. Every domain is both required and protected. The national/local split is not a division between domains but a way of balancing, within each domain, global, national and local concerns and opportunities; and it reflects the need for school, local authorities and communities, as well as government and its agencies, to play their full part in determining a significant part of what each domain contains.

We noted earlier the warning of former primary chief inspector Norman Thomas that the Rose Review appears to confuse curriculum and timetabling, and it is possible that some of the favourable responses to Rose may reflect a sense that timetabling six subjects (or what Rose calls 'areas of learning') each week is easier than timetabling 10 or 12. But while the lesson/session is the usual timetabling unit, and the week is its conventional frame, we would encourage more flexible use of the 798–893 hours of teaching time available annually. The term and year should be viewed as wholes and the advantages of demarcating less frequent but longer blocks of time for concentrated study within a domain should be carefully considered. The benefits of depth thus achieved would far outweigh the superficiality and fragmentation of one dutiful or scrambled lesson during a week in which teachers felt obliged to attend to every domain. This is the secondary model, and because most or all teaching in secondary schools is done by specialists the timetable there is perforce somewhat rigid. But primary schools have no need to mimic secondary timetabling assumptions or practices, and for as long as most teaching in primary schools is done by generalist class teachers, primary timetabling can be vastly more flexible.

There are certain exceptions. Where knowledge and skill need to be built up on the basis of memorisation, repetition and practice there is a case for regular and indeed daily activity. The error of the national strategies, which, according to this review's evidence, has been at considerable cost to the rest of the curriculum, has been the 'winner takes all' presumption that literacy and mathematics as a whole can be advanced only through daily activity. Some aspects of literacy require daily attention or frequent practice. Others do not.

We propose below that panels of independent experts should be convened to advise on the content of the national curriculum, having regard to the proposed aims and the earlier discussion about knowledge and culture. Part of their brief would be to recommend which aspects of a domain require regular – though not necessarily daily – attention, which can profitably be pursued on a less frequent basis and which lend themselves to handling in concentrated blocks of time.

Progression and transition

The framework needs to ensure a smooth progression from the foundation stage via primary to secondary. Accordingly, the domains are expressed in terms which it is hoped are compatible with the preceding and following stages of schooling while remaining true to themselves. However, there is a necessary debate about whether all domains, and/or all contributory aspects of each domain, should be included from Year 1. The proposed national domain panels would be asked to consider this, and to ensure continuity they would include representation from early years settings and secondary as well as primary schools.

Clearly, there cannot be one-to-one correspondence between the eight domains and the six EYFS areas of learning and development, any more than there is between the eight domains and the 14 subjects in the KS3 curriculum. However, it takes little effort to track the path from EYFS areas to primary domains and onward to secondary subjects, noting that in each educational phase the curriculum diversifies. In terms of the EYFS/primary interface, the crucial condition for progression is that the EYFS areas provide, as their name requires, a curricular foundation upon which primary schools can build. We believe that the framework encourages this.

Equally, we warn against the assumption that because the Rose model has the same number of areas – six – as the EYFS, and similar area names, this solves at a stroke the problem of progression. What matters, as we have stressed, is not the label but what is taught and learned in its name, and reactions to the Rose report suggest that among early years experts, at any rate, there remains considerable scepticism on this score.

The other warning to be heeded is Rose's own: 'While primary education must build upon the EYFS and prepare children for education post-11, it is far more than either a post-script to the early years, or a prelude to secondary education.'[42] Primary education is sandwiched between two phases with strong and contrasting identities. Historically, infant/KS1 education has sought to sustain itself by reference to a distinctive early years rationale while what shapes the education of juniors/children in KS2 has never been very clear, created as it was from the old elementary/lower secondary structure. Starting from evidence and belief about children, culture and the wider world, the Cambridge Review has devised first a set of aims and then a curriculum which it believes to be right for the primary phase as a whole, and as a phase which in developmental and educational terms has its own imperatives. Education, we have insisted, attends to today as well as tomorrow, to development no less than to preparation. This has been the central task. But it happens that what we have proposed for the primary phase also maps onto what precedes and follows it.

While the Rose report's warning is welcome, the coincidence of curriculum area numbers and names, and the lack of a rationale for the primary phase other than building on the EYFS and preparing for secondary, lend support to the view that the task has been viewed more in terms of rationalisation than reform, especially as the report proposes taking a set of primary school aims off the secondary school shelf.[43]

The domains

It is proposed that the primary curriculum be re-conceived as a matrix of the 12 specified aims together with eight domains of knowledge, skill, disposition and enquiry. The domains bring together the 14 areas in which, drawing on the Review's evidence, we have suggested that primary education should be pursued. Below, notwithstanding the centrality of language, oracy and literacy, the domains are listed alphabetically so as to discourage regression to a curriculum pecking order.

- arts and creativity
- citizenship and ethics
- faith and belief
- language, oracy and literacy
- mathematics
- physical and emotional health
- place and time
- science and technology

If this is compared with the recommendations of the Rose Review, two apparent omissions will immediately be noted: ICT and personal development. Both are extremely important, but neither, in our view, is best conceived as a separate domain. The child's personal development is a constant, and is pursued, as we explain below, through most or all of the domains; and indeed through generic pedagogy and the life of the school. In addition, more specific aspects of what is generally defined as PSE appear in *citizenship and morality, physical and emotional health* and *faith and belief*. Similarly, those aspects of ICT which are essential to a modern concept of literacy and to effective communication are within *language, oracy and literacy*. The many other applications of ICT are developed through the other domains.

What, then, is a domain? Though their characters differ – and this variety and complementarity is indeed the point – each also has:

- thematic and/or epistemological coherence and integrity;
- an identifiable and essential core of knowledge and skill which is contingent upon certain dispositions and modes of exploration or enquiry; in some cases the knowledge is recognisably disciplinary while in others it is more eclectic;
- capacity to contribute to the pursuit and achievement of one or more of the 12 proposed educational aims;
- strong *prima facie* justification for inclusion at the primary stage, the justifications ranging from the child's present developmental need, through acculturation to future instrumental relevance, as reflected in the 14 areas proposed earlier;
- potential to build on the EYFS and bridge to the secondary curriculum without being subservient to either.

A domain is *not*:

- a named slot in the school's weekly timetable – domains are curriculum categories, and how they are translated, terminologically, temporally and pedagogically, is for schools to decide;

- an invitation to low-grade topic work in which thematic serendipity counts for more than knowledge and skill.

Collectively, the domains are:

- the starting point for curriculum planning in which the proposed domain panels will consider how each domain is most appropriately elaborated by reference to the twelve aims and the outlines below, and schools will determine how the domains are reconstructed as a viable school curriculum and are then named, timetabled and taught. We make no proposals on such matters, for our task is to provide a framework for others to work within. But unless the distinctiveness of the framework is understood, the radicalism of an aims-driven curriculum will not be realised and we shall merely perpetuate the problems, as we have identified them, from which the primary curriculum most needs to escape.

Domains and aims: the curriculum matrix

The 12 aims for primary education are no less essential to this enquiry's conception of a primary curriculum than the eight domains. To underline this, we have departed from the usual practice of identifying what in earlier versions of the national curriculum were called 'cross-curricular themes, skills and dimensions' and have replaced these as the second axis of our curriculum framework by the aims themselves (Figure 14.3).

AIMS \ DOMAINS	Arts and creativity	Citizenship and ethics	Faith and belief	Language, oracy and literacy	Mathematics	Physical and emotional health	Place and time	Science and Technology
The individual								
Well-being								
Engagement								
Empowerment								
Autonomy								
Self, others and the wider world								
Respect and reciprocity								
Interdependence and sustainability								
Local, national and global citizenship								
Culture and community								
Learning, knowing and doing								
Exploring, knowing, understanding, making sense								
Fostering skill								
Exciting the imagination								
Enacting dialogue								

Figure 14.3 Aims and domains: the primary curriculum matrix.

The domains explained

Here we place within the eight domains of knowledge, skill, enquiry and disposition the 14 educational imperatives listed on pages 259–60. Because curriculum hierarchies and their concomitant anxieties are so deeply embedded, we probably need to add that the different lengths of the descriptions below reflect not their perceived importance but the challenges of reconceptualisation (particularly critical for language, oracy and literacy, the relatively new domain of citizenship, and for physical and emotional health).

Arts and creativity

This domain includes the arts, creativity and the imagination, with particular reference to art, music, drama and dance, each with its complementary dimensions of 'appreciation' (knowledge, understanding and disposition) and 'performance' (knowledge, understanding and disposition allied with executive skill). As argued earlier, we would wish to encourage a vigorous campaign aimed at advancing public understanding of the arts in education, human development, culture and national life, coupled with a much more rigorous approach to arts teaching in schools. The renaissance of this domain is long overdue.

Creativity, of course, is not confined to the arts, but also entails what the Robinson enquiry called the 'democratic definition' of creativity, which 'is equally fundamental to advances in the sciences, in mathematics, technology, politics, business and in all areas of everyday life' and which has four features: the pursuit of purpose, the use of the imagination, originality, and the exercise of discriminating judgements of value.[44] The arts are indelibly creative, and properly pursued they achieve the aim of 'exciting the imagination' which features in our list of 12. But we have also stressed that both creativity and imaginative activity can and must inform teaching and learning across the wider curriculum.

Citizenship and ethics

This domain includes the values, moral codes, civil customs and procedures by which humans act, co-exist and regulate their affairs. As noted above, it has local and global as well as national components.

Locating ethical questions in the curriculum is difficult. Though most religions have a moral element, moral questions and ethical standpoints are not dependent on religious belief. Equally, as – say – the Sermon on the Mount, the Ten Commandments or Sharia remind us – it makes no sense to detach morality from a religion to which it is so fundamental.

Once again, we remind ourselves of the 12 aims towards which we propose that not just the curriculum but also the entire conduct of primary education should be directed. Reflecting strong representation from the Review's witnesses and widespread concern about the ousting of mutuality and civic consciousness by selfishness and material greed, we highlighted 'encouraging respect and reciprocity' in the list of aims. This is interpreted not in the narrow, deferential or intimidatory way that the word 'respect' is sometimes used, but much more broadly, as an outlook of 'willing courtesy' towards ideas as well as people, and as the bedrock of relations within and between societies. Respect in this sense manifests a moral standpoint, and other aims – 'promoting interdependence and sustainability', 'celebrating culture and community', 'enacting dialogue' and indeed 'exploring, knowing, understanding and making sense' – all carry no less of a moral charge. For these reasons, it makes sense not only for private and public morality to be placed together within the communal domain of citizenship, but for citizenship to be mandatory rather than, as at present, optional.

We use the term 'ethics' in preference to 'morality' because of the normative overtones of the latter. It also encourages the questioning, exploratory approach to such matters which is captured in the Review's aim of 'enacting dialogue' and has been successfully developed through recent work on dialogic pedagogy and philosophy for children (P4C),[45] both of which have been taken up in many other countries, thus giving the global dimension of citizenship as proposed here particular resonance. These approaches, of course, have applications across the entire curriculum and are not specific to citizenship.

Faith and belief

On the question of religious education, we take the view that religion is so fundamental to this country's history, culture and language, as well as to the daily lives of many of its inhabitants, that it must remain within the curriculum, even though some Review witnesses argued that it should be removed on the grounds that England is a predominantly secular society or that religious belief is for the family rather than the school. However, while denominational schools see their mission as the advancement of particular religious beliefs and moral codes, non-denominational schools should remain essentially secular, teaching about religion with respect and understanding, but not attempting to inculcate or convert. Further, other beliefs, including those about the validity of religion itself, should also be explored. This approach helps us to resolve the quandary of moral education, for in teaching about a religion its ethical elements can be handled with the same sympathetic objectivity as we commend for the treatment of its beliefs and rituals.

The situation is complicated by the fact that religious education has a unique and perhaps anomalous place in law. Alongside religious education in the classroom, schools are still obliged, as they were under the 1944 Act, to hold a daily act of collective worship of pre-dominantly Christian character for all the school's pupils. However, in 2009 the cultural and religious character of England is such that for many schools this creates acute dilemmas, not just because a typical urban primary school has pupils from many religious faiths, and indeed from families with no religious faith, but also because the 'act of [Christian] worship' obligation sits uneasily with the more recent requirement that schools should promote inclusion and community cohesion. Mostly the dilemma simmers unresolved. Occasionally, as in Sheffield in February 2009, it explodes into the media with unhappy consequences for all those involved.

Although we argue that teaching about faith and belief should be part of the curriculum, for a non-denominational school to require pupils from different faiths (or none) to join an act of worship in just one of those faiths raises more difficult questions. Some might suggest that the act of worship contradicts the rationale for the 'faith and belief' domain as outlined both here and in many existing RE syllabuses, and that divested of its controversial 'act of worship' requirement the school assembly could more appropriately pursue other aims, as indeed in many schools it already does. Interdependence and sustainability, respect and reciprocity, culture and community, and citizenship are obvious candidates for such treatment from this review's proposed list of aims, and we have already argued that they should be pursued outside as well as inside the classroom. The matter arouses strong feelings. We believe it deserves proper debate.

Language, oracy and literacy

This domain includes spoken language, reading, writing, literature, wider aspects of language and communication, a modern foreign language, ICT and other non-print media. Though we dispense with the old core/non-core distinction, we do not hesitate to argue that the domain is the heart of the new curriculum. But it stands in considerable need of revision.

The importance of oracy

It is a recurrent theme of this Review that in England literacy is too narrowly conceived and that spoken language has yet to secure the place in primary education that its centrality to learning, culture and life requires, or that it enjoys in the curriculum of many other countries. The current national curriculum formulation, as 'speaking and listening', is conceptually weak and insufficiently demanding in practice, and we would urge instead that important initiatives like the National Oracy Project be revisited, along with more recent research on talk in learning and teaching, as part of the necessary process of defining oracy and giving it its proper place in the language curriculum.

Re-thinking literacy

Relatedly, the redesigning of this domain requires, as noted earlier, that the primary national strategy's literacy component be curtailed in its present form and that literacy – in the familiar sense of reading and writing – be re-integrated into the language curriculum. Further, the goal of literacy by the end of the primary phase must be more than functional. It is about making and exploring meaning as well as receiving and transmitting it. That is why talking must be part of reading and writing rather than an optional extra. And it is why engagement with the meanings made by others through literature, and with the language through which such meanings are conveyed, is no less essential. Literacy achieves our listed aim of empowerment by conferring the skill not just to read and write but to make these processes genuinely transformative, exciting children's imagination (another listed aim), extending their boundaries, and enabling them to contemplate lives and worlds possible as well as actual.

Which modern foreign language?

There is an obvious debate about which foreign language should be taught. The interim Rose report proposes that 'schools should be free to choose which language(s) that they wish to teach, however, as far as possible the languages offered should be those which children will be taught at key stage 3.'[46] Continuity from primary to secondary is certainly one criterion. A second is the likely use or usefulness of the language, and arguments divide over what might be termed 'vacational' use (which favours French, Spanish or Italian) and 'vocational' use (which favours languages of growing global economic importance such as Standard Mandarin, Russian or Hindi). A third criterion is the support which learning a foreign language gives to the advancement of the pupil's understanding and skill in English. Mindful of the roots of the English language this would support the teaching of French and/or German. Fourth, and less commonly heard, there is the argument that in communities which are linguistically diverse, cultural understanding and cohesion would benefit if the principle of English as an additional language (EAL) were reversed and native English speakers were to learn one of the prominent local languages. Like Rose, we see no alternative to the decision on such matters being taken locally.

The ubiquity – and challenge – of ICT

While ICT reaches across the entire curriculum, it should receive more explicit attention, and attention of a particular kind, within the language component. In this we differ from the Rose Review, which treats ICT as a neo-basic 'skill for learning and life', or as a tool without apparent substance or challenge other than the technical.

Within the space of a few years schools have advanced far beyond what used to be called 'computer-assisted learning', in which computers, like textbooks, were a pedagogical aid largely within the control of teachers. Now in such matters children are increasingly autonomous. Much of their out-of-school learning is electronic and beyond the reach of either parents or teachers. They exchange messages and information by texting on their mobile phones and through on-line networking sites such as MySpace, Facebook, Twitter and Bebo. They seek information from Google and Wikipedia. They download music, DVDs, games and other material pretty well at will, using the mobile phones, PCs and laptops which are increasingly standard property in English households. In such matters, as Hargreaves shows, they are not merely passive 'surfers' who read, watch and listen, but 'peerers' who use electronic media to share, socialise, collaborate and create.[47]

In as far as most such activities depend on the ability to read and write, they must be counted in part as variants or extensions of literacy. It no longer makes sense to attend to text but ignore txt. Yet the matter is not merely one of skill or access. In the Cambridge Primary Review's soundings and submissions, parents, teachers – and children themselves – expressed concern about the perils as well as the opportunities of the electronic communication and information-handling skills which today's children so effortlessly command and the material to which they have access. However, while policing the more unsavoury reaches of the web is clearly necessary, the issue is not so much what is extreme and self-evidently disreputable as what is mainstream and apparently to be taken on trust. The more fundamental task is to help children develop the capacity to approach electronic and other non-print media (including television and film as well as the internet) with the degree of discrimination and critical awareness that should attend reading, writing and communicating of any kind.[48] This, we believe, is an argument for treating ICT both as the cross-curricular informational tool which it obviously is, and as an aspect of the language curriculum which demands a rigour no less than should apply to the handling of the written and spoken word, and to traditionally-conceived text, information and evidence.

There is a further concern here. In April 2009, the Secretary of State found himself having to respond to headlines about the Rose Review's apparent advocacy of an approach to ICT which included teaching children about Wikipedia and social networking sites like Twitter, to the detriment of more familiar subjects like history. He said, 'We have a duty to ensure our children learn about history. We also have a duty to make sure they are not left in the technological dark ages.'[49] However, his apparently gung-ho approach took no account of concerns raised by neuroscientists about the risks of excessive exposure to screen technologies. In a debate in the House of Lords, Baroness Greenfield warned:

> The mid-21st century mind might almost be infantilised, characterised by short attention spans, sensationalism, inability to empathise and a shaky sense of identity … If the young brain is exposed from the outset to a world of fast action and reaction, of instant new screen images flashing up with the press of a key, such rapid interchange might accustom the brain to operate over such timescales … Real conversation in real time may eventually give way to these sanitised and easier screen dialogues … It is hard to see how living this way on a daily basis will not result in brains, or rather minds, different from other generations.[50]

These remarks caused a certain amount of controversy, and, in some quarters, ridicule.[51] But warnings about any technology which in an exceptionally short space of time becomes such a prominent and almost addictive aspect of young people's lives should not be lightly dismissed. Further, we believe that this debate confirms that it is right to locate ICT within the language curriculum rather than as a semi-detached and uncritically-fostered 'skill for learning and life' as in the Rose report, for placing it here enables schools to balance and explore relationships between new and established forms of communication, and to ensure that the developmental and educational primacy of talk, which is now exceptionally well supported by research evidence, is always maintained.

Revisiting language across the curriculum

Finally, we commend renewed attention to the Bullock enquiry's recommendation that every school 'should have an organised policy for language across the curriculum'[52] so as to underline four recurrent concerns of this review:

- Although language, oracy and literacy are conventionally located within the teaching of English, they are no less important in the other seven domains.
- The achievement of high standards in literacy requires not the narrowing of the primary school curriculum and the downgrading of other than 'the basics' which England has

witnessed periodically since the 1860s and with renewed force since 1997, but the pursuit of breadth, balance, challenge and high quality teaching across the entire curriculum.

- Language, and the quality of language, are essential to cognitive development, learning and effective teaching in all contexts. A policy of language across the curriculum therefore requires the mapping of the different kinds and registers of language, both spoken and written, which are intrinsic to each domain and for which each domain provides particularly significant development potential.

- If language unlocks thought, then thought is enhanced, challenged and enlarged when language in all its aspects mentioned here, and in every educational context, is pursued with purpose and rigour.

Mathematics

This includes both numeracy and wider aspects of mathematics. The boundaries of this domain remain broadly unchanged, provided that numeracy be taken out of the PNS and re-integrated with the rest of mathematics. Further, and mindful of the concern of some of our witnesses that primary mathematics escapes the critical scrutiny to which other domains are subject, domain panels and teachers should address with some rigour the question of what aspects of mathematics are truly essential and foundational in the primary phase.

We suggest that what is sometimes called 'financial literacy' be handled within this domain, even though financial literacy, properly conceived, is about much more than monetary computation. But placing it here is analogous to broadening the domain of science and technology to include their human and environmental impact, and it is right that such real-life applications of mathematics be explored alongside the acquisition of mathematical knowledge and skill.

Physical and emotional health

This deals with the handling of human emotions and relationships and with the human body, its development and health, together with the skills of agility, co-ordination and teamwork acquired through sport and PE as conventionally conceived. It is important that the significance of this reconfiguration be properly understood and that neither emotional/relational understanding nor health be treated as a mere PE add-on. We believe that it makes medical as well as educational sense to group together physical and emotional health, and indeed for health as such to be named as a mandatory component of the child's curriculum for the first time. However, unlike Rose, we do not go so far as to place well-being as a whole in the physical domain, for, as defined in our list of aims, well-being has aspects other than the physical, and although attending to children's physical and emotional well-being and welfare is an essential task for primary schools, well-being is no less about educational engagement, the raising of aspirations and the maximising of children's potential across the board.

As with several other domains, we wish to stress that what is required here is a complete reconceptualisation. In this case it would explore the interface between emotional and physical development and health and their contribution both to the more comprehensive concept of well-being which is signalled in our first nominated aim and to children's educational attainment. A strongly 'affective turn' was noted in one of the Review's commissioned research surveys, and is to be welcomed, as is that survey's caution about 'emotional literacy', 'emotional intelligence' and 'therapeutic pedagogy'.[53] But affectivity is not a subject, an area of learning or a domain. It is a state of mind which manifests itself in complex ways to which one-dimensional terms like joy, sorrow and anger may only approximate. Researchers and teachers are right to stress its importance as an influence on children's engagement, motivation and attainment and it is therefore with a certain ambivalence that we place the education of the emotions within any one domain. We do so to ensure that it is explicitly attended to as an aspect of the curriculum, but we remind readers also that it, like well-being more generally, is an aim for primary education as a whole which can be realised only if it pervades the wider life and relationships of the classroom and school, as well as the curriculum.

Place and time

This principally includes how history shapes culture, events, consciousness and identity and the lessons which it offers to our understanding of present and future; and the geographical study of location, other people, other places and human interdependence, locally, nationally and globally. Like the arts, this domain and its contributory disciplines stand in need of proper public and political recognition of their importance to children's understanding of who they are, of change and continuity, cause and consequence, of why society is arranged as it is, and of the interaction of mankind and the physical environment. In opening up children's understanding of these matters the domain may range beyond the boundaries of what is conventionally included in primary history and geography to draw, as Jerome Bruner's *Man a Course of Study* (MACOS) famously did during the 1960s, on anthropology and other human sciences. The domain is central to the advancement of a number of the proposed aims, notably *respect and reciprocity, interdependence and sustainability, local, national and global citizenship,* and *culture and community.*[54]

Science and technology

This includes the exploration and understanding of science and the workings of the physical world, together with human action on the physical world through both science and technology, and its consequences. It incorporates understanding of the key ideas about these areas and the skills of scientific enquiry, making and doing through which this understanding is progressively developed and applied. Although science is currently one of the three core subjects, our evidence shows that it has been increasingly squeezed out by the exclusivity of recent attention to literacy and numeracy. It is clearly of immense importance, and among our witnesses some – and not all of them scientists or science teachers – were prepared to argue that in the pervasiveness of its actual and potential impact on the individual and society it is considerably more important at the primary stage than mathematics. However, as we have insisted and shown that curriculum hierarchies are unhelpful, we do not wish to encourage such rivalry.

What is beyond dispute is that the educational case for primary science, as for the arts and humanities, needs to be re-asserted. This is now urgent, for there is evidence that from being one of the success stories of the original national curriculum during the decade 1989–99, primary science has increasingly been marginalized by the government's national strategies, retaining its place only because it continues to be tested at the end of KS2 but with reduced teaching time.

NEXT STEPS

Although we have urged a considerable reduction in central specification and prescription, we accept the value to heads and teachers of well-conceived guidance and exemplification. Moving from the outlines above to a sufficient level of detail to enable schools to move forward would seem to require something along the following lines.

The national component, or the national curriculum

Eight expert panels would be convened to define in greater detail the place of each domain in the new national curriculum, and to propose in broad terms the content, process and progression within the domain. By 'expert' is meant a combination of experienced primary heads or teachers together with early years and secondary representatives, and experts from the domain's contributory discipline(s) and their transformation into what American researcher

Lee Shulman calls 'pedagogical content knowledge'.[55] The panels would propose programmes of study and would indicate those aspects of learning where frequent or regular teaching is required, but they would not specify precise time allocations. In convening the panels it should be noted that several of the domains require radical planning or restructuring, and reading across from the existing programmes of study will certainly be helpful but will not suffice. In mapping the domains, each panel would work towards:

An expanded statement of the essential features of the domain (statutory)
- the overall rationale and scope of the domain
- those of the 12 aims for primary education which are most effectively pursued within the domain, and how they can be securely embedded within it
- the knowledge, skills, dispositions and modes of enquiry and exploration with which the domain is chiefly concerned
- what, in general terms, a child should be expected to encounter, experience, know and do within the domain by the time he/she moves on to secondary education.

Programmes of study (non-statutory)
- progression in the identified knowledge, skills and dispositions through the primary phase
- more precise intermediate and terminal indications of what children should encounter, experience, know and do, possibly year by year and certainly for the end of the primary phase
- particular aspects of the specified knowledge and skill which require regular attention and/ or practice
- how the domain builds on the EYFS curriculum and leads on to the secondary curriculum
- how the identified problems in current arrangements can be avoided
- priorities for ITT, CPD and resources.

A further whole curriculum panel would receive each set of domain proposals and ensure that they cover the specified field, avoid duplication and when taken together can be comfortably accommodated within the 70 per cent of the year available for the national component. This panel might need to exercise its responsibilities with a vigour which the architects of the first national curriculum avoided, for disciplinary loyalties tend to outweigh interest in the balance and viability of the whole.

There would be full national consultation on the draft domain statements and programmes of study.

The QCA has considerable experience in curriculum planning and in the drafting of curriculum guidance and exemplification. On that basis, and given its statutory responsibility, it is the obvious body to take forward the planning of the national component. However, the QCA and its predecessors (NCC and SCAA) are in part responsible for the perceived problem of curriculum overload which looms large in the Review's evidence, and in any case some view the QCA as lacking the intellectual, political and professional independence which the task requires. On balance, therefore, we would prefer to leave open the question of what body would co-ordinate the development of the national component. The conditions are:

- the work of the domain panels must be genuinely and visibly independent
- they should be properly resourced and supported.

The local component, or the community curriculum

Each local authority would convene a community curriculum partnership (CCP) to consider what might be included in the local component of each domain. The CCPs would include primary, secondary and early years teachers, domain experts and community representatives, and would have domain-specific sub-committees. The existing SACREs for religious education, expanded to meet the extended scope of this domain, would form one of these sub-committees, in effect making the SACRE a prototype for local curriculum planning across the board. Children would be involved in the consultations, probably through school councils.

The CCP would have equivalent responsibility to the whole curriculum panel at national level, ensuring that what is proposed is viable within the allocated 30 per cent of the year. The resulting guidance would be non-statutory.

This arrangement, we should add, is not an attempt to recover what was recommended in the 1993 Dearing Report and left unimplemented. On that occasion, the time (20 per cent) was to be entirely at each school's discretion. In contrast, the local component proposed here has an explicitly communal focus and both encourages a local orientation in those of the domains where this is applicable and gives life to aim 8, 'Celebrating culture and community'. It is for these reasons that we suggest that the local component be planned collectively, even though

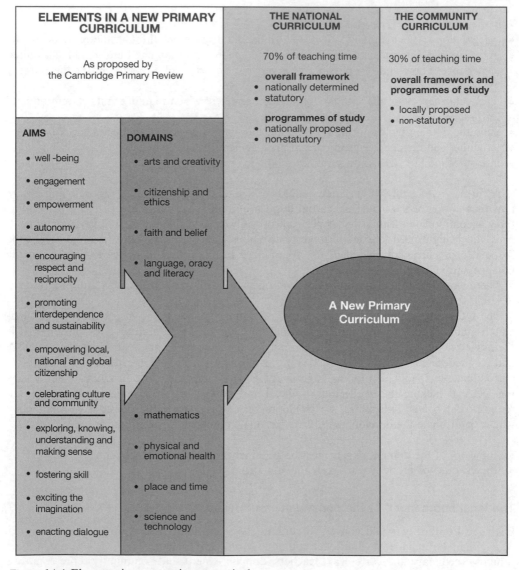

Figure 14.4 Elements in a new primary curriculum.

the outcome in terms of detail will be non-statutory. In a multi-ethnic inner city, schools and the local authority might work together to ensure that the curriculum as a whole genuinely engages with both the challenges of that environment and its possibilities in terms of the cultural diversity and richness that flow from plurality. It would also give close attention to the handling of faith and the teaching of language, including the choice of a foreign language. In a rural area, small and widely-dispersed primary schools might collaborate to enhance the study of a very different environment, to share resources, and to ensure that pupils have access to those cultural riches more readily available in urban settings.

Additionally, by building on children's knowledge and experience, by engaging children educationally with the local culture and environment in a variety of ways, and by involving children in discussion of the local component through school councils and the work of the CCPs, the community curriculum would both give real meaning to children's voices and begin the process of community enrichment and regeneration where it matters.

Many witnesses deplored the loss of community outside school and were grateful for what many schools offer by way of compensation. The community curriculum, allied to more flexible use of school premises, is a way to recover the idea of community in its fullest sense. It also offers a much-needed way to re-invigorate the creative potential and innovative partnership of schools, local authorities, colleges and universities, bearing in mind the contention by a senior witness to the Review, quoted earlier, that this is where many of the most significant educational innovations have originated.

The disposition of domains, national curriculum and community curriculum, and the roles of the planning bodies concerned, are shown in Figure 14.4.

CONCLUSION

The new primary curriculum proposed here:

1. Addresses and seeks to resolve the problems of present and past arrangements, especially: overload, micro-management from the centre, the distorting impact of testing and the national strategies, the dislocation of English/literacy, the qualitative imbalance between 'the basics' and the rest, the marginalisation of the arts and humanities, tokenism in respect of aims, and the muddled discourse of subjects, knowledge and skills.
2. Is planned and implemented with clear regard to principles of procedure which highlight and safeguard, for example, entitlement, quality, breadth, balance of attention to present and future needs, rights, equity, guidance not prescription, local responsiveness, and the pursuit of explicit aims and values.
3. Starts from an account of the aims of primary education which is grounded in analysis of the needs, capabilities and circumstances of children now, of their likely future needs as adults and lifelong learners, and of the condition of the society and world in which they are growing up. These aims are fundamental, and inform not only the curriculum but also wider aspects of pedagogy and the life of the school.
4. Builds on, and respects the appropriateness and integrity of, the EYFS curriculum.
5. Is conceived as a matrix of 12 educational aims and eight domains of knowledge, skill, enquiry and disposition, with the aims locked firmly into the framework from the outset.
6. Dispenses with the notion of the curriculum core as a small number of subjects and places all eight domains within the curriculum on a non-hierarchical basis, on the principle that although time will be differentially allocated, all the domains are essential and all must be protected.
7. At the same time acknowledges and celebrates the centrality of language, oracy and literacy, both to young children's development and to a properly-conceived curriculum in which breadth and standards go hand in hand.
8. Incorporates a significant and protected local component to the entitlement curriculum by differentiating the 'national' from the 'community' curriculum, though both include all

eight domains. Divides time between them on the basis of 70/30 per cent of the yearly teaching total.

9. Differentiates curriculum from timetabling, both to discourage the equating of domains with timetabled lessons and to encourage domain panels and schools to think carefully about which aspects might be taught separately and which combined, which need to preserve disciplinary integrity and which are amenable to thematic treatment.

10. Requires a radical re-think of most of the domains, especially language, oracy and literacy.

11. For the purposes of planning divides the national curriculum and the community curriculum into three segments:

    - a nationally-determined description and rationale which specifies in broad terms the knowledge, skills, dispositions and kinds of enquiry to be taught through the primary phase, an expanded statement for each domain (see 'the national component', above), and the standards of achievement and quality of learning[56] to be secured by the time a pupil transfers to secondary school (statutory);
    - nationally-determined programmes of study for each domain (for programme scope see 'the national component' above), which in combination should take no more than 70 per cent of the yearly time available (non-statutory);
    - a locally-determined community curriculum for those of the eight domains where this is appropriate and feasible, which also identifies the particular local needs which the curriculum as a whole should address and the distinctive educational opportunities which the local community and environment provide.

12. Is planned nationally by independent expert panels for each domain together with a whole curriculum panel. (The question of how such work should be co-ordinated should await a review of the remit and functions of the QCA and the other national agencies). Each panel includes school representatives and experts in the contributory disciplines and their classroom application. The national planners are charged with ensuring that the knowledge, understanding, skills and dispositions that are required and recommended attend closely to the specified aims and can be accommodated within the 70 per cent of time available for the national curriculum; and they are asked to identify those aspects of each domain which require regular attention and those where flexibility in timetabling is appropriate.

13. Is planned locally by community curriculum partnerships (CCPs) convened by each local authority, or where this is desirable and appropriate by local authorities acting together; each panel includes school representatives, community representatives and experts in the contributory disciplines, and its work must involve consultation with children. The community curriculum includes both those elements agreed collectively among schools and each school's response to ways that the lives of the children themselves can be respected and built upon.

14. Merges the existing SACREs within the new local framework, making them one of the eight domain sub-committees of each CCP, and ensuring that their membership is expanded to include the necessary perspectives on belief and morality outside the context of particular faiths.

15. Is implemented flexibly and creatively by each school, though having regard to the requirement to plan and teach all eight domains and to achieve high quality teaching and learning across the entire curriculum regardless of the amount of time allocated to each domain.

16. Is implemented in a way which pursues the aims in the overlapping contexts of (i) domain-specific content and activity (ii) generic pedagogy and (iii) the life of the school as a whole.

Conditions

Success in the enterprise of reconceptualising, planning and implementing the new primary curriculum would appear to depend on the following changes to current mechanisms, many of which are considered in later chapters of this report:

Reforming institutions, procedures and requirements

- Redefining the statutory functions, in respect of the curriculum, of the DCSF, QCA, local authorities and the national strategies.
- Reinvigorating local authorities as agents and facilitators in curriculum development.
- Winding up the primary national strategy in its current form, or merging it with the QCA, and combining the expertise and resources of both in the interests of producing the best possible advice to the domain planning groups and non-statutory guidance of the highest quality.
- Making what is non-statutory genuinely so, and changing those requirements or procedures formulated by the DCSF, Ofsted and the TDA which currently make the non-statutory in effect obligatory.
- Reforming national assessment, especially at age 11, so that it does its job without compromising children's statutory entitlement to a broad and balanced curriculum.

Building professional capacity

- Rethinking both primary ITT and CPD to ensure that all eight domains are properly attended to, and the potential of generic pedagogy in pursuit of the aims is properly understood.
- Ensuring that epistemology, pedagogy and discipline-based pedagogical content knowledge are given much greater prominence in primary ITT.
- Re-thinking teaching roles and staff deployment in primary schools, with particular reference to the balance of generalist, semi-specialist and specialist teaching, in order to ensure that every school has the necessary expertise to teach every domain well.
- Requiring collaboration between professionals in primary, early years and secondary settings in order to ensure smooth transition from foundation to primary and primary to secondary.
- Encouraging collaboration between schools in order both to share expertise and develop the community curriculum.
- Auditing the capacity of each local authority with a view to ensuring that it is able to take the envisaged lead role in co-ordinating the development of the community curriculum.
- Making the pursuit and proper use of evidence central to each of the above.

In arguing for national reform we envisage not the familiar scenario of government reaching for a new national strategy, initiative or task force, or national bodies telling local authorities and schools what to do, but the reform of those national bodies and requirements themselves. Without a combination of reform in this sense allied to rigorous professional capacity-building in schools and local authorities, the primary curriculum will continue more or less as it is, with its labels cosmetically adjusted but its most fundamental problems unresolved.

FINAL NOTE: THE CAMBRIDGE PRIMARY REVIEW AND THE ROSE REVIEW

At the beginning of these two chapters on the curriculum we compared the questions posed by the Cambridge Primary Review with those which the government's 2008–9 Rose review was required to address, and we have made other comparisons between the two enquiries. A more systematic comparison was published in the 2009 House of Commons Select Committee report on the national curriculum.[57]

NOTES

1   White (2010), *The Cambridge Primary Review Research Surveys*, Chapter 12; see also Chapter 12 of this report.
2   See, for example, the response to the interim Rose report from the Early Education Advisory Group, which has a distinguished membership of acknowledged early years experts (EEAG 2009, cited with the Group's permission).

3 Campbell (1993).
4 Ofsted (2002).
5 DfES (2003b).
6 DCSF (2008s).
7 DES (1978a, 1985b).
8 DES (1978a): para 6.12.
9 Dr Eric Midwinter led the ground-breaking Liverpool Educational Priority Area project during the 1970s.
10 Rose (2008): paras 2.23–2.27.
11 *Ibid.*: para 2.25.
12 Alexander (1984): Chapter 3.
13 Gulbenkian Foundation (1982).
14 Ofsted (2004c).
15 DES (1985a).
16 Board of Education (1931); CACE (1967); DES (1978a); Ofsted (1997b, 2002).
17 HM Treasury (2006).
18 Hours as specified in regulations currently in force: DfEE (1999a).
19 Richards (2009).
20 Rose (2008).
21 Both quoted in Alexander (1984): 18.
22 A 'leading primary school head teacher' applauding the Rose Review's interim report: quoted in *The Times*, 9 December 2008 (Aaronovitch 2008).
23 Charles Dickens, *Hard Times*, Chapter 1.
24 Luke and Carrington (2002).
25 Rose (2008): para 2.25.
26 Rose (2008): para 2.23.
27 QCA (2007a): 31.
28 Bayliss (1999).
29 DfEE (1998a).
30 Hargreaves (2004a).
31 OED definition.
32 For example, the 1999 Robinson Report (NACCCE 1999), commissioned by the then Secretary of State, David Blunkett.
33 Rose (2008): 48–54; Rose (2009): recommendation 14.
34 Dearing (1993b).
35 Hargreaves (1978).
36 Scottish Government (2008a).
37 Gardner (1999).
38 Rose (2008): 37–39.
39 *Ibid.*: para 2.23.
40 Goswami and Bryant (2010), Mayall (2010), *The Cambridge Primary Review Research Surveys*, Chapters 6 and 3.
41 LGA *et al.* (2008b): 8.1–8.79.
42 Rose (2008): para 1.31.
43 Rose (2008): paras 1.34–1.35.
44 NACCCE (1999): 27–30.
45 Lipman *et al.* (1980).
46 Rose (2008): recommendation 18.
47 Hargreaves (2008a).
48 For a detailed discussion of the role of film and television in the teaching of English see the report of the 1993 BFI/TES Commission of Enquiry into English (Bazalgette 1994).
49 For example, the *Daily Mail*, 6 April 2009.
50 Baroness Susan Greenfield, quoted in *The Guardian*, 24 February 2009.
51 For example, 'Baroness, you are being a complete twit about twitter', Catherine Bennett in *The Observer*, 1 March 2009.
52 DES (1975): 514.
53 Conroy, Hulme and Menter (2008) (Volume 2, Chapter 16). See also Chapter 7 of this volume.
54 'Place and time' is borrowed from – and a tribute to – two champions of the primary humanities, the late Joan and Alan Blyth.
55 Shulman (1987).
56 We have insisted that 'standards' and 'quality' are not necessarily the same, and the use of both words is intended to encourage debate about what, in the broadest sense, pupils should experience and achieve by the time they leave primary school. For more detailed discussion, see Chapter 17.
57 House of Commons (2009): Appendix 2

15 Re-thinking pedagogy

Good teaching makes a difference. Excellent teaching can transform lives. Our 12 aims for primary education place teachers at the forefront of the quest to enliven young minds, build knowledge and understanding, explore ideas, develop skill and excite the imagination, and through these to empower children to take control of their destinies and engage with others in pursuit of a productive life, a just society and a sustainable world. Our framework for the curriculum rejects the still prevalent belief that 'standards' in primary education are about the 3Rs alone and insists that if curriculum entitlement means anything, it is about excellence across the board, in every aspect of learning, regardless of how much or how little time is allocated to it.

So we have set our sights high – higher, we believe, than at present, for all the tough talk of standards, targets, zero tolerance, step changes, world-class schools and the rest – because while not giving an inch on standards as conventionally defined we want to encourage a vision of primary education which is broader and richer.

In all this, the teacher's expertise and commitment are crucial. Of course, the precise chemistry of the various influences on children's learning remains open to debate, especially in relation to the school effectiveness paradigms and measures which have been influential in policy circles since the mid-1990s and on which we comment later in this chapter. Thus, in assessing the relative impact on cognitive attainment of family, pre-school and primary education, the Effective Provision of Pre-School Education (EPPE) study – one of the largest of its kind – concluded that the 'academic effectiveness' of the primary school is a significant factor in accounting for variation in pupils' reading and mathematics attainment by Year 5; that the combination of pre-school quality and primary-school academic effectiveness 'are strongly associated with better "self-regulation" and "pro-social" behaviour'; and that 'raising the effectiveness and quality of both can help improve children's all-round development'.[1]

For some, the EPPE findings confirm that teaching makes a real difference, while others worry whether such studies really do prove what they claim. Yet that debate is less about education than about the limits of research conducted within a particular paradigm, and because using its methods it is difficult to show conclusively that schools do make a difference, that doesn't mean that they do not. Rather, what is important about studies like EPPE, which embed their analysis of teaching in contexts beyond the classroom, is that they remind us that schools achieve most when they are able to work with the grain of other influences, including those over which they may have little or no control. Conversely, although there are impressive examples of schools that succeed against the odds,[2] their task in situations where school, home and prior experience diverge is vastly more difficult. This is the insight which has yielded the government's 'contextual value added' measures for factors such as poverty, mobility, ethnicity and prior attainment – though, again, their validity and use provoke technical objections which must be heeded.[3] Similarly this insight has given rise to a succession of compensatory projects ranging from the educational priority areas and social priority schools of the 1970s and 1980s to education action zones in the 1990s and then Excellence in Cities, City Challenge and Narrowing the Gap.

It is thus fitting that the present chapter is located near the middle of our report, after discussion of childhood, parenting and caring, aims and the curriculum, and in anticipation of assessment, schools, teacher training, leadership, governance, funding and the policies that bear on all of these. For there is no theme in this report, or in the Cambridge Primary Review as a whole, which does not bear in some way on what goes on in classrooms; and if educational aims such as those adumbrated in Chapter 12 are to mean anything, they must be pursued with equal vigour in teaching, the curriculum, assessment and the wider life of the school.

It follows that to understand teaching – the particular focus of this chapter – we must not only be aware of the contextual influences and constraints to which the realities and possibilities of classroom life are subject; we should also find a way to frame teaching conceptually so that its scope and complexity can be meaningfully captured and explored.

This is what takes us from teaching to *pedagogy*, for if teaching is the classroom act narrowly defined, pedagogy is that act together with the ideas that inform it. Teaching is a skill, or a complex combination of skills, but it is much more than that, and the teacher's knowledge, dispositions, attitudes, values and interpersonal capacities are no less important. It is no longer acceptable to assert, as to their shame Britain's political leaders did during the 1990s (and, we fear, some still do), that teaching is just a matter of common sense and that everything else is 'barmy theory'. What the teacher knows and how the teacher thinks shape, for better or worse, how the teacher acts; and knowledge, deliberation, judgement and action pursue, or ought to pursue, clearly-articulated aims.

'Pedagogy' signals a much wider frame of reference than 'teaching', one which in many other countries has been taken for granted for centuries but in England has had to fight for a hearing.[4] Here, because it has been adopted, albeit modified, in contexts as different yet as authoritative as the government's Primary National Strategy and the Economic and Social Research Council's Teaching and Learning Research Programme (TLRP), it does not seem presumptuous to use the definition of pedagogy which originated within this review's team:

> Pedagogy is the act of teaching together with its attendant discourse of educational theories, values, evidence and justifications. It is what one needs to know, and the skills one needs to command, in order to make and justify the many different kinds of decision of which teaching is constituted.[5]

Something of that 'attendant discourse' emerges from what follows. Much more has already come from the preceding chapters. As to the 'act of teaching' more narrowly defined, we offer later both a framework for analysing it and principles by which it might be informed.

WHAT THE REVIEW'S WITNESSES SAID

Constraints on teaching

Almost one third of the submissions to the Cambridge Review commented on teaching directly. All agreed that effective teaching is of paramount importance but there was less agreement about what it looks like and how it should be achieved. Teachers and professional organisations readily acknowledged improvements brought about by recent national initiatives, but tended to say more about the constraints these imposed, though a few believed that they had retained some room to innovate and experiment. Viewing the situation from a secondary school standpoint, the Association of School and College Leaders believed that primary teachers were generally more effective, better trained and qualified than in the past. Parents and community representatives – in the soundings as well as submissions – concentrated less on teachers' working conditions and more on their tasks, arguing, among much else, that there should be a heavier emphasis on discipline, respect and responsibility.

Yet a picture of teachers and teaching hamstrung by recent policy dominated the submissions of almost every adult group consulted in the Review's soundings. The culprits were three, and they are already familiar from our discussion of the curriculum: an over-prescriptive national curriculum, high-stakes testing, especially at key stage 2, and the national strategies. The submission from the Association for the Study of Primary Education is representative:

If prospective teachers embark on a training course in the belief that they are entering a profession dedicated to the development of young minds through innovative and child-centred ideas, only to discover that most of their teaching is constrained by external demands, it is little wonder that they become disillusioned. If they decide to become teachers in the belief that a sizeable proportion of the work is dedicated to the social and moral development of children, only to discover that the role is largely one of imparting knowledge and boosting test results, nobody should be surprised by their loss of motivation. If they enter the profession in the belief that they will be free to use their creativity, personality and intuition to inject a sense of purpose into the classroom, only to discover that time constraints, paperwork, fear of inspection and obsession with targets dominates the agenda, their negative reactions can be forecast.

Head teachers at one community sounding said that the flexibility of 'excellence and enjoyment' promised in the Primary National Strategy launch document[6] had been 'stymied' by the continuing emphasis on SATs and the defensive or strategic rather than educational thinking which this dictated. One teacher wrote:

> At a staff meeting last year, I was appalled when the advice from the MIT [monitoring and intervention team] adviser was that the school should analyse the SATs results and from this focus teaching and resources in Year 5 and 6 on children who are likely to get a level 3 but could possibly get a level 4 so as to improve the school's league table performance. This ... would mean that the needs of the lower ability children are not addressed fully, leaving them further behind, and risking the higher ability children becoming switched off from learning because they are not being challenged enough. This advice is coming from people employed by the government to advise schools on how they should be running – the same government who are also promoting their strategy *Every Child Matters.* The two do not seem congruent.

But in the soundings some school senior management teams, heads and community groups suggested that teachers were too ready to blame the DCSF and Ofsted for problems which were partly self-inflicted. Teachers, they said, need to exercise their professional right to ask 'Why?' more often, assert their independence and concentrate on getting 'inside children's minds' and teaching 'from the heart'. However, such confidence grows from authority and experience. For a young teacher on the main scale, to challenge official orthodoxy requires a school culture which itself encourages this, and not all of them do. Youthful scepticism is quickly stifled by managerial conformity.

In any case, acceding to the plea for flexibility does not necessarily guarantee change. As Larry Cuban points out, there is an inherent conservatism, or perhaps caution, in the profession which means that even when constraints are removed little may change;[7] and while the well-massaged 'myth of progressivism'[8] portrayed English primary schools overwhelmed by rampant progressivism during the liberal 1960s, inspectors found that only 5 per cent of classrooms exhibited wholeheartedly 'exploratory' characteristics, and that didactic teaching was still practised in three-quarters of them.[9]

What good teaching looks like

We can extrapolate from all the submissions and soundings, including those from teachers and children, agreement that good teaching:

- is well-organised and planned
- is reflective
- is based on sound subject knowledge
- depends on effective classroom management

- requires an understanding of children's developmental needs
- uses exciting and varied approaches
- inspires
- encourages children to become autonomous learners
- facilitates children's learning
- stimulates children's creativity and imagination.

It might be suggested that this list is pretty self-evident. However, once one pauses to think about each of these conditions they become less a truism than a challenge. How do we translate the approbatory but casual 'sound', 'effective', 'exciting and varied' into meaningful operational criteria against which teaching can be judged? Precisely what kind of teaching 'inspires', 'encourages' and 'stimulates'?

There is also an interesting difference of perspective here between children and adults. The children we met during the community soundings were exercised by, among much else, the clarity, structure and subject knowledge that attends expertise. Good teachers, said our child witnesses, 'explain things in advance so that you know what a lesson is about', 'know a lot about their subject', 'make sure it's not in too big steps' and 'give us records of what we learn'. They are also 'firm but fair' and 'trustworthy', and 'understand how you feel but don't intrude'. The valuing of equity and empathy sits interestingly alongside an intuitive grasp of what elsewhere would be called advance cognitive organisation, pedagogical content knowledge, graduated instruction and formative feedback – conditions for effective teaching on which books have been written and careers have been made, though not, so far, by children. The common strand, and it should be closely heeded, is that children want and need to know what they are doing and why, to be brought inside the thinking that informs the teacher's decisions on their behalf. Children, too, are interested in pedagogy.

Improving teaching

Views on improving teaching ranged from wish-lists comprising the by now familiar calls for 'more creativity', 'greater flexibility' and 'less prescription', to detailed proposals for the adoption of specific teaching strategies. The prevailing requirement, however, was for teaching to be removed from political control. As the submission from the National Union of Teachers argued:

> The government has failed to understand that imposed transformation will fail. Teachers have to be motivated by, believe in and above all contribute to any Primary National Strategy … Professional development has to be developed and be owned by teachers. They must have a deeper understanding of the educational issues underpinning the NLNS frameworks if they are to be able to adapt them to meet the needs of their pupils. The long-overdue need to provide some degree of flexibility and to encourage teachers to modify the frameworks, using their professional judgement, has been recognised in the recent revisions to the frameworks, but it remains to be seen how far their impact on teaching and learning throughout the primary curriculum will change as a result.

Witnesses appeared to believe that once these conditions were met teaching would be free and able to:

- draw on the local community's knowledge and expertise
- respect and respond to the interests and needs of individual learners
- be based on clearer understanding of children's development
- use more exciting and varied approaches to engage children's interest
- include more opportunities for collaborative activities
- provide more opportunities to stimulate children's imagination and creativity

- do more to facilitate children's independence as learners and encourage lifelong learning
- involve dialogic teaching approaches to promote higher-order thinking skills.

But of course life is not like that. In any case, it could be argued that most of these are pre-conditions for teaching which is proficient rather than exceptional. On the other hand, if all teaching were genuinely exciting, stimulating, diverse, dialogic, collaborative and directed towards children's independence, imagination, creativity, higher-order thinking and lifelong learning, then this chapter would be unnecessary.

The submissions provided more detailed comment on a number of the ideals listed above. The National Education Trust and the National Primary Headteachers' Association were among many organisations pressing for an 'emphasis on active learning' and a more play-based approach in key stage 1. The Association for Science Education lamented that 'too much practice is dominated by teachers telling and pupils copying'. Children themselves, at one community sounding, advocated problem-solving as a surer way than transmission to engage and retain their interest. We need, though, to sound a note of caution. Ever since the 1931 Hadow Report commended 'activity and experience' as the basis for primary education, 'active learning' has been used with increasing frequency but a diminishing sense of what it means. The same goes for other current buzz phrases like personalised/individualised learning, creative/flexible teaching.

Speaking from their concern with the fate of small schools and the mainly rural communities they serve, the National Association for Small Schools argued that 'primary education needs to relate more directly to everyday life and experience' and urged that teachers should 'tap and exploit community talents and resources'. These concerns do not relate only to small schools, and in Chapters 12 and 14 we translated them into aims and an approach to curriculum planning which we believe constitute imperatives for primary schools everywhere.

Moves towards increasing children's active participation and voice were widely welcomed. 'Building on pupils' interests in designing and teaching units of work increases their engagement and supports their learning', asserted one inner-city local authority. The Universities' Council for the Education of Teachers urged teachers 'to learn to relate to pupils in such a way that they can make pupils' personal and social experience the starting point for their exploration of all that subjects have to offer'. Lessons and activities that give children opportunities to take the lead in their learning enable them to develop a sense of responsibility and self-confidence, according to some; and echoing this report's arguments about childhood capability (Chapters 5 and 7), one submission observed that 'pupils can often do more than adults think they can, especially if they are involved in the planning of a project and understand its aims'. This reinforces, too, our view that children need to be fully informed about what they are doing and why, and to be party to as much of the teacher's thinking about their learning and progress as is practicable.

Dialogue and dialogic teaching were highlighted in several submissions as an important means of developing children's intellectual capacities. SAPERE, an organisation which promotes philosophy for children along lines proposed by Matthew Lipman,[10] said that 'teachers should be given more encouragement and preparation in stimulating and managing classroom dialogue' and went on to argue that 'more opportunity should be allowed within curriculum for "open enquiry"'. In a similar vein, the Basic Skills Agency argued that 'pedagogy should be made in a constant dialogue'. We say more about this idea later in the chapter.

Standing back from advocacy of particular classroom approaches, some submissions concerned themselves more with what teachers need to know. The list was headed, as it has been since the 1930s, and as it was with renewed insistence from the late 1960s,[11] by knowledge of children's development and learning. One submission observed that at 'a time when schools have to collect so much empirical data on pupils' performance, so little of our teaching practice is based on sound empirical research as to how children learn most effectively'. Others called for research into children's cognitive development to be more fully integrated into educational practice, and for children's 'readiness' to learn to be taken into account in what, when and how they are taught. One local authority wanted 'high quality research to be quickly translated into what head teachers and teachers can do to make a difference to children's learning in the classroom'. Teaching organisations, heads, researchers and individual teachers all recommended that teachers should be given more time and support to consider research on children's learning and more flexibility to act on such research by adapting national strategies to fit their own pupils' needs and interests, especially in key stage 1.

Personalising learning

Government might respond that since 2004 these calls have been heeded, and that 'personalisation' is the way forward not just for education but for the full spectrum of public policy.[12] In 2006, the Teaching and Learning in 2020 Review Group characterised 'personalised learning' thus:

> Close attention is paid to learners' knowledge, skills, understanding and attitudes. Learning is connected to what they already know (including from outside the classroom). Teaching enthuses pupils and engages their interest in learning: it identifies, explores and corrects misconceptions. Learners are active and curious: they create their own hypotheses, ask their own questions, coach one another, set goals for themselves, monitor their progress and experiment with ideas for taking risks, knowing that mistakes and 'being stuck' are part of learning. Work is sufficiently varied and challenging to maintain their engagement but not so difficult as to discourage them. This engagement allows learners of all abilities to succeed, and it avoids the disaffection and attention-seeking that give rise to problems with behaviour.[13]

An earlier exposition had paid less attention to learners 'of all abilities' and more to 'intensive small group tuition in literacy and numeracy for those falling behind and extra stretch for the gifted and talented.'[14] Yet while many Review witnesses confessed to uncertainty about what 'personalised learning' meant or whether it offered anything new (a situation confirmed in a parallel survey of teachers undertaken by Judy Sebba and others[15]), many organisations nevertheless supported it. The submission from the Trades Union Congress (TUC) said:

> The development of a personalised teaching and learning approach for all pupils has wide support among trade unions and to some degree it is based on underpinning principles that the school workforce unions have been advocating for a number of years. And this is not a new agenda by any means, as teachers have always exercised their professional judgement and skills within the classroom in order to provide a tailored education for all their pupils.

But, the TUC went on to warn,

> There is a strong argument that the existing format and operation of the national curriculum makes it very difficult to see how a fully personalised teaching and learning agenda can co-exist with the current curriculum and associated structures in primary schools in England.

A rather different reservation, relating to demography rather than policy, was conveyed by a local authority:

> We aim to be responsive to all the learning needs of all pupils, but the challenge is the ever growing variety and quantity of learners from other cultures, which demands greater resourcing and professional knowledge from teaching staff.

Personalised learning was not universally welcomed. The charity Save the Children warned that 'personalisation implemented badly can succeed only in labelling children and damaging those who do not achieve'. A local authority argued that 'over-emphasising personalisation and differentiation are undermining advances in social pedagogy and interactive learning'. A teacher-training institution was worried about the 'possible isolation for a child following an entirely personalised curriculum'.

We have to say that, as advocated in government publications, 'personalised learning' remains either somewhat obvious or, more accurately perhaps, elusive because it is expressed in such self-evident terms that one assumes that there must be more to it than meets the eye. Thus a 2008 DCSF explication of personalised learning lists as its 'key features': 'high quality teaching and learning', 'ongoing evaluation', 'a variety of learning approaches', 'engaging with children', 'engaging with parents', 'joining with other providers', 'access to opportunities and activities outside the school day', and 'raising expectations of and for children and young people'.[16]

Fortunately, there are those – notably Professor David Hargreaves – who have shifted 'personalised learning' onto an altogether higher plane and have re-configured it as an idea which has real educational potency. We return to his work later in this chapter: our witnesses, however, had to make do with the official definition.

Managing behaviour

There was extensive concern in the submissions about classroom management and discipline in response to what was perceived as a worrying decline in children's standards of behaviour. The National Association of Head Teachers felt that newly qualified teachers had insufficient training in managing disruptive behaviour. Local authorities were among the organisations that suggested children should be taught how to behave via stricter systems of rules and 'boundaries'. According to children themselves, for teaching to be effective the classroom needed to be an orderly and 'safe' place.

Most insistent of all on this score were parents, who in the community soundings – as we note elsewhere – made more frequent reference to 'respect' than any other group. However, their concern was far from narrow, and they commended these guiding values for schools which helped shape one of the Review's 12 aims for primary education:

- respect for oneself
- respect for peers and adults
- respect for other generations
- respect for difference
- respect in the use of language
- respect for courtesy and good manners
- respect for the environment, both globally and locally.

The Review's community soundings report, from which this list is taken, also noted:

> Some parents saw the problem not just as disrespect as manifested in public rudeness or loutishness, but as a more subtle loss of the nuances of interpersonal dealings and the language which attends them, an all-embracing familiarity regardless of whether it is merited or welcomed.[17]

That said, many teachers believed that such values ought to be instilled by parents rather than themselves and were adamant that they were at the receiving end of tendencies which originated outside the school and which made their task much more difficult than it should be. They argued that children's lack of maturity and poor social skills aggravated the problem, and that parents must take responsibility for these. For their part, parents were no less ready to blame 'soft' teachers who lacked the skills to manage behaviour effectively.

Among teachers themselves, there were differences. In the 2008 NUT study by Maurice Galton and John MacBeath:

> Teachers newer to the profession tended to blame ... poor classroom discipline and ... the increase in the number of children with serious learning difficulties now entering school ... Longer serving teachers tended to attribute the decline to the pressures emanating from the 'performance culture'.[18]

This distribution or deflection of cause and responsibility mirrored the finding of the 1989 Elton Report:

> One of the most striking features of our evidence is the sheer variety of causes of, and cures for, bad behaviour in schools that was suggested to us. A few submissions fall into the single cause or single cure category, but the great majority are much more complex. ... The variety of causes and cures suggested to us represents an important finding in itself. It is clear that most of the individuals and organisations submitting evidence consider that bad behaviour in schools is a complex problem which does not lend itself to simple solutions. Taken as a whole the evidence submitted to us indicates that any quest for a single, dramatic remedy, such as a major piece of new legislation, would be futile.[19]

As to the extent of the problem, views were no less diverse. In 2005 Ofsted reported that standards of behaviour overall were improving,[20] but the 2008 NUT study said:

> In ... 2002 ... classroom disruption was not highlighted as a major problem. Five years on, teachers in the same schools regard it as a more significant priority ... Even in the early years of primary education [pupils] were reluctant to follow instructions ... and a minority could be extremely confrontational, use foul language and could even be physically aggressive.[21]

In a response to this Review's interim report on the primary curriculum (Chapters 13 and 14 in this volume), the think tank Civitas asserted

> No amount of tinkering with the national curriculum will improve academic standards until and unless a far more important cause of poor educational standards is addressed ... Too many schoolchildren today are being prevented from learning at school by the unacceptably high levels of disruptive and unruly behaviour of their peers.[22]

Civitas then provided some 'startling' but unsourced figures about the incidence of disruptive and violent behaviour in primary and secondary schools, adding:

> None of this early bad behaviour can be attributed to what teachers are attempting to teach pupils; practically all of it can be [put down] to lack of proper parental guidance at home ... The suggestion that it has been an uninspiring curriculum or over-testing that has caused the misconduct is ludicrous.[23]

This is a good illustration of the way this issue generates more heat than light, for the Cambridge Primary Review certainly did not make the 'ludicrous' claim which Civitas attributes to it. On the other hand, the capacity of the curriculum to engage and stimulate children is certainly one necessary element in the debate, and this is acknowledged in the government's Children's Plan.

The government's practitioner group on school behaviour, chaired by Sir Alan Steer, goes further, and directly challenges views of the kind that Civitas voices. One of its reports quotes pupils who attest to the positive impact of sport and the performing arts on their self-esteem and capacity to manage their own behaviour, and adds:

> The role that the arts can play in helping pupils with challenging behaviour and disaffection has a proven track record. Offering pupils the opportunity to shine in front of their peers and communities develops their self-esteem and status.[24]

More generally, the Steer group states as the first of its six 'core beliefs' that 'the quality of learning, teaching and behaviour are inseparable issues, and the responsibility of all staff.'[25] Merely blaming parents, then, is a counsel of despair, and the Steer group's balanced approach is to be applauded.

If Civitas wish to dismiss all causal links between behaviour and what teachers do, then they should ponder, alongside the advice of the Steer group, the implications of policies which separate the two entirely. Galton and MacBeath show that many primary schools are increasingly adopting secondary schools' use of 'zero tolerance', firm rules, 'time out' and immediate sanctions imposed without discussion.[26] This environment of high control is somewhat at odds with the parallel attempts, referred to later in this chapter, to foster collaborative learning and classroom dialogue in which, if pupils are encouraged to give reasons for their answers to questions, teachers must expect to model the same openness and accountability.[27] This means that while poor behaviour cannot be condoned, in such an environment teachers need to explore its reasons. Managing behaviour and managing learning are intimately connected. Indeed learning in classrooms extends to learning about behaviour and does not stop at the formal curriculum. Strategies for each of them need to be aligned and consistent, or at least if there is inconsistency (for example if pupil A is treated one way and pupil B another) it needs to be explained. At the heart of both classroom learning and behaviour, as both teachers and children understand – and as the children in our community soundings emphasised – are the nature and quality of the relationships which the teacher is able to foster with and among the pupils. Public discussion and media-directed political interventions tend to ignore this, focusing on rules rather than relationships, detaching behaviour from learning, and replacing interaction from which pupils learn to think by directives which teach them to comply.

ALTERNATIVE PERSPECTIVES: THE REVIEW'S RESEARCH SURVEYS

The submissions tend to dwell on constraints, problems and challenges arising from the practical situations that pupils and teachers find themselves in, and which frustrate their achievement of the ideals signalled under the headings 'what good teaching looks like' and 'improving teaching' in the previous section. Chief among such perceived constraints are the weight of externally-imposed requirements and expectations and the challenge of poor pupil behaviour. The Review's commissioned research surveys step back from all this and focus on conditions for teaching and learning which, like the 12 aims (Chapter 12) and the ideal of a rich, balanced and empowering curriculum (Chapter 14), need somehow to be kept in view whatever the circumstances. The evidence from the research surveys can be summarised under the following headings:

- children's experience before and outside primary school
- children's thinking
- cognitive prerequisites for learning
- social prerequisites for learning
- language in learning
- ICT in learning
- classroom organisation
- class size
- principles for effective learning and teaching.

Research on the pedagogical impact of children's experience before and outside primary school[28]

- The benefits of high quality pre-school experience remain evident until the end of the primary phase.
- Good early years pedagogy combines direct teaching, instructive learning environments and sustained shared thinking to develop children's learning.

- Funds of knowledge are embedded in the cultures of homes and communities and can be used to support learning in schools.
- Children are active agents in learning, in interaction with siblings and parents. They learn, through apprenticeship, the social, cultural and moral order of their home, and their responsibilities as moral agents. They learn at home that they are persons (rather than pre-social projects). They have more chance at home of being respected as persons than anywhere else. They participate in everyday household and neighbourhood activity. They learn speech that is adequate for communicating in the social environment of the family. They learn the health-related ideas and practices of their home. On all this schools can and should build, but they do not yet do so sufficiently.
- Knowledge-exchange activities can make teachers more knowledgeable about children's out of school lives, and parents more knowledgeable about what happens in school.

Research on children's thinking and how it can be advanced[29]

- Children think and reason largely in the same ways as adults, but they lack experience, and are still developing the ability to think about their own thinking and learning (meta-cognition) and to regulate their own behaviour and interactions. They need diverse experiences in the classroom to help them develop these self-reflective and self-regulatory skills. This is a key insight from recent research, and contrasts with the 1960s/1970s view that child and adult thinking are totally different.
- Recent research shows that learning depends on the development of multi-sensory networks of neurons distributed across the entire brain. Ideas such as left-brain/right-brain learning, or unisensory 'learning styles' (visual, auditory or kinaesthetic) are not supported by neuroscience.
- Children construct causal frameworks to make sense of their experiences. Knowledge gained through active experience, language, pretend play and teaching are all important for the development of these causal explanatory systems.
- Incremental experience is the key to learning. The brain learns from every experienced event, but because cognitive representations are distributed across networks of neurons, cumulative learning is crucial. This supports the value of multi-sensory approaches to teaching.
- Pretend play and the imagination are important for cognitive development in the early years of education, helping children to reflect upon and regulate their own cognitive behaviour, and to reflect upon and gain a deeper understanding of the mind. Pretending is more effective when carried out with other children and when scaffolded by adults.
- Learning in classrooms can be enhanced by developing metacognitive strategies, self-reflection and inhibitory control in children. These skills can be taught.

Research on cognitive prerequisites for learning[30]

- Symbol systems like the alphabet and the number system require direct teaching, but for both reading and number certain cognitive prerequisites facilitate learning.
- The cognitive prerequisites for reading and number depend on language development, perceptual development and spatial development, and can be enhanced by direct teaching (for example, using linguistic rhyme and rhythm games). For reading, the key cognitive prerequisite is phonological awareness, the child's ability to reflect upon the sound patterns of words in her mental lexicon at different 'grain sizes' (for example syllable, rhyme). For number, the main cognitive prerequisite appears to be recognition of numbers as approximations of quantity.

Research on social prerequisites for learning[31]

- Individual differences in the ability to benefit from instruction, identified by Vygotsky as the 'zone of proximal development', are large in the primary years. At the same time, children have much in common, and their learning is primarily a social activity which requires common goals and shared activities. This should be the teacher's starting point, and is the necessary context for individualising or personalising learning in response to specific needs.

- If learning in young children is socially mediated, then families, carers, peers and teachers are all important. Even basic perceptual learning mechanisms require social interaction to be effective. This limits the applicability of educational approaches such as e-learning in the early years.
- Social interaction and collaborative activity among children in class can provide valuable, complementary and distinctive opportunities for learning and conceptual development. Social development influences patterns of interaction, which in turn affect learning, the development of ways of thinking and social development itself.
- Encouraging children to pursue joint goals, explain their understanding, express different points of view and attempt to reach consensus through discussion have all been found to help learning and understanding. Observations in primary classrooms, however, suggest that children seldom have the opportunity to engage in productive social interaction.

Research on the importance of language in learning[32]

- Language is crucial for development but there is huge individual variation from an early age. Children who enter school with impoverished language skills require immediate support.
- Differential exposure (for example to spoken or written language) will lead to differential learning. As an example, one of the most important determinants of reading fluency is how much text the child actually reads, including outside the classroom.
- The ways in which teachers talk to children can influence learning, memory, understanding and the motivation to learn. Learning and memory benefit when the teacher adopts an elaborative conversational style, amplifying and evaluating what the child says. This elaboration helps children to make sense of temporal and causal aspects of their experiences.

Research on the use of ICT to enhance learning[33]

- Effective teaching and learning with ICT involves building bridges between 'idiosyncratic' learning, arising from extended periods of individual engagement, and 'intended' learning that often needs to be supported by the teacher.
- Young children's encounters with ICT are enhanced when practitioners use guided interaction (questioning, modelling, praising, supporting) and balance child-initiated and adult-led activities.
- Guided interaction with ICT can enhance dispositions to learn, knowledge of the world and operational skills, as well as hand-eye coordination.
- Providing a broad range of ICTs, including digital still and video cameras, mobile phones and electronic keyboards and toys, as well as computers, promotes more opportunities for learning.
- There is a two-way exchange of knowledge between home and school use of ICT and this impacts on school learning, but the teacher remains key to the successful use of ICT for learning.

Research on classroom organisation[34]

- Teachers should encourage exploratory talk, argumentation and participative discussion. Effective learning is developed in relationships between staff, children and peers rather than the individual child.
- Groups in classrooms are often formed without a strategic view of their purpose, and there is little support for pupil-pupil interactions within groups. Pupils often struggle to work together successfully in groups.

- Recent pressures relating to the curriculum and the classroom context have resulted in an increasingly heavy emphasis on whole-class teaching with little room for group work. Pupils are likely to be seated in an arrangement that does not facilitate their learning. Pupils usually sit in groups but rarely interact and work *as* groups.
- Effective group work has a positive effect on pupils' academic progress, higher conceptual learning, behaviour and relations with others, provided that teachers take the time to train pupils in the skills of group working.
- Schools need to look more deeply at their current practices regarding differentiation (especially setting and inflexible within-class grouping) and identify best practice on the basis of actual effects on pupil learning rather than rhetoric.
- Varying pupil within-class grouping for different activities offers more flexibility, facilitates movement between groups structured by ability, and avoids limiting the opportunities for some children.
- However: the evidence suggests there are no consistent effects of structured ability grouping, such as setting, on attainment, although there can be detrimental affects on social and personal outcomes for some children. Teaching quality seems to be the most important factor in determining outcomes, although pupils in the top groups can have an enhanced educational experience.

Research on class size[35]

- Pupils' age is important when considering class size effects. There is a clear case for small classes in the reception year, but research also shows where resources could be further targeted: that is, on achieving classes of fewer than 25 for those children with most ground to make up in literacy. Another important implication is to maintain smaller classes from one year to the next where possible.
- Some have argued that money is better spent on teachers' professional development than on reducing class sizes, but these should not be placed in opposition. Rather, professional development should be used to help teachers exploit the learning opportunities of small classes, while developing strategies for realising their educational objectives in large classes.

Research on the relationship between pupil and teacher voice[36]

- Pupil consultation benefits children by enhancing engagement with learning, their sense of agency and of themselves as learners. It benefits teachers by deepening their insights into children's abilities and learning preferences, leading to more responsive teaching and willingness to give pupils more responsibility. And it benefits schools by strengthening school policy in substantive ways.
- However, ingrained habits can prevent pupils being heard. Many barriers to pupils' participation and learning stem from teachers' misplaced assumptions about what children can and cannot do. These assumptions can be changed if teachers engage collectively with evidence about pupils' experience of school and their own practice.
- There is a relationship between the way teachers think about their own practice and how pupils learn. Classroom-focused professional enquiry by teachers is a key condition of promoting autonomous learning by pupils. The schools that embed assessment for pupil learning are those which also make support for professional learning a priority. Pupils whose teachers are committed and resilient are likely to attain more than pupils whose teachers are not, but teachers in schools serving more disadvantaged communities are more persistently challenged than others.
- Assessment for learning helps teachers promote learning how to learn; however, it is difficult to shift teachers from reliance on specific techniques (the letter of AfL) to practices based on deep principles integrated into the flow of lessons (the spirit of AfL).

- Educational networks are much talked about but little understood, and electronic tools for professional development purposes are not well used; however, the intellectual capital of schools can be built on the social capital developed through teachers' personal networking practices.

A 'STATE THEORY OF LEARNING'? POLICY AND PRIMARY TEACHING SINCE 1991

To return to the Review's submissions and soundings:

- They concerned themselves more with what is wrong with the current situation than with what is right.
- They more readily identified problems than proposed solutions.
- Though some were studiously even-handed, accepting that teachers have more freedom in the classroom than conventional wisdom admits, a much larger number accused recent government policies of creating circumstances in which teachers feel excessively constrained and controlled.

The general air of pessimism and powerlessness could be an accurate reflection of how people feel, anywhere, when their freedom of action and thought in the area which lies at the heart of their work is reduced. It is, after all, 17 years since a government emphatically announced that 'questions about how to teach are not for Government to determine',[37] and a decade since this final taboo was no less emphatically broken by the national literacy and numeracy strategies – technically non-statutory but regarded everywhere as obligatory. Since then, in the view of two commentators, English primary schools have been expected to conform to:

> a state theory of learning ... based on the idea that a combination of the repeated high stakes testing of pupils, a national curriculum, and in primary schools mandated pedagogy in literacy and numeracy, will raise standards ... There is little doubt that the machinery of surveillance and accountability makes it difficult for schools to deviate from focusing on test performance.'[38]

The Stalinist overtones of a 'state theory of learning' enforced by 'the machinery of surveillance and accountability' are as unattractive as they are serious. The charge needs to be proved or refuted. Since it depends in part on a view of what preceded the era of government centralisation and micro-management, we should say immediately that talk of a 'golden age' of autonomous and creative primary teaching is almost certainly wide of the mark, except perhaps for some teachers in a few local authorities. We would also note that it is now 20 years since the introduction of the national curriculum and national testing, and the shift of educational control from local to national government 'in a manner without parallel in the western world'.[39] The teaching profession has meanwhile become younger[40] and those teachers with experience of the pre-1989 'golden age' will soon be a fast-dwindling minority.

It is true, as we have noted, that national governments held back from intervening directly in pedagogy until 1997. However, others were only too happy to do so. The period before the 1988 Education Reform Act was not one of benign professional freedom, still less of the professional anarchy portrayed by the Black Paper authors, but of firm local authority control, and the power wielded by LEA advisers and inspectors, not to mention their patronage in staff appointments and promotion, could be considerable. In many LEAs there were clear expectations of what good classrooms and teaching should look like, from the structuring of the curriculum to the organisation of groups, and older teachers retain their folk memory of advisers' aesthetic preferences during the 1960s and 1970s for tastefully arranged teasels (Oxfordshire), rolls of corrugated cardboard (Hertfordshire) and fabrics (West Riding), not to mention weightier matters like creative writing and 'the new mathematics'. In those days, too, heads had – and were expected to have – firm views. This was the era of 'my school', 'my teachers', 'my children', 'my governors' and even 'my parents'.

One study of teachers at work during this period shows them struggling to reconcile the competing pedagogical imperatives of external expectation and professional experience: the expectation that planning be loose, flexible and 'open' and their need for structure and predictability; the insistence that they should stand back and 'facilitate' when they needed to intervene; the requirement that they should treat group work as an organisational panacea even though at times they needed to work with whole classes or individuals,[41] and even though the potential of group work was rarely realised in genuinely collaborative activity.[42] These teachers did their best to make things work; yet despite being experienced, they felt they could not question what was expected. Another study shows an entire local system of 230 primary schools and 2,400 primary teachers under instructions to emulate the layout, decoration and use of the LEA's single 'model classroom'.[43]

However, then as now, local authorities could be very different, and this qualification is emphasised lest we be accused of generalising. For every LEA advisory team that laid down directives about ideologically-grounded 'good practice' there were others keen to explore with teachers the implications of classroom research, seeing their role as encouraging rather than controlling teachers' development.

At issue, therefore, is not the presence or absence of pressure to conform before and after the arrival of the national curriculum and national strategies, but its source and justification. For prescription of some kind has usually been there. Before 1989, it might stem from advisers, heads or teacher trainers, always subject to the variability in professional culture noted above. Today, however, prescription comes from the DCSF, Ofsted, QCA, the national strategies and the culture of performativity that these bodies in their different ways represent. Then, the culture had a personal edge to it, for the head and adviser were familiar figures and advancement depended on their approval; today, at least, it is more impersonal. A further difference of some importance in this discussion of pedagogy is that the localised pressure was more likely to stem from belief than evidence and justification. With 'my school' came 'my values and ethos', and it was often deemed sufficient for the authority figure to define pedagogy by reference to belief alone, and indeed it was sometimes assumed that the more unshakeable the belief, the better the teaching. Now, 'evidence-informed practice' is the watchword (the reliability and interpretation of the evidence cited are another matter). Interestingly, conviction pedagogy was ousted by the arch-proponents of conviction politics.[44]

One potentially significant but so far under-investigated aspect of the shift from local authority to national control has been that many of those in local authorities retained their power over teachers' lives by moving from town and county hall to the DCSF, the national strategies, QCA and Ofsted. There is a great deal in the tone, language and mindset of documents emanating from these bodies over the past decade, not to say the attitude to ideas, evidence and citation, which resonates much more strongly with the culture of some former local authority advisory and inspection teams than the career civil service. The career paths of many key government advisers may well confirm the hypothesis. No less striking – as is illustrated by comparison of, say, the 1985 White Paper *Better Schools* and the 2003 Primary Strategy manifesto *Excellence and Enjoyment* – is the replacement of clear prose and reasoned argument by jargon, over-simplification, and appeals to what one can only describe as the lowest common denominator of professional understanding.

'Three wise men' and after

With this qualified correction to current claims of an unprecedented loss of professional ownership of pedagogy, let us track the changes in a little more detail. The ostensible shift from belief to evidence in policy perspectives on pedagogy, and perhaps even the start of the associated shift from local to national direction, came with the 1991–92 'three wise men' enquiry. This was commissioned by government to review 'available evidence about the delivery of education in primary schools ... particularly in key stage 2',[45] and it had at its disposal not just inspection data and the results of the first international surveys of educational achievement but also the findings of the first generation of large-scale school and classroom studies in the British primary sector, from Neville Bennett, Maurice Galton, Peter Mortimore, Barbara Tizard, Robin Alexander and their colleagues,[46] and the earlier secondary school effectiveness research study by Michael Rutter in which Mortimore had been involved and on which his primary-school study built.[47]

Combining such evidence with HMI inspection data, some of it unpublished, the enquiry's report immediately debunked political and media claims of a 'progressive' takeover of primary classrooms (though this was not what some wished to hear and it is a truth which some journalists and politicians still refuse to acknowledge), arguing that the problem was not Plowden but what had been done in its name, often misguidedly. The result, the 1992 report claimed, had been not revolution but, all too often, mediocrity. It argued for teaching to be framed by high expectations and proper diagnosis, and to be grounded in a repertoire which combined the broad organisational strategies of whole-class teaching, collaborative group work and individualised attention with generic techniques such as observation, questioning, explaining, assessing, providing formative feedback and managing behaviour, all of which were essential whatever pattern of organisation was used; and that these should be deployed on the basis of 'fitness for purpose'. The report also urged greater attention to what children have in common and what they can learn from each other, and stressed the limits to the individualisation of teaching to which many teachers at that time aspired. It noted from the research that the level of cognitive challenge provided by teachers, especially through carefully-structured classroom interaction informed by good subject knowledge, was both a critical factor in the gains noted in process-product studies and was confirmed in research on children's development and learning which at this time was beginning to shift towards the socio-cultural perspectives discussed in Chapter 7.

Overall, the message was *repertoire, balance,* and *fitness for purpose* – different methods of organisation, a range of techniques, a mix of thematic and subject teaching – and judgement grounded in aims, needs and circumstance rather than doctrine. The report urged avoidance of the highly complex patterns of organisation inherited from the 1970s, in which one might find six or eight groups pursuing tasks in as many curriculum areas at the same time, overstretching most teachers' capacity to diagnose, assess and meaningfully interact, and forcing many of them into a state of perpetual crisis management.[48] Nevertheless, because the findings were instantly politicised, the 'three wise men' report became highly controversial, often portrayed not as a plea for balance but as the replacement of one extreme position by another. Yet the report framed a succession of studies from the newly-founded Ofsted,[49] and the very first phase-specific national criteria for primary initial teacher training.[50] Its findings remain readily detectable in more recent documents, for example the 2007 professional standards for teachers from the Training and Development Agency,[51] and the primary and secondary national strategies' document *Pedagogy and Personalisation,*[52] which lists a 'teaching repertoire of skills and techniques' which includes 'the generic skills of questioning, explaining, guiding and organising group work', which, though over-simplified, is taken almost verbatim from the 1992 report.

The search for panaceas: interactive whole-class teaching

One of the messages of the 'three wise men' study was that more and better – though definitely not exclusive – use could be made of whole-class teaching. This, combined with a growing recognition of the need for interaction of the kind that would empower children cognitively, paved the way for 'interactive whole-class teaching', an approach which was imported from continental classrooms during the mid 1990s. Its arrival was mainly thanks to the advocacy of Professor Sig Prais at the National Institute of Economic and Social Research and Roger Luxton and his inspectoral colleagues in Barking and Dagenham, whence – in a move which was then novel but is now more common – many teachers were taken to schools in Germany and Switzerland to observe and learn from continental practice.

Though they did make extensive use of whole-class teaching, and pioneered the horseshoe arrangement that was later taken up by the national strategies, Prais and Luxton readily understood that the pedagogical potential of these changes lay less in the pattern of organisation than in the character of the interaction which it encouraged.[53] The horseshoe layout enabled all pupils to see each other as well as the teacher, and facilitated the collective approach to teaching and learning which has always been significant in the classrooms of central and Eastern Europe; but the layout also permitted both individual work and pupil-pupil collaboration. Yet of itself the arrangement guaranteed nothing, for everything depended on the kind of talk which teachers were able to model and promote. Politicians, though, saw matters differently. Ignoring the interaction they focused on the organisation alone, which for them sat neatly (not to say obediently) with their repeated calls for 'back to basics', and epitomised the order and discipline of their own golden age, which was the era not of Plowden but of the one that preceded it, the 1950s.

Towards national strategies

Meanwhile, the second wave of international achievement surveys, in which England fared none too well, prompted policy-makers to look to this country's educational and economic competitors for answers, especially in continental Europe and south-east Asia. In the *Worlds Apart* review which Ofsted commissioned from David Reynolds and Shaun Farrell,[54] the authors warned that England's 'long tail of underachievement', already marked by the end of key stage 1, would continue to grow unless teachers opted for teaching which was more goal-focused and organisationally less complex, and which maximised opportunity to learn and time on task. What would secure these changes was a combination of high expectations, interactive whole-class teaching and well-structured textbooks which saved teachers from the time-consuming task of preparing worksheets. The report acknowledged the impact of culture on attitudes to education, though it reduced culture to just one factor among many when others believed it to be what mattered most. Generally, though, *Worlds Apart* was taken as a further endorsement of the efficacy of whole-class teaching. It cut little ice that, as the commonest method world-wide, whole-class teaching could be made to correlate as readily with low-performing education systems and low GDP national economies as with high. As if to confirm the frailty of the reasoning, several Pacific Rim economies whose success supposedly lay in high standards delivered by whole-class teaching collapsed shortly after the publication of the Ofsted study.

By this time, the then government was piloting national projects to raise standards in literacy and numeracy, and with the change of government in 1997 these became the national literacy and numeracy strategies. At their heart were highly structured lessons with a significant and mandated component of whole-class teaching, supported by centrally-produced texts and other resources.

The shift was significant in two other respects. First, it marked the end of the understanding that politicians could say what they liked about teaching but would stop short of telling teachers how to do it; second, it replaced eclecticism by a single paradigm. The 'three wise men' report of 1992 had reviewed a wide range of research from different sources and traditions. *Worlds Apart* embraced the lone, new and controversial paradigm of school effectiveness research, and it was eagerly taken up by the incoming government.

Mixed messages, conflicting paradigms?

We noted in Chapter 14 that with the introduction of the national strategies in 1998–99, literacy and numeracy were defined by government as 'standards, not curriculum' in order to justify their direct control from DfES/DCSF, which was and is responsible for standards and which established a Standards and Effectiveness Unit for this purpose. 'Standards', then, were defined as – and strictly limited to – performance in the tests at key stages 1 and 2, while 'effectiveness' meant only what school effectiveness research allowed it to mean: measured gains in tests of a narrow range of educational outcomes correlated with such classroom process factors as themselves are measurable, which is not many. Meanwhile, as we showed in Chapter 14, the rest of the curriculum, including aspects of English and mathematics not defined as literacy or numeracy, remained the responsibility of the QCA, and the government displayed no obvious interest either in standards in this rump of the curriculum nor in the effectiveness of schools and teachers in achieving them.

We have criticised this policy, the thinking behind it and its adverse impact on both the curriculum and children's statutory curriculum entitlement, and have urged the government to make the necessary changes. In this chapter, though, our concern is the teaching through which the curriculum is enacted. Here we note the possibility of a similar dissonance between the DCSF and other agencies.

Initially, the literacy and numeracy strategies were pedagogical monoliths: a four-part daily literacy hour comprising three parts whole-class teaching (15, 15 and 10 minutes) and one part group and individual work (20 minutes). The three-part daily numeracy lesson included whole-class teaching at the beginning and end (a 5–10-minute introduction and a 10–15-minute plenary) and a central section which allowed whole-class, group and/or individual or paired work (30–40 minutes).

The relatively greater flexibility of the numeracy lesson, combined with a larger measure of consensus over its content, explains why, as we saw in Chapter 13, it met with rather more professional approval and support than the NLS. Even so, the approach which was advocated – or, as teachers saw it, required – by the two strategies was a long way removed from the focus on repertoire, principle and professional judgement supported in the 1992 report. The criteria for 'successful teaching' in accordance with the literacy strategy were that it should be unswervingly framed by the four-part daily literacy lesson and be, within that structure, 'discursive', 'interactive', 'well-paced', 'confident' and 'ambitious'.[55] For the numeracy lesson, teachers were told that they should 'aim to spend as much time as possible in direct teaching and questioning of the whole class, a group of pupils, or individuals.'[56] The repertoire was more open organisationally in the latter case, but direct teaching is only one of the several kinds of interaction which are available.

The emphasis in the literacy strategy on pace, which was defined as 'a sense of urgency, driven by the need to make progress and succeed',[57] was taken up by Ofsted and generated considerable anxiety among teachers. Like the approach to lesson structure, the definition of pace was monolithic, and it has been argued that to focus on organisational pace as an end in itself was probably counter-productive. The pace that matters in classrooms is 'interactive pace' ('the pace of teacher-pupil and pupil-pupil exchanges, and contingent factors such as maintaining focus and handling cues and turns'), 'cognitive pace' ('the speed at which conceptual ground is covered') and 'learning pace' ('how fast pupils actually learn'). 'The critical issue ... has to be the relationship of interactive pace to cognition and learning' and international research shows how a more studied interactive pace, with longer teacher-pupil exchanges, is more effective cognitively than the rapid-fire sequence of brief exchanges which the national strategies and Ofsted required.[58] The danger of the NLS approach is confirmed in one of the government's own studies, which attributes to it 'a rash of lessons and closing plenaries characterised by fast and furious closed questions and superficial answers rather than exploratory discussion and reviewing learning that was the aim.'[59]

The race-track version of pace remains one area where all sides follow the same line. It frequently appears in school inspection reports, as Ofsted readily accepted the new pedagogical orthodoxies of the NLS and NNS and expected to see them implemented in schools. This is one example among many where Ofsted does not fulfil the proper function of a national inspectorate and reserve judgement on the efficacy of policy, but merely polices schools' compliance with it. This ensures that the flaws become embedded alongside the benefits, and indeed possibly counteract them. At the same time, Ofsted appeared to retain the notion of repertoire inherited from the 1992 report and consolidated through its follow-up studies and pre-NLS/NNS inspection criteria. Similarly, the TDA advocated repertoire, just as its pre-decessors had done. Thus, the TDA professional standards for newly-qualified teachers applicable at the time of going to press expect them to:

> use a range of teaching strategies and resources ... demonstrate the ability to manage the learning of individuals, groups and whole classes, modifying their teaching to suit the stage of the lesson ... make effective use of a range of assessment, monitoring and recording strategies.[60]

Taken at face value, this may seem to encourage teachers and teacher trainers to abandon their sense that the literacy and numeracy strategies are obligatory, and to redefine them as just two of 'a range of teaching strategies and resources' among many. However, the prevailing complexion of accountability seems to preclude this interpretation. Both schools and teacher-training providers, according to their evidence to the Cambridge Review reported here and in Chapter 13, feel obliged to implement the national strategies as they stand. In any case, those responsible for the strategies might well wish to argue that, as now modified, they do precisely what the TDA expects, and the circle of repertoire and 'one right way' has been squared; that is, that the strategies themselves are as diverse, eclectic and flexible as any alternative framework. We would not dismiss this claim out of hand, for our evidence shows that there are many teachers whose professional vocabulary has been greatly enlarged by the strategies and its associated CPD. But to presume that pedagogy and the strategies are one is empirically and conceptually unacceptable and educationally dangerous. Unacceptable, because of flaws we have exemplified and the much larger deficiency in respect of pedagogical principle which we discuss later in this chapter; dangerous, because it makes the act of teaching and the professional knowledge of teachers subservient to political and electoral calculation. In any event it is inconsistent with the principles and aims of primary education set out in Chapter 12.

'Principles of good learning and teaching'

In 2003, the government consolidated the NLS and NNS within a single Primary National Strategy (PNS) which it launched in the document *Excellence and Enjoyment*.[61] The consolidation was not just about ensuring that literacy and numeracy were taught as required, but more fundamentally about using them as a pedagogical template for the entire curriculum:

> The literacy and numeracy strategies have, according to all those who have evaluated them, been strikingly successful at improving the quality of teaching and raising standards in primary schools. But we need to embed the lessons of the literacy and numeracy strategies more deeply ... In the best schools, teachers are using their understanding of the principles behind the literacy and numeracy strategies ... We want a new approach that will help more schools and teachers to ... apply the principles of good learning and teaching across the whole curriculum.[62]

These 'principles of good learning and teaching' arising from the NLS and NNS were then specified. They should:

- *Ensure that every child succeeds:* provide an inclusive education within a culture of high expectations.
- *Build on what learners already know:* structure and pace teaching so that students know what is to be learnt, how and why.
- *Make learning vivid and real:* develop understanding through enquiry, creativity, e-learning and group problem-solving.
- *Make learning an enjoyable experience:* stimulate learning through matching teaching techniques and strategies to a range of learning styles.

- *Enrich the learning experience:* build learning skills across the curriculum.
- *Promote assessment for learning:* make children partners in their learning.[63]

It has to be said that we are once again in the realm of the obvious. The only item here which advances beyond sentiment is the final one.[64] Conversely, the popular notion of 'learning styles' in the fourth item (now also an essential part of the government's personalisation agenda) has been challenged by research surveyed for this review.[65] Other terms – 'learning skills' and 'pace', for example – are no less problematic. The above list was slightly modified for the 2007 DCSF document *Pedagogy and Personalisation*, but not sufficiently to attend to these concerns.[66]

In our attempt to test Maria Balarin's and Hugh Lauder's proposition about a 'state theory of learning', this is a worrying combination, for here is proposed the extension of the DCSF-controlled NLS/NNS pedagogy across the rest of the curriculum, redefined as a set of principles which either amount to very little or are empirically questionable. The move is justified by the government's claim, quoted above, that the literacy and numeracy strategies 'have been strikingly successful at improving the quality of teaching and learning and raising standards in primary schools'. Unfortunately, as we shall see in later chapters, this claim can and has been contested, and even the government's officially-commissioned evaluation admitted that 'it is difficult to draw conclusions about the effect of the strategies on pupil learning'.[67]

This does not look at all like a safe basis on which to extend the pedagogical hegemony of the national strategies.

Personalised learning

There is an immediate paradox in the conjunction of 'personalised learning' with a policy framework which aims for greater uniformity in teaching. For a time after its initial launch the term remained opaque and, rather like the PNS 'principles of good teaching and learning' cited above, was insufficiently incisive to make a difference. By 2008, preparing the ground for the 2009 White Paper, the DCSF headed its list of 'key features of personalised learning' with 'providing high quality teaching and learning'.[68] What this might mean was explained in a further document, *Personalised Learning: a practical guide*, which lists as the 'key characteristics of quality first teaching':

- highly focused lesson design with sharp objectives
- high demands of pupil involvement and engagement with their learning
- high levels of interaction for all pupils
- appropriate use of teacher questioning, modelling and explaining
- an emphasis on learning through dialogue, with regular opportunities for pupils to talk both individually and in groups
- an expectation that pupils will accept responsibility for their own learning and work independently
- regular use of encouragement and authentic praise to engage and motivate pupils.[69]

The origins of some of this will be apparent to those familiar with the recent literature on classroom talk and dialogic teaching,[70] though overall the 'characteristics' remain disappointingly vague.

The official definitions veer between personalisation for all (as above) and for some. The TDA says: 'The term "personalised learning" means maintaining a focus on individual progress, in order to maximise all learners' capacity to learn, achieve and participate'.[71] However, the DCSF confuses its own apparent endorsement of this position by indicating that personalisation is less about all children than those with 'additional needs' arising from 'health needs, [special] educational needs or an unforeseen event in their lives which causes them to need some extra support.'[72] On the other hand, this qualification makes personalisation more obviously an arm of *Every Child Matters* and the 2007 Children's Plan and couched thus has perhaps greater purchase, since teachers might retort that 'maintaining a focus on [the] individual progress' of all learners is what they do as a matter of course.

Overall, no sources are cited, for in this as in other such material, the DCSF and the national strategies tend to appropriate and adapt without acknowledging. This generates two problems:

- There is no warrant, empirical or otherwise, for the ideas and claims presented, other than that they have official approval.
- The ideas are invariably presented in a generalised and simplified form, but because their source is not acknowledged, teachers are unable to pursue them to the level of detail required if they are to be properly understood and discussed, let alone applied to their existing practice.

A 'state theory of learning'?

We said that we would examine the proposition of Balarin and Lauder, in their research survey for the Cambridge Review, that English primary teachers are now expected to conform to a 'state theory of learning'. We also reminded readers, by way of a corrective to rose-tinted views of the period before the national curriculum and the national strategies, that primary teachers have always been subject to external pressure to conform to particular views of what constitutes good teaching, locally if not nationally.

Having said that, the proposition of Balarin and Lauder appears to be confirmed by what has happened since the mid 1990s. For, leaving aside (though certainly not discarding) the essential argument about the position of professionals within a democracy, it is the *quality* of the ideas and prescriptions on teaching and learning which have emerged since 1997 which gives most cause for concern. The amount of such material is now vast – far more than teachers can hope to accommodate. Much of it is pitched at the bland and generalised level illustrated here, rarely advancing beyond sentiment and assertion into argument and justification. Evidential sources are seldom cited, and some of the material could attract accusations of plagiarism. Such unacknowledged ideas are frequently distorted beyond recognition in order to fit the policy agenda. Teachers are placed in the position of having to take everything on trust, yet if the prescriptions do not deliver the promised improvements in standards, the prevailing trajectory of educational accountability means that it is they, rather than the policies which they struggle to implement, who are called to account.

Added to all this, the evidence on the impact of such prescription on the character of teaching and the quality of learning is mixed. In Chapter 17 we consider the important question of what has happened to standards in primary education over the past two decades. Here we note a finding which is both important and consistent across a large number of research studies: that although the layout and organisation of English primary classrooms and teaching practices have changed considerably since the mid-1990s, as has the structure of lessons,[73] such change is more superficial than it may seem or than its architects may wish to acknowledge.

We noted earlier the TLRP finding that 'it is difficult to shift teachers from reliance on specific techniques (the letter of AfL) to practices based on deep principles integrated into the flow of lessons (the spirit of AfL).'[74] Similarly, the long-term follow-up studies of Galton and others have shown that 'deep structure' pedagogical change is extremely slow in the vital realm of that interaction which shapes (or frustrates) children's understanding, and that basic interactive habits are highly resilient,[75] for they are deeply embedded, historically and culturally.[76] This is confirmed in a series of more recent studies of the impact of the national literacy and numeracy strategies. Here, the new formalism of highly structured lessons, whole-class plenaries and focused group work, coupled with a much greater emphasis on the hitherto neglected national curriculum attainment target of 'speaking and listening', might appear to provide a recipe for the empowerment of children as talkers and thinkers. Yet the work of Fay Smith,

Frank Hardman, David Skidmore, Debra Myhill, Richard Eke and others confirms, in the words of one major study, that:

> Traditional patterns of whole-class interaction have not been dramatically transformed by the strategies … In the whole-class section of literacy and numeracy lessons, teachers spent the majority of their time either explaining or using highly structured question and answer sequences. Far from encouraging and extending pupil contributions to promote high levels of interaction and cognitive engagement, most of the questions asked were of a low cognitive level designed to funnel pupils' response towards a required answer.[77]

This is extremely unsatisfactory, and it lends further support to our argument in Chapter 14 that the national strategies stand in need of radical overhaul. More than that, we suggest that the case against government intervention in pedagogy is now abundantly clear.

EXTENDING THE MAP OF PEDAGOGY

We return now from policy interventions in pedagogy to our initial question about how pedagogy might be conceived. Here are some possibilities.

A framework from the national strategies

The DCSF national strategies' document *Pedagogy and Personalisation* attempts what we argued is essential to the debate about teaching but often missing from it: to provide a framework for analysis and action which engages with rather than circumnavigates classroom action. 'It is helpful,' says the DCSF, 'to consider pedagogy as four interrelated categories or domains: subject and curriculum knowledge, teaching and learning models, teaching repertoire of skills and techniques, conditions for learning.'[78]

On closer examination, however, this is essentially a prescriptive rather than descriptive framework. Under each heading are listed things that, in the view of the national strategies, teachers need to know, and each heading ends with outcomes which the listed attributes are expected to produce. Thus, 'well-founded and secure subject and curriculum knowledge' are claimed to yield 'decisions … about achievement and the next steps in learning … learning [which is] vivid and real … individuals [who are] partners in their own learning, understanding what they are learning and why'. Or, from 'the consistent use of specific teaching and learning models' come 'learning [which is] an enjoyable and challenging experience … learners [who] develop the learning and thinking skills they need'.[79]

There are three difficulties with the national strategies' framework for pedagogy: it is prescription in the guise of description; the elements are arbitrary and – the familiar problem – have no explicit warrant from research or other evidence; and the cause-effect relationship between elements and outcomes is asserted rather than demonstrated, and indeed (as exemplified above) the cause-effect relationship is clouded by non-sequitur.

A framework from school effectiveness research

Early editions of the influential American Educational Research Association (AERA) *Handbook of Research on Teaching* show how the preoccupations of researchers and the methods available to them came to define the nature of teaching itself.[80] The attempt to identify what aspects of teaching make a difference, using the then popular statistical procedures which were seen as essential to the aspiration of making educational research a true science, produced a model which ran in an apparently logical, linear or temporal line from *presage* and *intention* to *context*, *process* and *outcome* or *product*. This yielded six sets of variables whose relationship is theoretically amenable to scientific analysis: context-process, context-product, presage-process, presage-product, context-presage and process-product. As the late Nate Gage of Stanford

University explicated this kind of analysis, it was based on the principle that to discover the elements of teaching that made a difference to any outcome, one needed to identify observed differences between effective and less effective practitioners and relate these as far as possible to presage variables. In principle, the 'product' could be anything (for example, specific kinds of teaching). However, as Gage also noted, policy-makers were chiefly interested in only one of these relationships, that between the variables of process and product, and the latter was invariably defined as measured pupil attainment.[81]

This model has generated a truly vast research literature and has proved remarkably durable, even though the current version of the AERA *Handbook* is methodologically and conceptually much more eclectic, explores the interface of quantitative and qualitative research and attends to culture, context and educational content.[82] Yet the model's current variant is exemplified in the school effectiveness research of David Reynolds, Bert Creemers and their colleagues which uses (their words) 'a classic input-process-output model' in which inputs are defined as 'pupil [but not teacher] inputs', processes are divided into 'teacher' and 'school', and outcomes are listed as 'maths achievement, attendance, attitudes to school, self-conception, democratic attitudes and locus of control'.[83] An earlier literature review commissioned by Ofsted produced from an aggregation of similar studies 11 'key characteristics of effective schools' whose classroom elements included 'concentration on teaching and learning', 'purposeful teaching', ' high expectations', 'positive reinforcement', and 'monitoring progress'.[84]

For all that it yields apparent school and classroom 'effects', this approach is in its way as limited a basis for understanding teaching as the framework proposed by the national strategies. It is logical and linear, which in real life teaching rarely is. It deals only in what can be measured, for 'effectiveness' is defined strictly and simply as a statistical calculation of the gain in output over input.[85] It therefore 'is unable to engage with the purposes, meanings and messages which elevate teaching from mindless technique to considered educational act. Teaching is presented as value-neutral and content-free.'[86] It produces lists of 'what matters' or 'what works', such as 'opportunity to learn', 'time on task' and 'pace', which have a surface objectivity which belie how problematic they are methodologically (for example, the difficulties of 'pace' have already been exposed and to say that pupils are 'on task' when they are looking at a textbook or at the teacher ignores the possibility that their minds may not be engaged). What emerges is fundamentally and inescapably random. It is there, and it assumes importance, because it can be measured. What is measurable in terms of 'input' or 'process' may correlate with what is measurable as 'outcome', but what is highlighted in this way may or may not be important, and what escapes this mode of analysis may be at least as significant.

Yet the model has proved immensely seductive in policy circles, especially under the patronage of New Labour. With school 'effectiveness' go school 'failure' and 'improvement', and all three are fuelled by the same assumptions about what matters and 'what works', how its impact can be judged and what are available as 'levers' for improvement. We saw in Chapter 14 how the primary curriculum has been distorted by treating test scores in the 3Rs as exclusive measures of educational standards and as proxies for the curriculum as a whole. In an important critique of school effectiveness research, Gaby Weiner cites a growing consensus that government simply fails to understand its limits and weaknesses. In turn, school effectiveness researchers have been too eager to accommodate to government's preference 'for simple solutions to complex issues' and to allow their work to be adopted to provide academic legitimacy for a market culture which pits school against school on the basis of indicators which are of doubtful validity.[87]

From the parts to the whole: synoptic frameworks

In addition to such methodological and political reservations about models of teaching which arise from the still dominant process-product paradigm, there is a further objection. Such models fragment teaching into its constituent parts but convey no sense of how these might be reconstituted. Or rather, unlike a jigsaw puzzle which presents all the parts for re-assembly, school effectiveness frameworks provide only some of them, mislay the rest but still expect teachers to see the full picture.

An alternative approach to understanding teaching, and hence to making better sense of what goes on in primary classrooms, and what ought to go on, is to consider frameworks which aim to be comprehensive or at least synoptic, starting with the whole and then examining the parts. We briefly exemplify three of these.

Example 1: universals for understanding pedagogy

The first example is the double framework devised by Alexander to structure data collected as part of a large-scale comparative study of culture, policy and pedagogy in primary education in five countries. The framework needed to be stable across time, place and culture, which ruled out normative models of the kind exemplified above. Instead, the framework started with two irreducible propositions about teaching in any setting or culture.

- Teaching, in any setting, is the act of using method x to enable pupils to learn y.
- Teaching has structure and form; it is situated in, and governed by, space, time and patterns of pupil organisation; and it is undertaken for a purpose.

These were then translated into a model containing three broad analytical categories – the immediate context or *frame* within which the act of teaching is set, the *act* itself, and its *form* – and a set of elements within each such category. The core acts of teaching (*task, activity, interaction* and *judgement*) are framed by *space, pupil organisation, time* and *curriculum,* and by *routines, rules and rituals.* They are given form, and are bounded temporally and conceptually, by the *lesson* or teaching session (Figure 15.1).

It is not appropriate to go into detail, but if we take 'the act of using method x' from the first proposition we see how it provokes four questions, each of which yields an element for the 'act' section of the framework:

- In a given teaching session or unit what learning tasks do pupils encounter?
- What activities do they undertake in order to address these learning tasks?
- Through what interactions does the teacher present, organise and sustain the learning tasks and activities?
- By what means, and on the basis of what criteria, does the teacher reach judgements about the nature and level of the tasks and activities which each pupil shall undertake (differentiation), and the kinds of learning which students achieve (assessment)?

The same procedure leads to the four elements under 'frame', which derive from 'to enable pupils to learn y' in the first proposition, together with the larger part of the second proposition. Although not watertight, this kind of framework is helpful in three ways beyond the context of its original use as a research tool. First, it focuses on teaching as it is – as an activity that takes place within the constraints of time and space and concerns itself, however it is

Frame	Form	Act
Space		Task
Pupil organisation		Activity
Time	Lesson	
Curriculum		Interaction
Routine, rule and ritual		Judgement

Figure 15.1 Pedagogy as the act of teaching.

Alexander (2001b): 325.

undertaken, with certain decisions and actions which are necessary to all teaching, anywhere. It may be schematic, but it has common-sense validity. Second, it enables us to spot emphases and gaps in other ways of looking at teaching. Third, it provides a starting point for planning and evaluating teaching.

The framework for the act of teaching is accompanied by one which attempts to map the main elements in the surrounding discourse, in other words to facilitate the shift from an apprehension of the scope and essentials of teaching to a pedagogy which engages with these in a principled manner. The second framework defines three levels and 11 domains of ideas through which the act of teaching is enabled, formalised and located (Figure 15.2). Each of these also features prominently in the present report and, in this sense, the entire Cambridge Review maps and explores a new pedagogy for primary education.

Classroom level: ideas that enable teaching

Concerning
    children and childhood
    learning
    teaching
    aims and curriculum as transacted

System/policy level: ideas that formalise and legitimise teaching

Concerning
    schools as organisations
    aims and curriculum as conceived / specified
    assessment criteria and procedures
    professional roles, responsibilities and expertise

Cultural/societal level: ideas that locate teaching

Concerning
    family and community
    culture and society
    individual and collective identity

Figure 15.2 Pedagogy as ideas (theories, values, evidence and justifications).

Adapted from Alexander (2008b): 47–49.

Example 2: principles for improving teaching

These principles arise from the Teaching and Learning Research Programme (TLRP). This programme comprised nearly 70 projects, 22 of them relating to schools. It was launched in 2000 and was completed in 2008, with some outliers continuing until 2011. The Cambridge Review commissioned from the TLRP a survey of all its projects relevant to the primary phase. They cover: learning in or through specific areas (English, mathematics, science, ICT) and across the curriculum; environments for better learning (for example, group work, home-school knowledge exchange, provision for gifted and talented pupils, effective pre-school provision); and school conditions for the improvement of teaching and learning (for example, consulting pupils about teaching, learning and assessment, developing inclusive school practices, learning how to learn).

At the same time, the TLRP has distilled from all its projects 10 'evidence-informed principles to guide policy and practice'. These do not describe teaching in the way attempted above, but they do convincingly extrapolate from peer-reviewed research what matters most in the quest to improve it and are thus the logical next step. Each principle starts with a proposition which is then expanded into recommendations. Thus, the TLRP concludes, effective teaching and learning:

1. *Equips learners for life in its broadest sense.* Learning should aim to help individuals and groups to develop the intellectual, personal and social resources that will enable them to participate as active citizens, contribute to economic development and flourish as individuals in a diverse and changing society. This may mean expanding conceptions of worthwhile learning outcomes and taking seriously issues of equity and social justice for all.

2. *Engages with valued forms of knowledge.* Teaching and learning should engage learners with the big ideas, key processes, modes of discourse and narratives of subjects so that they understand what constitutes quality and standards in particular domains.

3. *Recognises the importance of prior experience and learning.* Teaching and learning should take account of what the learner knows already in order to plan their next steps. This includes building on prior learning but also taking account of the personal and cultural experiences of different groups of learners.

4. *Requires the teacher to scaffold learning.* Teachers should provide activities and structures of intellectual, social and emotional support to help learners to move forward in their learning so that when these supports are removed the learning is secure.

5. *Needs assessment to be congruent with learning.* Assessment should be designed and implemented with the goal of achieving maximum validity both in terms of learning outcomes and learning processes. It should help to advance learning as well as determine whether learning has occurred.

6. *Promotes the active engagement of the learner.* A chief goal of teaching and learning should be the promotion of learners' independence and autonomy. This involves acquiring a repertoire of learning strategies and practices, developing positive learning dispositions, and having the will and confidence to become agents in their own learning.

7. *Fosters both individual and social processes and outcomes.* Learners should be encouraged and helped to build relationships and communication with others for learning purposes, in order to assist the mutual construction of knowledge and enhance the achievements of individuals and groups. Consulting learners about their learning and giving them a voice is both an expectation and a right.

8. *Recognises the significance of informal learning.* Informal learning, such as learning out of school, should be recognised as at least as significant as formal learning and should therefore be valued and appropriately utilised in formal processes.

9. *Depends on teacher learning.* The need for teachers to learn continuously in order to develop their knowledge and skill, and adapt and develop their roles, especially through classroom inquiry, should be recognised and supported.

10. *Demands consistent policy frameworks with support for teaching and learning as their primary focus.* Institutional and system level policies need to recognise the fundamental importance of teaching and learning and be designed to create effective learning environments for all learners.[88]

Of particular significance for the Cambridge Primary Review is the way these principles, which were reached without reference to our work, chime with so much that the Review has found and said: the emphasis on broad social objectives such as citizenship, equity and social justice in the overarching aim, alongside economic development (principle 1); the balancing of interdependence and mutuality with independence and autonomy (principles 1 and 6); the endorsement of the importance of knowledge, even down to the use of the term 'domain' (2); the need to respect and build on children's prior and informal learning outside as well as inside school, and to respect what they think and say (3, 7 and 8); the essentially social, collective, interactive and dialogic view of learning and teaching (4, 6 and 7); the importance of assessment which is in tune with, and part of pedagogy, rather than an accountability add-on (5).

The objection to this list is that it is less a framework than a post-hoc rationalisation based on a number of disparate projects, whose selection and funding themselves were based on non-pedagogical criteria. On the other hand, empirically-grounded principles give life to a conceptually-grounded framework of the kind provided in Example 1.

Example 3: gateways for transforming teaching

The first framework provides a basis for describing and analysing teaching, however and wherever it takes place. The second extrapolates principles for effective practice from teaching and learning as they happen – here, now and in Britain. In contrast to both (though in fact the three frameworks are complementary) our third framework, from Professor David Hargreaves' work with the ASCL and the Specialist Schools and Academies Trust (SSAT), is consciously transformatory. It takes the government's policy of personalised learning but elevates 'personalisation' into something much more ambitious, bringing together potent ideas from the wider discourse of teaching, learning and leadership. It also changes the phrase to 'personalising learning' to signal that this is work in progress rather than a done deal. Hargreaves seeks nothing less than a new approach to both teaching and leadership within schools which are designed and organised on the basis of very different relationships among teachers and students to those inherited from earlier centuries, and indeed different views of what knowledge and what kinds of learning are of greatest worth.

Hargreaves identifies a sequence of nine 'gateways' to personalising learning:

1. student voice
2. assessment for learning
3. learning to learn
4. the new technologies
5. curriculum
6. advice and guidance
7. mentoring and coaching
8. workforce development
9. school organisation and design.[89]

Each of these is developed by reference both to recent research and examples from schools, thus giving the framework a double validatory onward nudge. Most are familiar from other contexts. Student voice, assessment for learning and learning how to learn, for example, all feature in other chapters of this report. The originality here lies in what Hargreaves has chosen to identify as the key gateways, and how he explores their applications and relationships. Cutting across the nine 'gateways' are six core themes predicated on the belief that student engagement is the key to successful learning:

- engagement with learning and life
- responsibility for learning and behaviour
- independence in and control over learning
- confidence in oneself as a learner
- maturity in relationships with staff and fellow students
- co-construction in the design, delivery and assessment of learning.[90]

The theory is extended further as interactions between the gateways in pursuit of the 'four deeps':

1. deep learning
2. deep experience
3. deep support
4. deep leadership.[91]

So, for example, 'deep learning' brings together the gateways *student voice*, *assessment for learning* and *learning to learn*, and among the conditions for deep learning proposed are 'meta-cognitive control', 'growing learner autonomy' and 'learning conversations'. Meanwhile, innovation in these and other areas takes place in schools and networks which are:

- decentralised
- disciplined

- distributed
- dialogical.[92]

Once again we find resonance with what the Cambridge Review has found and said, not just on those aspects of teaching, assessment and leadership highlighted in this chapter and elsewhere in this report – decentralisation, distributed leadership, student voice, learning to learn, assessment for learning, co-construction, dialogue (see below) – but also on the principles and aims for primary education which we discussed in Chapter 12, especially those relating to engagement, empowerment and autonomy. If there is a common thread, it is the challenging of old assumptions about where authority in a modern system of education should reside in the classroom, the school and the system as a whole. Transmission teaching, top-down school organisation, and government micro-management of curriculum, assessment and pedagogy are viewed as equally unsuited to the promotion of education and lifelong learning in a world where knowledge has been dramatically and irreversibly democratised by the internet.[93]

The elements in an alternative to the 'state theory of learning' are beginning to crystallise.

A point of pedagogical convergence: classroom interaction

This chapter is not an exhaustive review of research on teaching but an account of such evidence on teaching and related matters as was received by the Cambridge Primary Review and an attempt to find a way to situate this rather disparate body of material and concerns within research-based frameworks. Using the three examples above – and they are only examples, without prescriptive intent – we have suggested that if we broaden our frames of reference as illustrated, we shall have a more secure basis for identifying the gains and omissions in the current discourse on teaching and learning, and for achieving a better understanding of pedagogy in order to improve and perhaps transform it.

So the chapter does not isolate 'best buys' from recent research, though it is not hard to nominate some of them: assessment for learning; teaching for scaffolding, metacognition and self-regulation;[94] the importance of repertoires both organisational and technical; balancing cognitive, social and emotional aspects of learning; using teaching to model and shape positive behaviour and understanding how to handle the interdependence of learning and behaviour; encouraging pupil voice; understanding the relationship between the learning of teachers and their pupils; recognising, on the 'horses for courses' principle, that different kinds of learning demand different kinds of teaching – declarative and procedural knowledge require direct teaching, while conceptual and metacognitive knowledge require co-construction and dialogue.[95]

Having said that, if there is a single point where a great deal of the research converges, it is the character and quality of interaction that takes place in schools and classrooms. We have seen that interaction is highlighted in the Review's submissions and soundings as a powerful and indeed essential tool for engaging and sustaining children's attention and promoting their higher-order thinking. Language, and especially spoken language, is identified in the research on children's cognitive development (see Chapter 7) as one of the keys to thinking, understanding and learning from the earliest age and throughout the primary phase. Early years experts know it to be the cornerstone of all that they do. It is argued for in the reviewed research on children's social development as essential to both productive relationships and collaborative learning, enabling pupils to learn from each other as well as from teacher and text. It is what gives effect to pupil voice. It is the basis for at least five of the 10 TLRP 'principles for effective teaching and learning' listed above and themselves derived from some 22 major research projects: scaffolding, active learner engagement, learning as a social activity, informal learning, and assessment for learning. It is what unites five of Hargreaves' nine 'gateways' to personalising learning: student voice, assessment for learning, learning to learn, advice and guidance, and mentoring and coaching; and is one of his keys, through dialogue, to successful innovation.

Interaction is also pivotal to the curriculum as proposed in Chapter 14, especially to the reconfigured domain, now reaching across the whole curriculum, of language, oracy and literacy; and it is manifest in six of the 12 aims for primary education proposed in Chapter 12: engagement, empowerment, respect and reciprocity, citizenship, community, and of course 'enacting dialogue', which sums up the case thus:

> To help children grasp that learning is an interactive process and that understanding builds through joint activity between teacher and pupil and among pupils in collaboration, and thereby to develop pupils' increasing sense of responsibility for what and how they learn. To help children recognise that knowledge is not only transmitted but also negotiated and re-created; and that each of us in the end makes our own sense out of the meeting of knowledge both personal and collective. To advance a pedagogy in which dialogue is central: between self and others, between personal and collective knowledge, between present and past, between different ways of making sense.

Yet classroom research also shows that, in England, teacher-pupil and pupil-pupil talk are under-exploited as tools for learning and understanding, and that their potential in teaching for much more than transmission is rarely fulfilled. Both British and American researchers point to the resilience, notwithstanding change in other aspects of teaching, of recitation as the default pattern of exchange – closed 'test' questions, competitive or strategic bidding for teacher attention, brief recall answers, minimal feedback, talk for replaying the teacher's thinking rather than enabling children to think for themselves, even in the ostensibly novel context of 'interactive' whole-class plenaries.[96] Talk – at home, in school, among peers – is education at its most elemental and potent. It is the aspect of teaching which has arguably the greatest purchase on learning. Yet it is also the most resistant to genuine transformation.

For all these reasons, we would nominate classroom interaction as the aspect of pedagogy which most repays investment by teachers and those who support them through research, teacher training and CPD.

There is no shortage of workers in this field: Vygotsky, Bruner, Bakhtin, Halliday and Wells provide the psychological, philosophical and linguistic fundamentals.[97] Cole, Wertsch and Bruner[98] enlarge and enrich the scope of psychology by injecting culture into the study of mind. Engeström and Daniels use activity theory to revisit and update Vygotsky, one of the founding fathers of the movement.[99] Barnes, Cazden, Galton, Sinclair and Coulthard, Edwards and Westgate pioneer revealingly diverse observational studies of classroom talk.[100] Alexander, Mercer, Mortimer and Scott build on all this work, add their own perspectives and construct a variety of frameworks for promoting dialogue in classrooms, both between teachers and pupils and among pupils themselves.[101]

One of these takes forward this chapter's emphasis on *repertoire*, setting out separate repertoires of teaching talk, learning talk and classroom organisation, and combines these with classroom indicators and – most important – *principles* by which decisions on the use of these should be guided. Crystallising the core messages of the research on children's development and learning and the conditions for effective teaching, these propose that teaching which is 'dialogic' and which begins to exploit the true potential of talk, is:

- *collective:* teachers and children address learning tasks together, whether as a group or as a class
- *reciprocal:* teachers and children listen to each other, share ideas and consider alternative viewpoints
- *supportive:* children articulate their ideas freely, without fear of embarrassment over 'wrong' answers and they help each other to reach common understandings
- *cumulative:* teachers and children build on their own and each others' ideas and chain them into coherent lines of thinking and enquiry
- *purposeful:* teachers plan and steer classroom talk with specific educational goals in view.[102]

An increasing number of local authorities, including that earlier pioneer of interactive whole-class teaching, the London Borough of Barking and Dagenham, are exploring work such as this with teachers. It has penetrated the national strategies, though there it remains imperfectly understood, while 'speaking and listening' in the national curriculum provides the palest of imitations.

The groundwork is established for the much-needed improvements in classroom interaction, but here we have perhaps the textbook example of the limits to central prescription in the domain of pedagogy, for it is hard to see how learning as dialogue can sit other than uncomfortably with teaching as compliance. Dialogue is the antithesis of a state theory of learning, and its antidote.

CONCLUSION

Pedagogy is the heart of the enterprise. It gives life to educational aims and values, lifts the curriculum from the printed page, mediates learning and knowing, engages, inspires and empowers learners – or, sadly, may fail to do so. In this chapter we have summarised the Review's evidence on pedagogy from the submissions, soundings and research surveys. We have examined the trajectory of national policy on teaching and learning from the era of local authority dominance to the current phase of national prescription. We have tested the claim that England's primary teachers are now subjected to a 'state theory of learning', and have found that it can probably be sustained. We have raised questions not just about the appropriateness of this extent of government intervention in the day-to-day work of teachers and pupils, but also about its quality and effectiveness.

We have also tried to expand the map of the narrow territory of teaching into the much larger domain of pedagogy in order that teaching can be as well grounded as it needs to be in professional understanding of its essential elements and of reliable evidence about children, learning and classroom life. We have illustrated complementary frameworks which may help us to understand teaching, improve it and perhaps transform it. We have found that much of the research evidence surveyed, and many of the views expressed by the Review's witnesses, converge on the importance of high quality interaction between teachers and pupils and among pupils themselves; yet though – or perhaps because – such interaction is so crucial to effective learning and teaching, it does not always have the profile and rigour it needs. This, we argue, requires even more sustained attention than it has begun to receive.

There is one aspect of pedagogy we have said little about so far: the relationship between teaching and learning in the general senses explored here and the specific kinds of knowledge and understanding represented by the curriculum domains proposed in Chapter 14 and the disciplines and other ways of making sense that inform them. In continental Europe this branch of pedagogy is called didactics. In Anglophone countries, following Lee Shulman's work, it raises questions about what he calls 'pedagogical content knowledge' – what the teacher needs to know about each aspect of the curriculum in order to restructure it as successful learning encounters and experiences.[103]

This omission is deliberate because we wish to place discussion of pedagogical content knowledge within a broader consideration of the expertise needed for primary teaching, the way primary teachers are trained and deployed, and their career cycle from novice to expert. These matters are dealt with in Chapter 21.

We conclude that government intervention in pedagogy, whether through the national strategies or by other means, may have helped some teachers but in general it has been excessive and often ill-founded conceptually and empirically. Historically, primary teachers have always been placed in a position of excessive dependence on others for their ideas, and in pursuing its goals of raising standards the government should have understood that this was an indefensible and probably sexist legacy of the old elementary system. It should have stepped back from pedagogy, and the prospects for its renewal promised by research, rather than seize control and then politicise it to the point where electoral calculation began to compromise educational judgement.

For while teachers complain about the loss of the 'creativity' and 'flexibility' which experienced professionals expect and value as a matter of course, the true problem is more fundamental than this. Mature teaching (as opposed to teaching to cope or survive) requires:

- command of a repertoire of knowledge, strategies and skills
- understanding of the evidence on which each element in the repertoire draws in order to justify its inclusion
- the judgement to weigh up each pupil need and classroom situation and determine how the repertoire should be deployed and translated into everyday decisions and actions
- a framework of well-grounded principles of learning and teaching, whereby the decisions and actions taken can be known to be right
- a set of educational aims and values to steer and sustain the whole.

The 1992 'three wise men' report proposed an approach to teaching in which a comprehensive classroom repertoire is deployed on the basis of fitness for purpose. However, though this formula kept aims firmly in view, it rather lost sight of pedagogical principles, which of course are not the same as educational aims, and implied that classroom judgements are essentially pragmatic, rather in the manner of the current vogue for 'what works'.

That, we now argue, is an insufficient basis on which either to teach or to know that how one teaches is educationally sound. The current situation is even more reductive. The national strategies commend repertoire, but reduce that repertoire to what has official approval. At the same time, such principles as can be adduced to justify what is prescribed or commended are anodyne or tautologous, and have no explicit grounding in evidence. In their approach to pedagogy the national agencies assert and require but do not argue or justify. The teacher, then, is left in the position of being expected to make complex judgements and decisions without knowing why; or whether the procedures have any warrant other than that they are commended by government and its agencies.

We need instead to move to a position where the repertoire is established through initial training and refined and extended through experience and CPD, and teachers acquire as much command of the evidence and principles which underpin the repertoire as they do of the skills needed in its use. The test of this alternative view of professionalism is that in relation to anything he or she does a teacher is able to give a coherent justification citing (i) evidence, (ii) pedagogical principle and (iii) educational aim, rather than offer the unsafe and undemocratic defence of compliance with what is required. Anything less is not just professionally demeaning; it is also likely to be educationally unsound.

This is the force of that key TLRP finding that there is a necessary relationship between how teachers think about their practice and how pupils learn, or David Hargreaves' argument that the 'learning conversation' is a condition of professional development and innovation no less than of pupil learning. In teaching, as we have said, dialogue is indivisible. Pupils will not learn to think for themselves if their teachers are expected to do as they are told. That being so, there is a crucial connection between this chapter's discussion of pedagogy and the nature and development of professional expertise. These matters are explored further in Chapter 21.

NOTES

1 Sammons *et al.* (2007b, 2007c).
2 As documented, for example, in DES (1977b), NCE (1995) and Ofsted (2009).
3 Gorard (2006, 2008).
4 Simon (1981); Alexander (2004a, 2008b).
5 Alexander (2004a).
6 DfES (2003b).
7 Cuban and Tyack (1995).
8 Simon (1981).
9 DES (1978).
10 Lipman *et al.* (1980).

11 That is to say, following the Hadow and Plowden reports of 1931 and 1967, both of which placed child development centre-stage (Board of Education 1931: paras 25–47; CACE 1967: paras 9–74).
12 Miliband (2004a).
13 Teaching and Learning in 2020 Review Group (2006): 6.
14 DfES (2005b).
15 Sebba *et al.* (2007): 125.
16 DCSF (2008b): 5–6.
17 Alexander and Hargreaves (2007): 24.
18 Galton and MacBeath (2008): 109.
19 DES (1989).
20 Ofsted (2005b).
21 Galton and MacBeath (2008): 109.
22 Civitas (2009).
23 *Ibid.*
24 DfES (2005c): 52.
25 *Ibid.*: 2.
26 Galton and MacBeath (2008).
27 Watkins and Wagner (2000).
28 James and Pollard (2010), Mayall (2010), *The Cambridge Primary Review Research Surveys*, Chapters 20 and 3. See also Chapters 5 and 11.
29 Goswami and Bryant (2010), *The Cambridge Primary Review Research Surveys*, Chapter 6. See also Chapter 7.
30 *Ibid.*
31 Goswami and Bryant (2010), Howe and Mercer (2010), Blatchford *et al.* (2010), *The Cambridge Primary Review Research Surveys*, Chapters 6, 7 and 21.
32 Goswami and Bryant (2010), *The Cambridge Primary Review Research Surveys*, Chapter 6.
33 James and Pollard (2010), *The Cambridge Primary Review Research Surveys*, Chapter 20.
34 Blatchford *et al.* (2010), James and Pollard (2010), *The Cambridge Primary Review Research Surveys*, Chapter 21 and 20.
35 Blatchford *et al.* (2010).
36 James and Pollard (2010).
37 Secretary of State Kenneth Clarke, in 1991, cited in the so-called 'three wise men' report on primary teaching (Alexander, Rose and Woodhead 1992: para 1).
38 Balarin and Lauder (2010), *The Cambridge Primary Review Research Surveys*, Chapter 26.
39 The then opposition shadow secretary of state, Jack Straw (see Chapter 3).
40 GTCE (2008).
41 Alexander (1995): 8–44.
42 As also recorded in the ORACLE research of the mid-1970s (Galton, Simon and Croll 1980b).
43 Alexander (1997): 65–66.
44 Prime Ministers Margaret Thatcher and Tony Blair.
45 Alexander, Rose and Woodhead (1992): 1.
46 Bennett (1976); Bennett *et al.* (1984); Galton, Simon and Croll (1980a, 1980b); Mortimore *et al.* (1988); Tizard *et al.* (1988); Alexander (1997).
47 Rutter *et al.* (1979).
48 As recorded in the studies by Bennett, Galton and Alexander noted above, and in the Ofsted *Worlds Apart* review of Reynolds and Farrell (1996).
49 Ofsted (1993a, 1993b, 1994, 1995).
50 DfE (1993).
51 TDA (2007a).
52 DCSF (2007f): 5.
53 Prais (1997); Luxton and Last (2000).
54 Reynolds and Farrell (1996).
55 DfEE (1998b): 8.
56 DfEE (1999b): 11.
57 DfEE (1998b).
58 Lesson pace is unpacked in Alexander (2001b): 418–26, from where these quotations and alternative definitions are taken.
59 Cordingley *et al.* (2003): 4–5.
60 TDA (2008e): 9.
61 DfES (2003b).
62 DfES (2003b): paras 3.2–3.5.
63 *Ibid.*: 29
64 Black and Wiliam (1999); Black *et al.* (2002).
65 Goswami and Bryant (2010), *The Cambridge Primary Review Research Surveys*, Chapter 6.
66 DCSF (2007f): 2.
67 Earl *et al.* (2003b): 3.
68 DCSF (2008b): 5–6.
69 DCSF (2008ab): 12.

70 For example, Mercer and Hodgkinson (2008), Alexander (2008b).
71 TDA (2007a): 4.
72 DCSF (2008b): 9.
73 Webb and Vulliamy (2006).
74 James and Pollard (2010), *The Cambridge Primary Review Research Surveys*, Chapter 20.
75 Galton *et al.* (1999); Alexander *et al.* (1996); and, in the United States, Nystrand *et al.* (1997).
76 Alexander (2001b).
77 Smith *et al.* (2004). See also Hardman *et al.* (2003); Moyles *et al.* (2003); Myhill (2005); Eke and Lee (2004); Alexander (2008b).
78 DCSF (2007e): 3–4.
79 *Ibid.*
80 Gage (1963).
81 Gage (1978).
82 Richardson (2001).
83 Reynolds *et al.* (2002): 30–31.
84 Sammons *et al.* (1995).
85 Creemers (1994): 189–206.
86 Alexander (2001b): 38.
87 Weiner (2002). Similar objections are raised by Pring (1995), Elliott (1996) and Hamilton (1996).
88 James and Pollard (2010), *The Cambridge Primary Review Research Surveys*, Chapter 20. See also Hofkins (2008b): 5.
89 Hargreaves (2004b).
90 Hargreaves (2006b).
91 Hargreaves (2006a).
92 Hargreaves (2008b).
93 Hargreaves (2008a).
94 A central theme of Galton's 2007 research-based discussion of primary teaching (Galton 2007).
95 For a fuller list, see Good and Brophy (2002).
96 Galton (2008); Nystrand *et al.* (1997).
97 Vygotsky (1962); Bruner (1983, 1996); Bruner and Haste (1987); Bakhtin (1981, 1986); Halliday (1989); Wells (1986).
98 Cole (1996); Wertsch (1985); Bruner (1996).
99 Engeström (1996); Daniels (2001).
100 Barnes, Britton and Rosen (1969); Sinclair and Coulthard (1975); Cazden (2001); Galton, Simon and Croll (1980a); Galton *et al.* (1997); Edwards and Westgate (1994).
101 Alexander (2001b, 2008b); Mercer (2000); Mercer and Littleton (2007); Mortimer and Scott (2003); Mercer and Hodgkinson (2008).
102 Alexander (2008b).
103 Shulman (1987, 2005).

16 Assessment, learning and accountability

Children in England, as is well known, are among the most tested in the world. As is also well known, the Year 6 SATs, the culmination of many years of testing, put pupils and their teachers under considerable pressure. The results are seen as a judgement on schools while children often see them as a judgement on themselves. But is this fair or accurate? Do the results really tell pupils and teachers, parents and politicians what they need to know? And, perhaps even more fundamentally, do the tests help or hinder pupils' learning?

This chapter is about the nature, methods, purposes and uses of assessment. First, it clarifies some terms, particularly distinguishing testing, which is only one form of assessment, from assessment in general. It then outlines the current arrangements in England and some other countries at the time of the Cambridge Primary Review. Consideration of what high quality assessment entails is followed by a critique of tests in terms of validity, reliability, impact on the curriculum and teaching, and use of resources. The same criteria are applied to the main alternative to tests – greater use of teachers' judgements for summative assessment. A particular advantage of this alternative is the potential impact on the use of assessment to help learning – a key factor in the government's drive to quicken the rate of progress in children's learning. Finally we propose some recommendations for change in assessment policy pertaining at the time of the Primary Review.

WHAT IS ASSESSMENT?

The word 'assessment' is often used in two senses: as a process carried out to provide data about something or someone, and as a product, as in referring to 'teachers' assessments'. In this chapter we use the word in the first sense and refer to products as 'assessment results'. Assessment in education involves making judgements about pupils' attainments. It involves deciding what information is relevant, how to collect it, how to come to a judgement and then how to report or communicate the judgement to those who want to know what pupils are achieving. All of these decisions depend on the reason for conducting the assessment. Many people and organisations have reasons for needing assessment results: pupils to help them in their learning, parents to know how their children are progressing, teachers to regulate their teaching and to diagnose problems; school governors, local authorities and central government to indicate the effectiveness of schools.[1]

Assessment also needs to be distinguished from *evaluation* and from *testing*. Here we take evaluation to mean making judgements, not about children's learning, but about educational programmes, institutions and policies. In some countries the words evaluation and assessment are used interchangeably – and in some languages there is only one word for both – and the context is used to decide whether the process is about pupils' achievement or the performance of programmes, schools and so on. Similarly, the words testing and assessment are sometimes used loosely for the same thing, and in this case the distinction is important and fundamental to this chapter. Throughout it is essential to be clear that assessment does not mean testing, as we now explain.

No shortage of data

Almost anything that a pupil does can reveal some ability or attribute.[2] So regular work is a source of data, which can be collected in various ways; for example, by observation by the teacher or by gathering samples of work in a file or portfolio (which can include photographs, tape-recordings, or videos of performance or artefacts). This evidence would, of course, vary from class to class, even child to child, and for some uses of the results this might lead to unfairness. One way to avoid this problem is to ensure that pupils perform the same tasks in the same conditions, that is, to use tests. In tests, the tasks, the conditions and the time for under-taking them are specified. In addition, the way in which the pupils' responses are marked, either by the teacher or an external agency, are prescribed. In between the unstructured observation by a teacher and the formal test are various other approaches, such as having special tasks, designed to require certain skills or knowledge, embedded in normal work. The children do not identify these tasks as special but they provide the teacher with a rich source of information.

Tests, then, are one way of conducting assessment and, in common with other ways, have strengths and weaknesses, to be discussed later. Tests, however, are not all the same. They can be 'paper-and-pencil', 'practical', 'multiple choice', 'fixed response', 'open response', according to the type of task and the way in which pupils are asked to respond.

Why is assessment needed?

This question is frequently confused with the question of whether testing is needed. For instance, the 2008 enquiry into testing and assessment by the House of Commons Children, Schools and Families Committee in 2008 answered only the latter question and summarised the answers drawn from the evidence it gathered (mostly from government) as being that testing is required in order to:

• ascertain and recognise levels of pupil achievement on a standardised basis
• hold schools and teachers to account
• assess the quality of education available to children across the country.[3]

However, in its submission to the Review, the National Association for Primary Education (NAPE) argued that these three needed separate approaches. Several submissions pointed out that, in the case of the second and third of these uses, assessment of pupils should be only part of the data considered. Organisational representatives at the Review's national soundings argued for the use of multiple, linked assessment approaches, using different methods for different purposes. In the case of ascertaining pupils' levels of attainment, parents and teachers in the community soundings[4] suggested abandoning formal external tests and making greater use of assessment by teachers. These are some of the key matters considered in this chapter.

What happens in primary schools?

In 2009, assessment by teachers as part of teaching and to help learning is encouraged throughout the foundation stage and primary years. As discussed later, information for this purpose does not need to be collected in a uniform way as it does not have to be used to compare pupils or report levels of achievement. More formal assessment was introduced into the early years in 2000, when the foundation stage profile was used to summarise what children had achieved as they entered Year 1. The profile was based on teachers' observations in relation to nine points on 13 scales, covering personal, social, emotional and physical as well as cognitive development. In both submissions and soundings for the Review, teachers were sharply divided on the profile with some finding it 'excellent' and others 'excessive'.[5] Certainly, if teachers did not build up the profile over time, as intended, the labour involved in complet-ing it could well be seen as onerous.

In 2008, Year 2 pupils sat internally-marked tests and tasks in English (reading, writing and spelling) and mathematics at the end of key stage 1. Teachers used the results to inform their judgement of national curriculum levels achieved by individual pupils, which was expected to be based on wider evidence collected throughout the key stage. At the end of key stage 2, Year 6 pupils sat externally-marked national tests (SATs was the unofficial title) in the core subjects of English, mathematics and science. The results of the tests were reported separately from teachers' judgements of levels. Teachers also reported to parents at least once a year on performance in all subjects of the national curriculum and often did this in terms of levels, using optional tests in the core subjects for pupils in Years 3, 4, and 5.

Single level as well as SATs?

On the horizon were more tests, initially proposed in Making Good Progress[6] and later built into The Assessment for Learning Strategy.[7] Described as single-level tests, they were designed to decide whether or not a pupil had achieved a particular national curriculum level. This contrasted with the end-of-key-stage SATs which identified which of several levels a pupil had achieved. Single-level tests, developed initially in reading, writing and mathematics, were intended to be used to confirm a teacher's judgement that a pupil had reached a certain level. It was clear in the government's response to the Select Committee report on testing and assessment that these were intended to supplement, rather than replace, SATs at key stage 2.[8] Schools would be set 'progress targets' relating to the number of pupils advancing by a certain number of levels within a key stage, as well as end-of-key-stage targets.

There were many concerns about these new tests,[9] which, it was feared, would mean that teaching to the test would 'permeate the entire key stage rather than the final year, as it does now'.[10] In its submission to the Review, the National Association of Head Teachers affirmed that 'our children are over-tested'[11] and these tests were 'not the way forward'. Instead it called for the key stage 2 SATs and their reporting arrangements to be scrapped.

The position of single-level tests was mentioned, but not clarified, in the Secretary of State's statement on national curriculum tests to the House of Commons on 14 October 2008. Following unsatisfactory results from pilots of single-level tests at key stage 3, Ed Balls announced the end of these trials. However, results of trials at key stage 2 were described as 'encouraging'[12] and the decision as to their adoption left open.

What happens in other countries?

Comparisons with other countries, both within the UK and beyond, show that in England at the time of the Review there was far more testing and assessment than elsewhere – even if we include only what is statutory. Between 2007 and 2009, changes were being implemented in the assessment systems in Scotland, Wales and Northern Ireland.[13] Wales and Northern Ireland abandoned testing, or were in the process of so doing, relying instead on teachers' judgements, with optional tests in Wales to support teachers in their decisions during the transition. In Scotland, tests continued to be available as an option to be used at any time to confirm teachers' judgements. No other UK country used assessment results to compile 'league' tables of schools, a process which, as we see later, added to pressure on schools to improve levels artificially.

Outside the UK the picture is varied but the summary table of primary-school assessment arrangements in 17 countries, given by Kathy Hall and Kamil Øzerk in their research survey for the Review, led them to conclude that 'England is unusual in its high incidence of assessment. It is exceptional in its emphasis on statutory external standardised assessment of children at ages seven and 11'.[14] Further, while several other countries monitor pupils' learning to keep track of national levels of achievement, they do so by assessing representative samples, not by assessing every pupil as in England. As we see later, sampling yields potentially richer and more valid information.

USES OF ASSESSMENT: STRENGTHS AND WEAKNESSES

What's it all for?

There is a sense in which all assessment should help learning. This can be through the direct use of data to inform the actions of pupils and teachers on a day-to-day basis, or through a more indirect route, where information about the performance of groups affects policy and the learning opportunities of future learners. Whether the indirect impact actually helps learning depends on the nature of policy decisions, however. Leaving aside the longer-term use, it makes sense to identify two kinds of purpose:

- helping learning and teaching
- reporting on what has been learned

These are not different *kinds* of assessment, but different ways of using the data that assessment provides. The first is described as formative or assessment for learning. Information gathered for this purpose has only one use; by definition if it is not used to help learning then it cannot be described as formative. In contrast, assessment for the second purpose, described as summative since the results provide a summation of learning at a point in time, is used in several ways. The results for individual children are used within the school for recording pupils' progress, reporting to parents and to pupils, and in some cases for grouping pupils. In secondary schools, assessment is additionally used to inform decisions about optional courses. Summative assessment is also carried out for use outside the primary school, to meet the requirements of statutory national assessment and in some cases for selection.

The recognition of the various purposes of assessment and the possibility of using the same information to serve different purposes was a feature of the 1988 report of the Task Group on Assessment and Testing (TGAT) which advised the government during the development of the national curriculum in England and Wales. The report argued that assessment to support learning should be at the heart of the assessment system up to the age of 16, since 'if assessment were designed only for summative purposes, then formative information could not be obtained'.[15] Based on that, the report went on: 'It is realistic to envisage, for the purpose of evaluation, ways of aggregating the information on individual pupils into accounts of the success of a school, or LEA, in facilitating the learning and achievements of those for whom it is responsible'.[16] However the emerging policy focused on this evaluative use and the recommendation for a system designed for formative use was effectively ignored.[17]

In England, in 2008, the results used to report the learning of individual pupils were also aggregated for groups and used for several other purposes. For example, these included:

- internal school monitoring and evaluation
- external evaluation of schools and local authorities
- monitoring levels of achievement to identify changes in 'standards' (see Chapter 17 for a discussion of this term).

These were just some of the uses made of assessment results; the Qualifications and Curriculum Authority identified 22 uses. In his evidence to the Select Committee enquiry on testing and assessment, Ken Boston, the QCA's chief executive, commented that 'when you put all of these functions on one test, there is a risk that you do not perform any of these functions as perfectly as you might'.[18] Similar comments have been put more forcefully in submissions to the Review and in national soundings of organisations. However, Dr Boston also pointed out that 'it would be absurd to have 22 different sorts of tests in our schools',[19] and argued for restricting the functions and types of tests to three or four. The Committee strongly disagreed, seeking instead to promote plurality and innovation in tests so that types of outcomes not so far assessed could be included. It recommended that 'national tests should be reformed in order to decouple the multiple purposes of measuring pupil attainment, school and teacher account-ability and national monitoring'.[20] However, the government's response to this was to assert that 'test result data is fit to support each of these three important uses'.[21]

This position was again confirmed by the Secretary of State in announcing changes to assessment and testing at key stage 3. He referred to three principles underpinning the approach: that it should give parents the information they need to compare schools, enable head teachers and teachers to secure the progress of every child, and allow the public to hold national and local government and governing bodies to account on the performance of schools. These same principles were invoked as reasons for ending national tests at key stage 3 and for retaining them at key stage 2, arguing that 'externally-marked KS2 national curriculum tests are essential to give parents, teachers and the public the information they need about the progress of each primary-aged child and of every primary school. Some argue that we should abolish the tests, but that would be the wrong thing to do.'[22]

All in favour of formative assessment

The use of assessment to help learning has been widely recognised as a key component of effective teaching. As noted above, it was recognised before the introduction of the national curriculum and assessment, but largely ignored in the subsequent legislation. This formative use was possibly the single aspect of assessment for which there was unanimous support from all sources of evidence in the Review. It enjoys theoretical and empirical support and has been embedded in new curricula and assessment systems throughout the UK and in many other countries.[23] It fits modern views of how learning takes place, particularly in building on children's initial ideas and skills and strengthening their engagement with and responsibility for learning. Empirical support derives from research, reported in several reviews, most notably that conducted by Professors Paul Black and Dylan Wiliam.[24] In a brief summary of findings in 1998, they described the impact on learning of implementing formative assessment as being greater than for any other innovation, capable of improving 'performance of pupils in GCSE by between one and two grades.'[25] Further, they said that 'improved formative assessment helps the (so-called) low attainers more than the rest, and so reduces the spread of attainment whilst also raising it overall'.[26]

The definition of assessment for learning given by the Assessment Reform Group has been widely quoted, being originally published in a poster sent by the QCA to every school in England:

> The process of seeking and interpreting evidence for use by learners and their teachers to decide where the learners are in their learning, where they need to go and how best to get there.[27]

What this involves for teachers is best described as a cyclic process, in which they gather data about pupils' current understandings and skills by observation, careful questioning, gathering children's views and studying pupils' work, then interpret this information in relation to the lesson goals to decide the next steps in learning. The cycle is repeated by gathering more data in the next activity, having the effect of regulating learning so that the pace of moving forward is adjusted to ensure the active participation of the learners. The value of children's participation at all stages in this cycle is widely recognised.[28] It requires that children as well as teachers have a clear idea of what they should be aiming for, thus enabling them to take a part in assessing their work and gaining some independence in learning.

A child is more than a level

It seems reasonable to expect that the records and reports of children's attainments should reflect the full range of their educational goals – as the foundation stage profile sets out to do.

In contrast, primary schools' records and reports in 2008 tended to be dominated by pupils' performance in curriculum subjects and summarised in terms of levels, even though reporting a level was only required at the end of key stages. Arriving at a level involves scanning a variety of evidence from children's regular work, special tests or tasks, teacher-made tests, commercial tests and occasionally pupil self-assessment. This is brought together and compared with the description of the most likely level, using a 'best-fit' approach. Reducing this rich range of data to a 'level' serves to label children rather than to enlighten parents and other teachers about the range of their achievements. The Review's community soundings found that parents, for instance, wanted not only to know if their children were progressing satisfactorily but also whether there were problems and whether they were happy.[29]

The existence of SATs and optional tests in the core subjects for other years tended to narrow the information used in reporting. Moreover, teachers emulated these tests when making their own.[30] The narrowness of the range of pupil achievements reported was regretted in submissions to the Review from the National Primary Headteachers' Association, the Association for the Study of Primary Education and the National Association of Head Teachers. The SATs results, particularly at the end of key stage 2, acquired such importance in the eyes of parents and children[31] as well as schools that they came to dominate reporting practice in the primary school. We now look at how this came about.

Using SATs to evaluate schools

What children achieve in relation to the attainment targets of the national curriculum is clearly central to the work of teachers and schools, but whether they are wholly accountable for it is arguable. In 2008 the percentage of pupils reaching level 2 at the end of key stage 1 in English and mathematics and level 4 at the end of key stage 2 in all three core subjects were used to evaluate primary schools. (Similarly, the percentage of students achieving certain grades at GCSE was used in evaluating secondary schools.) We take up later the matter of what proportion of pupils reached the target levels and how this has changed. Our concern here is with the principle of using national test results to evaluate schools by publishing these results and setting targets in terms of levels derived from tests.

It is not difficult to understand why comparison of schools on the basis of raw test scores is criticised as unfair. Strong opinions on this matter were expressed in submissions from all professional associations. Typical of these was the NAPE statement that: 'Data gained from unsound measures of children's performance on tests should not be used to define the success or failure of schools or to predict future progress'. Schools do not start off on a level playing field. Their pupils vary in prior learning, and in many influences and conditions that affect their learning – and these factors need to be taken into account when judging effectiveness. One approach is to use 'contextual value-added' scores, which take account of pupils' prior attainment. But these are only as accurate as the test scores from which they are derived and the assumptions of the model used in computing them. The House of Commons Children, Schools and Families Committee recommended that both raw results and value-added results ought to be considered in relation to other information about the school and a wider view of its performance.

Meanwhile, because of the high profile of test results, the pressure to do better had a massive impact on schools. Teacher witnesses in the Review's community soundings reported that SATs:

- put children and teachers under intolerable pressure
- were highly stressful
- constrained the curriculum, especially in respect of the arts and humanities
- subverted the goals of learning for its own sake
- undermined children's self-esteem
- ran counter to schools' stated commitments to a full and rounded education

- turned the final year of primary schooling into the wrong kind of educational culmination – a year of cramming and testing
- disadvantaged those children whose parents cannot afford to pay for private SATs coaching.[32]

All these claims have been backed by research.[33] While they might be taken to lead to the conclusion that all would be well with the national tests if only the results were not published, this does not take account of the less than perfect nature of the tests, which we consider later.

However, despite the research evidence and the confirmation by Ofsted that preparing for tests had affected the experience of Year 6 pupils,[34] the government disclaimed responsibility. Instead, it claimed that: 'There is no reason for testing to result in an unbalanced, narrow curriculum or uninspiring teaching. The breadth of the curriculum and the quality of teaching are both entirely within the control of the school and the teacher.'[35] The government called for guidance to help schools and emphasised that 'excessive time spent on test preparation would be unacceptable'. However, it also appeared to reject suggestions to avoid this misuse of time made by MPs in their report on testing and assessment.

The government's proposals for School Report Cards,[36] the subject of consultation in spring 2009, could address the criticisms arising from the use of test results as the sole basis for the accountability of schools. The proposals suggest that the new report would contain information about performance in categories in addition to academic attainment, such as wider outcomes, pupil progress, parents' and pupils' views of the school and Ofsted inspection judgments where available. However the extent to which this will reduce the focus on test results will depend on decisions about the weight to be given to the various categories of performance.

Using SATs to monitor national performance

Monitoring national achievement using SATs results takes the aggregation of results one stage higher than the school or LEA. What it means is that the information used to judge whether the educational system as a whole is producing adequate results is only as broad as the range of items included in the national tests. Contrast this with the breadth of information that was collected in the Assessment of Performance Unit (APU) surveys when these were in operation in England, Wales and Northern Ireland during the 1970s and 1980s.[37] Each of these annual surveys involved about 2.5 per cent of the age group and any one pupil took only a fraction of the large number of tests used in the whole survey. Sampling of this kind, where only a small proportion of pupils are selected and each takes a small sample of test items, means that the curriculum is covered more adequately than by a single test taken by all pupils. For instance, in the science surveys of 11-year-olds, the APU assessed inquiry skills both on paper and in performance, practical problem solving and the application of knowledge in everyday contexts. Moreover, since in any class few pupils are involved, and there will be many different tests, any 'teaching to the test' must cover a broad range and so becomes closer to 'teaching to the curriculum'.

National surveys such as the APU's have greater validity on account of covering more of the curriculum, though only needing a small sample of the population. The current practice of using the results of SATs for this purpose under-samples the curriculum and over-samples the population. Sampling of the APU-type is used in international surveys (such as PISA and TIMSS) and in national surveys in Scotland, New Zealand and the USA. The reintroduction of sample surveys in England was strongly advised by the MPs investigating testing and assessment[38] and was among the recommendations submitted to the Review by the National Union of Teachers and by Cambridge Assessment. The arguments appeared to have been accepted by the Secretary of State[39] in relation to 14-year-olds, but there is marked reluctance to make similar changes at age 11.

ACHIEVING HIGH QUALITY ASSESSMENT

Defining quality

The definition of assessment at the start of this chapter indicated that it involves questions of what information is to be used, how it is to be collected and how it is to be judged and reported. Answers to all these questions depend on the purpose that the results are to serve. Nor are they easy questions, since the quality of the result will depend not only on what is assessed but on how. But first we must define quality.

There are certain properties that are necessary in some degree for all types and purposes of assessment. An obvious question to ask of the results of any assessment is whether it is valid for its purpose. That is, does it assess what it purports to assess? Another is whether the results are reliable: are they accurate enough to be trusted? Then it is also important to know the impact of assessment: does it serve its purpose and does it have unintended as well as intended consequences? Further, the resources it requires have also to be considered: what time and other resources are needed? These four questions translate into four properties of high quality assessment: validity, reliability, impact and use of resources.

Assessment to help learning

In the case of assessment for learning, validity requires that the information gathered must relate to the goals of a lesson or series of lessons. This should be the case if teachers gather information as part of teaching; opportunities for learning are then identical with opportunities for assessing progress. Reliability is not important in assessment for learning since, in the cyclic process, information is constantly gathered and later decisions can correct any errors in earlier ones. Impact, though, is all important, since the whole purpose is to assist learning. Research evidence suggests that the strategies which help learning include open questioning and dialogue, feedback, and peer and self-assessment.[40] For self-assessment, pupils need to know the goals of their work and how to judge its quality. The strategies alone, however, may not have the desired impact unless they are underpinned by a focus on enhancing learning rather than teaching.

In relation to resources, materials and professional development may be needed to provide understanding of the strategies and rationale and to give teachers a clear idea of the nature of progression in learning, but once up and running, the costs are negligible. At first using assessment in this way may seem to take extra time but in fact it means that time is used differently.[41]

Assessment used to report attainment

High validity is also important for good summative assessment, if only because what is assessed will be taken as indicating what it is important to learn. Ideally it should provide information about the full range of learning goals. Whether this is possible depends on how the information is gathered. For instance, external tests which are administered to large numbers of pupils are in practice limited to what can be assessed using paper and pencil, thereby restricting validity, while considerations of reliability mean that there is a preference for test items that can be marked with minimum error. Both of these factors tend to reduce the range of what is included and hence the validity of the results. This causes a tension between reliability and validity, which means that, in practice, an assessment cannot have both high validity and high reliability. There has to be a trade-off between the two, which applies in whatever way the assessment is carried out, and which depends on its purpose.

Reliability v validity

Take tests, for example. No test or examination can cover all the learning in the curriculum; what is tested can only be a sample of the goals. Reliability is of concern since fairness to pupils is important. Increasing reliability, as just noted, favours questions which can be unequivocally marked, likely to be ones assessing factual knowledge and the use of a closed format (multiple-choice, for example), as opposed to questions requiring application of knowledge and the use of more open-ended tasks. Thus the limitation on what is covered in a test affects its validity; increasing reliability decreases validity. Attempts to increase validity by widening the range of questions, say by requiring more open-ended responses demanding more judgement in marking, will mean that the reliability is reduced.

The same arguments apply to the use of teachers' judgments instead of tests for summative assessment. While validity can be high, since the data can potentially include all outcomes, reliability will be low unless effective moderation procedures are applied. When assessment is used to help learning, reliability, as noted earlier, is not of concern, so validity need not be limited. But when teachers give grades or levels, based on a broader range of evidence and so having greater validity, it is still important that these mean the same for all pupils – in other words, reliability needs to be as high as possible.

The impact of summative assessment

Summative assessment pleases some pupils but makes others anxious.[42] This happens not only when they are given formal tests, but when their work is marked which is why teachers' comments rather than grades or levels are important in assessment for learning. Given that pupils in England were the most tested of any country, there is an urgent need to reduce the frequency of testing and indeed of marks where comments would be more useful. Research[43] shows that using grades to engage or reward pupils may ultimately demotivate them and reduce the quality of their work. It will become increasingly more important, as technology makes possible almost daily reporting[44] of children's activities, to ensure that what is reported helps rather than narrows their learning. The impact of high-stakes external testing on teachers and teaching also has implications for the validity of the results.

We now look more closely at tests and testing, and alternative approaches to assessment, in terms of the four properties – validity, reliability, impact and use of resources.

THE DEBATE ABOUT TESTS AND TESTING

What are we testing?

The concern about what is being tested relates to validity, the extent to which it is reasonable to take a test result as a true indication of the skills and knowledge that it aimed to assess. Although many of the points here relate to tests in general, our focus is inevitably on the SATs on account of their serious impact on primary education.

In evidence to the Select Committee's enquiry on testing and assessment, the National Foundation for Educational Research, while admitting the omission of speaking and listening from the English tests, of scientific enquiry from the science tests, and of using and applying from the mathematics tests, considered that otherwise the coverage of the curriculum was good. It also saw value in changing the tests every year so that different aspects were covered from one year to another. More typical of the evidence, though, was that of the Association for Achievement and Improvement through Assessment (AAIA), which criticised SATs on grounds of validity for assessing only a narrow part of the national curriculum. It also complained of bias towards pupils with good recall and neglect of skills and achievement that cannot be assessed through written tests. The QCA, too, acknowledged that tests can only assess a narrow range of achievement. Witnesses from primary-school senior management teams in the Review's community soundings expressed strong opposition to SATs on grounds, among others, of low validity. Parents shared this view and teaching assistants were concerned that children with special needs are not well catered for in the SATs.

Much of the criticism of the tests[45] related to the impact on teachers and pupils. The NAHT evidence to the Select Committee suggested that the problems lay not with the tests themselves but the high-stakes use of the results. This raises the question, hinted at earlier, of whether, without the high stakes, the tests would have a less restricting impact on children's experience. The answer is probably 'yes' and the research carried out in relation to science teaching in Wales, after compulsory SATs were scrapped gives some confirmation of this.[46] Many teachers in Wales continued to revise in Year 6 and chose to use tests that were still available, but their purpose was to improve learning rather than test scores. The status of teachers' assessment would no doubt rise to equal that of SATs if the high-stakes were removed, raising a further question of whether SATs would then be needed at all.

Really reliable?

Reliability is a property of tests relating not to what is measured but to how well. Since all measurement is subject to error, it is impossible for a test to be 100 per cent reliable. Black and Wiliam[47] identify the main sources of possible error in a test result as arising from:

- variation in a pupil's performance according to the particular items chosen for the test
- pupils performing better or worse on different days on the same test
- marks awarded for the same answer varying from one marker to another.

The last of these can be reduced by refining and checking marking, as much as resources allow, and selecting questions which rely less on markers' discretion (which is likely to infringe validity). This source of unreliability can never be eliminated as long as human beings are involved. The regrettable delay in marking and announcing the SATs results in 2008 for KS2 and 3 reflected the serious problems in ensuring reliable and timely marking of several papers from each of about 600,000 children at each key stage. This event was widely condemned as an indication of the failure of the system of national tests – 'another nail in the coffin of the tests,' as one union leader[48] put it. However, rather than criticising the policy, the company responsible for organising the marking was blamed. Subsequently QCA's chief executive himself accepted responsibility. He was subsequently sacked.

It is hard for tests such as SATs to take into account the fact that the same pupil can take the same test on different days with very different results. Variation can only be reduced by spreading the testing over several occasions. And fluctuations as a result of the questions chosen are also unavoidable and much larger than generally realised. They arise because a large number of possible questions could be included in a test for a curriculum domain. Test constructors take pains to ensure that a particular selection is a balanced sample. Nevertheless, it is still a sample and pupils will respond differently to different samples: the shorter the duration of the test, the larger the sampling-error.

For SATs, Dylan Wiliam[49] calculated how the sampling-error influences the level allocated to pupils by SATs at all key stages. Assuming an overall reliability of a properly constructed test to be about 0.80, the sampling-error meant that 19 per cent of pupils at KS1 and 32 per cent at KS2 were likely to be given the wrong level. These percentages could have been reduced by having a longer test, providing a larger sample of the possible questions, but the gain is not in proportion to the test length, which would need to have been about 30 hours to reduce the misclassification to 10 per cent.

In order not to over-react to this unavoidable error, it is useful to quote from the evidence to the Select Committee from Black and colleagues:

> ... the above is not an argument against the use of formal tests. It is an argument that they should be used with understanding of their limitations, an understanding which would both inform their appropriate role in an overall policy for assessment and which would ensure that those using the result may do so with well-informed judgement.[50]

Tested by testing

Since testing became a required part of primary education, there has been a growing body of evidence of its impact on pupils, teachers and teaching, as documented in several of the Review's research surveys and in other research reviews.[51] Although some studies are small scale, together they combine to provide a picture which has rarely shown testing having a positive impact. Nevertheless the government continued to claim that it is through testing that levels of attainment can be raised (as in the 2008 proposals for single-level tests and progression targets for schools[52]).

The evidence of impact on teaching and teachers revealed was that many teachers felt impelled, because they considered they were being judged on the SAT results, to spend a good deal of time in Year 6 and sometimes earlier in revision and practice tests in order to maximise the test levels. The effect was described in the Review's community soundings as 'demoralising' and 'detrimental' by school senior management teams.[53] The impact was on teaching styles as well as the content. Teachers have been observed to adopt a 'transmission' style even though this was not what they believed to be the best for helping children's understanding and development of skills.[54] Other research has shown that teachers' day-to-day assessment became mainly summative and concerned with assigning levels rather than being used to help learning. In addition, disproportionate time was spent on the subjects tested at the expense of creativity and personal and social development. Typical of statements to the Review from teachers' associations, the NAPE reported that 'in a great many schools coaching for test performance has replaced education ...' There was also a strong call in national soundings for organisations for school accountability to be separated from pupil progress.

In terms of impact on pupils, the matter of whether measured attainment changed over the first two decades of the national curriculum and the role of testing in any change is left until Chapter 17. In terms of feelings and motivation, the research shows that pupils' attitudes to reading, mathematics and science tend to become more negative with age in any case and this happens in countries where there is no testing. In the case of mathematics there does not appear to have been a greater rate of decline during or since the 1990s. For reading[55] and science[56] however there is some evidence of a greater than usual decline in the attitudes of 11-year-olds over that time. While there are many factors that could account for this, it is known that the quality of their educational experience is a major one and, as we have seen, this has been affected by the high-stakes SATs.

Evidence in relation to aspects of motivation for learning has accumulated to suggest that testing lowers the self-esteem of the lower-achieving pupils and gives all pupils a rather narrow view of learning, in which test performance is more highly valued than what is being learned. The NAHT submission to the Review identified the emphasis on those children who fail to make the grade at the end of key stages as creating 'the conditions for disengagement from education (which) promotes low self-esteem'. One head teacher pointed out that 'you can't teach confidence but you can destroy it completely by negative experience'. It was not only teachers who put pressure on pupils. Parents in our community soundings admitted to putting pressure on their children when the test result meant getting a place – or not – at a preferred secondary school.

The best use of resources?

It is almost impossible to answer the question of whether using tests as frequently as was the case in English primary schools in 2008 was making the best use of resources. It depends on value judgements about whether the information that the testing yielded was worthwhile. The government clearly thought so, claiming in evidence to the House of Commons Children, Schools and Families Committee that the current testing system 'equips us with the best data possible to support our education system'.

So what does testing consume, in terms both of costs and teaching and learning time? Estimated costs[57] for administering the annual SATs were almost £19 million at each key stage in 2007, borne by the QCA. This figure excluded the preparation and trial of items for SATs and optional tests. The QCA commissioned a survey of costs of all tests and examinations from PriceWaterhouseCoopers in 2003, but no breakdown of direct costs has been published, only the overall figure of £370m for all key stage tests, GCSEs, AS and A levels.

For schools it is perhaps the indirect cost of teachers' and pupils' time that is the important resource to be considered (although schools were spending a considerable amount of the funds on purchase of tests, which increased rather than decreased when SATs were introduced). Wynne Harlen[58] drew on several surveys of time used in activities relating to assessment to conclude that:

- for pupils in Year 6, time spent on practising and taking tests, in addition to other assessment activities, occupied the equivalent of 13 school days.
- teachers of Year 6 spent on average 165 hours in test-related activities across the year.

Figures for Year 5 were lower but considerably greater than for Years 4 and 3. So, without testing, pupils and teachers could have been spent several weeks in other ways, easing the pressure to 'cover the curriculum'.

WHAT ARE THE ALTERNATIVES?

According to Keith Bartley, chief executive of England's General Teaching Council:

All the evidence points towards the negative impact of high-stakes testing. We need to have the courage of our convictions and look at new ways of supporting and measuring pupils' learning which allows a more positive experience for them and their teachers.[59]

Teachers' judgements: pros and cons

The severe criticisms of SATs for their narrowness and inevitable inaccuracy – quite apart from the effect of high-stakes use of the results – has forced consideration of alternative ways of providing for the summative assessment of pupils' achievements. The most obvious way, and one which has attracted support of teachers and researchers alike, is to make more and better use of teachers' judgements. Recommendations that teachers' assessment should predominate in national assessment appear in submissions to the Primary Review from the NPHA, ATL, NUT and ASPE. National soundings from organisations and practitioners endorsed the development of a system of summative assessment based on teachers' judgements.

There are clear advantages for the validity of the assessment results since teachers can collect information about a wider range of achievement and learning than formal testing allows. The whole curriculum can in theory be assessed, so eliminating the special focus on those parts included in a test. Further, pupils are not subject to the anxiety that accompanies tests and which can affect the outcome, reducing validity. Other aspects of impact of the assessment process favour teachers' summative assessment:

- there is no need to distort teaching methods to focus on what is needed for a test, so teachers can pursue learning goals in ways that suit their pupils
- information gathered during teaching can be used to help learning as well as being summarised at times when achievement is to be reported
- pupils can have some role in the process through self-assessment, encouraging them to identify learning in a different way than as performance in tests.

Resources used in testing, as discussed above, are released for learning activities, and teachers have more time for conducting their summative assessment reliably. This point is the key to the acceptability of assessment by teachers, since the results are often perceived as being unreliable and subjective. The use of test scores only and not the results of teachers' assessment in league tables is tacit confirmation of this. There is indeed research evidence to show that teachers' judgements can be biased and influenced by irrelevant aspects of pupils and their work. However, this is only from reports in situations where nothing has been done to improve the reliability of their judgements.[60] Moreover, the popular notion that tests are necessarily more reliable fails to take account of the errors in tests that we have noted above.

Making teachers' judgements more reliable

When teachers conduct summative assessment, the process, as mentioned earlier, involves scanning a range of information and comparing it with criteria indicating performance at certain levels. The main causes of low reliability in this process are the inclusion of irrelevant information (such as neatness, when this is not part of the task), variation in interpretation of the criteria, and the problem of relating performance in specific contexts to general criteria. However, as the submission from the Association of Teachers and Lecturers pointed out, well-written assessment criteria and teacher training can lead to an appropriate level of reliability in teacher assessment, and this can be reinforced through a rigorous moderation process.

The degree of specificity of the criteria is a key element. Too specific and the process becomes rather like using a check-list. Too broad and it becomes difficult to discriminate between levels. At the time of the Primary Review the national curriculum level descriptions were used in the teacher assessment required for reporting at the end of key stages. However, in developing the Assessment of Pupil Progress materials, the QCA created more specific criteria in 'a structured approach to teacher assessment', based on 'assessment focuses' derived from the programmes of study and the attainment targets. The criteria at each national curriculum level for these focuses were rather more detailed than level descriptions, with two or three level-related criteria[61] for each focus.

Providing worked examples of how criteria apply to specific pieces of work helps in the interpretation of criteria by indicating what aspects are significant in arriving at a judgement and what aspects are not. Most materials designed to support teachers' assessment include such exemplars. It is best if they contain several examples of any one pupil's performance and discourage 'levelling' of separate pieces of work. Some schools develop their own portfolios of assessed work for this purpose and also use them in communicating with parents about how their children's work is assessed.

There are three further ways of improving the reliability of teachers' judgements. One is to use a reference test, which is given to a pupil when the teacher judges a particular level has been reached. This is one of the methods of quality assurance used in Scotland, and recommended for introduction in England in Making Good Progress.[62] However, in Scotland, as of 2008, tests were not obligatory and pupils' levels were not centrally collected. Moreover each test was a random sample drawn from the relevant sections of a bank of items to encourage teaching 'to the curriculum' rather than to the test. Access to a bank of questions for teachers to use as they choose was among recommendations submitted to the Review by the NUT.

A second means of increasing reliability is through group moderation. When national assessment was introduced, time and resources were provided for teachers to meet and share their interpretations of the level descriptions and discuss their judgements of specific sets of work. However, when resources were redirected elsewhere, the opportunities for such group moderation were reduced and in many schools disappeared.[63] Experience of group moderation and of other countries where teachers' judgements are used, suggests that it has benefits beyond improving the quality of assessment. It has a well-established professional development function and indeed the practice of teachers meeting to discuss the conclusions that can be drawn from studying pupils' work has been described as 'the most powerful means of developing professional competence in assessment.'[64]

A third approach, suggested in submissions[65] as part of a national assessment package, would involve all pupils taking a different sample of questions from a large bank. This would provide wide coverage of the curriculum and reduce the tendency to teach to the test since different pupils would have different tests. The average performance across the school would provide information for school evaluation and a basis for moderation of teachers' assessment of individual pupils for reporting purposes.

In search of synergy

One of the most damaging reported impacts of national testing was on the use of assessment more widely defined to help learning. This was serious because, while the claim that 'testing raises standards' is hotly contested, no one disagrees about the benefits of using assessment to help learning. Under a testing regime, children and their teachers are aware that classroom assessment, rather than being formative in function, has become a series of mini-summative tests. It is important to consider, then, whether, given the difference in the nature of summative and formative assessment, it is possible to create synergy between them. Can summative assessment data help learning and can information used for formative assessment provide summative data?

Classroom tests can be used to identify children's strengths and weaknesses and help teachers to plan action based on the results, providing feedback to the teacher as well as the child. In general, however, tests are designed to summarise learning and lack the detail needed to diagnose particular problems. Starting the other way round, however, with the more detailed information used in formative assessment, it is certainly possible to bring this together as required for summative assessment. It is important to realise that this is not a simple summation of the judgements used in day-to-day teaching, but rather a reinterpretation of the evidence in terms of the criteria used in reporting achievement. This is usually a matter of judging 'best fit' to the criteria and, since this judgement is made by the teachers, it requires some moderation, as discussed earlier. It is not necessary to do this more often than once or twice a year when reporting is required, as is indeed recommended by the QCA.[66]

There is, however, as important caveat. If teachers' assessment becomes as high stakes as SATs, the pressure that creates teaching to the test may create 'teaching to the criteria'. The criteria are turned into a check-list and what ought to be formative assessment into a series of mini-summative episodes. Hence the importance, underlined by teacher and governor participants in community soundings[67] and by organisations in national soundings, of pupil assessment being detached from school accountability.

CONCLUSION

The world of assessment has changed radically since the time of Plowden. In 1967, the discourse was dominated by assessment for selection, and was mostly concerned with the pros and cons of non-verbal IQ tests. In 2009, while testing is very much to the fore, there is recognition that assessment has purposes other than selection, particularly for helping learning, and that it can be conducted in many different ways. The government's publication of an assessment for learning strategy in 2008,[68] despite its proliferation of tests and targets, recognises the role of assessment in learning and of teachers' judgements in assessing pupils' progress.

That said, the evidence collected in the Review identified the frequency, form, properties and uses of tests as of major concern. Thus:

- Primary pupils in England are tested more frequently and at an earlier age than in many other countries.
- In public and political discussion, testing is frequently equated with assessment. This is a serious error – linguistically, technically and educationally. It generates excessive faith in the power and outcomes of tests and diminishes the use of other kinds of assessment which have greater diagnostic and pedagogical value. Testing is just one kind of assessment among several.
- Assessment is an overarching term for the process of judging children's attainment and progress. It may involve the use of tests but can also be carried out in other ways. There is

an urgent need to enlarge the vocabulary and practice of assessment, for it is without doubt an essential tool in both teaching and educational accountability. At the same time there is a strong need to place testing in its proper context and to be realistic and honest about its strengths and weaknesses. Conversely, there needs to be a much fuller understanding of the centrality to good teaching and to pupils' progress of assessment for learning which is intrinsic to pedagogy rather than detached from it.

- It is often claimed in defence of national tests that they raise standards. In fact, at best the impact of national tests on standards is oblique. The prospect of testing, especially high-stakes testing undertaken in the public arena, forces teachers, pupils and parents to concentrate their attention on those areas of learning to be tested, too often – as the evidence of this and other enquiries shows – to the exclusion of much activity of considerable educational importance. It is this intensity of focus, and anxiety about the results and their consequences, which make the initial difference to test scores. But it is essentially a halo effect, which does not last; for it is not testing which raises attained standards but good *teaching*. The point is obvious to the point of banality but apparently it needs to be underlined. Conversely, if testing distorts teaching and the curriculum, which our own and other evidence on SATs clearly shows that it does, it may actually depress standards properly defined.

- Contrary to some claims about testing, it produces results which have lower validity and reliability than is generally assumed; their excessive use consumes resources and time that could be used more effectively to support pupils' learning.

- Another myth about testing is that it objectively compensates for teachers' over-favourable judgements about their pupils. In fact, the evidence shows that teachers' ratings of their pupils' attainment, based on a far wider range of evidence, are likely to be lower than their test scores.

- Use of SAT results to evaluate teachers, schools and local authorities puts pressure on teachers which is transferred to pupils to the detriment of their learning experiences. The process also places heavy and perhaps excessive demands on teachers' and pupils' time, and on local and national resources. What may fairly be called the fiasco of the marking of the 2008 SATs – which left thousands of papers unmarked even after the results had been announced – raises serious questions about cost-effectiveness and feasibility as well as reliability and validity.

- Test results are not the best source of data for the multiple functions they perform – measuring pupils' attainment, school and teacher accountability and national monitoring. Despite government claims to the contrary, the use of aggregated test results as a basis for evaluating schools does not provide a fair picture, even when the disputed 'contextual value-added' scores are used. This high-stakes use of test results leads to practices that not only have negative impact on pupils but fail to provide valid information, being based on what can be assessed in time-limited written tests in at most three subjects. The use of the same data for national monitoring also means that we have extremely limited information, collected under stressful conditions, which provides little useful data about national levels of performance and even less about how to improve them. The aggregation of SAT results for monitoring national levels of performance fails to reflect achievements in the full range of the curriculum. It is difficult to understand how these arguments can be accepted in relation to key stage 3, according to the Secretary of State's statement of 14 October 2008,[69] but not in relation to key stage 2.

These problems, identified by many professional organisations, based on research, and replicated in other enquiries besides the Cambridge Primary Review, have within them some solutions. Foremost is to stop using the assessment results of individual pupils for multiple purposes. The main purpose of individual pupil summative assessment should be to report on and monitor the progress of these individuals. Any aggregation of results should be for internal school purposes and as just one, and not necessarily the most significant, part of external school evaluation (a matter we consider in the next chapter). At the same time, the nature of this summative assessment needs to be reviewed. Recognising the inherent limitations of tests means that a far wider range of evidence relating to the whole curriculum should be taken into account when assessing any child. This can only be achieved by making greater use of teachers' judgements, which can cover a much larger range of what is taught. Teachers also have the potential to use information gathered in the course of teaching both to help learning and to report on it. If the results are used for reporting achievement, some form of moderation of teachers' judgments, perhaps through the use of calibrated tests or tasks, is needed. In relation to national monitoring, the alternative to depending on aggregated individual test results is to use surveys of representative samples of pupils and a bank of test items that can include performance and practical tasks.

There is an urgent need for a thorough reform of all aspects of the assessment system in England, providing a coherent set of practices and procedures suiting the goals of education in the 21st century and meeting the needs for information about the performance of individual pupils, schools, local authorities and the nation as a whole. At the heart of this should be the use of assessment to help learning, leading to the development of lifelong learners. This should be supported by a system for summarising, reporting and accrediting children's performance that provides information about all aspects of learning. As we have argued here and recommend later, separate systems are also required for the external evaluation of schools and for monitoring national standards of performance.

NOTES

1 Brooks and Tough (2006).
2 Harlen (2007): 17.
3 House of Commons (2008a): 13.
4 Alexander and Hargreaves (2007).
5 *Ibid.*: 19.
6 DfES (2007d).
7 DCSF (2008c).
8 House of Commons (2008b).
9 Harlen (2010), *The Cambridge Primary Review Research Surveys*, Chapter 19.
10 Professor Dylan Wiliam, quoted in the House of Commons Children, Schools and Families Committee (2008a): 68.
11 Quoted in the *Times Educational Supplement*, 29 February 2008.
12 Hansard debates (October142008): column 674.
13 Hall and Øzerk (2010), Harlen (2010), *The Cambridge Primary Review Research Surveys*, Chapters 19 and 15.
14 Hall and Øzerk (2010), *The Cambridge Primary Review Research Surveys*, Chapter 15.
15 DES/WO (1988): para 25.
16 DES/WO (1988): para 25.
17 Daugherty and Ecclestone (2007): 155; Black (1997).
18 House of Commons (2008a): 99.
19 *Ibid.*: 100.
20 House of Commons (2008a): Recommendation 21.
21 House of Commons (2008b): Appendix 1, paragraph 9.
22 Hansard reports (14 October 2008): column 674.
23 Hall and Øzerk (2010), *The Cambridge Primary Review Research Surveys*, Chapter 15.
24 Black and Wiliam (1998a).
25 Black and Wiliam (1998b).
26 *Ibid.*
27 ARG (Assessment Reform Group) (2002).
28 Stiggins (2001); Black, Harrison, Lee *et al.* (2002).
29 Alexander and Hargreaves (2007): 25.
30 Pollard and Triggs (2000).
31 Pollard, Triggs *et al.* (2000); Reay and Wiliam (1999).
32 Alexander and Hargreaves (2007): 19–20.
33 Wyse *et al.* (2010), Harlen (2010), *The Cambridge Primary Review Research Surveys*, Chapters 29 and 19.
34 House of Commons (2008b): Appendix 2.
35 House of Commons (2008b): Appendix 1.
36 DCSF (2009a).

37 The APU was established to monitor national standards in language, mathematics, science, aesthetic development, personal and social development, and physical development. It did so in a systematic way for language, maths and science before being superseded by the national testing system introduced following the 1988 Education Reform Act.
38 House of Commons (2008b): Recommendation 23.
39 Hansard reports (14 October 2008): column 680.
40 Black and Wiliam (2006).
41 Harlen (2010), *The Cambridge Primary Review Research Surveys*, Chapter 19.
42 Alexander and Hargreaves (2007): 15; Assessment Reform Group (2002).
43 Harlen (2010), *The Cambridge Primary Review Research Surveys*, Chapter 19.
44 Somaiya (2008).
45 Wyse *et al.* (2010), *The Cambridge Primary Review Research Surveys*, Chapter 29; Mansell (2007).
46 Wellcome Trust (2008).
47 Black and Wiliam (2002).
48 Curtis (2008).
49 Wiliam (2001).
50 House of Commons (2008a): 24.
51 Hall and Øzerk (2010), Wyse *et al.* (2010); Harlen (2010); Tymms and Merrell (2010); Cunningham and Raymont (2010); *The Cambridge Primary Review Research Surveys*, Chapters 15, 29, 19, 17 and 28; NUT (2006).
52 Harlen (2010), *The Cambridge Primary Review Research Surveys*, Chapter 19.
53 Alexander and Hargreaves (2007): 21.
54 Wellcome Trust (2005).
55 Sainsbury and Schagen (2004).
56 Osborne, Simon and Collins (2003).
57 Tymms and Merrell (2010), *The Cambridge Primary Review Research Surveys*, Chapter 17.
58 Harlen (2007).
59 GTC Website (29 February 2008).
60 Harlen (2005).
61 See http://www.standards.dfes.gov.uk/primaryframework/assessment/app/waaf/
62 DfES (2007d).
63 Hall and Harding (2002).
64 Maxwell (2004).
65 Green *et al.* (2007).
66 QCA (2003).
67 Alexander and Hargreaves (2007).
68 DCSF (2008c).
69 Hansard (14 October 2008).

17 Attainment, standards and quality

Are schools better than they used to be? Are pupils better educated? Such questions are easily asked but less easily answered. Any hint of a decline – or rise – in standards provokes more heat than light. Yet the questions must be addressed and in this chapter we attempt to do so. We consider the evidence on what has happened in recent years to pupils' attainment and to the quality of education in England's primary schools. We also examine how evidence on such matters is collected and reported.

The chapter falls into four parts. We start with some ground clearing in relation to the meanings of 'standards' and 'quality' as these are applied to the performance of pupils and schools. Next, we examine what the research and other evidence collected by the Review has to say about levels of pupil attainment from national test results and from other measures, including international surveys of pupils' performance. We then consider conceptions of quality and processes of quality assurance in relation to schools. Finally we present some broad conclusions on all these matters.

WHAT DO WE MEAN BY STANDARDS?

Few people discuss education without mentioning 'standards', and the word permeates the evidence collected for the Cambridge Primary Review. Only in a few instances is its meaning made explicit, yet it is used in at least two distinct ways and users sometimes slide from one to another in the same discussion. On the one hand, 'standards' refers to 'measured levels of performance', that is, *what is actually achieved* by pupils, teachers or schools. On the other hand, it refers to levels of performance *that ought to be achieved*, that is, something to be aimed for. Before talking about whether or not standards in schools have changed, we need to sort out this ambiguity.

Standards as 'what is attained'

In this sense, standards are identified with judgements about actual performance or behaviour. In everyday life we may talk about 'letting standards slip' in various contexts, such as levels of hygiene in hospitals, or the general efficiency of certain services. There is an implicit notion of what has changed, even though it may not always be explicit. But we know it means a change in the level of service experienced, not changes in our expectations of service levels. In the Review's research survey of evidence about how standards and quality have changed over time the word *standards* is used in this way, while *quality* is used to describe how 'attained standards' compare with 'expected standards'.[1]

Defining standards as attainment begs the further question of precisely how and in relation to what aspects of learning such attainment is defined and judged. Much of the discourse about standards in education concerns children's attainment as measured by their scores in tests that examine only a relatively narrow range of what has been taught. Equating attainment with scores and levels runs into difficulties in the face of the recognised deficiencies of tests. As discussed in Chapter 16, there is evidence that tests are not capable of assessing some important learning outcomes and that what they do assess is subject to unavoidable and large errors. It means that using changes in children's scores and percentages of pupils reaching various levels to measure the rise or fall of 'standards' over time is flawed, for the changes are often small compared with the margins of error in the scores. In other words, we do not know whether 'standards', in this sense of the word, are rising or falling, a point repeated by many who have studied the detail of the measures involved[2] and reiterated in the Review's national soundings of organisations.

There remains, though, a need to identify where improvement has and has not taken place. As argued in Chapter 16, this would be most dependably measured at the national level by a survey of a national sample of pupils using a range of questions and tasks that cover the majority of the curriculum. Such an approach, dissociated from individual pupil assessment, was supported by submissions to the Review from the National Union of Teachers and the Association of Teachers and Lecturers. But however it is done, what is assessed would be best described as 'attainments' rather than 'standards', reserving the latter term for desired attainment. It would then make sense to talk about how attainments compare with standards, and being 'up to' or 'below' standard would have some meaning. In absence of consensus on this matter, however, we will here use the term 'attained standards' when this is what is meant.

Standards as 'what to aim for'

Used in this sense, 'standards' indicate levels of behaviour or performance considered to be desirable. It is often implicit that the level described by the standard is what constitutes quality in the performance or attributes. So unless there is a change in what is considered to be 'good behaviour' or desired levels of performance, it makes no sense to talk about 'letting standards slip'. This conception of standards disconnects 'the standard' from attained levels of performance.

Consistent with this meaning, we have, for instance, professional standards for teachers,[3] standards for classroom assessment practice[4] and standards which schools use for self-evaluation.[5] The government's targets, set in terms of percentages of pupils reaching certain national curriculum levels in core subjects, are standards of this kind. In the Review's community soundings with teachers[6] and in the submissions from professional organisations, the opinion was widespread that holding teachers, schools or local authorities responsible for reaching standards expressed in terms of test outcomes is unjust and leads to the widely recognised distortion of learning and teaching. What is preferred and regarded as more just is for schools to be held accountable for the quality of their work. It is this for which they are responsible, whereas test results depend also on the nature of their pupil intake and on the out-of-school influences that affect children's learning.

But it is not just these other factors that influence what schools can do. Targets also determine priorities. Without the targets and without the national tests, it would be reasonable for the government to claim, as it does, that 'the breadth of the curriculum and the quality of teaching are both entirely within the control of the teachers'.[7] There is a lack of consistency between what the government claims teachers are responsible for and what they are in practice holding them responsible for. A greater emphasis on the quality of provision in the evaluation of schools would address this imbalance. This requires that we are clear about the meaning and measuring of quality in this context.

As noted earlier, we take quality to mean how what we get compares with what we expected to get – how actual performance or conditions compare with criteria or levels of expected performance or conditions. In the case of pupil assessment this is the difference between standards attained and standards expected, or target levels. In the case of provision for learning it is the difference between observed standards of the curriculum, teaching, relationships and so on, and the criteria taken as indicating good quality in these areas. This cannot be measured in any meaningful way, only judged or appraised in relation to criteria. Such judgements may be informed by, but are not reducible to, quantitative data such as test results. They are inevitably subjective and partial in the sense of being incomplete. Because they have to be expressed in everyday language which can be unclear or ambiguous these judgements can, and will, sometimes be interpreted in different ways by different people.[8] These are inevitable limitations but those involved in making and reporting judgements of quality or on the receiving end of these may often fail to recognise such limitations. The inevitably subjective nature of the criteria and their application forces us to give attention to the value judgements that are unavoidable in setting standards or criteria when they are conceived as 'what ought to be' rather than 'what is'.

Judgements about standards

Decisions about standards, whether in the 'what is' or 'what ought to be' meaning, involve value judgements of different kinds. First, there are judgements about the kind of attainment. For instance what is to be taken into account in evaluating a school? In the case of standards of pupils' attainment, one example is the national test results in the core subjects. There is, of course, a wide range of different kinds of evidence that could be included instead of, or in addition to, SATs levels. These judgements concern the aspects taken as indicators of desired performance.

Second, there are decisions about what levels or aspects of performance in the indicator(s) are to be specified. (These apply only in the sense of standards as 'what to aim for'.) Why 85 per cent of pupils reading at level 4 at the end of key stage 2; why not 95 per cent or 75 per cent? What kinds of teacher-pupil relationships are expected? What types of records are teachers expected to keep? In practice these decisions, which may appear to be arbitrary, are influenced by norms. The levels are set with a view to what is found in the most favourable circumstances and is judged to be within the reach of all schools. Standards of this kind do not have to be expressed quantitatively, of course. They can be communicated through examples of performance captured on video (say of dance or the conduct of a scientific inquiry or teaching that exemplifies the use of formative assessment) or audio (playing a musical instrument or speaking a foreign language). The kinds of performance depend on the indicators used in deciding what aspects are taken into account; the standards describe the judgement as to what constitutes quality in relation to these indicators.

Applying a standard or criterion involves a third kind of judgement – how closely the relevant evidence matches the stated criteria for different levels of performance. When using qualitative data for pupil assessment a 'best-fit' approach is applied, comparing the evidence with the description at the most likely level and with the levels above and below. Such judgements are an unavoidable part of assessment in education. To try to avoid them by turning the standards, and therefore the evidence, into numbers (90 per cent at level X) leads, as is clear from Review witnesses, to reducing the quality of education to what can be measured and counted. Moreover the numbers convey little meaning in terms of the quality of performance.

HOW HAS THE ATTAINMENT OF PRIMARY PUPILS CHANGED?

What do national test results tell us?

In 2008, national assessment data were reported to the public as the percentages of children reaching level 2 or above at the end of key stage 1 and of those reaching level 4 or above in the tests at the end of key stage 2. Such testing began earlier for KS1 (1992) than for KS2 (1995). During that time several changes were made to the KS1 tests. Other changes to the English tests were made in 2000 and from 2005 the basis of reporting performance at the end of KS1 became teachers' assessment informed by tests and tasks. These changes, summarised in the Review's research survey by Dominic Wyse, Elaine McCreery and Harry Torrance on national reforms and initiatives,[9] accentuate the difficulties in measuring trends over time when different tests are used on each occasion.

The figures for the KS1 tests indicate that for English (reading and writing combined) a slight fall from 1992 to 1995 was followed by a steep rise to 2000, after which there was hardly any change up to 2008. The plateau occurred at about 83 per cent after which there were slight fluctuations including a decrease of one percentage point a year from 2005 to 2007. For mathematics the percentage at level 2 in 1992 was similar to that for English (about 78 per cent) but after 1995 it rose more steeply, levelling off at about 90 per cent in 2000, where it remained until 2007. (Note that from 2005 the figures for KS1 are based on assessment by teachers.)

Very similar trajectories are found in the KS2 results for all three subjects tested: a steep rise from 1995 (1996 in the case of science) to 2000, with only small changes thereafter. The percentage of pupils reaching or exceeding level 4 in English rose from 75 per cent in 2000 to 79 per cent in 2005, increasing by one percentage point each year to 81 per cent in 2008. For mathematics the figure rose from 72 per cent in 2000 to 75 per cent in 2005 and again by one percentage point per year to 78 per cent in 2008. For science, 85 per cent achieved level 4 or above in 2000 and this figure rose more slowly to 88 per cent in 2007 and 2008. Thus science is the only subject where the government's target of 85 per cent has been reached.

Whether or not these results are the cause for celebration or hand-wringing depends entirely on expectations and on what is valued. As the 2008 report on testing and assessment by the House of Commons Children, Schools and Families Committee pointed out, when the national curriculum levels were developed they were identified with the average attainment of children at particular ages/stages.[10] Setting a target level of 85 per cent (the national target for KS2 performance in 2008) is expecting a very high proportion of children to achieve what was previously set as an average. It may well be reasonable for the government to expect that improved teaching and extra resources, such as teaching assistants, make this possible. However, the figures and past experience suggest that there is a limit to the extent to which attainment (attained standards) can be raised with current provision.

The early steep rise probably encouraged the government of the day to raise the targets. However, there have been various explanations for the increase in test scores which throw doubt on to what extent they reflected a real increase in attainment. Some explanations are technical and refer to how the tests are made comparable from year to year.[11] Others suggest it was the result of schools becoming more familiar with formal external tests or of factors that come under the label of 'teaching to the test', discussed in Chapter 16. Further, basing targets on the percentages of children reaching a specified level encourages schools to focus on borderline pupils. Former Education minister Jim Knight is quoted in the Children, Schools and Families Committee report as admitting that: 'At the end of KS2 there is too much focus in some schools on people on the margins of a level 4 and not on the rest, because that is where the measure is.'[12] The evidence from the Review's community soundings of pupils showed that they were aware that teachers concentrated on some groups more than others.[13]

This is as much as the national test results tell us about the attainments of primary children. However, it should not be forgotten, as Colin Richards has pointed out, that this information is about attainment in *tests*, which is not necessarily the same as attainment in the national curriculum, even in the limited range of subjects tested.[14] For that to be true, the tests need to be shown to be a valid reflection of the national curriculum attainment targets and level descriptions. There appears to be a dearth of evidence as to how far the SATs represent the level descriptions of the parts of the curriculum they purport to test.

Reactions to the rising test scores varied from welcoming them as indicating the success of primary education – as, for example, in the Association of School and College Leaders' submission to the Review – to concern that the overall figures masked a large gap between the lower and higher achieving pupils and between the 'best and worst providers'. It was also claimed, for example in the submission from the Association for the Study of Primary Education and in the national soundings for organisations, that targets, as currently conceived, stifle creativity and the development of a broad range of skills. At the same time, head teachers pointed out that exciting and creative lessons do more to advance basic skills than any narrow focus on them. Similarly, from the late 1970s HM Inspectors and Ofsted have consistently reported that schools providing a broad, balanced and well-managed curriculum perform well in the 'basics' of literacy and numeracy.[15]

National tests vs the rest

In the years before national testing, the main sources of performance data were the surveys of the Assessment of Performance Unit (APU), the body set up in 1974 to monitor national standards in language, mathematics, science, aesthetic development, personal and social development, and physical development. Longitudinal studies and international surveys (discussed in the next section) also supplied data and there were other more restricted studies providing some relevant data from individual local authorities over varying timescales and generally concerning mathematics and reading only. However, as the so-called 'three wise men' report of 1992 showed, it is certainly not the case, as the government has claimed, that before 1997 there was no useful information on national standards. That report listed six significant and viable sources of data on pupil achievement including APU tests, local authority tests, inspection reports, international achievement surveys and data from the National Foundation for Educational Research.[16] The NFER data included the results of tests in reading and mathematics administered in 1976 and 1977 and collected as part of the 1978 survey by HMI. In the case of reading, the test for 11-year-olds was the same as that administered in surveys in 1955 and 1970. The results showed a 'rising trend in reading standards between 1955 and 1976'[17] but this was not confirmed by other reading test results which remained largely unchanged during this period.[18] No trend data for mathematics could be reported.

The Assessment of Performance Unit surveys

It is worth paying some attention to the APU surveys since many of the Review's witnesses wanted sample surveys of this kind to replace national test results as a means of monitoring change over time. The APU surveyed samples of pupils at age 11 (in mathematics, English language and, unusually, science), at age 13 (science and foreign languages) and at age 15 (in mathematics, English language, science and design and technology). Surveys in mathematics were conducted annually from 1978 to 1982 and then again in 1987. In English they took place from 1979 to 1982 and in 1988 and in science from 1980 to 1984.[19] As discussed in Chapter 16, the surveys involved small but representative samples of pupils taking different tests which were then combined to provide the overall picture. An extensive range of questions and tasks (known as items) covered the curriculum far more validly than a single test taken by all pupils. In the science surveys, samples of pupils tackled random selections of items from large banks created for the six main categories of science performance.

The APU surveys were terminated when the government decided to use the national test results to monitor trends. During its brief existence, the APU could actually do little more than establish a firm and informative baseline and begin regular monitoring. However, the APU surveys provided rich information not just about whether overall attainment was changing, but about performance in different aspects of subjects, and among different sub-groups of pupils in relation to conditions of learning.

In science, for example, while overall levels of performance were stable over the period of the surveys, at more detailed levels it was possible to detect differences. Six main categories were assessed, including three involving children using equipment and manipulating real objects. Performance in the category 'using graphical and symbolic representation' was higher than in other categories though pupils increasingly struggled as they moved from using tables, through to bar charts and then to graphs and grids.[20] Gender differences were particularly illuminating and informative for classroom practice. Girls were more willing to write extended answers and more proficient at planning investigations while boys were more adept at 'applying science concepts' and more willing to undertake investigations.

The APU results for mathematics showed a slight but steady improvement with, as for science, interesting differences between aspects of the subject. For instance the 'number' category was the only one where there was a decline in performance. In English, trend results were available only for reading where performance levels were stable across the years. Assessment procedures and instruments were also developed and used for writing, spoken English and oral comprehension. This provided valuable descriptions of pupil performance but no information about trends was reported.

Era of change

After the publication of the APU findings there were no national data on the performance of 11-year-olds until the national test results in 1995. There were, however, data from other studies which, although not using national samples, were carefully controlled. One reported a drop in reading scores of eight-year-olds between 1987 and 1991,[21] another (conducted in a small number of schools in one local authority) a drop between 1989 and 1995[22] while a third reported that in 1995 reading performance had returned to 1987 levels.[23] The early 1990s coincided with the introduction of the national curriculum and other changes in schools arising from the Education Reform Act, which were known from other evidence to have overloaded teachers. So it is not unreasonable to suggest that reading and mathematics test scores were at depressed levels around 1995 and performance might be expected to rise as teachers came to grips with the changes.

In their research survey for the Review, Peter Tymms and Christine Merrell compared SATs results with those from several other studies of children at the end of KS2.[24] They reported that for mathematics there was evidence of a rise in scores between 1995 and 2000 but that it was smaller than that indicated by the SATs results. For reading, a similar analysis of other data suggested that the rise was also less than in the SATs, going from 48 per cent reaching or exceeding level 4 in 1995 to 58 per cent in 2000 rather than the 74 per cent reported. Indeed, taking into account the dip after the introduction of the national curriculum, Tymms and Merrell concluded that reading attainment had changed little since the 1950s.

Records from teachers' assessment of pupils' levels, collected separately from national test results, largely supported the finding of much lower rises in percentages reaching the target levels. In 2005 Richards reported:

> At key stage 1 teacher assessments mirror the national test results in showing a small but steady rise in performance in English and mathematics from 1996 to 2001 with a levelling off thereafter. Both test data and teacher assessment data report a 6 per cent rise in the proportion of pupils achieving level 2 in English at the end of key stage 1 and a 7 per cent rise in mathematics. Teacher assessment data in science show a similar pattern, though with a 5 per cent rise. This close correspondence between test and teacher assessment data is not surprising given the procedures governing the assessment and reporting of children's performance at the end of KS1.[25]
>
> At key stage 2 teacher assessments rose steadily from 1996 to 2001 (plateauing thereafter) but at a rate of improvement considerably less than that recorded in the test results – 12 per cent more pupils achieving at least level 4 according to teacher assessments compared with 18 per cent in the tests. In mathematics there is a similar pattern with teacher assessments again recording a lower rate of improvement (14 per cent) compared with 17 per cent in the tests. In science a similar pattern occurs but at a higher level – with a 17 per cent improvement recorded by teacher assessments compared with a 25 per cent rise reported in the tests.[26]

International comparisons

Although there have been several international surveys of pupil achievement since the first study of mathematics in 1964, not all have included primary pupils. For instance the most recent addition to the surveys which allow comparison over time – the OECD's Programme of International Student Assessment (PISA) – has carried out surveys of reading, mathematical and scientific literacy at three-yearly intervals from 2000, but only for 15-year-olds. In their research survey for the Review, Chris Whetton, Graham Ruddock and Liz Twist examined six international studies which involved primary pupils, four of these having taken place since 1990.[27] The authors were at pains to point out the many sources of inaccuracy in these studies and the caution with which the results need to be treated. With this in mind the main results can only be stated at a very general level. These are:

- For *mathematics*, the performance of English pupils was poor compared with other countries surveyed before 1995. From 1995 to 2003 it improved considerably but not enough to bring it up to the level of countries in the Pacific Rim and also the Netherlands and Flemish Belgium.
- For *reading*, the surveys providing the most valid data were those of the Progress in International Reading Literacy Study (PIRLS) in which 10-year-olds were assessed. These placed English pupils high in the international pecking order, performing particularly well in reading stories and somewhat less well in reading factual texts.
- For *science*, prior to 1995, the only evidence placed England in the middle group of countries. But from 1995, performance of nine- and 10-year-olds increased significantly, placing England in a group with only Singapore and Chinese Taipei scoring at a higher level. The evidence also indicated considerable progress for this age group from 1995 to 2003.

Comparing these results with SATs and other within-country results is unproductive, since they did not attempt to assess the national curriculum and were not all carried out with the same age group. The general trend, however, did suggest some improvement in attainment since 1995, just as did the SATs results. For science, particularly, the results seem to support the general high level achieved by about the year 2000.

There was a further finding of some importance, concerning the spread of scores for English pupils compared with other countries. In all three subjects the range of attainment from the lowest 5 per cent to the highest 5 per cent of pupils in England was among the very largest of all countries. This wide gap was present in earlier, pre-1980s, surveys and persisted as a feature in all international surveys since. In the PIRLS study, the highest 5 per cent of pupils scored more highly than the highest 5 per cent in any country. This was also true for the higher scoring 50 per cent when compared with some other countries with a similar overall score. But the lowest 5 per cent scored lower than many other countries including France, the Netherlands and Sweden. There is evidence from the PISA surveys that the difference increases as pupils get older. In the 2006 PISA survey the spread of 15-year-olds' scores for England were the largest among 29 OECD countries. The persistence of this wide range in attainment since the introduction of the national curriculum and SATs-based targets suggests that these have done little to raise the relative performance of our lowest attaining children.

HOW WELL ARE WE DOING?

At the start of this chapter we distinguished between standards as measured attainment and standards as what ought to be attained. The evidence from national tests and surveys relates only to the first of these, that is the 'attained standards'. It is easy to be drawn into the detail of changes in terms of percentages, leaving aside the hard questions of whether we should be expecting more, or indeed, whether these tests give us the information to make judgements about the quality of primary education. The percentages of pupils reaching certain levels of attainment rose between 1995 and 2000 in mathematics and science, but changed little in reading. Just what does this mean in terms of children's education?

If, instead of looking at what has been achieved, we consider what ought to be achieved (standards in the second sense) there are two aspects of attainment to consider – range and level. In terms of range, the breadth of education to which schools should aspire in the 21st century was frequently mentioned in Review evidence. For example, in commenting on changes from 2000 to 2006 in several countries including England, Maha Shuayb and Sharon O'Donnell noted a continued 'focus on raising standards, citizenship education and multi-culturalism' and increased emphasis on 'pupil enjoyment and participation, pupil safety, healthy eating and lifestyles, and sustainable development'.[28] The government's own 2004 plan, the *Five Year Strategy for Children and Learners*,[29] aimed to ensure 'a richer curriculum'. Yet at the same time it gave priority to 'high standards in reading, writing and mathematics' and the government continued to use measures in these subjects as the basis for judging the effectiveness of primary schools. As long as this narrow base is used as a measure, so the narrow curriculum will continue, rendering talk of developing thinking, problem solving, creativity and learning to learn, empty rhetoric. Whilst there is potential for acknowledging 'wider outcomes' in the government's proposals for a School Report Card,[30] it is not yet possible to judge whether this will in practice lead to more appropriate attention to a broader range of goals.

What is clearly needed is a better match between the standards we aim for and the standards we actually measure. Assessment by teachers can provide this for individual children and it can be done at the national level by sample surveys of the kind used by the Assessment of Performance Unit. The APU showed that it was possible to assess a much wider range of concepts and skills within literacy, mathematics and science and began to make inroads into other areas of the curriculum. Such surveys, separated from the assessment of individual pupils, can provide the rich qualitative as well as quantitative information that is needed to decide whether aimed-for standards are being achieved.

Turning to the second aspect of 'standards to aim for', the level of attainment to be expected is a matter for judgement based on the quality and range of learning and not just on higher levels of achievement in tests. What price more children reaching the target level in reading if more children dislike reading? In fact we do not have more children achieving more highly in reading but we do have more turning against it. There is clear evidence, noted earlier, that the government's targets set in terms of percentages of pupils reaching a certain level has led to a focus on those just below the target, resulting in less attention to others and arguably associated with the large and increasing gap between the highest and lowest achieving pupils. Setting targets in terms of the progress of all children (as in *Making Good Progress*[31]) is an attempt to meet this criticism, but at the cost of even more testing.

In searching for ways to narrow the large gap between higher and lower achievers, we might look at other countries where the gap is much smaller, although other differences make it tricky to suggest causes. A hypothesis that pressure of testing has widened the gap received some support from the PIRLS results for attitudes to reading. At the individual pupil level, being good at reading correlated strongly with enjoying it. For lower attaining children, frequent testing equals frequent failure, inevitably reducing their liking for reading. England had a high level of pupils with negative attitudes to reading as did other countries, such as the United States, where testing was prevalent. In Sweden, with no external testing in the primary years, negative attitudes to reading were less common and there was a much smaller gap between the higher and lower achieving children.

As suggested at the beginning of this chapter, value judgements in relation to standards in education cannot be avoided. There are alternatives to turning to percentages of what has been achieved and ignoring what children ought to be able to do. Instead, examples of what children can actually do might be put before all those who use assessment results, who could then comment on which examples should be taken as the standard to aim for at that time. A report could then be made of attained standards set beside different views of what ought to be achieved. Such a report would make clear the value judgements involved, as in reporting on the quality of education in schools arising from inspections, to which we now turn.

JUDGING THE QUALITY OF SCHOOLS THROUGH INSPECTION

Since 1839 schools funded by the state have been scrutinised by government-appointed inspectors. Between that year and 1992, inspections evolved in different ways in a variety of social and cultural contexts.[32] Periodically, judgements of the overall quality of primary education were rendered. For example, as part of the evidence collected for Plowden and published in 1967, HMI subjectively rated all English primary schools in terms of nine problematic categories and concluded that 'a third of the schools were pretty good, about a half were more or less average, and the remaining sixth were not very good.'[33] Eleven years later, operating with a sample of schools and rather different inspection criteria, HM inspectors again provided an overall assessment of quality, though in more nuanced and less generalised terms than previously.[34]

Similarly, since its inception in 1992, Ofsted has regularly revised its inspection procedures as circumstances have changed. It too has made periodic statements about overall quality. For example, in 1997, using different criteria from HMI and focusing on reporting progress, it reported that pupils made good and consistent progress in about 30 per cent of primary schools and reasonable progress in about 60 per cent of schools.[35] However, progress was considerably worse than expected in about 10 per cent of schools at key stage 1 and about 12.5 per cent at key stage 2. In 2008, using yet another revised set of criteria, Ofsted reported that 63 per cent of schools inspected were judged to be good and 4 per cent inadequate.[36] It is important to note the changing nature of Ofsted criteria and the changing ways these overall judgements were reported before attempting to use such evidence to assess any changes in the overall quality of English primary education.

The Ofsted inspection regime featured in many of the Review's submissions and soundings. As far as teachers, parents, politicians and the public are concerned, quality assurance in English schools has come to be identified with inspections carried out by Ofsted inspectors working to Ofsted criteria. It is important to acknowledge that inspection can give a valuable independent evaluation of the quality of education in a school at a particular time, provided Ofsted's criteria are accepted – a very important proviso. It can give a professional, though subjective and tentative, assessment of a school's strengths and weaknesses. Many schools can attest to this; equally a considerable number cannot. Its value for teachers, parents and others depends on a variety of factors including the professional experience of the inspectors, their sensitivity to the peculiarities of context, their interpersonal skills, their ability to make judgements related to agreed core principles and values, their sensitive use of data to inform (not determine, their judgements and their employment of suitable tentative language given the limitations of the inspection process. It is clear from the evidence to the Review that these factors do not always obtain and that policy and practice need to be kept under continuous (and in particular independent) review in order in order to add optimum value to the inspection process. A local authority submission expressed a view shared by many other witnesses to the Review:

> Without losing accountability, a culture is required that continues to raise teachers' status, minimising explicit and implicit criticism through over-reporting of unrefined data.

THE PROCESS AND QUALITY OF SCHOOL INSPECTIONS

In Chapter 16, certain properties were identified as being the basis for 'good quality' in relation to the process of pupil assessment. Similar criteria can be applied to the process of school inspection. Major questions to ask include:

- How valid are the judgements made of a school's provision for learning?
  (Do the aspects of provision and performance that are included serve the purpose of informing stake-holders about overall quality? What aspects require more or less emphasis in inspections in order for fair inferences to be drawn about the school's effectiveness?)
- How reliable are the judgements that are made?

(Would the same team of inspectors make the same judgements if the inspection were to be repeated? Would a different team arrive at similar conclusions? How well defined are the criteria used in making judgements?)

- What is the impact of the inspection process and outcomes?
  (How does the inspection affect teachers and pupils prior to, during and after the inspection? Is there a lasting positive or negative impact? Does the inspection result in school improvement?)
- What does the inspection cost in terms of time and other resources?
  (What time is spent on the preparation and follow up by those in the school? What is the cost of travel and salaries of inspectors? Does the inspection provide value for money?)

It may be helpful to have these questions in mind as we describe the process of school inspection and reactions to the form it takes at the time of the Cambridge Primary Review.

Inspection involves more than observing, collecting evidence and reporting findings. Inspectors are not simply the equivalent of mindless, value-less cameras providing snap-shots of schools and classrooms. Inspection involves the interpretation, not just the reporting, of activities. Centrally too, it involves making judgements as to whether what is observed, collected and reported is worthwhile. To be reliable interpretations such qualitative judgements need to be made in relation to explicit and agreed criteria. It is to Ofsted's credit that it has published its criteria (or more accurately, a series of changing criteria) but the nature of these criteria can be challenged. To be valid the criteria should relate to the core principles and values of the schools being inspected and to the core principles and values of the educational system itself. For example, unless it is tied into explicit principles and values, a judgement that a particular aspect of a school's work (for example, the curriculum) is of 'good quality' means nothing apart from conveying a general sense of approval. Yet as Richards pointed out, the inspection framework outlining Ofsted's criteria makes no explicit reference to either principles or values – in part, perhaps, because of the lack of national consensus as to what these should be, as noted in a number of the submissions made to the Review.[37]

In addition to a number of HMIs within Ofsted who regulate the system, inspectors are former, or occasionally current, heads and teachers under contract to commercial inspection agencies who are themselves under contract to Ofsted. As with any large organisation the expertise of inspection teams varies from outstanding to inadequate, notwithstanding the training which is supposed to even out such differences. In the Review's community soundings, several groups raised doubts about the competence of inspection teams – a view echoed in those submissions which questioned the ability of some inspectors to make valid assessments of the quality of teaching and learning. Others, including former HMIs, have expressed concerns about the quality and thoroughness of the inspectors' training and about the limited support they receive. Ofsted maintains that the competence of its inspectors, their training and support are assured by HMI but no independent evidence has been made public about the quality of that assurance. Some national soundings participants and submissions argued for replacing Ofsted by a re-formed inspection system relying on a combination of inspection, support and advice. The role of HMI in the reformed system was not commented on.

Following the Education Acts of 2005 and 2006 inspectors are required to report on:

- the quality of education provided in the school
- how far the education meets the needs of the range of pupils
- the educational standards achieved
- the quality of the leadership and management
- the spiritual, moral, social and cultural development of the pupils
- the contribution made by the school to the well-being of those pupils
- the contribution made by the school to community cohesion.[38]

This is a wide-ranging set of requirements for what is inevitably a time-limited process – and one which garnered a mixed response in the Review's submissions and soundings. While recognising in principle the importance of being judged on a wide range of aspects of provision, many teachers and schools claimed that in practice there was undue emphasis on some aspects (especially standards as defined by national curriculum tests and quality of teaching in literacy and numeracy) to the detriment of other areas of schools' work. There was concern that inspectors no longer reported on standards across the range of subjects and that educational standards were construed too narrowly in terms of pupils' test results at the end of key stages – the latter claim voiced too by MPs on the Children, Schools and Families Committee but rejected, though not rebutted, by Ofsted.[39] Inspections were seen by witnesses to the Review as more or less consciously controlling teachers as well as schools[40] and resulting in a degree of curriculum distortion, a limited range of teaching methods and a disincentive to innovation on the part of both teachers and pupils.

Inspectors have to use qualitative terms when expressing their judgements but critics have pointed out how terms such as 'good', 'outstanding', 'inadequate' or 'satisfactory' are interpreted differently by inspectors and by teachers despite Ofsted's ultimately vain attempt to define them precisely in its guidance. Questions have also been raised about the feasibility of inspecting something as difficult to pin down as 'spiritual and cultural development' or a school's contribution to 'community cohesion'.

Judgements of teaching quality need to be central to any inspection. By their expertise and experience inspectors should be able to make such judgements and the vast majority can. However, very importantly, Ofsted's claim that its inspectors can evaluate the quality of teaching, judged in terms of its impact on pupils' learning during lessons, has been shown to be too far-reaching and in reality limited in its application to a range of observable responses by pupils. Except in a minority of cases (largely involving the acquisition of observable skills) it is impossible for inspectors to make reasonably reliable and valid assessments of pupils' progress in knowledge and understanding during lessons, unless radical, and probably impractical, changes are made to enable inspectors to become fully acquainted with pupils' understanding before and at the end of lessons.[41] Nevertheless Ofsted has maintained that 'first-hand observations of pupils' current progress in developing their skills, knowledge and understanding will always be a key part of the inspection process'.[42]

Witnesses to the Review also worried about schools and inspectors being over-burdened by continual additions to the inspection agenda. Paradoxically, however, there were also arguments for widening the scope of inspections to include aspects such as happiness or enjoyment, suggested in the submission from the Association of School and College Leaders, or for addressing more closely equality and equity in education through monitoring factors such as gender, race, poverty, and special needs for their impact on achievement.[43]

The evidence Ofsted inspectors gather to back up their judgements comes from a variety of sources: schools' self-evaluations, test data, classroom observations, discussion with parents and children and scrutiny of children's work and of other documentation. However, in the soundings, submissions and professional literature there were concerns about the balance of evidence from these sources. Witnesses commented that too little emphasis was placed on classroom observations (especially in 'light-touch' inspections), most of which related to just literacy and numeracy. Similarly, it was argued that in judging schools' overall effectiveness inspectors place undue emphasis on test data, especially contextual value-added data, and fail to acknowledge its weaknesses.[44] The Review's national soundings of practitioners revealed support for more emphasis on self-evaluation as part of the inspection process – provided this met the school's own needs for evaluation to inform its improvement agenda and not simply Ofsted's requirements. The present system of self-evaluation prior to inspection was seen as an imposition, limiting evaluation to those aspects deemed important to Ofsted, but not necessarily to the school. The submission from the National Union of Teachers was particularly emphatic, arguing that 'there should be one single form of institutional evaluation: school self-evaluation'. Possibly anticipating the criticism that this might be regarded as a professionally self-serving soft option, the NUT also argued that such school self-evaluation should be quality-assured by HMI. Greater scope for research-based self-evaluation was seen as important too in the Review's research survey on quality assurance.

The manner in which classroom observations are undertaken proved contentious; some teachers felt their practice had been affirmed while many others felt undermined. The term 'punitive' was used to describe Ofsted inspections in a significant number of the submissions. Research findings revealed the differing effects of inspection on teachers' sense of professional fulfilment and on the maintenance of a broader view of their role in relation to the 'whole child'.

There was no clear consensus as to the degree of notice (if any) that Ofsted should give schools of forthcoming inspections or of the interval between inspections. There were mixed views about the duration of inspections and whether inspection should be proportionate in the light of evidence such as performance data. The NUT submission reported that their members 'support shorter, sharper focused inspections, although they are opposed to a narrow focus by inspections on the core subjects'.

In order to influence school policy and practice, inspection judgements are reported back to those with an interest. As well as involving limited verbal feedback to heads and teachers, inspections result in reports for parents and others produced in hard copy and on the internet. In addition a brief summary of a school's last inspection is likely to appear in the new School Report Card, which the government plans to introduce from 2011.[45] There was no opposition in principle to the publication of inspection reports but in the community soundings several groups expressed concern that there was no right of reply. Nor is such a right of reply envisaged in the proposals for the School Report Card

Probably most contentious of all was the issue of how Ofsted inspection findings are used. At a national level, the chief inspector of schools reports annually on quality and standards of the system as a whole. This invariably attracts headlines as in 1996 when the chief inspector, ignoring inspection evidence to the contrary, claimed that educational standards were unsatisfactory and needed to be raised in about half of primary schools, or, as in 2008, when a different chief inspector claimed that standards had 'stalled' without acknowledging her narrow interpretation of the word 'standards'.[46]

At school level, inspection findings have been used both to 'showcase' outstanding schools but also, through the use of categories such as 'special measures,' to highlight schools judged to be providing an inadequate standard of education. The deleterious effects of categorisation have been widely disseminated in the educational press and documented through research. A strong thread running through many of the Review's submissions was the view that overall, Ofsted inspections were unhelpful and counter-productive as a means of evaluating quality in primary education. A re-established and modified HMI system of inspection combining external evaluation with help and guidance found considerable support.

Lastly, there is the issue of how the Ofsted quality assurance system is itself quality assured: that is, 'who guards the guardians?' – an issue which has engaged, and continues to engage, both Ofsted itself and MPs on the Children, Schools and Families Committee.[47] Ofsted inspections carried out by contractors are monitored for quality by HMI, but the inspections HMI lead or carry out themselves are monitored by their colleagues. Although HMI investigate complaints about the judgements arrived at in Ofsted inspections, their own judgements cannot be challenged by anyone outside Ofsted. There is no outside body to whom complainants can appeal. Ofsted reports to the select committee periodically but this is not an appropriate forum in which to debate the details of quality assurance procedures, criteria or judgements.

ALTERNATIVES TO OFSTED INSPECTION

When it comes to assuring the quality of education, there are alternatives both to Ofsted inspection in particular and to school inspection in general. For example, inspection is carried out somewhat differently elsewhere in the UK and has not aroused the same degree of professional concern as in England. In the Channel Islands, a process of 'validated school self-evaluation' has been developed which has included a 'framework' for development and review influenced by Ofsted but drawn up with the agreement of working parties. Finland, the Netherlands and the Australian state of Victoria also employ self-evaluation unaccompanied by the 'heavy hand' of external evaluation by a government agency.[48] In England there has been limited use of self-evaluation frameworks developed by local authorities but all within the context of the high-stakes Ofsted inspection regime.[49] In reality, since 1992 there has been little or no opportunity for English primary schools to engage with other forms of quality assurance independent of the influence of Ofsted. The latter has virtually monopolised that function.

HAS THE QUALITY OF ENGLISH PRIMARY EDUCATION CHANGED OVER TIME ?

Despite the limitations of Ofsted, the collation of evidence from inspections can be used to provide a reasonably valid, if partial, assessment of the quality of English primary education nationally at a particular time provided that Ofsted's own criteria and procedures are accepted. However, can such evidence address the issue of how the overall quality of English primary education has changed over time? We conclude that it is impossible to say with any confidence whether that overall quality has improved, deteriorated or remained the same over any period of time since Plowden. It is the case that, at both national and school levels, Ofsted has claimed to detect changes in quality and standards over time. For example, Peter Matthews and Pamela Sammons claimed a clear link between inspection and improvement in their provocatively titled report Improvement Through Inspection: an evaluation of the impact of Ofsted's work.[50] Again, in her response to the Children, Schools and Families Committee report on testing and assessment, the chief inspector said that her 'annual report for 2006–7 states that the overall quality of the primary curriculum has improved'.[51]

Ofsted reports all refer to progress (or its reverse) that schools have made since their previous inspections. But these claims are highly questionable. Ofsted's ability to report progress or its reverse is severely, probably fatally, compromised by the successive changes it has instituted in inspection criteria and methodology, and by its employment of different teams of inspectors from one inspection to the next of the same school. Ofsted's temporal comparisons are thus highly problematic. We comment further on this problem in the context of claims about long-term trends in the quality of teachers and teacher training made by Ofsted, the Training and Development Agency and the government (Chapter 21).

CONCLUSION

This chapter has looked at the kinds of information which are used to evaluate the performance of pupils and of schools. At issue is how well they furnish valid, reliable, effective and efficient information for these purposes. We have emphasised the important distinction to be made between attained standards and standards to aim for as criteria for judging quality. The role of value judgements in setting target standards is evident, even when they are expressed in such definite terms as 85 per cent of pupils gaining level 4 at the end of KS2. But values are equally involved in reporting data and findings about attainment and provision, since they are embodied in decisions about what information to gather, and about how to gather, report and use it. One of our key conclusions is that in presenting information about standards and quality the basis for decisions about what to include must be made clear and full acknowledgement should be given to the inevitable limitations of the data presented and hence of the conclusions to which the data lead.

At the national level, the assumption that aggregating individual pupils' test results enables trends in attained standards to be identified is highly problematic. Although the statistics can be computed, their meaning in terms of changes in attainment is brought into question by the limited range of what is tested and by the impact of using the results for high-stakes judgements. We are left with little sound information about whether pupils' attained standards have changed. The position with regard to quality of education is equally problematic. While the evaluation of quality at a particular time can be informative, differences from year to year in inspection procedures, in the criteria used and in the consistency of their application from team to team mean that no reliable conclusions can be reached about change over time.

Schools acknowledge the importance of being held accountable for their work and accept periodic inspection. However, Ofsted's procedures attracted a good deal of criticism which can be summarised in relation to the questions of validity, reliability and impact, raised earlier. In relation to validity, Ofsted's claims to be able to make valid judgements about some aspects of schooling are problematic. It is difficult, perhaps impossible, to envisage how, for example, inspectors can possibly evaluate 'spiritual development' or how they can possibly 'tell parents, the school and the wider community ... whether pupils achieve as much as they can'.[52] There are limits, too, to how far inspectors can validly evaluate progress in lessons or over time using their current methods. Many witnesses have noted that to increase validity inspectors should give greater attention to aspects that reflect schools' own priorities and to schools' self-evaluation. The relative emphases given, for example, to test results and to classroom observation in coming to inspection judgements, were also frequently mentioned.

Points raised about reliability indicate criticism of the expertise and training of inspection teams, with concern particularly expressed about variation in interpretation of criteria both by different inspectors on the same inspection and by different inspection teams in different schools. The impact on schools and teachers of the inspection process, like the impact of targets based on SATs results, depends on how sensitively the inspection is conducted and its findings are reported, and on how the findings are used. According to many submissions there should be more opportunity for schools to respond publicly to inspection reports and there should be more post-inspection advice and support. In this regard it is worth noting that back in 1999 the House of Commons Education and Employment Committee concluded that 'Ofsted has a clear opportunity to consolidate its achievements by working in partnership with the education profession to maximise the benefits that can flow from inspection'.[53] A decade later, judging from our evidence, it has still a considerable way to go to create that partnership and that confidence and trust in the inspection process.

An overarching theme that emerges from consideration of the evidence is that teachers and schools can and should have a greater role in the assessment of their pupils and in the evaluation of their provision for learning. In the case of pupil assessment, there is an overwhelming case for extending the range of aspects of attainment that are included in reporting attained standards and in identifying the standards to aim for. At present the pupil attainment data reflect only a small part of the curriculum and within that only aspects easily measured by written tests. Greater use of information that teachers can collect as part of teaching can help learning and, suitably moderated, can provide information which is a better reflection of the curriculum. Similarly there is a strong case for moderated school self-evaluation across a wide range of provision. Such evaluation should help the school's own improvement agenda and not simply be instituted to meet Ofsted's requirements.

The evidence collected in relation to this part of the Review confirms the need for agreed procedures that enable the work of schools to be evaluated and for these to include the collection of information about pupils' achievements and the use of inspection through first-hand observation. The findings also emphasise that these procedures need to be seen by all concerned as fair, open, informative and effective or, to put this in more technical terms, as valid, reliable, transparent and efficient. It is not the principle of accountability that is in question but the means by which it is rendered, a point reflected in our recommendations for change in Chapter 24.

NOTES

1 Tymms and Merrell (2010), *The Cambridge Primary Review Research Surveys*, Chapter 17.
2 Wiliam (2001a); Tymms (2004).
3 Training and Development Agency for Schools (2007).
4 Assessment Reform Group (2008).
5 DfES / Ofsted (2004).
6 Alexander and Hargreaves (2007).

7 House of Commons (2008c): para 15.
8 Richards (2001b).
9 Wyse, McCreery and Torrance (2010), *The Cambridge Primary Review Research Surveys*, Chapter 29.
10 House of Commons (2008b).
11 Tymms and Merrell (2010), *The Cambridge Primary Review Research Surveys*, Chapter 17.
12 House of Commons (2008b): para 74.
13 Alexander and Hargreaves (2007): 14–15.
14 Richards (2005).
15 HMI (1978); Ofsted/DfES (1997); Ofsted (2002).
16 Alexander, Rose and Woodhead (1992): paras 24–50.
17 DES (1978a): 164.
18 Tymms and Merrell (2010), *The Cambridge Primary Review Research Surveys*, Chapter 17.
19 Foxman, Hutchinson and Bloomfield (1991).
20 DES, Welsh Office and DENI (1988).
21 Gorman and Fernandes (1992).
22 Davies and Brember (2001).
23 Brooks, Schagen and Nastat (1997).
24 Tymms and Merrell (2010), *The Cambridge Primary Review Research Surveys*, Chapter 17.
25 Richards (2005).
26 Richards (2005): 19–20.
27 Whetton, Ruddock and Twist (2010), *The Cambridge Primary Review Research Surveys*, Chapter 18.
28 Shuayb and O'Donnell (2010), *The Cambridge Primary Review Research Surveys*, Chapter 13.
29 DfES (2004c).
30 DCSF (2008v).
31 DfES (2007d).
32 For changes see Dunford (1998); Lawton and Gordon (1987); Maclure (2000).
33 Maclure (2000).
34 DES (1978a).
35 Ofsted (1997a).
36 Ofsted (2008a).
37 Richards (2001b).
38 Ofsted (2008e).
39 Ofsted (2008b, 2008h).
40 Cunningham and Raymont (2010), *The Cambridge Primary Review Research Surveys*, Chapter 28.
41 Richards (2001b).
42 Ofsted (2008b).
43 Cunningham and Raymont (2010), *The Cambridge Primary Review Research Surveys*, Chapter 28.
44 Oates (2006).
45 DCSF (2008v).
46 As reported in the *Times Educational Supplement* (May 23, 2008).
47 See for example House of Commons (1999a).
48 See Cunningham and Raymont (2010), *The Cambridge Primary Review Research Surveys*, Chapter 28.
49 Davies and Rudd (2001).
50 Matthews and Sammons (2004).
51 Ofsted (2008b).
52 Ofsted (2008e).
53 House of Commons (1999a).

18 Schools and communities

A primary school is many things. For children, it is central to their daily lives: a place for learning all sorts of important 'grown up' things and somewhere to make, and be with, friends. For adults, a primary school might be a workplace, or it might be the provider of their children's education and (in some cases) childcare, or it might simply be a place they look back on, fondly or not, from their own childhood days. In this chapter we look at primary schools from two angles: as physical spaces in which teachers teach and children learn and as communities with their own particular ideas and values. We consider how primary schools have come to be as they are; what those who use them think about them and what primary schools might become. Although this chapter examines each angle separately it is important to remember that they are inextricably linked. Discussion of professional and pupil organisation in primary schools can be found in Chapter 19.

THE PHYSICAL CONTEXTS OF LEARNING

Formal learning happens in school buildings and their grounds. The significance of this physical environment has been highlighted in research demonstrating the influence of space and place on human behaviour. Schoolworks, an independent organisation promoting better school design, has described how this environment affects learning:

> First, and crucially, a school building symbolises a set of values and acts as a metaphor for the ways in which society and the community value education. Secondly, environmental conditions have a direct impact on teaching and learning. Thirdly and equally important, but less researched, are the indirect effects of the building. The design of a school affects the way pupils and staff interact, and their motivation and self-esteem. These factors in turn have an effect on learning.[1]

Schools are not only places for formal teaching and learning, they are also important social spaces for both children and adults. They are public or semi-public spaces and often mimic other civic and commercial architecture in conveying statements about society's aspirations and values.

In this section we look at the following aspects of the physical contexts for learning:

- school buildings and playgrounds
- other spaces and places for learning
- educational resources and materials.

School buildings and their grounds

A school's physical environment has an appreciable, and sometimes unexpected, influence on those who use it. As the Review's research survey by Karl Wall and colleagues notes, there are identifiable effects, both positive and negative, on children and staff and on learning.[2] The quality of the built environment relates, in part, to its physical structures – the walls, roof (the built 'envelope') and its layout. A fifth of school buildings in use at the beginning of the 21st century were built before 1945. Nearly three-quarters were more than 30 years old, reflecting the design, construction and purposes of earlier times. It is useful, therefore, to look briefly at the evolution of English primary school buildings and the perspectives and priorities that have shaped their architecture and use.

From 1870 to 1967

Prior to the 1870 Education Act, most children were taught in large communal rooms that housed an entire school. The Act prompted a wave of construction throughout England, with a large number of schools built to a fairly standardised design in a relatively short time. In London and Birmingham, for example, extensive building programmes resulted in very large schools built to a new 'civic' style. Board schools, built during this period, were created to provide the clean, 'healthy' premises then considered a priority.

The Edwardian era heralded a re-thinking in school design with an emphasis on the need for daylight and fresh air. The 'veranda school' design, pioneered by architects in Staffordshire and Derbyshire before World War I, became popular. Rows of classrooms were built around an open courtyard, often with glazed, folding doors instead of side walls, to provide maximum light and cross-ventilation. The assembly hall – a central feature in the Victorian era – was relegated to the side or became detached. Later on, the inter-war period saw further changes in school buildings, reflecting new social and political conditions: free kindergartens and nursery schools appeared and single-storey elementary schools sprang up on spacious sites on the fringes of towns.[3]

Responding to the conditions of post-war Britain led to further changes in primary school design, most radically in the development of 'open-plan' schools. The prototype 'semi-open-plan' school opened in 1958 in Amersham, beginning a movement that remained in vogue for 20 years. These compact styles reduced circulation space to a minimum. They reflected new trends in educational thinking, such as a more integrated school day, and new ways of organising pupils such as vertical and mixed-ability grouping. These more flexible teaching methods required equally flexible space and movable interior walls became common. However, echoing the concerns of many teachers, an NFER/Schools Council report, published in 1980, commented that open-plan schools were often poorly designed and noted that 'complaints were rightly made against practical areas or teaching areas being necessarily used as major thoroughfares, causing additional noise and distraction as well as resulting in loss of teaching space'.[4]

The Plowden Report relied on evidence drawn from a 1965 Department of Education and Science report on the condition of primary schools three years earlier. This report highlighted major shortcomings: 25.1 per cent of primary schools had no central heating; 26.3 per cent lacked hot water and 66.5 per cent had outdoor toilets. Moreover, the buildings were getting old.

Statistical foundations

Number of schools. Since 1967 there has been a steady reduction in the number of primary schools: from 22,831 in 1967 to 17,361 in 2007.[5]

Size of schools. The average number of pupils rose from 193[6] in 1965 to 224 in 2007/8.[7]

Types of schools. It is important to note that although we generally refer to primary schools, there were many types of maintained school catering for primary-aged children in England (see Table 18.1). In 2008, these included:

- all-through primary schools (from reception to Year 6, with or without nursery classes)[8]
- infant schools (from reception to Year 2, with or without nursery classes)
- junior schools (Years 3 to 6)

Table 18.1 Maintained primary schools: number of schools and numbers (headcount) of pupils by mode of attendance, by type of school

Type of school	Number of schools	Number of full-time pupils	Number of part-time pupils
Infant schools	1,705	291,890	47,260
First schools	1,115	167,180	15,580
All-through primary schools	12,845	2,915,980	195,430
First & middle schools	68	20,670	1,150
Junior schools	1,542	425,560	20
Primary deemed middle schools	86	26,960	10

Source: DCSF (2007b).

- joint first and middle schools (from reception to Year 7 or 8, with or without nursery classes)
- first schools (from reception to Years 3 or 4, with or without nursery classes and the first part of a three-tier 'middle school' system)
- middle schools (from Years 4 or 5 to 7 or 8)

Early years settings include state-funded nursery schools, as well as private playgroups, day nurseries, children's centres and kindergartens.

Age of school buildings. Government figures showed that in 2007 around 70 per cent of primary schools were built before 1976. Of the 30 per cent built since 1976, more than half were built between 2001 and 2007.[9]

The politics of construction

Although many aspects of education have been subject to extensive policy change, primary school buildings and grounds were generally ignored by policy-makers until the turn of the 21st century. Most schools and their sites are owned by local authorities and the lack of capital funding in local government since the 1970s curtailed any major re-development. However, during this period many local authorities instigated programmes for replacing infant and junior schools with one-site primaries, raising capital funding for new building through selling existing school sites.

The New Labour government's focus on education heralded a change. The devolved formula capital grant, introduced in April 2000, gave schools direct access to centralised funding for renovating buildings and improving ICT. Subsequently, the Every Child Matters guidance provided a further impetus to ensure that school premises were 'fit-for-purpose'. Established under the ECM remit in 2006, the Primary Capital Programme acknowledged, and set out to remedy, shortcomings in primary school buildings.[10] Under this ambitious programme, a £1.9 billion investment was promised, with the aim of renewing at least 50 per cent of primary schools by 2022/23, although this funding was targeted at particular areas, rather than being universally available. Allocations were made on a formula basis, depending on school numbers and levels of deprivation, but local authorities were also required to draw on existing capital funding streams. In 2006, 23 local authorities became 'pathfinders' in the programme's first phase and all local authorities were required to submit strategies for change by June 2008.

Questions were raised about differences between the secondary school building programme, *Building Schools for the Future* (BSF),[11] and the Primary Capital Plan.[12] The House of Commons Education and Skills Committee observed:

> The Government clearly has significant ambitions for this programme as for BSF, but it is not so wide-ranging (not all schools will be affected) nor is an equivalent amount of money being made available. This may be because primary schools are much smaller than

secondary schools and may not be expected to have the same specialised features as secondary schools. On the other hand, there are in the region of 20,000 primary schools, so 10,000 schools are expected to benefit, which is a very large number. A crude calculation gives a figure of £700,000 per primary school in the programme. There will clearly be a wide variation on that, with some rebuilt and some refurbished, but it is a marked contrast to the £20 million that is likely to be spent on a new secondary school.[13]

In terms of building design and construction, regulations were established through a series of statutory and non-statutory documents: these included statutory health and safety regulations for public buildings and specific guidance for educational premises laid out in Building Bulletins issued by the Department for Children, Schools and Families (and its predecessors). In 2002, the government document, 'Assessing the net capacity of schools' laid down procedures for calculating minimum space requirements. For primary schools, the net capacity was calculated on the basis of the number and size of spaces designated as 'class bases' which was then checked against the total usable space to ensure that 'there is neither too much nor too little space available to support the core teaching activities'.[14] The regularly published and updated Building Bulletins also offered guidance on many aspects including structural requirements, acoustics, lighting, ventilation, temperature control, carbon emissions and fire safety.

School buildings and playgrounds

The Review's evidence demonstrated that the physical context of learning is both important and topical. The following section examines the Review's four strands of evidence on the condition of school buildings, playgrounds and resources, and considers what changes are necessary to ensure that the physical conditions provide effective support for teaching and learning.

Sound and vision

The Review's research survey on the built environment of primary schools considers published research on the effectiveness of the school sites, buildings and grounds as infrastructures for teaching and learning.[15] The survey concludes that there is a relationship between the quality of the physical environment and educational outcomes. The researchers point out that poorly managed and badly maintained settings could have some measurable effects on pupils and teachers. In particular, the survey highlights the importance of considering classroom acoustics to ensure that children and teachers are not exposed to harmful levels of noise, and that children with hearing impairments or who have English as an additional language are not disadvantaged by poor sound quality.

Ventilation is another concern: the lack of appropriate ventilation or heating can sometimes affect children's performance. Research also shows that lighting can have a noticeable effect on children and teachers' well-being, health and learning. Although much is known about the relationship between good lighting and eyesight, it is less commonly acknowledged that poor lighting can affect people's mental well-being. There is increasing evidence, for example, that low levels of exposure to natural light are associated with reduced concentration, disturbances in sleep patterns and depression.

Spatial awareness

The Review's submissions and soundings brought to light a rather different set of concerns about school buildings and playgrounds. Although the National Association of Head Teachers (NAHT) pointed out that funding for school buildings had risen significantly and applauded the announcement of the Primary Capital Programme, the majority of comments were critical. Teachers, heads and parents felt that primary schools were often too small, in poor condition, and lacked suitable space for learning, both inside and outside. Some head teachers and local authorities suggested that schools and play facilities hindered the achievement of the Every Child Matters objectives. Local authorities expressed concern that initiatives concentrated on the 'first wave' of schools to the detriment of schools in later waves. One submission from a group of head teachers raised the issue of Private Finance Initiatives and warned that these schemes may impose contractual constraints on the use of school buildings, restricting, for example, community access.

The relationship between pedagogy and the physical environment was widely acknowledged in the Review's evidence. The need for 'flexibility' was frequently mentioned in comments on the physical environment and it was suggested that limited space unduly restricted teaching and learning activities. Unsurprisingly, several organisations and local authorities said that primary-school buildings failed to meet 'the needs of teaching in the 21st century'. One local authority ascribed these inadequacies to government guidance on the use of space, arguing that the 'national net capacity assessments do not address this flexibility of need for personalised learning'. A few submissions from practitioners were more specific in their recommendations of what schools needed, including this head teacher:

> Don't be obsessed by iconic design. Schools don't need gimmicks. They need spacious classrooms, big halls for indoor sports, an all-weather sports pitch, good toilets and spacious cloakrooms, a library, low maintenance and energy costs, an IT suite with 30 computers, not one between two. We need space!

However, some researchers and architects argued that educational design should not only be functional but also inspirational and imaginative. Architect and designer Mark Dudek emphasised that spaces for children should be conceived as rich and multi-faceted 'worlds within worlds'.[16]

Outside interests

The importance of learning outdoors was raised in many submissions. Sports, physical play and opportunities for learning about the natural environment featured strongly in children's submissions. Children offered imaginative suggestions for outside play in future schools, including adventure playgrounds, water play, trampolines and bouncy castles. But outside areas were not only regarded as being for play: for example, a Year 5 boy called for 'lots of shady areas where you can sit down and read a book'. Many children talked about the importance of learning about nature through conservation areas, butterfly houses, greenhouses and ponds, or small farms and zoos. Adults also described the benefits of outside learning: for example, practitioners in the national soundings emphasised the need for better facilities for outdoor play to ensure that children can exercise. Many others shared this view. Reflecting similar concerns regarding children's health, several submissions from parents also drew attention to inadequacies in schools' catering facilities. It was felt that, in keeping with the aims of Every Child Matters, on-site school kitchens should be revived to provide children with balanced diets, including freshly-prepared hot meals. In this they were in accord with the DCSF which announced in 2007 that £150m was to be spent on building or refurbishing school kitchens, both primary and secondary.

Security

Feeling secure was a surprisingly prominent feature in children's thoughts on the school environment and there were frequent requests in children's submissions for CCTV cameras, burglar alarms, security gates, entry-card systems and even a policeman on the premises. However, some adults lamented that heightened security measures, introduced since the 1996 shooting of 16 children and one teacher at Dunblane primary, had effectively cut schools off from their communities. Children also suggested having quiet areas and 'chill-out rooms' where they could relax and feel safe, an indication that, in some schools, the levels of noise and distraction were too much for some. The submission from Futurelab, the charity that supports innovation in education, cited research indicating that children want schools to be of:

> ... a size they can relate to; that is safe and welcoming rather than austere and intimidating; that gives them a sense of belonging not just to the school itself but also to a 'family' or community grouping with which they can identify; and a place in which their views and needs are valued, listened to and acted upon so that they feel empowered. Learners may also want to have a fixed base and want an area that they can customise and make their own.

For many children the school hall was a focal point, establishing a feeling of community and belonging. Children's drawings suggested that the hall remained a prominent feature of school life, providing a venue for whole-school activities like assemblies and performances. As Robin Alexander pointed out in 2001, this communal space holds a special prominence in British schools in comparison with other countries.[17]

The school library featured in children's submissions as a favourite area. Optimum Education expressed concern that school libraries were often 'under-used or inaccessible' because of timetabling and space problems. In a similar vein, Ofsted noted that, in many primary schools, children were often not able to access the library and concluded that there were significant weaknesses in their funding, accommodation, resources, staffing and management.[18]

The inclusion of pupils with special educational needs in mainstream schools placed new demands on school facilities that were not always recognised or met by local authorities, according to the Review's submissions evidence (see Chapter 9). Some head teachers pointed out that the implications of special school closures had not been adequately considered and they felt that mainstream primary schools did not always have the specialised facilities to support children with particular special needs.

OTHER PLACES FOR LEARNING

Home educating

Home education was once the prerogative of the wealthiest families who employed governesses and tutors to teach their children. Today's home-educating families come from a wide range of social and ethnic backgrounds and include professional and non-professionals, low and high earners, and those with strong religious beliefs or with none.[19] There are no reliable statistics on how many people educate their children at home: some have estimated that 50,000 children are home educated[20] but one study noted that up to 65 per cent of home-educating families were unknown to their local authority.[21] A Times newspaper survey of 35 local authorities in 2009 reported that the number of home-educated children registered in each authority ranged from 10 (in Hartlepool) to 430 (in Norfolk).[22]

Parents are not obliged to send their child to school but they do have a legally enforced responsibility to ensure that their children are educated. The 1996 Education Act stipulates that:

> The parent of every child of compulsory school age shall cause him to receive efficient full-time education suitable–
> (a) to his age, ability and aptitude, and
> (b) to any special educational needs he may have, either by regular attendance at school or otherwise.[23]

However, as the following DCSF guidance makes clear, whilst there are few restrictions imposed on parents wishing to educate their child at home, there is little official support either:

> Parents do not need to be qualified teachers to educate a child at home. Children are not obliged to follow the national curriculum or take national tests, but parents are required

by law to ensure they receive a full-time education suitable to their age, ability and aptitude. Any special educational needs a child may have must be recognised. Parents do not need special permission from a school or local authority to educate a child at home, but they do need to notify the school in writing if they are taking a child out of school. Parents need to notify the local authority if they are removing a child from a special school. Parents do not need to observe school hours, days or terms, or to have a fixed timetable, or give formal lessons. There are no funds directly available from central government for parents who decide to educate their children at home. Some local authorities provide guidance for parents, including free national curriculum materials.[24]

Local authorities can make 'informal inquiries' about the arrangements parents make for educating their children out of school but they are not under a statutory obligation to record, inspect or advise on home education. Nevertheless many local authorities do check that children are receiving a suitable education if they are not in school, although it is emphasised that parents do not have to accept home visits or submit forms and reports on their home-educating arrangements. For children with statements of special educational need, however, the local authority must ensure that the child's needs are being adequately met, whether in the home or at school.[25]

In practice there appears to a wide variation in local authorities' responses to home education.[26] An NFER research report on home-educating parents' views of the support they received from their local authorities noted that:

> Some local authorities were reported to have been encouraging and helpful in directing parents to useful sources of information, but it was asserted that some lacked sufficient knowledge about home education (particularly its legal status) and were often deemed unsympathetic, rendering any contact a negative process.[27]

In January 2009 the government launched a review of home education in response to local authorities' concerns that not being registered in a school meant some children could be at risk of harm. Some home education organisations raised strong objections to the review's remit: Education Otherwise, a group representing home educators, called for 'a halt to the review of home education, launched despite the fact that the previous four consultations affecting home educators consistently supported the view that existing laws are sufficient to the task of protecting home educated children'.[28]

The experience of home educating

How parents chose to educate their children at home varies widely. Some parents adopt a formal, 'school at home' approach with a timetable of lessons and a set curriculum, whilst others prefer a more unstructured, 'learning through living' style in which children learn through informal, unplanned activities. Alan Thomas, a leading researcher on home education, observed that:

> Many parents started out using the familiar structured approach of schools but without the external compulsion to continue in this vein, found themselves drawn towards more informal methods. Children themselves often resisted the 'school at home' approach and besides this, parents found that children were learning spontaneously and effectively outside their planned lessons. The degree to which families gave up formal learning varied. Some felt more comfortable retaining a varied amount of structured input but others abandoned formal learning altogether.[29]

Some parents chose to educate their children at home for a few years and then return to the school system.

Several home educators submitted evidence to the Cambridge Primary Review. Some wrote to explain why they had chosen to remove their children from primary school, citing reasons such as bullying, large class sizes and lack of individual attention. All the home educators who contacted the Review felt that home educating had been a positive experience for them and for their children. Teaching children at home offered a genuinely personalised education, according to some parents, because children could explore their own interests in depth, without the constraints imposed through timetables and tests. Most found little difficulty in arranging social opportunities for their children as home education networks were available in many areas and they took part in local children's clubs and sporting activities.

The accessibility of resources through the internet and the establishment of local family networks had made home educating easier, according to our witnesses. Some suggested that the availability of these new resources, coupled with increasing concern about state education, had led to an increase in the number of home-educating families but this was impossible to confirm. It was also acknowledged that there were drawbacks to home education. Parents spoke of the financial implications as many were dependent on one income and there were additional costs for educational resources, clubs and specialist tutors. Several parents expressed concern about the increasing state involvement in home educating and they were worried that local authorities would be obliged to exert more control.

Home education clearly offers a viable alternative to school for some families. Attainment figures and outcomes measures, both in the UK[30] and internationally,[31] suggest that home education can be an effective way of learning and for many of the parents and children who contacted the Review, home-based learning was evidently a rewarding and happy experience. Home educators' experiences suggest that where children are free to choose activities, to spend extended periods of time on things that fascinate them and they have opportunities to engage in 'real world' activities, they often learn more easily and effectively.

Supplementary schools

The government estimated in 2006 that there were more than 5,000 supplementary schools nationally and these schools were run by, for example, Chinese, African Caribbean, Afghan, Somali, Jewish, Turkish and Iranian community groups.[32] According to research, supplementary schools provide support in national curriculum subjects, as well as teaching the ethnic community's first language, culture and traditions.[33] Supplementary schools operate after school and at weekends and are generally staffed by volunteers, some of whom are qualified teachers, as well as community representatives, parents and carers. A study carried out for Bristol City Council concluded that supplementary education could play an important role in raising educational achievement, as well as helping to maintain cultural traditions in ethnic communities.[34] Government support for supplementary education was reflected in the opening, in 2007, of the National Resource Centre for Supplementary Education. Sunday schools, mosque schools and other faith-based education also provide supplementary education in some areas.

Home truths

We know that supportive homes have a considerable influence on children's learning and attainment. That being so, it is pertinent to mention some of the facilities and resources that children have at home.

In the community soundings and submissions, children talked about the kinds of learning they experienced at home. They enjoyed opportunities for learning independently at home where they could follow their own interests, explore things that they found fascinating and be creative. Television could be a source of ideas. Children described how they used ICT for gathering information and for playing games. While home offered quiet space for reading or creative writing for some children, in more crowded households it was difficult to find suitable places for homework. The submission from the charity Shelter argued that children living in overcrowded, substandard accommodation were seriously disadvantaged. One London head teacher advocated loans to enable deprived children to have computers and other ICT equipment at home. However, researchers Clare Pollock and Leon Straker made the point that it is not only availability of ICT equipment in the home that matters but also how the family as a whole understands and makes use of these facilities.[35]

Field trips

Many submissions commented on the importance of providing children with educational experiences that take them out of their everyday environments. Field trips, for example, gave valuable opportunities for children to discover museums, galleries, nature reserves, historical buildings, theatres and concert halls, as well as more unusual venues such as factories, famous football grounds and design studios. Children said that they would like more field trips – a clear indication that they valued these events.

There was concern that school trips had been cut back in response to worries about children's safety and schools' fears regarding legal action following accidents. The government published the *Learning Outside the Classroom* manifesto in 2006 to reassure teachers of its support for out-of-school learning.[36]

The 'forest school' idea also featured in submissions to the Review. Children at one school taking part in the community soundings talked about their own forest school and their enthusiasm for these first-hand experiences of learning about nature. Forest schools, which originated in Scandinavia in the early 20th century, aim to develop children's and adults' awareness and understanding of the natural environment. Teachers and teaching assistants were trained as accredited forest school leaders by the Forest Education Initiative, a partnership of eight government, community and commercial organisations.

EDUCATIONAL RESOURCES AND MATERIALS

Educational resources and materials have expanded beyond a level that would have seemed incredible even 20 years ago. In 1967, a child writing in Edward Blishen's book, The School that I'd Like ... fantasised about having a box on their desk that would allow them to communicate with others around the world. By 2008, the dream was a reality. The interactive whiteboard, colour printers, digital video, plasma screens and many other technological wonders opened up new possibilities for teaching and learning. However, although the whiteboard rapidly became a more common feature of the classroom than its traditional counterpart, books, pencils and other traditional resources remained familiar features in primary classrooms. Three types of educational resources featured strongly in the Review's evidence: books, ICT and specialist resources.

Expenditure on books and other printed materials increased between 2002–3 and 2007–8 by 8.6 per cent in primary schools, each school spending on average £4,140 on printed resources in 2007.[37] According to the government agency, Becta, in 2007 primary schools had, on average, one computer to every 6.6 pupils and these figures were similar to those published in 2005. However spending on computer software decreased by 9.3 per cent between 2006 and 2007.[38,39]

Books

In spite of rapid developments in educational technology, books continued to be the main resources used in primary classrooms. Children's submissions indicated that they enjoyed books and, as we saw earlier, the school library was often a cherished space. However, there were indications that books faced competition with other resources, particularly ICT, in schools' budget decisions. Steve Hurd and colleagues calculated in 2006[40] that spending on books in primary schools was little more than £16 per pupil per year though more recent data from Ofsted suggested that this had risen slightly to an annual £20 per pupil. The National Union of Teachers felt that spending on books was inadequate: they were often out-of-date or worn; children had to share textbooks and, in some cases, parents had to buy essential books. The UK Literacy Association's submission argued that the question was not simply one of buying more books but of providing a rich and diverse range of texts, both printed and digital.

The National Literacy Trust argued that it is also important to build on children's reading interests and experiences outside school. The trust's submission cited evidence from its Reading Connects survey in 2005 that children read a wide range of texts outside schools including magazines, websites and text messages, and that schools should examine their materials to ensure they cater for children's interests. The trust went on to say that its evidence offered ideas for motivating reluctant readers:

> This [evidence] is important in the light of Ofsted's finding in Reading for Purpose and Pleasure (2004) that schools rarely build on pupils' own reading interests as a starting point to further their reading in school and improve their motivation. Most additional support was focused on raising attainment, but did not address improving the attitudes of reluctant readers. The survey therefore suggests that schools examine the materials they provide in order to guarantee that children's interests and choice of reading materials are reflected in the reading opportunities in school. Children's reading for enjoyment could also be increased if teachers or support staff (particularly any who are involved with school libraries) were able to receive more training in knowledge of children's literature.

Given that complaints about resourcing for school libraries coincide with concern about declining levels of use of many public libraries, one of the many lessons from Finland is the extent to which the latter are used by schools. The 2003 comparative study of the education of six-year-olds in England, Denmark and Finland noted that the relatively modest collections of books within school settings 'must be set in the context of the more extensive and extensively used municipal libraries outside them.'[41] The Ofsted team visited thriving public libraries to which children from local schools made weekly visits and which were real communal focal points, bringing together in an attractive setting not just children, books and other media but also – and of considerable importance socially – different generations.

Computers

From its first appearance in primary classrooms in the early 1980s, the computer's potential as a tool for learning was obvious and information and communication technology now embraces a vast array of resources. It is important to note that the role of ICT in schools extends beyond classroom learning applications and, as its name suggests, it is about both information and communication. In information gathering, data storage and analysis, computers provide efficient means of record-keeping and data processing for monitoring and assessment. In communication, information technologies allow opportunities to explore the world. In some cases, the school website has become a shop window, advertising services to prospective parents; a display case for children's work and a noticeboard, displaying information for parents and the local community. Yet, in spite of ICT opening up so many hitherto undreamt-of possibilities, there are many questions about the use of these innovations in classrooms and homes.

Our evidence suggests that most teachers and pupils were enthusiastic about using ICT in the classroom: for example, teachers in the Review's community soundings thought that ICT and interactive whiteboards captured children's imagination. However, they were concerned that there was not enough training in the use of new technologies and they were sometimes bewildered by the choice of equipment and pace of change. The General Teaching Council for England argued in its submission:

For sustainable and effective innovation to take place primary teachers need greater engagement with the learning potential of ICT in education. New pedagogies need to develop in line with new technologies and teachers need structured supported opportunities to enquire into effective and creative use of these technologies for learning, and to develop their teaching practice accordingly. Alongside introducing standards for common software, tools and services, expansion in ICT for schools should also be supported by the provision of framework agreements in which practising teachers can acquire broadband access and appropriate equipment where they need it – in the school and in the home.

Many submissions called for more ICT in classrooms. The National Advisers and Inspectors Group for Science pointed out that the amount of computer hardware available varied from school to school and that not every classroom had an interactive whiteboard. Local authority submissions placed a high priority on the development of ICT.

Requests for more ICT hardware appeared frequently in children's comments, too. One Year 6 boy explained: 'If every child had a laptop or interactive pad, then children could do more of their own research – when we find things out for ourselves we learn more.' Another boy saw ICT as a way of linking work at home and school: 'If you're doing your homework you could just put it on a memory stick and bring it into school.'

Some submissions looked ahead. Futurelab included ideas about using new technologies to allow children to learn anywhere, at any time:

Developments in mobile technologies can change the ways in which we access information. Increasingly, they are becoming networked and have greater capacity and functionality than ever before. Greater portability and also personal ownership of mobile devices increase the likelihood of learning being able to take place in a range of spaces, with more opportunities to access, capture, manipulate and publish information in these locations. Mobile devices not only allow us to learn in more varied locations, they also enable the transformation of learning experiences to become more inspiring, dynamic, relevant and creative activities. Commercial technology such as GPS, for example, is already increasing the potential for such learning. If the system knows where the user (or learner) is, it can deliver information directly to them.

In its contribution to the Rose Review, Becta envisaged that personalisation would become an important facet of ICT in the classroom:

Technology makes greater personalisation of learning possible. When pupils work online, and their work is assessed and managed online, it is possible for each learner in a class to experience his or her own personal route to learning success. Teachers can have immediate access to rich information on each learner's progress, and can potentially direct each learner to the appropriate materials to support his or her learning journey. Some learners, in some contexts, need their learning to be carefully paced. Others will want to go faster. Less secure learners may wish to practise and revisit skills and knowledge quite often. It can be practically and emotionally easier for a young learner to take risks and make mistakes when they are working online, with technology, than when they are working on paper and face to face with the teacher. Personalisation is also useful in helping the educator and the institution to address the needs of a wider range of learners, including those from different ethnic and social backgrounds, or with different personal and special needs. Use of technology as a tool for personalisation is not yet fully developed in education in this country. Developing more sophisticated personalisation will require considerable development of resources and increasing sophistication of learning platforms and content management systems, as well as support and professional development for teachers to extend the range of pedagogical approaches.[42]

Although many felt that ICT provision was crucial, there were also words of caution. One head emphasised the need for a balanced approach: 'There is a need to resist the notion that primary education can ever be restricted to online learning. It is essential that young children learn to socialise, work within teams and develop personal skills.' Others shared this concern about younger learners' use of ICT: it was widely argued that children spent too much time in front of screens and that ICT should not displace more 'hands-on' learning. Schools have a responsibility for teaching children how to make selective and critical use of material accessed through new technologies, according to some submissions. In a published submission to the review, Terry Freedman called for a stronger focus on developing children's 'digital literacy':

> Digital literacy should not be seen only in defensive terms. A digitally-literate person will be able to express herself by creating a presentation, a podcast or a video. She will be able to validate data before putting it into a model, and then verify the results of the modelling process in terms of the accuracy and plausibility of the data. A digitally-literate person will be able to use software applications in elegant and efficient ways, and even perhaps in ways that could not have been foreseen by the program's creators.[43]

Home use of ICT raised concerns about access to social networking sites, their child protection implications, and fears about access to inappropriate 'adult' material. These matters were addressed in the Bryon Review for the DCSF which made recommendations for ensuring 'e-safety' including that it becomes part of the curriculum and is a training priority for new and existing teachers.[44]

It is not only pupils who can benefit from e-networking. Teachers' use of e-forums to discuss ideas with other practitioners featured in the submissions while responses to the Review's website indicated that some teachers were keen to access up-to-date research evidence. The national soundings of organisations also drew attention to the use of ICT as a way of connecting schools in 'e-networks', although it was argued that this should not replace face-to-face networking.

The importance of ICT as a means of monitoring children's progress was highlighted in submissions from some organisations. A Becta report on schools removed from special measures, concluded that their increasing use of ICT played a crucial role in helping them monitor pupils' attainment, attendance and progress more effectively.[45]

In our proposals on the curriculum in Chapter 14, we recognise the pervasive and important role of ICT and the need for schools to help children to explore and master its possibilities. But we also argue for a balanced and critical approach, noting warnings from neuroscientists about the cognitive and social risks of over-exposure, and criticising the glib and indeed dangerous claim that ICT has made books and even knowledge redundant. That is why we place ICT within the domain of language, oracy and literacy, so that its informational and communicative possibilities can be placed in their wider context, and its uses can be explored comparatively rather than in isolation.

Specialist resources

The availability of specialist resources raised concerns in several submissions. The National Network of Science Learning Centres (SLC) noted inadequacies in primary schools' provision for science:

> In our work with science co-ordinators in the SLC network we are often dismayed by the low levels of funding that are available in schools for science resources. Many schools allocate less than a few hundred pounds annually to science, insufficient even to replace consumables such as batteries.

Storage and access to specialist resources were also problematic in many schools. As one organisation pointed out: 'Specialist resources for science, art, music, mathematics, etc., may be distributed around the school – impossible to access quickly or sometimes even find.' Resources for children with special educational needs were cited as another area that requires further investment and one local authority called for extra funding to buy, for example, multi-sensory equipment for pupils with specific learning difficulties.

IMPROVING SPACES AND RESOURCES FOR LEARNING

The Review's evidence highlighted three possible approaches to improving school buildings, playgrounds and resources for learning:

- users should be involved in design
- design should support teaching and learning
- schools should be more sustainable

Be user friendly

The Review's research survey on workforce management and reform by Hilary Burgess argues that school buildings should be designed interactively, with designers working with the people who use them and have an interest in what goes on in them. In particular, school designers need to know more about how children learn and develop across the primary years: research evidence drawn from fields such as psychology and ergonomics can provide important information for improving the 'fit' between school building design and users. It was suggested in several submissions that architects and designers should collaborate closely with educational professionals – one head teacher recommended that designers shadow primary teachers to enable them to understand the design implications of their working practices.

In their report for School Works, Barbara Annesley and colleagues suggested that:

> The process should go beyond consultation which invites stakeholders to react to pre-conceived ideas. Rather the community should be involved in the initial creative process. A process of participation of this kind does not just result in better buildings; it can act as a catalyst for change within the school. It can empower people, encourage innovation and, ultimately, contribute to improved learning for all.[46]

Kenn Fisher, an expert on the design of learning spaces, said that designing new schools, or revamping old ones, must start with a clear vision of teaching and learning shared by designers and stakeholders.[47] Hannah Jones, of the National College for School Leadership, argued that the Primary Capital Plan and Building Schools for the Future programme present an opportunity 'to completely rethink their educational provision and learning environments. At school level the first and most important question to ask is 'what sort of learners would we like? It's a question to share as soon as possible with all staff, pupils and the local community'.[48]

Involving pupils in design can have many advantages. It can create more child-friendly, imaginative environments and establish a more participative culture in the school. Offering pupils opportunities to experience the world of design is also valuable, as in the Sorrell Foundation's Joinedupdesignforschools project.[49,50] This enabled children to work with professional designers and architects, leading not only to some innovative designs but also to some exciting learning experiences for both the children and adults involved.

Optimum Education's submission to the Review quoted head teacher Derek Wise: 'If you are serious about learning you need to redesign the school around it and added, 'Absolutely right and it has never been done before.' Many people called for school buildings and resources to reflect new styles of teaching and learning but, beyond vague suggestions about the need for 'space' and 'flexibility', there were few indications of what the optimal conditions for teaching and learning might be.

Green shoots

By 2016 all new schools should be carbon neutral while all schools should be sustainable by 2020 if government targets are achieved. Already, more than half of all primary and secondary schools in England are registered as eco-schools, according to the Department for Environment, Food and Rural Affairs. A report from the British Council for School Environments pointed to three reasons why schools should be at the forefront of sustainable development:

- socially, so that they can be a major asset, not just in the education they provide, but as a wider resource for the community and an example of sustainability principles and practices in action
- economically, in being long-lasting assets which can both add value directly and indirectly; and which as buildings are easy to use and to adapt, and affordable to operate and maintain
- environmentally, not just by minimising the adverse impacts of their construction and operation, but in taking positive steps to improve the environment locally, nationally and globally.[51]

'Green' primary schools already exist, of course – schools where sustainability has become part of the ethos, influencing activities often undertaken in partnership with the local community. Eastchurch primary school, on the Isle of Sheppey in Kent, is one. It has installed solar panels and children monitor energy and water usage as well as producing energy-saving leaflets for local households. The school's success has won it two major awards, including £30,000 from The Green Fund, sponsored by EDF, to pay for four wind turbines.

SCHOOLS AS COMMUNITIES

The learning environment is not just shaped by physical buildings and resources, but also by social factors. The physical and social are interwoven: physical conditions constrain, shape and support the activities within them and, more subtly, they influence people's attitudes and feelings. Conversely, actions and purposes determine how spaces and facilities are used and adapted: teachers adjust classroom layouts to suit particular teaching purposes and make decisions about what happens where, and when. This section explores schools as communities, investigating the relationships, rules and routines which create particular cultures for learning. It focuses on the notion of school ethos and the question of how schools as communities create and convey values, beliefs and purposes. And it goes beyond the gate to examine the relationships between schools and their communities. Then we add the final dimension to our exploration of the world of primary schools by focusing on the issue of time.

The invisible influence of ethos

School ethos can be described as a set of values that shapes a school's day-to-day life and culture. Although it may lack the quantifiable substance demanded by those seeking measurable indicators, ethos is recognised as exerting a profound influence on many aspects of school life, including relationships between teachers, pupils and parents, and pupils' attitudes and behaviour. Governors often influence a school's ethos and their membership is determined by its status as either a maintained school (foundation or community) or as a faith school whose governors include representatives of a particular faith or denomination (see Tables 18.2 and 18.3).

Ordered, calm and positive

Submissions to the Review frequently referred to the importance of school ethos in significantly influencing the quality of schools. Parents looked for a positive ethos when selecting a school, though how they judged this was not often spelt out. Although schools often declare

Table 18.2 Maintained primary schools: number of schools by their status and religious character in 2007

	Community	Voluntary Aided	Voluntary Controlled	Foundation	Total
Total	10,726	3,731	2,542	362	17,361
No religious character	10,726	15	43	322	11,106
Church of England	0	1,956	2,446	39	4,441
Roman Catholic	0	1,696	0	0	1,696
Methodist	0	2	24	0	26
Other Christian*	0	28	29	1	58
Jewish	0	28	0	0	28
Muslim	0	4	0	0	4
Sikh	0	1	0	0	1
Other	0	1	0	0	1

* includes schools of mixed denomination or other Christian beliefs.
Source: School Census and Edubase, January 2007.

Table 18.3 Maintained primary schools: number (headcount) of pupils by the status and religious character of their school in 2007

	Community	Voluntary Aided	Voluntary Controlled	Foundation	Total
Total	2,799,440	785,840	414,130	108,270	4,107,680
No religious character	2,799,440	2,470	8,400	99,210	2,909,510
Church of England	0	361,960	396,520	8,840	767,320
Roman Catholic	0	404,350	0	0	404,350
Methodist	0	420	4,070	0	4,490
Other Christian*	0	6,180	5,130	220	11,540
Jewish	0	8,690	0	0	8,690
Muslim	0	1,150	0	0	1,150
Sikh	0	300	0	0	300
Other	0	330	0	0	330

* includes schools of mixed denomination or other Christian beliefs.
Source: School Census and Edubase, January 2007.

their aims in carefully positioned posters in the entrance hall, these statements are not necessarily a true reflection of ethos. However, the system of rules and codes for behaviour was something that parents, in particular, regarded as important in both conveying and shaping ethos. According to some submissions, a good school was one where standards of discipline maintained an atmosphere of order and calm. Similarly, witnesses in the community soundings repeatedly called for clear systems of rules that are fair and consistently applied. Some also felt that teachers were not authoritative enough and were no longer able to instil respect and establish discipline.

Community spirit

One of the most frequent comments on ethos in the submissions evidence was that schools should engender a strong sense of community. The Association of RE Inspectors, Advisers and Consultants argued that: 'A shared, articulated ethos which underpins the life of the school and which is "lived" by all the members of its community is at the heart of good primary education.' This view of shared community was echoed by parents at one junior school:

Once children feel confident in their environment and share a sense of belonging and ownership of the school structure and ethos, they make much better 'learners'. There is a very positive feeling of citizenship and good discipline, observable in the playground through lining up, during assembly and in attitudes towards staff and adults.

As well as embodying a sense of community, it was often suggested that school ethos should embrace the *Every Child Matters* philosophy. One head teacher argued that schools need to devote more time to making personal contact with children to ensure that they feel welcomed and valued as individuals. Children taking part in the Review's community soundings said that a good school is one where people 'care for each other' and make you feel part of a community. Children also described how listening to each other helps to create a positive environment for learning and they liked to hear 'what's on other people's minds'. Having opportunities to express their views and having those views taken seriously was also seen as contributing to a good school ethos.

Although specifically discussing children with special educational needs, Harry Daniels' and Jill Porter's argument that schools should establish an 'ethos of provision where learners have the security and self-esteem to reflect on their relative strengths and difficulties in a process of self-determination'[52] applies equally to other pupils and to primary schools in general. One teacher felt that ethos can help children to appreciate their responsibilities as members of a community:

> ... the primary school is a community where children learn to act as responsible citizens. They recognise their place within the group, class, school and wider community. Children are provided with freedom to make choices and the responsibility to build up the community. This happens through class and school councils and in many less formal ways. Community is at the heart of the learning that takes places formally and informally in a primary school.

Some submissions regarded school ethos as crucial in shaping children's moral development and saw a key role for schools in combating intolerance through positive messages and behaviour models. The need to respect individual differences was also highlighted in many submissions. One institution called for primary schools to celebrate diversity through encouraging an ethos of tolerance – promoting, for example, the equality of lesbian, gay, bisexual and transgender people as part of a broader whole-school ethos that challenges inequities of all kinds.

At odds over faith

Witnesses to the Review were sharply divided regarding the place of religious codes and values in education. Some community representatives expressed their concern that the ethos of some schools reflected society's aims, seeking 'success at all costs' and relegating faith to the background. However, those who thought that state education should not promote particular belief systems argued that it was important for schools to create an atmosphere where different world views, values and ideas are embraced. In its submission, the Universities' Council for the Education of Teachers suggested that primary schools should adopt an approach which recognises that England is a multi-ethnic society:

> We must continue to recognise and celebrate our rich cultural diversity, taking culture, ethnicity and heritage as starting points for learning in school and classroom ... However, within the context of cultural diversity we must not lose sight of the values that affirm our membership of a broad and coherent community. It is in the primary school that we must begin to reinforce the values of a cohesive, tolerant, just, and inclusive community. These values should be the focus of study and exploration as part of the primary school's formal curriculum and should be implicitly asserted by every primary school's whole mode of operation.

Submissions from parents reflected the wider dichotomy in views of faith schools, with some staunchly opposed to the existence of such schools on the grounds that they could be divisive, while others felt equally strongly that faith schools were necessary foundations for children's spiritual and moral development. Some parents sought places at the local faith school because it had a good reputation or simply because faith was respected, even if it was not their faith. Some parents, however, had little option:

> Personally I couldn't get my son into a non-faith primary unless I wanted to bus him half way across the county. So, even though that is what I would have preferred, he attended a C. of E. primary. Many teachers 'have faith' of some sort. That's OK by me. Teaching seems to be a 'lay vocation' for many Christians. But institutionalised faith? I'd prefer not.

From classroom to community

Several local authority submissions proposed that primary schools should equip children to become future members of their communities. Academics at one higher education institution took the argument a step further in proposing that education should provide 'the skills to build strong communities in which optimism is able to flourish, relationships are strengthened and regeneration can take place'.

The Review's community soundings suggested that in many areas primary schools had established positive relationships with their communities, including those in areas with a very diverse cultural mix. Community witnesses were impressed with schools' achievements in fostering both common goals and a respect for difference. However, at one sounding, police and other community representatives portrayed their city as being physically divided along ethnic lines, and were deeply concerned about cohesion and relationships across this ethnic split. Some witnesses at this sounding spoke of a climate of growing fear and suspicion. Yet, somehow, primary schools themselves were felt to be steering a sensible course in a situation of considerable sensitivity, and the educational values and purposes commended in such circumstances were broadly similar to those we encountered elsewhere: a strong emphasis on community, mutual respect and concern, and on generic skills for learning, for employment and for life.

This theme is taken further in Chapter 14's discussion of the community dimension of the curriculum.

Rural schools

In rural areas, the Review found rather different concerns regarding schools and their communities. Rural schools were often part of local clusters providing support and sharing resources, including staff. However, recent policies, such as *Every Child Matters*, posed new challenges for small schools said to be lacking adequate local infrastructure and support to implement the policies. Clustering could also bring its own problems, according to head teacher witnesses. Educationally, the closest school may not be the most appropriate one with which to work, while the most compatible school may be too far away. Heads were sometimes wary of enforced, rather than voluntary, clustering or federating – village schools tend to be genuinely community schools and the relationship between the two may be tight, subtle, complex and long-standing. Competition between schools, promoted directly or indirectly by aspects of government policy, also served to undermine efforts to encourage co-operation through networking and federations.

The community soundings reminded us that smaller primary schools, and the rural communities which most serve, face their own challenges. It is important to note that these are not minority issues – 44 per cent of England's primary schools had fewer than 200 pupils and nearly 15 per cent fewer than 100 (see Chapter 19).

Worldly wise

Many submissions expressed the view that schools should look outwards, beyond the boundaries of local and national interests, to teach children about global concerns and foster greater understanding of the world as a global community. Children's submissions suggested that they wanted to know more about global issues, such as climate change, and many were also curious about other countries and cultures. Some parents and practitioners felt that schools must recognise and respond to the increasingly globalised culture that children encountered, either through the media or as a consequence of international migration. One local authority suggested that schools should encourage children to see themselves as global citizens and to feel that they can help solve world problems. UKOWLA, the charity that promotes global community links, made the case in its submission for primary schools to link with international partner schools. It argued that:

> It is essential that children at primary level understand the global context in which they are living and the many different social, economic and faith environments in which their contemporaries are living and/or from which they have come.

In its submission, the Development Education Association recommended that schools should adopt individual approaches in responding to globalism:

> A more explicit focus on the global dimension can lead to a deeper understanding of the school as a community and the school in the community when localities are seen as meeting points for global interaction as described by expressions such as 'the world in our neighbourhood' and 'the global in the local'. The way that schools respond to this cannot be prescribed nationally.

TIME

What primary schools are and what they do reflects the communities and society of which they are part. This chapter has looked so far at schools as physical spaces and social places but there is another dimension – time. We begin with the school year.

The school year

In 2008, the school year comprised a minimum of 190 teaching days and ran from August or September to July. In 2004 the Local Government Association and the teacher union NASUWT established a set of principles for agreeing standardised school terms. Under these principles the school year was divided into six terms of approximately equal length and, in some years, Easter did not fall in the school holidays. According to the LGA, 63 per cent of the 125 local authorities in England had adopted the six-term system by 2008.

A flexible, virtual calendar

Some submissions called for a re-thinking of the way schools operate to allow for more flexible access to learning. Some thought that in the future learning would no longer be tied to a particular place or time. Round-the-clock and year-round access to learning was commended in some organisations' submissions. One head teacher argued: 'As a resource schools must explore ways to become "on demand".' One way might be to work on the concept of virtual schooling, so that pupils can work across many spaces and locations and at times that best suit their learning clock.' Thursday's Child, a report by the Institute for Public Policy Research, recommended a revision of the school year:

We inherited the long summer holiday from a time when the school year was structured around the agrarian summer picking season. There are currently strong arguments for rethinking the structure of the school year. Some groups of young people are spending more time than ever before unsupervised, especially those from disadvantaged backgrounds yet we now have an increased understanding of the greater structure and provision children and young people need in their spare time. A long summer holiday can be an impediment to children's learning, again particularly for children from lower socio-economic backgrounds [...]. We should move towards a nationally set, standard school year for all publicly funded schools with a more even spread of time in school throughout the school year.[53]

Perhaps unsurprisingly, some children said that they wanted longer, or more frequent, holidays. In one community sounding session, children said they disliked the fact that their older siblings, who were at local secondary schools, had different holidays. Some local authorities had consulted parents, teachers and employers about changing school terms and holidays. Their survey findings generally indicated that parents were mainly concerned about the impact of these changes on their work and childcare arrangements. Local employers felt that a more co-ordinated system of school holidays could potentially mean staff shortages as all their employees would request the same weeks off. Some teachers taking part in the survey thought that children's learning could be adversely affected by longer holidays and saw some benefits in having shorter but more frequent breaks in the school term.

The school day

In England, the length and structure of the primary-school day was often determined by social and economic needs – and these influences were still apparent in 2008 with most state schools deciding on their timings based on local needs. In 1990, government guidelines, which gave responsibility for timings to governors, divided the day into two sessions 'separated by a break in the middle of the day unless exceptional circumstances make this undesirable'.[54] However, it was up to individual schools to decide whether they preferred a longer morning session with a short afternoon session but a break in the middle of the day was the expected norm. Each morning and afternoon session must allow enough lesson time to cover the statutory curriculum and religious education and the following timings were suggested:

Suggested minimum weekly lesson times:[55]

Age	Lesson hours
5–7	21 hours
8–11	23.5 hours

Under the government's 'power to innovate' scheme, schools could be exempted from certain legislation, including regulations on the timing of the school day.[56] A few primary schools have successfully applied for 'power to innovate' status, allowing them to adjust timings to provide enrichment sessions for pupils. Grinling Gibbons primary school in Southwark, London, for example, switched to an 8.30am start and 2.30pm close, liberating the period from 2.30 to 3.30pm for optional clubs and activities, including learning languages and creative arts. In 2005, the introduction of the extended schools programme encouraged all primary schools to offer childcare from 8am to 6pm, meaning that some children could spend up to 10 hours a day in school.

The long and short of it

Several submissions noted that extended schools and other initiatives encouraged parents to leave their children in school for longer periods of time, potentially contributing to the 'scholarisation' of childhood commented on in Chapter 5. One education consultant's submission argued:

There are too many mixed messages from government ministers concerning the provision for children. On the one hand, the primacy of family life and the contribution that parents have as the child's first educators is stressed, whilst on the other, there is an enthusiasm for extended services that encourage parents to spend less time with their children. A more cohesive approach is needed.

However, some saw extended schools as an 'experimental arm', offering teachers time and space to find out what excites and motivates individual children in an informal, relaxed setting. Researcher Anna Craft pointed out that there had been little investigation into the transition from the formal part of the day to the more informal learning offered in extended schools. Other submissions warned that extended provision for children with special educational needs had been overlooked. The British Association of Teachers of the Deaf suggested that extended schools could offer a valuable resource for developing deaf children's thinking skills but this required funding for resources, specialist training for staff and, in some cases, transport for pupils.

In spite of the extended schools programme and the availability of breakfast and after-school clubs in many areas, some parents' submissions referred to difficulties in coping with staggered or irregular school start and finishing times. One local authority submission argued that children and parents or carers need to be given a greater say in considering the length and structure of the school day. Encouraging parental involvement also required re-thinking of access to schools. One teacher-training institution argued that: 'Parents need to be made more welcome into settings and not restricted by gates, times and culture.' According to another submission, schools should also think carefully about the routines and rituals of the school day and the impact of these on relationships and children's autonomy and self-esteem. Autonomy was also a theme in children's comments: they liked 'golden time' or 'privilege time' where they had a 'free' choice of activities and materials.

CONCLUSION

Although this chapter has looked at each dimension separately, the physical and social contexts of primary schools and the resources provided within them are woven together in the fabric of primary education. In combination they reflect and shape the conditions of learning that children experience. As we think of the future, we must look more closely at schools as spaces and as communities of learning and ensure that they can adapt to the challenges of 21st century teaching and learning. Investment in the infrastructure of primary schools is essential – investment not only of money but also of time, thought, debate and research. Attention should focus not only on what happens within the school walls but outdoors, too: ensuring that children have access to outside areas that stimulate physical activity and imaginative play. We must consider how primary schools are accommodating the demands of the extended schools programme and lifelong learning as education moves beyond the boundaries of the traditional school day and school career. The evidence presented in this chapter indicates that involving children, teachers, parents and communities in the design and operation of schools is a fundamental step in this important task of creating better schools.

Moreover, the task of improving schools also requires us to consider how schools function as communities, both within their own walls and as part of the local and global communities they serve. The development of citizenship education and the movement for children's voices and children's participation represent positive steps but our evidence suggests that there is still a long way to go in re-conceptualising the school as a collaborative, inclusive community for learning. As our proposals on the aims of primary education (see Chapter 12) emphasise, there is a need for children to experience and engage with the culture and life of their community, to develop meaningful relationships with others, and to participate as active members of the local and the global community.

At the beginning of the 20th century, even in the most deprived inner-city areas, local elementary schools stood out among the rows of terraced houses as resounding statements of their local community's civic pride and faith in the value of education. At the beginning of the 21st century, new primary schools are often elusive. Some are hidden away on suburban estates or tucked into a corner of a secondary school playing field, and housed in featureless blocks fronted with aprons of car park. In villages, the local school may have vanished altogether. We need to ask ourselves if these changes should be seen as progress or whether they are, in effect, isolating communities and children, to the detriment of both. If we believe the latter to be the case, then the Primary Capital Plan offers an opportunity to remedy this situation and to create schools that embody the principle that every child and community matters. If, that is, the Primary Capital Plan survives the recession.

NOTES

1 Annesley *et al.* (2002): 1.
2 Wall *et al.* (2010), *The Cambridge Primary Review Research Surveys*, Chapter 22.
3 Seaborne (1971).
4 Bennett *et al.* (1980).
5 DCSF (2007i).
6 Source of figures: DES (1965).
7 DCSF (2008z).
8 For readers from outside England, the primary-phase pupil classification is as follows: reception (R) ages 4–5, Year 1 (Y1) ages 5–6, Y2 ages 6–7, Y3 ages 7–8, Y4 ages 8–9, Y5 ages 9–10, Y6 ages 10–11. R is within the Early Years Foundation Stage, while the applicable key stages are KS1 (Y1–2) and KS2 (Y3–6).
9 DfES (2007a).
10 DfES (2006b): 4–5.
11 http://www.teachernet.gov.uk/management/resourcesfinanceandbuilding/bsf/
12 DCSF (2008ac).
13 House of Commons (2007): 28.
14 DfES (2002a): 2.
15 Wall *et al.* (2010), *The Cambridge Primary Review Research Surveys*, Chapter 22.
16 Dudek (2006).
17 Alexander (2001a).
18 Ofsted (2006c).
19 Rothermel (2004).
20 Meighan (1997).
21 Rothermel (2004).
22 *The Times*, 20 January 2009.
23 Great Britain (1996).
24 http://www.direct.gov.uk/en/Parents/Schoolslearninganddevelopment/ChoosingASchool/DG_4016124 [accessed 13 March 2009].
25 DCSF (2007c): 12.
26 Kendall and Atkinson (2006).
27 NFER (2007).
28 Education Otherwise (2009): 1.
29 Thomas, 1998, cited in Thomas and Pattison (2008): 2.
30 Rothermel (2004) *op cit.*; Thomas and Pattison (2008).
31 Rudner (1998).
32 DfES (2006c).
33 Minty *et al.* (2008).
34 Bristol City Council (2005).
35 Pollock and Straker (2008): 786.
36 DfES (2006b).
37 Figures from NERP/EPC (2007).
38 Becta (2007).
39 BESA (2007).
40 Hurd *et al.* (2006): 78.
41 Ofsted (2003a): para 98, and additional information from the team involved in this study.
42 Becta (2009): 19.
43 Freedman (2009).
44 DCSF (2008b).
45 Hollingworth *et al.* (2008): 32.
46 Annesley, Horne and Cottam (2002).
47 Vision (2008): 3.
48 Vision (2008): 3.
49 Sorrell and Sorrell (2005).

50 http://www.thesorrellfoundation.com/judfs.html
51 Bunn (2006).
52 Daniels and Porter (2010), *The Cambridge Primary Review Research Surveys*, Chapter 9.
53 Sodha and Margo (2008): 14.
54 DES (1990): 2.
55 DES (1990): 6.
56 Through the Power to Innovate, the Secretary of State for the Department for Children, Schools and Families (DCSF) is able, temporarily, to suspend or modify education legislation that may be holding back, or even stopping, innovative approaches to raising standards (DCSF 2008m).

Part 4
The system of primary education

19 Structures and transitions

The structures, stages and transitions of England's primary-school system – some contentious, some taken for granted – exert an influence on the child's education which in some cases may be as powerful as the curriculum. It is therefore important that we examine their strengths and weaknesses in order to be able to ponder the possibility of more effective alternatives.

Many questions arise with regard to the landmark stages of primary schooling. The crucial one of when it should start is tackled in Chapter 11 but there is also the question of when it should end. Is there an optimum age at which children should transfer to secondary school? And what of the key stage divisions – perpetuating historical divides between infants, juniors and seniors, do they promote or impede contemporary continuity of learning? How smoothly, for example, do very young children move from pre-school into reception and on into key stage 1? How do they fare in the transitions between key stages 1 and 2 and from KS2 to secondary school?

Also important are questions concerning how children are grouped within these phases. Is there, for example, an ideal size for a school and for classes within a school? How should those classes be organised? Are mixed-age preferable to single-age classes? Is the recent extension of setting pupils by ability to be welcomed or are the majority of teachers correct in preferring mixed-ability classes? Many of these questions provoke emotional responses – small schools, small classes, and mixed-ability teaching, for example, all have passionate supporters. But are they right?

STAGES AND TRANSITIONS

Young changelings

In 2008, five-year-olds in England, unlike most of their European peers, adapted to new places and faces three times in their journey from home through pre-school and reception and into the formal schooling of Year 1. As they progressed through the year groups, they also travelled through three official phases – from foundation to key stage 1 to key stage 2. Some also changed schools, from infant to junior or from first to middle, but the majority moved on at age 11, with the rite of passage represented by transfer to secondary school. By contrast, children in Sweden, Finland and Russia attended the same school from age seven through to 15 or 16 and usually had the same teacher for the first few years.

Of England's 17,361 primary schools, 12,845 took children from ages four/five to 11. This model was in the ascendancy, but the others still accounted for more than 4,500 schools. In 2007, there were 1,115 first schools, 1,705 infant schools, 1,542 junior schools, 68 combined first and middle schools, and 86 middle schools (ages nine to 12).[1] All varieties could exist in one authority. Consider, for example, Suffolk. In 2008, alongside its all-through schools, it had schools for five to seven-year-olds, for five to nine-year-olds, for seven to 11-year-olds, for nine to 12-year-olds, and for nine to 13-year-olds.[2]

Key stages locked in the past

Such an assortment of ages, stages and transitions resulted from decades of often conflicting influences on education. Political, religious and economic pressures shaped the school system, frequently reflecting social prejudices and local demography as much as educational theory. The apparent recency of key stage 1 conceals deep roots. The Elementary Education Act of 1870 formalised a distinct phase for five to seven-year-olds. Infants were taught separately and were also exempt from the 'payment by results' system that qualified schools for grants depending on how many children passed inspectors' tests. The Act was following the practice, if not always the developmental spirit, of Robert Owen's pioneering New Lanark school which opened in 1816 and aimed to ameliorate the effects of poverty on the children of cotton-mill workers. Catering for three to seven-year-olds, it was much concerned with children's health and moral welfare and was wary of 'overburdening' young minds. Another pioneer, David Stow, opened his own infant school in Drygate, Glasgow, in 1828. Victorian educational thinking was heavily influenced by Stow's division of pupils by age. Two to three-year-olds enrolled in an 'initiatory' department, moving on at age six into the juvenile department which was sub-divided into juniors (six to 12-year-olds) and seniors (12 to 14-year-olds). Although not widely adopted at the time, the pattern of infant, junior and senior had become the norm by the 1930s when the Hadow committee was producing its reports.

Similarly, key stage 2 had its origins in the 1926 decision of the Hadow committee to make 11 the age at which elementary pupils moved from junior into senior school. Eleven was chosen because it was the minimum school-leaving age at the time, and the committee considered it coincided with adolescence. In selecting 11, they created another divide that, according to Plowden, became 'as firmly fixed in Englishmen's minds as 1066'.[3]

A middle way

The traditional infant and junior ages were challenged in the 1960s when Alec Clegg, the innovative chief education officer of West Riding, suggested infant schools take children up to age nine and middle schools up to 13. While one motive was financial, there were also educational arguments including the belief that middle schools offered young adolescents better support than large secondaries, an argument which re-surfaced in evidence to the Cambridge Primary Review. Plowden, a supporter of three tiers, chose to make the breaks at ages eight and 12. Three years at infant school would, the report said, allow children and teachers to 'work steadily and without anxiety'. And with middle schools freed from the 'dreaded landmark' of the 11-plus, transfer at 12 cut the risk of pupils suffering from 'premature emphasis on class instruction, adult systematisation and precision in secondary schools'.[4]

For a while, it seemed as though there might be a flourishing alternative structure to those of infant, junior and primary. For funding purposes, middle schools for eight to 12-year-olds were 'deemed' by the 1964 Education Act (which actually preceded Plowden) to be primary while those for nine to 13-year-olds were 'deemed' secondary, and inspectors reported on the quality of education in both variants in survey reports published in 1983 and 1985.[5] But these alternative ages and stages, also introduced in New Zealand and the USA, never became dominant and the arrival of the national curriculum in 1988, with its 5–7, 7–11 key stages, dealt them a possibly fatal blow. In 2007, there were 334 middle schools (transferring at both 12 and 13) compared with their peak of 1,813 in 1983, when 22 per cent of 11-year-olds were in some type of middle school.[6]

The Review's community soundings included an area with middle schools where parents and teachers were waging a strenuous campaign against the local authority's decision to change to the two-tier system. By the time the Review went to press this campaign had been lost, and the tale had been repeated elsewhere. Thus, the tide in 2008 appeared to be flowing against three tiers, and even two tiers appeared to be questioned by the government's professed desire to see a 'significant rise' in the number of all-through academies. Five opened in 2008 bringing the total to 14 with five more in development. Approval was also given for the first 'matrix' academy in Ashington, Northumberland, where three failing primaries and a secondary school will combine under one management team, though remaining on separate sites. All-through is a tried and tested model in Sweden, Finland, Russia and elsewhere and, closer to home, in the English private-school sector. However, research to support the move to all-through academies remains elusive. In 2007, the government admitted that it had not commissioned a review of the benefits or otherwise of all-through schools, saying merely that 'the small number of open all-age schools in England presents a generally positive picture'.[7] In the same year, by contrast, Ofsted applauded the performance of separate nursery and infant schools, indicating, to adapt an early mantra of New Labour, that attempts to raise standards by changing structures risks jettisoning the good as well as the not-so good.[8]

Barriers to the flow of learning?

The ages and stages of primary education vary across the world. In New Zealand, the primary years run from ages five/six through to 12/13, in France and Italy from six to 11, in Germany from six to 10 or 12, and in Sweden and Finland from six/seven through to 16. Generally, the phases of each country's curricula reflect school structure. In Sweden, for example, there is a pre-school curriculum from birth to age six/seven and a lower secondary curriculum from six/seven to 16. In England, most local authorities aim to align school structure with the key stages of the national curriculum. While the Review's research survey in this area did not find any conclusive strengths or weaknesses associated with any particular structure, it highlighted concerns that in England the historical divisions between infant, junior and adolescent education deepened after the introduction of the national curriculum.[9] The key stages risked creating a lack of continuity and flow in learning, compartmentalising early years, primary and secondary curricula and teachers – divisions accentuated by phase-related teacher training. Certainly, children's difficulties moving into and between the key stage 'compartments' were raised as significant problems in submissions to the Review from schools, local authorities and national organisations. One teacher commented that:

> The rigidity of the age bands can be a problem, especially as formal education starts so (increasingly) early. It is often the case that a child is clearly not ready for the next class or phase, especially the summer-born children ... Yet it is often difficult to hold them back or keep them in an appropriate class as this can affect the numbers in classes as required by local councils. However, mixed-age classes are often unpopular with parents.

Strict adherence to the key stage structure was cited by some local authorities as a barrier to sustaining the momentum of learning. The submission from the Association for the Study of Primary Education argued that:

> The artificial separation of primary education into two distinct phases following the foundation stage was originally brought about in order to re-classify what used to be called infants and juniors. It was also intended to bring about greater clarity in the classification of pupils in first schools as an alternative to separate infant schools. It was also fuelled by the obsession with testing children at the end of each key stage. With moves to trust teachers' own assessments more at the end of key stage 1 and the movement towards personalised learning there is now an argument in favour of blurring the edges and seeing the primary phase as one continuum; a system that provides learning approaches which reflect the increase in maturity of pupils as they move through the primary phase.

From Reception to key stage 1

Two transitions at the start of a child's school life merit urgent attention, according to the Review's community soundings and submissions. Worries about how well children transfer from pre-school to reception classes mirrored fundamental concerns about England's early starting age, dealt with in Chapter 11. However, children who have attended high-quality pre-school settings generally cope well, particularly if there are strong links between pre-school, primary school and family, concludes the Review's research survey on classes, groups and transitions by Peter Blatchford and colleagues.[10] They also report that pastoral support for children arriving in reception classes is now generally good, but the mechanisms to ensure progress in learning remain less effective.[11]

The submissions expressed fears that, once in school, some infants, particularly summer-born children and those with special needs, struggled in the transition from the early years foundation stage to the more formal teaching of key stage 1. Research evidence also indicated that parents' and children's worries about this transition had been glossed over.[12] Reception pupils interviewed in England in 2005 reported unhappiness at the loss of play and worries about workload.[13] One girl said she expected Year 1 to be 'no toys' and 'just work, work, work'. One Year 1 boy described sitting on the classroom carpet as 'wasting your life'.

As we noted in Chapter 11, this matter was taken up by the government's 2008–9 Rose review of the primary curriculum, and we commented on it both there and in our later discussion (Chapters 13 and 14) of the relationship between the EYFS and the KS1 national curriculum. However, Rose's solution – that all children should enter school the September following their fourth birthday – provoked considerable opposition from early years experts, mainly on the grounds that in terms of space, resources, training and the quality of provision many reception classes do not offer appropriate provision for such young children. This report's final chapter makes specific recommendations on this matter.

Curriculum discontinuity troubled teachers as well as pupils. While they mostly succeeded in sensitively introducing subject-based teaching, there was a tension caused by having to knit together two very distinct phases. Inspectors commented on a sense 'of provision which swung heavily and suddenly, for all pupils at the beginning of Year 1, towards literacy and mathematics'.[14] Only two of the 10 local authorities visited by Ofsted in 2007 had clear guidance for schools on managing the transition from the foundation stage to key stage 1.[15]

Schools managed the transition most effectively when it was part of 'a broader whole-school approach to achieving good curricular continuity and progression in pupils' learning,' said the inspectors. Researchers recommended that transition be regarded as a process and reception-class routines and play activities be extended into Year 1, an approach supported by the interim report of the Rose Review in 2008.[16] Parents needed more guidance and teachers needed to offer more support to summer-born pupils, those with special needs or with English as an additional language.

The importance of a smooth move into school and on into Year 1 was also indicated by research evidence suggesting that the effects of transition may be cumulative – that the legacy of a badly-managed move early on could damage children's abilities to make successful transitions throughout their school career.[17]

Set against the prevailing anxiety about foundation stage/key stage 1 transition in England, it is instructive to look abroad. After all, wherever there is pre-primary provision of some kind, transition is potentially a problem.

The Ofsted comparative study of the education of six-year-olds in England, Denmark and Finland set out to examine this issue by comparing the character of the care and education received by six-year-olds in primary schools (England) and pre-school settings (Denmark and Finland) and relating the similarities and differences in provision to the expectations of parents, teachers and governments, and to cultural values. The Ofsted report noted:

> Much more importance is attached in Finland and Denmark to the way six-year-olds develop as people, rather than what they should know and be able to do. Although literacy and numeracy and other areas of learning are important in the Danish and Finnish programmes, personal and social development, learning to learn, developing self-control, and preparation for school are given a higher priority … In England, literacy and

mathematics lessons filled most mornings ... There was a pronounced sense of curriculum pressure to squeeze in all that was required, and to achieve national, local and school-specific targets. In Denmark and Finland there was no such pressure. Here, too, the curriculum, in its important personal and social aspects at least, spilled out of the classroom into other aspects of school life, while in England it was more tightly confined to the classroom.[18]

Crucially, in the context of that concern with accountability which drives the British government's preoccupation with literacy and numeracy targets, Danish and Finnish parents were happy with their countries' approach:

> Parents in Denmark were unanimous in the belief that [the setting] was about socialisation [and] the encouragement of positive attitudes to school and to learning was a high priority ... The views of parents in Finland mirrored those in Denmark.[19]

All this also provides an important alternative perspective on the debate about literacy goals in the early years foundation stage already discussed in Chapter 11.

Learning dips in Year 3

The learning dip observed in Year 3 was also commented on in submissions to the Review and there was research evidence suggesting that the Year 2 national tests lead pupils and teachers to perceive Year 3 as less important. (An alternative view was that progress in Year 2 was artificially inflated as a result of pressure to do well in the national tests.) While research conducted in 2002 found that although head teachers recognised the importance of Year 2/Year 3 liaison and parental involvement in helping to sustain pupils' progress in Year 3 only a minority of schools were addressing these areas.[20]

For some children the transition from key stages 1 to 2 coincided with transfer from infant to junior school. Awareness of what this entailed was raised by a project involving 24 infant and junior schools in West Sussex.[21] For example, there was recognition that for some children leaving their school was akin to a bereavement, and an appreciation of the need for information about pupils to flow back to the infant school as well as forward to the junior. Despite a focus on standards, including continuous assessment records that bridged the key stages, more work on curriculum continuity was regarded as a priority.

The troublesome transfer: from primary to secondary

Some local authorities and teachers' submissions said the bumpy path between primary and secondary school had much improved and research evidence confirmed that better organisation of the personal and social aspects of induction had eased children's fears. However, many remained. Parents interviewed in the community soundings revealed anxieties that their children were too young, that their confidence would be dented and their behaviour deteriorate. Children worried about losing their friends, and their way, in this 'intimidating' change. Teachers, too, expressed concern about the stress caused to young people. The submission from Human Scale Education talked of a 'significant and damaging disjuncture between primary and secondary schools', while an argument put forward in the Review's national soundings for organisations was simply that transitions were always problematic and should be minimised.

The 'hiatus' in some pupils' academic progress after a change of school, highlighted in 1999, continued to be a serious concern, according to schools, local authorities and national organisations.[22] The consensus from the Review's research evidence and submissions was that curriculum discontinuity and variations in teaching practice tripped pupils up while they were adjusting to the new social environment of secondary school. Many started to feel the work was too easy, reflecting a failure to exploit prior learning. Communication between schools, parents and pupils still needed attention. Some primary teachers and heads said their secondary colleagues underestimated what children could do and had little interest in, or respect for, what happened in primary schools. Similarly, the 2008 interim report of the Rose Review warned that secondary schools appear to pay too little attention to reliable information on primary pupils' progress and stressed the need for greater curricular continuity.[23]

There was evidence that cross-phase units of work and more collaboration between KS2 and KS3 teachers improved continuity of learning. Other suggested solutions from the submissions included a national transition week in July, the appointment of local authority transition advisers, phased entry to secondary school, and funding for more contact between staff. Some children and one head teacher wanted primary and secondary schools to combine as all-through institutions, thus hopefully bypassing the 'intimidating' experience altogether. Other children echoed Plowden in expressing a preference for a gradual progression via middle schools which offered better resources than primaries in Years 6 and 7. However, the submission from the Association of School and College Leaders commented that middle schools also suffered a learning dip, though between Years 4 and 5, rather than in Years 7 and 8. This view is supported by evidence from the USA and New Zealand as well as England.[24]

Concentrate on communication and continuity

Communication and continuity of learning appear essential to breaking down barriers between infant, junior and secondary phases. More communication with parents eases fears and helps maintain relationships that often evaporate at secondary level. Communication with pupils is also vital as their anxieties and expectations need to be expressed. More communication between teachers of all ages and stages aids continuity of learning and less abrupt curricular and pedagogical changes, such as those occurring between reception and Year 1 and between Years 6 and 7.

Greater standardisation of the primary curriculum would help secondary teachers whose Year 7 pupils come from a variety of schools, as would standardising the quality and quantity of information passed on about a transferring pupil. Many examples of innovative and successful induction programmes could be built on, particularly those that strengthened academic links, for example, exchanging Year 6 and 7 teachers for some lessons. Cross-phase units of work also needed to encompass subjects such as PE and languages as well as literacy, numeracy and science.

School clusters and federations should aid communication and continuity. However, all-through schools, able to mix and match pupils and teachers across all ages and phases, appear to have the best chance of achieving smooth progress. Sweden's all-through schools are often held up as a model, though it is worth noting that, outside the cities, many only cater for 200 pupils. Transition is the 'biggest unsolved issue facing education', according to the former head of one of England's few all-through schools. However, he also counselled that: 'All-through isn't a one-size-fits-all solution. Each community needs to find its own solution.'[25] Arguably, all-through does not automatically eliminate the problems of transition, particularly in split-site schools such as the proposed 'matrix' academy in Ashington, and it is an expensive answer.

For some communities, the answer is the middle school, as it was for Plowden and Clegg. While three tiers entail two transfers, clearly some middle schools are confident that they are successfully bridging their divides. Learning how to manage change is as valid an answer as trying to eliminate it altogether. But middle schools, as we have already noted, are a fast-declining species.

SCHOOL SIZE

In 1965, four million children attended 20,789 English primary schools. Each had, on average, 193 pupils. By 1991 this average had risen slightly to 199. Since then the average school size has risen more steeply to 224, putting England ahead of Scotland (128 pupils), Germany (185), New Zealand (188), Sweden (217) and the Netherlands (222).[26]

School size relates in part to organisation. Plowden commended the two-form entry school as being the ideal size organisationally, educationally and communally. In 2008 this would produce, using average class sizes and adding a nursery class, a school of nearly 400 pupils. The national average of 224 reflects the dominance of one-form entry schools.

While overall pupil numbers dropped by 25,974 between 1965 and 2008, school numbers fell by 3,428. Small schools suffered the greatest – and most contentious – losses. At the time of Plowden, there were 6,272 schools with fewer than 100 pupils. In 2007, there were 2,605, a fall of more than 3,600. Numbers of schools with 301–400 pupils also fell, down by 203 since 1965. Those with between 101–200 pupils saw their numbers decrease slightly by 13. Schools with 400–600 pupils saw the most substantial rise – up by 342. The majority of primaries – more than 10,300 out of 17,361 – had 100–300 pupils. At the same time, the size of the largest primary schools increased to approximately 1,000 pupils.[27]

Questions of viability

Debates about school size continued to swirl around whether small was viable, on educational and financial grounds. Opponents argued that, like village post offices, village schools were desirable, but maybe not cost-effective. Others worried that they could not offer pupils a broad and stimulating curriculum. Plowden recommended 240 pupils as the ideal number for a first school and between 300–450 for a middle school. But, despite being a champion of separate first and middle schools, Plowden proposed that they be combined to safeguard small village schools. This option was pursued only in respect of 8–12 middle schools 'deemed primary' and by 1981 there were 388 combined 5–12 schools in 26 local authorities.[28]

Recognition of fierce local commitment to village schools persuaded the government to announce its 'presumption against closure' in 1998. Despite this, small schools remained vulnerable. Pressures on local authorities to cut surplus places at a time of falling rolls and in difficult economic circumstances provoked battles with rural communities in, for example, Shropshire and the Isle of Wight. In 2008, Herefordshire withdrew proposals to shut or merge 37 small schools, citing concern about damaging rural communities, as well as the cost and environmental impact of transporting pupils to alternative schools. Also in 2008 the Scottish government launched a consultation on how best to protect its rural schools, arguing that: 'Local schools are an important part of ensuring vibrant local communities and local economies in villages across rural Scotland ... This government wants their future safeguarded.'[29]

Small wonders?

In 2000, Ofsted reported that primary schools with fewer than 100 pupils achieved markedly better test results at key stages 1 and 2 than larger schools. Even after adjusting for the children's socio-economic backgrounds, small schools remained, marginally, ahead. Quality of teaching was praised as generally better than in larger schools and inspectors said they had 'a positive ethos with a family atmosphere, close links between staff and parents, an important place in the local community, and good standards of behaviour'. Overall, they concluded that 'a good case emerges for the place of small schools in the education system as a whole, when the quality of their educational performance is added to the broader contribution they make to their communities'.[30] This pattern of higher achievement at key stage 2 continued – government figures for 2004 quoted by the Commission for Rural Communities confirmed that schools with fewer than 100 on roll obtained the best results.[31]

From achievement to economics: one estimate was that schools with 80–100 pupils cost 16 per cent more per child than larger schools, while costs escalated substantially for those with fewer than 50 on roll.[32] However, as the Scottish government was told in 2007 there was not 'necessarily a conclusive argument for closure on financial/economic grounds as the wider recurring costs of transport, boarding and the resultant, often unquantified, loss to the community are difficult to cost in full economic terms, particularly in the long term'.[33]

Cost was a factor raised in the Review's national soundings for organisations, as was the need for small schools to attract good teachers and offer pupils a rich and varied curriculum. The drive towards extended schools was seen as likely to exacerbate these problems as small schools might find it hard to provide what the government terms the 'core offer' of clubs for children, childcare, family support, access to specialist services and community use of facilities. Federation, whereby small schools share a governing body and pool some resources, was suggested as a possible solution, though the submission from the National Association for Small Schools (NASS) argued that this was often just a slow route to closure. In 2008, the National College for School Leadership suggested small schools should federate under an 'executive head' able to shoulder some of the burdens weighing down individual head teachers. This would provide, said the NCSL, 'a sustainable model that will preserve our small schools, their individual character and their place in our communities'.

The NASS argued in its submission that 'the evidence has been moving towards us for the past 10 years'. It would be hard to disagree. In terms of ethos, many small schools were excelling through close links with parents and the community, their family atmosphere and their high standards of behaviour. In terms of educational achievement and quality of teaching, they had been more than vindicated by Ofsted. Also, other characteristics such as a teaching head, mixed-age classes, flexibility and innovation in teaching, and clustering – while often adopted out of necessity – had been shown to have advantages. Even in financial terms, higher unit costs had to be balanced against the transport bill in times of high fuel prices, and against the longer-term social costs of dying villages and alienated children. Certainly, Herefordshire took these into account when it withdrew plans to shut or merge 37 small schools, and countries such as Sweden appeared happy to maintain small schools in exchange for sustainable rural communities.

There were some contrary notes. An 'idealised' view of a rural past could provoke baseless fears of the death of a community, according to a study of the impact of small school closures on culture, community and language undertaken in Wales in 2007.[34] It could also lead people to ignore the many advantages of larger schools. 'The needs of children – not their parents, communities or any other public interests – should be considered above all others,' said former government adviser David Reynolds who led the research and concluded that the impact of the closures he had studied had been 'overwhelmingly beneficial'.

Size and the pressure to compete

Small schools do face challenges. They are vulnerable to being thrown off course by the departure of a dedicated head or a key teacher. Clustering may yield imaginative and cost-effective sharing of resources and expertise, but it can also impose a heavy administrative load. There is also a tension, which surfaced during the Review's community soundings between the pressure (and desire) to collaborate and the need to compete. Since inter-school collaboration and parental choice – which fuels competition between schools for pupils – are in 2008 both matters of policy, it might be suggested that government has placed schools in a no-win situation. For small schools – where the advantages of professional collaboration are most obvious yet the consequences of even a marginal drop in pupil numbers can be catastrophic, this double bind is deeply unsatisfactory. It should be resolved in such a way that professional collaboration, and hence the improvement of educational quality, are never compromised.

Finally, small schools – again – reported that they were often warned that the 'extended schools' agenda, with its emphasis on community use and longer hours, would prove beyond them. Yet the NASS argued that the concept is rooted in the type of relationship that could exist between a village and its school. There were imaginative examples of community use of small schools: one had opened a shop, another a community-managed nursery classroom, and another, bucking national trends, a post office.

CLASS SIZE

Politics, parents and pupil numbers

In 2008, there were, on average, 25.6 pupils in a key stage 1 class, and 27.2 in a key stage 2 class.[35] The overall average was 26.2, which put England near the top of the class-size league when compared with the average of 21.5 across the 30 countries belonging to the Organisation for Economic Co-operation and Development.[36] Also, unusually among OECD countries, classes in England tended to be larger in primary schools than in secondaries. In 2008, the average secondary class in England contained 21.2 pupils.[37]

At the time of Plowden, 59 per cent of children were in classes of more than 30 and 17 per cent in classes of more than 40.[38] In 2007, less than 2 per cent of five- to seven-year-olds (23,210 children) were in classes of more than 30. At key stage 2, however, 23 per cent of pupils (448,989 children) remained in large classes. Across the country there were 730 KS1 and 13,837 KS2 classes with more than 30 pupils.[39]

The educational effects of different class sizes have been long debated. In 1993, the Conservatives denied any link between class size and quality of education and in 1995 Ofsted reported that quality of teaching was more important. Yet, in 1997 New Labour capped infant class sizes at 30 in an election pledge that tapped into teachers' and parents' preference for smaller classes. In 2008, the Liberal Democrats argued that cutting 'over-sized' classes was more important than changing the curriculum while in Scotland the SNP was accused of backtracking on its election pledge to 'work towards' classes of just 18 pupils in the first three primary years.

Almost all of Plowden's witnesses believed 'in the value of smaller classes' and the committee acknowledged that they were a key factor in persuading parents to opt for private schools. Forty years later, teachers, parents, children's organisations and unions were still pushing for smaller classes and they remain one of the private sector's strongest selling points.

Are 30 pupils still too many?

The impression gained from the Review's submissions and soundings on class sizes was that, in the words of one local authority, '30 is still too big'. A parent and former middle school teacher recommended limits of 15 in reception and Year 1. A head teacher demanded no more than 20 in all primary classes, as did the National Union of Teachers. The National Association of Head Teachers sought classes 'small enough to enable a personal focus on the learner'. While infant classes were capped at 30, the size of key stage 2 classes, not limited by law, was a concern commented on in many submissions.

Two substantial and influential studies, examined in the Review's research survey by Peter Blatchford and colleagues,[40] made the link between class size and attainment, particularly in the early years. The Tennessee STAR project followed more than 7,000 pupils for four years from kindergarten through to grade 3, beginning in 1985. Children and teachers were randomly assigned to either small classes (13–17 pupils) or to larger classes (22–25 pupils) both with and without a teaching assistant. Researchers found that children in the smaller classes, particularly those from minority-ethnic backgrounds, performed better in reading and maths. This finding stood the test of time, though subsequent re-analysis revealed that the children made the greatest gains in the kindergarten year.[41]

The more sophisticated CSPAR (Class Size and Pupil Adult Ratios) project, run by London University's Institute of Education, tracked 10,000 children in 300 schools from reception through to Year 6. Like STAR, it found clear improvements in reception children's literacy and maths when they were taught in classes of under 25. The greatest gains were made by the children who had the most ground to make up. However, researchers noted little long-term effect on maths attainment. Literacy gains were evident two years later, but only if the children continued in small classes.

Research also consistently showed that the smaller the class, the more personalised the teaching. Relieved of the stress of managing large numbers of children, teachers had more time to actually teach, spot problems, give feedback and set targets. Larger classes were prone to more disruptive behaviour,[42] and children's concentration and quality of work could suffer as a result of working in larger groups. Nevertheless, CSPAR found no evidence that children in smaller classes made more progress in maths, English or science at key stage 2. As the Review's research survey indicated, smaller classes only give teachers the opportunity to be more effective. Simply taking away pupils does not make a mediocre teacher better.

Smaller classes: an expensive luxury?

Reducing class sizes is expensive, though cost – and cost-effectiveness – is often disputed. In Scotland, the Association of Education Directors said infant class sizes of 18 would require an extra £62 million a year for new teachers, with £360m needed for 900 new classrooms. Professor Dylan Wiliam estimated that reducing pupil numbers by 30 per cent would cost £20,000 per class per year.[43] Instead, he said, the emphasis should be on improving the quality of teaching and increasing the use of formative assessment.

Education professionals and parents continue to press for substantially smaller classes at key stages 1 and 2. Acting on their wishes would be costly and their conviction that smaller was better was only partly supported by the evidence. Some submissions to the Review pointed out that reducing some class sizes can have an unforeseen impact on school organisation. The number of mixed-age classes may increase while smaller classes on entry means more parents are denied their choice of school.

That said, there appears to be a strong case for reducing some class sizes further – to below 25 for reception and Year 1 and for those children with most ground to make up, a position backed by the Welsh inspectorate Estyn in 2003. However, whether infants in Scotland would gain any more as a result of the decision to move towards classes of 18 was questionable, though, significantly, the STAR project compared small classes of 13–17 with 'large' classes of 22–25.

CSPAR evidence that the gains infants made in smaller classes 'washed out' when they moved into larger ones was worrying, suggesting that investment early on might be wasted. While smaller classes through to Year 6 are an obvious answer, more cost-effective solutions, such as formative assessment, have also been proposed. Certainly, in terms of raising standards, proof of the value of small classes through to Year 6 was elusive. One commentator argued strongly that beyond the age of six 'small classes served as a convenient slogan for unions and politicians, because they were easily understood and accepted by the public as self-evidently a good thing. It is time we moved beyond them and thought more creatively about how we use educational resources.'[44]

Yet should what parents, teachers and unions considered 'self-evidently a good thing' be dismissed? Classes of under 25 allow teachers to get to know their pupils better and to give them more attention. Smaller classes tend to be better behaved and require less marking and planning from teachers. All these factors matter to teachers and parents – for whom education is not just about results. As one teacher's submission to the Review said: 'It is not just that fewer children may lead to better test results, but that the whole atmosphere of a class, the quality of the relationships between adult and child, and child and child, is affected by numbers.'

CLASS STRUCTURES

Streaming and a stratified society

After the Second World War, primary education operated as a 'sorting, classifying, selective mechanism'.[45] Despite the increasing influence of theories of child development, discussed in Chapter 7, school organisation reflected a stratified society and was shaped by the belief that intelligence was fixed from birth. Schools streamed children in classes based on ability, but ability usually correlated with social class. At the age of seven most working-class children were set 'on a path towards the secondary modern school and low-level occupations for the rest of their lives'.[46]

Selection and streaming were in rapid decline by the end of the 1960s, their disappearance hastened by a successful campaign backed by research showing that while not raising attainment, except among those in the top band, streaming lowered expectations, pupil self-esteem and hence attainment among the rest. Plowden accepted both the campaign's arguments and the evidence: 'We welcome unstreaming in the infant school and hope that it will continue to spread through the age groups of the junior school.'[47] The abolition of the 11-plus test and the spread of comprehensive schools following DES Circular 10/65 did the rest. By the 1990s mixed-ability classes were the norm, with only about 3 per cent of primaries large enough to stream actually doing so.[48]

Yet the debate about streaming persisted, and it was included in the remit of the 1991–92 'three wise men' enquiry into primary teaching. Their report, however, confirmed the Plowden judgement while adding a further objection, to its inflexibility:

> Research into the effect of streaming on pupils undertaken in the 1960s showed that streaming could benefit the achievement of some pupils, notably the most able, but that there could be a significant and negative impact on the self-image of those pupils who, placed in lower streams, came to see themselves as failures. But the fundamental problem with streaming is that it is a crude device which cannot do justice to the different abilities a pupil may show in different subjects and contexts. For this reason grouping ... is a more flexible device.[49]

Soon, however, the government was urging primary and secondary schools to set children in ability-based classes for some subjects as a route to higher standards. While setting is a more discriminating and sensitive practice than streaming, it is still more controversial than within-class grouping by ability. It was illegal in Sweden, for example, at the time of writing and in Italy pupils could not be set before age 15. In primaries, the spread of setting was slow and concentrated mainly in Years 5 and 6, but continued to grow. By 2003/4, Ofsted reported that 28 per cent of schools set pupils for maths, 15 per cent for English, and 2 per cent for science.

Primary classes were traditionally organised by age as well as by ability. Infant schools, Plowden observed, had been experimenting since 1933 with mixed-age, or vertically-grouped, classes, largely to iron out the effects of fluctuating pupil numbers resulting from termly intakes. By 2002, about 1 million children, a quarter of primary pupils, were being taught in mixed-age classes and numbers were rising, according to the government. They existed in all local authorities, though the majority were found, arising from necessity rather than choice, in small schools in rural areas

Setting and streaming versus mixed ability

'The adoption of structured ability groupings has no positive effects on attainment, but has detrimental effects on the social and personal outcomes for some children,' according to the Review's research survey by Peter Blatchford and colleagues. Submissions to the Review revealed a sharp division on the pros and cons of setting. Some teachers and local authorities strongly advocated mixed-ability teaching, while others maintained that ability grouping offered a more manageable and effective structure for teaching. A typical view from the pro-setting lobby was expressed in a teacher's submission:

> Children should be taught for English and maths in small groups of no more than 20 similarly able pupils (yes, put them in sets). There does not need to be an attitude of shame about it, it is a question of expecting and celebrating progress. Regularly allow for movement of children between groups if rate (or lack) of progress requires.

A submission from a researcher made an equally powerful plea for an end to setting:

> Children spend too much time in fixed pupil groupings, in which those who find learning difficult are thrown back on their own limited resources and lack the role models, the language experience and the scaffolding that would be possible if they spent more of their time working in mixed-ability collaborative groups. Research has shown that the reading curriculum is stratifying children at a very early stage ... This early stratification can create a downwards spiral as boys avoid and resist learning due to early experiences of being classified as poor readers.

In 2001, researchers studied key stage 2 pupils in Barking and Dagenham.[50] The 1,000 pupils taught in mixed-ability maths classes showed an average gain in test scores (of up to 7 per cent) over the 200 in set classes. Not only did the mixed-ability children maintain their lead over two years, but the range of attainment in the classes narrowed. In 2006, a study of 12 primaries showed that those using setted classes rarely achieved results higher than the local authority or national average.[51] The setted schools' value-added scores, a measure of how much they helped children to progress, were negative in comparison to the positive scores of non-set schools.

In the era of streaming prior to the 1970s, schools usually allotted the most experienced and best-qualified teachers to the A-stream pupils in order to maximise their prospects in the 11-plus test and hence the school's standing. Similarly, in 1998, Ofsted reported that the most effective teachers were consistently found in the higher sets, concluding that setting polarised teaching quality.[52] And, as was also the case with streaming, social class was a significant indicator of a child's set, irrespective of their prior attainment. In 2007, 40 per cent of children in lower sets qualified for free school meals compared to 15.9 per cent nationally.[53]

The social and psychological consequences of setting are significant. Children are alert to whatever method of grouping their school adopts. Those in higher and lower sets have been shown to be vulnerable to being teased or stigmatised. However, only 3 per cent of lower-ability children were found to have high self-esteem when taught in setted classes, compared with 29 per cent in mixed-ability classes.[54] 'In ability-based grouping, pupils in lower groups were vulnerable to making less progress, becoming demotivated and developing anti-school attitudes.'[55]

Categorise with caution

'Why can't we have streaming and setting, to help all children reach their potential?' asked Conservative leader David Cameron in 2005. 'Treating every child as if they are the same fails the child who is struggling and the child who is not.'

The issues within this plea need to be unpacked somewhat. Streaming and setting are of course very different procedures, and in this sometimes heated debate that needs to be remembered. Far from treating every child as the same, the term which is used for the alternative to both arrangements – 'mixed-ability teaching' – actually accentuates their differences. In contrast, a consistent and repeatedly verified problem of streaming is that while it certainly does not treat all children as the same, it does not treat them as individuals either, classifying them instead as falling into (usually) three categories from which there is little chance of escape.

In this sense, as research going back to the 1960s clearly shows, streaming may benefit the able but fail the child who is struggling and do little for the child who neither struggles nor shines. Setting may offer greater flexibility, but it may also lead to the social stereotyping of pupils and polarise teaching quality, with no obvious improvement in outcomes – except, again, for the higher attainers.

Such devices, then, need to be used with due caution. In this debate the lessons of English educational history need to be heeded; so too do those of other countries, in many of which mixed-ability classes at the primary stage are the norm. There, the assumption is that during their early years of schooling children can and should work together towards common goals, and that it is the task of the teacher to ensure that they stay together – rather than drift apart and having so drifted are forced further apart by differential treatment.[56]

Mixed-age and single-year

Children's submissions to the Review indicated that they were generally happy with age-based classes, though several local authorities reported that strict age banding created problems for summer-born pupils. However, they added that flexibility was constrained by budget considerations and that parents preferred single-year groups, fearing that older children would be held back and younger ones isolated in mixed-age classes. One authority said local discretion and school size should determine how classes were organised, though mixed-age was an option schools should consider. The organisation Optimum Education argued in its submission that: 'Age differentiation is a blunt organisational instrument.'

In 1967, Plowden saw advantages in mixed-age, or vertically-grouped, classes for infants with older children acting as role models to newcomers and teachers having more time to build relationships with their pupils. Subsequent research continued to associate social and emotional strengths with vertical grouping and a review of all such investigations concluded in 2003 that children's social development was probably helped and certainly not hindered by the mixing of ages.[57]

Vertical grouping was dealt a blow in 1978 when inspectors criticised large schools that had deliberately opted to mix the years. Attainment was suffering, they said, and teachers had difficulty selecting appropriate tasks for children. However, subsequent national and international reviews of achievement have generally found no significant difference in attainment between mixed- or single-age classes.[58] Furthermore, as noted earlier in this chapter, small schools which have no alternative to mixed-age classes do well academically.

Stage not age

Mixed-age classes, in a secondary context, were given a fillip in 2004 when the chief inspector declared: 'Teaching by age could in time be replaced by teaching for stage, allowing students to progress at their own rate.'

Serlby Park school near Doncaster took this vision to heart. An all-through 3–18 school, it mixed and matched its pupils on the basis of need, organising mixed-age literacy in early primary right through to mixed-age GCSEs. In 2008, its then head, David Harris, had high expectations of such projects. For him there was 'no educational basis for separating children solely by age'.

This appears to be the case – judging by research evidence on attainment and social development, and the outstanding work produced by many small primaries with mixed-age classes. Certainly parents have little grounds for regarding mixed-age as an economy measure, particularly those with summer-born children who were more likely to flourish in a class where they were not always the 'baby'.

However, David Harris acknowledged that the 'stage, not age' concept needed 'a very imaginative timetable, and lots of goodwill'. And perhaps there is the rub. Mixed-age classes require considerably more from teachers in terms of preparation and planning. Perhaps not surprisingly then, research in 2006 found that most teachers preferred single-age classes, though nearly as many had no preference.[59]

As one of the Review's research surveys pointed out, the challenges of mixed-age classes are similar to those of mixed-ability.[60] Teachers carry a heavier burden, but they have more options in terms of personalising learning. They can extend younger children's learning and social development as Vygotsky would have wished, while older children profit from rising to the challenge of being role models and peer mentors.

CONCLUSION

This chapter tackles some contentious and important questions arising from how primary schooling is structured. Clearly, some aspects of the structure are more in need of repair than others. As the evidence reveals, of most pressing concern is the age at which children enter formal schooling – dealt with in Chapter 11. Another issue capable of arousing high emotion is school size or, more precisely, the future of small schools. Judging by campaigns waged across the country, small schools are often deeply treasured by the usually rural communities they serve. In many respects people feel they are the community. As environment ministers talk up the need to create sustainable communities and education ministers urge parents and schools to forge ever stronger links, it seems perverse that many small schools once again feel under threat of closure. As the evidence shows, most do very well by their pupils, educationally as well as socially. They are fragile, vulnerable to being knocked off course by the departure of an experienced head, but that is surely a reason to promise them a secure future rather than a motive for shutting them down.

This chapter also highlights problems caused by another major structural weakness – a flaw that has persisted for decades. Concerns about children's loss of educational momentum at certain points in their school careers have been commendably high on school, local authority and political agendas for many years, and they were prominent in the Review's own evidence. Yet the many transitions and transfers that primary pupils make still have the potential to derail their learning – particularly at age 11. The sudden curricular and pedagogical changes that mark their moves between schools and between key-stage 'compartments' need to be eased. Transition must become a process, rather than an event. Many local authorities, teachers and teacher trainers are aware of how crucial communication and continuity are to ensuring successful transitions and avoiding learning 'dips'. However, schools need time and resources if they are to break down the walls of artificial compartments, through, for example, more cross-phase teaching. All-through schools may find it easier to manage transitions, but only if their structure facilitates communication and continuity rather than the creation of new compartments.

Unusually, in this chapter at least, parents and teachers part company with research evidence in relation to class size. Like transfers and transitions, class size is an education perennial. However, while there is consensus as to what helps ease transitions, there is less so on the subject of the ideal number of children in a class. Teachers and parents value smaller classes – and they are correct in assuming that smaller means more individual attention for each pupil. However, there appears no clear correlation between size and success. Up to age six, and for children who have fallen behind, the evidence points to limiting class sizes to 25. Beyond six there may be more cost-effective ways of raising attainment.

That said, a 2008 OECD finding does give pause for thought.[61] The UK has 'very large' primary classes and stands out as the developed country with the greatest difference between state and private sectors – on average, state primary classes have 13 more pupils than private-sector classes. While the OECD commented that this could be an efficient use of an education budget, clearly doubts remain. At the very least, it is vital that the impact of the introduction of smaller classes in Wales and – possibly – Scotland is monitored.

Finally, this chapter looked at evidence in relation to how schools organise their pupils into classes. With regard to mixed-aged classes, a practice common in smaller schools, the evidence overall appeared to be in favour of the flexibility it gave teachers to mix and match pupils within lessons and the social and emotional opportunities it opened up for children. More contentious was the issue of grouping whole classes by ability. Setting is divisive, not just of children, but of teachers and local authorities. Some are strongly in favour; the majority are strongly opposed. While setting has been shown to benefit the very gifted, for most children it runs the risk of demotivating them by pigeon-holing them in categories determined as much by social background as by any true assessment of their ability.

In brief, the findings of this chapter indicate that there are cracks in the structure of primary education into which some children fall – through poor management of transitions and transfers, for example. There are walls where perhaps only movable partitions are needed – between the key stages and between classes strictly divided by age or ability. And there are some delicate structures in the form of small schools that merit strong buttresses.

NOTES

1 DCSF (2007h).
2 Suffolk County Council (2007).
3 CACE (1967): para 365.
4 *Ibid.*: para 371.
5 HMI (1983, 1985).
6 HMI (1983): para 1.1.
7 House of Lords Hansard reports (19 February 2007).
8 Ofsted (2007a).
9 Alexander (1995).
10 Blatchford *et al.* (2010), *The Cambridge Primary Review Research Surveys*, Chapter 21.
11 *Ibid.*
12 *Ibid.*
13 Sanders, White, Burge, Sharp, Eames, McCune and Grayson (2005).
14 Ofsted (2003c).
15 Ofsted (2007b).
16 Sanders *et al.* (2005).
17 Ofsted (2007b).
18 Ofsted (2003a): 5, 38.
19 Ofsted (2003a): 19.
20 Doddington and Flutter (2002).
21 Gibbs (2004).
22 Galton, Gray and Rudduck (1999).
23 Rose (2008).
24 QCA (2006).
25 *Times Educational Supplement* (2008) April 4.
26 Riggall and Sharp (2010), *The Cambridge Primary Review Research Surveys*, Chapter 14.
27 CACE (1967); DCSF (2007g).
28 HMI (1985): para 1.3.
29 Scottish Government (2008b).
30 Ofsted (2000).
31 Commission for Rural Communities (2007).
32 http://www.teachernet.gov.uk/
33 Wilson (2007).
34 Reynolds (2007).
35 DCSF (2007h); DfES/National Statistics (2006).
36 OECD (2007).
37 DCSF (2007h).
38 CACE (1967): Table 19.
39 DCSF (2007h).
40 Blatchford *et al.* (2010), *The Cambridge Primary Review Research Surveys*, Chapter 21.
41 Goldstein and Blatchford (1998).
42 Finn, Pannozzo and Achilles (2003).
43 Dylan Wiliam, in a speech to the annual Chartered London Teachers Conference, 25 February 2008.
44 Wilby (2008).
45 Galton, Simon and Croll (1980).
46 Blatchford *et al.* (2010), *The Cambridge Primary Review Research Surveys*, Chapter 21.
47 CACE (1967): recommendation 100.
48 Blatchford, Hallam *et al.* (2010), *The Cambridge Primary Review Research Surveys*, Chapter 21.
49 Alexander, Rose and Woodhead (1992): para 85.
50 Whitburn (2001).
51 Kutnick *et al.* (2006).
52 Ofsted (1998).
53 Children and Young People Now (2007). However, please note that this figure refers to secondary school pupils.
54 Devine (1993).
55 Kutnick *et al.* (2005).
56 Reynolds and Farrell (1996); Alexander (2001b).
57 Wilson (2003).
58 Blatchford *et al.* (2010), *The Cambridge Primary Review Research Surveys*, Chapter 21.
59 Berry and Little (2006).
60 Blatchford *et al.* (2010), *The Cambridge Primary Review Research Surveys*, Chapter 21.
61 OECD (2008b).

20 Schools, local authorities and other agencies

Before considering the relations between schools and other agencies, we must assess the challenges that they face. We need an insight into the totality of children's needs in England in order to be able to judge how well the public services, the private and voluntary sectors and families are meeting them. The interconnectedness of these needs – the justification for moves to integrate services – has been underlined repeatedly. As the Secretary of State for Children, Schools and Families said in 2008:

> Every head teacher I meet wants the very best for the pupils at their school, but they all tell me they can't do it alone. They tell me that if a child arrives at school hungry, or they have speech and language needs that are not being met or if they don't have a stable home to go back to at the end of the day, then it can have a really damaging impact on their learning.[1]

The Review's evidence places the plight of such individuals in the larger social and economic context:

> The contrasts in children's lives were thought [by our witnesses] to be massive and widening. Those born into familial stability and economic comfort fare well, exceptionally so in many cases. For others, deprivation is profound and multifaceted: economic, emotional, linguistic, cultural. Our community witnesses believed that the accident of birth profoundly and often cruelly divides the nation's children.[2]

Anguished headlines followed the 2007 Unicef report which concluded that children in the UK were the most deprived, at risk and insecure of all young people surveyed in 21 economically-advanced countries.[3] Save the Children warned that three million British children – 25 per cent – were growing up in poverty, with one in 10 enduring severe deprivation, one of the worst rates in the industrialised world.

In relation to health matters, profound anxieties surround children's states of mind, with 10 per cent of five-to 15-year-olds reported to be suffering from mental health problems.[4] Obesity is rising faster than anywhere else in Europe, with a third of 10- to 11-year-olds either overweight or obese.[5] More children are being diagnosed with developmental disorders such as autism[6] and ADHD.

With regard to social concerns, worries persist about the strain long working hours place on families. Of Unicef's 21 countries, relations between children and their parents were at their worst in the UK. And in 2008 the World Health Organisation's final report on international health equity showed how closely enmeshed are health, life expectancy, and inequalities in income and education. As indicated earlier, this is a matter for nations like the UK which are rich but strikingly unequal as well as for the more familiar cases in the 'third world'.[7] The WHO reported:

> A child born in a Glasgow suburb can expect a life 28 years shorter than another living only 13 kilometres away. A girl in Lesotho is likely to live 42 years less than another in Japan. In Sweden, the risk of a woman dying during pregnancy and childbirth is 1 in

17,400; in Afghanistan, the odds are 1 in 8. Biology does not explain any of this. Instead, the differences between – and within – countries result from the social environment where people are born, live, grow, work and age ... (The) toxic combination of bad policies, economics and politics is, in large measure, responsible for the fact that a majority of people in the world do not enjoy the good health that is biologically possible ... Social injustice is killing people on a grand scale.[8]

Clearly such dire circumstances as these represent a nexus of complicated and long-standing social problems. However, it is important to recognise that many children and their families face challenges that reflect their own unique, and often complex, difficulties and needs, and responding to these poses rather different problems for schools and other agencies.

This chapter examines how those concerned with children respond to such immense challenges. In this era of integrated children's services, how successfully does the work of teachers, health and social care professionals articulate and cohere? Are government policies effective and providing value for money? Are professional barriers being broken down and are all families being reached? What is being done to help the most vulnerable children and narrow the gap in life chances? How might the relationships between those who work with children be differently conceived? It goes without saying that every child matters – the challenge is to give that principle meaning in the daily life of schools.

TOWARDS INTEGRATION

The Sixties: calls for collaboration

The Plowden committee recognised that schools could not offer everything some children needed. Any who required additional help from the state were seen as 'deprived ... prevented from following [their] proper developmental path by adverse social circumstances.'[9] In order to help them, the report called for investment in the school health service and in social workers, educational psychologists, psychiatrists, speech therapists, probation officers and education welfare officers.

Striking what we shall see are some perhaps depressingly contemporary notes, the Plowden Report recommended:

> Co-operation between family doctors, school and public health services and hospitals should be closer.[10]
>
> Information collected by health visitors, clinics and the School Health Service could be used to warn other medical and social workers of families in danger arising from social circumstances. The information should be treated as confidential and be given only to those who are likely to deal directly with a family.[11]

and, foreshadowing *Every Child Matters* and the re-organisation of local authority children's services:

> The principal need is for a grouping of existing organisations within a comprehensive plan of action.[12]

Other reports also backed improved coordination. The 1968 Seebohm Report,[13] which created unified social services departments, sought simply 'one door to knock on', a phrase close to the 'one-stop shop' of the 1990s. Similarly, Plowden's recognition of the difficulties of achieving closer collaboration could have been written in 2008:

> Co-ordination is not simply an administrative or procedural problem. It demands a reappraisal of family needs and of the skills required to help those in difficulty. It requires a greater measure of training common to all the services.[14]

While the education welfare officers say in their evidence to us that they work closely with other agencies, they also complain that others neglect them, and that teachers and education officers sometimes fail to understand their role. Health visitors give evidence of the need for improved connections between the social services affecting the primary schools, and one of our own studies strongly implies that health visitors themselves are sometimes unwilling to make contact with social workers.[15]

One of the notable outcomes of Plowden was the establishment of a small number of educational priority areas – to target help at schools in deprived districts 'where educational handicaps are reinforced by social handicaps'.[16] The committee recommended that such schools needed smaller classes, teachers' aides, and, of relevance to this chapter, school-based social workers, links with colleges of education and better parent-school-community relationships.

The Seventies: selective services

In the 1970s, schools' links with other services were driven by a desire to protect children from threats from within and beyond the family.[17] Parents were held increasingly responsible for their child's failure to thrive and where home life was judged inadequate, the state was expected to compensate.

Plowden's EPAs achieved only partial success; money was short and the priority areas only crudely correlated with need. So agencies outside schools began to target specific groups of children, such as those with special needs, in what has been described as a 'drift' from universal services to selective ones.[18] Yet 'mismatches' between cultural practices of home and school were 'frequently interpreted as deficits to be remedied by school or, at worst, by family services, social work or speech therapy'.[19] Class and ethnicity often swayed decisions about which families were in need of help.

The lack of coordination between services, as observed by Plowden, remained an issue. In 1973 seven-year-old Maria Colwell was killed by her stepfather despite warnings from neighbours and teachers and 30 calls to social services. The enquiry criticised poor communication and liaison between the agencies responsible for the child. Area child protection committees were set up to improve coordination, but, despite their efforts, the involvement of social and health services with schools was characterised as 'rogue meteors diving in and out of the school atmosphere at odd times'.[20]

As one commentator pointed out in retrospect, the Colwell enquiry recommendations 'established a pattern that has been wearily repeated, with the need for better training of staff, increased co-operation and co-ordination between statutory services and the demand for yet more resources'.[21]

The Eighties: children of the market place

With the election of the Conservative government in 1979, the construction of childhood changed again. In the words of one of our research surveys, a child growing up in the 1980s and 1990s was an 'individualised "market child" … whose opportunities were shaped for good or ill by the consumerist choices of her parents'.[22]

The Conservatives did not implement the findings of the Black Report which highlighted, nearly 30 years before the WHO report, the poor health of working-class children in comparison with that of those growing up in wealthier families.[23] The Black Report 'concluded that early childhood is the period of life at which intervention could most hopefully weaken the continuing association between health and class.' It emphasised the importance of children's diet, recommending that school dinners be free. Instead, the school meals service was privatised and cost, rather than nutrition, generally appeared to be the main criterion on which contracts were awarded. It was only recently, largely thanks to the high-profile media campaign of chef Jamie Oliver and concerns about child obesity, that the need for schools to provide children with nutritious food was once more the target of government policy.

The view that promoting child health was not the business of the state was encouraged by a 1992 government report, 'Health of the Nation'. Any sense of collective responsibility for children's health and well-being was hampered by power being split between different government departments. 'The health care of children during their days at school has been neglected by the policy-makers ... parents remain the principal people deemed responsible,' according to researchers.[24] Nevertheless, education and health authorities were urged to liaise for the sake of children with special needs, and in 1994, a new code of practice defined the roles of local authorities, social services, health services and school governors.

State, schools and parents in partnership: 1997 onwards

The many tendrils with which poverty chokes children's prospects were firmly in New Labour's sights. 'Joined-up thinking' was the phrase of the moment and the Social Exclusion Unit, launched to help what some call the deprived 'underclass', was urged to promote joint action between Whitehall departments. The Sure Start early years initiative and Behaviour and Education Support Teams, both considered later in this chapter, were early examples of attempting to shape services to met need, rather than needs being defined in the light of what services could offer. The links between poverty and ill-health were spelt out in the 1998 Acheson Report which recommended extra help for schools in deprived areas, the development of health-promoting schools and improvements in school food.

Then in February 2000, eight-year-old Victoria Climbié was starved and tortured to death by her great aunt and the woman's boyfriend. Lord Laming's subsequent enquiry exposed the breakdown of the multi-agency child protection system set up after Maria Colwell's death in 1973. In response to the enquiry, the government published the Every Child Matters framework in 2003. Its overriding purpose was to improve children's lives by providing joined-up universal services, including children's centres and extended schools. Achieving the five 'outcomes' for children – to be healthy, stay safe, enjoy and achieve, make a positive contribution, and achieve economic well-being – was seen to rest on:

- more support for parents and carers
- better early intervention and protection
- greater accountability and integration at both local and national levels
- workforce reform.

There was to be a national child database, made up of information hubs in 150 local authorities. Integrated services were seen as crucial for children in need of additional support. The common assessment framework was developed to encourage the early and holistic appraisal of their needs, with a lead professional appointed to co-ordinate provision and be a single point of contact.

The pressure for partnership working was maintained as was the insistence that public services, including schools, were to be shaped by children's needs rather than professional preoccupations. In 2004 the government backed the spread of extended schools as a way of 'integrating service delivery and ensuring that services are delivered closer to where children and their families spend most of their time'.[25] Similarly, the strategy for inclusion, Removing Barriers to Achievement, reflected the government's determination to develop a 'partnership' approach, although this was not a new idea.

AGENCIES WORKING WITH CHILDREN AND SCHOOLS

By 2008 many agencies were working with children and schools, their number, roles and responsibilities having expanded greatly under the auspices of *Every Child Matters*. Broadly, the agencies intersecting with primary education were concerned with:

- health care
- social welfare and housing
- family law and criminal justice
- the arts, recreation and sports

It is beyond the scope of this chapter to review in detail the myriad public, private and voluntary agencies working in each of these fields and we focus on the key public bodies with responsibility for primary-age children and their families (local authorities, children's trusts, primary care trusts). We also take a brief look at the roles of agencies in the private and voluntary sectors and how these work with public agencies.

Local authority children's services

Local authorities had long borne responsibility for providing education, social care and recreational amenities for children and young people. The 2004 Children Act, the legislation that brought *Every Child Matters* to life, obliged authorities to integrate these services, previously spread across various departments, and to embrace previously disconnected purposes and roles. Under the Act local authorities also had to appoint a director of children's services and designate a lead member with responsibility for education and children's social services. To encourage partnership local authorities and 'other relevant partners' were placed under a 'duty to co-operate'. As we shall see later in this chapter, these changes have not been straightforward or universally welcome but in 2008 they were relatively new and their impact was only beginning to be assessed.

In 2005, the government announced that Ofsted was to start inspecting local authorities' children's services – a further step towards a more 'joined-up' approach.[26] At the same time the children's workforce strategy came into being, running in parallel with school workforce reform, with the objective of raising standards across all agencies working with children. As part of the strategy, the Children's Workforce Development Council was set up and charged with promoting workforce excellence through training, career development and improved workforce mobility, as well as encouraging better integration.[27]

Children's trusts

In 2004, local partnerships, in the form of 35 'pathfinder' children's trusts, were launched to bring together all agencies concerned with children and families. Underpinned by *Every Child Matters*, the 2004 Act and the National Framework for Children, Young People and Maternity Services, the children's trusts shared a common foundation, although their membership and functions were tailored to meet local needs. However, the government insisted on some 'essential features':

- outcome-led vision – a focus on results, informed by the views of children and their families
- integrated front-line delivery – professionals freed from departmental constraints working together to meet children's needs
- integrated processes – better assessments, information sharing and improved referrals to ensure quick access to services
- integrated strategy – joint commissioning of services and pooling of budgets and resources to drive multi-agency working
- inter-agency governance – a clear framework for strategic planning, resource allocation, and accountabilities.[28]

In 2007, research showed that the 35 pathfinder children's trusts had taken some steps towards developing more integrated, cohesive services though it also noted some significant obstacles.[29] One difficulty was the time it was taking for 'managerial enthusiasm and written protocols to be extended to service delivery', suggesting that this 'top-down' model had not yet led to significant improvements in practice.

As children's trusts were set up across the country, there was a recognition that these new structures were not a 'quick fix' to the problem of fragmented services. While maintaining a predictably upbeat view of the strategy, revised statutory guidance for children's trusts observed:

> In the past few years local partners in many areas have made significant improvements in the extent and impact of partnership working through children's trusts. Real progress has been made in implementing the structural and systemic changes needed to drive improved outcomes. This has been variable across the country, however, and the cultural changes needed to drive these changes through to demonstrable improvements in outcomes have yet to be sufficiently embedded.[30]

In 2007 the Children's Plan heralded a strengthening of the children's trusts and included proposals for further legislative backing. Following the death of 'Baby P', in November 2008 the government announced that children's trust boards,[31] comprised of representatives from local authorities, the police, health and other services and schools, would co-ordinate and be held accountable for child protection measures.

Primary care trusts

Primary care trusts (PCTs) were introduced in 2000 as part of the restructuring of the National Health Service, in effect replacing the committees and primary care groups of the former health authorities. By 2006 there were 152 PCTs with responsibility for providing and managing local primary health care services.[32] PCTs had their own budgets and were able to adapt services according to community needs and priorities, within parameters set by their strategic health authorities and the Department of Health. The government increasingly encouraged PCTs to commission some services from the private and voluntary sectors but PCTs were also obliged to work closely with local authorities under the umbrella of children's trusts.

PCTs' work with children, families and schools is multifaceted. Individual trusts offer many community-based services for children including:

- school nurses
- children's community nurses
- disabled children's teams and special school nurses
- child development teams
- co-ordination of vaccination and immunisation
- health visitors
- health education programmes
- children's occupational therapists
- speech therapists
- physiotherapists
- parent educators and 'community parent' schemes
- children's weight management teams
- children's mental health teams
- dentists
- chiropodists
- opticians.

Health services offered within primary schools had notably declined since their heyday in the inter-war period. By 2008, routine child development and health checks, dental screening and hearing and vision tests were no longer common features of primary-school life. Although this decline largely pre-dated the PCTs, it was a trend that continued under their auspices. For example, routine dental screening for six- to nine-year-olds had become a rarity, although the Department of Health had recommended that PCTs should consider adopting these programmes.[33] However, many PCTs had established school health services, though their remits and practice varied. In London, Tower Hamlets PCT's school health service, for example, was part of the community nursing service. Staff checked children's height and weight, as well as their eyesight and hearing, and advised on conditions such as asthma, eczema and epilepsy.[34] They also offered advice on being healthy and on drugs and alcohol as well as supporting schools in relation to issues such as child protection, domestic abuse and bullying. Some PCT school health services worked with teachers to develop health education as part of the national curriculum.

Private and voluntary agencies

By 2008 the number of private and voluntary agencies offering children's services had grown exponentially, driven by social, political and economic changes. The political trend for 'marketisation' in public services was one element but social trends also played a part. More mothers with young children were working full-time, for example, and their need for childcare was met largely by private nurseries, childminders and nannies. Private and voluntary agencies had also sprung up, or expanded, in response to new directions in policy: the children's rights agenda (see Chapter 10), for example, gave rise to voluntary bodies such as the Children's Legal Centre. In many arenas – education, health, social care, housing, the law, the arts, sports and recreation – private and voluntary agencies became increasingly important providers of services for children, their families and primary schools.

Some private agencies operated locally: catering companies, for example, delivered meals to clusters of schools, either in collaboration with the local authority or commissioned directly by schools themselves. Some voluntary agencies came into being in response to local needs and interests, such as community associations, support networks for parents and sports clubs. These voluntary and community agencies had certain advantages over public agencies, as commented on in a report commissioned by the Local Government Association and others:

> The voluntary and community sector often works in partnership with, but is independent of, the statutory sector and can operate with fewer political constraints. Their independence brings both strengths and challenges. On the one hand it allows the sector to be far-seeing and innovative, flexible and lacking in bureaucracy, often spotting trends and needs before they have been statistically identified. Its services are often perceived by service users as being non-stigmatising and it therefore often finds it easier to reach the most vulnerable children and young people.[35]

As noted in Chapter 18, private agencies were also being courted to work with local authorities in order to construct new schools under the government's private finance initiative. Local authorities were also turning to national companies and charities for support with social services, including fostering, adoption and children's homes. Moving key public services for children and families into a complex arrangement of shared responsibility with the private and voluntary sectors was inevitably controversial and the results have been mixed.

We now turn to examine in detail the impact on schools of Every Child Matters.

EVERY CHILD MATTERS

Every school matters – now

Perhaps surprisingly, schools were not at the heart of the 2004 Children Act that provided the legal underpinning of ECM. There was professional anxiety about additional duties being pushed onto hard-pressed schools and eventually only strategic bodies such as councils and primary care trusts became 'relevant partners' bound by the duty to co-operate on the children's trusts. Subsequently, however, most schools became eager to get their voices heard. The 2007 Children's Plan proposed extending the duty to co-operate to schools, seeking a 'step-change' in their involvement with the trusts. The aim was to give head teachers more influence over the planning and commissioning of services and ensure pupils with additional needs received better support.

In doing so, the plan was in accord with the submission to the Review from the National Association of Head Teachers:

> The relationship between adult and child established at school often provides the security and constancy around which additional agencies work. The ECM strategy was initiated with schools at the margin. We believe this was a significant strategic mistake. The potential of ECM will only be realised if schools are at the core of all multi-agency activity for children and their families.

The education service is universal, and comes into contact with all children. This is not true of social or medical services, which only come into contact with children or families who have problems that fall within their remit. Despite this, there are still concerns in schools that they are not always informed of medical or social problems that affect a child or family, that are likely to have an impact on the child's education.

The Review's national soundings of practitioners struck a similar note as to the pivotal role of schools in the achievement of ECM goals: 'If schools are a point of stability in a troubled society, then they require responsibility and power for decision-making so that they can take a primary role in bringing together teachers, children, parents, local community and others ... '.

The submission to the Review from the National Union of Teachers welcomed ECM, adding that it rightly recognised and sustained the idea that schools were at the heart of their communities. Head teachers in the community soundings said it was an important and positive development, as did community representatives. Witnesses from statutory and voluntary bodies concerned with children's well-being, and from groups not directly involved with the initiative, all told the Review that they believed ECM was a significant development. Some wished to make multi-agency working an even more fundamental part of primary school life. Arts organisations stressed the value of schools working with artists, theatres and musicians, as did schools themselves, though they were distressed that neither time nor funding permitted them to take full advantage of what was on offer. The benefits for children with special needs were commented on by heads and in local authority submissions. The charity I CAN said parents welcomed the move to a single children's service so that they no longer felt 'juggled' between different agencies.

Slow steps to integration

So has *Every Child Matters* succeeded in integrating the work of schools with that of other children's services? In 2008 the answer was only a partial yes. Ofsted reported that when judged against the five ECM outcomes, 'the majority of children's services are improving and that partners are working well together to secure better outcomes for children and young people in their areas'. However, it conceded that considerable challenges remained with regard to closing the gap between the most vulnerable children and the rest, and in securing strong partnership working. When this was achieved, inspectors said, for example through basing social workers in schools, results were impressive.[36] But ECM, they concluded, was essentially still 'a work in progress'. Similarly, the Local Authorities Research Consortium reported that: 'Steady progress has been made and there are good signs of impact on outcomes, but there now needs to be a step change in the pace and consistency of that progress.'[37]

Schools were positive about their links with health services. In 2007, 74 per cent of primaries rated their 'accessibility of support' as either good or excellent.[38] The police and leisure services were also praised with more than 70 per cent of schools rating accessibility as either good or excellent. Certainly community representatives in Yorkshire welcomed having a local police officer attached to each school.

However, as Ofsted indicated, the picture was far from one of complete satisfaction. Lord Laming criticised the 'rather patchy' implementation of the policy his enquiry had helped create,[39] adding that schools were clearly 'immensely important' if ECM's five outcomes were to be achieved. Many submissions to the Review agreed that reality was far from matching up with the rhetoric. According to the NAHT:

> The quality of joint agency working is very patchy. Setting this up takes time; best practice tends to be found in those authorities which had developed joint working in the past. The result is that there is not a uniform level of service available to all children and families, and schools cannot always be confident of accessing social services support quickly, should it be required.

Staffordshire County Council commented that there were too many agencies now, that processes took too long and children were passed around until the problem returned to schools. Submissions from head teachers and teachers concurred, saying that accessing and communicating with outside agencies, particularly social services, remained difficult, in spite of improvements. One head teacher reported that:

> ... despite joined-up thinking, there is little real cohesion in children's services. Social services are overburdened and under funded. It would be immensely helpful if health professionals worked with us – we are often kept in the dark about things that would help us to meet children's needs more effectively. Some doctors are incredibly rude when approached.

A 2007 survey by the National Foundation for Educational Research[40] found that only 40 per cent of primary schools rated their accessibility to social services as good or better, though this was a 9 per cent improvement on the previous year. Echoing the submission above, another head told researchers that 'the lack of staff in social services results in poor communication and a huge emphasis on schools (head teachers!) to work with families'.

Distrust of children's trusts

In terms of schools' involvement with children's trusts, the NFER reported that a third of primaries shared information with their trust, but more than half had no contact. As John Dunford, general secretary of the Association of School and College Leaders, commented: 'Most of my members have yet to discover what a children's trust is, let alone what services it offers. Schools do not yet feel local authorities are getting them the services they require.'[41]

The creation of children's services departments from the merger of social services and education departments caused tensions in some areas. Heads' unions reported that the emphasis on delivering what children needed was at the price sometimes of what schools needed. Mick Brookes, general secretary of the NAHT, warned in 2008 that the quest to provide joined-up services had in fact created a 'growing divide' between children's services departments and schools. The loss of education experts from these departments, he added, had left schools not knowing where to look for support.[42] The NUT's submission to the Review reflected similar concerns. It urged that, while the initiative for new services should come from schools, local authorities must still be in a position to provide them. The union stressed its belief in the importance of maintaining 'second-tier' officers for education so that schools could be sure that strategies, once agreed, would be implemented.

Exhausted and confused ...

Head teachers interviewed in the community soundings reported that Every Child Matters, welcome as it was, did create considerable extra work – in one extreme estimate, 90 per cent of a head's time might be spent on 10 per cent of pupils. Community soundings in rural schools revealed that while they welcomed ECM – and extended schools – in principle, they worried about the lack of support to enable the policy to be properly implemented in small schools, already struggling with earlier initiatives.

Achieving joined-up services remained 'complex and highly problematic,' according to the Review's research survey by Ian Barron and colleagues.[43] It added: 'Early research suggests that barriers to communication and collaboration across professions are deep-seated and resistant to change.'

Gillian Pugh, chair of the National Children's Bureau and of the Review's advisory committee, described the move to multi-agency working as a 'massive cultural shift'.[44] She said:

> The ECM agenda has been broadly welcomed, but the blizzard of new initiatives and strategies and pilot projects is proving exhausting as well as confusing for many practitioners. So some stability would be welcome, and would enable all concerned to embed these important changes.[45]

Organisations consulted during the Review's national soundings emphasised the importance of time and training.

> We must modernise the discourse on children's services and social services, to reflect the many changes. Many new organisations are now working in new ways in new partnerships with schools and all sides have to learn how to do this. There needs to be time and resources to evaluate these new ways of working and allow them to become embedded in the organisations.

They agreed that communication between schools and other agencies needed to be strengthened and that all employees should be trained in how to work together and share knowledge. 'There can be conflict due to role definitions, expectations and appropriate activities in any multi-disciplinary or multi-agency system. These all need to be clearly defined.' Evidence reported by the 2020 Children and Young People's Workforce Strategy acknowledged, however, that training for multi-agency work, 'can be difficult to fund, organise and deliver unless it is prioritised by all partners'.[46]

Successful integration

BEST practice

In 2002 Behaviour and Education Support Teams (BESTs) were launched to work in partnership with schools. These were multi-agency teams, bringing together professionals from the social care, health and education sectors to promote emotional well-being, positive behaviour and school attendance with an emphasis on early intervention. (A similar multi-agency team approach – known as the Team around the Child – was backed in the 2007 Children's Plan.) Evaluated in 2006, BESTs gave an early indication of the rewards and challenges inherent in linking up schools with other services. Evidence gathered by the Review supported the researchers' view that: 'Multi-agency teams are complex structures to set up and operate. Bringing together a broad spectrum of professionals to form a cohesive unit, with a remit that is clearly understood by schools, other agencies and team members, inevitably takes time to establish'.[47]

BESTs helped with children's attainment, attendance, behaviour and well-being. The teams eased parents' and schools' access to specialist services, positively influenced parenting skills and forged more effective links between home and school, particularly where relationships had broken down. They also helped school staff understand and support children with challenging behaviour and emotional difficulties. Interestingly, the teams saw passing on skills and strategies to manage behaviour as their most important contribution, while school staff rated access to services more highly – suggesting a difference in the way each party perceived the BEST's role and, possibly, schools' anxieties about being handed ever increasing amounts of responsibility for difficult children – an anxiety reflected in evidence to the Review.

There was other evidence of the advantages of an integrated approach in relation to vulnerable children. As the Review's research survey on learning needs and difficulties reported, school-based family social work services substantially cut intervention costs while collaboration with school nurses in organising cognitive behavioural therapy reduced anxiety and depression in primary pupils.[48] The research survey concluded that 'collaborative forms of practice, with professionals working together across boundaries both within and outside school, ... has been found to be particularly effective for children with conduct disorders and those at risk of mental health problems, two groups which are most at risk of exclusion'.[49]

Vote of confidence from children

Three groups of vulnerable children surveyed in 2008 praised the difference integrated services had made to their lives. Looked-after children, children with autistic spectrum disorders and those who had missed large amounts of schooling said they were getting on well with school work and felt safer and happier. Their parents and carers talked of ongoing, respectful and reliable support, easy access to services and information as well as early identification and greater understanding of the children's needs. However, they also wanted greater understanding and involvement by schools and GPs, suggesting that teachers be trained 'to understand and support these children'.[50]

These parents' desire for greater involvement by schools was echoed by local authority staff who worried about the lack of sign-up from all agencies, but particularly schools, GPs and health services. They also expressed concern about how hard it was to organise multi-agency panels, and about communication and leadership.

Are schools reluctant to integrate?

The subtext here appears to be that, contrary to views expressed in the Review's submissions, it is schools that are resisting integrating with other services. According to Infed, a group backing informal education: 'Schools have tended to be little fiefdoms, isolated to a significant extent from the direct interventions of other professionals outside the schooling system. Where schools have had to work with other agencies their relative size, statutory nature and high degree of control over what happens within their walls have often made them difficult partners.'[51]

Resolving tensions at the heart of policy

Schools can perceive a contradiction between policies that push them to raise standards and those that press them to create a genuinely inclusive education service, according to the Review's research survey on learning needs and difficulties.[52] The researchers urged ministers to resolve the tension between 'competitive education markets based on school league tables and narrowly-conceived measures of pupil attainment and ... a broadly-based account of inclusive schooling within the "whole child" remit of local authority children's services'.

Furthermore, as London's Institute of Education warned in 2008, ECM is not immune to the target-setting culture of the standards agenda. 'Every Child Matters with its current emphasis on blunt and predetermined outcomes may become – or risk being seen as – another means for governing children, parents and the children's workforce.'[53] It warned that the initiative 'intended as a holistic approach to education, may fail because of too much emphasis on predetermined outcomes'.

A submission from a head teacher pointed to the pressure caused by having to spend considerable amounts of time on ECM work that 'does not raise standards' and in which heads had not been trained. For that head teacher, the answer lay in the initiative operating through supportive federations of schools under a director, leaving individual heads free to concentrate on learning. Other agencies such as social services and health would work directly with the federation.

A contrary note, however, was sounded by the staff of six extended schools, including two primaries, interviewed in 2007. Perhaps these schools were further advanced in terms of embedding ECM in their activities for they did not perceive any contradictions between ECM, extended schools (see later section) and the standards agenda. 'Where tensions did exist they were usually based on early misconceptions about the implementation of extended schooling,' according to the staff, who also said that achieving the five outcomes would ultimately raise standards. The researchers urged school leaders to gather evidence to reinforce the argument that ECM could raise attainment, and this link should be promoted widely in schools and their communities, securing everyone's commitment.[54]

EXTENDED SCHOOLS

Early hubs of the community

The Cambridge Primary Review posed many questions as to what a primary school should be like. Few of the answers were as wondrously multifaceted as that supplied in a different context by one pioneering Bolton head teacher. According to Teddy O'Neil, who led Prestolee school from 1918 to 1953, a school should be:

> ... a place for lectures and teaching; a workshop for young and old – of both sexes; a den of hobbies and indoor games; a studio for drawing, painting and plastics; a music studio; a hall for song and dance; an educational shop-window; a reference library; a picture gallery; a museum; a reading room; a book-stall for magazines and newspapers; a club; a place for parties; a refreshment bar; an orchard; a zoo; an aquarium; a vivarium; a home for pets; a playing field; a gymnasium; a bathing place; a fair garden; a kitchen; a dining place; a laundry; a first aid post; a cleansing department; store sheds for raw materials.[55]

In the evenings Prestolee transformed into the 'Palace of Youth', a community centre that accommodated up to 400 people for dances and other cultural activities. The playground, which had been built by the children, boasted a windmill, water gardens, fountains, a well and a large paddling pool. Clearly Prestolee was, in some respects, an early 'extended' school. It opened its doors to the community and organised activities far beyond formal education and long beyond the traditional school day.

There were earlier examples. In 1816, Robert Owen declared that the lower rooms of the New Lanark's Institute for the Formation of Character 'be thrown open for the use of the adult part of the population, who are to be provided with every accommodation requisite to enable them to read, write, account, sew or play, converse or walk about. Two evenings in the week will be appropriated to dancing and music, but on these occasions, every accommodation will be prepared for those who prefer to study or to follow any of the occupations pursued on the other evenings'.[56] Similarly, some Victorian ragged schools decided to appeal to adults, opening club rooms and hostels, and adding savings clubs and holiday schemes to their programmes of classes. Coffee and reading rooms, Bands of Hope, Penny Banks, refuges, men's clubs and sewing and knitting classes were depicted on the branches of S.E. Hayward's illustration The Ragged School Tree.

Schools with multiple uses became more common during the second half of the 19th century. There were schools that hosted social activities, adult education programmes and 'return-to-learning' classes. Second-hand clothes shops, health clinics, meals, and summer play programmes edged their activities into the realm of welfare services.

Another version of 'extended' schooling was set up in 1930s Cambridgeshire where Henry Morris made real his vision of schools as the springboard and centre of lifelong community education. His village colleges

> ... would take all the various vital but isolated activities in village life – the School, the Village Hall and Reading Room, the Evening Classes, the Agricultural Education Courses, the Women's Institute, the British Legion, Boy Scouts and Girl Guides, the recreation ground, the branch of the County Rural Library, the Athletic and Recreation Clubs – and, bringing them together into relation, create a new institution for the English countryside.[57]

In the USA, which had its own community school movement, a more radical concept was developed in the late 1970s. 'Full service' schools provided integrated health and social services to support families bringing up children in disadvantaged areas.

In 2008, a combination of the 'full-service' concept and the vision of O'Neil and Morris lived on in what the government called the extended schools' 'core offer'. Seen by government as central to the success of Every Child Matters and a key component in the push for multi-agency working, the aim is that by 2010 all primaries are to ensure children have access to a variety of clubs – for example, study support, sport, art, chess and music. Parents are to be offered high-quality childcare and support. Community services will include adult education classes and use of the school's facilities. Crucially, schools should also offer 'swift and easy access' to specialist services such as speech therapy and mental health services and parenting support. In these ways, making an explicit requirement to link up with health and social services, extended schools go even further than Prestolee and the village colleges. In 2008, the government estimated there were 8,700 extended primary schools, about 50 per cent of the total.[58]

A good idea – or not?

Extended schools attracted a mixed response in evidence gathered by the Review. In one community sounding, head teachers in a former coalmining town in Yorkshire now suffering high unemployment and social deprivation, were generally unimpressed with the concept. The expectations of the policy, with its demands for multi-agency working, were unrealistic, they said, and had been foisted on them without adequate discussion. They also believed that a day lasting from 8 am to 6 pm was far too long for both children and teachers. In this there was little change since 2006, when heads surveyed by the NFER said that while extended schools offered benefits to pupils, parents and the wider community, the price was a heavier workload and longer hours for school staff.[59] Similarly, a poll for ICM conducted in 2006 found only 11 per cent of primary and secondary teachers fully supported extended schools.

The issue of long working hours for parents, commented on in Chapter 6, is also relevant here. One teacher questioned the extent to which schools should be expected to compensate for society's deficiencies and the wisdom of 'forcing' parents out to work and then having to fund schools to look after children for long hours. Some submissions to the Review said that extended schools represented an excessive encroachment on children's time. Extended schools had accelerated the pace at which their lives were becoming scholarised, a problem discussed in Chapter 5.[60] A similar warning as to the risk of extended schools producing 'institutionalised' children followed research in the West Midlands.[61] If after-school activities were offered by school-based staff, rather than run by people from outside, children perceived them as a rather unrelaxing extension of class – registers were taken and they were directed by adults as to what and when to play. This, according to the Joseph Rowntree Foundation, was of particular significance to disadvantaged children unlikely to have any other access to out-of-school activities. What was needed, according to the foundation, was an 'imaginative range of activities in which children are able to develop positive relationships with supervising adults and feel more in control of learning than they do at school'.[62]

However, other submissions were more positive. The charity 4Children wholeheartedly supported the extended schools agenda, saying the benefits of the core offer could not be underestimated, particularly in deprived communities. Both 4Children and the General Teaching Council believed that extended schools had the potential to identify children's needs early on – and to do something about them. ContinYou, the community learning charity, commented that the policy should 'make it easier for universal services like schools to work with the specialist or targeted service that some children and families need so problems are spotted early and handled effectively'.

Another positive note was struck by the NUT, though it insisted that, properly implemented, extended schools must liberate teachers to concentrate on teaching:

> The concept of extended schools, in particular the siting of health and social services in primary schools, would be particularly beneficial in areas of disadvantage. Multi-agency approaches to children's services could facilitate access to services amongst local communities and could also have the advantage of freeing teachers in schools to focus on educational achievements rather than the wider social needs of pupils that could be better met by others.

Extended schools and multi-agency working

Clearly, extended schools need good relations with health and social services, with sporting and leisure providers and with the voluntary sector. As responses to the Review indicated, this was not easy, with the potential for professional defensiveness existing in every service. The NAHT's submission summed it up thus:

> Schools are keen to work in partnership with other social services, but in many places these arrangements have failed to reach fruition. Progress is required on two different levels. Strategic planning needs to be put in place to overcome the complexities caused by differing pay scales, conditions of employment, professional standards and working practices across medical, social and education services. Secondly, personal contacts need to be developed between the people working locally in each service, by means such as joint training and seminars, to promote greater understanding and commitment to the process.

The importance of the relationships built between professionals working together and the need for training was also stressed by 4Children. 'Many teachers will need additional training in the identification and recognition of types of problems experienced by children and families, and it is essential that they receive support from health or social care services via the school should they identify concerns.'

Heads stay in charge

The question of who decides what activities and services an extended school should offer was tackled by witnesses to the Review. 4Children put heads firmly in the driving seat:

> Head teachers need to take a lead to encourage and develop integrated practices, welcoming the working together between different professionals with backgrounds in social care, health and education. Effective 'commissioning' of services must ensure that professionals with the relevant skills and experience are employed to support children and families who are referred or who seek additional help themselves.

Likewise, the NUT's submission insisted that schools should remain in charge and not be subsumed into a larger community organisation. 'Initiatives for the development of extended schools should come from schools themselves. Audits should be conducted of additional services needed at school-level by schools in conjunction with local authorities.' If a children's centre was located in a primary school, careful management was needed if it was not to be seen as an imposition. 'Such developments must be determined and led by schools, taking into account both the needs of the local community and the school's capacity to implement such a development,' said the union. It also warned that schools not able to offer the full package might need protection against, for example, a drop in admissions.

In 2008, the National College for School Leadership reported that ECM and extended schools had widened the head teacher's role.[63] An effective school leader, it said, needed to share responsibility with all professionals within a school, to collaborate with other schools, agencies and services, and to accept a leadership role that was moving beyond the school into the wider community.

A different perspective was supplied by Infed, discussing the Scottish experience of community schooling:

> In Scotland the impact of new community school policies has been to insist upon collaboration – often on the school site – and this has shifted the balance a little away from principals and heads. They now need the co-operation of other professionals in order to reach the standards or performance by which their schools are judged. Just how the extended schooling model develops in England is a matter of some speculation. Certainly there has been a tendency for heads in a number of schools to insist on the new cadre of workers, assistants and mentors being responsible to them rather than to some outside agency. However, when it comes to managing medical and child protection staff they are far more likely to leave management to others.[64]

Short of cash to reach out?

As the Joseph Rowntree Foundation pointed out, extended schools can give poorer children a taste of the activities and clubs enjoyed by better-off children. (Although, in these increasingly 'scholarised' times, it might be said that the foundation's finding that poorer children's free time was dominated by unsupervised street play and socialising with friends should not be viewed as entirely negative.)

Certainly, for children interviewed in the Review's community soundings, out-of-school activities such as sport, music and drama were a source of pleasure. Ofsted also reported that children enjoyed after-school clubs. The inspectors praised schools which were involving vulnerable pupils, for example 'by arranging for a mentor to act as a bridge to the extended activity or designing a breakfast club or an after-school club as an extension of the inclusive approaches during the day. Extra intervention made a considerable difference to small numbers of the most vulnerable, especially when combined with family support'.[65]

However, while some schools had overcome social and psychological barriers to the participation of deprived children, there was also evidence of financial barriers. In 2007 the charity New Philanthropy Capital reported that after-school clubs were often run on a shoestring or relied on the energy and goodwill of a few volunteers. And, according to The Times Educational Supplement: 'After-school clubs offering homework, chess and activity classes are being shut down in some of the poorest parts of the country, while the children of middle-class parents, who can afford to subsidise them, are reaping all the benefits of the scheme'.[66] The economic downturn of 2008 made it unlikely that these financial constraints would decrease and as unemployment, debt and house repossession made their impact felt more widely, the pressures on schools would inevitably increase.

Any results yet?

While 'the joined-up architecture of the most recent reforms represented a major move towards "extended" provision and fuller collaboration ... its effectiveness in serving the interests of children remained to be established', according to the Review's research survey on schools and other agencies.[67]

This lack of proof of effectiveness has been a concern to Ofsted. In 2006, inspectors concluded that extended services boosted children's self-confidence and helped them become more positive about learning and about what they might achieve. However, it added that any impact on standards and achievement was not always monitored.[68] Two years later, the chief inspector reported that extended schools, and children's centres in particular were making 'good progress overall', but again, 'monitoring and evaluating the impact of these services is an area for improvement – especially in relation to the academic attainment of children and young people'.[69] Clearly monitoring is vital – without it extended schools simply will not be able to tell if they are identifying and meeting needs and ultimately improving children's lives. Moreover, there has been serious concern expressed about Ofsted's own methodology for evaluating children's services: a criticism highlighted in the case of 'Baby P' where Ofsted admitted that shortcomings in Haringey children's services department had not been picked up in its inspection data.

The government's three-year evaluation of extended schools did conclude, tentatively, that they were raising attainment, particularly that of disadvantaged children. Families and local people suffering hardship were also benefiting, and while costs were high, they were either equalled or outweighed by the benefits. In relation to multi-agency working, the evaluation reported that while difficulties of partnership working remained after three years, enough schools had found solutions to suggest the problems were not insuperable. It identified some 'promising developments in terms of the stable and productive partnership arrangements ... the beginnings of genuine pupil and community involvement'.[70]

As Gillian Pugh said in 2008:

> As far as hard evidence from research studies is concerned, it is early days for conclusive results. But studies of some of the first extended schools have found improvements in children's educational attainment and their attendance, motivation and behaviour. Smaller scale studies have shown a range of outcomes, including earlier assessment and response to children with additional needs, reductions in bullying, healthier lifestyles, and schools being better able to tap into the resources of their local communities. The key measure of success will be the extent to which a more integrated approach will narrow the gap between those who do well and those who do not.[71]

Narrowing the gap was seen by many submissions and by ministers as a raison d'être of extended schools. As the government's evaluation indicated, the services offered by extended schools can help vulnerable families – but only if they use them.

Involving fathers in their children's education was a problem, according to some witnesses in the Review's community soundings. Their worries were supported by evidence from Ofsted. Extended schools and Sure Start children's centres 'were not always sufficiently active in reaching out to groups, including fathers and some minority ethnic groups. Some schools recognised that services were not used enough by the families beyond the immediate school neighbourhood, but they were not effective enough in widening participation'.[72]

Similar problems had been identified in relation to children's centres two years previously. Managers agreed then that they needed to do more to identify and provide outreach services to deprived families.[73] The leadership team in one children's centre had worked hard to employ staff from local minority ethnic groups to encourage wider engagement. Another centre used a 'parents' crew', which included other carers, to knock on doors in the community, as the centre had found that word of mouth was the most effective way of reaching people.[74] Language barriers, cultural and religious insensitivities, cost and concerns about quality were further deterrents identified by the Daycare Trust in 2008.[75] Minority ethnic parents reported that they did not know where to find out about services and that sometimes the services did not seem relevant or were not available when they needed them.

NARROWING THE GAP

By now it will be apparent that one of the more fundamental and recurrent concerns of the Review is the gap in children's attainment that mirrors gaps in wealth, health, familial stability, risk, housing and other indicators which in England are more pronounced than in many other countries. A distillation of the Review's submissions and soundings raised the question as to whether the problem was beyond the scope of schools, demanding a proper alignment of educational and social policies, and action to reduce the gross inequalities in wealth.

The submission from the NUT dealt with the issue in terms of what schools could do and how links between schools and other agencies could make a difference:

> Although schools do make a difference in even the most challenging circumstances, a testament to the profession's dedication and expertise, teachers and schools alone cannot address all the problems of primary schools which serve disadvantaged communities. The quality of life in these areas has a direct impact on the educational prospects of children. Whilst one in seven children lives in poverty ... there will always be barriers to children achieving their true potential ...
>
> Within the primary education system, there should be a sustained attack on the root causes of social and economic deprivation ... Early years initiatives, such as Sure Start, are both an important recognition of this fact and a real contribution to tackling a persistent and damaging feature of our society. Social class still has a powerful influence on the achievements of children. To its credit, the government has recognised this. There needs to be, however, joined-up thinking, on how initiatives in communities to tackle social and economic deprivation can link up to primary education locally.

Why so 'hard to reach'?

As children's centres and extended schools have found, some deprived children and families remain stubbornly 'hard to reach'. Yet the involvement of these groups is crucial if Every Child Matters is to achieve its aims and, ultimately, England's achievement gap to be narrowed. Part of the problem, suggested the Review's research survey on schools and other agencies, is that being targeted for additional help implies failure. 'The selective targeting of "insufficient" children and families as recipients of services perpetuates a climate of stigma and censure that fails to mesh with the diversity of contemporary life and may impede uptake and effectiveness.'[76] Certainly some submissions to the Review commented that referral to outside agencies stigmatised families experiencing difficulties. Children in the Birmingham community soundings considered it important that teachers knew if children were in care or were having difficulties at home. However, in an indication of the sensitivity of emotions involved, they also believed children should have a choice about disclosing such information.

In 2004, the Home Office defined three types of 'hard to reach' families: minority groups (the marginalised, disadvantaged or socially excluded such as some ethnic minorities; members of Gypsy, Roma and Traveller communities;[77] migrant workers; asylum seekers); those who 'slip through the net' (carers or people with mental health problems); and the 'service resistant' (families 'known' to social services, those with a history of drug use, alcohol abuse or criminal behaviour).[78] It stressed the importance of talking to the families – surprisingly, direct consultation only occurred in a quarter of all interventions – and that any assessment of their needs should be non-stigmatising.

One way to reduce stigma is to make public services as universal and as easily accessible as possible. There is evidence that 'universal population level approaches do contribute to preventing child maltreatment because they normalise and destigmatise attendance at parenting programmes ... because they provide opportunities for support networks to be established within communities and because they provide parents with a positive experience of professional help.'[79] However, attempting to make a service universal obviously risks diluting what is on offer. And, as indicated by the experience of Sure Start children's centres, providing a universal service does not guarantee universal uptake. Furthermore, work is needed to ensure that families regard services positively – too much provision is 'built on deep-seated notions of children as incompetent, credulous, powerless or incomplete'.[80]

Clearly public services are recognising the need to become attuned to social and cultural diversity in terms of poverty, class, ethnicity and disability, but there is a long way to go, as the following examples illustrate.

Travellers: marginalised, bullied and segregated

The plight of Traveller children, as an example of a marginalised group, was recognised in the Review's community soundings, one of which included meetings with Travellers and those who work with them. The Traveller representatives said that they and their children faced discrimination, bullying and segregation, both inside and outside school, and reported disturbing instances involving teachers as well as other parents. This sense of isolation was reinforced by community representatives who said they believed some teachers were frightened of Travellers and did not know enough about them. Traveller parents also reported that their own lack of education made it hard for them to support their children's learning, especially now that homework had become a more prominent feature of primary education. They also pointed out that there were obvious reasons – technical as well as financial – why many Traveller families could not meet the education system's tacit expectation that all today's children had ready access to a computer and the internet. On the other hand, as a family-based culture they warmed to the idea of family-based learning.

The allocation of statements of special needs revealed a high percentage awarded to Traveller and Roma/Gypsy children, as discussed in Chapter 9, and one authority has suggested that 'special education continues to fulfil its traditional function vis-à-vis the mainstream sector of containing troublesome individuals and depoliticising educational failure.'[81]

The Review's national soundings stressed the need for services to listen to marginalised groups and for teachers to be trained in how to work with them. It was felt to be particularly important that teachers and others should reach out to the different groups, rather than wait for them to come to school. The findings on disproportionate statementing and the fact that the 2007 Equalities Review final report found a striking and disturbing correlation between marginalisation and under-achievement, combine to give this recommendation both authority and urgency.[82]

Mental health: slipping through the net

Children with mental health problems or those who look after mentally ill parents are another hard-to-reach group. The British Medical Association has estimated that 1.1 million children under 18 would benefit from specialist mental health services.[83] It warned that those from deprived homes, looked-after children, young asylum-seekers as well as those who have witnessed domestic violence, were all at particular risk. The association called for more flexible access to services, a holistic approach that supported the child and the family, and possibly combining mental health services with general medical and sexual health services to reduce stigma.

In its submission to the Review, ContinYou, the community learning charity, also urged that primary pupils suffering from mental health problems should be quickly referred to the specialist services provided through extended schools. By contrast, in 2008 Young Minds proposed that teachers be trained in spotting mental health problems, pointing out that 80 per cent of seven-to 13-year-olds said they would rather go to their teacher for emotional support than to a health professional.

Stigma also clouded the prospects of another group of largely invisible children – those with a parent in prison – estimated in 2008 to be more than 160,000 in the UK every year (there were no official records). Families preferred to keep what has happened secret, so the children, at increased risk of aggressive behaviour, depression, anxiety, truancy and under-achievement, were often left without support. In 2007, Action for Prisoners Families called on the Department for Children, Schools and Families to 'recognise children of prisoners as a potentially vulnerable group and ensure that its policies, practice and practitioner training reflect their needs'. The Cabinet Report 'Think Family' acknowledged the difficulties in meeting the complex needs of some families and recommended a 'whole family' approach which:

> stresses the importance of looking at the family as a unit and of focusing on positive interdependency and supportive relationships. This approach takes the family's resilience and social capital as the foundations for achieving positive outcomes.[84]

THE NARROWING THE GAP PROGRAMME

So what can schools and local authorities do to help narrow the gap? Ideas and case studies were provided by a two-year programme of considerable potential significance, which was funded by the Department for Children, Schools and Families and the Local Government Association. It aims

> to make a significant difference, on a national scale, to the performance of Children's Trusts in 'narrowing the gap' in outcomes between vulnerable and excluded children and the rest, against a context of improving outcomes for all.[85]

Its particular focus is on children aged 3–13, making the programme of special relevance to this review, given the evidence that the programme's first report cites of the positive impact of early intervention on cognitive outcomes, educational attainment, social development, behaviour, health and well-being. The project is valuable in the first instance for identifying from national datasets those groups of children and young people who are most vulnerable in respect of the ECM outcomes and most likely to fall behind:

- children from poorer socio-economic groups, including White working-class boys
- looked-after children
- children with disabilities
- children with special educational needs, with and without statements
- children excluded from school
- children with records of poor school attendance
- children from different ethnic backgrounds
- young offenders
- young carers
- children at risk from significant harm
- children living with 'vulnerable' adults
- children not fluent in English
- children who are asylum seekers or refugees.[86]

In its first year, the programme recommended:

- close links between primary schools and early years settings to support children when they transfer
- access to the services of extended schools for all children and families
- schools to engage effectively with parents and develop preventative services for those with particular needs. Parents to be helped to understand and support their children's development and learning

- schools to have access to a range of staff and programmes to provide a speedy response to serious and urgent needs
- priority to be given to the needs of children in care with children's centres and schools working in partnership with adoptive parents, foster carers and residential care staff
- schools to work with wider children's services and other partners to provide, as early as possible, coordinated personalised support for children with additional needs or at risk of poor outcomes
- governing bodies to ensure that multi-agency staff working in and with children's centres and extended schools are co-ordinated, supported and receive joint training and supervision from their relevant professional organisation.

Narrowing the Gap, like the 2007 Children's Plan, stressed the key role of schools and the need for close links with other services 'as a critical means of improving outcomes for children and narrowing the gap'. However, it said, echoing concerns expressed earlier in this chapter, that 'surveys of head teachers, particularly in secondary schools, suggest we have so far failed to secure their full buy-in to this idea of the role of the school ... If the gap is to be narrowed everywhere, the notion of the school as a community asset and all that implies, must be driven through.'[87]

In 2008, the project's final report suggested that if the principles underpinning *Every Child Matters* were now implemented, outcomes for children would be improving and the gap would be narrowing everywhere. Nevertheless, it concluded that 'the overriding approach and central components of ECM, expanded and built on in the Children's Plan, were broadly the correct policy prescription'. And schools, children's centres and other services had made significant progress in their ability to work together effectively. The project found outstanding examples of integrated working with children's centres and schools right at the heart. 'Their capacity to act as an accessible, non-stigmatising resource for children and families is manifest in many of these case studies, as is the positive impact on children's attainment and readiness to learn as one of many benefits resulting from working more effectively with children's services.'

A key message to emerge from the project was the importance of a strong and consistent focus on the needs of all children, but particularly the most vulnerable. Another was the need for good relations with parents – an area, discussed in Chapter 6, where schools are still falling short. 'Professionals, including teachers, should be encouraged to go out more and talk to people – parents especially – because face-to-face communication is always more effective in building relationships than letters and leaflets'. A third vital ingredient was strong leadership amid a culture where 'everyone shares a sense of common purpose and contributes to a single vision and message that is constantly reinforced and promoted by leaders and practitioners, using a common and shared language'.

During 2008, the project tested practical and strategic guidance on narrowing the gap with 101 local authorities and their children's trust partners, publishing revised guidance, backed by 114 case studies, in November of that year. The guidance recommended that 'local authorities and their partners [should be held] firmly to account for achieving improvements in outcomes and for narrowing the gap.'[88] This emphasis on localism in one vital aspect of children's education and care contrasts with the continuing centralism in respect of the national curriculum, national assessment and national strategies for raising standards. It might be suggested that our own approach, which provides for a strong and protected local component to the curriculum, is more consistent with the government's strategy for narrowing the gap in educational outcomes between the most vulnerable and disadvantaged children and the rest. Indeed, the Review's proposed community curriculum might take its place as one of the key strategies in the Narrowing the Gap pantheon.

CONCLUSION

This chapter has looked at the relations between schools and other agencies, for a child's chances of flourishing at school rest not just on the broad shoulders of the education service but also – of course – on parents and carers and on other public services. The need for these services to start with the child – to be shaped by the needs of young people and their families irrespective of professional boundaries – has been accepted for decades. Yet perhaps only now is the political, organisational and professional will strong enough to make the massive cultural shift that genuine joined-up, integrated working requires. Judging from evidence submitted to the Review and other research findings, there is consensus that policies such as *Every Child Matters* and Narrowing the Gap, which necessitate an integrated approach, are the right way to go. But there was also consensus that the process is complex and progress is slow and the challenges to primary schools very demanding. The reality for many primary schools is that the quality of joined-up working remains patchy.

There are tensions. 'Barriers to communication and collaboration across professions are deep-seated and resistant to change,' as one of the Review's research surveys puts it.[89] Sometimes schools blame other services for the barriers. Sometimes the services blame schools. At a strategic level, some barriers would be removed by tackling a well-known source of resentment: the differences in pay and working conditions between all those who work with children. At a personal level, giving staff from the different services at a local level the chance to get to know each other, perhaps through joint training, will also speed their disappearance. Professionals from various backgrounds need to learn to speak the same language, but to work in different ways. The message that integration needs more time came through strongly in the evidence to the Review.

Many teachers, under tremendous pressure to raise standards and wary of becoming auxiliary social workers, have been reluctant to embrace integrated working. Nevertheless, schools are now getting on board. As hubs of their communities, the one place where all children go, they must be central to decisions about what services their pupils need. Teacher unions, while agreeing with this key role, worry about local authorities' ability to deliver. Paradoxically, in an era of integration some schools feel more isolated from local authority support than previously. Their contacts in the defunct education departments have perhaps moved on and they have yet to feel at ease with the new children's services departments. However, there is a sense that they are slowly finding their feet and the Narrowing the Gap programme reported considerable progress in integrated working in just the first six months of 2008.

In the light of this, calls to the Review for a period of stability to allow the new ways of working to be evaluated and become embedded seem sensible. Instead, however, the Children's Plan seeks a 'step-change' in schools' involvement with children's trusts and to drive them into closer relationships with a greater number of partners. More may need to be done to ensure there is the vision and leadership within the children's sector to rise to this challenge. There is also a risk of tension between top-down and bottom-up: between government and local authority control of services and recognition that effective change occurs when schools and communities are in charge of their own destinies. Forcing heads to co-operate with the local children's trust will be futile unless their assessment of pupils' needs is allowed to shape a school's relations with other agencies.

There are other tensions. Evidence to the Review suggests that some schools feel caught in a policy contradiction. On one side, *Every Child Matters* requires them to co-operate, integrate and support – encouraging them to reach out to difficult or troubled families. On the other, there are the standards agenda, choice and competition – forces that tend to marginalise families for whom choice is not an option and competition means defeat. Every child does matter, but in terms of test results some children appear to matter more than others. As the evidence revealed, some heads see ECM as a distraction from what they perceive to be their key role of raising academic standards. Yet the success of Behaviour and Support Teams were an indication of the potential benefits of a holistic approach to a child's needs. Such multi-agency teamwork is expanding hugely. Even more encouragingly, there is also evidence from schools well advanced along the ECM road that concentrating on its five goals also raises standards – a message that needs to be strongly trumpeted.[90] Early evidence from some 'core offer' extended schools also reveals improvements in children's attainment, behaviour, motivation and attendance. And children's charities have high hopes for extended schools' ability to identify pupils' problems early on.

Heads also worry about workload and the long hours that an extended school operates. Such anxieties might be eased by findings that children actually prefer their after-school clubs not to be run by teachers. And the schools praised by Ofsted for the quality of their integrated services were the ones that had set up multi-agency teams to support vulnerable pupils. Similarly, the NUT sees the proper implementation of the extended schools policy as one that can liberate teachers to concentrate on teaching, leaving other professionals to concentrate on other needs. As the National College for School Leadership has said, heads must accept their leadership role has broadened into the community, but they must also be adept at sharing responsibility.

While evidence indicates that a multi-agency approach can help all pupils, gaps have also been revealed. The children still most likely to slip through the net are those in greatest need. Sure Start has been slow to make an impact, not surprisingly given the deep-seated problems of deprivation that it faced. Early evaluations showed that it was failing to reach the most vulnerable families. Similar criticisms have been made of extended schools. Again, though, there appears to have been progress – the most recent evaluation of Sure Start children's centres found that they were helping all the three-year-olds in their areas. And there is greater clarity about what schools need to do to reach marginalised families. First, they have to identify which parents are not engaging so they need to monitor attendance at, for example, after-school clubs. Second, they must understand the kind of needs they are dealing with. Teachers told the Review that they lack the confidence to approach some marginalised groups such as Travellers – clearly training is needed. And third, they need to make contact, which means being given the time to go out and talk to parents. Parents and carers are the key. The government knows this and has launched many parenting initiatives. Some schools have already appointed parent support advisers. The children's centre that used a 'parents' crew' to knock on doors showed the way. It is not easy, but as Narrowing the Gap has found, face-to-face communication is better than official letters. Disaffected families with little money or hope rarely open them.

As the potential hub of the community – even more so if our proposed aims and curriculum are implemented – primary schools are in an ideal position to respond to challenges arising from the complexity and diversity of modern children's lives. But they cannot do it alone. Heads who are wary of the integrated approach probably do not need to be persuaded as to the undoubted benefits of having schools embedded in their community, providing – without stigma – parental support and access to specialist services such as speech therapy and mental health. What they do need is a commitment that teachers' workload will not increase beyond reasonable limits, and that teachers are not expected to fix all society's ills. We believe that schools struggling to build bridges to other services should be given the time, resources and staffing to help make it happen. Those in deprived areas need money to run good after-school clubs and the staff to monitor attendance. All schools need advice on how to improve relations with hard-to-reach families so that the families gain the confidence to access services of use to them. Teachers need help in spotting children's mental health problems – and support from specialists when they spot them. Schools need training in how to work with marginalised groups to ensure they respect religious and cultural sensitivities and that these groups have a voice. Progress in these areas on the part of schools and other agencies will help challenge the negative perception of vulnerable families and go some way to narrowing the gap through which too many children currently fall.

NOTES

1 Balls (3 July 2008).
2 Alexander and Hargreaves (2007).
3 Unicef (2007).
4 Office for National Statistics (ONS) (2004).
5 National Child Measurement Programme (2006/07).

6 Baird (2006).
7 World Health Organisation (2008a).
8 World Health Organisation (2008b).
9 *Ibid.*
10 CACE (1967): para 215.
11 *Ibid.*: para 209.
12 *Ibid.*: para 255.
13 See Bohm (1968).
14 *Ibid.*: para 231.
15 *Ibid.*: para 232.
16 *Ibid.*: para 153.
17 Barron *et al.* (2010), *The Cambridge Primary Review Research Surveys*, Chapter 5.
18 Mayall and Storey (1998).
19 Barron *et al.* (2010), *The Cambridge Primary Review Research Surveys*, Chapter 5.
20 Fitzherbert (1980).
21 The Observer, January 26, 2003, article by Dr C. Hanvey, director of operations, Barnardos.
22 Barron *et al.* (2010), *The Cambridge Primary Review Research Surveys*, Chapter 5.
23 DHSS (1980).
24 Mayall and Storey (1998).
25 DfES (2004e).
26 The reorganised Office for Standards in Education, Children's Services and Skills drew together the Commission for Social Care Inspection (CSCI), the Children and Family Court Advisory and Support Service (CAFCAS), the inspection remit of Her Majesty's Inspectorate for Court Administration (HMCIA) and the remit of the Adult Learning Inspectorate (ALI).
27 DfES (2005d).
28 DCSF (2008g).
29 University of East Anglia/National Children's Bureau (2007).
30 DCSF (2008g): 4.
31 DCSF (2008n).
32 Originally there had been over 300 PCTs but in 2005 the government reduced their number by 50 per cent.
33 Department of Health (2007).
34 Tower Hamlets PCT School Health Service website: http://www.thpct.nhs.uk/your-services/school-health-service/
35 King (2004): 9.
36 Ofsted (2007c).
37 Lord *et al.* (2008).
38 Lewis, Chamberlain *et al.* (2007).
39 Ward and Milne (2008), *Times Educational Supplement.*
40 Lewis, Chamberlain *et al.* (2007).
41 Ward and Milne (2008), *Times Educational Supplement.*
42 General Secretary's address to NAHT annual conference (4 May 2008).
43 Barron *et al.* (2010), *The Cambridge Primary Review Research Surveys*, Chapter 5.
44 Pugh (17 March 2008).
45 GTC *Teaching* magazine (1 July 2008).
46 DCSF (2008a): 39–41.
47 Halsey *et al.* (2006).
48 Daniels and Porter (2010), *The Cambridge Primary Review Research Surveys*, Chapter 9.
49 *Ibid.*
50 Lord *et al.* (2008).
51 www.infed.org
52 Daniels and Porter (2010), *The Cambridge Primary Review Research Surveys*, Chapter 9.
53 Institute of Education, University of London press release (22.07.2008) (online: http://ioewebserver.ioe.ac.uk/ioe/cms/get.asp?cid=1397&1397_1=20824).
54 Kendall *et al.* (2007).
55 Prestolee Primary School, Bolton: www.prestolee.bolton.sch.uk
56 Owen (1816).
57 Morris (1925).
58 TDA (2008g).
59 Chamberlain *et al.* (2006).
60 Mayall (2010), *The Cambridge Primary Review Research Surveys*, Chapter 3, quoted in Barker (2007), *Times Educational Supplement.*
61 Arnold *et al.* (2006).
62 Joseph Rowntree Foundation (2007).
63 NCSL (2008).
64 www.infed.org
65 Ofsted (2008f).
66 Marley (2007), *Times Educational Supplement.*
67 Barron *et al.* (2010), *The Cambridge Primary Review Research Surveys*, Chapter 5.

68 Ofsted (2006b).
69 Gilbert (2008) Ofsted press briefing, 23 January.
70 Cummings *et al.* (2007).
71 GTC *Teaching* magazine (July 1, 2008).
72 *Ibid.*
73 National Audit Office (2006).
74 Ofsted (2008f).
75 Daycare Trust and Esmée Fairbairn Foundation (2008).
76 Barron *et al.* (2010), *The Cambridge Primary Review Research Surveys*, Chapter 5.
77 Further references to Gypsy/Roma and Travellers of Irish Heritage communities, individuals or young people will be encompassed under the ethnic group of 'Travellers'.
78 Doherty *et al.* (2004).
79 Sanders *et al.* (2003).
80 Barron *et al.* (2010), *The Cambridge Primary Review Research Surveys*, Chapter 5.
81 Armstrong (2005).
82 The Equalities Review (2007).
83 British Medical Association (2006).
84 Cabinet Office (2007): 28.
85 LGA, DCSF, Improvement and Development Agency (IDeA) (2007): 2.1.
86 LGA, DCSF and IdEA (2007): 2.2.
87 LGA, DCSF and IdEA (2007).
88 LGA, DCSF and IdEA (2007): 2.1.
89 Barron *et al.* (2010), *The Cambridge Primary Review Research Surveys*, Chapter 5.
90 http://www.dcsf.gov.uk/childrensplan/downloads/ECM%20outcomes%20framework.pdf

21 Teachers

Expertise, development, deployment

Nearly one million adults work in England's schools. Of that one million, 198,200 are primary teachers and 172,600 are primary school support staff.[1] This amounts to about one adult for every 11 primary pupils, and represents growth as well as investment on a remarkable scale. When the Plowden Report was published in 1967, though pupil numbers were similar to today's, there were only 140,000 teachers and an unspecified but far smaller number of 'ancillary helpers'. Indeed, the massive increase in support staff is a recent phenomenon, and a cornerstone of the current government's strategy for workforce reform (see Chapter 22).

The workforce has diversified as well as expanded. At the time of Plowden, primary schools operated with a simple 'flat' organisational structure of heads, deputy heads (in schools with more than 100 pupils) and class teachers. In a section of their report grandly entitled – with a disarming lack of gender awareness and a somewhat proprietorial view of headship – 'The Head Teacher and His Staff', Plowden noted that some of the latter had 'graded posts' often for little more than long service and good conduct. It suggested that some of these 'graded' staff might be used as 'consultants', 'to raise the quality of work' in specific subjects, even taking over a class for part of the week.[2]

The 1978 HMI primary survey, undertaken in line with Plowden's recommendation that there be a follow-up survey of the state of English primary education every decade or so, expressed more direct concern about inconsistencies in curriculum coverage and quality within and between schools. Like others before and since, the inspectors were persuaded of the common-sense view that teachers' knowledge of a subject and the quality of their teaching are closely linked, and showed how inadequate subject knowledge led to poor planning and low levels of 'match' between task and pupil.[3] Taking its cue from Plowden, HMI recommended the appointment of cross-school subject co-ordinators to lead curriculum planning and help plug gaps in individual teacher's subject expertise. During the next decade the nomenclature drifted between curriculum/subject 'co-ordinator', 'consultant', 'leader' and 'adviser', but the idea was the same: in each school, some teachers would combine the role of generalist teacher of one class with that of specialist co-ordinator of planning and support in a particular area of the curriculum across the school as a whole.

In 2008, the Training and Development Agency (TDA) listed the following roles and responsibilities typically found in today's primary schools:

- *Head teacher*: leads and manages the school, its staff, its pupils and the education they receive.
- *Deputy head teacher* (all but the smallest schools): manages the school in the absence of the head teacher.
- *Assistant head teacher* (large schools only): supports the head and deputy head with the management of the school.
- *Early years co-ordinator*: responsible for children in the EYFS and for leading the team of foundation stage teachers, nursery nurses and teaching assistants.
- *Key stage co-ordinator*: leads and manages either key stage 1 or 2. Usually also has a class teaching commitment.

- *Special educational needs co-ordinator (Senco)*: responsible for the day-to-day provision for pupils with special educational needs, including the implementation of the SEN code of practice.
- *Subject leaders and curriculum co-ordinators*: responsible for the leadership and management of a particular curriculum area; usually combined with responsibility for a class.
- *Classroom teachers*: plan, prepare and deliver lessons to meet the needs of all pupils, setting and marking work and recording pupil development as necessary. Many combine this with roles listed above.
- *Supply teachers*: substitute or temporary teachers usually employed by a supply agency or local authority to take classes when teachers are in training or absent due to sickness.[4]

Alongside these, according to another study, may be found:

- *Teaching assistants and equivalent* (teaching assistant, learning support assistant, nursery nurse, therapist)
- *Pupil welfare workers* (education welfare officer, home-school liaison officer, learning mentor, nurse and welfare assistant)
- *Technical and specialist staff* (ICT network manager, ICT technician, librarian, science technician and technology technician)
- *Other pupil support staff* (bilingual support officer, cover supervisor, escort, language assistant, midday assistant and midday supervisor)
- *Facilities staff* (cleaner, cook, and other catering staff)
- *Administrative staff* (administrator/clerk, bursar, finance officer, office manager, secretary, data manager and personal assistant to the head teacher)
- *Site staff* (caretaker and premises manager).[5]

This chapter concentrates on the central educational function of primary schools and for that reason will say little about many of the people listed above. This in no way denies their importance to the successful running of primary schools, as any teacher will immediately confirm. However, even an enquiry as broad as the Cambridge Primary Review cannot do justice to the range of professional and support roles currently undertaken. In the narrower context of schools' strictly educational tasks, the key staff are head, deputy head, class teacher, key stage year/subject/special needs co-ordinator and teaching assistant, and it is on these that we shall concentrate in the present chapter and the one that follows. Even more specifically, we leave discussion of leadership in its various forms to Chapter 22, and focus here on teachers and teaching. Chapter 22 will also look in greater detail at the work of teaching assistants, who of course do have an educational role, and an important one.

We add to this introduction a historical point which has profound and complex ramifications for all that follows. The defining teaching role in primary schools is that of the generalist class teacher who teaches most or all of the curriculum to one class for the whole year, and in some cases remains with that class is it moves up through the school. This contrasts with the typical secondary-school subject specialist who teaches one or two subjects to pupils in different years and in a given day will encounter a large number of children whose ages, theoretically, may range from 11 to 18.

The class teacher system creates two obvious imperatives, encapsulated in the phrases 'whole child' and 'whole curriculum' which many primary teachers are happy to use to define the essence of their work. The first is to develop a comprehensive and rounded view of each pupil in the class. The second is to plan, teach and have mastery of all the subjects, areas of learning or domains in the curriculum, except those where specialist support is provided.

The class teacher system is so familiar, so much taken for granted, that few pause to ask whether, educationally, it best serves primary pupils' needs. Yet it arose not for educational reasons but because, for the Victorian founders of mass public elementary schooling, it combined cheapness and efficiency in the context of large classes, a very basic curriculum and a view of teaching as little more than the drilling of facts and skills. Since then, less functional justifications – usually pivoting on the idea of 'the whole child' and the stability and security the arrangement offers young pupils – have been added *post hoc* to the role. Yet the class teacher system is now regarded by many as inevitable, right and proper. It attracts considerable loyalty, generates a particular kind of job satisfaction, and is staunchly defended – so much so that when in 1992 the 'three wise men' report suggested that schools might care to explore the extension of primary teaching roles to include specialists and semi-specialists as well as class teachers and curriculum co-ordinators,[6] many teachers rounded on the suggestion as tantamount to sacrilege.

We regret to say that we cannot allow ourselves to be deflected from the question of how well the class teacher system serves children's needs, and the related matter of how well initial teacher training serves the needs of class teachers. The world has moved on: classes may now be smaller, but since 1870 the curriculum has expanded and become more complex and professionally demanding, while teaching – as we saw in Chapter 15 – is now understood to entail a great deal more than transmission. Further, it is our view that some of the problems which have been projected onto the curriculum – the claim that since 1989 it has been inherently unmanageable, for example – may be less about the curriculum than the expertise of teachers, and specifically the limits to what a class teacher can reasonably be expected to know and do. This possibility has already been hinted at (in Chapter 14), though the government's 2008–9 Rose Review entertained no such thoughts and presumed that the problem is the curriculum and only the curriculum – or, as Rose put it, 'quarts into pint pots'.[7]

We also need to consider how far the role of curriculum co-ordinator / subject leader makes up for any deficiencies in the curriculum expertise of the class teacher. In doing so we must note that it, too, has fallen foul of the sometimes intense loyalty surrounding the class teacher system. Titles like 'consultant' were deliberately chosen to imply a territorially less invasive role than that of 'co-ordinator' as originally envisaged or 'subject leader' as later used by the TDA's predecessor, the Teacher Training Agency (TTA).[8]

EXPERTISE FOR PRIMARY TEACHING

These comments on generalists and specialists beg a key question, not just for this chapter but for the Cambridge Review as a whole in its quest to improve the quality of primary education: in the context of primary teaching, what do we mean by 'expertise'?

Head and heart

A clear and simple message which emerged from the Review's soundings and submissions was that teachers need to be qualified and knowledgeable but also caring. Children, in particular, had little doubt about the qualities they wanted teachers to possess and we summarise them elsewhere as equity, empathy and expertise. The 'expertise' in question was in the subjects to be taught, and in this important respect our child witnesses differed from many primary teachers who argued that subject knowledge at this stage is much less significant than dispositions and relationships. Interestingly, the children's views align with the principle, propounded by the Teaching and Learning Research Programme, that effective teaching 'engages with the big ideas, facts, processes, language and narratives of valued forms of knowledge'[9] (Chapter 15) and with Chapter 14's insistence that knowledge is a central component of the curriculum – any curriculum – and that the debate has been ill-served by a reductionist discourse that equates knowledge with arid or obsolete information.

Behind this pattern of responses are two assumptions. First, that teaching, like learning, is both a cognitive and an affective activity and that teachers need therefore to engage both head and heart, recognising that what in a professional sense may be matters of quasi-clinical judgement may be no less about the quality of the relationships they establish with their pupils, individually and collectively, as persons. That is certainly the way pupils themselves tend to see matters.

The other assumption is a variant on the old slogan 'We teach children, not subjects'. In one sense this is an indefensible dichotomy of the kind we objected to in Chapter 2, since teachers do both of these things. When it leads, as sometimes it still does, to the assertion that the only knowledge a primary teacher needs is about child development, and curriculum knowledge is of little importance, it is clearly a polarisation too far. However, in the other sense – that a teacher will not get very far without a deep understanding of what motivates and engages children, and what discourages, unsettles or alienates them – the slogan voices a significant, albeit partial, truth.

In this simple formulation, heart and head, child and subject are intersecting axes in a matrix. Knowledge of *children* is both generalised (see Chapter 7) and specific; derived from research and from everyday experience (though we noted earlier that research-informed practice is rarer than it should be); of children in general and of the particular children one teaches. Knowledge of *subject*, or what in light of Chapter 14 we prefer to call domain knowledge, includes both the intellectual grasp of content and its classroom application that we discuss below, and the sense of excitement and enthusiasm which a teacher feels for particular kinds of knowledge and understanding and the capacity to generate it in others.

The evidence reported in earlier chapters adds a third dimension to this – for the moment – basic model of expertise: knowledge of context, especially of children's lives outside school. It also brings the model within reach of the kind of pedagogical framework explored in Chapter 15, where, for example, pedagogy was proposed as comprising ideas, values, evidence and justifications (heart and head again, though who is to say which corresponds to which?) about children and childhood, aims and curriculum, family, community, culture and society, as well as teaching and learning (Figure 15.2).

Expertise as standards

A second source of insight into the nature of primary teaching expertise is policy, and specifically what teacher trainers are expected to attend to while taking trainees to the point where they can assume full-time responsibility for a class. The clearest current statement of such expectations is provided in the TDA's 2008 *Professional Standards for Qualified Teacher Status and Requirements for Initial Teacher Training*. This document frames expertise in terms of *professional attributes, professional knowledge and understanding* and *professional skills*:

Professional attributes
- relationships with children and young people (high expectations and positive values)
- frameworks (awareness of duties and policies)
- communicating with others (capacity to communicate with relevant others and commitment to collaboration)
- personal professional development (reflection on practice, identification of professional needs, openness to innovation and advice).

Professional knowledge and understanding
- teaching and learning (knowledge of repertoire)
- assessment and monitoring (knowledge of formal requirements and resulting information, and of other approaches to assessment)
- subjects and curriculum (knowledge of subjects to be taught and related pedagogy; knowledge of statutory and non-statutory curricula and frameworks, national strategies and other government initiatives)
- literacy, numeracy and ICT (as tested as a condition of entry, together with knowledge of their applications in teaching and the curriculum)
- achievement and diversity (knowledge of individual development and cultural diversity; ability to 'personalise' provision, including for SEN or for children with English as an additional language; knowledge of roles of other professionals working in areas such as SEN)

- health and well-being (knowledge of current policies and legal requirements, and of how to support children experiencing personal difficulty).

Professional skills
- planning (for progression in the curriculum, in literacy/numeracy/ICT, and for homework)
- teaching (use a range of teaching strategies and resources; build on prior knowledge and enable learners to apply new knowledge, understanding and skills; adapt own language to learners and 'use explanations, questions, discussions and plenaries effectively'); manage the learning of individuals, groups and classes)
- assessing, monitoring and giving feedback (use range of strategies, assess pupils' learning needs, provide feedback, help learners to reflect on their learning)
- reviewing teaching and learning (evaluating and modifying)
- learning environment (establishing a purposeful and safe environment and a clear disciplinary framework)
- team working and collaboration.[10]

On this list we might make a number of observations, starting with a brief but necessary historical excursion.

Expertise as knowing, doing – and perhaps much more

The TDA standards demonstrate a significant shift from the *content* of initial teacher training (ITT) courses – which was how such matters were defined under the ITT validation and accreditation procedures which operated during much of the post-war period, through the decade of the Council for the Accreditation of Teacher Education (CATE, 1984–94) and into the era of TTA/TDA (since 1994) – to their *outcomes*.

This shift of focus has been accompanied by an adjustment in the balance of concern from a broad range of knowledge on which teaching is held to be contingent to teaching expertise more narrowly defined. Until the 1990s, the expertise of the newly-qualified teacher (NQT) was viewed – albeit obliquely, via the specified content of ITT courses – as a combination of subject engagement (at the student's own level, undergraduate courses only), subject 'applications' (knowledge of the subject(s) as and how taught in school), professional studies (classroom-related knowledge and skill) and educational studies (the knowledge about education in which teaching was thought to be embedded). These derived ultimately from the 1944 McNair Report's distinction between 'general' and 'professional' subjects, its underpinning belief that the trainee's personal education and professional preparation were intimately and necessarily linked, and its view that the NQT should have mastery of both 'principles of education' and 'such a knowledge of the subjects he proposes to teach as can justify his claim to teach them.'[11]

Following moves to make teaching a graduate profession, heralded by the introduction of the Bachelor of Education degree (BEd) in 1963, the nodal points of initial teacher training became educational studies and subject studies, the former structured round the 'big four' education disciplines of psychology, sociology, philosophy and history of education. This was a conscious exercise in academicisation in order to prove that the BEd was a 'real' degree rather than a lengthened teaching certificate. What the teacher knew, then, was now deemed more important than what he or she could do. This was seen by some as a necessary injection of academic rigour into teacher training allied to a conviction that to educate others teachers themselves needed to be well-educated, able to stand back from the job, place it in its larger social and epistemological context, and reflect autonomously and knowledgeably upon it. To the critics, though, the change was seen as making teacher training needlessly and – for students – bafflingly theoretical. Meanwhile, they objected, classroom-focused study had receded further and further into the background, and for primary trainees, 'curriculum' or 'professional' studies had low status, limited practical value and were given far too little time. Not surprisingly, complaints about the divergence of 'theory' and 'practice' were rife, and it was partly out of this experience that education theory earned the poor press which it continues to suffer. (There are other and more complicated reasons, having to do with the lowly status of training colleges/ colleges of education and the national intellectual climate, but we cannot go into them here.)

During the 1970s and early 1980s there were lively and often heated debates about the proper focus and structure of initial training for primary teaching, with parallel enquiries into the PGCE and BEd commissioned by the Universities Council for the Education of Teachers (UCET) and the Council for National Academic Awards (CNAA). The latter was by then was loosening the universities' control, through the post-war area training organisation system, of teacher training in colleges and polytechnics.

Both the UCET and CNAA reports insisted that professional study needed to be reinstated and upgraded.[12] The UCET report identified 'five elements in the professional equipment of pre-secondary teachers: classroom technique, curricular knowledge, professional knowledge, personal and interpersonal skills and qualities, constructive revaluation.'[13]

These developments were overtaken by what was in effect the first national curriculum, though it was for ITT rather than schools. A government circular paved the way for a single set of criteria in relation to which all ITT providers were to be inspected and all courses accredited. Professional studies were prominent, but particular attention was paid to subject knowledge, on the grounds that the HMI primary and secondary surveys of 1978–79 had 'demonstrated the overwhelming importance of teachers' knowledge base and confidence in the subjects which they teach'.[14]

Viewed in light of these developments, we see that the current TDA standards have a clear and indeed elaborated focus on executive classroom skill, but that subject knowledge has once again receded, while the independence of mind and broader understanding which were deemed so important during the 1970s and early 1980s have all but disappeared. Such contextualising knowledge as is listed is mostly about policy, and even evaluative capacities like 'reflection on practice', 'openness to innovation and advice' and 'reviewing teaching and learning' are tacitly policy-directed, because national curriculum, assessment and pedagogically-oriented strategies frame the entire operation.

This also explains the absence of attention to questions of value and purpose such as we explored in Chapter 12, and which in Chapter 14 we argued must be sorted out as a pre-condition rather than appendage to curriculum reform. Conspiracy theorists may claim that trainees and NQTs are denied a chance to explore and debate such matters because to do so may render them more likely to rock the boat as their school strives to do what is expected of it. It is more likely that the possibility of including exploration of aims and values did not occur to the drafters of the TDA standards simply because they assumed that the purposes of primary education are for government, rather than teachers, to determine.

Such matters, together with the conformist thrust of Ofsted inspections, lie behind the deep concern expressed in many of the Review's submissions and soundings that expertise for primary teaching is now more about compliance than the exercise of independent judgement. Head teachers taking part in the community soundings applauded the quality and dedication of their teachers but many believed that they were becoming de-skilled by over-reliance on official prescription, and that younger teachers, in particular, were trained merely to implement national strategy requirements and lacked the skill, or will, to improvise.

There was a clear age-related element in this: younger teachers, who had known no world outside the national curriculum and the national strategies, seemed content to 'comply and implement', while older teachers – partly because of the memory of different times and partly because they had advanced beyond the novice stage of professional development (see below) – talked more about creativity and autonomy. During the Review's national soundings there were many calls for teachers to have more time for reflection, research and study in order to meet these challenges, and for autonomy and creativity to be encouraged. The Association of Teachers and Lecturers warned: 'The national bank of expertise in curriculum and assessment will decline unless changes are made to encourage teachers to make their own judgements …'.

During the 1980s and 1990s, Schön's idea of the 'reflective practitioner'[15] provided the ostensible rationale for most initial teacher training courses (though it some cases it was more of a fashion accessory). However, whereas practice at that time was believed to require reflection, now the drive for highly-focused practical training may actively discourage it.

The new instrumentalism is not restricted to government and its agencies. The Institute for Public Policy Research (IPPR), source of many New Labour ideas and recruiting ground for advisers and even ministers, criticises the TDA's distinction between 'attributes', 'knowledge and understanding' and 'skills' as 'too vague to be useful', and proposes instead that 'today's teachers need to be:

- *Subject specialists*: able to teach in specialised subject areas.
- *Life coaches*: able to equip pupils with financial, communication, psychological, social and behavioural skills.
- *Pedagogical experts*: able to deliver personalised learning in increasingly mixed ability classes, in which some pupils may not have English as a first language; able to assess pupils diagnostically and create supportive environments for them.
- *Curriculum designers*: able to be flexible, making the curriculum relevant to pupils.
- *Professionals*: committed to teaching and interested in learning and using pedagogical techniques that work.'[16]

Actually, once one gets past the decisive-sounding categories, this is even more vague than the TDA standards, and even more imbued with uncritical adherence to the policy of the moment. If the TDA teacher is not encouraged to reflect, the IPPR teacher is positively discouraged from doing so. The IPPR also makes clear its view that effective teaching depends on government asserting even tighter control of curriculum, testing, schools, children's services and the 'measures and mechanisms' of accountability.[17] And what teacher, we have to ask, would conceivably be interested in using pedagogical techniques that do *not* work?

Expertise, pedagogy and didactics

If a reminder of the post-war development of primary teacher training allows us to assess some of the preoccupations and omissions in the TDA's version of expertise, a brief overseas trip enables us to locate it within the context of international debate. For what seems clear is that the endlessly oscillating discussion about the nature of expertise for teaching stems in part from that very English failure to engage with teaching in a principled rather than pragmatic manner which prompted Brian Simon's famous question 'Why no pedagogy in England'[18] (see Chapter 15). If we cannot define teaching then we are unable to say what kinds of expertise it requires.

In contrast, in continental Europe the one word *pedagogy* confidently sweeps together within a single concept the act of teaching and the body of knowledge, argument and evidence in which it is embedded and by which particular classroom practices are justified. Thus, at a typical Russian pedagogical university, pedagogy encompasses: 'general culture' comprising philosophy, ethics, history, economics, literature, art and politics; together with elements relating to children and their learning – psychology, physiology, child development and child law. Also included are aspects relating to the subjects to be taught, or *didaktika* and – linking all the elements – *metodika*, or ways of teaching them. The subject element, *didaktika* in Russia, *la didactique* in France, *die Didaktik* in Germany, subdivides variously into, for example, *allgemeine Didaktik* and *Fachdidaktik* (general and specialist or subject didactics) in Germany, *didactiques des disciplines* and *transpositions didactiques*, or *savoir savant* and *savoir enseigné* (scholarly and taught knowledge) in France.[19] These are equivalent to what Lee Shulman calls 'content' and 'pedagogical content knowledge' (PCK)[20] and what TTA/TDA's precursor body, CATE called 'subject' and 'subject applications'.

But only up to a point, for didactics in countries like Germany is a highly-developed branch of professional study and training, framed by concepts and theories which are as far removed from the homeliness and improvisatory quality of much English subject study as it is possible to imagine.

However, for some commentators the continental approach is too exclusive in its attention to knowledge as codifed in the disciplines, and this criticism has been levelled at Schulman too. For him, pedagogical content knowledge embodies:

> The aspects of content most germane to its teachability ... the most useful forms of expression of those ideas, the most powerful analogies, illustrations, examples, explanations and demonstrations – in a word, the ways of representing and formulating the subject that make it comprehensible to others.[21]

What this does not allow for is what we tried to capture in our discussion of knowledge and the cultural role of the school in Chapter 12, the idea that knowledge is personal as well as public, dynamic rather than static, and to an extent recreated in every learning encounter. Or, as Jerome Bruner said many years ago:

> A curriculum reflects not only the nature of knowledge itself but also the nature of the knower and of the knowledge-getting process ... We teach a subject not to produce little living libraries ... but rather to get a student to think mathematically ... to consider matters as an historian does, to take part in the process of knowledge-getting. Knowing is a process, not a product.[22]

If didactics is missing from both the TDA and IPPR versions of expertise, so too are versions of knowledge other than those 'out there'. To teach well surely dictates an understanding of how the learner comes to know, in order that the key pedagogical notion of 'scaffolding' can be realised and new knowledge can be more speedily and securely assimilated to what the pupil already knows. If England has, or has had until recently, no pedagogy in the sense we coined in Chapter 15, it may equally be suggested that while subject knowledge and subject applications have long been central to teacher training, they have not acquired the coherence that marks out mainstream European didactics. Indeed, David Hamilton's oblique tribute to Brian Simon is entitled 'Why no didactics in England?'[23]

Domain knowledge and craft knowledge

The fact that we have dwelled on the vexed issue of domain and pedagogical content knowledge should not be taken to imply that this is the only kind of knowledge for teaching that either exists or matters. This report's earlier chapters on childhood, aims and values, pedagogy and assessment more than hinted at the broader extent of the territory, as did the pedagogical models and principles discussed in Chapter 15 and the excursion into continental European didactics above. Lee Shulman himself, who coined the influential phrase 'pedagogical content knowledge', made it just one of seven categories of a knowledge base for teaching:

- content knowledge
- general pedagogical knowledge
- curriculum knowledge
- pedagogical content knowledge
- knowledge of learners and their characteristics
- knowledge of educational contexts
- knowledge of educational ends, purposes and values.[24]

To these, Pam Grossman adds – and in view of what we say below about professional development it is an important addition –

- knowledge of self[25]

These are not only different categories but also different kinds of knowledge. Knowledge of learners is, as has been noted, part generalised, public and research-informed and part rooted in each teacher's experience. Knowledge of educational ends, purposes and values encompasses both the public debates this Review's Chapter 12 (on aims) seeks to provoke, and the personal values of each teacher. In teaching, as in children's learning and indeed in virtually any situation one cares to nominate, public and personal ways of knowing and making sense are both influential and significant. It is out of the encounter between them that learning arises – by teachers as well as by children. It is not surprising, therefore, that the literature on knowledge for teaching includes a great deal on teachers' beliefs and values and on their experientially-acquired craft knowledge:

> Craft knowledge is vastly different from the packaged and glossy maxims that govern 'the science of education' – at the very least, the expectation that rules and maxims can drive practice. Craft knowledge has a different sort of rigour, one that places more confidence in the judgement of teachers, their feel for their work, their love for students and learning, and so on, almost on aesthetic grounds.[26]

It is no less surprising that there is much discussion about how such craft knowledge can be accessed and validated, for it is 'embedded in practice and not readily articulated, which accounts for teachers' talk which fails to measure up to the complexity and subtlety of the craft knowledge that they deploy in their practice.'[27]

Expertise and development: ways of conforming

In attending to the nature of expertise we would not wish to imply that it remains fixed throughout a teacher's career. Teachers grow and develop, they reach deeper understandings and higher levels of skill. Experience shapes them as people and hence as professionals. In this sense, though the domain headings of expertise may be the same for all teachers, what these entail as ways of thinking and acting in classrooms varies considerably, depending partly on teachers' personal qualities and values and partly on their experience and proficiency. Most conspicuously, when teachers start their first job, their craft knowledge is restricted to what they have briefly experienced on a few school placements and the sense they have managed to make of it. By the time they retire, with any luck, they have a store of 'richly elaborated knowledge about curriculum, classroom routines and students that allows them to apply with dispatch what they know to particular cases'.[28]

In 1972, the famous James 'tricycle'[29] conceived of three levels of training and thus, in effect, just three stages of development: pre-service, induction and in-service. It did not differ-entiate the latter, even though it can cover 40 years or more in comparison with one to four years for initial training and one year for induction. With that vast span of age and experience in mind, it is hardly surprising that prominent in the Cambridge Review's submissions from teachers are complaints about 'one size fits all' continuing professional development (CPD), and about being patronised by providers who know and have experienced less than those whose expertise they are charged with developing.

In 2007, the TDA set out professional standards for teachers at five career points:

- newly-qualified (Q)
- core (post-induction teachers on the main pay scale) (C)
- post-threshold (teachers on the upper pay scale) (P)
- excellent teachers (E)
- advanced skills teachers (A)

The same overall framework of 'attributes'. 'knowledge and understanding' and 'skills' as is used for NQTs (see above) is applied to the other career stages, as are the various sub-categories listed above, but the standards are presented as progressing from basic to advanced. They are spelled out in detail in separate documents and then mapped together within a single framework.[30]

It is instructive to examine how the TDA perceives different levels of expertise by comparing core and advanced skills standards in our two nodal (and contested) areas of what the agency calls 'teaching and learning' and 'subjects and curriculum'. In terms of 'professional knowledge and understanding':

> All teachers (C) should (Standard C10): Have a good up-to-date working knowledge and understanding of a range of teaching, learning and behaviour management strategies and know how to use and adapt them, including how to personalise learning to provide opportunities for all learners to achieve their potential.
>
> Excellent and advanced skills teachers (E and A) [in this matter the two are not differentiated] should (Standard E3): Have a critical understanding of the most effective teaching, learning and behaviour management strategies, including how to select and use approaches that personalise learning to provide opportunities for all learners to achieve their potential.[31]

A difference is certainly intended: C teachers have an 'up-to-date working knowledge of a range' while E and S have a 'critical understanding of the most effective'. However, since all three are expected to secure identical outcomes ('personalise learning to provide opportunities for all learners to achieve their potential') it is not clear whether the difference amounts to much.

Similarly, under 'professional skills', all teachers are expected to do pretty well the same things listed for NQTs above (use a range of strategies, build on prior learning, use appropriate language, manage the learning of individuals, groups and classes) but for E and A teachers the difference is the decidedly opaque 'demonstrate excellent and innovative pedagogical practice.' Again we must ask whether this takes forward our understanding of the difference between ordinary and outstanding levels of expertise.

Rather different problems attend the standards for knowledge and understanding in literacy, numeracy and ICT. There, in an area which since 1997 has attracted policy initiatives and massive levels of public money, the standards for all teachers are identical:

> (Standard C17) Know how to use skills in literacy, numeracy and ICT to support their teaching and wider professional activities.[32]

Although listed under 'knowledge and understanding', the standard deals only with the application of skill. The knowledge remains either tacit or, presumably, as codified in the national strategy documentation. The difference between basic and outstanding teaching in this vital area remains a mystery which is all the more curious when we note that large numbers of teachers have moved to the advanced skills stage on the basis of their supposed excellence in teaching literacy and numeracy (by 2008 the total number of 'A' teachers was 4,300).[33] On exactly what basis, one is entitled to ask, have they been judged to be in possession of 'advanced skills'? This is not to belittle their achievement, simply to raise a question about criteria and procedure.

Although, as argued above, differentiating stages of professional development is essential to a dynamic account of expertise for teaching, the TDA framework is mostly unhelpful in the matter of discovering wherein the differences truly lie. This is because they focus on the teacher's possession of approved but vaguely-expressed information and skill, rather than on how the teacher might think; and on whether the teacher conforms rather than demonstrates originality. The possibility that expert teachers might not demonstrate their expertise in identical ways isn't entertained. The question of who defines 'the most effective teaching, learning and behaviour management strategies', and in relation to what evidence the strategies are deemed 'the most effective' is not addressed. This, then, is a framework for codifying not levels of development but degrees of compliance.

Expertise and development: ways of thinking

There is an alternative way of approaching the challenge of tracking the development of expertise in teaching, and it emerges from a mostly American literature. Hubert and Stuart Dreyfus[34] propose five stages:

- novice
- advanced beginner
- competent
- proficient
- expert

Robert Glaser[35] identifies three cognitive stages applicable across a wide range of professional activities:

- externally supported
- transitional
- self-regulatory

Glaser's model pinpoints the essence: the transition from dependence to autonomy. Exceptional teaching, like exceptional performance in any sphere, lies beyond mere competence and adds a high degree of artistry, flexibility and originality whose precise features may be hard to pin down as measurable indicators; but we certainly know it when we see it.

However, reviewing work such as this – and the literature is extensive – Professor David Berliner argues:

> Expertise is specific to a domain, and particular contexts in domains, and is developed over hundreds of thousands of hours …[36]

This is an important corrective to the view, tacit in the TDA standards, that if a teacher achieves the requisite standard it will be demonstrated in most or all contexts. On the contrary, argues Berliner:

> Exemplary performance by a teacher at the 10th grade does not automatically mean that exemplary performance will be seen at the 4th grade if the teacher were to switch grades … Expert teachers working in the suburbs, or the inner city, may be much less competent should they attempt to switch environments.[37]

What are the stages of development, as proposed and tested in American school environments? Berliner summarises them thus:

- *Novice* teachers stick to context-free rules and guidelines, are relatively inflexible, and demonstrate limited skill.
- *Advanced beginners* start to build practical case knowledge, both positive and negative, on the basis of which decisions can be made. They also develop 'conditional and strategic' understanding which qualifies what at the novice stage are unbending rules about how or how not to act.
- *Competent* teachers make conscious choices about what they are going to do; are able to discriminate between what is and is not important, what has to be attended to and what can safely be ignored, when to stay with an idea and when to move on. Competent teachers are more in control of events than novices or competent beginners, though not yet 'fast, fluid or flexible'.
- *Proficient* teachers have acquired from their accumulated case knowledge and successful choices a degree of intuition. 'Out of the wealth of experience … comes a holistic way of viewing the situations they encounter. They recognise similarities among events that the

novice fails to see.' Proficient teachers, then, can predict how pupils will behave and respond, even in novel situations.

- *Expert* teachers. 'If the novice is deliberate, the advanced beginner insightful, the competent performer rational, and the proficient performer intuitive, we might categorise the expert as being arational.' Expert teachers appear to act effortlessly, fluidly and instinctively, apparently without calculation, drawing on deep reserves of tacit knowledge rather than explicit rules and maxims. Yet when problems are encountered, they revert to a more deliberate and analytical mode of problem solving.[38]

If Berliner, Dreyfus and Dreyfus, Glaser, Shulman and other researchers in this field are right, the TDA continuum from newly-qualified to advanced skills teacher is not only unhelpful in the way it focuses on propositional knowledge rather than ways of thinking; it is also, in fundamental ways, wrong. For example, in proposing that teachers at every level draw on the same basic repertoire it runs contrary to the American researchers' finding that novices need a relatively restricted repertoire in order to operate successfully. In specifying that the NQT/novice, in common with teachers at more advanced developmental stages, knows how to adapt strategies for particular circumstances, the TDA framework disregards the finding that novices tend to be rule-bound – that is to say, relatively unable to adapt. At the other end of the spectrum, the expectation that 'excellent' and advanced skills teachers deploy the same knowledge and skill as those at earlier stages effectively suppresses the intuition and fluidity noted in the American research and denies the extent to which outstanding teachers draw on craft knowledge which is tacit and grounded in their unique experience rather than public and codified. This, too, sets limits to the TLRP's claim, which also underpins the national strategies, the TDA standards and Ofsted inspections, that pedagogy comprises knowledge which must be 'collective, generalisable and open to public scrutiny'.[39]

This alternative way of looking at expertise helps us to understand the Review's findings that young teachers are happier with the national strategies than their more experienced colleagues, and that the latter chafe at the bit of prescription. For the national strategies are all about rules, and this is precisely what novice professionals are more likely to need. Experienced teachers are experiencing conflict between the way their level of expertise and their accumulated craft knowledge enable and encourage them to act and what the government's national strategies and the TDA standards tell them to do. They have reached the stage where they not only want a high degree of autonomy to achieve job satisfaction, but they also need it in order to be effective. Further, in seeking so tightly to circumscribe the process of professional development, the TDA and DCSF may have scored an own goal, *for teachers who are unable to operate in the way which best suits their stage of development are likely to be less effective not just in relation to the pursuit of their own goals, but also in fulfilling the government's agenda of 'driving up standards'*. That being so, it is also possible that the unique talent of some of the country's most gifted teachers is so at odds with 'excellence' and 'advanced skills' as officially defined that it remains unrecognised. In the current performance standards regime there is little room for the inspirational idiosyncrasies of those teachers who in newspaper articles about 'my best teacher' are recalled as seminal influences on some of Britain's great and good.

Of course, it could be argued that novice and expert teachers may operate in different ways but if the TDA standards are successful in identifying, at least some of the most promising and effective teachers this does not matter overmuch. However, American research has also taken the necessary next step, implicit in the italicised objection above, and has examined how far the research-based accounts of expertise relate to learning outcomes. In the Greensboro study, which sought to validate the standards proposed by the National Board for Professional Teaching Standards (NBPTS), Lloyd Bond and his colleagues devised measures for 13 prototypical features of expertise:

- better use of knowledge
- extensive pedagogical content knowledge, including deep representations of subject matter

better problem-solving strategies

better adaptation and modification of goals for diverse learners including better skills for improvisation

- better decision-making
- more challenging objectives
- better classroom climate
- better perception of classroom events including a better ability to read cues from students
- greater sensitivity to context
- better monitoring of learning and providing feedback to students
- more frequent testing of hypotheses
- greater respect for students.[40]

These were correlated with measures for the outcomes of teaching in areas such as students' higher levels of achievement, deep rather than surface understanding of subject matter, higher motivation to learn and feelings of self-efficacy.[41] The results, concludes Berliner, are 'remarkable': teachers who are defined as expert in terms of the model derived from research achieve significantly more on these student outcome measures than those who are not, especially – and doubly significant in the context of both this Review and government policy on narrowing the gap – with younger and low-income pupils. Further:

> The features with the greatest ability to discriminate between the expert/non-expert teachers were the degree of challenge that the curriculum offered, the teachers' ability for deep representations of the subject matter, and the teachers' skillfulness in monitoring and providing feedback to their students.[42]

This puts firmly into the frame not just classroom interaction and assessment for learning (Chapter 15) but also teachers' subject/pedagogical content knowledge; and it underscores the concerns expressed in Chapter 14 about the divided curriculum and the quality of teaching and learning in the non-core subjects where many primary teachers' curriculum knowledge may be least secure – especially perhaps in key stage 2 (the Greensboro study included teachers working with the equivalent grades). It also reminds us that while testing may be the elephant in the curriculum, where teaching expertise is concerned the elephant may be subject knowledge. That has hugely significant implications for primary teacher training, the way teachers are deployed in schools and the future of the class teacher system. Meanwhile, there is an apparently unbridgeable gulf when it comes to delineating expertise. On one side is the TDA standard for the professional knowledge and understanding in the 3Rs of excellent and advanced skills teachers – 'Know how to use skills in literacy, numeracy and ICT to support their teaching and wider professional activities'. On the other are the research-based criteria of 'extensive pedagogical content knowledge, including deep representations of subject-matter' and the ability to 'act effortlessly, fluidly and instinctively, apparently without calculation, drawing on deep reserves of tacit knowledge rather than explicit rules and maxims'.

These radically different ways of characterising teachers' developing expertise also prompt two questions. The provenance of the NBPTS standards is clear, but where did the TDA standards come from? And was any attempt made to validate them by reference (a) to research and (b) to pupil learning outcomes?

Such questions are necessary in respect of any policy, but especially one which seeks to align standards of teaching, standards of pupil attainment and teachers' career development and pay. Reviewing strategies for recruiting, developing and retaining effective teachers across 25 countries, the OECD argues, as all those years ago did the James Report:

> The stages of initial teacher education, induction and professional development need to be much better interconnected to create a more coherent learning and development system for teachers …

but adds:

> A statement of teacher competencies and performance standards at different stages of their career will provide a framework for the teacher development continuum.[43]

The case that defined competencies are a necessary basis for teacher development is asserted but not argued. Our discussion here suggests that the matter should be approached with a good deal more caution and understanding than is evident from the OECD report, to whose views governments in an increasing number of countries subscribe. We note also that the need for caution appears to be better understood in some other Anglophone countries than in England – as the research on expert teachers undertaken for the NBPTS shows. In the United States, Australia and New Zealand, moreover, teachers themselves have been more involved in the process of developing their professional standards.[44]

As a leading professional body, the General Teaching Council for England (GTCE) has a good record of offering robust and independent comment on government policy. However, in the matter of defining a code of conduct for teachers, which in effect is a list of the behaviours through which expertise is demonstrated, it stays very close to the government and TDA line. The second of its 'eight principles of conduct and practice' starts promisingly with 'reflect on their own teaching' but immediately curtails such reflection with the sub-item 'registered teachers meet the professional standards for teaching relevant to their role': that is, the TDA standards, which are taken as given and not available for reflection, let alone research-informed critique. Similarly, under the same heading of 'reflect on their own teaching' we find 'registered teachers develop their practice within the framework of entitlement set out in the national curriculum'.[45] That framework, as Chapters 13 and 14 show, is flawed and cannot therefore be exempted from professional reflection. More seriously, the item limits teachers to developing their practice *within* the national curriculum framework and discourages them from going beyond it. Once again, one size fits all; and the size to be fitted is not that of the experienced or expert teacher who needs and deserves the right to think 'outside the box' of policy.

THE RECRUITMENT, TRAINING AND DEVELOPMENT OF PRIMARY TEACHERS

Routes: proliferation and acceleration

Training for teachers and other adults working in schools was a key area of concern for the Plowden Report. In 1967 despite an acute shortage of primary teachers, the idea of employing untrained staff drew sharp condemnation:

> The employment of unqualified teachers is to be deplored and should be discontinued as soon as possible.[46]

So training remained, for the time being, a requirement. However, it was also true that at that time a graduate without formal teacher training was deemed acceptable by virtue of having a degree (that loophole was closed only during the 1980s); and that there have been several occasions since then when government ministers, no less, have advanced the view that to teach requires the possession of little more than a modicum of subject knowledge, common sense and the capacity to maintain 'control'. Such a view, it scarcely needs to be added, displays depressingly limited understanding of what it takes to engage children's motivation, secure their learning, advance their knowledge and understanding, achieve and maintain high standards of attainment, and combine these with the development of balanced and rounded personalities.

However, although the importance of well-qualified, suitably trained staff has remained a key priority since Plowden, the range of teaching roles and the expectations of them, as we have seen, has expanded. From 1984, CATE effectively oversaw the introduction of Britain's first national curriculum. Validation of diverse courses in what were then colleges of education (the former teacher-training colleges) and polytechnics – the two majority providers of primary teachers at this time – was until then undertaken by university-based area training organisations and the Council for National Academic Awards (CNAA). With the establishment of CATE, the government introduced the accreditation of all courses in accordance with a single set of national criteria. In 1994 CATE was disbanded and replaced by the Teacher Training Agency, which in turn gave way to the TDA. Whereas CATE concentrated exclusively on initial teacher training, both CPD and the vital matter of teacher supply were dealt with elsewhere. TDA took on all these functions and much more besides.

During this period, then, new approaches to teacher training were introduced, together with a complex framework of training and accreditation for teaching assistants, support staff and those undertaking a variety of leadership roles within and across schools.

According to the 2007 McKinsey Report, there are now no fewer than 32 routes into teaching in England.[47] These include the familiar four-year undergraduate (BEd/BA/BSc) and one-year postgraduate (PGCE) programmes, and minority routes such as SCITT (School-Centred Initial Teacher Training) run by schools and EBITT (Employment-Based Initial Teacher Training) for graduates who want to train 'on the job' rather than through a prescribed course of study. Training via this route also offers a wage and may therefore be attractive to mature entrants who are changing careers or who have families to support. The government initiative, Teach First, established in 2003, aims to recruit high-achieving graduates into secondary teaching in challenging areas but is not currently available for primary schools, although it is under consideration.

Clearly the range of training options has expanded but what is perhaps less clear is the rationale which underpins them. The situation is complicated by the speed of change. Since the arrival of CATE and national accreditation criteria in 1984, the requirements for initial teacher training have changed with almost dizzying frequency. Each incoming Secretary of State has been determined to make his or her mark, and teacher training providers have offered a conveniently soft target, caught as they are between teachers' suspicion of 'theory', government scapegoating of left-leaning academics, and mainstream academics' disdain for education as a marginal discipline. All this is captured in the endlessly repeated neo-Shavian 'those who can, do; those who can't, teach; those who can't teach, train teachers'.

But the pace of change has not only proved unsettling for all concerned; it has also meant that initiatives have come and gone without proper evaluation. Tracking this process from 1984 to 1998, Robin Alexander noted:

> New criteria for accrediting four-year and one-year teacher training courses, each set superseding the previous one, were promulgated by the UK government in 1984, 1989, 1992, 1993, 1996 and 1998. (DES, 1984, 1989; DFE 1992b, 1993; DfEE 1996; TTA 1998). On each occasion government justified the changes on the grounds that existing courses were not good enough. In fact the timescale made a proper judgement on this matter impossible, especially for the four-year undergraduate courses. In any case, by the 1990s the government's consistently negative claims about the state of teacher training had to be a comment on their own criteria and procedures as much as the courses themselves, for by then all the courses were run in accordance with government requirements and all had been inspected and accredited by HMI or Ofsted. Naturally, this did not stop them from blaming teacher training providers for much that was wrong with schools.[48]

Clearly, this is a highly unsatisfactory scenario, and although justified repeatedly in the name of progress and improved standards, it is as likely to yield the opposite.

Mapping careers

In 2007, as the latest such major initiative, the TDA published the professional standards spanning five designated stages of the teacher's career which we discussed above. The framework requires teachers to demonstrate they have met the standards at each stage before being considered eligible to move on to the next. Assessment is carried out either by an external body, as in the case of excellent teacher and AST status, or within schools. After the induction year, newly qualified teachers are 'expected to continue to meet the core standards and to broaden and deepen their professional attributes, knowledge, understanding and skills within that context'.[49] This process then continues, attracting increments on the pay scale at each stage. However, not all teachers move on to the following stages but it is emphasised that these standards should 'support teachers in identifying ways to broaden and deepen their expertise within their current career'.

All qualified teachers in maintained schools and non-maintained special schools must also register with the GTCE and abide by its code of conduct and practice.[50] Qualified teacher status (QTS) and registration with the GTCE are conferred by the NQT's initial teacher-training provider following assessment demonstrating that the QTS standards have been achieved.

During the induction period, NQTs are not expected to be able to meet core standards fully. The stages take a progressive path and teachers at later stages should be in a position to 'provide role models for teaching and learning, make a distinctive contribution to raising standards across the school, continue to develop their expertise post threshold and provide regular coaching and mentoring to less experienced teachers'.[51] Those who reach excellent teacher status should 'provide an exemplary model to others through their professional expertise, have a leading role in raising standards by supporting improvements in teaching practice and support and help their colleagues to improve their effectiveness and to address their development needs through highly effective coaching and mentoring'.[52] Similarly it is envisaged that ASTs will contribute to school improvement initiatives and the continuing professional development of colleagues in their own and other schools.

The five key outcomes outlined in *Every Child Matters* and the six areas of the *Common core of skills and knowledge for the children's workforce* provide the underpinning principles for the TDA's standards. New legislative requirements relating to teachers' work are also evident, including the Children Act 2004, the Disability Discrimination Acts 1995 and 2005, the special educational needs provisions in the Education Act 1996 and *Special Educational Needs: Code of Practice*, the Race Relations Act 1976 as amended by the Race Relations (Amendment) Act 2000, and the DfES guidance *Safeguarding Children in Education*.

Primary ITT: some pressing issues

Teacher education and training is a field in its own right, as vast and complex as primary education itself. The research survey commissioned by the Review from Olwen McNamara, Mark Brundrett and Rosemary Webb fills out the statistical and demographic detail touched on above and explores some of the important issues.[53] Having reviewed recent research and policy, McNamara and her colleagues conclude:

> The last 25 years have seen a period of sustained and increasingly radical reforms to initial teacher education (ITE)[54] as successive governments have progressively increased prescription and control through the regulation of courses, curriculum content and the assessment of standards. The resulting changes to training provision have been both practical and ideological and have aligned primary ITE with wider education reform agendas. The result of these fundamental and comprehensive changes, and the rigorous inspection regime which has been mobilised to ensure compliance with them, has been to:
> - Improve standards in ITE and increase the quality and preparedness of newly qualified teachers, as measured by the Ofsted inspection framework.
> - Increase the level of intensification of primary programmes, refocusing them to engage with subject and pedagogic knowledge as it is situated in primary classrooms and target course content on the core curriculum, particularly English and mathematics; but leave

little time for previously key aspects of curricular and professional learning such as non-core subjects, especially on postgraduate routes.

- Embed partnership as a core principle of provision but cause, as a result, short-term acute concern over the capacity in the system to deliver quality school-based training and continuing chronic capacity problems in key stage 1 in certain geographic areas.
- Render peripheral many fundamentally important debates about ITE because of the sheer weight and intrusiveness of policy requirements, bureaucracy and accountability.
- Reduce the undergraduate sector of the market from 53 per cent to 37 per cent overall (1998 – 2005), increase the proportion of undergraduates taking shortened three year degrees (with QTS) to 40 per cent, and expand the diversity of postgraduate provision to school-centred and employment-based routes.
- Increase primary training numbers by 30 per cent, and attract a somewhat more diverse population in terms of age and ethnicity, although not in terms of gender, the proportion of primary male trainees remaining a consistently low 14 per cent (with marked variation across routes and Government Office Regions).
- Create staffing problems in university/college education departments as a result of age demographics and the difficulty of attracting new recruits with QTS from senior management positions in primary schools; the latter resulting from relative pay differentials and the perceived challenge of making the transition between cultures and acquiring the necessary range of knowledge and skills, particularly in respect of research and scholarly activity.
- Create a schism between research active staff and teacher educators which, exacerbated by the drive for increased research selectivity particularly in research intensive universities, has meant that most teachers are trained in departments with no core research funding.
- Fail to capitalise upon the significant contribution ITE can make to teacher development and school improvement, despite increasing emphasis on mentoring as a vehicle for professional learning. Analysis of all primary Ofsted reports (1999–2005), for example, reveals that fewer than 6 per cent made any reference to schools' involvement in ITE.[55]

Two of these points deserve further comment.

The quality and content of training

We have referred elsewhere to Ofsted's 2003 claim that today's teachers are the 'best-trained ever',[56] and have been forced to challenge it:

- At best it can relate only to the few years of Ofsted NQT inspections, and 'ever' therefore counts as no more than a rhetorical flourish. 'The best trained since 1998' sounds rather less exciting.
- The claim presumes that compliance with TDA standards, as judged by Ofsted inspections, equates in an absolute and indisputable sense with quality. We have already said enough to query that assumption.

The adequacy of Ofsted judgements of quality is called immediately into question by the research findings on the intensification and content of courses. If the non-core subjects are squeezed out, with the consequences for pupils' education which we examined in Chapter 14, then the judgement that NQTs are well-trained is remarkably selective in its focus. In our view, if teachers embark on their first post without appropriate basic training in aspects of the curriculum which they are obliged by law to teach, they are not by any definition well trained. The least that can be expected of professional training is that it should match the role towards which it is directed. In this fundamental sense the training of many primary teachers does not.

To this omission we can add others. It is clear from our examination of the NQT standards that trainees are not expected to explore questions of educational purpose and value. It is equally clear that they are expected to take the prescriptions of the national strategies at face value. Of course, given what we have said about professional development, it might be argued that it is safer to start teaching armed with rules and a degree of certainty rather than excessive choice aggravated by doubt, and the argument has something to commend it. However, if the seeds of open enquiry, scepticism and concern about larger purposes are not sown, it is possible that teachers will find it more difficult to progress even to Berliner's third developmental stage, since 'competence' is defined there as the exercise of choice and discrimination. The point is well made in the submission to the Review from UCET:

> In the public statements about the competences that must be demonstrated prior to becoming a teacher, there has been a tendency to represent teaching as a matter of mastering a restricted repertoire of practical techniques and the teacher as a mere technician with little responsibility for exercising professional discretion. Such representations fail to acknowledge that there is a great deal of knowledge that teachers need to acquire if they are to be effective mediators of learning. That knowledge is neither inert nor a mere intellectual embellishment, but represents the kind of cognitive capacity that issues in intelligent action. We make a plea that the Cambridge Primary Review makes reference to the need for teachers to exercise critical reflection, for that is at the heart of effective teaching. It needs to be publicly and officially endorsed that becoming a teacher is to be inducted into a community of reflection, enquiry and debate, and that the capacity to engage in such reflection underpins the teacher's classroom decision-making, the evaluation of practice, the adjudication between alternative lines of professional action, and ultimately gives point to the endeavour to facilitate and enrich learning, enabling the teacher to evolve a rationale for his or her classroom and school work by locating it within a broader social and human context.

Moreover, precisely what is the process by which the repertoire of the novice expands to the point where he or she is in a position to make informed choices? In part it comes from experience, contact with colleagues and learning on the job. But such opportunities vary markedly from school to school, and may need to be supplemented from other sources. Unfortunately, since the TDA standards specify more or less the same repertoire for every level of professional development, the difference being in its use rather than its content, it is hard to see how prevailing conceptions of CPD can meet the need, except possibly award-bearing advanced courses where the teacher moves out of his or her school into an environment where the critical examination of options, evidence and argument is required; or the government's new but so far untried Masters in Teaching and Learning (MTL).

Evidence is central to this process: evidence about what is available and possible, and evidence about what is, or is likely to prove, effective. UCET again:

> The capacity to draw on and exploit evidence needs to be nurtured from the beginning of the teacher's professional preparation. All of those who embark on such programmes should be encouraged to see themselves from the outset as researchers of their own practices, with the resourcefulness to adjust their teaching strategies in the light of the evidence they generate about their engagements with learners. We would expect teachers to display a disposition to self-scrutiny, and in addition to be able to draw on evidence on the most appropriate ways of engendering learning.

In their submissions, ITT providers told us they were unhappy that the constraints of time, especially on the PGCE, made inadequate training almost unavoidable. But even if we accept the developmental argument for providing NQTs with security and confidence in a limited array of executive skills – though UCET provides a powerful counterblast – we must ask whether in three particular areas providers make, or are forced into making, choices where choices should not be available.

The first of these is pedagogy. In Chapter 15 we showed that, properly conceived, the act of teaching depends for its effectiveness on various kinds of knowledge, of learners and learning no less than of curriculum. But the range of pedagogical knowledge attended to is often very limited. This may lead to skill without understanding, or rather – since, properly conceived, skill presupposes knowledge – a facility to operate in a particular way which may barely be counted a skill.

The second area, inevitably, is subject and pedagogical content knowledge where, once again, the UCET submission expresses both the need and the problem:

> There is a need to re-affirm the importance of subject knowledge in teacher education. However they may evolve in response to advances in human understanding or technology, or to fluctuations of intellectual fashion, these domains of knowledge will continue to constitute the principal vehicles through which the educational objectives of schools and other settings are realised. However, the approach to subject teaching now required calls for a more explicit recognition of the psycho-social and other educational aims that are to be pursued. That is, teachers need to understand, analyse, apply and, importantly, demonstrate in their interactions with learners, just how subjects can be exploited as resources for addressing the needs of children, for equipping them with the tools of autonomous living, for nurturing their affective as well as their cognitive development, and for cultivating a wide range of social and practical skills. They need to learn to relate to pupils in such a way that they can make pupils' personal and social experience the starting point for their exploration of all that subjects have to offer.

Except possibly in the case of literacy, numeracy and a curriculum specialism where this is on offer, the chances of achieving this are limited. Yet primary teachers' subject and pedagogical content knowledge emerges with absolute and predictable consistency from research and inspection going back many decades as their point of greatest vulnerability, so much so that 'we teach children, not subjects' is more likely to be a defensive than a positive account of what they do. If this is so, not only will NQTs be underpowered in relation to their immediate task, but their prospects for moving on to the more advanced stages of development, whether defined by the TDA or the American research discussed above, will be compromised. In the latter case, we remind readers, the 'expert' teacher combines 'deep representations of subject matter' with challenge in the way pupils are encouraged to engage with it.

The third area relates to the distinctive character of generalist class teaching and the way it requires a perspective on the curriculum as a whole and on the different ways of knowing and understanding that it embodies. In Chapter 14 we argued and demonstrated that debate about the primary curriculum has become infected and weakened by a muddled and reductive discourse about subjects, knowledge and skills. Discussion of the place of subjects, we said, is needlessly polarised; knowledge is grossly parodied as grubbing for obsolete facts; and the undeniably important notion of skill is inflated to cover aspects of learning for which it is not appropriate. There is an urgent need for key curriculum terms to be clarified and for the level of curriculum discussion and conceptualisation to be raised.

This is a task for CPD as well as initial training. Yet it is surely not acceptable that someone whose professional role centres in a fundamental way on knowledge and coming to know should deem it acceptable to caricature and dismiss all knowledge as an obsolete irrelevance. The task therefore starts with ITT, where curriculum study, in its broadest sense and including basic epistemology, is arguably an essential accompaniment to pedagogical content knowledge (PCK) in the domains to be taught. Indeed, if domain-specific PCK is not embedded in broader questions about knowledge and the curriculum, it hinders as much as helps the prospective primary teacher, for whom, as a generalist, such embedding is essential to the holistic nature of his or her role.

However, the problem of subject and pedagogical content knowledge, and its classroom ramifications, is so serious that it may well be that we should be reaching for structural solutions rather than castigating ITT providers. Of these, two present themselves immediately:

- lengthening the course of initial training so that it is better able to do what it must;
- developing alternative patterns of staff deployment in primary schools, and reducing the dominance of the generalist class teacher, so that initial training no longer has to attempt, or fail to attempt, the impossible.

The first will be proposed in this report's conclusion as a possibility requiring careful examination. We return to the second later in this chapter.

Training, research and quality

The Review's research survey from McNamara, Brundrett and Webb spoke of 'a schism between research active staff and teacher educators', and noted that 'most teachers are trained in departments with no core research funding.' This, in the training for any higher-order profession, is serious. In medical training it would be unthinkable that training should not be properly grounded in evidence from research and other kinds of enquiry, and in evidence whose interpretation, applications and limits are as well understood by the providers as they are intelligently considered by the trainee. Teaching is not usually a matter of life and death, but teaching can enhance or diminish the quality of an individual's life, and well-being is rightly prioritised both in this Review as a core aim for primary education and in recent government policy. It matters as much for teachers as for doctors that the decisions they take and the judgements they reach can, where appropriate and possible, be justified on empirical grounds.

Some would argue that it is sufficient for providers to be aware of, rather than actually engage in, relevant research. Unfortunately, the evidence suggests that this may not be enough. Using an analysis of TTA/TDA data,[57] John Furlong shows – at the top and bottom of the scales at least – a correlation between teacher-training quality (as defined by Ofsted grades) and research quality as measured in the higher education research assessment exercise (RAE). Furlong speculates on reasons: research-intensive university departments attract better students (as, in terms of A-level grades, they do); they attract better staff (whatever that means); they have more money for staff and facilities because they can cross-subsidise from research; they build on historical institutional privilege; a research culture somehow pervades the wider institutional culture, encouraging a mindset in which sights are set high in all spheres of activity.[58]

Induction

The importance of the induction period has long been understood. At the time of Plowden, the first year of teaching was a 'probationary' year, and the report's concern was mainly with the need to place NQTs in 'suitable' schools and classes.[59] With the 1972 James Report attention shifted from probation to 'induction' and the need for NQTs to be appropriately and systematically supported as well as sympathetically placed.[60] Yet progress was slow. A DES circular published 20 years after James, and based on an HMI report criticising induction in many schools and LEAs, felt the need to reassert:

> Induction should be a planned extension of initial teacher training ... it should refine the skills and build on the knowledge new teachers have gained in this pre-service training. It is clear from the HMI report that statutory probation does not guarantee induction.[61]

A statutory induction period of three terms was introduced in 1999[62] and the regulations sought to ensure that NQTs were not overburdened in their first posts and that they would have opportunities for professional development. Thus:

NQTs should have
- regular teaching of the same classes;
- similar planning, teaching and assessment processes to those in which qualified teachers working in substantive posts in the same school are engaged;
- a 10 per cent reduced timetable to allow for professional development activities such as observing other teachers.

NQTs should not be presented with
- classes of pupils presenting mainly very challenging behaviour;
- additional non-teaching responsibilities without the provision of appropriate preparation and support;
- teaching outside the range and subject(s) for which they have been trained.[63]

It is worth noting, however, that in 2007[64] only 58 per cent of those primary NQTs in employment had secured the permanent post needed to access this entitlement. Revised induction regulations were introduced in September 2008 requiring for each NQT:

- reduced timetable (no more than 90 per cent);
- a named contact outside the school to advise in case of concern about the induction programme;
- an individualised programme of monitoring, support and assessment planned and implemented in conjunction with an induction tutor, and focusing on strengths and development opportunities identified towards the end of ITT as part of the career entry and development profile (CEDP) process;
- development opportunities including observing and working alongside experienced colleagues and participating in more formal events and activities;
- regular observation of teaching by the induction tutor and/or others;
- three formal assessments, the final one leading to recommendations on whether the core standards (C) have been achieved.[65]

In one sense, the nettle of induction appears at last to have been grasped, and the DCSF, TDA and GTCE are to be commended for this. However, it is too early to judge the impact of the new regulations, though it is pertinent to sound two notes of caution. First, many submissions to the Review expressed anxiety about the viability of the mentoring role taken on by the induction tutor, which is easier to organise in large secondary schools than in small or even medium-sized primary schools. The NQT's time is protected: that of the induction tutor – who, according to TDA, is likely to to the deputy head or key stage co-ordinator – needs to be protected, too. Second, successful transition at the end of the induction year is defined in relation to the TDA standards on which we have already commented. We are not convinced that these standards provide a sufficiently discriminating or adequately researched tool to use in assessment. Third, the TDA rightly requires that induction tutors should 'have the skills to fulfil the role … be able to make rigorous and fair judgements on performance',[66] but training for what is in fact a complex role is not mentioned, and it certainly cannot be assumed that simply by being on a school's senior management team a teacher has the capacities needed.

Continuing professional development

As we saw in Chapter 3, CPD became increasingly centralised from 1983 onwards, when funding began to be earmarked to support government priorities. Following the Education Reform Act in 1988, the modality of CPD shifted from individual development by attendance at external courses to school-based training aimed at meeting national needs. Secondments for advanced award-bearing courses all but dried up, and the capacity of local authorities to deliver their own in-service training was substantially reduced by the delegation of budgets to schools.

Changes in the funding, competition from courses leading to vocational qualifications, and more lucrative overseas markets also led to higher education institutions greatly reducing their CPD provision. Increasingly, professional associations, consultants and other commercial agencies entered the market.

In the 'new professionalism' promoted by New Labour, participation in CPD was recognised as important, albeit with the main purpose of equipping teachers to implement government reforms and tightly circumscribed within progression through the TDA standards and competences.

Surveying research and policy in this area for the Review, McNamara, Brundrett and Webb summarise the main developments over the past decade as:

- the tightening of government control of the agenda and forms of CPD through the national literacy, numeracy and primary strategies;
- the establishment of the General Teaching Council for England (GTCE) in September 2000 with a specific remit to promote teachers' professional development;
- the introduction of the government's CPD strategy in 2001 together with the GTC's *Teachers' Professional Learning Framework* setting out teachers' CPD entitlement and responsibilities; and
- the TDA assuming responsibility from 2005 for the national co-ordination of CPD for all school staff.

However, McNamara, Brundrett and Webb cite research showing the teachers' access to CPD may be constrained by:

- lack of time, heavy workload, financial cost and distance from training opportunities;
- overemphasis on meeting system needs to the detriment of the learning and career development needs of individual teachers; and
- inadequate evaluation, particularly in relation to value for money, of school CPD policies, pupil effects and teacher morale.[67]

Many of those who submitted evidence to the Review identified as central the CPD tension between meeting individual teachers' developmental needs and advancing school and national goals (the latter two were often synonymous since schools' own priorities were in the first instance determined by national requirements) and believed that the balance had tipped too far towards the servicing of policy. Further, while the Teachers' International Professional Development programme provided 2,500 short-term study visits abroad a year, a number of other promising developmental schemes had ceased. These included Best Practice Research Scholarships and sabbaticals for experienced teachers in challenging schools. Like advanced course secondments until the mid-1980s, such experiences were highly valued by teachers and the submission from GTCE argued that serving teachers needed to re-engage during their careers with research and theory, especially in the areas of children's development and learning, and this was identified as a priority in many other submissions. Teachers participating in the Review's national soundings identified the following professional development priorities:

- working with parents and community
- understanding and building on children's learning outside school
- fostering effective teacher-pupil and pupil-pupil interaction
- preparing children for school transfer
- improving professional confidence and expertise in the use of new technologies
- gaining access to research on teaching and learning, and learning how to evaluate and apply it
- developing the capacity to be creative and improvisatory in teaching
- acquiring strategies to cope with children's behavioural difficulties

- developing skills for teaching English as an additional language
- learning about school leadership and governance
- pursuing study and research both for their classroom application and for their own sake.

There remains, then, a hunger for CPD which addresses not just government priorities but also day-to-day professional needs and challenges as teachers themselves define them.

During 2008, a major 'state of the nation' study of CPD was undertaken for the TDA by David Pedder, Anne Storey and Darleen Opfer. This addressed questions about:

- the benefits, status and effectiveness of CPD
- its planning and organisation
- access to and take-up of different kinds of CPD (in-school, out-of-school, accredited courses, study groups and so on).

As it progressed, the study also identified a number of key cross-cutting themes:

- teachers' values and purposes in undertaking CPD
- the quality of provision
- the organisation of CPD
- the context of professional standards and performance management
- the school context
- barriers to engagement
- accreditation and the Masters in Teaching and Learning (MTL) programme.

The study identified a number of issues arising from CPD as currently conceived and organised:

- Too little CPD focuses on classroom-contextualised practice, professional collaboration and research-informed professional learning.
- There is insufficient CPD of a kind which is active and sustained.
- Despite hopes and expectations, CPD has no obvious impact on raising standards of pupil attainment or narrowing the gap.
- The benefits of CPD depend too much on the circumstances of individual schools.
- School leaders believe that school-based and classroom-based CPD provide better value for money than CPD which takes place elsewhere.
- However, most in-school CPD entails passive rather than active professional learning.
- Schools' CPD planning does not meet schools' full range of professional development needs.
- There is an unhelpful divergence between school and CPD leadership, and the CPD potential of excellent and advanced skills teachers is under-exploited.
- CPD evaluation is inadequate.
- The range of CPD opportunities on offer is too narrow.
- Participation in CPD can be compromised by unfavourable school conditions and teacher attitudes.[68]

To these we might add, in light of this and earlier chapters:

- The prioritising of CPD aligned to the national strategies confirms teachers' belief that the strategies may be non-statutory but they are not optional.
- The failure to allocate significant CPD resourcing to supporting the non-core subjects confirms the divided curriculum as discussed in Chapter 14 and makes it difficult for schools to break out of the historical cycle of low valuation and inadequate provision.
- Even where approved CPD provision is school-based and thus has the potential to respond to individual developmental needs and circumstances, it appears not to do so. Instead, it remains pitched notionally toward the middle or lower end of the developmental continuum.

- It is thus not surprising that a recurrent objection of teachers in the Review's submissions and soundings is that CPD related to national initiatives tends to lack challenge, deals in the obvious and patronises those to whom it is directed.

Whether the Masters in Teaching and Learning can break the mould remains to be seen. Announced in March 2008, it reflects the government's aim, set out in the 2007 Children's Plan, to make teaching a Master's level profession. But another purpose of the MTL is to fill a recognised gap in the professional development of teachers early in their careers. The programme is to be mainly school-based, validated by higher education institutions and provided by them jointly with schools, by trained coaches and tutors, and through self-study.[69] The government has said it wants every teacher to complete the MTL at some stage[70] but intends that it should first be offered to teachers in 'struggling' schools.

In 2008, TDA undertook regional consultations on the MTL. These identified as content priorities for the new programme:

- teaching and learning
- assessment for learning
- subject knowledge for teaching
- curriculum and curriculum development
- children's development and learning, and the management of behaviour, special educational needs and English as an additional language
- leadership, including curriculum leadership
- working collaboratively.[71]

These resonate with our own findings, but with one crucial difference. The TDA consultation highlighted matters relating to the curriculum – subject knowledge, curriculum development, curriculum leadership. This Review's national soundings with teachers did not. That suggests the possibility of a significant difference of opinion over how far curriculum expertise really matters in primary education. We have shown that over several decades HMI, Ofsted and independent researchers have agreed that it is a problem, and one which has serious consequences for the scope and quality of children's primary education, and that the aspect of professional expertise covered by the terms subject knowledge, subject applications, pedagogical content knowledge and didactics is vital to successful teaching at any stage. We therefore hope that school and higher education partners in the new MTL can reach agreement on how to tackle the problem with due seriousness but also in a manner which attends closely to the international research on professional development. The warning of UCET, that the MTL could all too easily become 'Master in Teaching Lite', should be heeded.

CONCLUSION

This chapter started by noting that despite the diversification of professional roles within primary schools, the generalist class teacher remains the default and the Review believes (Chapter 14) that it is a complicating factor in the debate about the manageability of the primary national curriculum.

This prompted a discussion of the nature of expertise for teaching in which we contrasted policy-led models of the kind exemplified by changing requirements for initial teacher training since the 1960s, and TDA's 2007 'professional standards', with those which have emerged from research. The views from these sources of what teaching entails are very different. Teacher-training requirements have shifted from a specification of the kinds of knowledge which it is assumed that teachers need, to instrumental but not very specific accounts of skill allied to policy-driven information which teachers are expected to know and with which they are expected to comply. In contrast, European comparisons open up the well-developed fields of pedagogy and didactics, while transatlantic research has produced taxonomies which include both different domains of professional knowledge (of children, curriculum, pedagogy, pedagogical content, aims, contexts and so on) and professional knowledge of different kinds (public and personal, disciplinary and craft).

Noting that professional expertise is dynamic, experiential and changing rather than static, we turned next to how such expertise develops as teachers move through their careers. Once again, policy and research provide telling contrasts. On the one hand we have development conceived as the five career points, from newly-qualified (Q) to advanced skills (A), introduced as part of the government's workforce reforms; on the other, a developmental progression from 'novice' to 'expert' which derives from research.

Here too there was considerable dissonance. The government's professional standards sequence is context-neutral whereas research stresses the power of context. The government's model proposes the same basic repertoire at every stage when research shows many teachers at the start of their career operating, and needing to operate, within a limited repertoire governed by rules. Conformity to rules, or at least to approved versions of what good teaching entails, is fundamental to the government model, but its problem is that the teacher is expected to remain subservient to these throughout his or her career. In contrast, research shows expert teachers not only acting differently from novices but also thinking in fundamentally different ways. These advanced modes of professional thinking are also tacit and less readily codified and generalised. Just as many novices need rules and a bounded repertoire, so experts need to be freed from rules and prescriptions and given the liberty to operate autonomously, creatively and instinctively.

We say 'need' advisedly: for what emerges with some force from these comparisons is the worrying possibility that TDA standards for teachers aimed at raising standards of pupil learning may actually depress them: first, by expecting too much of NQTs; second, by so constraining experienced and talented teachers that they cannot operate as effectively as they are able; third, by allowing the unique and idiosyncratic talent of some of our very best teachers to go unrecognised because it lies beyond the understanding of those whose job it is to assess and grade teachers' competence.

The various mismatches led us to ask, bluntly, exactly where the TDA standards came from and why they were apparently not validated by reference either to research or to pupil learning outcomes. In contrast, in both the United States and Australia, considerable efforts have been made to come up with professional performance standards which bear empirical scrutiny and can be shown to relate indicators of professional excellence to high levels of pupil attainment.

Also notable was the research finding that 'deep representations of subject matter' grounded in pedagogical content knowledge most conspicuously discriminates expert teachers from non-experts. In the context of our recurrent question about the capacity of the generalist class teacher system to deliver what a modern curriculum requires, this is a finding of some significance.

These two broad concerns – about the nature of teaching expertise and the trajectory of teacher development – framed our discussion of initial teacher training, induction and continuing professional development. They prompted us to challenge Ofsted claims about the 'best ever' quality of ITT on the grounds that so much that is essential has been squeezed out, particularly in respect of pedagogy, pedagogical content knowledge in other than the national curriculum core subjects, wider engagement with matters of curriculum and epistemology at a level which will help raise the quality of discourse as required by our analysis in Chapter 14, and the development of respect for evidence, open debate and a sense of the problematic.

For as long as ITT is directed at the role of generalist class teacher, it will be hard pressed to provide what is required, especially on the one-year PGCE route. The possibility of a two-year PGCE, as discussed during the 1980s, should be revisited. At the same time, the content should be refocused so as to ensure that the training and NQT's classroom role are properly aligned. Urgent questions also arise about the relationship between training and research, and about providers' capacity in respect of the latter.

We drew on both submissions and published research to confirm just how far CPD has moved from its former goal of helping teachers to develop as individual professionals and hence make a better contribution to the work of their schools. Now CPD is largely dominated by the policy agenda of the day and this is presumed to define the needs of schools and teachers too. Again, this model sits uneasily with the research-based accounts of professional development and professional excellence that we explored earlier. While such a model may be apposite for less experienced teachers it appears not to serve the needs of more advanced practitioners. In the Review's submissions and soundings, teachers themselves endorsed this criticism, finding much policy-informed CPD insufficiently challenging.

It is time, therefore, to revisit the old question about the proper balance of professional development conceived as personal growth, and professional development as mastery of an agenda set by others. This sets a considerable challenge for the MTL, not least since it remains framed by the TDA standards of which this Review is somewhat critical.

Finally, we return to this chapter's big question. In a world of ever-expanding demands on primary teachers' knowledge and skill, is the generalist class teacher system inherited from the 19th century still up to the job?

We have seen that initial teacher training, especially the one-year PGCE, cannot realistically provide adequate preparation in all areas of the curriculum which the generalist must expect to teach and to which primary pupils are entitled. That goes, incidentally, for what is concealed by the six 'areas of learning' proposed in the Rose Review, since Rose has insisted that regardless of his teacher-friendly labels subjects are here to stay. In Chapter 14, we ourselves made what we trust will be seen as a strong case for knowledge, generously defined and conceived, in primary education. We have also seen that the use of CPD which favours policy over free-ranging professional development has exacerbated the unevenness of curriculum-related provision.

Over the past 30 years or so, there have been four critical moments in the evolution of national policy in relation to the role of the primary teacher. In 1978, picking up Plowden's cue, HMI linked pupil progress to teachers' levels of subject expertise on the one hand and whole-school curriculum planning on the other. They proposed that every primary school should appoint curriculum co-ordinators to cover the main areas to be taught, concentrating on whole-school planning and leadership.[72] In 1986 the House of Commons Select Committee reinforced the message, but found that most teachers simply did not have the time to combine the full-time teaching of a class with a major cross-school responsibility. It proposed that 15,000 extra teachers be appointed to provide all but the smallest schools with some flexibility to free teachers for curriculum co-ordinator roles. This proposal was not implemented.[73] Meanwhile, the DES and CATE had made it a requirement of all new ITT courses that each primary trainee should follow a curriculum specialism alongside their generalist training. Trainees on undergraduate courses were also required to undertake two years of study, at higher education level, of a relevant subject, and PGCE trainees were required to offer subjects from their degrees which had demonstrable relevance to the primary curriculum.[74]

By 1992, after the introduction of the national curriculum, it was clear that this combination of modified teaching roles and adjusted ITT was not delivering what was needed, especially as during the 1980s HMI had been rather cautious on whether curriculum co-ordinators should do more than lead from outside their colleagues' classrooms. At issue, then, was the fiercely-defended territory of the class teacher (the 'my class' counterpoint to the 'my school' of the primary head). The 'three wise men' enquiry, commissioned by the government, proposed that the established role of generalist class teacher and the emergent role of curriculum co-ordinator be supplemented by those of subject specialist and semi-specialist. These would teach their subjects, full or part time, rather than merely co-ordinate them, and would thereby extend schools' repertoire of staffing possibilities. (The 1978 HMI primary survey had entertained this possibility too, particularly in relation to science which at that time was seen as one of the weakest areas of primary provision.[75]) However, the 1992 report warned that change depended, first, on the ending of the primary/secondary funding differential, so that funding between the phases could be rebalanced more in favour of primary and schools would be able to appoint extra staff; second, on primary teachers' preparedness to moderate their loyalty to the class teacher system and entertain alternatives.[76]

In 1994, a further report from the House of Commons Select Committee took up the primary/ secondary funding anomaly, found it unacceptable, and came off the fence on which HMI had sat throughout the 1980s, arguing that classroom intervention by specialist subject co-ordinators – not just whole-school planning – was essential to generalists' effective delivery of the curriculum.[77] Subsequently, give or take some mixed messages, the newly-established Ofsted shifted this classroom-based part of the co-ordinator role from guidance to monitoring and evaluation, in later publications increasingly emphasising the teaching function as well.[78]

By 1998, this consensus appeared to be breaking up. The TTA stuck somewhat timidly to the mainstream definition of cross-school curriculum leadership.[79] Ofsted displayed increasing pessimism about the class teacher system's capacity to raise standards and argued instead for direct intervention and specialist teaching by subject leaders/co-ordinators.[80] But the government, introducing its flagship literacy and numeracy strategies, revealed a general loss of confidence in primary schools' ability, whatever roles their teachers adopted, to deliver both high standards in the 'basics' and a broad, balanced and consistently well-taught curriculum. David Blunkett, when he was Secretary of State, relieved primary schools of the obligation to do other than vaguely 'have regard to' the programmes of study in the non-core subjects. His intention was to give the literacy and numeracy strategies the best possible start, as he saw it (the DfEE press release was headed 'Blunkett strengthens curriculum focus on the basics')[81] but the result was a decade in which the historic split between what in Chapter 14 we called 'curriculum 1' and 'curriculum 2' became a chasm, and in many schools the 1988 Education Reform Act's vision of curriculum entitlement receded even further into the distance.

This is where, in 2009, the system still is. In English primary schools, generalist class teaching remains the default mode of staff deployment. True, schools have their subject leaders, and there is a certain amount of specialist teaching, notably of music, sport and modern foreign languages. Teachers also have considerably more non-contact time than in the 1960s-1980s, but Planning, Preparation and Assessment time (PPA) is intended to support their own teaching rather than free them to undertake work across the school in their specialist subject. Indeed, viewed against this background, the Rose Review of the curriculum tacitly confirms both the professional status quo and the traditional perception of the nature of the problem to be addressed. It has approached curriculum reform as a problem of curriculum management, what Rose calls 'quarts into pint pots'. It has decided that of the two possibilities which that phrase presents – curriculum and management – it is the curriculum which is the problem, not management. But this, as we showed from a long string of inspection-based studies and official reports, is an incorrect analysis, for many schools provide the full range of subjects, teach them well, and achieve high standards in KS2 tests.

In this context, the real problem, then, is not the curriculum but its management. We say 'in this context' since the more fundamental curriculum problem, tackled only in part by the Rose Review but considered in depth in this report, concerns the aims and content of the curriculum, to which questions about management should be subsidiary. Instead, in 2009, as in 1998, the government has used the curriculum as the safety-valve for a problem which at root is about the mismatch of schools' tasks and their resources of teachers and curriculum-related expertise. Thus, 150 years on from Robert Lowe's promise for 'the education of the poor, or primary education' that 'if it is not efficient it shall be cheap',[82] a curriculum is made 'manageable' by trimming the education rather than increasing the resources.

The principle proposed by the Cambridge Review on this matter is straightforward: *every primary school must have access to the range and depth of curriculum expertise which is needed in order to plan and teach, with consistent quality across the full curriculum range, the curriculum that 5- to 11-year-olds need and deserve.*

How is it to be done? We make formal proposals on this matter in this report's final chapter, but the essential ingredients are:

- Acceptance that the much-discussed problem of curriculum manageability in the primary phase, especially since the introduction of national tests and strategies, is as much about management as curriculum.

- A willingness by primary schools to think beyond the class-teacher default and accommodate a continuum of teaching roles, for which the 1992 proposal of *generalist – generalist/ consultant – semi-specialist – specialist* remains appropriate.[83]
- Rejection of the assumption that the solution lies with teaching assistants. It does not: this is about the expertise of teachers, not TAs.
- A preparedness to learn from those schools which successfully secure breadth, quality and standards.
- Exploration of the potential of partnership between schools which involves the sharing and exchange of curriculum-related expertise, and indeed of teachers.
- Re-alignment of ITT and CPD to train for a broader range of teaching roles, giving particular attention to the domain and pedagogical content knowledge of both generalists and specialists.
- A re-assessment of the staffing assumptions which underpin primary-phase funding (see Chapter 23).
- A repertoire of properly-costed strategic options based on the above, and including the possibility of expanding the number of primary teachers.

Identifying options is essential, for the debate on this matter needs to move beyond the simple opposition of 'generalists' and specialists' and we wish it to be clearly understood that we are not proposing the summary curtailing of the established system of primary school staffing. Thus, a fully generalist approach might be maintained for the early primary years with a generalist/ specialist mixture in upper primary. Capacity could be strengthened by having more than one model of initial training, say (i) fully generalist, (ii) generalist with specialism as, with many ITT programmes, at present, (iii) combined-domain specialist (perhaps two or three domains), (iv) single-domain specialist.

The discussion would also need to encompass the relationship between the curriculum domains proposed in Chapter 14 and the notions of both generalist and specialist, and indeed the academic base on which newly-conceived or modified domains like citizenship and ethics, or personal and emotional health, might build. One domain, paradoxically, requires both generalists and specialists through the primary years. As described in Chapter 14, the extended domain of language, oracy and literacy is so fundamental to the curriculum as a whole that it needs to be part of the professional repertoire of every teacher – hence our reminder of the Bullock Report's concept of 'language across the curriculum'. At the same time, the drawing up of a school-level curriculum in this domain requires considerable specialist knowledge, while parts of the domain such as a modern foreign language might in any event require specialist teaching. The case made in the Williams report for strong specialist support for primary mathematics[84] surely applies, *a fortiori*, to language, oracy and literacy.

The key to progress is – as was argued by the 1992 'three wise men' report – a national primary school staffing and funding policy which gives schools the flexibility to make their own decisions on these matters. The 1986 Select Committee proposed injecting a modest degree of flexibility into the system by appointing 15,000 extra teachers. Had this been accepted by government it would have made some difference but not enough, especially in large schools, where it would have had negligible impact on curriculum quality (and many schools would have used their additional teacher to reduce class sizes rather than strengthen the curriculum). Some countries staff their primary schools on the basis of one extra teacher for a given number of classes, and this, we believe, is the more sensible approach. We were impressed, during the community soundings, by the school whose entrepreneurial use of school premises out of hours had generated sufficient income to allow it to appoint four teachers for every year group of three classes, and to ensure thereby that it had teachers with real specialist strength in every aspect of the curriculum (and in other areas too, for 'specialist' teaching can relate to needs other than the curriculum), and the flexibility to deploy them in any of a number of ways. This kind of model, we suggest, allied with school partnerships and more diverse patterns of initial training and CPD, deserves to be explored and costed for its potential to be scaled up into a national strategy for genuine curriculum renewal. Partnerships – including between primary and secondary schools as well as within primary school clusters – have a potential which as yet is under-exploited.

We add, as grounds for modest optimism:

- We have been informed by DCSF that a 'quiet revolution' in primary school staffing has begun to take place, and that specialist activity is more prominent than a decade ago. For the moment it tends to be confined to music, sport, modern foreign languages (MFL) and ICT. Through CPD provided by Trinity College of Music and the Open University and initiatives like Sing Up (the National Singing Programme), DCSF believes that generalist class teachers are gaining the necessary confidence to teach primary music at the level specified in the national curriculum. At the same time music specialists are supporting the government's drive to encourage children to learn an instrument. Meanwhile TDA is training primary modern foreign language teachers and nearly 5,000 will have been through that programme by the end of 2009.[85] Once the benefits of such schemes become apparent, schools may be more willing to countenance movement towards the above generalist/specialist professional continuum for all domains, not just those which have always been accepted as requiring specialist expertise. However, specialist teaching of music was noted as a regular arrangement as far back as the 1978 HMI primary survey, so the revolution may be leisurely as well as quiet.
- The Review's proposal (Chapter 14) for a protected local component to the curriculum, developed on a non-statutory basis by community curriculum partnerships, provides an ideal forum for opening up the staffing debate. Indeed, the task of supporting schools in the effective delivery of both the national and local component might be added to the partnerships' remit for exploring the potential for locally-specific content. Again, DCSF reports the benefits of local activity, citing its School Sport Partnership scheme and links between primary and secondary schools in support of foreign language teaching.

However, apart from a welcome increase in instrumental tuition, which necessarily involves full specialists, the emphasis in most of the initiatives mentioned is on strengthening the capacity and confidence of generalist class teachers rather than extending specialist teaching as such. Further, the initiatives remain confined to curriculum domains which are regarded as special cases. The real breakthrough will come when schools accept that the argument made by the Williams report for using specialists to enhance the teaching of mathematics[86] could be made for all curriculum domains, including those outside the current core which it tends to be assumed that 'anyone can teach'. For the case of mathematics is not unique. Until there is acceptance that domain expertise is so crucial to educational quality that it directly challenges the historical basis of primary teachers' professional identity as generalists, this Review's definition of curriculum entitlement as the highest possible standards of teaching in all domains, regardless of how much or little time each is allocated, will remain a pipe dream.

NOTES

1   DCSF (2008w).
2   CACE (1967): paras 929–37.
3   DES (1978a).
4   TDA (2008f).
5   Adapted from Blatchford *et al.* (2006): 7.
6   Alexander, Rose and Woodhead (1992): paras 139–50.
7   Rose (1998).
8   TTA (1996).
9   James and Pollard (2010), *The Cambridge Primary Review Research Surveys*, Chapter 19.
10 TDA (2008e): 5–10.
11 Board of Education (1944): para 224.
12 UCET (1982); CNAA (1983). The UCET enquiry was chaired by the late Alan Blyth, and the CNAA enquiry by Robin Alexander.

13 UCET (1982): 42.
14 DES (1978a, 1979, 1983b: 5).
15 Schön (1983).
16 Margo *et al.* (2008): 7.
17 Margo *et al.* (2008): 13.
18 Simon (1981b).
19 Moon (1998); Alexander (2001b).
20 Shulman (1987).
21 Shulman (1987).
22 Bruner (1963): 33.
23 Hamilton (1999).
24 Shulman (1987).
25 Grossman (1995).
26 Grimmett and MacKinnon (1992): 437.
27 Mumby, Russell and Martin (2001): 889.
28 *Ibid.*
29 DES (1972).
30 TDA (2007a, 2007b, 2007c, 2007d).
31 TDA (2007e): 9.
32 TDA (2007e): 12.
33 Source: DCSF Schools Research Team.
34 Dreyfus and Dreyfus (1986).
35 Glaser (1996).
36 Berliner (2004): 13.
37 Berliner (2004): 18.
38 Paraphrased (except for the direct quotes) from Berliner (1994, 2004). His five stages are adapted from Dreyfus and Dreyfus (1986).
39 Hofkins (2008b): 27.
40 Bond *et al.* (2000).
41 Bond *et al.* (2000).
42 Berliner (2004): 24–25.
43 OECD (2005): 13.
44 NBPTS (1994); Ingvarson and Hattie (2008).
45 GTCE (2008): 10.
46 CACE (1967): para 884.
47 Barber and Mourshed (2007).
48 Alexander (2001b): 591.
49 TDA (2007b): 2.
50 GTCE (2007).
51 TDA (2007b): 3.
52 TDA (2007b): 3.
53 McNamara, Brundrett and Webb (2008), *The Cambridge Primary Review Research Surveys*, Chapter 24.
54 The authors quoted here use 'ITE'. There is a long-standing debate about whether we should talk of teacher 'training' or 'education' which started long before the now-defunct teacher training colleges became colleges of education. This report sticks to 'ITT', even though the Cambridge Review holds firmly to the views that teachers need to be highly-educated as well as thoroughly trained.
55 McNamara, Brundrett and Webb (2008).
56 Ed Balls, 'Why Britain has the best teachers ever', *The Guardian*, 23 October 2007; Michael Day of TDA, quoted in *The Guardian* on 16 May 2006: 'Ofsted has found that today's newly qualified teachers are the best trained ever, and there are rigorous inspection procedures in place to ensure that the award of qualified teacher status only goes to those who have met the required standards.'
57 Smithers and Robinson (2008).
58 Furlong (2009).
59 CACE (1967): paras 999–1012.
60 DES (1972).
61 DES (1992).
62 DfEE (1999c).
63 Ashby *et al.* (2008): 42.
64 Hobson *et al.* (2007).
65 TDA (2008d).
66 TDA (2008a).
67 McNamara *et al.* (2010), *The Cambridge Primary Review Research Surveys*, Chapter 24.
68 Pedder, Storey and Opfer (2008).
69 TDA (2008b).
70 DCSF (2008d).
71 TDA (2008c).
72 DES (1978a).

73 House of Commons (1986).
74 DES (1984).
75 DES (1978a): para 8.42.
76 Alexander, Rose and Woodhead (1992), paras 139–150.
77 House of Commons (1994).
78 Ofsted (1994, 1996).
79 TTA (1996).
80 Ofsted (1996, 1997c).
81 DfEE (1998).
82 See Simon (1964): 349.
83 Alexander, Rose and Woodhead (1992): paras 139–50.
84 P. Williams (2008).
85 Information provided by the DCSF Schools Research Team, April 2009.
86 P. Williams (2008).

22 Professional leadership and workforce reform

The working environment of the primary school has been radically transformed over the past 20 years. The profession's career structure has been reformed, performance-related pay introduced, the workforce 'remodelled', and national qualifications and standards brought in for head teachers. All these changes have impacted on senior management's scope for making decisions. Head teachers, once the undisputed and independent leaders of their schools,[1] now operate in a culture of compliance and one that, borrowing the language of business, exhorts them by turns to be 'visionary', 'invitational', 'democratic', 'strategic', 'instructional' or 'transformational'. The importance of their leadership is emphasised, as is what is expected of them – and who can call them to account if they falter. Just as their roles and responsibilities have become more complex and demanding, so the work of teachers has been circumscribed by government strategies regarding what and how they teach. Many now, thanks to the huge rise in support staff numbers, manage small teams of classroom co-workers and have extended roles as middle managers. They are thus increasingly cast in a supervisory role – and they are also increasingly being supervised.

Against this background of two decades of change, the Cambridge Primary Review asked some key questions. How well are our primary schools led and managed? How can we ensure that we secure – and retain – the best professionals for the job? How should schools balance and make best use of their mix of professionals and para-professionals? Such questions were rendered particularly important by fears that teachers have been de-professionalised, de-skilled and demoralised by political micro-management, a heavy workload and negative media coverage. The newly elected government of 1997 had set out to raise teachers' 'image, morale and status', though few would have predicted how it would attempt to achieve this. Certainly its designation of teachers, an all-graduate, professionally-trained body of people, as part of the 'workforce' sat uneasily with this aim, undermining the formal recognition of their professional status alongside doctors and lawyers in the 2001 census[2] – the culmination of a 130-year struggle. To what extent is the profession still disheartened and constrained? Or are heads, teachers and support staff finding a route forward that balances not only work and life but also the often conflicting, and sometimes overwhelming, external demands of a competitive, results-driven culture with their professional commitment to the education of the whole child?

This chapter sketches the principal reforms affecting the primary professional environment since 1988 and considers the evidence to the Review about their effects on school leadership, classroom teachers and teaching assistants. It explores the extent to which reforms have affected the work of primary teachers, including their sense of professionalism and status. First, however, we look briefly at the major policy reforms of the past decade.

KEY POLICIES IN AN ERA OF ACCOUNTABILITY

New policy relating to the professional environment of primary schools has proliferated since the mid-1980s (see following section). Local financial management, introduced by the Education Reform Act of 1988, not only radically altered the nature of head teachers' work, it also increased and broadened governors' responsibilities. The policy of budgetary delegation rendered these volunteers more formally accountable to parents and government for the services their school provided. Teachers too were increasingly being held answerable within the educational 'market place' and had to reconcile this accountability – to parents, the public, Ofsted, local authorities and government – with their professional commitment to the welfare of children.

In 1998, a DfEE Green Paper, *Teachers: meeting the challenge of change*, combined a professed desire to see the 'hard work and commitment of classroom teachers recognised' with an insistence on the need for a 'modern professional structure' which included the introduction of performance-related pay.[3] The national literacy and numeracy strategies, also in the Green Paper, were designed to raise standards by equipping teachers with a wider repertoire of tools and strategies, but were, as we have discussed, nonetheless a constraint. While the 2003 primary national strategy promised to restore some professional autonomy to teachers, allowing them a degree of flexibility and scope for creativity, it remained closely tied to the literacy and numeracy framework.[4] Its promise of 'excellence and enjoyment' sought to disguise the fact that the status quo of a divided and unbalanced curriculum would be maintained, while the underlying message was that primary teachers were to comply with a view of 'best practice' in classrooms defined by government and its agencies and not on the basis of free-thinking professional research and debate.[5] National strategy course and documentation, and the DfES/DCSF school standards website, became the expected source of accredited professional wisdom. As a consequence, and thanks to the continued control exerted by targets, national assessment and inspection, teachers carried on much as before.[6]

Policy initiatives and statements with significant implications for teachers and school leaders appeared annually after 2000. The government renewed its emphasis on raising status in return for increased accountability within a new model of professionalism for all public service personnel. *Every Child Matters* and the Children's Plan extended the range of people who could contribute to the realisation of goals embracing enjoyment, safety, health and well-being. As the Children's Plan declared: 'The single most important factor in delivering our aspirations for children is a world-class workforce able to provide highly personalised support …'.[7]

THE CHANGING FACE OF PRIMARY LEADERSHIP

Some policy milestones

- 1998: Qualification for headship introduced by the Teaching and Higher Education Act.
- 2001: Head teachers given control of 85 per cent of school budget under proposals in the White Paper *Schools Achieving Success*, which subsequently formed the basis of the 2002 Education Act.
- 2004: Head teachers given greater say in school self evaluation and improvement planning under 'covenant' proposed in the *New Relationship with Schools* which also introduced more participative and lighter-touch inspections. *Every Child Matters* conferred responsibilities for liaison with multi-professional teams and external agencies.
- 2005: Parents win right to set up new schools, close 'failing' ones and dismiss head teachers under proposals in the White Paper *Higher Standards, Better Schools for All*.[8]
- 2007: Additional workload and responsibilities conferred on head teachers and senior management teams by the Children's Plan.

Primary head teachers: by number, age and gender

In 2008 there were 17,100 primary head teachers in England, but only 11,900 deputy and 5,900 assistant heads. Five per cent of heads had no deputy or assistant head, and 14 per cent had only one of either grade.[9] Vacancy rates for nursery and primary heads and deputies remained relatively stable between 1997 and 2008. In January 2008, there were 110 unfilled headships in primary and nursery schools and 180 vacancies for deputy or assistant heads.[10] Around two-thirds of heads managed schools with fewer than 250 pupils, with about 14 per cent in charge of fewer than 100 pupils.[11] In small schools, heads also taught, as did deputies in all but the biggest schools.

Meanwhile, in stark contrast to the mainly male 'grandparent' heads of the 1960s,[12] 61 per cent of new heads in 2007 were under 45 and three-quarters were women (see Table 22.1). Some see this as a process of feminisation likely to deter men and, in these still gender biased times, undermine the status of the profession. The tiny proportion (1.5 per cent) of Black or minority ethnic head teachers remains significantly under-representative of the ethnic composition of school populations today and raises serious questions about commitment to social justice within the profession.[13]

The emergence of 'leadership'

Over the past four decades what it means to lead a primary school has changed significantly. The Plowden Report's conclusion that: 'The independence of the head teacher within his school is great' and that 'the intervention of local authority or managers in the curriculum and organisation is no more than nominal'[14] would, in 2009, be met with scepticism. Ofsted's power to issue 'notices to improve' and to put schools in special measures, as well as the creation of school improvement partners (SIPs), with a direct line of accountability through the local authority to the government, provides a stark contrast with Alan Blyth's depiction of headship in the 1960s. Blyth characterised the formal structure of the primary school as a 'three-generation family', the head figuring as grandparent, the teacher as parents, and the children as children, in which 'the head, one stage removed from the heat of the classroom, takes a detached and less critical view of children than do the class teachers'.[15] By the early 1980s, Robin Alexander showed that the traditional 'flat' model of primary school management, with its two zones of influence and autonomy – 'my school' (head) and 'my class' (teacher) – was beginning to give way to three-tier departmentalism with the appointment of curriculum and year leaders in place of the old 'graded posts' given essentially for long service and good conduct.[16] At the same time, Jim Campbell noted the beginnings of a move from the absolutism or paternalism of traditional primary headship ('my school' again) to more collegial professional relations.[17] What hastened these shifts was the recommendation in the 1978 HMI primary survey that schools should appoint subject-specific curriculum co-ordinators in order to reduce the considerable unevenness in curriculum planning and practice between schools, which made pupils' curriculum experiences something of a lottery.[18] Both heads and class teachers were now forced to accept the limits to their expertise and to acknowledge how much they could learn from each other.

Table 22.1 Profile of candidates appointed as head teachers in 2007

Age (years)	Successful applicants (%)
<35	13
35–39	24
40–44	24
45–49	20
>50	19
Gender	
men	27
women	73
Ethnicity	
minority ethnic background	1.5

Adapted from NCSL (2007): 2.
Source of statistics EDS (2008) (from Howson 2007).

Since then, the homely image of the primary-school family has faded further, as have head teacher absolutism – and indeed, with the changing gender profile of primary headship – paternalism. In the 1980s, a school leadership discourse began to emerge in policy circles, in part prompted by a Conservative government which saw the business sector as a model for emulation within education. The head teacher became less grandparent, more manager. Decision-making powers were progressively devolved and accountability for achieving the government's targets progressively increased. But heads were still clearly in charge, despite the changes ushered in by the Education Reform Act. School effectiveness research, an increasingly strong influence on policy through the 1970s and 1980s, highlighted leadership as the key to school quality and improvement. 'Professional leadership' was given pride of place among 11 key indicators of effectiveness in a meta study in 1988.[19] As John Gray commented: 'The importance of the head teacher's leadership is one of the clearest of the messages in school effectiveness research.'[20] What was less well understood, as this model of school effectiveness winged its way to other Anglophone countries, was this was by no means the international norm, and in some countries schools operated successfully without so much being invested in one person.[21]

Yet in England, as the above comments illustrate, primary heads, once grandparent figures, then managers, were now leaders. The extent to which this changed the character of headship in primary schools was questioned in one submission to the Review. The authors remarked:

> ... the term 'leadership' has been adopted relatively recently. In the early 1980s, educational 'administration' was the well-worn vocabulary, so terms such as 'educational leadership' and 'school leadership' were much more muted than is the case at present (Gronn 2003). For us a key question is what changes, if anything, when commentators begin to privilege words such as 'leader', 'leading' and 'leadership' as discursive modes for representing reality, instead of previously favoured terminology such as 'manager', 'management' and so forth?

The creation of a National College for School Leadership and the change in terminology from senior management teams to senior leadership teams signalled a shift, not only of language but also in focus. But the question remains pertinent in a climate where heads are held accountable in so many ways and have to manage their workforce to meet government targets.

Heads and senior leaders now test their degree of autonomy within a nexus of multiple and complex accountabilities and a need to collaborate with statutory and voluntary agencies which whom they share responsibility for the achievement of the five Every Child Matters outcomes. The highly visible nature of leadership and the high stakes involved in school performance bring with them a need to keep a watchful eye on the media and require new skills in media management. The need for vigilance across competing and conflicting accountabilities is compounded by the need for internal accountability, to fellow members of the leadership team, to teachers and to the many other staff with roles created by workforce remodelling.

Perhaps unsurprisingly, given the expansion in head teachers' work and responsibilities, leadership is no longer seen as the sole prerogative of one individual in the way that it clearly was until the 1980s:

> Such an outlook limits leadership to one person and implies lone leadership. The long-standing belief in the power of one is being challenged. Today there is much more talk about shared leadership, leadership teams and distributed leadership than ever before.[22]

Quality assurance and the 'big cats'

The market-oriented management philosophy used by governments since the 1980s to reform their public sectors, brought with it into schools in England the concept of quality assurance, or QA. This meant both a new vocabulary and a new perspective on the work of school leadership. In education, QA has been seen primarily as the role of the inspectorate, linking school improvement with external accountability. Ofsted brought a sharper edge to the process while the pursuit of a more rigorous system of holding schools to account was famously described in 1992 by one Secretary of State as a need for 'big cats prowling the educational landscape'.

By 1999, however, MPs were urging the chief inspector 'to improve morale and promote confidence in the teaching profession', and recommending that inspectors should 'take account of self-evaluation procedures used by the school'.[23] Five years later, the government-commissioned Gershon Report[24] on public spending transferred around £400 million from Ofsted to front-line services. While school self evaluation was presented as integral to improvement, the natural accompaniment of local school management, it was underpinned by a strong economic rationale. Lighter touch inspections would save money.

The case for self evaluation had long been argued by, among others, the National Union of Teachers, the General Teaching Council and local authorities, many of whom had their own distinctive approaches. During the 1970s it also began to emerge in what was then the non-university sector of higher education (colleges and polytechnics), as the Council for National Academic Awards (CNAA) encouraged institutions to move from external to internal accreditation of their courses.[25] While the movement gathered pace in higher education, in the school sector these often homegrown methods became submerged in the New Relationship with Schools (NRwS). This was heralded in 2004 by the then Secretary of State, David Miliband, as a 'covenant that will give schools the time, support and information they need to focus on what really matters'.[26] It may have ignited hope among school leaders that they would have greater power to tailor programmes to their school's developmental history and social context but, in fact, the new relationship did little to counteract the constraining influence of performance tables, government targets and inspection reports.

The introduction of the self-evaluation form (SEF) in 2005 immediately gave schools a template and parameters for assessing quality, reinforcing a view of self evaluation as an event preceding inspection rather than as a way of thinking deeply embedded in the day-to-day work of teachers and senior leaders. Virtually all the 400 head teachers consulted in a series of school leadership workshops said they had completed their SEF (typically during their summer holidays) in anticipation of an inspection. The vast majority regarded it as mandatory, despite Ofsted guidelines clearly stating that schools could use their own approaches. It was a brave and unusual head who did not hurry to complete the SEF in case of an unexpected visit from an Ofsted team.[27]

So, however friendly the rhetoric, the bottom line was clearly articulated by David Miliband: 'Accountability drives everything. Without accountability there is no legitimacy; without legitimacy there is no support; without support there are no resources; and without resources there are no services'. It is within this political imperative that school leaders and inspection teams have to negotiate, exploring where trust and support reside, what those words mean and how they are tested.

The challenge facing the 'new relationship' is the legacy of 15 years in which the 'big cats' had become all too real.[28] Teachers and head teachers interviewed in a 2005 NUT study had a substantial list of concerns, including inspectors' excessive focus on accountability, the blame culture and pressure from national exams and SATs. They worried about school league tables, negative publicity, inaccurate inspection reports and lack of genuine consultation with teachers. Increasing and oppressive paperwork was another complaint, together with ambiguity about the purposes and scope of self evaluation.[29]

Reluctant to step up?

Given the challenges of the head teacher's role, the need to seek out, 'incentivise' and retain talented leaders has been accorded high priority – particularly in the light of a shortage of suitable candidates. In 2006 the House of Commons Public Accounts Committee noted that

Progress is being made in increasing the professionalism of school leaders and improving the training and support they receive, but much more is needed to make head teacher posts attractive to good candidates and to develop potential leaders, for example by increasing the emphasis of initial teacher training on opportunities for developing a career in school leadership.[30]

One recruitment expert pointed out that: 'Although the market for head teachers remains out of balance, most schools have fewer problems recruiting either a deputy or an assistant head teacher. This suggests that there is no real unwillingness to take on a leadership role'.[31] The burden of office as ultimate decision-maker is, however, less attractive.

While acknowledging problems with headship recruitment, the DCSF insisted that difficulties tended to be associated with particular areas and schools in challenging circumstances:

A high proportion of schools going into special measures have had leadership problems. Between September 2007 and April 2008, 51 out of 73 primary schools newly requiring special measures had experienced significant turbulence in leadership ... Several schools have significant difficulties in recruitment. Patterns are not consistent around the country. There is emerging evidence that more needs to be done to attract the best teachers to the most challenging areas and keep them there. Some areas, such as parts of Cumbria and the Yorkshire coast, have a high proportion of failing schools – this could be associated with isolation and difficulty in recruiting quality middle and senior managers.[32]

What makes a good leader?

In 2002, the government outlined its expectations of school leaders:

Our determination is to ensure that every head is able to do more than run a stable school. Transformation requires leadership which:

- can frame a clear vision that engages the school community;
- can motivate and inspire;
- pursues change in a consistent and disciplined way; and
- understands and leads the professional business of teaching.

To achieve their full potential, teachers need to work in a school that is creative, enabling and flexible. And the biggest influence is the head. Every teacher is a leader in the classroom. Every head must be a leader of these leaders. And the head's greatest task is the motivation and deployment of their key resource: staff.[33]

'England is rapidly moving towards creating one of the most systematic portfolios of programmes for leadership in education in the world', conclude the authors of the Review's research survey on leadership development,[34] a reference to the major investment in the National College for School Leadership. Political support for raising the quality of school leadership through professional programmes is strong and seen as a prerequisite for improving schools and raising standards. Evidence for the impact of NCSL on the day-to-day work of schools is, nonetheless, hard to gauge given the increasing complexity of head teachers' commitments and the impact of workforce reform.

The Review's research survey on the professional environment by Ian Stronach, Andy Pickard and Liz Jones suggests that by 2008 primary schools had the potential to develop leadership models that served their own needs and purposes while at the same time responding to external expectations.[35] Effective school leaders were coming to be seen as 'enablers' rather than 'controllers'. While it was argued that such leaders would be likely to carry teachers with them, there was an undertone of scepticism in the research survey's conclusions. National bodies and educational theorists were in agreement that 'the compliance of teachers is most effectively accomplished by securing their commitment', the authors note. This survey also cited evidence that primary head teachers' preference for a 'hands-on' approach to educative or pedagogical styles of leadership had become more difficult to sustain in the face of the expansion of their management, marketing, and financial responsibilities – and in a political landscape filled with talk of 'turning round' schools and 'delivering excellence' via highly proactive 'visions' and leadership 'mission' strategies.

Head teachers are faced with a proliferating selection of leadership styles, many direct imports from business. Despite a political climate that appears to value compliance above all, heads are enjoined to be 'visionary, 'invitational', 'democratic', 'strategic', 'instructional', 'moral', situational', 'transformational'. 'Distributed leadership' is currently in vogue with policy-makers, though it carries within it a variety of meanings. A 2004 study for the NCSL identified six variations, from distribution as formal delegation to distribution as a sponta-neous exercise of agency within a culture which blurs the boundaries of status and institutional authority.[36] However, as that study also found, a genuinely distributive sense of agency and initiative was high risk, particularly in schools where raising attainment standards was a strategic and tactical focus.

The advocacy of a more distributive approach to leadership is allied to a move away from officially sanctioned competition between schools to greater collaboration through networked learning communities, and through other approaches to knowledge sharing. It is, however, left to individual school leaders to resolve the tensions between collaboration and competition.

SCHOOL LEADERSHIP: WHAT THE REVIEW'S WITNESSES SAID

Head teachers' submissions to the Review painted a vivid picture of primary-school life. It was often a wide-angle view, reflecting their many roles, and one coloured with mixed emotions. Many complained about the pressures they faced as they sought to cope with multiple demands: 'pushy parents', unruly children, burdensome bureaucracy, inspections, school league tables, and keeping up with the latest swathes of initiatives. As a result,

> as far as head teachers are concerned, many are now demoralised, posts are harder to fill and in the main, they are fed up with the constant interference, mindless paperwork, lurches in policy, daily announcements of gimmicky initiatives and a daily diet of condemnation by the press who seem to pursue a vendetta, depicting a Britain of failing schools and falling standards. Most heads will retire within the next five to ten years and unless the climate changes, no amount of financial rewards will make the job attractive. This is a shame, because most of us love the job, love the children and are totally dedicated to our schools. But many are burning out fast!

Head teachers who took part in the community soundings confessed to feeling under similar pressure, but their chief concern was that this diverted their attention from their proper tasks of educating children and leading a school. Heads, particularly those in large urban schools, felt that they had become ever more distant from the classroom. Rural heads pointed out that while colleagues in large schools were able to delegate some of their responsibilities, they were obliged to undertake all the work themselves. Distributed leadership was seen as a strength in the community soundings – in the sense that parents, for example, can consult any senior member of staff – as was the mutual support schools gained through clustering.

There was a common feeling that the title 'head teacher' described their role and commit-ment to pedagogy. Such a commitment sat uneasily, however, with satisfying the requirements of Ofsted, the local authority and other agencies, as well as processing all the paperwork. Though welcoming Every Child Matters in principle, it was seen as diverting senior leaders even further from the classroom.

A 2007 NUT survey estimated that a third of head teachers' time was spent on paperwork and just 15 per cent on strategic educational leadership.[37] The union, in its submission to the

Review, was 'unequivocal that the potential head teacher shortage facing primary schools in particular is government manufactured, rather than one which is endemic to the role itself'. It cited additional research evidence to support this view, arguing that the government needed to cut back urgently on the number of initiatives in order to make the role of head teacher more manageable and sustainable. In the same year the NCSL also warned the Secretary of State about the heavy workload of many primary heads and their continuing difficulties despite, and sometimes because of, workforce remodelling. This was especially the case in small schools. 'Head teachers have engaged in the process of workforce remodelling to try to achieve a more manageable workload for staff but have not always achieved this for themselves'.[38]

Recruiting the best school leaders raised different concerns. Solutions suggested by management consultants PricewaterhouseCoopers in 2007 – school federations or hiring people from outside education[39] – were not met with unequivocal enthusiasm. Such moves were unlikely to be in the best interests of schools or the education system, argued the NUT in its submission to the Review.

Some submissions pointed to the head teacher's important role in shaping the relationships between community and school. Heads, it was suggested, had a key part to play in communicating not only with parents but with the community at large. Understanding and responding to local needs should be part of their brief, it was argued. Extended schools are one way of achieving these aims and recent NCSL research found evidence of senior leaders' time in extended schools becoming increasingly directed to inter-agency work and community initiatives.[40] Representatives of the wide range of voluntary agencies and organisations which contributed to the Review's national soundings said if teachers were to meet the particular needs of their children and their community, head teachers should have greater power over the curriculum. We have pursued this issue in our proposals for curriculum reform, though we argue there that the 'community curriculum' should be developed through collaboration between schools, the local authority and indeed the community itself, rather than by schools acting in isolation (Chapter 14). What we should perhaps be wary of is harking back to pre-national curriculum days, leapfrogging not just the era of compliance but also the era of collegiality. Inspection and research during the 1970s and 1980s clearly exposed the limits to the assumption that in curriculum matters the head teacher knows best.

Finally, school self evaluation was welcomed as a way forward by head teachers, who saw it as playing a key role in the creation of a positive school culture in which pupil autonomy, voice and participation are valued and the quality of leadership is highlighted. One submission suggested that consideration should be given to the routines and rituals of the school day and how they impact on relationships and on children's sense of autonomy and self-esteem. Several submissions suggested that schools should create more opportunities for children to be consulted, to take responsibility and to help in decision-making within the school.

One significant challenge for head teachers recently has been to implement the 2003 workforce agreement in their schools, and so we devote the next section of the chapter to this endeavour and to relevant research and evidence presented to the Review.

WORKFORCE REFORM

Teacher workloads and an 'understandable anxiety'

The 1998 Green Paper *Teachers: meeting the challenge of change* had three basic aims, according to the Review's research survey on workforce management and reform.[41] First, to strengthen teaching and learning by using 'the full potential of teaching assistants and school support staff'; second, to increase the number of teaching assistants by 20,000 by 2002; and third, to produce guidance for teachers on how to use assistants effectively.[42] The rise of the teaching assistant – seen both as radical and as a potential threat to teachers' professional status – had been mooted by the Plowden Report 30 years earlier. Extolling the underused skills of teachers' aides and classroom ancillaries, Plowden had proposed that 'a national agreement between the authority and teachers' organisations on the functions of teachers, aides is desirable', adding 'but we hope that a good deal of discretion will be left to the head teachers'.[43] The committee anticipated concern about professional roles: 'Constructive suggestions in this field, more than in any other, are apt to be blocked by the understandable anxiety of the teaching profession to avoid dilution'. There were also fears about potential exploitation: 'On no account should children be in the charge of untrained helpers without supervision by a qualified teacher.'[44]

By the end of the 1990s, there was increasing concern about teachers' workloads following the Education Reform Act. As Hilary Burgess recounts in her research survey for the Review, the government commissioned PricewaterhouseCoopers to investigate, following pressure from the School Teachers' Review Body. The finding that workloads were excessive justified the launch of the 'Time for Standards' reform of 2002.[45] This was built on four principles: standards and accountability; devolution and delegation; flexibility and incentive, and expanding choice. Support staff were to be 'recognised for their contribution to raising standards and have more opportunities to take on wider and deeper roles in support of teaching and learning, supported by the right training and new career paths, with numbers growing to deliver reform.'[46]

In 2003, the national workforce agreement was signed. The NUT, alone among professional organisations, refused to add its name, concerned that the government would attempt to save money by replacing teachers with support staff. The 'understandable anxiety' predicted by Plowden was perhaps justified by the publication in 2004 of the professional standards for higher level teaching assistants (HLTAs). Standards related to planning, monitoring and assessment, as well as teaching and learning, closely paralleled those for teachers, including, for example, 'that they advance learning when working with whole classes without the presence of the assigned teacher'.[47] Such standards challenged assurances made in the HLTA guidance for schools; that higher level assistants would always work under the supervision of a qualified teacher, and that the roles were not interchangeable.[48]

The rise and rise of support staff

Between 1997 and 2008, the total number of support staff in primary and nursery schools in England rose 250 per cent from 75,700 to 172,6000 (see Table 22.2).

While the most dramatic rise has been in teaching assistant numbers, the ranks of what the DCSF labels 'other education support staff' have also swelled (see Figure 22.1). This group includes librarians, welfare assistants, learning mentors and other regularly employed non-teaching staff. Their numbers almost doubled from around 14,000 in 1997 to more than 27,000 in 2008.

The effects of workforce reform

Workforce reform was phased in between 2003 and 2006.[49] In January 2004, following the transfer of 24 non-teaching tasks from teachers to TAs, the workforce agreement monitoring group (WAMG) said that the first 'wave' had produced positive effects 'where it counts – in the classroom'. While claiming that 87 per cent of schools had either made the changes or planned

Table 22.2 Numbers of teaching assistants and other support staff in English primary and nursery schools 1997–2008 (numbers given in thousands)

Nursery and primary schools	1997	2000	2001	2002	2003	2004	2005	2006	2007	2008(p)
Teaching assistants	41.9	53.4	65.5	71.8	82.3	89.2	97.9	99.0	105.8	115.0
Other support staff	33.9	39.1	42.5	51.0	45.3	45.0	46.6	55.3	57.4	57.6

p: provisional
DCSF (2008w)

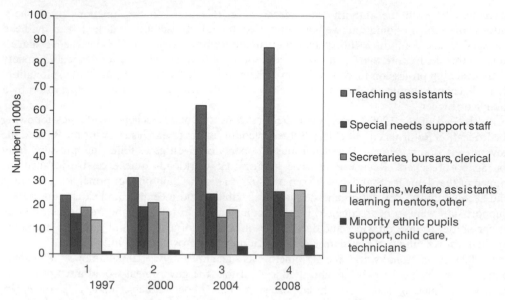

Figure 22.1 The changing profile of support staff in primary and nursery schools in England, 1997–2008 (Source: DCSF 2008w).

to, the group admitted that there was 'real work ly[ing] ahead … in a cultural change that will raise the status and professionalism of teachers, create new opportunities and greater recognition for support staff and enable schools to focus on the individual needs of every child.'[50]

In 2006, most schools were still at the 'developing' stage and concerned about what would happen when the extra funding dried up, according to the National Foundation for Educational Research.[51] Nevertheless, teachers identified benefits such as planning, preparation and assessment (PPA) time, flexible team working and the use of 'remodelling' as a way of managing the changes. Given the parallel introduction of *Every Child Matters* in 2004, there was a view that schools needed more support in seeing how these various agendas linked together. Teachers in the pathfinder Transforming the School Workforce project identified as problems 'too much bureaucracy and paperwork, planning, government initiatives, unrealistic targets and discipline in schools'. Asked for solutions, they suggested 'deployment of more support staff, more non-contact time, reduction in paperwork, development of ICT and smaller classes.'[52]

Another evaluation by Rosemary Webb and Graham Vulliamy reported positive attitudes to some aspects of workforce reform such as the increase in numbers of adults, and TAs' contributions to improving children's 'self-esteem, motivation and achievement' in the classroom.[53] At the same time the prospect of TAs taking whole classes to release teachers for PPA was widely rejected. As Burgess puts it: 'Workforce remodelling was viewed as both a threat to teacher professionalism and as a means of enhancing it by opening up new possibilities'[54] as teachers developed new skills in co-operation, monitoring and delegation.

Webb and Vulliamy's evidence of change in teachers' perceptions of their work was corroborated to some extent by the large-scale government-funded Deployment and Impact of Support Staff in School (DISS) project.[55] TAs were observed to work mostly with small groups, focusing on children seen to have greatest need. However, as children's individual interactions with TAs increased, so their individual interactions with teachers decreased. While impressionistic evidence suggested that schools, through their use of support staff, were succeeding in improving attitudes, behaviour and attainment, the research team concluded that 'the problem head teachers faced was proving it'.[56]

In 2007, Ofsted confirmed and extended many of these findings, both positive and negative. It boldly claimed 'a revolutionary shift in the culture of the school workforce', with 'teachers' time and work more directly focused on teaching and learning, and a substantial expansion of the wider workforce at all levels'.[57] It presented numerous examples of how schools (both secondary and primary) had adopted and adapted the opportunities provided by remodelling to suit their own requirements. Positive results, Ofsted concluded, came when workforce reform was linked to other government initiatives such as *Every Child Matters*, or was used to focus on teaching and learning, or to give head teachers dedicated 'headship' time. In particular, it highlighted how the 'wider workforce' had both expanded and become more diverse. Classrooms in England were welcoming volunteers such as parents and carers, retired experts, career changers, recent graduates gaining school experience before training to teach, or paid workers. These included counsellors, medical staff, personnel managers, data managers, premises managers, a variety of business staff, student mentors, trainee teachers, work experience students, and the caretaker (or school keeper or site manager) and school meals supervisors (or kitchen supervisors).[58] Support staff might be organising breakfast clubs, after-school study support, a summer play scheme, information meetings for parents, or a 'fun for fathers' club between 5 and 7pm. However, Ofsted also noted that few schools were collecting any hard evidence of how time was being used, or its effects on pupils' attitudes, attainment or engagement, though this had improved by 2008.[59]

Work and life still out of balance

While evidence in support of the positive effects of workforce reform emerged from several studies, undeniable difficulties were identified by the DISS project and three other contemporary large-scale studies.[60] These included a dependence on the goodwill and extra hours worked by support staff; widespread concern that teaching assistants were badly underpaid; extra and more demanding work for teachers now filling the 'space' created by PPA; and the use of TAs to cover PPA time, so excluding them from planning meetings with teachers. Thus, ironically, opportunities for joint planning that had previously enhanced TA skills and sense of professionalism could be one of the casualties of the workforce reform. Maurice Galton and John MacBeath summed it up as having

> proved something of a palliative for a system on the verge of implosion, but has not affected an improvement in work-life balance, most categorically not for head teachers, neither for increasingly put upon teaching assistants, [nor] ... from our sample, for the majority of school staff.[61]

Further, they found no discernible effect on pedagogy, despite Ofsted's claim that teachers were able to focus on teaching and learning. Thus, where a better adult-child ratio could potentially improve the quality of pupil-adult interactions, instead, 'lessons appear more than ever to be delivered rather than becoming a genuine dialogic process'.[62]

WORKFORCE REFORM: WHAT THE WITNESSES SAID

The Review's community soundings – of children, parents, governors and other community representatives as well as teaching professionals – offered a broader perspective on workforce reform than much of the research literature. We begin with teaching assistants.

We met groups of TAs in each of the schools visited. Their common message was that they know the children, and their parents, as individuals and so are able to liaise between school and home (perhaps better than teachers, although this was implied rather than stated). Teaching assistants in a London school, for example, said: 'We care for children, missing lunch if we see children in trouble. We look for them on the way home and may bring children back to school [if concerned for their safety].' Their aim was to make school a secure environment where 'staff and children could leave home troubles at home', making school 'an extended home'. In other words, these TAs took on caring responsibilities. Although caring is also valued by primary teachers there is a degree of ambivalence about their pastoral role as it may, according to some sources, detract from their professional status.[63]

Teachers valued the part played by TAs, wondered how they managed before workforce reform, and acknowledged them as full members of schools' professional teams. While the TAs recognised that teachers appreciated their contribution, they wanted better training now that they were part of the teaching team, as membership was a very variable experience. While TAs in Devon said that they had lost their planning time, one pointed out that PPA had made 'no difference ... the nature of job is not to know exactly what's going on'. In Yorkshire a TA said, 'Planning with the teachers – Wonderful! Wonderful! If our teacher is out I can just, say, move that [task] there, and then make sure they get what she wants'. Her colleague, who supported the school's rapidly growing number of children with English as an additional language, told a different story however: 'Often I don't get planning time – often the activity is given to me in the morning, or often I don't get anything – and I have to go back to basics. If I don't get the planning – I can't help them with what the teachers ask. By the time you have done your intervention groups, then you have admin tasks, registers and [then] you don't get the planning.' As research mentioned earlier intimated, PPA time, though welcomed now by teachers, may be excluding TAs from the planning process and denying them the planning time they once had, as they cover classes.[64]

The TAs confirmed that they were frequently assigned to support children deemed to need extra support, as the DISS project found. This worked in different ways however. In one outer London primary, for example, the TAs explained that they tried to '[be] accessible for everyone; you must be inclusive' so that children with special needs could integrate and interact with other children. In a Devon school with a relatively large proportion of children with behavioural difficulties, the TAs 'support the teacher in teaching the majority while we help groups with behavioural difficulties'. TAs in a school which catered also for children with various physical needs, however, had had their roles changed from 'integration assistants', who looked after the disabled pupils, or general 'classroom assistants', to all being TAs. They unanimously preferred the previous system, as now they were confronted by dilemmas such as whether to support the teacher or the child. Their priority was clearly the child.

Teaching assistants had serious concerns, too, about being given 'responsibility without authority', as when they were left alone with a class. Higher level assistants were, they claimed, being used as cheap teachers. It was also said that there were still not enough TAs and that, in certain areas, more bilingual assistants were needed. Community representatives in Devon argued for more TAs with specialised skills.

Several organisations praised improvements in the quality of the teaching workforce. This was attributed not only to continuing professional development but also to TAs' contributions to work in the classroom. PPA time was seen as a significant benefit, in submissions from consultants, advisers and head teachers. Although not specifically cited by teachers (who may simply take it for granted), evidence from elsewhere suggests that PPA time has been warmly welcomed by primary staff.

There were, however, two major concerns. First, that neither TAs nor teachers had the relevant knowledge and expertise to support children with more complex learning needs. This was particularly worrying given that TAs were most often deployed in working with these children. Second, some national organisations objected to the increasing use of non-qualified TAs in classroom teaching. These concerns were echoed in the community soundings, notably by TAs themselves. While anxiety about assistants taking whole classes had receded between 2002 and 2007,[65] teachers were still very aware of the gap between responsibility and remuneration.[66]

TEACHERS' ROLES, PROFESSIONALISM AND STATUS

Teachers have been under 'increasing pressure to do more in less time, to be responsive to a greater range of demands from external sources, [and] to meet a greater range of targets'.[67] They have been criticised by politicians, the media and the inspectorate. The growing complexity of their roles and responsibilities, the stream of new tasks and deadlines have been documented widely in recent years.[68] Compelled to comply with government prescriptions for curriculum and, to a large extent, pedagogy, teachers have warned that their creativity, imagination, expertise and confidence have all been constrained. Although there is now one teaching assistant for every 1.7 teachers, compared to one to every 4.6 teachers in 1997, this may have achieved only a short-term reduction in workload, though there are signs that teachers are at least able to devote more time and energy to pedagogical processes,[69] even if improvements remain elusive.

From flat to stepped: teachers' career structure

The primary teacher's career path was once relatively straightforward, with opportunities for promotion limited by school size. After a probationary year, promotion opportunities consisted of a 'graded post', a managerial role as, say, head of infants, a deputy headship and ultimately a headship. From 1988, the national curriculum gave rise to roles such as curriculum co-ordinator or manager, but the career structure for most teachers was relatively 'flat', with years spent at the same grade and no possibility of further reward for those who wished to remain class teachers with little or no management responsibility.

We noted earlier how the 1978 HMI primary survey prompted the growing departmentalisation of primary schools, with the rise of curriculum and year leaders in place of the old relatively random array of 'graded posts'. Pay structures began to accommodate this change, but not completely, and in many primary schools there was a mismatch between the jobs that needed doing and the posts available. The 1998 Green Paper (see policy milestones at the beginning of this chapter) proposed a more stepped career structure: first, a pay and performance threshold to be reached, typically after five years in post, and, second, the possibility of promotion to 'excellent teacher' or advanced skills teacher (AST) for those who rejected the management route. 'Excellent' and 'advanced' were to be defined within the government's prescribed instructional models (see Chapter 21), and measured in terms of pupil performance in the national tests. ASTs, subject to successful external assessment of their classroom practice, were to be rewarded with extra pay and required to support other teachers, in their own and other schools, for the equivalent of one day a week.

These performance management proposals provoked a storm of protest from a variety of agencies, in particular from teachers' associations.[70] Some pointed out the irony of the government's statement that 'what counts is what works' and its determination to pursue performance management 'despite the weight of evidence which points to its negative potential'.[71] Nevertheless, a pay threshold was introduced and teachers were required to present a portfolio of evidence including pupil performance data to justify their crossing it. While head teachers were the ultimate judges of who should or should not cross, governors exercised a degree of oversight over the process, and in some cases assisted in the process of selection.[72]

Teaching by numbers ...

Plowden reported that there were 140,000 full-time equivalent teachers in primary schools in 1965. By 2008, there were 198,200 FTE teachers, of whom 192,900 had Qualified Teacher Status. Of the 130,300 classroom teachers in nursery and primary schools, about 10 per cent had become advanced skills teachers. Table 22.3 shows the change in the total number of nursery and primary school personnel in the past decade. The improved ratio of teaching assistants to teachers has been achieved by a steady increase in the number of TAs, while the number of teachers, and other support staff in primary and nursery classes, has increased only slightly.

... and by gender

In 1965, women outnumbered men by three to one in primary schools, and five to two in junior schools, while 'in infant schools in 1965, there were only 97 brave men out of a total of

Table 22.3 Full-time equivalent number of teachers and support staff in local authority maintained schools in England : January 1997 to January 2008

Nursery and primary schools	1997	2000	2001	2002	2003	2004	2005	2006	2007	2008(p)
All regular teachers	191.7	193.1	195.0	197.4	197.4	196.6	196.3	198.2	197.1	198.2
Total support staff	75.7	92.4	108.0	122.8	127.6	134.1	154.4	154.4	163.1	172.6
Total workforce	267.4	285.5	303.0	320.2	325.0	330.8	340.8	352.6	360.2	370.8

(*p: provisional*)
DCSF (2008w)

33,000 teachers'.[73] While half of the head teachers were male, 40 per cent of primaries had no men on the staff. By 2006, five out of six primary teachers were women, as were three out of four heads, and half of England's primaries had no men on staff. As regards ethnicity, in 2008 89 per cent of teachers were White British, 5.1 per cent Other White, 2.5 Asian/Asian British, 1.7 per cent Black or Black British, and 0.1 per cent Chinese. Clearly, primary teaching is dominated by White British women. However, recent evidence suggests that a teacher's gender or ethnicity does not affect children's attitudes and attainment in primary schools.[74]

The question of professionalism

> The job became less fun for teachers and pupils alike. The remorseless pursuit of grades had unhealthy effects on other educational goals; the impact of these degradations took a few years but by 2001 Secretaries of State were beginning to talk a new language of 'creativity', of 'emotional intelligence', 'personalisation' and 'self-esteem'. Standards were still important but there had to be more flexibility ...[75]

These words, from the Review's research survey on the primary professional environment, vividly express the perceived effects of the policies of the 1990s. Many teachers stopped enjoying their work, and by the mid-1990s resignations outnumbered retirements. The change in the texture of their work, wrought by the 'remorseless pursuit of grades,' was accompanied by research exploring the meaning of 'professionalism' in relation to teaching.

What exactly is meant by professionalism? Andy Hargreaves and Ivor Goodson, in their book on teachers' professional lives, accept that: 'What it means to be professional, to show professionalism or to pursue professionalisation is not universally agreed or understood'.[76] They offer six classes of definition, from what they call 'classical' professionalism – exemplified by medicine and law and characterised by specialised knowledge, extensive training, self-regulation and a strong commitment to meeting clients' needs – through examples of 'practical', 'flexible', 'extended', 'complex' and finally 'postmodern' professionalisms. The last of these embodies, in relation to teaching, the power to use one's own judgement, to work in partnership with pupils, parents and the community, to collaborate with colleagues in solving problems – rather than simply implementing external mandates – and a commitment to continuous professional learning that is self-determined rather than externally prescribed.

Various interpretations of teacher professionalism are identified in the Review's research survey by Stronach, Pickard and Jones.[77] They note, however, that much of the discourse is conducted in terms of binary oppositions. Teachers' autonomy and/or authority to make decisions about teaching and learning is contrasted with the high degree of regulation and accountability and the requirement to 'deliver' a ready-made curriculum in a certain way. Drawing on their previous analysis of the field, they reject any single, simple construct of professionalism, arguing instead that teachers' professionalism is 'more fluid, more plastic, more dynamic'.[78] They contend that 'ambiguity and uncertainty [are] at the heart of professional identity' and the many, often contradictory, images of primary teachers – pressured individuals, subject specialists, coerced innovators, sceptical pragmatists – are the 'shards' or fragments that make up these identities, also often influenced by their own memories of good teachers. They quote Alexander's observation that the discourse on primary professionalism fails to recognise the 'more nuanced and dilemma-conscious private conversations of primary teachers, where feelings matter ... and where subtlety and realism puncture the notions of "one-size fits all" and "good primary practice"'.

At the core of this alternative view of professionalism, teachers believe, is the 'ability to motivate and develop children's learning and to boost their confidence and self image,' according to Webb and Vulliamy.[79] Similarly, a national survey in 2003 found that teachers chose the career because they enjoyed teaching, wanted to work with children and to give them the best start in life. More than half the participants in the government-commissioned VITAE project, a four-year study of teachers' work, lives and their effects on pupils, also referred to making a difference to children's lives. Teachers referred to special, trusting relationships, making children feel secure, and to children's social and affective development, not just their academic work. In other words, teachers seemed intrinsically motivated to support all aspects of children's development, not solely the academic.

Comparisons with early years practitioners are illuminating. Jayne Osgood's studies found that being forced to work in a market place had undermined their common ethic of care and replaced it with 'a constructed professionalism that emphasises rationalisation, competitiveness, and individualism'.[80] She calls for EY professionals to re-assert their 'ethic of care and emotional labour' and establish a different kind of professionalism which acknowledges the unique nature and complexity of their work, in the face of the government's new model of professionalism. Announced in 2002, this 'professionalism for the modern world' explicitly emphasised high standards, 'what works best', regular rigorous training and professional development, and an assumption that 'what is in the best interests of [pupils and parents] will be susceptible to procedures of measuring accountability and performance'.[81] Adherence to this model would apparently earn the government's trust. Greater autonomy would be granted in return for evidence of improved pupil performance, and the profession's status would rise.

The question of status

In 2002, the government, concerned about low morale and recruitment, sponsored a four-year research project into the profession's status.[82] It concluded:

> Very few teachers enter their profession for its status or image: most become teachers to work with children, to give children a good start in life and/or to give something back to society. In the Teacher Status Project, having lamented the trials and tribulations of the teacher's life, the stress, the workload, the unprecedented levels of accountability and the erosions of professional autonomy, teachers' common refrain was '... but I love it.'

Teachers, TAs, parents and governors believed that the status of teaching had been in sharp decline during the decades since Plowden, though it had begun to level out in 1997, the project reported. Another finding was that teachers were not overly concerned about their standing in society, 'gaining positive status when they felt trusted, appreciated and rewarded by parents and through collaborative work with other professionals'. Supportive leadership and time for personal development also increased their sense of self worth, while they believed the quality of their working conditions affected how others regarded them.

While teachers insisted they were not too concerned about status, the project found they consistently underestimated the esteem in which they were held by the public, parents, governors and support staff. They perceived a chasm between themselves and those they regarded as high-status professionals. Teaching, in their eyes, was characterised by low pay, little respect and too much external control and regulation – although newly qualified teachers were typically more positive than their more experienced colleagues and 49 per cent of the public considered teaching an attractive career. Teachers consistently blamed their low status on a 'bad press', but analysis of print media going back to 1991 found that recent years had seen a shift to a balanced and arguably more positive coverage, in which, if anything, teachers were portrayed as a profession under siege from a hostile government.[83] Perhaps teachers' conviction that they will always be blamed by the media has militated against any improvement in their status.

The project also found that 30 per cent of the public considered teachers' social status to be on a par with social workers, with the same proportion saying that the need to control a class of children was an unappealing aspect of the job.[84] This echoed Professor Eric Hoyle's earlier proposition that the achievement of high status is hampered by the fact that teachers 'care' as well as teach.[85] Their standing is undermined by this ambiguity of function and the public perception that their 'clients' might get out of control. Hoyle also suggested that the high proportion of women in the profession may deter men, and the lack of subject specialists may deter academic high flyers, both of which may impact on status. The lower academic threshold for entry in England as compared with countries such as Finland and Taiwan, is also a factor, according to a recent report on the status of teachers around the world.[86]

ROLES, PROFESSIONALISM AND STATUS: WHAT THE WITNESSES SAID

A high proportion of the submissions we received referred to teachers' work and professionalism and how recent policies had affected these. Practitioners frequently spoke of the damage inflicted on professional autonomy and status by political micro-management, and the uneasy relationship between political pressure for higher academic attainment and professional commitment to the 'whole child'.

For example, when asked about their priorities, teachers' principal concerns were to develop children's social, communication and critical thinking skills, and their ability to make reasoned choices. They also wanted children to have self-respect, and to be rounded personalities with an awareness of their community. Teachers at one sounding, for example, thought that too great an emphasis was placed on basic skills, rather than creating 'rounded people'. The curriculum was seen unanimously as being too narrow, rigid and prescriptive, over-emphasising content rather than learning skills, and literacy and numeracy at the expense of play.

Head teachers, commenting on what made a good teacher, did not mention targets, attainment and inspection criteria, indicating that they saw their colleagues not as datasets but as people, bringing professional motivation, effort and skill to their work as a matter of course. In fact, head teachers and children valued very similar qualities in staff, appreciating those who were flexible, reflective, who made learning fun, who could 'get inside a child's mind', were able to scaffold learning, take risks, and be both caring and approachable.

Children's organisations argued that pupils were well catered for in spite of restrictions on professional autonomy. They felt teacher quality was improving, which many put down to improvements in initial training, while curriculum organisations commented on the 'formidable force' of experienced teachers. Many of the other groups who gave evidence, especially consultants and head teachers, saw workforce reform, PPA time and the new roles of teaching assistants as a great benefit.

However, the erosion of professional autonomy and status as well as constant changes in policy were condemned in numerous submissions from heads, teachers and governors. The profession was being demoralised, they said, and frustrated by micro-management. One teacher expressed this in terms of a case for 'personalised teaching – recognising [that] teachers have different strengths, different ways of working and different personalities, so must be allowed to do things in different ways ... in the best interests of children'. The inspection system was seen by many head teachers as undermining professionalism by public denigration of individual staff and schools. There were calls for the improvement of the image and status of teaching, as one local authority pointed out:

> Without losing accountability, a culture is required that continues to raises teachers' status, minimising explicit and implied criticism through over-reporting of unrefined data. The

prevailing sense is of a profession beset by change over which they have minimal control, which acts as a further indicator of low status.

These submissions reflected a wider concern about the politicisation of education. Individuals and organisations, both within and outside education, shared similar concerns about political interventions that appeared to lack knowledge and understanding of children's needs, and about waves of policies introduced so rapidly that they could neither be implemented nor evaluated effectively.

A submission from one group of head teachers called for more 'trust and respect' because teachers know 'what children need and when they need it, not when a strategy says it should happen'. The submission from 'Heading for Inclusion', a group of heads and senior leaders committed to the ideal of inclusion, argued that political pressures and media portrayals had undermined the public's trust in teachers, spreading a 'national disrespect' of the profession. Other countries, they pointed out, valued their teachers:

> Those of us who come from or who have visited other countries note the high regard in which teachers are held, as represented in their professional status, income, conditions of service and treatment by politicians and the media – even free entry to galleries and museums! Teachers continue to be paid considerably less than other professionals – doctors, solicitors, engineers, senior civil servants. Our qualifications are being slowly eroded and our work is being devalued by passing it to less qualified people.

There were concerns both inside and outside the profession regarding the impact of school 'league tables' on public perceptions of teachers and consequently their status. Presenting 'unrefined data' on pupil attainment was widely regarded as damaging status and morale and one organisation suggested that, although public accountability was important, there was a need to ensure that 'explicit and implied criticism' was minimised. Constant political scrutiny and intervention in education signalled to the public that teachers could not be entrusted with the task of educating children without the steering hands, and watchful eyes, of government policy-makers. If the government was seriously committed to its stated aim of re-establishing teacher professionalism, it clearly needed to demonstrate its faith in teachers. The submission from the Association of Teachers and Lecturers called for a firm line to be drawn between the responsibilities of government and those of teachers:

> We certainly accept the need for accountability and continuing professional learning. We also understand the government's need to promote higher standards in both teaching and learning and we are happy to work with them to see our vision for a New Professionalism materialise. But, authority over the curriculum and pedagogy must reside with those who have the expertise.

Whilst teachers felt they were losing control in their traditional domain, at the same time they were assuming new responsibilities outside the classroom. With the expansion of multi-agency working and the challenges posed by *Every Child Matters*, their workloads had increased. However, the submission from the Universities' Council for the Education of Teachers (UCET) argued that these developments were likely to enhance status:

> Some fear that the effect of these changes will be to threaten the teacher's professional identity. On the contrary, UCET holds that the effect of these changes will be to reinforce the role of the teacher as the specialist in human development through learning.

In this chapter we have considered the effects of recent reforms on the professional environment of the primary school, taking into account workforce reform, new concepts of leadership and the ambiguous state of teachers' professionalism and status. We turn now to try to bring these threads together.

CONCLUSION

How then might we characterise the relationships between leadership, workforce reform and teacher professionalism? How might we tease out the story of what it means to lead, to teach and to support and improve teaching in primary schools?

The rhetoric, vocabulary and literature of leadership have expanded over a decade and more, but in practice it is still the individual head teacher who is burdened with a proliferating range of responsibilities and accountabilities. When the price of these pressures is too often paid in physical and mental health, it is no longer tenable for any one person to assume such a complex portfolio of tasks. Distributed leadership has therefore commended itself to policy-makers and others as the answer to the problem. Yet the term conceals more than it reveals. It may be interpreted as a matter of delegating tasks in accordance with role and status, or less mechanistically, as an organic process in which all staff feel free to take the initiative.

Both interpretations are, nonetheless, problematic within a remodelled workforce. The first with its clearly demarcated roles may be efficient but at the same time frustrate initiative, creativity and teamwork. Teaching assistants may adhere religiously to their 24 tasks while teachers may no longer put up displays of children's work despite this being, for many, a deeply satisfying activity. The second interpretation which encourages a free flow of activity and shared responsibility, blind to status and hierarchy, may also be blind to professional qualifications and identity. So, for example, a TA with greater interpersonal skills than a teacher may enjoy license to play to those strengths and prove highly effective in a pastoral or even a teaching role. Yet, however intuitive and skilful that TA, they may have no formal qualifications and their pay and conditions would be unacceptable to teachers and to their professional associations. Such concerns pervaded our evidence, with soundings and submissions resonating with the research findings that while workforce reform has been broadly welcomed, its effects appear to be mixed. The contributions made by teaching assistants and other support staff are valued, but the workload respite for teachers has been short lived as they have had to take on new tasks; their focus on teaching and learning has not yet resulted in pedagogical improvements; and TAs have concerns about the responsibilities they are expected to shoulder, and their lack of training.

Evidence to the Review also revealed serious concerns about low status, loss of professionalism and lack of trust by government as indicated by the relentless tide of often contradictory initiatives and expectations. Unsurprisingly, as teachers try to solve 'the irresolvable contradiction of excellence and enjoyment',[87] many find their professional identity in a state of continual flux.[88] Yet, while many teachers have come to value the structures and methods they have been forced to adopt – and may be beginning to use these more flexibly[89] – the strategies and reforms have not brought about engagement with fundamental pedagogical issues, as discussed in Chapter 15. As long as there are SATs, league tables, and national strategies which are to all intents and purposes obligatory, the professionalism that seeks to encourage children's creativity, curiosity and well-being is likely to remain enfeebled by intense demands for accountability. Fortunately for many, but not all, their colleagues provide the positive ethos, mutual support and encouragement that maintains their self esteem and personal sense of status.

We are no less concerned by evidence to the Review which suggests a split in the primary force between those who welcome the prescriptions of the national agencies and their local authority counterparts, and those who resent being told what to do and how to think, and deplore both the compliance culture and the dependence on others for ideas that it has fostered. To some extent this split is age-related: in the Review's evidence, younger teachers, by and large, were more likely than their more experienced colleagues to value and rely on the national strategies and to be happy to download ready-made lessons and materials from DCSF and other websites. However, if teachers now operate within a system which may discourage or even prevent many of them from progressing beyond the stage of external support or dependence to self-regulation or autonomy, and if there are experienced teachers who are content not to move beyond the first stage, then that should give everyone, not just the teaching profession, cause for considerable concern.

The challenge to leadership, then, is to take advantage of what may be a source of creative opportunity while avoiding a professional minefield. The test comes at moments of crisis, a high level of teacher absence, a flu epidemic, an unforeseen event or accident. It is in such circumstances that leadership requires a blend of pragmatism and an unswerving set of professional standards. These are accompanied by a strong sense of collegiate, or 'internal' accountability which respects and nurtures teachers' professional expertise. At the same time the needs and careers of support staff are catered for, fostered by an organisational intelligence and an alertness to the potential of high calibre people who may be encouraged and supported to further their qualifications. Capacity building and succession planning are to the fore, led by a commitment to recruit teachers, middle and senior leaders of the highest quality. These are people who understand the issues and bring a blend of pragmatism, vision and collective accountability to their role.

Workforce reform has created the chance to foster a staff with complementary skills and the capacity to deal creatively with challenges from the community on the one hand and policy directives on the other. In response to the widespread perception of recruitment crisis, the 2001 McKinsey Report[90] advocated a 'war for talent'. It was premised on the assumption that the talent existed somewhere else and had to be found and captured to effect institutional change. Author and journalist Malcolm Gladwell's rejoinder[91] was that 'great organisations create talented leaders'. These apparently oppositional stances can be reconciled by prescient leadership which attends to developing the talent within while also having a keen eye for the potential beyond the school.

'Learning: the treasure within', the title of the Delors Report[92] in 1996, framed the challenge to leadership as recognising and cultivating not only the incipient agency of teachers but also of children and young people. In the complex mix of workforce remodelling there is a danger that pupils' voices may be lost or subdued. As Suzanne SooHoo wrote 16 years ago, pupils are the school's largest untapped knowledge source, 'the treasure in our very own backyard',[93] arguing that a school which overlooks that source is inevitably poorer as a consequence. Historically they have been the last to be consulted about school quality and effectiveness, the last to be commentators on learning, the last to assume leadership roles, yet, as a developing literature attests, they may get closest to the heartbeat of the school.

NOTES

1 CACE (1967): para 929.
2 Hoyle (2001).
3 DfEE (1998c).
4 Webb (2007); Galton and MacBeath (2008).
5 Alexander (2004a).
6 Webb and Vulliamy (2006).
7 DCSF (2007b): 11.
8 DfES (2005a).
9 PwC (2007).
10 DCSF (2008w).
11 NCSL (2007).
12 Blyth (1965).
13 Cunningham and Hargreaves (2007).
14 CACE (1967): para 929.
15 Blyth (1965): 165, citing Wilson (1962).
16 Alexander (1984).
17 Campbell (1985).
18 DES (1978a).
19 Mortimore *et al.* (1988).
20 Gray (1990): 214.
21 Alexander (2001b).
22 Southworth (2002).
23 Parliamentary Select Committee on the Work of Ofsted.

24　Gershon (2004).
25　Adelman and Alexander (1982).
26　Miliband (2004b).
27　MacBeath (2006).
28　Learmonth (2000).
29　MacBeath and Oduro (2005).
30　House of Commons (2006): 5–6, paraphrased in DCSF (2008h): 126.
31　Howson (2008).
32　DCSF (2008h): 126.
33　DfES (2002b): 26.
34　McNamara *et al.* (2010), *The Cambridge Primary Review Research Surveys*, Chapter 24.
35　Stronach *et al.* (2010), *The Cambridge Primary Review Research Surveys*, Chapter 23.
36　MacBeath *et al.* (2004).
37　NUT (2007).
38　NCSL (2007).
39　PwC (2007).
40　NCSL (2008).
41　DfEE (1998c).
42　DfEE (1998c): para 19–20.
43　CACE (1967): para 925.
44　CACE (1967): para 926.
45　DfES (2002b).
46　DfES (2002b): 4.
47　TDA (2004).
48　ATL *et al.* (2004).
49　Detailed in Burgess (2010), see *The Cambridge Primary Review Research Surveys*, Chapter 25.
50　WAMG (2004).
51　Easton *et al.* (2006).
52　Burgess (2010), *The Cambridge Primary Review Research Surveys*, Chapter 25.
53　Webb and Vulliamy (2006).
54　Burgess (2010), *The Cambridge Primary Review Research Surveys*, Chapter 25.
55　Blatchford, Bassett *et al.* (2008) surveyed 76 schools and conducted systematic classroom observations and case studies in 49 schools.
56　Blatchford, Bassett *et al.* (2008): 13.
57　Ofsted (2007d): 1.
58　Compiled with help from NAHT.
59　Ofsted (2008c).
60　Day *et al.* (2006); Hargreaves *et al.* (2007); Galton and MacBeath (2008).
61　Galton and MacBeath (2008): 114.
62　Galton and MacBeath (2008): 114.
63　For example, Hoyle (2001); Lortie (1975).
64　Galton and MacBeath (2008).
65　Galton and MacBeath (2008).
66　See, for example, Hargreaves *et al.* (2007).
67　Galton and MacBeath (2002): 13.
68　For example, Woods *et al.* (1997); Woods and Jeffrey (2002); Mahony and Hextall (2000); Revell (2005); Webb (2006); Day *et al.* (2006).
69　Webb (2006).
70　Mahony and Hextall (2000) provide a detailed account.
71　*Ibid.*: 65.
72　Governors' interviews for the Teacher Status Project, Hargreaves *et al.* (2007).
73　CACE (1967): para 881.
74　Francis *et al.* (2008).
75　Stronach *et al.* (2010), *The Cambridge Primary Review Research Surveys*, Chapter 23.
76　Hargreaves and Goodson (1996): 4.
77　Stronach *et al.* (2010), *The Cambridge Primary Review Research Surveys*, Chapter 23.
78　Stronach *et al.* (2010), *The Cambridge Primary Review Research Surveys*, Chapter 23, quoting Stronach *et al.* (2002): 114.
79　Webb and Vulliamy (2006): 126.
80　Osgood (2005).
81　Morris (2001).
82　Hargreaves *et al.* (2007).
83　Analysis by Anders Hansen of the Department for Communication and Media University of Leicester. See Hargreaves *et al.* (2007).
84　Hargreaves *et al.* (2007).
85　Hoyle (2001).
86　Barber and Mourshed (2007).

87 Brchony (2005)
88 Stronach *et al.* (2002)
89 Vulliamy (2006)
90 Michaels *et al.* (2001)
91 Gladwell (2002)
92 Delors (1996)
93 SooHoo (1993)

23 Governance, funding and policy

The Cambridge Primary Review has taken place against a backdrop of constantly changing national education policy. Since 2006, when the Review was launched, policy has changed with such speed and frequency that even full-time policy experts, let alone teachers, have been hard pressed to keep track of what has been going on.

In every policy a great deal is invested by way of both hard political calculation and genuine principle, and for every policy a great deal – often too much – is claimed. The stakes are high and the turbulence for those at the receiving end is often considerable, so it is not surprising that most policies also have their critics. To such criticism, heightened as it often is by media coverage whose sensationalism is matched only by the hype with which the policies themselves are launched, government these days tends to respond in what it calls a 'robust' manner. Too often, a 'robust' response ridicules the critics, dismisses their arguments out of hand and counters evidence with denial rather than refutation.

Centralisation of policy making allows politicians to present themselves to voters as being firmly in the driving seat, taking charge and no longer letting matters drift. This accrues electoral capital – with more to come if the policy is successful. However, when things go wrong the finger usually points at government, and at government only. This is not always fair, since the line from policy creation to implementation is long and meandering, and even in totalitarian states government cannot control everything; but in a system where so much power has shifted so rapidly to the centre, blaming government is an understandable reaction. Small wonder, then, that government's instinct is to neutralise the criticism and, if necessary, discredit the critic. No holds are barred when the electoral consequences of acknowledging failure are serious. Even to enter into discussion about the evidence from which critique arises is to run the risk of exposing weaknesses in the evidential basis of policy itself.

We shall consider the policy process in greater detail in the second part of this chapter, for it bears not just on the condition and prospects of primary education, but also on the progress and impact of the Cambridge Primary Review. The Review's evidence shows that the policy record of the past two decades is mixed. Some policies have been highly successful, others rather less so; some may have even been counter-productive. This evidence – and the Review's experience of attempting to engage with policy-makers about it – also suggests that the policy process is in certain respects flawed.

Before we enter such contentious territory, it is as well to remind readers of how, formally and officially, England's system of primary education works, and what the Review's witnesses said about it, bearing in mind the questions we posed in 2006:

- How adequately is the system of primary education in England funded and how efficiently is it controlled and administered?
- Does it have the right balance of control and responsibility between national government, local government, local communities and schools?
- What has been the impact of the post-1988 drive to a more centralised system?
- Through what system of school governance are the interests of children, teachers, parents and local communities most effectively and equitably addressed?
- How might matters be differently ordered?

THE GOVERNANCE OF PRIMARY EDUCATION

At the national level

Her Majesty's Government, based at Westminster, is responsible for the public system of primary education in England (though not for education in other parts of the United Kingdom). The relevant government department is the Department for Children, Schools and Families (DCSF), created in 2007. The DCSF:

- plans and monitors educational services for children and young people in England;
- ensures the provision of integrated services for children;
- co-ordinates policy directives relating to children, young people and families;
- produces guidance to assist local authorities (LAs) and educational establishments to implement legislation and other regulations;
- publishes statistical information, commissions research and publishes reports on aspects of the education system and other provision for children and young people.

The department is staffed by permanent civil servants and led by a Permanent Secretary who reports to the Secretary of State for Children, Schools and Families. The latter represents schools, children and young people and their families in the Cabinet and is responsible for all the department's policies. The DCSF also contains political advisers, and there are close links with the Prime Minister's Strategy Unit in the Cabinet Office and the Policy Unit at 10 Downing Street.

Working closely with the DCSF are 12 non-departmental public bodies and agencies (NDPBs), of which the following have particular relevance to primary education:[1]

- *The British Educational Communications and Technology Agency (Becta)* promotes the effective and innovative use of technology in learning.
- *The National College for School Leadership (NCSL)* provides training, research, development and resources for school, college and children's centre leaders, and advises the DCSF on these matters. At the time of going to press it is proposing to change its name to the National College for School and Children's Leadership in order to support serving and aspiring local authority directors of children's services.
- *The Office of the Children's Commissioner (OCC)* promotes awareness of the views and interests of children and young people. It works closely with schools, the police, hospitals and voluntary groups.
- *The Office of the Qualifications and Examinations Regulator*[2] *(Ofqual)* regulates qualifications, examinations and tests in schools and colleges.
- *The Office for Standards in Education, Children's Services and Skills (Ofsted)* inspects schools, day care and children's services, together with adult education and teacher training, and reports on these to the government and – via its freely accessible reports – parents and the public.
- *The Qualifications and Curriculum Authority*[3] *(QCA)* develops and reviews the curriculum (other than those areas covered by the national strategies), providing curriculum advice and support to schools, assessing pupils of compulsory school age, and overseeing assessment tests and tasks.
- *The School Teachers' Review Body (STRB)* advises the Secretary of State on the pay and conditions of employment of England's 550,000 school and college teachers.
- *The Teachers TV Board of Governors* oversees the work of Teachers TV, which provides independent educational news and CPD for teachers.
- *The Training and Development Agency for Schools (TDA)* is charged with maintaining standards of teaching and learning through the supply, training, induction and continuing development of teachers and other professionals, supporting workplace reform and

promoting multi-agency working. Its remit is now framed by a single professional development strategy for the whole children's workforce.

Also linked with the DCSF, but not an NDPB:

- *The General Teaching Council for England (GTCE)* is the regulatory body for teachers and offers advice on issues affecting the quality of teaching and learning.[4]

In addition:

- The cross-party *House of Commons Children, Schools and Families Committee*[5] examines the administration, expenditure and policy of the DCSF and its NDPBs.
- *The Audit Commission* independently assesses the 'value for money' of public services, monitoring and reporting on their economy, efficiency and effectiveness.

At the local level

Local education authorities (LEAs) came into being under the 1902 Education Act, taking over from the school boards which had been established by the 1870 Elementary Education Act, and later assuming other responsibilities such as school meals provision (in 1906) and medical inspection (in 1907). Their role and their relations with local institutions, government and the teaching profession remained largely unchanged until 1988 when, as a result of the Education Reform Act, they entered into a series of 'precariously balanced partnerships involving, to various degrees, parents, central government ... the scrutineers of local government, employers, private business, the community'.[6]

After 1988, LEAs became the local mechanism through which the national educational agenda was to be realised and they were charged with implementing school improvement directives. In 1997 the White Paper, *Excellence in Schools*, assigned them the task of setting an improvement agenda for each school, requiring them to

- analyse recent test, examination and inspection data
- compare results and progress with data from other schools
- monitor parental and local concerns
- agree annual targets
- check that the school's approach to improvement planning meets national standards.[7]

Felicity Fletcher-Campbell and Barbara Lee argue that while LEAs had 'given broad-based support for the government's policy intentions, and welcomed the clarity of role following a period of uncertainty', they were also concerned about 'the significant increase in central control and the reduction of scope for local flexibility, discretion and innovation implied by the new arrangements'.[8] Their new responsibilities also fell under the scrutiny of Ofsted and their effectiveness in raising standards was benchmarked against inspection criteria. The chief inspector's annual reports frequently cited weaknesses and criticised the variable quality in LEA services.

Following the 2003 *Every Child Matters* proposals and the Children Act of 2004, the renamed local authorities (LAs) were required to establish departments of children's services which co-ordinated the work of all agencies concerned with children's education and well-being (as discussed in Chapter 20). Each local authority also appointed a director of children's services and a lead member 'who must have direct responsibility and provide a clear line of accountability for local authority education and children's services'.[9] The School and Inspections Act 2006 led to further changes in the responsibilities of local authorities, reflecting the over-arching objectives of the *Every Child Matters* agenda. Their key duty became a strategic one to 'promote choice, diversity, high standards and fulfilled potential for every child'.[10] Their methods were also to change. Local authorities, once *providers* of children's services, were instead to prepare to *commission* them:

> One of the roles of the local authority is to commission services for children and young people, acting on their behalf and on behalf of their parents and carers, to secure the best provision possible. This basic principle applies just as much to securing the provision of school places as it does, for example, to securing services that meet the needs of individual children … Commissioning is about raising standards and giving parents a real choice of good schools. Local authorities are very well placed to champion the needs of local communities, and to make the strategic decisions on how to meet those needs.[11]

With such a wide-ranging and challenging new remit, local authorities are clearly facing a further period of turbulence and readjustment.

At school level

Ultimately, of course, schools bear the immediate, day-to-day responsibility for educating the children in their care. In discharging this responsibility schools are subject to local governance arrangements, which vary according to which of the five legal categories they belong:

- *community* primary schools are wholly owned and maintained by the LA;
- *voluntary aided* primary schools are maintained by the LA but a foundation (usually of a religious character) owns the land and buildings, employs the staff, has primary responsibility for admissions and appoints most of the governors;
- *voluntary controlled* primary schools are maintained by the LA, which employs the staff and has primary responsibility for admissions, but a foundation (usually of a religious character) appoints some of the governors;
- *foundation* primary schools are maintained by the LA but have more discretion than community schools to manage their affairs and may decide on their own admissions policy;
- *trust* primary schools are state funded and supported by charitable trusts; established under the Education and Inspections Act 2006, they involve schools working with charitable partners and often other schools.

Every primary school, whatever its legal status, is required to have a governing body with members drawn from parents, staff, the local authority, the community and (where applicable) the foundation. The governing body has a duty to set out the school's mission and ethos whilst fulfilling various statutory requirements,[12] and discharging other legal responsibilities which include:

- setting the school's strategies, direction, objectives and policies
- reviewing progress against plans and targets
- approving budgets
- securing accountability
- appointing and supporting the head teacher

In practice, governors delegate the day-to-day curriculum and administrative responsibilities to the head teacher and senior management/leadership team. With the shift towards school self-governance, governors have, theoretically at least, become more important. Modelled on private-sector boards of directors, they are expected to promote the development of more strategic forms of school management.

Since 1997, central government has instigated and/or encouraged a number of alternative models of school administration. In the secondary sector, the controversial academies have considerable autonomy with respect to admissions, governor appointments, and choice of specialism(s). The role of charitable trusts has been strengthened through trust schools, while the government has also encouraged the expansion of the faith schools sector.

CHANGING PATTERNS OF GOVERNANCE[13]

There has been a fundamental shift in the educational balance of power, as Maria Balarin and Hugh Lauder note in their research survey for the Review.[14] Where schools were once substantially under local authority control, now they have more autonomy in some matters but in others are tightly constrained by central government. These changes were initiated by the Conservative government during the late 1980s and 1990s and have been built upon since 1997 by New Labour. In this context, the place of education in the remit of local authorities has also changed while new agencies have been introduced and parents have been given a more prominent place. The focus has been on fiscal efficiency and raising educational standards as defined and supposedly measured by the national tests at ages seven and 11.

Changes at the national level

New agencies and actors have come to occupy the education policy arena: public bodies such as Ofsted, the TDA and the QCA, as well as private companies such as CfBT and Capita which have managed key initiatives including the primary national strategy. Each of the public bodies has been given more extensive powers than its predecessors, and their links to the DCSF are such that they are in effect arms of government, regardless of any independence they claim.

At the same time, the government has strengthened its hand through what Balarin and Lauder call a 'state theory of learning'. This posits that a combination of the repeated high stakes testing of pupils, a national curriculum, and mandated pedagogy in numeracy and literacy will raise 'standards'. Schools are judged by their performance in national tests of pupil attainment and their resulting standing in league tables. The validity of the 'state theory' claim is assessed in Chapter 15.

Centralisation/decentralisation

There is a tendency to talk of 'centralisation' and 'decentralisation' in monolithic, all-or-nothing terms. This is unhelpful, because except in the most extreme national cases, important decisions are made, and will continue to be made, at different levels. England's education system is more centralised than it was during the period from 1944 to 1989, but not comprehensively so. Thus, Roger Dale differentiates the activities of *funding*, *regulation* and *delivery* in public education and this allows greater discrimination in the way decision-making is mapped.[15] For its comparison of national systems the Organisation for Economic Co-operation and Development (OECD) differentiates both *levels* (national, regional, local and school) and *domains* of decision-making (organization of instruction, personnel management, planning and structures, resources).[16]

On this basis we can see that while the overall control of funding remains with national government, day-to-day budgetary control has shifted from local authorities to schools. Meanwhile, regulation is tightly controlled from the centre and this shapes, constrains and polices delivery, even though the 'organisation of instruction' is ostensibly in the hands of schools. Hence the paradox (see Chapters 14 and 15) of national strategies which are non-statutory but obligatory; or of schools' freedom to buy into an 'open' CPD market which is dominated by the same national strategies. Put more simply, England's education system is now much more centralised than it used to be in as far as government and its agencies control what, in strictly educational terms, matters most: curriculum, assessment, pedagogy, teacher training and inspection. In the process, as we see below, power at the local authority level has been most conspicuously reduced since 1989, though latterly local authority responsibility and culpability have been greatly increased, especially in the area of children's services. LAs are also required to act as agents of national government in relation to its standards agenda (see below).

Local changes

By devolving resources and related decision-making powers to schools the 1988 Education Reform Act radically altered the definition of local authority functions. Several policies were introduced as part of the move towards school self-management. Local authorities had to hand a large proportion of their budget over to schools, their control over pupil selection was undermined by open enrolment, and they lost their inbuilt majority on school governing bodies as more places were given to parents and local business people. More recently, and in line with the government's commitment to 'joined-up' policy under the 2004 Children Act, education and social services have been merged into the wider brief of children's services.

A key change for local authorities, however, is that they have become part of the process of monitoring standards, generating data by which schools' performance can be judged and developing strategies for intervention in cases where schools are not considered to be performing well.

Policy making in the new environment

Today the balance of power lies between central government, NDPBs and schools. Compared with their period of dominance before 1988, local authorities are shadows of their former selves in respect of their influence over what goes on in schools, though their remit remains considerable and indeed has expanded since the 2004 Act. Government control is exercised through the curriculum and strategies for setting and monitoring standards, with Ofsted playing a key reinforcing role through its inspections of schools, local authorities and teacher training. The national strategies in literacy and numeracy, now consolidated within the primary national strategy, have extended the control of content via the national curriculum into the realm of day-to-day classroom practice and decision-making, thus greatly reducing teachers' autonomy.

Michael Gove, who as this report goes to press is the (Conservative) shadow secretary of state, writes:

> Under Labour there is only one relationship which matters: the relationship between the individual and the state. The Labour conception of society is a thin and impoverished one in which there appear to be only two primary centres of decision-making. The central state organises and the individual is expected to respond appropriately. Individuals are assessed by the state as economic units in need of upskilling, taxing, monitoring or redeploying as appropriate – according to priorities set, and policed, centrally ... Local government is no longer an autonomous centre of decision-making, with its primary responsibility the nurturing of community strength and its primary accountability to local people. Increasingly, councils are instruments for delivering on policies set and monitored centrally ... Local councils are treated as simply branch offices of the central state.[17]

In 2009, decentralisation is a matter of policy for both main opposition parties. Here are the Conservatives:

> We will introduce a radical programme of decentralisation and deregulation to give communities more say over how they are run, including the removal of central controls over local government.[18]

and the Liberal Democrats:

> The central Whitehall department [DCSF] would be dramatically reduced in size – by around 50%. The 18% of the education budget held nationally would be devolved to

schools and local authorities. Central initiatives would be scrapped ... Local government would have new and more powerful strategic powers to enable councils to deliver their statutory role as strategic commissioners for services to children in their locality.[19]

GOVERNANCE: WHAT WITNESSES SAID

Control

No fewer than 10 of the Review's 31 published research surveys, notably those dealing with curriculum, assessment, inspection, teacher training and workforce reform, as well as with governance itself, cited empirical evidence showing a considerable strengthening of state control over primary education since 1988, and especially since 1997.[20] This trend was also remarked on in the submissions and soundings and met with considerable criticism. Parents and governors called for centralised intervention and political influence in primary education to be greatly reduced. While accepting the case for a national curriculum, teachers argued that central government's grip on its content should be loosened. Schools called for greater freedom to tailor their practice to suit their pupils and communities. There was a common thread of argument that the balance of control between national government, local authorities and schools should be comprehensively re-assessed and re-configured (as we argued in Chapter 14) in favour of local and school-level decision-making and innovation.

Much of this has already been reviewed, and indeed is reflected in our proposals on the curriculum. As far as this Review's evidence is concerned, then, the two opposition parties would seem to be pushing at an open door, though while arguing for decentralisation they do not necessarily accept in full our diagnosis of what has gone wrong. Thus, drawing on witness views, Chapters 14 and 16 highlighted the damaging consequences for children's educational entitlement of the national tests and strategies and argued that government assumptions about the relationship between the curriculum and standards were both wrong and counter-productive, as was the Rose Review's take on the 'problem' of curriculum manageability. Chapter 15 challenged the versions of pedagogy emanating from the national strategies and the resulting mis-direction of teachers' efforts. Widespread concern was reported in Chapter 16 about recent policies on assessment and testing and their adverse impact on curriculum, pupils and teachers; and in Chapter 21 about the corrosive impact on professional self-esteem and effectiveness of the culture of compliance. Chapter 21 also found the official account of professional development, which informs initial teacher training and workforce reform, to be at odds with the findings of research. Chapter 22 found teachers' working lives increasingly constrained and to a degree de-professionalised.

As well as objections to the degree of government control and its impact, there was also concern that policy is not always consistent. Chapter 13 records teachers' frustrations at changes, about-turns even, in national strategy requirements, especially in respect of the literacy strategy. Chapter 21 used the example of initial teacher training to show how such changes may happen in such rapid succession that they cannot be properly bedded down or evaluated before being superseded; yet reform is usually based on the claim that existing procedures are not working – a bogus claim in view of the telescoped timescale and the absence of evaluation. Head teachers criticised a lack of cohesion in what reached their desks from the different national agencies. Local authorities deplored schools' lack of autonomy, particularly in the face of government initiatives that were inadequately funded and supported.

The role of local authorities

There was support in the submissions for the view that 'decentralised-centralism'[21] had left local authorities with insufficient power to carry out their responsibilities. Unless local authorities have more control over admissions, it was argued, they cannot ensure that children with the greatest need have the chance to attend the best schools for them. LAs themselves were unhappy with having their role reduced to delivering and policing national policy and drew attention to their considerable innovatory potential.

School governors expressed the most divergent set of opinions about the role of LAs, with some welcoming authority support and others sharply critical. One group of governors taking part in the Review's community soundings felt that their authority had reduced school support to the point where its continuing effectiveness was in doubt, although they also noted that it continued to exert its power by withholding resources for children identified with special educational needs. Two predominantly rural LAs were believed to be structurally and attitudinally incapable of responding to pockets of real and substantial urban deprivation (or, as governors put it, 'inner-city circumstances in a rural environment'). Here the consequences, in terms of financial support, were perceived as direct and serious because the LAs lacked both the infra-structure and funding formulae to respond effectively to social and educational disadvantage. It must be added that elsewhere governors' views of local authorities were less combative and the division of responsibility between them and governors appeared to work well.

In its submission the National Union of Teachers (NUT) suggested that LAs no longer held the power to discharge some of their responsibilities because they were required to commission rather than provide services. The NUT argued that this change, particularly problematic when it came to *Every Child Matters*, effectively undermined the local authority's role of 'providing expert and knowledgeable advice to schools' because its staff would no longer have the neces-sary expertise. Others complained that some local authority advisers were now so tied to national policy implementation that they had lost both the ability and the will to offer the independent advice which teachers needed.

School governing bodies

The National Governors' Association (NGA) pursued these concerns into the arena of school governance. Although *Every Child Matters* was seen as a positive development, the NGA believed that it might also undermine schools' autonomy because governance structures in other areas of children's services were very different to those in education. The association raised the question: 'On whose behalf is the governing body operating?' Valued roles such as making leadership appointments and being guardians of the school's ethos were effectively 'heavily constrained by central diktat', it was said. However, the NGA acknowledged that local management of schools had increased governors' responsibility in some areas but it also called for more and better training of governors. The NGA disputed claims that weakness in gov-erning bodies was widespread, pointing to Ofsted evidence to the contrary.

In its submission, the NUT emphasised the importance of the stakeholder model of school governance, with representation from the school and community, 'rather than allowing them to become the ownership of individual business people or sponsoring trusts.' It proposed that incentives such as childcare payments should be offered to ensure that all sections of the community are represented. The need to safeguard local democratic accountability at school level was generally recognised as important in the submissions.

Teachers were divided on the value of governing bodies. For some, their combination of power and lack of educational knowledge made them a hindrance. Some heads felt governors' expectations were unrealistic. One children's organisation suggested that the current system amounted to little more than anachronistic and irresponsible collections of well-meaning amateurs who contributed little to their schools' effectiveness. However, some schools valued their governing bodies as bulwarks against unreasonable local authorities.

In talking with governors during the Review's community soundings, it was evident that some of them held strong and strategic visions for their schools and were keen to fight for the school's interests against the local authority or any other body which they believed threatened those interests. In separate discussions, several heads expressed gratitude and admiration for the vigour and political skill with which their chair of governors pursued such campaigns. In many cases governors knew their schools and many were frequent visitors and participants. In one school visited by the Review there was nothing dutiful about the affectionate farewells of the children for the chair of governors who had been elevated to be Dean of the nearby cathedral: indeed the pupils were the stars at his installation ceremony. Overall our evidence showed that governing bodies served their primary schools well, both as friends and supporters.

There were suggestions that despite the aspiration that governing bodies should represent all sections of local communities, they remained too middle class. The National Association of Teachers of Travellers (NATT), for example, pointed out that Gypsy, Roma and Traveller parents were inadequately represented and that the system of elections and committees deterred those who were wary of schools.

THE FUNDING OF PRIMARY EDUCATION

Funding mechanisms

Both central and local government determine how much money a primary school receives and how it receives it. However, as Philip Noden and Anne West point out in their research survey for the Review, the last 10 years have seen major changes in England's school funding system aimed at providing a fairer distribution of resources.[22] The balance of control between central and local government has ebbed and flowed, as has the influence of historical patterns of spending and the degree of stability in school funding.

Since 2006, the majority of funding for the day-to-day running of schools (that is, revenue funding) has been provided from central government through the dedicated schools grant (DSG). The level of DSG given to a local authority is based on projected pupil numbers, projected delegated budgets for individual schools and projected budgets for other services for pupils provided by local authorities, such as special educational needs provision and pupil referral units. Local authorities retain autonomy over the distribution of the DSG to schools in order to reflect local needs and priorities. Noden and West comment that the DSG 'is largely driven by historical patterns of spending and with its introduction, control over spending on schools has become more centralised than ever.'[23]

In late 2007, the DCSF announced the first three-year funding settlement for every local authority in England for the period 2008/09 to 2010/11. This new settlement is intended to enable local authorities to plan for the long term and to use their budgets more efficiently and strategically over the three years.

The DCSF also provides local authorities with grants which must be spent on specific education priorities. In England, the Standards Fund is the government's main channel for targeting money at national education priorities. The majority of grants are allocated at 100 per cent but some require a contribution from the LA. Standards Fund grants include:

- the school development grant
- the school standards grant and school standards grant (personalisation)
- the new area-based grant (ABG).

Schools are free to spend their devolved Standards Fund money in any way that improves teaching and learning, providing they deliver the outcomes and outputs agreed under the grant's allocation. The aim is to ensure that schools have the flexibility to use the money to meet their own priorities for improvement. The only exceptions to this are two 'ring-fenced' grants made under the Standards Fund scheme: the ethnic minority achievement grant (EMAG) and the school lunch grant. EMAG is allocated on a needs-based formula to all local authorities to support minority ethnic pupils and children for whom English is an additional language. The lunch grant aims to help schools provide healthy and affordable food.

The revenue funds actually received by schools depend on a formula agreed by each LA. Pupil numbers and age (the latter particularly adversely affecting the funding of pupils in KS2) are the most common factors considered when determining a school's allocation. Additional criteria which may be taken into account include pupils' special educational needs; numbers of children for whom English is an additional language; turnover of pupils; prior attainment of pupils entering a school; size and condition of a school's buildings and grounds relative to other schools; salaries at a school; and numbers of newly qualified teachers (NQTs). Local authorities must also take account of the degree of deprivation affecting the community served by a school.

Funding for capital projects is a complex area which falls outside the normal school budget arrangements. New build projects may involve various agencies and private funding initiative (PFI) schemes as well as central and local government. In 2005 the government announced a major programme of funding to improve the primary school buildings across England through the Primary Capital Programme (see Chapter 18). This funding started in 2008 and is expected to run for 14 years.

Funding and expenditure levels

Figure 23.1 shows changes in school-based expenditure per pupil in England's primary and secondary schools since 1993.[24] Although there are some problems with the interpretation of these figures they indicate that the level of school expenditure per pupil was relatively stable from 1992 to 1998 but that it increased very substantially thereafter – the direct result of changes in government policy.

The data also reveal a long-standing, indeed perennial, feature of educational funding – more has always been spent on secondary pupils than on primary pupils.[25] Indeed, although the primary-secondary 'gap' narrowed from 1992–93 to 1998–99 it widened thereafter. It is a consistent feature across all English LAs but there is a significant variation among them in terms of the ratio of spending on primary and secondary pupils, with expenditure per primary pupil ranging from 66 per cent to 94 per cent of the level of expenditure per secondary pupil. In 2006–7, the average school-based expenditure per pupil was £3,360 for primary and £4,320 for secondary.

This disparity in funding was criticised as early as the Hadow Report of 1931 and featured prominently in the final chapter of Plowden, which stressed that 'a higher priority in the total educational budget ought now to be given to primary education' and went on to make the

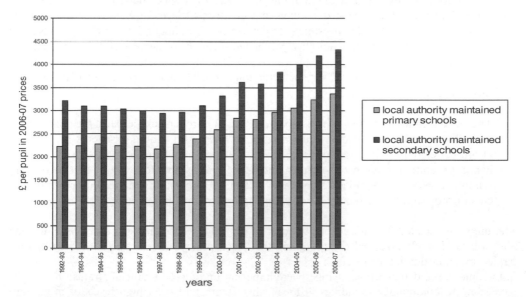

Figure 23.1 School based expenditure per pupil in real terms 1992–93 to 2006–07 in England. DCSF and DIUS (2008)

commonsense (but unheeded) observation that 'a good deal of money spent on older children will be wasted if more is not spent on them during their primary school years'.[26] A plea for more equitable treatment in order to facilitate greater use of specialist expertise was made in the government's primary education enquiry of 1991–92.[27] The House of Commons Education Committee also highlighted the disparity in 1994.[28]

Despite powerful advocacy the disparity remains – a disparity which many in primary education find unjustifiable given that success in secondary education and subsequently is highly dependent on what happens and what is provided earlier in a child's educational career. It also means that while secondary schools have the freedom to deploy specialist curriculum expertise as they see fit, most primary schools do not. This, we argued in Chapters 14 and 21, may directly and adversely affect the quality of curriculum provision.

Funding: what witnesses said

Witnesses recognised that to a considerable degree who controls the money controls the system. Many local authority submissions pointed out that they were financially constrained by government, while schools complained that they did not receive adequate funds from local authorities.

While there was general recognition that English primary schools are better funded now than ever before, many submissions deplored the persistence of the disparity between the primary and secondary phases.

Some respondents said that, while the money for primary education was generally adequate, few schools had enough to be creative in funding new ventures, especially initiatives carrying significant financial risk. Support for children with special needs was the area most often cited in soundings and submissions as needing more money. Other areas mentioned included equal opportunities, ICT, music, teacher and TA professional development, PPA time and mentoring. There was, however, particularly among local authorities, a clear recognition that there was a limited 'pot' of money. Equality, fairness and even distribution had to be balanced against targeting specific needs. LAs in particular pointed out that the sustainability of funding was often more important than the amount.

The Association of School and College Leaders (ASCL) suggested that funding needed to reward those 'that take on children with the greatest need rather than ... the easiest children'. Some organisations argued that the creation of children's services departments within local authorities had further complicated funding, but children had yet to experience the benefits. One submission argued: '... the investment of time, effort, funding and resources that has gone on over the past three years may not have percolated through to the very children the changes were planned to protect.'

The NUT advocated a needs-led system of funding, which would respond to identified needs in disadvantaged communities.

> The current funding system, which is based on pupil numbers, exacerbates the polarisation of intake experienced by many urban schools. Successful, popular schools are able to afford better pupil facilities and resources, all of which may help to improve performance, hence generating even better results and more pupils the following year. Struggling schools, however, lose money from their budget as pupil numbers decline, necessitating cuts in provision which reduce the chances of performance improvement.

The union also called for an audit of the cost of central government's statutory requirements and policies, including capital costs, arguing that 'each policy introduction should be accompanied by an evaluation of its cost'.

In some areas, demographic changes were imposing unforeseen financial strains on schools. According to community soundings in areas where there had been high levels of migration, schools were facing particular difficulties. Funding was not keeping pace with fast-changing pupil numbers as a result, they said, of seriously inadequate government data on migration.

Local authorities proposed that financial management should be under their control because they have an overall view of a local community or region. Head teachers welcomed the degree of financial control that local management of schools offered – a positive outcome of the 1988 Education Reform Act. However, some found financial management very burdensome and felt that they lacked the time and expertise. Certainly governors experienced in financial management were highly valued by head teachers. The advantages of placing financial control in the hands of those with knowledge of local needs was evident but schools need more help in managing this additional responsibility.

There was strong evidence of the disruption caused by successive changes aimed at creating a fairer funding system for those needing the most help. Subsequently, attempts to stabilise the system had penalised the worst off and made it more difficult to respond to demographic changes. Our evidence demonstrated the challenges of attempting to balance stability of funding with providing for changing needs. Funding based primarily on pupil numbers, as the NUT argued, worked against those schools which were already in difficulty, disadvantaging their pupils further. The historically-based funding formula also ensured that primary children continued to be less well-funded than secondary students.

In responding to our commissioned research survey on funding from Noden and West, the DCSF said, 'We don't specify centrally a ratio of primary to secondary funding in each local area. This is decided locally by local authorities in consultation with local schools and heads.'[29] This is true, and participants in the community and national soundings contrasted the varied application of funding formulae in different local authorities. However, the general assumption in local authorities that primary pupils merit lower funding than secondary is deeply rooted, as is the view that pupils in key stage 2 require less resource than those in key stages 1 or 3. This, which started with the introduction of age-weighted pupil units, is held to disadvantage junior schools in particular, because unlike 4/5 11 primary schools they cannot vire funding across key stages.[30]

THE POLICY BALANCE SHEET

In Chapter 3 we identified a series of policy 'milestones' in English primary education since 1944 (Figure 3.3). If we take the more recent period (1988–2009) with which the Cambridge Review has been particularly concerned, we find policy-makers' attention devoted mainly to six broad areas:

Children and families, including
- early childhood care and education
- children who are vulnerable, at risk or excluded
- children's care and well-being generally
- parents' rights and responsibilities

Curriculum, including
- literacy
- numeracy
- citizenship
- modern foreign languages
- whole curriculum review

Pedagogy, including
- lesson structure, content and teaching methods in literacy and numeracy

Standards and accountability, including
- testing, standards and targets
- inspection and quality assurance
- school performance and accountability

Teachers, including
- initial teacher training and continuing professional development
- school leadership
- workforce reform

National and local infrastructure, including
- local re-organisation
- national re-organisation: government departments and NDPBs
- funding and budgetary control.

Recent policy: the judgement of the Review's witnesses

All of the areas listed above feature in the present report, together with accounts of how the Review's witnesses responded to specific initiatives under each heading and what our commissioned research surveys had to say about them. We do not need to reiterate these judgements. However, it is useful to summarise in broad terms the popularity and impact of the most prominent policies before we turn to the vital question of how well the current policy process works. First, then, in terms of witness response through the submissions and soundings, we find:

- *Policies which have been broadly welcomed, albeit with some reservations*
  o *Every Child Matters*
  o The Children's Plan
  o Sure Start
  o Narrowing the Gap
  o The expansion of early childhood care and education

- *Policies about which there is ambivalence and some unease*
  o Special educational needs
  o The re-organisation of local authorities

- *Policies on which opinion tends to be sharply divided*
  o Workforce reform

- *Policies which are seen as sound in principle but unsatisfactory in practice*
  o The early years foundation stage
  o The national curriculum

- *Policies provoking mixed reactions, but leaning more towards hostility than support*
  o The numeracy strategy
  o The literacy strategy (less favourably viewed than the numeracy strategy)
  o The primary strategy

- *Policies provoking widespread opposition, albeit with residual support in some quarters*
  o National targets and testing
  o Performance tables and the naming and shaming of schools
  o Ofsted inspection

Ministers might respond that in the field of policy unpopularity does not signal ineffectiveness (the reverse is also true: a popular policy is not necessarily an effective one). Thus, in respect of national testing, the government has countered every objection from teachers, parents, researchers and the House of Commons Select Committee with the insistence that the national tests are an essential tool of accountability, that parents want them – a questionable claim (see below) – and that they are here to stay (despite summarily abandoning the key stage 3 tests in 2009). It is true that the efficacy of a policy cannot be judged by its popularity. On the other hand, if a policy is disliked by those who have to implement it, it will be less effective; and ultimately it is on the basis of their popular appeal that political parties are elected into and out of government.

THE STANDARDS AGENDA: EVIDENCE AND ASSUMPTIONS

For the Cambridge Review, however, what matters for the longer-term quality of primary education is evidence, and this is why it is pertinent to ask whether those policies towards which there is greatest hostility – which, broadly, are those central to the government's standards agenda – are more or less effective than their reputation suggests. Earlier chapters contain detailed presentation and discussion of the relevant evidence, so here again matters are summarised rather than repeated. This time we draw mainly on the 'hard' data reviewed in the 28 commissioned research surveys and in earlier chapters, especially those on curriculum (13 and 14), pedagogy (15), assessment, accountability and standards (16 and 17), teachers (21) and workforce reform (22). Readers will recall that this evidence includes, alongside independent research, the findings from Ofsted inspections and surveys and from studies undertaken or commissioned by the DfES/DCSF itself.

'Standards': a problem of definition

Looming over the standards drive and the balance sheet which follows is the highly problematic nature of the term 'standards' itself. Warwick Mansell warns:

> The word 'standards' is central to New Labour's policy on school improvement. The term, as cited in the government's 1997 White Paper and used repeatedly since, has been routinely abused in the last few years, by politicians and others. 'Raising standards' ... is implied to stand for improving the overall quality of education in our schools. That, in the public mind, I would venture, is what the phrase means. The reality in schools, however, is that 'raising standards' means raising test scores, as measured by a set of relatively narrow indicators laid down more or less unilaterally by ministers, and often subject to disproportionate influence by the performance of a small group of schools. These scores represent only a sub-set of schools' work. Therefore it is not clear that they stand, reliably, for schools' overall quality. The two meanings are not interchangeable, and should not be treated as such.[31]

This review has already judged (Chapter 14) that the pursuit of an overly-exclusive concept of 'standards' at the primary stage has compromised children's legal entitlement to a broad and balanced curriculum and that it may even have had the opposite result to that intended. Standards in primary education, we would argue, should be redefined as the quality and outcomes of learning in the entire curriculum to which children are entitled by law – a definition which in fact is closer to what Warwick Mansell takes to be the public perception.

Positive evidence on standards (Chapters 16–17)

Subject to the reservations noted, the following positive claims about standards appear to be reasonably secure:

- Within the limitations and variations of the measures used, standards of tested attainment in primary education have been fairly stable over time, with some changes up or down.
- Pupils' attitudes to their learning in the tested areas are generally positive (though, as is generally found internationally, they appear to decline as pupils approach the end of primary education).
- The national data show modest improvements in primary mathematics standards, especially since 1995, though different datasets tell different stories.

- The international data also show substantial improvements in primary mathematics from 1995 to 2003.
- The international data from 2001 show high standards in reading among English pupils by comparison with those from other countries, but the more recent data (from 2006 onwards) suggest that the 2001 results may have been misleading. England appears to be above the international average but not exceptionally so.
- The international data show considerable improvements in primary science by comparison with other countries, though there have been methodological reservations about the studies in question.[32]

Negative evidence on standards (Chapters 4–6 and 16–17)

Subject to the same reservations, the following negative claims about standards appear to be reasonably secure:

- The national strategies have had, of themselves, a less pronounced impact on reading standards than might have been expected from the level of investment.
- The evidence is not clear cut, but it suggests that gains in reading skills have sometimes been at the expense of pupils' enjoyment of reading.
- Similarly, there is some evidence of an increase in test-induced stress among primary pupils, especially at key stage 2, and much firmer evidence of pressure on their teachers.
- The primary curriculum has narrowed in direct response to the perceived demands of the testing regime and the national strategies, to the extent that children's statutory entitlement to a broad and balanced curriculum has been seriously compromised.
- The historically wide gap between high and low attaining pupils in reading, mathematics and science has persisted. It is already evident at a very young age and widens as children move through the primary phase.
- The attainment gap maps closely onto indicators of inequality in other aspects of children's lives, notably income, health, housing, risk, ethnicity and social class. This confirms that tackling inequalities in educational outcome requires action across a broad range of public policy, including much which lies outside the remit and control of schools.
- There is no reliable evidence on national standards in areas of children's learning outside those aspects of literacy, numeracy and science which have been tested, other than that in many schools such learning appears to have been compromised by the standards drive itself.

Methodological or interpretative problems with the evidence on standards (Chapters 16–17)

- Taken as a whole, and noting the many changes made since its inception, the national system of assessment up to 2000 had a low level of dependability both in relation to results for a given year and as a basis for tracking trends over time. Since 2000, the quality of the data and its usefulness for tracking trends over time have improved considerably. Overall, however, this means that any claims about long-term trends must be treated with scepticism (see below).
- Similar reservations must be voiced about data from Ofsted school and teacher-training inspections, where the methodology has changed too frequently to allow year-on-year comparison, and there are problems of validity in relation to what is inspected and of reliability in the inspection process.
- Though in some respects the international comparative evidence on trends in pupil attainment is encouraging, overall it is rather thin, and there are considerable challenges in the devising of international measures and the interpretation of international data.
- The concept of 'standards' is highly problematic yet is routinely presumed to be straightforward.

**Questionable claims and assumptions relating to the standards agenda
(Chapters 14–17 and 21–22)**

Assumption / claim	Comment
In 1997, England's system of primary education was at a 'low state' and primary teachers were 'professionally uninformed'.	The first part of the claim has rhetorical rather than evidential force. The second can readily be exposed as myth (see next two sections of this chapter).
Testing of itself drives up standards.	Formative assessment can be shown to have a greater impact on pupils' learning than summative; at best, the impact of national tests on standards is oblique, for what drives up standards is good teaching.
Parents support testing.	Many parents are as worried as teachers about tests and testing.
Tests of pupil attainment are the best or only way to hold schools to account and monitor the performance of the system as a whole.	Sample surveys do the job as well or better, and pupil assessment is distorted if it is made to serve other purposes; further, schools should be judged on the full contribution they make to their pupils' education.
The pursuit of standards in the 'basics' is incompatible with a broad, balanced and enriching curriculum.	Curriculum breadth/balance and standards in the 'basics' have been shown to be related, and many high performing schools achieve both; the downgrading of the wider curriculum in policy, initial teacher training and inspection may thus be counter-productive in terms of standards as well as a denial of children's statutory curriculum entitlement.
Literacy and numeracy are valid proxies for standards in primary education as a whole.	Numeracy and – above all – literacy are indeed essential foundations for current and later learning, but the curriculum also includes knowledge and understanding of wholly different kinds which in their own way are no less essential.
Standards in literacy are best achieved by concentrating on reading and writing.	Quite apart from the point above about the relationship between literacy/numeracy standards and curriculum breadth and balance, there is a necessary relationship, in terms of both the quality of learning generally and children's literacy development, between reading, writing and the spoken word, and between the spoken word and children's learning across the board. Literacy and oracy should therefore go hand in hand.

The national strategies are an effective way to ensure deep, positive and permanent changes in pedagogy.	The national strategies have generated substantial organisational and attitudinal change, but at the deeper level of the discourse on which the quality of learning more decisively depends, there has been limited movement away from the cognitively-restricting interaction noted in classroom studies of the 1970s, 1980s and 1990s; in any event, the account of pedagogy underpinning the national strategies has limited empirical provenance. Where the quality of classroom talk improves dramatically, credit may not lie with the national strategies.
Teaching assistants are essential to the standards drive.	Teaching assistants make a difference, but the quality and expertise of teachers count for much more.
The standards in teaching which are essential to the improvement of standards in learning are accurately mapped in the TDA professional standards for career development from NQT to advanced skills.	The TDA standards are too vague to be useful, have no obvious empirical foundation, and are at odds with both research on teacher development and other countries' efforts to validate performance-based professional standards.

Frequently-voiced claims which can be neither proved nor refuted

- England has the best teachers ever.
- England has the best-trained teachers ever.
- England's pupils are achieving the highest standards ever.
- Recent improvements in primary education are a direct consequence of the government's standards drive.

On one occasion, a minister combined such claims with assertions about professional freedom and partnership which the country's largest teaching union might wish to contest and which in any event are contradicted by the Review's evidence:

> Our partnership with the teaching profession has led to radical improvements in working conditions and has recently led Ofsted to conclude that we have 'the best trained genera-tion of teachers ever'. Schools and teachers have the freedom and autonomy to do what they do best – teach. We make no apologies for delivering the highest standards ever.[33]

THE POLICY PROCESS: MODEL AND REALITY

Public service reform

It is time, then, to consider the model of reform which has underpinned the standards drive. In 2008 the Cabinet Office published a blueprint for the reform of public services, including education.[34] This explained that since New Labour came to power in 1997, public service reform (PSR) has included two distinct stages:

> The first stage used the explicit introduction of clear national standards and targets to drive up performance while increasing investment. Standards rose in primary schools,

hospital waiting lists began to fall ... As services improved from their low state, there was a growing recognition of the need for more flexibility and innovation if progress was to be sustained. So from around 2001, the second stage of reform complemented these top-down targets and standards, with clearer incentives to improve, generated from within the public services themselves rather than imposed from Whitehall ... Standards have continued to rise. Primary and secondary school results are now better than ever before.[35]

The first sentence is unarguable: the standards drive and the target regime have been prominent themes in the Review's submissions and soundings, and the evidence also shows a considerable and welcome increase in investment in primary education. But the rest is open to dispute. Whether public services really were at a 'low state' in 1997 will be contested by some, assuming that a 'low state' can be defined. Standards as measured by key stage tests rose after 1997, but with the exceptions and reservations noted above and in Chapter 17. After 2001, the rate of improvement slowed markedly. Phrases like 'better than ever before', as we suggest above in respect of claims about teacher training, have a purchase on reality which is rhetorical rather than empirical. Many witnesses to the Review would not know that after 2001 they had entered a second stage of reform, because the top-down pressure, the targets and the league tables were all sustained; and when in 2008 leading academics Professors Stephen Ball, Frank Coffield, Richard Taylor and Sir Peter Scott complained in the press that 'government policy is no longer the solution to the difficulties we face but our greatest problem',[36] they wrote of the present, not the past.

Yet even if the strategic shift did not take place, as claimed, as early as 2001, there was at least a recognition in government that the initial approach may have gone too far:

> The Government needs to apply the lessons we have learned through this period ... We know that services need clear standards but that, following our first phase of reform, persisting with too many top-down targets may be counter-productive; we know services must value professionals if we are to foster innovation and excellence; we know that while government must be a key player in driving better public services there are limits to what it can achieve and if it seeks to do too much it will stifle local initiative.[37]

The key word here is 'counter-productive'; the key phrase is 'stifle local initiative'. This Review has received evidence of both of these adverse conditions, and the research by Frank Coffield and his colleagues[38] provides a persuasive analysis from the skills sector which applies equally to the primary phase:

> Top-down policy and micro-management from the centre have brought high costs and are not creating a coherent, self-improving skills system ... The pace of change and the proliferation of initiatives have been intense, and changes to targets, funding rules and paperwork ... have diverted staff away from the central task of teaching.[39]

Having learned the lessons of stage one the authors of the Cabinet Office paper move to stage two. This has three components:

> *Citizenship empowerment* ... Public services should reflect the preferences and needs of those who use them, not those who provide them ... In world-class systems citizens have clear information about the performance of services and the power to ensure that their needs and aspirations are met.
> *New professionalism* ... Innovation, consistency, continuous self-improvement and responsiveness are driven from within by the public services themselves ... Sometimes in the past our reform programmes have discouraged professionals from developing or sharing new ideas or innovations. Energising the workforce is a key element of the next phase of our reform programme.

Strategic leadership ... World-class public services depend on governments providing leadership by setting a clear vision, a stable framework, adequate resources, effective incentives, as well as accessible and consistent information on performance. Only government can take this broad overall view. This means rejecting the temptation for government to micro-manage from the centre. It also means rejecting the laissez-faire option of an absentee administration.[40]

Given that PSR phase 2 is claimed to have started in 2001, and it is now 2009, questions again arise about the seriousness of the government's intentions and the accuracy of its claims, at least in respect of the evidence on primary education. Here chronology is important. The government might argue that the objections to central control and top-down micro-management which are prominent in the Review's evidence relate only to the first phase of public service reform, and that since then everything has changed and the evidence has become obsolete. However, the Review did not begin to collect data until late 2006, five whole years into phase two of PSR, and its most recent evidence dates from 2009, when professionals were continuing to complain that the policy framework was far from 'stable', about being 'discouraged ... from developing or sharing new ideas' and about the apparent inability of the DCSF to resist 'the temptation ... to micro-manage from the centre'. If after eight years of a supposedly new phase of public service reform there is little discernible difference in the culture and processes of policy-making in the primary education sector, then it is not unreasonable to ask, during the year before a general election, whether the changes are ever likely to happen.

Policy, information and myth

The 2008 Cabinet Office declaration stresses that information, and access to information, are central to the empowerment of citizens and professionals in relation to public service reform. The paper also argues that the success of information-sharing depends on the perceived independence of the information in question.[41] In the reform of primary education, however:

- We have shown that the information provided by government and public bodies on the performance of the system, as judged by pupil testing and school inspection, has been less comprehensive, valid and reliable than it should be.
- Policy and information about its impact are a sealed and self-reinforcing system in which, although Ofsted does comment broadly on the impact of particular policies, individual inspections tend to check only on compliance, while local authorities receive substantial funding to ensure that the national strategies are implemented as promulgated. Meanwhile, NDPB and many local authority publications readily fall into line with government language and assumptions and display no obvious capacity or will to regard these as problematic.
- The word 'independent' is attached to government initiatives which are subject to tight central control.
- Genuinely independent information is often viewed with suspicion by the DCSF or rejected out of hand.
- Government has relied heavily upon the creation and/or perpetuation of myths about the period preceding its reforms, and through these myths it has been able to present its actions and achievements in the best possible light.

The myth that governments have most conspicuously perpetuated is that of the 1960s and 1970s as an era of feckless progressivism, when, supposedly, the 3Rs were neglected, standards plummeted and 'trendy' teaching prevailed. There is certainly a problematic legacy from this period, and we showed (in Chapters 7, 14 and 15) that part of it is a less than rigorous discourse on curriculum and pedagogy coupled with a belief in the fixed nature of children's developmental stages and ages which depressses teacher expectations. However, the larger claim has been dispensed with by both research and inspection, as we have also shown. To be fair, the myth of a progressive takeover was used even more devastatingly in the 'discourse of derision' fostered by governments before 1997,[42] but it continues to surface in policy documents and the media, for example in response to proposals on the primary curriculum from both this enquiry and the Rose Review. As Warwick Mansell points out, rather than engage with adverse evidence, policy makers and advisers sometimes prefer to adopt the less demanding course of abusing those who present it, and the charge of being a 1970s ideologue is one of the insults of choice.[43]

One educational myth which government has actually created – as opposed to recycled – concerns information itself. Here, for example, is the head of the Prime Minister's Delivery Unit during the first phase of New Labour's programme of public service reform (his italics):

> Until the mid-1980s what happened in schools and classrooms was left almost entirely to teachers to decide ... Almost all teachers had goodwill and many sought to develop themselves professionally, but, through no fault of their own, the profession itself was uninformed ... Under Thatcher, the system moved from *uninformed professional judgement to uninformed prescription*. The 1997–2001 Blair government inherited a system of *uninformed prescription* and replaced it with one of *informed prescription* ... The White Paper signals the next shift: from *informed prescription* to *informed professional judgement* ... The era of informed professional judgement is only just beginning ... The era of informed professional judgement could be the most successful so far in our educational history ... It could be the era in which our education system becomes not just good but great.[44]

For the record, during Barber's 'era of uninformed professional judgement' the teaching profession had ready access to:

- HM Inspectorate reports on individual schools
- HMI national surveys on primary and secondary education
- The chief inspector's annual reports
- Official and independent reports on primary, secondary, further, higher and teacher education, and on English, mathematics, the arts and special needs[45]
- HMI and government documents on the curriculum
- Local evidence on standards of attainment from local authority annual tests administered in a high proportion of primary schools
- Local authority curriculum schemes and guidelines, and courses for teachers
- Public examination results
- National evidence on pupil attainment in English, maths and science at the ages of 7, 11 and 15 from the sampled assessment programmes of the Assessment and Performance Unit
- Reports from the House of Commons Education Select Committee
- Curriculum guidance and other materials from the Schools Council and its successors
- Courses of initial and in-service teacher training and development
- Information provided by professional and subject associations through their in-house courses, journals and other publications
- The weekly offerings of the educational press
- Published research and other writing on education, some of it arcane but much of it readily accessible to teachers.

Even on the more limited matter of information about *standards* in primary education, the 1991–92 'three wise men' enquiry on primary education was able to interrogate six major domains of published data dealing with standards, most of them annual and cumulative. These included local authority and APU tests, NFER tests and surveys, inspection reports, national curriculum assessment and international achievement studies.[46] The report cited nearly 100 separate sources of published evidence as well as the extensive pre-Ofsted HMI database and research material in the pipeline.[47] There was, then as now, a glut of information. Significantly, a much larger proportion was genuinely independent.

The myth of 'the era of uninformed professional judgement' has allowed government to claim that it was obliged to step in and save the teaching profession from itself, and the nation's children from ignorant teachers, by setting targets, prescribing in detail what and how teachers should teach and creating a vast canon of approved information on the basis of which teachers could enter 'the era of informed professional judgement'.[48] Gemma Moss's research shows what this comprised: between 1996 and 2004, the DCSF and the public bodies and agencies issued 459 documents on the teaching of literacy alone, the equivalent of one every week.[49]

Elsewhere, both myths are combined in the complaint that 'It's the road back to the 1970s to say that each teacher knows best in their own classroom,'[50] an anarchic condition which is contrasted with teachers' subsequent acceptance that government knows best:

> Standards stayed the same for 50 years before rising sharply in the late 1990s ... Positive feedback [on the national literacy strategy] began to pour in ... teachers may not have liked being told what to teach, but they found that their children learnt more, and faster.'[51]

Myth-making is not unique to educational governance in England. David Berliner and Bruce Liddle exhaustively chart and dispose of a long catalogue of myths about the achievement of American school and college students and the work of American public-sector schools, on the basis of which the Reagan and first Bush administrations were able to declare the American school system to be in crisis and unleash a programme of reforms of the kind with which England has now become familiar.[52]

Policy, media and mediation

The frailty of the information base for education policy was underlined when former Secretary of State Estelle Morris told BBC Radio 4 listeners that ministers do not have time to read important documents and are forced to rely for their information partly on their officials and partly on the press.[53]

It is no criticism of the press to suggest that this is an extremely unsafe way for government to do business. However informed, accurate and perceptive a journalist may be, deadlines and shortage of page or programme space mean that his or her account of a substantial document cannot be other than highly selective. As to the reliability of official digests, only those party to both them and the original documents can judge whether such mediation does justice to the latter.

It was with this problem in mind that the Cambridge Review adopted a dissemination strategy which accompanied every published report by a briefing of under four pages, every group of reports published together by a three-page overview briefing, and all these by short though more than usually informative press releases. The result, we hoped, was to provide precisely the kind of digest which would meet the needs of even the busiest people, whether teachers, politicians, officials or journalists. All four versions of each report, incidentally, were sent to the DCSF, as a matter of courtesy, a week before publication. In the case of the February 2009 special report on the curriculum, of which the DCSF was no less dismissive than of the Review's other interim reports, the department was sent the final draft a whole month before publication and was invited to comment.

However, at our meetings with senior DCSF officials and advisers it became apparent that the full reports were rarely opened and even the briefings were unlikely to have been read. Much more influential than either, as Baroness Morris implied, was the media coverage.

This immediately presents a problem, because if a published document contains the merest hint of criticism of government a journalistic eye will spot it. The criticism, rather than the document in the round, will then become the story. Having not read the document in question, or even its authors' own briefing or summary, ministers then find themselves having to defend government from attack, or rather, relying on their officials to provide such a defence. But the officials may not have read the document either, so the entire sequence from report to response is in effect steered by the media. Unintentionally confirming this situation, a DCSF official said to the Review:

> The DCSF aims to be balanced in our responses to the hundreds of stories that are put to us each month. If media wish to highlight recognition of government achievement, we will celebrate. If they wish to highlight the negative to criticise government achievement, we will of course defend our reputation.[54]

This portrays government departments as being capable only of reaction. Here, the DCSF responds not to published reports and briefings of the kind this Review has provided, but to 'stories' – that is, press accounts of those reports. And a DCSF response can hardly be 'balanced' if the story is not. But one former Secretary of State told us that she expected officials to provide a proper summary of all documents on which the department might be asked to comment by the press or opposition parties, always starting with the positive. On this basis, government could remind journalists or political opponents that their 'story' was unbalanced and that the report in question included significant positive findings, thus retaining the initiative rather than sounding merely defensive or cantankerous. It would seem that subsequent secretaries of state have not followed this example.

While the inability of ministers to read everything is understandable, less understandable or indeed acceptable is their preparedness to make confident pronouncements about documents or events which may be of considerable policy significance on the basis of hearsay which is not only unchecked but which may be doubly biased: first by the initial media 'story'; and then by an official's concern to provide the ammunition needed to see the story off. It would seem that in such cases, judged by the sensible standards cited above, officials are not adequately serving either their ministers or the advancement of properly-informed policy. Jenni Russell goes further, and suggests that in feeding ministers with the kinds of riposte which we exemplified in Chapter 2, officials are actually protecting their own interests:

> Since then [the tenure of an earlier Secretary of State] every education secretary and minister has been distinguished by an almost wilful determination to ignore the mass of research that does not suit their agenda. Politically, that is the easiest choice. They are encouraged in this by their senior civil servants, whose careers have been built around delivering a particular agenda, and who have nothing to gain by seeing it change course.[55]

Sometime a subtler process is at work, as evidence reaching the department is publicly rejected but privately sifted for what can be assimilated to policy. But such assimilation may not be acknowledged, for as one senior official candidly told us, a simple test is applied: 'Not invented here'. If an idea does not originate within the department it is either dismissed as 'not invented here' or appropriated, re-packaged and put out under the department's name.

The complete record of the Review's dealings with government, if published, would provide useful illustrations of the fundamental weaknesses in the policy process as described here, and of the startling gulf between private and public government responses to the Review's work. As Appendix 5 shows, Review personnel had no fewer than 27 meetings with government and NDPBs between October 2006 and March 2009. The tenor of these meetings was usually cordial, and in most cases the issues under discussion were constructively explored. Yet when government commented publicly on the Review it was as if the meetings had never taken place.[56]

Education policy and the democratic deficit

In 2006, the Joseph Rowntree Trust published *Power*, the final report of its independent enquiry into the condition of democracy in Britain. *Power* reported 'high and widespread alienation' towards politicians, the main political parties and the political system's key institutions. Dismissing claims that the public had voluntarily disengaged from formal political processes out of apathy, Power concluded that 'citizens do not feel that the processes of formal democracy offer them enough influence over political decisions ... the main political parties are widely perceived to be too similar and lacking in principle ... people feel they lack information or knowledge ... The main political parties are widely held in contempt ... Voting is simply regarded as a waste of time.'[57]

No less seriously, *Power* identified risks to British democracy from this 'crisis of disengagement': a 'loss of mandate and legitimacy' [all recent governments have gained power on the basis of a minority of the potential electoral vote, which means that the system effectively disenfranchises the majority]; a 'loss of dialogue between government and governed'; the growth of a 'quiet authoritarianism' ... where 'policy is made in consultation with a small coterie of supporters ... and general elections become empty rituals.'[58] As further symptoms of the malaise, *Power* reported that the Executive, and especially the Prime Minister's office, have become more powerful at the expense of MPs; central government departments have become more powerful at the expense of local government; quangos and NDPBs have gained extra powers; and political decision-making has become more opaque, hidden and complex.[59]

The analysis is widely shared. Anthony Sampson compares his celebrated 1962 analysis *The Anatomy of Britain* with the situation in 2004 and finds real substance to complaints about

> the centralisation and concentration of power, the clout of bureaucracies and the politicisation of the public service ... how decisions are actually taken by small groups of people, most of them unelected and unaccountable.[60]

He goes on:

> Looking back on the landscape of power which I have surveyed ... I find it hard to recognise it as belonging to the British democratic tradition, with its small clusters of self-enclosed, self-serving groups on the peaks and the populace on the plains below. The retreat of both the old Establishment and the rebels on the left has left a vacuum which has been filled by the masters of the market-place who can evade responsibility and pass the buck to each other.[61]

From an even longer perspective, Eric Hobsbawm contrasts the decline in trust of formal government with the growth of rival centres of political activity and information exchange:

> The striking centralisation of an already strong decision-making power has gone hand-in-hand with a demotion of the House of Commons and a massive transfer of functions to unelected institutions, public or private ... A good deal of politics will be negotiated and decided behind the scenes. This will increase the citizens' distrust of government and lower their opinion of politicians. Governments will fight a constant guerrilla war against the coalition of well-organised minority campaigning interests and the media. These will increasingly see as their political function the publication of what government would prefer to keep quiet.[62]

This confirms the Power enquiry's finding that disengagement from formal politics reflects not apathy but active rejection of the way that Westminster goes about its business and a belief that there are more effective ways to get things done.[63] By May 2009, disengagement had hardened into public disgust at evidence of widespread abuse, at taxpayers' expense, of procedures whereby members of the UK Parliament claim for their expenses. In this matter, Eric Hobsbawm's words were prophetic indeed. Public opinion of politicians sank to an all-time low. Parliamentary officials fought long and hard to prevent publication of the information in question, which was secured only through leaks to assiduous journalists.[64] Only after considerable grass-roots constituency pressure were some of the more egregious offenders called to account. Belatedly sensing the mood, party leaders promised 'root and branch reform' and 'a new democratic settlement', but their anger and contrition were widely viewed as synthetic and their assurances provoked little confidence that what was promised would address systemic problems of the kind which the Power enquiry, political analysts, historians and this Review have identified.

CONCLUSION

This penultimate chapter has reviewed the institutions and processes of governance, funding and policy which frame the work of primary schools. Though the narrative is dominated by one theme – centralisation – it would be wrong to infer that government intervention is never justified. We have seen that the case for a national curriculum is generally accepted, that in the balance sheet of policy the government's childhood agenda is warmly applauded and its obligation to step in to protect vulnerable children is understood, and that some key educational standards as defined and measured by the national tests have risen.

But we have also reported widespread and growing disenchantment with both the degree and the manner of centralisation since 1997, the extent to which the power of government and its agencies has reached ever more deeply into the recesses of professional action and thought, and the evidence that flagship interventions like the standards agenda have not only proved unpopular but may have been less successful and more problematic than government is willing to admit.

Thus, we showed how the undeniably positive evidence on standards is countered by significant negative findings, how the evidence may be compromised by methodological weaknesses in the testing and inspection procedures, and how many of the assumptions and claims underpinning the standards agenda are open to challenge of a fundamental kind. Such reservations raise a further question: given hostile reaction to several key initiatives, the modest gains of others when set against their considerable costs, and the erroneous assumptions and faulty evidence on which several initiatives have been based, might standards have risen, and indeed have risen further and faster, if government had not intervened in the way it did? In the catalogue of the problematic are interventions ranging from the key stage tests, the national curriculum and the literacy, numeracy and primary strategies, to the professional standards for teachers.

These questions took us inexorably from the content and outcomes of policy to its processes. Despite the fact that from 2001 the government's first phase of public service reform was replaced by one which ostensibly balanced top-down pressures with pressures from below, the Review's 2007–9 data shows little evidence or perception of change in the way policies are evolved or in the way policy-makers behave.

In this, education mirrors what some see as wider problems in Britain's political culture, and an erosion of the country's democratic processes. The prosecution of policy relating to primary education does not stand apart from the trends characterised by Sampson, Hobsbawm and the Power enquiry. Indeed, it convincingly exemplifies many of them: centralisation, secrecy and the 'quiet authoritarianism' of the new centres of power; the disenfranchising of local voice; the rise of unelected and unaccountable groups and individuals taking key decisions behind closed doors; the 'empty rituals' of consultation; the replacement of professional dialogue by the monologic discourse of power; the politicisation of the entire educational enterprise so that it becomes impossible to debate ideas or evidence which are not deemed to be 'on message', or which are 'not invented here'; and, latterly coming to light, financial corruption.

These trends appear to be endemic to England's political system in 2009. In addition, the Review and its witnesses have highlighted variations on this larger theme of democratic deficit, many of them centring on the nature and quality of the information on which both sound decision-making and effective education depend: the less than complete reliability of official information, particularly in the crucial domain of standards; its lack of independence; the creation and/or dogged perpetuation of educational myths in order to underwrite an exaggerated account of political progress; the key role of the media in shaping the information that reaches government as well as the information that flows from it; the reluctance of decision-makers to countenance or come to grips with alternative information on which better policies could be founded; the use of misinformation to marginalise or discredit ideas running on other than approved lines, and evidence from other than approved sources.

This, surely, is not the way that education policy should be made.

NOTES

1 NDPBs and other bodies are listed at http://www.dcsf.gov.uk/ndpb/
2 Currently operating under the auspices of QCA but during 2009 it will become the regulator of qualifications as outlined in the Apprenticeships, Skills, Children and Learning Bill 2008–9.
3 During 2009–10 QCA will become the Qualifications and Curriculum Development Agency (QCDA) following recommendations in the government's Confidence in Standards Review in 2007.
4 Established by the Teaching and Higher Education Act 1988
5 Established in November 2007.
6 Fletcher-Campbell and Lee (2000): 1.
7 DfEE (1997).
8 Fletcher-Campbell and Lee (2000): 1.
9 DCSF (2008aa): 1.
10 Improvement and Development Agency (2009).
11 Teachernet (2009).
12 The Education School Governance (Constitution) (England) Regulations 2003 (SI 2003/348).
13 This section draws heavily on Balarin and Lauder (2010) *The Cambridge Primary Review Research Surveys*, Chapter 26.
14 *Ibid.*
15 Dale (1997).
16 OECD (1998).
17 Gove (2008): 1–2.
18 Conservative Party (2009): 8.
19 Liberal Democrat Party (2009): 22.
20 Especially Hall and Øzerk (2010), Wyse, McCreery and Torrance (2010), Harlen (2010), Tymms and Merrell (2010), Cunningham and Raymont (2010), Stronach, Pickard and Jones (2010), McNamara, Brundrett and Webb (2010), Burgess (2010), Riggall and Sharp (2010), Balarin and Lauder (2010), *The Cambridge Primary Review Research Surveys*, Chapters 15, 29, 19, 17, 28, 23, 24, 25, 14 and 26.
21 Karlsen (2000).
22 Noden and West (2010), *The Cambridge Primary Review Research Surveys*, Chapter 27.
23 *Ibid.*
24 DCSF and DIUS (2008), which explains: 'School based expenditure includes only expenditure incurred directly by the schools. This includes the pay of teachers and school-based support staff, school premises costs, books and equipment, and certain other supplies and services, less any capital items funded from recurrent spending and income from sales, fees and charges and rents and rates'.
25 Interestingly, Noden and West point out that the United Kingdom (not England) is a mid-ranking country among OECD members in terms of the level of expenditure on primary schools, in the proportion of the GDP spent on primary schools and also in the level of spending on pupils in primary education relative to secondary education: Noden and West (2010), *The Cambridge Primary Review Research Surveys*, Chapter 27.
26 CACE (1967): para 1231.
27 Alexander *et al.* (1992).
28 House of Commons Education Committee (1994).
29 DCSF spokesperson, quoted in *The Guardian*, 29 March 2008.
30 Alexander and Hargreaves (2007): 35–36.
31 Mansell (2007): 26.
32 This adds to the points in Chapter 17, drawing on Tymms and Merrell (2010), *The Cambridge Primary Review Research Surveys*, Chapter 17.
33 Lord Adonis, Schools Minister, quoted in *The Guardian*, 18 April 2008. The country's largest teaching union (the NUT) remains outside the 2003 Social Partnership agreement.
34 Cabinet Office (2008).
35 *Ibid.*: 9.
36 Letter to *The Independent*, 2 June 2008.
37 Cabinet Office (2008): 11.
38 Coffield *et al.* (2007).
39 Coffield *et al.* (2008).
40 *Ibid.*: 13–14.
41 *Ibid.*: 28.

42 See Chapter 2.
43 Warwick Mansell, 'Time to move on, Conor', http://www.educationbynumbers.org.uk/2009/03/
44 Barber (2001a): 13–14.
45 Plowden, Newsom, Crowther, Robbins, James, CNAA, UCET, Bullock, Cockcroft, Gulbenkian, Warnock.
46 Alexander, Rose and Woodhead (1992): paras 24–50.
47 Alexander, Rose and Woodhead (1992): paras 55–62.
48 Barber (2001a).
49 Moss (2007).
50 Barber (2007): 242.
51 *Ibid*: 188 and 34.
52 Berliner and Biddle (1995).
53 Week in Westminster, BBC Radio 4, 4 April 2009.
54 Email from a DCSF official to the Cambridge Review, 18 April 2008.
55 Russell (2008).
56 See www.primaryreview.org.uk for examples of official responses to the Review's interim reports.
57 Joseph Rowntree Trusts (2006): 16–17 and 29.
58 *Ibid.*: 33–35.
59 *Ibid.*: 125–26.
60 Sampson (2004): 365–66.
61 *Ibid*: 366.
62 Hobsbawm (2007): 111–12.
63 Joseph Rowntree Trusts (2006): 16.
64 A series of articles in the *Daily Telegraph*, running daily for several weeks during May and June 2009, and followed up by the other media.

Part 5
Conclusions and recommendations

24 Conclusions and recommendations

This final report from the Cambridge Primary Review ends, as such reports should, with conclusions and recommendations. The conclusions, by and large, are broad-brush statements. They do not summarise systematically the detail contained in previous chapters, and there are fewer recommendations than might be expected from previous reports of comparable length. Plowden, for instance, listed 197 and the 1975 Bullock Report as many as 333. Plowden's recommendations ranged from far-reaching matters of national policy like the universal provision of nursery education to the availability of telephones and typewriters and other fine details of school organisation.[1] Here we have 153 statements, of which 75 are recommendations. At the end of the chapter, these are compressed into 17 thematic signposts.

Our approach has been dictated by three aims. First we wish to concentrate attention on the problems, changes and improvements which in our judgement matter most. Readers can then turn back to the relevant chapters for detailed findings and recommendations relating to the matters thus prioritised. Second, we hope to encourage readers to consider the substance as well as the outcomes, to follow the plot rather than skip to the denouement. Third, it is essential that any changes which result from an enquiry such as this are firmly grounded in proper analysis of the problems that the changes seek to address. All too often, as the Review's evidence has shown, policy seems to have been introduced on the assumption that ministerial effectiveness is measured by the number of 'tough new' initiatives launched; or without proper evaluation of last year's shake-up; or – worst of all because policy then heads entirely in the wrong direction – on the basis of incorrect diagnosis. These are risks we would prefer to avoid.

Below, conclusions are in normal type and recommendations in **bold**.

THE OVERALL PICTURE

1. The Review has been undertaken against the background of a growing public sense of crisis in relation to each of its three perspectives – childhood, society and education. Children have been portrayed alternately as innocents in a dark and menacing world or as celebrity-obsessed couch-potatoes stirring themselves only to text their friends or invade the streets and terrorise their elders. British society has been characterised as 'broken', terminally divided by wealth, class, race and religion and severed from the traditional bonds of family, community and morality. The wider world, too, is perceived as divided and dangerous, polarised by income and ideology, ravaged by the passionate intensity of the worst, and now living on borrowed time because of nations' collective refusal to address climate change with the urgency it requires. To this apocalyptic vision is added a sense that teachers are fighting a rearguard action against social forces they cannot be expected to control, while detractors complain, as they always have, that standards are falling, that schools are neglecting the 3Rs and that education is not what it used to be.

2. Though this dismal account contains some grains of truth, the real situation is very different. As we note below, there are legitimate concerns about children's lives today, but the 'crisis' of modern childhood has been grossly overstated. Britain is certainly a complex and in many respects divided and unequal society, and for too many children this, rather than the

cult of celebrity, is the real and shameful crisis. And in 2009 perhaps we must add worries about what the global recession has revealed about the frailty of the country's economic system and the values by which it is driven, for these values exploit and exacerbate inequality, and they relate directly to the wider global problems which so exercised many of the Review's witnesses.

3. As for primary education, what we must emphatically report is that primary schools appear to be under intense pressure but in good heart. They are highly valued by children and parents and in general are doing a good job. They do not neglect and never have neglected the 3Rs, and those at Westminster and in the media who regularly make this claim are either careless with the facts or are knowingly fostering a calumny. The debates about starting ages, aims, curriculum, pedagogy, assessment, standards, expertise and staffing remain open, as they should, but the condition of the system is sound. Indeed, as was noted by many witnesses, primary schools may be the one point of stability and positive values in a world where everything else is changing and uncertain. For many, schools are the centre that holds when things fall apart.

CHILDREN'S LIVES (CHAPTERS 4, 5 AND 6)

4. So, in pursuit of balance, we have identified an impressive list of positives relating to the lives of today's children: life expectancy, health, income, housing, support, unprecedented access to information and entertainment, heightened cultural and global awareness, and vastly expanded educational opportunity.

5. On the downside, we have noted concerns about the undesirable values and material expectations to which children are exposed by those same media which can otherwise expand their horizons beneficially. We have reported anxieties about physical risk, especially in the major cities, the impact of the changing demography of parenting and family life, about children's emotional growth and well-being, and the loss of children's freedom to play and just be themselves. In this, witnesses believe, the premature pressures of formal schooling itself are partly to blame.

6. Yet, for most children, feared or perceived risk is much greater than actual risk. Conversely, for a significant minority the risks and deprivations are at least as severe as they are portrayed, and it is here that attention needs to be focussed, as indeed in recent policy it rightly has been. Britain remains a very unequal society. Child poverty persists in this, one of the world's richest nations. Social disadvantage blights the early lives of a larger proportion of children in Britain than in many other countries, and this social and material divide maps with depressing exactness onto the gap in educational attainment.

7. What happens to children at home vitally affects what happens to them at school. The roles of parents and teachers overlap, and the division of responsibility for children's socialisation and education is blurred. The relationship of parenting to educating is subtle and multifaceted, and demands not only close collaboration between parents/carers and teachers but also mutual understanding and respect. Whether the quality of parenting/caring has declined is open to question, and adults can over-control as well as under-control. The introduction of parenting programmes is not straightforward: they demand the utmost sensitivity. What is beyond question, however, is that many parents and families are under acute pressure, and that the impact of poverty is particularly profound when it is associated with family instability.

8. **While recent concerns should be heeded about the pressures to which today's children are subject, and the undesirable values, influences and experiences to which many are exposed, the main focus of policy should continue to be on narrowing the gaps in income, housing, care, risk, opportunity and educational attainment suffered by a significant minority of children, rather than on prescribing the character of the lives of the majority. The government's efforts to narrow the gap in all outcomes between vulnerable children and the rest deserves the strongest possible support.**

UNDERSTANDING CHILDHOOD (CHAPTERS 5, 7 AND 10)

9. The report's approach to primary education has been shaped not only by concerns about the quality of children's lives, but by changes in the way childhood itself is viewed and understood.

10. First, arising from converging attention to children's rights and voices, and from recent developments in child psychology and sociology, children's capacity and right to influence the direction of their own lives is increasingly acknowledged, as are their right to be consulted about matters affecting their lives and learning and their competence to make meaningful judgements on such matters from an early age. The Review is convinced by the evidence that a sense of agency is vital for both learning and well-being, and this features prominently both in our proposed aims for primary education and in our account of pedagogy.

11. Second, it is recognised that there is much more to children's lives than school, that what children do out of school can be valuable in itself, and that in the home and community children can develop understanding and skill of distinctive kinds on which schools can and should build. This is in sharp contrast to the 'blank slate' view of early childhood on which primary schooling has sometimes been based, and the belief that the home exists merely to support the school.

12. Third, recent research modifies our understanding of children's development and learning in a number of important directions. Cognitive research suggests that children think and learn not that differently from adults, but differ from them in having less experience through which to make sense of what they encounter. There is greater recognition of the inter-relatedness of the biological, social, emotional and intellectual aspects of children's development and of the consequent need to understand learning as a psycho-social process for which talk, collaborative activity and emotional security are both preconditions and ongoing requirements. Creativity is understood not only in terms of exposure to artistic and imaginative endeavour but as contributing to the quality and capacity of children's thinking, and to their perseverance and problem-solving abilities. Earlier notions of fixed developmental ages and stages have been jettisoned, as have those about left and right brain functions and 'learning styles'. Children are now viewed as competent and capable learners, given the right linguistic and social environment and teaching which engages, stimulates, challenges and scaffolds their understanding.

13. **The UN Convention on the Rights of the Child should be the accepted framework for all policies relating to young children and their education. Childhood should be understood in terms of children's present as well as future needs and capabilities, and their right to a rich array of experiences which will lay the foundations for lifelong learning, as well as prepare them for secondary schooling. Children should be actively engaged in decisions which affect their education, and attention to 'children's voices' should never be tokenistic.**

14. **The worth and impact of children's lives outside school should be respected, as should the right of parents and carers to bring up children in their own way, and home-school relations should be seen as respectful and reciprocal rather than unilateral. The funds of knowledge embedded in homes and communities should be fully used to support learning in schools. At the same time, there should be effective strategies to identify and support parents/carers in challenging circumstances, and all parents should have access to information about how children learn and develop and the kinds of early childhood experience which make a difference to their learning and future lives.**

15. **The evidence of research on children's development and learning, and of different cultural and gender-related perceptions of what makes for educational and personal success and failure, should inform all who work with primary-age children, and all who advise on policy for this age-range. In particular, teachers' initial training and continuing professional development should devote greater attention than at present to the pedagogical implications of psychological, neuroscientific and socio-cultural research on young children.**

CHILDHOOD, DIFFERENCE AND DIVERSITY (CHAPTERS 8 AND 9)

16. Britain is unequal, but it is also very diverse culturally and linguistically. Acknowledging this diversity means that primary schools are called on to serve not just the traditional centre of society but also its boundaries and margins. Even the centre is more variegated than politicians' appeals to 'middle England' imply. And what now drives all this diversity, to an extent which at the time of Plowden would have been unimaginable, is migration. The transience and unpredictabilility of migration, the inadequacy of local information and the mismatch of resource and demography all add to the pressure on schools over and above their task of attending properly to the needs of the children in question.

17. Sometimes those at the margins of society are further marginalised by education itself, and in this sense education appears not to have caught up with the full extent of diversity. The implications of mainstream differences in culture, gender, ethnicity and religion are reasonably well understood, and considerable steps have been taken locally to attend to them, but there remain too many children and families who for different reasons are viewed as 'hard-to-reach'. In this matter, there is a tendency to cast such families in a negative light, thus accentuating perceptions of difference and creating further barriers to learning. The Review encountered evidence of discrimination against marginalised groups, within the education system as well as in society.

18. Nearly a fifth of all primary pupils are identified as having special educational needs, 1.4 per cent of them severe enough to merit an official statement of those needs and how they should be met. The Review identified serious concerns about how well the system identifies and caters for these children. Too often, needs classifications appear arbitrary rather than considered, and result in stereotyping and discrimination. There is excessive local variation in funding and provision for children whose needs are defined as 'special', and deep frustration among parents and teachers, and in some local authorities, about the adequacy of available support. There is also a serious and long-standing tension between the desire to respond effectively to particular needs and a reluctance to label or pigeon-hole such children. Acceptance of the basic rights and principles of inclusion has not always been matched by appropriate knowledge, skills and attitudes.

19. **Efforts should be made to ensure that local information about migrant families and children is accurate and up to date, and that resources and needs (for example in relation to language support) are properly and promptly aligned. There should be improved systems for tracking, monitoring and communicating with transient and marginalised groups.**

20. **Teachers' initial training and continuing professional development should devote greater attention than at present to the facts, dilemmas, opportunities and challenges of diversity and difference. They should seek to promote equal valuing and treatment of all children at school, especially in relation to ethnicity, gender and special needs, and to counter stereotyping and prejudice. Equity should be fundamental to professional consciousness and action, as well as to public policy.**

21. **In the light of serious concerns about statementing and the limitations and constraints of the current system of providing for children identified as having special educational needs, and in the context of efforts to create a genuinely inclusive and personalised approach to learning for all children, we endorse the view of former Secretary of State Estelle Morris that there should be a full SEN review. This should cover definitions, structures, procedures and provision in the field of special educational needs, and proper debate on the meaning and practicality of inclusive education.**

FOUNDATIONS AND STAGES (CHAPTER 11)

22. Although the Review's remit did not include the pre-school years, a report on primary education which did not acknowledge the critical importance of early childhood and of laying secure foundations for later learning would make little sense.

23. There is widespread appreciation of the government's huge investment in early childhood services since 1997. The ideal of a children's centre in every community is to be applauded, and could help unify a system still divided between nursery education on the one hand and day-care on the other. But there remain challenges in ensuring that early years services are of a sufficiently high standard to be effective. Quality is too variable, and too many staff are under-qualified or poorly paid.

24. The early years foundation stage (EYFS) for children aged 0–5 has been broadly welcomed, especially for its underpinning principles and six areas of learning. But there is evidence, particularly in reception classes, that the well-intentioned requirement to narrow the gap in outcomes for the most vulnerable children is leading to pressure to skew an otherwise holistic and balanced curriculum in order to meet goals that are not all appropriate for all children. There is also concern that the reception year in many schools is responding less to the principles of the EYFS (in which it is located) than to downward pressure from key stages 1 and 2. Transition from the EYFS to KS1 is a major challenge. Many witnesses wish to see the EYFS extended upwards to age six or even seven. Some schools are already doing this and report that it pays dividends in terms of later learning.

25. Children in England start their formal schooling at a younger age than in most other countries, and there is strong support for the view that England should conform to international practice by starting formal school at age six or seven. However, with almost all three to four-year-olds already receiving at least 12.5 hours of early education a week, the issue becomes not so much when children should 'start school' as when they should move from play-based learning to a domain-based curriculum such as this Review proposes. The central issue here is the character and quality of what our youngest children encounter, whether in pre-school or school settings. What matters is that the provision is right. At the moment, according to our evidence, in reception classes it often is not.

26. **The introduction of the early years foundation stage is welcomed. It should be renamed the foundation stage and extended to age six. This would give sufficient time for children to establish positive attitudes to learning and begin to develop the language and study skills which are essential to their later progress. The challenge now is to ensure that the EYFS principles and commitments are implemented. The emphasis must be on securing the most appropriate early learning experiences for young children in all settings, and on ensuring a smooth transition from the foundation stage to mainstream primary education.**

27. **Once a proper early learning entitlement is secured for three-to six-year-olds, it should be extended to age two in areas of social disadvantage and for children with particular needs.**

28. **With the foundation stage extended to age six, key stage 1 becomes redundant. Instead, we propose that the national curriculum for the primary years be conceived as a single stage, building carefully and coherently on the foundation stage, and starting at age six. Following this change, the current structure should be simplified to foundation (0–6) and primary (6–11).**

29. **There should be a full and open debate about the starting age for compulsory schooling. Logically, ages and stages should be aligned, and this would point to raising the starting age to six, in line with many other countries. However, if recommendations 26 and 28 are implemented, starting age is less critical.**

30. **New and better ways should be devised to ensure that outcomes in early childhood improve and gaps in the learning and achievement of different groups are reduced. Provision and tracking of children's progress should focus on the areas which are known to make a positive difference to their all-round learning: language for thinking and communication, personal, social and emotional development, physical development and creative development.**

31. **Children's well-being in the foundation stage and success in the primary stage are strongly linked to the quality of the practitioners who support them in their earliest years. The current drive to raise the level of qualifications in the early years sector should be maintained. There should be a unified children's workforce strategy which brings together the responsibilities of the Training and Development Agency for Schools and the Children's Workforce Development Council.**

AIMS FOR PRIMARY EDUCATION (CHAPTER 12)

32. Policies on the curriculum, assessment, standards, inspection, teacher training and much else relating to primary education are incomplete and lack direction unless or until we ask what primary education is for. However, official attempts to define aims for the education system have a poor track record. The result, all too often, is a statement so brief or anodyne as to be pointless, and when it is devised separately from the curriculum its function may be no more than cosmetic. In defining aims, values and principles, therefore, there are two challenges: first, to produce a meaningful and viable statement which can command reasonable support in a plural society; second, to ensure that the statement's function is more than rhetorical and that it really does shape what children experience at school.

33. Although it is desirable to have a single set of aims for the whole of compulsory schooling, as proposed in the interim and final reports of the Rose Review, the distinctive character and needs of middle childhood and primary education require additional and specific aims with a different emphasis to those for pre-school and secondary education. Primary education, as we have already asserted, is not merely a preparation for secondary. It has its own imperatives and opportunities.

34. The Cambridge review has grounded its proposed aims for primary education in the totality of its evidence: that is to say, in analysis of children's development, needs and capabilities, what witnesses said about the condition of the society and world in which today's children are growing up, and predictions and fears about the future. We reject the claim in the final Rose review report that there is a 'considerable match' between our aims for primary education and the QCA secondary aims which Rose proposes should now apply to primary education as well.

35. **Accordingly, we recommend that the work of primary schools as a whole – that is to say, the curriculum, pedagogy and the wider life of the school – should enact and pursue the 12 aims for primary education proposed and elaborated in Chapter 12. These relate to the individual (*well-being, engagement, empowerment, autonomy*); to the wider world (*respect and reciprocity, interdependence and sustainability, local, national and global citizenship, culture and community*); and to learning (*knowing, understanding and making sense, fostering skills, exciting the imagination, enacting dialogue*).**

36. **In addition to these aims, the work of primary schools and the national and local bodies which support and/or are responsible for them should be guided by procedural principles such as those set out in Chapter 12 in order that aims for children's education are not negated by the way schools are run. The proposed principles are: entitlement; equity; human rights; quality, standards and accountability; balancing preparation for what follows with fulfillment here and now; continuity and consistency between phases; democratic engagement; respect for evidence; guidance not prescription; adequate resources and support.**

37. **The headings in recommendations 35 and 36 may convey little as they stand, and a careless reading of them may well lie behind the Rose report's claim that the aims proposed by the Review are little different from the QCA secondary aims.[2] Chapter 12 attaches descriptions to each aim which should be studied before they are commented on. In any case, our purpose in proposing the aims and principles is not to secure their wholesale adoption but to encourage the same kind of discussion that the exercise has forced upon us.**

THE CURRICULUM (CHAPTERS 13 AND 14)

38. The Review finds widespread acceptance of the need for a national curriculum, and the promise of entitlement which it embodies. It finds significant gains from the current national curriculum since its introduction in 1989, notably in science, citizenship and the handling of values and children's personal development. The national primary, literacy and numeracy strategies (especially the NNS) have their supporters, and younger teachers in particular welcome the structure and guidance which they provide. The early years

foundation stage (EYFS) areas of learning and development provide an appropriate platform for primary education.

39. However, as children move through the primary phase, their statutory entitlement to a broad and balanced education is increasingly but needlessly compromised by a 'standards' agenda which combines high stakes testing and the national strategies' exclusive focus on literacy and numeracy. It is regrettable that the Rose Review's remit excluded examination of these issues. The most conspicuous casualties are the arts, the humanities and those kinds of learning in all subjects which require time for talking, problem-solving and the extended exploration of ideas. Memorisation and recall have come to be valued more than understanding and enquiry, and transmission of information more than the pursuit of knowledge in its fuller sense. Worryingly, primary science, which was one of the success stories of the national curriculum's first decade, has also been squeezed by the national strategies, retaining its albeit reduced place only because it was tested at the end of key stage 2 (from 2010 this ceases too). Science is far too important to both a balanced education and the nation's future to be allowed to decline in this way.

40. Fuelling this loss of entitlement has been a policy-led belief that curriculum breadth is incompatible with the pursuit of standards in 'the basics', and that if anything gives way it must be breadth. However, evidence going back many decades, including reports from HMI and Ofsted, consistently shows this belief to be unfounded. Standards and breadth are often positively related, and high-performing schools achieve both. This is one of several modern manifestations of the historic divide between 'the basics' (protected) and the rest of the curriculum (viewed as dispensable). Now recognised by many contributors to the Review as a threat to standards as well as entitlement, this split is exacerbated by the relative neglect of the non-core curriculum in initial teacher training, school inspection and professional development. This produces a primary curriculum which, as Ofsted has acknowledged, is often two-tier in terms of quality as well as time.

41. Separate development and management of the national strategies (by DCSF) and the national curriculum (by QCA) have dislocated the teaching of mathematics and – especially – English. The latter is in urgent need of re-conceptualisation. Micro-management by the DCSF, the national agencies and national strategies is widely perceived to be excessive and to have contributed to the problems above.

42. Curriculum debate, and thus curriculum practice, are weakened by a muddled and reductive discourse about subjects, knowledge and skills. Discussion of the place of subjects is needlessly polarised; knowledge is grossly parodied as grubbing for obsolete facts; and the undeniably important notion of skill is inflated to cover aspects of learning for which it is not appropriate. There is an urgent need for key terms to be clarified and for the level of discussion and conceptualisation to be raised. Simply re-naming components of the curriculum 'skills', 'themes' or 'areas of learning' does not of itself address the fundamental question of what primary education is about; nor does it necessarily make the curriculum more manageable in practice.

43. The government's Rose review of the primary curriculum, whose final report was published as this volume went to press, addresses some of these problems, but excludes several that are fundamental. Further, it is premised on the assumption that the main challenge is curriculum time and manageability, or, in Sir Jim Rose's own words, helping 'primary class teachers solve the quarts-into-pint-pots problem of teaching 13 subjects, plus religious education, to sufficient depth, in the time available'.[3] Since some schools already succeed in teaching the full national curriculum to a high standard, despite being under intense pressure from the national strategies and tests, the current national curriculum cannot be regarded as inherently unmanageable. The clue to the true problem is in Sir Jim's added assumption that this is a job for the class teacher alone – an assumption which it is all too easy to miss, because history and habit have embedded the primary class teacher system so deeply into professional and public consciousness. We believe that both premises are contestable, and that though there is room for curriculum simplification, the more

fundamental problem is the growing gap between (i) primary schools' historic staffing patterns (which used the class teacher system to meet the Victorian imperatives of a narrow curriculum, large classes, transmission teaching and rote learning, all provided as cheaply as possible), (ii) the breadth and complexity of the tasks primary teachers are now expected to undertake and (iii) the expertise these tasks require.

44. Like others, we believe that the national curriculum should confine itself to setting out children's minimum curriculum entitlement. At issue, however, is what 'minimum' should entail. For reasons which by now will be clear, we do not agree with those who restrict primary pupils' minimum curriculum entitlement to literacy and numeracy.

45. **The curriculum needs to be reformed, but for educational rather than managerial reasons. The curriculum should be re-conceived for the 21st century. How it is planned, managed and taught should be dealt with separately.**

46. **The new primary curriculum framework proposed by the Review seeks to resolve the problems summarised at 39–42 above, while later recommendations respond constructively to the vital but neglected matter of the mismatch between task, expertise and resources (para 43). The Review's curriculum framework starts from, and is driven by, a clear statement of the aims of primary education grounded in analysis of children's present and future needs and the condition of the society and world in which children are growing up. It has regard to principles of procedure which highlight entitlement, quality, equity, breadth, balance, local engagement, and guidance rather than prescription. It respects and builds on the EYFS curriculum.**

47. **The curriculum is conceived as a matrix of the 12 recommended educational aims (para 35) and eight domains of knowledge, skill, enquiry and disposition, with the aims locked firmly into the framework from the outset. It dispenses with the notion of the curriculum core as a small number of subjects and places all eight domains within the curriculum on the principle that although teaching time will continue to be differentially allocated, all the domains are essential to young children's education and all must be taught to the highest standards. At the same time it insists on the centrality of language, oracy and literacy, both in their own right and as enabling learning across a curriculum in which breadth and standards go hand in hand. This domain also includes a modern foreign language and a carefully-judged approach to ICT, which is clearly also central. The framework reconceptualises other key curriculum areas too, notably citizenship and personal education. It vigorously defends science, the arts and humanities as essential to a proper primary education. It provides for a strong local component, differentiates the *national* and *community* curriculum, and divides time between them on the basis of 70/30 per cent of the yearly teaching total.**

48. **The proposed curriculum domains are: *arts and creativity*; *citizenship and ethics*; *faith and belief*; *language, oracy and literacy*; *mathematics*; *physical and emotional health*; *place and time*; *science and technology*. (As with the aims, these headings convey relatively little without their descriptors: see Chapter 14.)**

49. **For the purposes of planning, implementation and professional support the new curriculum has three segments: a nationally-determined description and rationale for the curriculum as a whole and for each domain (*statutory*); nationally-proposed programmes of study for the national component of each domain (*non-statutory*); locally-proposed programmes of study for the community component of each domain (where applicable) which also identify local needs and opportunities across the curriculum as a whole (*non-statutory*). The framework, then, shifts the statutory/non-statutory balance away from detailed prescription to a clear mandatory framework which offers considerable scope for professional flexibility and initiative.**

50. **Nationally, the curriculum would be planned by independent expert panels, supported and resourced by the QCA or another appropriate national body. Locally, the task would be undertaken by community curriculum partnerships (CCPs) convened and serviced by local authorities but not under their direct control. School-level implementation would be flexible, but schools would be required to teach all eight domains to a consistently high standard regardless of the amount of time each is allocated. The national panels would consider how**

each domain is most appropriately elaborated by reference to the 12 aim and eight domain descriptions. The CCPs would identify local needs and opportunities within and across the domains. Schools would determine how, thus elaborated, the domains are reconstructed as a viable school curriculum and are named, timetabled and taught, with the aims providing a constant point of reference throughout.

51. The primary national strategy (PNS) should be wound up and literacy and numeracy should be re-integrated with English and mathematics. Concern with standards should be extended to cover the whole curriculum rather than just 'the basics'. National assessment should be reformed (see next section) so that it does its job without compromising children's legal entitlement to a broad and balanced curriculum. [For update see pp. 513–4].

52. Successful development and implementation require the reform of institutions, procedures and requirements, and a major programme of capacity-building. The statutory and advisory curriculum functions of the DCSF, QCA, local authorities and the national strategies should be re-assessed. Local authorities will need to shift from their current role of co-ordinating and policing the delivery of the PNS on behalf of DCSF, supported by 85 per cent of the strategy's annual £200 million budget, to helping schools to make their own decisions on curriculum and pedagogy. Local authorities will need to enter into a new relationship with both government and the schools.

53. In order to build teachers' curriculum capacity, their training and their professional development should ensure that all eight domains are properly attended to and that curriculum matters are treated more rigorously than hitherto. Teaching roles and staff deployment in primary schools will need to be re-thought, in order that every school has the necessary expertise to advance the 12 aims and teach all eight domains well. This will require honest reappraisal of the strengths and limitations of the generalist class teacher system (see recommendations 126–29). Local collaboration between professionals in primary, early years and secondary settings should be encouraged in order to ensure smooth transition from foundation to primary and from primary to secondary, and in order to share curriculum expertise and develop the community curriculum.

PEDAGOGY (CHAPTER 15)

54. In 1998–99, the government abandoned a convention respected by all its post-war predecessors, that – in the words of an earlier Secretary of State – 'questions about how to teach are not for government to determine.' The government's national literacy and numeracy strategies, ostensibly non-statutory but regarded by nearly all teachers as obligatory, imposed on every primary school single models of teaching, with lesson structure, content and method specified in detail. Literacy and numeracy were detached from the rest of the curriculum, with adverse consequences noted in Chapter 14, teacher training and inspection were re-aligned to ensure compliance, and the national tests effectively reinforced the prescribed content and teachers' priorities. In 2003, the primary national strategy sought to consolidate this approach and extend it across the rest of the curriculum.

55. The Review has assessed the charge that this combination of initiatives amounted to the imposition of a 'state theory of learning'. The national strategies provided necessary support to inexperienced teachers, and have generated a body of valuable resource material, but many experienced and able teachers resented this degree of control of their work, its inflexible and monolithic character, and the overt politicisation of the act of teaching in which the strategies were routinely wielded as an electoral weapon. Further, examination of their empirical provenance, especially that of the literacy strategy, has found them in certain respects misconceived and out of step with recent research, while their adverse impact on the rest of the curriculum has already been noted. The case of 'interactive whole-class teaching', in which politicians wrongly saw increased whole-class teaching as the way to raise standards, rather than the improvement of classroom interaction whatever the pattern of organisation, illustrates the dangers of ill-informed political intervention in pedagogy.

56. In contrast, the Review has examined the views of teachers and children on what constitutes good teaching, and has juxtaposed these with the now substantial body of evidence from research, setting both bodies of data in the wider framework of an account of pedagogy which holds that teaching demands reflection, judgement and creativity, and is necessarily grounded in sustainable theories, values, evidence and justifications. The relevant research evidence summarised by the Review covers the importance of children's experience and learning outside school; children's thinking and how it can be advanced; cognitive and social prerequisites for learning; the importance of language in learning; the use of ICT; classroom organisation; class size; and the relationship between pupil and teacher voices. This represents a sounder foundation for effective teaching than prepackaged lessons. Research from the ESRC Teaching and Learning Research Programme and other sources reviewed in Chapter 15 shows that good teaching proceeds from teachers' grasp of principles grounded in evidence, together with the appropriate pedagogical content knowledge and a broad repertoire of strategies and techniques.

57. The Review encountered considerable concern about children's behaviour in schools and classrooms. It also found no clear agreement on the causes, though social trends, poor parenting and the performance culture were all frequently blamed. However, public and political discussion of the problem tends to focus on rules rather than relationships, detaching behaviour from learning, and replacing interaction through which pupils learn to think for themselves by directives which expect them to replicate the thinking of others.

58. **The Review strongly supports the view of Sir Alan Steer's group on pupil behaviour that 'the quality of teaching, learning and behaviour are inseparable' and the principle that the management of behaviour and the management of learning should be aligned and consistent.**

59. **Government intervention in pedagogy, whether through the national strategies or by other means, may have helped some teachers but in general has been excessive and sometimes ill-founded conceptually and empirically. Earlier governments were correct in their insistence that 'questions about how to teach are not for government to determine'. Central prescription of teaching methods and lesson content should now cease. Teaching should be taken out of the political arena and given back to teachers. There is a necessary relationship between how teachers think about their practice and how pupils learn. Pupils will not learn to think for themselves if their teachers are expected merely to do as they are told.**

60. **We need now to move to a position where research-grounded teaching repertoires and principles are introduced through initial training and refined and extended through experience and CPD, and teachers acquire as much command of the evidence and principles which underpin the repertoires as they do of the skills needed in their use. The test of this alternative view of professionalism is that teachers should be able to give a coherent justification for their practices citing (i) evidence, (ii) pedagogical principle and (iii) educational aim, rather than offering the unsafe defence of compliance with what others expect. Anything less is educationally unsound.**

61. **We do not nominate any 'best buys' from recent pedagogical research, and indeed would strongly discourage the chasing of pedagogical fads and fashions. At the same time, we note the extent to which research from many different sources converges on language, and especially spoken language, as one of the keys to cognitive development, learning and successful teaching, and indeed to the learner's later employment and democratic engagement. In many classrooms, notwithstanding the greater emphasis now given to the national curriculum's somewhat weakly-framed 'speaking and listening', talk remains far from achieving its true potential. We urge all concerned, especially teachers and researchers, to act together to effect the pedagogical transformation which is needed, and which in some schools and local authorities has already begun.**

ASSESSMENT AND TESTING (CHAPTERS 16 AND 17)

62. The world of assessment has changed radically since the time of Plowden. In 1967, the discourse was dominated by assessment for selection, and was mostly concerned with the pros and cons of IQ tests. In 2009, while testing is very much to the fore, there is recognition

that assessment has purposes other than selection, particularly for helping learning, and that it can be conducted in many different ways. The government's publication of an assessment for learning (AfL) strategy in 2008, despite the proliferation of tests and targets, recognises the role of assessment in learning and of teachers' judgements in assessing pupils' progress. However, questions have been raised about the interpretation of AfL in the context of current policy, and it is important that the research-informed principles enunciated by the Assessment Reform Group remain to the fore.

63. That said, primary pupils in England are tested more frequently and at an earlier age than in most other countries, and in public and political discussion testing is frequently equated with assessment. This is a serious error – linguistically, technically and educationally. It generates excessive faith in the power and outcomes of tests and diminishes the use of other kinds of assessment which have greater diagnostic and pedagogical value. Testing is just one kind of assessment among several.

64. It is often claimed in defence of national tests that they raise standards. In fact, at best the impact of national tests on standards is oblique. The prospect of testing, especially high-stakes testing undertaken in the public arena, forces teachers, pupils and parents to concentrate their attention on those areas of learning to be tested, too often to the exclusion of other activities of considerable educational importance. It is this intensity of focus, and anxiety about the results and their consequences, which make the initial difference to test scores. But it is essentially a halo effect, and it does not last; for it is not testing which raises standards but good teaching. The point is obvious but needs to be underlined. Conversely, if testing distorts teaching and the curriculum, as evidence from the Review and elsewhere shows that it does, it may actually depress standards properly defined.

65. Contrary to some claims about testing, it produces results which have lower validity and reliability than is generally assumed. Another myth about testing is that it objectively compensates for teachers' over-favourable judgements about their pupils. In fact, the evidence shows that teachers' ratings of their pupils' attainment, based on a far wider range of evidence, are likely to be lower than their test scores.

66. Use of SAT results to evaluate teachers, schools and local authorities puts pressure on teachers which is transferred to pupils to the detriment of their learning experiences. The process also places heavy and perhaps excessive demands on teachers' and pupils' time, and on local and national resources. What others have called the fiasco of the marking of the 2008 SATs – which left thousands of papers unmarked even after the results had been announced – raises serious questions about the cost-effectiveness and feasibility of the current system, as well as its reliability and validity.

67. Test results are not the best source of data for the multiple functions they perform – measuring pupils' attainment, school and teacher accountability and national monitoring. Despite government claims, the use of aggregated test results as a basis for evaluating schools does not provide a fair picture, even when the disputed 'contextual value-added' scores are used. This high-stakes use of test results leads to practices that not only have negative impact on pupils but fail to provide valid information, being based on what can be assessed in time-limited written tests in at most three subjects. The use of the same data for national monitoring also means that we have extremely limited information, collected under stressful conditions, which provides little useful data about national levels of performance and even less about how to improve them. The aggregation of SAT results for monitoring national levels of performance fails to reflect achievements in the full range of the curriculum. It is difficult to understand how these arguments can have been accepted in relation to key stage 3, according to the Secretary of State's statement of 14 October 2008,[4] but not for key stage 2.

68. There is an urgent need for a thorough reform of the assessment system in England, going well beyond the May 2009 report of the DCSF 'expert group', to provide a coherent set of practices and procedures suiting the aims of education in the 21st century and to meet the needs for information about the performance of individual pupils, schools, local authorities and the system as a whole. At the heart of this should be the use of assessment to help

learning, leading to the development of lifelong learners. **This should be supported by a system for summarising, reporting and accrediting children's performance that provides information about all aspects of learning, and work on the report card proposals contained in the 2009 White Paper should acknowledge both this need and the methodological challenges involved. Separate systems are also required for the external evaluation of schools and for monitoring national standards of performance.**

69. **No single assessment procedure, including statutory assessment, should be expected to perform both formative and summative functions. Assessment for learning, as defined by the Assessment Reform Group, should be uncoupled from assessment for accountability.**

70. **Children's learning across all aspects of the curriculum, including their developing capacity to learn, should be assessed formatively throughout the primary phase and summatively before transfer to secondary school. This is not straightforward technically, and on the basis of past experience the dangers of a simplistic and reductionist approach are all too evident. Moving to valid, reliable and properly moderated procedures for a broader approach to assessment will require careful research and deliberation.**

71. **The Review fully accepts the need for summative assessment at the point where pupils move from primary to secondary education. But while the assessment of literacy and numeracy is essential, a broader, more innovative approach to summative assessment is needed if children's achievements and attainments across the curriculum are to be properly recognised and parents, teachers and children themselves are to have the vital information they need to guide subsequent decisions and choices. Work is now urgently needed on the development of a comprehensive and coherent framework of summative assessment that can be administered unobtrusively and with minimum disruption towards the end of the primary phase.**

72. **The use of the results of statutory assessment at key stage 2 for monitoring national performance in primary education should be replaced by sample testing using a bank of varied items covering the curriculum as a whole.**

73. **The practice of publishing primary school performance tables (now known as primary school achievement and attainment tables) based on the results of statutory assessment in English and mathematics at the end of key stage 2 should be abandoned.**

74. **At the time of going to press, it is rumoured that in response to pressure from the House of Commons Select Committee, several of the teaching unions, the Assessment Reform Group and this Review, the key stage 2 tests may be replaced by procedures more in line with what we have recommended. We shall be delighted if our earlier published concerns have been heeded and the recommendations above prove to be superfluous. [For update see pp. 513–4].**

QUALITY, STANDARDS AND ACCOUNTABILITY (CHAPTERS 17 AND 23)

75. The official evidence on whether standards in primary education have improved is unsafe. At its heart are two areas of difficulty: the validity and reliability of the chosen measures and procedures; and the historical tendency to treat test scores in limited aspects of literacy and numeracy as proxies for standards in education as a whole.

76. At the national level, the assumption that aggregating individual pupils' test results in only three subjects enables trends in attained standards to be identified is problematic. Although the statistics can be computed, their meaning in terms of changes in attainment are brought into question by the limited range of what is tested, by limitations in test technology and by the impact of using the results for high-stakes judgements. We are left with little sound information about whether pupils' attained standards have changed.

77. Subject to these substantial caveats, analysis of national test scores and international achievement surveys appears to show that standards of tested attainment in primary education have been fairly stable over the short period that usable data have been available, with some changes up or down. Pupils' attitudes to their learning in the tested areas are generally positive (though, as is generally found internationally, they appear to decline as pupils approach the end of primary education). There have been modest improvements

in primary mathematics standards, especially since 1995, though different datasets tell different stories. The international data from 2001 show high standards in reading among English pupils by comparison with those from other countries, though the more recent data (from 2006 onwards) suggest that the 2001 results may have been misleading. England appears to be above the international average but not exceptionally so. The international data also show considerable improvements in primary science by comparison with other countries, though there have been methodological reservations about the studies in question.

78. However, gains in reading skills may sometimes have been at the expense of pupils' enjoyment of reading. Similarly, there is some evidence of an increase in test-induced stress among primary pupils, especially at key stage 2, and much firmer evidence of pressure on their teachers. The primary curriculum has narrowed in direct response to the perceived demands of the testing regime and the national strategies, to the extent that in many schools children's statutory entitlement to a broad and balanced curriculum has been seriously compromised; yet the national strategies have had, of themselves, a less pronounced impact on reading standards than might have been expected from the level of investment. The historically wide gap between high and low attaining pupils in reading, mathematics and science has persisted: it is already evident at a very young age and widens as children move through the primary phase. There is no reliable evidence on national standards in areas of children's learning outside those aspects of literacy, numeracy and science which have been tested, other than that in many schools such learning appears to have been compromised by the standards drive itself.

79. Schools acknowledge the importance of being held accountable for their work and accept the need for periodic inspection. Ofsted produces useful annual reports on the condition of the system as a whole and surveys on particular issues, on many of which the Review has drawn to its considerable benefit. The collation of evidence from inspections can be used to provide a reasonably valid, if partial, assessment of the quality of English primary education nationally at a particular time, assuming that the Ofsted criteria and procedures are accepted. However, Ofsted's school inspection procedures attract a good deal of criticism in relation to their validity, reliability and impact; and because of frequent changes to inspection criteria and procedures, allied to the subjective nature of the process, it is much more difficult to say with confidence whether the overall quality of primary education has improved, deteriorated or remained the same over time. The same difficulty attends Ofsted inspections of individual schools. Such judgements are compromised by the successive changes Ofsted has instituted in inspection criteria and methodology and by its employment of different teams from one school inspection to the next. Temporal comparisons and claims about long-term trends based on Ofsted data are thus highly problematic.

80. **Teachers and schools can and should have a greater role in the assessment of their pupils and in the evaluation of their provision for learning. In the case of pupil assessment, there is an overwhelming case for extending the range of aspects of attainment that are included in reporting attained standards and in identifying the standards to aim for. At present the pupil attainment data reflect only a small part of the curriculum and within that only aspects which are easily measured by written tests. Greater use of information that teachers can collect as part of their teaching can help learning and, suitably moderated, can provide information which is a better reflection of performance acoss the full range of the curriculum. Similarly there is a strong case for moderated school self-evaluation across the full range of provision. Such evaluation should help the school's own improvement agenda and not simply be instituted to meet Ofsted requirements.**

81. **Current notions of 'standards' and 'quality' should be replaced by a more comprehensive framework which relates to the entirety of what a school does and how it performs. The Review's proposed statement of aims for primary education might provide the overall criteria for progress and success, combined with appropriate indicators for each of the proposed new aims and curriculum domains. However, we warn against moving from indicators of what can fairly be observed and judged to so-called measures of what cannot in fact be measured.**

82. Monitoring the performance of the national system of primary education is technically challenging and requires a form of data collection which is different from that which is optimal to promote school and classroom improvement. New provision is recommended, using robust national sampling and building on the lessons of the Assessment of Performance Unit and work in Scotland.

83. A new model for school inspection should be explored, with a substantially increased focus on classroom practice, pupil learning and the curriculum as a whole, and within a framework of accountability which directly reinforces processes of school improvement.

84. Every effort should be made, at school, local and national levels, to ensure that curriculum, pedagogy, assessment, inspection and teacher training all pull in the same direction and are clearly informed by educational aims and procedural principles such as those proposed in Chapter 12.

85. We take it as axiomatic that in a public system of education teachers and schools should be fully accountable to parents, children, government and the electorate for what they do. We reject any suggestion that our proposals for the reform of assessment and inspection imply otherwise. For us, the issue is not whether schools should be accountable, but for what and by what means, and the evidence shows that current approaches are in certain respects unsatisfactory. By insisting on a concept of standards which extends across the full curriculum rather than part of it, we are strengthening rather than weakening school accountability. It is no less important that others involved in primary education, including central and local government, are fully accountable for their part in the process. When responsibilities are shared, accountability should be shared too in order that the precise cause of problems can be speedily and accurately diagnosed and appropriate remedial action can be taken. Governments and policy advisers have been too inclined to blame teachers and a mythical 'educational establishment' for problems which are as likely to have their roots in policy.

PRIMARY SCHOOLS (CHAPTERS 18 AND 19)

86. Children of primary age in England are educated in 17,300 schools varying in size, organization and status: schools of over 1,000 pupils and fewer than 20; infant, junior, primary, first, middle, combined and a few all-age schools; community, foundation, voluntary aided, voluntary controlled and trust schools; buildings erected in the past year or two and buildings dating back to the mid-19th century (and in a few cases to centuries earlier). In addition, some of the nation's children are educated in the 5,000 supplementary schools and at home, while education also takes place in theatres, concert halls, museums, sports stadia and forest schools.

87. Schools are buildings, patterns of organisation and communities of people and ideas. One of the great strengths of English primary education is its interweaving of these elements, and its desire to make schools much more than places where children gather and are taught. This idea resurfaced with added poignancy when witnesses reflected on the condition of contemporary society outside the school gates. If communities are in decline, then schools can help to counter the trend. They both provide a focal point for their locality and embody what 'community' at best entails: shared values, a sense of interdependence, mutual concern and support, and a preparedness to show collective solidarity when the need arises.

88. The potential of schools both *in* and *as* communities has been highlighted in our list of proposed aims for primary education, where we argue that schools should 'enact the behaviours and relationships on which community most directly depends, and in so doing counter the loss of community outside the school.' But we have gone further, proposing that schools should see themselves as sites for cultural celebration and regeneration. Policy, we suggest, 'has paid little attention to the cultural and communal significance of primary schools and their pupils, except perhaps in the context of decisions about rural school closures, and then only after the event, as it were. This is a grave omission. To establish itself as a thriving cultural and communal site should be a principal aim of every school.'

89. Yet if we add to this mix recent developments in citizenship education, children's voice and communities of learning, we find that while the affective and interpersonal dimensions of community have long been cherished in primary schools, there may be some way to go before this newer democratisation of school life is fully achieved. School councils and the current interest in dialogic modes of teaching are important first steps. When to this we add the idea of extended schools and the integration of schools and other local children's services in accordance with *Every Child Matters* and the Children's Plan, it is clear that the very concept of a school must change.

90. The Review's evidence includes expressions of considerable concern not just about the current condition of school buildings, but also about the lack of fit between design and function. Space formulae were often viewed as inadequate and there was particular criticism of the loss of appropriate external space not just for sport and play but also for study.

91. Witnesses also complained of the limited availability of specialist facilities for science, art, music and children with special needs. Primary schools have traditionally been built to a very simple brief: classrooms for generalist teaching; a multi-purpose hall for assembly, music, physical education and dining; offices, cloakrooms and so on. As the functions of schools diversify, additional specialist facilities become more necessary.

92. There is growing concern that school libraries are becoming a casualty of the modernisation drive, with their place being taken by banks of computers. The Review's curriculum proposals underline the importance of ICT, but to see screens as the 21st century replacement for books is a grave mistake. Books and ICT are complementary, not alternatives.

93. The government's extended schools programme has given new impetus to old debates about the length of the school day and term, and the structure of the school year. Schools now have 'power to innovate' with the length and form of the day, and an increasing number of local authorities have moved to a year containing six terms of roughly equal length. Yet the long summer break remains a throwback to a more rural past, and witnesses were concerned that this leaves many of today's predominantly urban children unattended for long periods of time.

94. Like the class teacher system and the structure of the school year, the ages and stages of primary education have historical provenance rather than, necessarily, contemporary currency. The old infant/junior structure persists largely unchallenged, but the more recent experiment in 8–12 and 9–13 middle schools seems already to be in terminal decline. However, we heard strong arguments in favour of the latter arrangement from teachers, and from parents who were worried about their children growing up too soon. (The considerable concern about the starting age for compulsory schooling has already been discussed.)

95. Though primary/secondary transfer may remain a cause for anxiety, commendable steps have been taken in recent years to secure effective pastoral liaison between schools and years, to enlist teachers, parents and carers in support of successful transfer, and to involve pupils themselves as fully as possible in discussion about what transfer entails. Curriculum continuity, however, remains problematic.

96. There is considerable debate about the ideal size of primary school, and the point below which in terms of pupil numbers a school ceases to be viable. Paradoxically however, while large schools may offer a broader array of resources and pedagogical possibilities, and their per-pupil unit costs are considerably lower than those of small schools, schools with fewer than 100 pupils appear to achieve better key stage test results. Ofsted evidence suggests that this difference is cultural – reflecting the way they are run, how they relate to parents, and the kinds of community they serve – rather than the result of size alone. On the other hand, as their supporters insist, the size and culture of small schools are related. In any event, the Review heard powerful advocacy for smaller primary schools on educational grounds, as well as the more familiar arguments against the closure of village schools because of their contribution to community vitality and indeed viability.

97. The debate about class sizes also persists, and the Review's witnesses unite in pressing for smaller classes than the current norm. However, research suggests that class effects are most evident with the youngest pupils, particularly for those pupils with most ground to make up in literacy, and that smaller classes may be advantageous immediately after transfer from one educational phase to the next.

98. Primary schools tend to resist forming classes according to children's 'abilities', preferring within-class grouping. Most primary pupils are taught in mixed-ability classes with within-class ability groups for some subjects. Setting may occur in larger schools, in the higher year groups and for those subjects that are subject to national assessment, particularly mathematics. The evidence suggests no consistent effects of structured ability grouping on attainment, though there may be detrimental social and personal effects for some children. The quality of teaching is more important.

99. Government initiatives have increased the amount of whole-class teaching. It remains the case, as in the 1970s, that while pupils may sit *in* groups they are much less likely to work *as* groups, despite powerful evidence now available on the learning potential of well-structured collaborative tasks and the wider consensus, mentioned earlier, on the need to maximise the interactive possibilities of teaching.

100. **The government's Primary Capital Programme intends to close or rebuild the five per cent of primary schools which are in worst condition, and by 2023 will rebuild, refurbish or remodel at least 50 per cent of the rest. Assuming that PCP does not fall victim to the current recession, it is important that it reflects changing views of the purpose and character of schools, and that it involves, in line with the recognition of the significance of children's voices, consultation with learners as well as teachers. It should be taken as axiomatic that schools should become as far as possible environmentally sustainable.**

101. **In refurbishing and rebuilding schools, government, local authorities and governing bodies should note their increasing need not only for generalist classrooms but also for dedicated specialist space and better outdoor facilities. If staffing patterns change in the way the Review's evidence suggests that they should, then this kind of flexibility will become even more important and should be built into models for costing.**

102. **The Review supports the concern expressed by some of its witnesses and by distinguished figures elsewhere about the reduction or demise of school libraries, whether on grounds of cost or in pursuit of a misconceived notion that computers are all that a child needs. Books make a unique and irreplaceable contribution to children's development, education and inner lives, and the Review strongly opposes moves to reduce children's access to them.**

103. **Discussion should be re-opened on the length and structure of the school year, paying attention to the length of holidays as well as terms.**

104. **Initiatives like *Every Child Matters* and the Children's Plan are changing the remit of primary schools, while this Review has argued for schools' enhanced role both in and as communities. At the same time there are pressures to extend schools' specialist space and resources, outside as well as inside the school building. For all these reasons, and to avoid piecemeal initiative-specific development, there should be a full discussion on the concept of a primary school for the first part of the 21st century. This should articulate with the Primary Capital Programme rather than be separate from it. Such discussion should avoid futurist gimmickry.**

105. **There should be a presumption against the closure of any school exclusively on the grounds of size, especially when against higher unit costs can be set a record of higher pupil attainment in the KS2 tests or good quality as judged by Ofsted inspectors. This applies particularly to small rural schools, which are an irreplaceable community asset and are highly valued by those they serve.**

106. **Arguments about school character and viability tend to look at each school in isolation. Recent trends towards between-school co-operation helpfully discourage this and should be pressed further. Co-operation and the pooling or exchange of resources, including staff, can work across phases (for example between primary and secondary) as well as within them.**

The potential of clustering, federation and all-through schools should be fully explored, not just at the level of headship – for this is not just about the streamlining of management – but also to ensure the best possible use of professional expertise in support of children's entitlement to exemplary teaching across the full curriculum, in accordance with recommendation 125.

107. Local authorities responsible for England's remaining first and middle schools should not lightly dismiss the case for their retention based on the developmental benefits for their pupils.

108. The distinctive educational uses of whole-class teaching, group, paired and individual work need to be better understood. The collaborative potential of group work should be more fully exploited.

109. While considerable steps have been taken to ease pupil transfer from primary to secondary school, greater consideration should be given to a co-ordinated, systemic view of children's schooling through all its statutory phases. The reduction of the pre-secondary phases from three to two (foundation and primary) would help (recommendation 28). Achieving this kind of coherence is entirely consistent with the Review's belief that the distinctiveness of each phase must be preserved.

SCHOOLS AND OTHER AGENCIES (CHAPTER 20)

110. A child's chances of flourishing at school rest not just on the broad shoulders of the education service but also – of course – on parents and carers and on other public services. There is broad professional agreement that policies such as *Every Child Matters* and *Narrowing the Gap*, which necessitate an integrated approach, are the right way to go, and those children who have been surveyed about the changes believe this too. But there is also concern that the process is complex, progress is slow and the challenges to primary schools are very demanding. The reality for many primary schools is that the quality of joined-up working remains variable, particularly in rural areas.

111. Thus, the Review received evidence that services are sometimes nominally linked but not 'joined up' in any meaningful sense; that contact between schools and children's trusts may be limited; that barriers to communication and collaboration across professions are deep-seated and resistant to change. Schools and teachers' associations complained of a conflict of agendas between local authority children's services and schools, and about the loss from local authorities of genuinely educational expertise. They identified tensions between raising standards of pupil attainment and achieving a genuinely inclusive system, and warned that children with special educational needs are at risk from this. They also warned against inappropriate extension of the target culture. The message that integration needs time and a period of stability came through strongly in the Review's evidence.

112. There are also concerns about where the centre of gravity for the changes properly lies. As the hub of their communities and the one place where almost all children go, schools expect to be central to ECM and to decisions about what children need. Yet they complained both of being pushed to the margins and, paradoxically, in an era of integration some schools felt more isolated from local authority support than previously. Extended schools produced a mixed response. There were concerns that 8am to 6pm is too long, and that it may represent an excessive encroachment on children's time and lives.

113. While a multi-agency approach can help all pupils, gaps remain. The children still most likely to slip through the net are the ones in greatest need: under any system this is bound to be so. Early evaluations showed that Sure Start was failing to reach the most vulnerable families. Similar criticisms have been made of extended schools. Again, though, there appears to have been progress – the most recent evaluation of Sure Start children's centres found they were helping other three-year-olds in their areas. And there is now greater clarity about what schools need to do to reach marginalised families.

114. **The Review strongly supports the aims and implementation of *Every Child Matters*, and the vision of genuinely joined-up services for children's education and care which it offers. It supports the policy of developing primary schools as community hubs, as providers of extended services and effective multi-agency working. However, the complexity and challenges of translating policy into practice in an area involving so many different agencies, professionals and traditions will require constant vigilance, together with a review of resource allocations and their deployment at a local community level.**

115. **Primary schools need stronger support in ensuring that the range of professionals working in schools to meet the additional needs of pupils, particularly those in vulnerable families and those with mental health needs, are working as a cohesive team, in partnership with parents, in order to improve outcomes for all and to narrow the achievement gap for more vulnerable children.**

116. **The operation and viability of the extended schools initiative should be kept under close review.**

117. **Research should be undertaken and effectively disseminated into the still novel field of professional collaboration in a multi-agency world, in order to help those concerned overcome barriers and achieve productive working relations. The government, understandably, wishes to achieve a 'step change' in this area, especially in light of recent tragic cases involving vulnerable children. But its policies will be more effective if the views of all involved are elicited and properly heeded, and the problems they identify are tackled in a way which balances progress with the widely-urged need for stability.**

TEACHERS: EXPERTISE, TRAINING AND DEPLOYMENT (CHAPTERS 14, 15 AND 21)

118. Though in recent years the range of professional roles in and around primary schools has diversified, and the introduction of teaching assistants has spearheaded a welcome and much-needed expansion of professional support, the core roles remain those of class teacher and head. The generalist class teacher system was introduced in the 19th century as the cheapest way of delivering a narrow curriculum to large classes. Now, classes may be smaller, but the curriculum has expanded and become much more complex and professionally demanding, while teaching is understood to entail a great deal more than transmission and rote learning. While we respect the loyalty which the class teacher system attracts, and the prospects for a holistic approach to children's education which it offers, it would be irresponsible for an enquiry such as this to avoid the question of how far the class teacher system remains able to serve the full range of children's educational needs, and the related question of how well initial training serves the needs of class teachers. Evidence from enquiries undertaken by HMI and Ofsted going back to 1978 shows a system under increasing stress and in need of appropriate expert support.

119. Such questions beg others about the nature of expertise for primary teaching. Here the views from policy and research are somewhat different. Teacher training requirements have shifted from a specification of the kinds of knowledge which it is assumed that teachers need to instrumental but not very specific accounts of skill, allied to policy-driven information which teachers are expected to know and with which they are expected to comply. In contrast, European comparisons open up the well-developed fields of pedagogy and didactics, while transatlantic research has produced taxonomies which include both different domains of professional knowledge (of children, curriculum, pedagogy, pedagogical content, aims, contexts and so on) and professional knowledge of different kinds (public and personal, disciplinary and craft). What is beyond question is that a primary teacher, like any other teacher, needs a deep understanding of what is to be taught and how, and this is precisely the point of sharpest vulnerability for both the class teacher system and current patterns of initial teacher training, especially the one-year PGCE.

120. But individuals' expertise is dynamic, experiential and changing rather than static. The government's approach conceives of teachers' development as progress through five career points, from newly-qualified (Q) to 'advanced skills' (A), introduced as part of the

recent workforce reforms. Once again there is dissonance between policy and the evidence from research. The government's model proposes the same basic repertoire at every stage, while research shows many teachers at the start of their career operating, and needing to operate, within a limited repertoire governed by rules. Conformity to rules, or at least to approved versions of what good teaching entails, is fundamental to the government model, but its problem is that the teacher is expected to remain subservient to these throughout his or her career. In contrast, research shows expert teachers not only acting differently from novices but also thinking in fundamentally different ways. These advanced modes of professional thinking are also tacit and less readily codified and generalised. Just as many novices need the security of rules and a bounded repertoire (hence their greater support for the national strategies), so experts need to be freed from rules and prescriptions and given the liberty to operate autonomously, creatively and instinctively.

121. What emerges with some force from these comparisons is the worrying possibility that TDA standards for teachers aimed at raising standards of pupil learning may actually depress them: first, by so constraining experienced and talented teachers that they may not operate as effectively as they are able; second, by allowing the unique talent of some of our very best teachers to go unrecognised because its idiosyncrasy places it beyond the reach of the approved narrow account of excellence. We have to ask where the TDA standards came from and why they were apparently not validated by reference to professional development research or pupil learning outcomes. In contrast, in both the United States and Australia considerable efforts have been taken to come up with professional performance standards which bear empirical scrutiny and can be shown to relate indicators of professional excellence to high levels of pupil attainment.

122. In light of these concerns about the nature of teaching expertise and the trajectory of teacher development, we must question Ofsted claims about the 'best ever' quality of ITT not only on methodological grounds. So much that is essential to professional 'standards' is missing, particularly in respect of pedagogy, pedagogical content knowledge in other than the national curriculum core subjects, wider engagement with matters of curriculum and epistemology at a level which will help raise the quality of curriculum discourse, and the development of respect for evidence, open debate and a sense of the problematic.

123. Continuing professional development has moved away from its former goal of helping teachers to develop as individual professionals and hence make a better contribution to the work of their schools. Now CPD is largely dominated by the policy agenda of the day and this is presumed to define the needs of schools and teachers too. Again, this model sits uneasily with research-based accounts of professional development and professional excellence. While such a model may be apposite for less experienced teachers it appears not to serve the needs of more advanced practitioners. In the Review's submissions and soundings, teachers themselves endorsed this criticism, finding much policy-informed CPD insufficiently challenging.

124. When we return to the matter of the future of the class teacher system, we have to accept the possibility that the government's 'quarts into pint pots' remit for the Rose curriculum review has fundamentally missed the point, and has used the curriculum as the safety-valve for a problem which at root is about the mismatch between schools' educational tasks and professional resources. Thus, 150 years on from Robert Lowe's promise for 'the education of the poor, or primary education' that 'if it is not efficient it shall be cheap', a curriculum is made 'manageable' by trimming the education rather than increasing the resources.

125. **The long-standing failure to resolve the mismatch between the curriculum to be taught, the focus of teacher training and the staffing of primary schools must be resolved without further delay. The principle to be applied is the one of entitlement adopted throughout this report: *children have a right to a curriculum which is consistently well taught regardless of the perceived significance of its various elements or the amount of time devoted to them.***

126. **Primary schools should be staffed with sufficient flexibility to allow the above principle to be applied. This will require an increase in staffing along the lines recommended in previous**

enquiries, though alternatives to the models proposed in the 1978 HMI survey, the 1986 Select Committee report, the 1992 DES report and the 2008 Williams report should also be explored, as should curriculum- and activity-led staffing models.

127. The urgency of this task, and its potential cost, require a full national primary staffing review on the relationship between (i) the curricular and other tasks of primary schools as they are now conceived, (ii) the roles and numbers of teachers and other professionals required, (iii) the expertise and training/retraining which this analysis dictates, (iv) the recruitment of appropriately-qualified graduates to primary PGCE courses (bearing in mind, for example, the Royal Society's evidence on a sharp decline in the number of mathematics and science graduates entering these courses). The potential to tackle this problem through clustering, federation, resource-sharing, teacher exchange and all-through schools should also be examined.

128. Identifying options is essential, for the debate on this matter needs to move beyond the simple opposition of 'generalists' and 'specialists' and we wish it to be clearly understood that we are not proposing the summary curtailing of the established system of primary-school staffing. Thus, a fully generalist approach might be maintained for the early primary years with a generalist/specialist mixture in upper primary. Capacity could be strengthened by having more than one model of initial training, say (i) fully generalist, (ii) generalist with specialism as, with many ITT programmes, at present, (iii) combined-domain specialist (perhaps two or three domains), (iv) single-domain specialist.

129. For as long as initial teacher training is directed at the role of generalist class teacher, it will be hard pressed to provide what is required, especially on the one-year PGCE route. The possibility of a two-year PGCE, as discussed during the 1980s, should be revisited. At the same time, the content should be refocused so as to ensure that the training and the NQT's classroom role are properly aligned.

130. Initial teacher training and continuing professional development should move from models premised on compliance with national strategies and received official wisdom to critical engagement, on the basis that this not only makes for better teaching, but is a minimal position from which to advance the empowerment, autonomy and citizenship of the pupil. This principle should be noted by those responsible for developing the new Master's in Teaching and Learning programme (MTL). Initial teacher training should give greater attention to (i) pedagogy as discussed in this report, (ii) recent research on the social, emotional and developmental contexts of, and strategies, for learning, teaching and assessment, (iii) developing expertise in all aspects of the curriculum to be taught, (iv) understanding of the wider discourse of curriculum, knowledge and skill.

131. The TDA professional standards should be reviewed. They are empirically unsafe as well as too vague to be useful. If there are to be standards relating to different points in teachers' professional development (and that is debatable), they should be properly validated by reference to research on professional development and to pupil learning outcomes. If teachers now operate within a system which may discourage or even prevent many of them from progressing beyond the stage of external support or dependence to self-regulation or autonomy, and if there are experienced teachers who are content not to move beyond the first stage, then that should give everyone, not just the teaching profession, cause for considerable concern.

132. While the recent and considerable expansion of teaching assistants has proved a boon to many schools, liberating teachers from some of the more routine tasks which diminish time spent with children, it should be clearly signalled that the use of TAs as teachers is unacceptable. Auxiliary staff should not be regarded as an alternative to the expansion of high-level teaching expertise, and therefore teacher numbers.

133. To date, evidence suggests that TAs have little discernible effect on children's achievement, while TAs report being under-prepared for their tasks. They need training for the situations they most commonly encounter, especially working with small groups and with children with special educational needs.

TEACHERS: STATUS, LEADERSHIP AND WORKFORCE REFORM (CHAPTER 22)

134. The working environment of the primary school has been radically transformed over the past 20 years. The profession's career structure has been reformed, performance-related pay introduced, the workforce 'remodelled', and national qualifications and standards brought in for head teachers. All these changes have impacted on senior management's scope for making decisions. Head teachers, once the undisputed and independent leaders of their schools, now operate in a culture of compliance, yet one that, borrowing the language of business, paradoxically exhorts them by turns to be 'visionary', 'invitational', 'democratic', 'strategic', or 'transformational'.

135. The rhetoric, vocabulary and literature of leadership may have expanded, but in practice it is still the individual occupant of the head teacher's office who is burdened with a proliferating range of responsibilities and accountabilities. When the price of these pressures is too often paid in physical and mental health, it is no longer tenable for any one person to assume such a complex portfolio of tasks. Distributed leadership has therefore commended itself to policy-makers and others as the answer to the problem. Yet the term conceals more than it reveals. It may be interpreted as a matter of delegating tasks in accordance with role and status or, less mechanistically, as an organic process in which all staff feel free to take the initiative. Both interpretations are problematic within a remodelled workforce. The first with its clearly demarcated roles may be efficient but at the same time frustrate initiative, creativity and teamwork. The second encourages a free flow of activity and shared responsibility, but may also be impervious to professional qualifications, status and identity.

136. Evidence to the Review reveals serious concerns about low status, loss of professionalism and lack of trust by government as indicated by the relentless tide of often contradictory initiatives and expectations. As teachers try to resolve 'the irresolvable contradiction of excellence and enjoyment', many find their professional identity in a state of continual flux. Yet, while some teachers have come to value the structures and methods they have been forced to adopt – and may be beginning to use these more flexibly – the strategies and reforms have not brought about engagement with fundamental pedagogical issues. As long as there are SATs, league tables, and national strategies which though non-statutory are to all intents and purposes obligatory, the professionalism that seeks to encourage children's creativity, curiosity and well-being is likely to remain enfeebled by intense demands for accountability. [For update see pp. 513–4].

137. We are no less concerned by evidence to the Review which suggests a split in the primary workforce between those who welcome the prescriptions of the national agencies and their local authority counterparts, and those who resent being told what to do and how to think, and deplore both the compliance culture and the dependence on others for ideas that it has fostered. To some extent this split is age-related. Its persistence may limit what schools and their leaders can achieve.

138. **There must be a continued effort to improve the prestige of primary education and the status of its teachers by increasing public awareness of their qualifications and their professional parity with secondary teachers. Raising the qualification ceiling and giving more primary teachers opportunities to engage in professionally-related research would help this process.**

139. **Primary head teacher posts will only be made more attractive to potential school leaders when their clear priority is on pupil, professional and organisational learning. The focus needs to be one which enables school leaders to develop a culture in which internal school accountability for the quality of teaching and learning precedes and shapes external accountability. This rests on the development of trust, and openness to collegial support and challenge. For primary headship to be genuinely attractive it requires tangible evidence that policy makers value pedagogy informed by research, and allow latitude for leadership to motivate and inspire those who want the very best for children and their families.**

140. **Primary head teachers should benefit from a quality of support which on the one hand allows them to create optimal conditions for learning and teaching and, on the other, which promotes effective collaboration with external agencies, recognising that barriers to learning very often lie in the interface of school and home, peer group and neighbourhood. Inter-agency work cannot be simply mandated, as it is an area fraught with competing priorities, languages and conventions, and micropolitics. Sensitivity to those difficulties needs to be supported by opportunities for professional (and inter-professional) development.**

141. **Some larger primary schools have diversified their management support roles to include bursars and business managers, where funding permits. Just as busy general medical practices now have practice managers to help them cope with the expanding array of tasks outside basic patient care which GPs are required to undertake, so this model should be explored in the context of schools, and funded if appropriate. We repeat: heads should not be distracted from the job for which they are most needed – leading learning.**

142. **Recruitment of head teachers needs to be alert to the often hidden potential of classroom teachers and the leadership activities in which they currently engage. This presumes sources of support which help head teachers to recognise ways in which inherent talent may be nurtured and how to put in place sequential and structured pathways to headship ('entering from the shallow end'). Consideration should also be given to ways of extending the conventional pool of potential recruits if senior leaders are to meet the growing complexities, responsibilities and accountabilities of their roles.**

GOVERNANCE, FUNDING AND POLICY (CHAPTERS 3 AND 23)

143. England's system of primary education has three main levels: national, local and school. At the national level there are government, the DCSF and the non-departmental public bodies such as Ofsted, QCA, TDA, the National College for School Leadership and, at one stage removed, the General Teaching Council for England. Locally, local authority children's services combine their traditional responsibilities for schools with children's well-being and protection. At the point of delivery are the schools and their governing bodies. The balance of control and responsibility between these different levels was initially just one theme among 10 in the Review's remit. But what has emerged as a meta-theme, surfacing time and again in the Review's evidence and in each of this report's chapters, is centralisation: the provable fact that since 1989, and especially since 1997, national government has tightened its control over what goes on in local authorities and schools; and the perception that the power of government and its agencies has reached far more deeply into the recesses of professional action and thought than is proper in a democracy or good for schools themselves.

144. It would of course be wrong to infer that government intervention is never justified. Since 1997, funding for primary education has increased massively. The policy prospectus has included ambitious initiatives relating to children and families, early childhood, curriculum, pedagogy, standards and accountability, teachers and workforce reform, and national and local infrastructure. In the policy balance sheet the case for a national curriculum is generally accepted; the government's childhood agenda is warmly applauded; its obligation to step in to protect vulnerable children is understood; the move to integrated services for education and care, first recommended by Plowden in 1967, is welcomed, though like the EYFS it is viewed as sounder in principle than in practice (which could reasonably be put down to teething problems).

145. However, opinion is divided on workforce reform and the national strategies, and such division escalates into deep and widespread hostility when we move into the remainder of the flagship 'standards' agenda – national targets, testing, performance tables and the current practices of external inspection (as opposed to the principle, which is generally supported). However, we emphasise that the debate is not about the pursuit of standards as such – and indeed this Review proposes an even more rigorous concept of standards,

covering the entire curriculum, than the one currently in operation – but about the way they have been defined and measured, and the strategies through which government has attempted to improve them.

146. Ministers might respond that popularity is less important than effectiveness, and that teachers may not like pedagogical prescription or testing but at least these have delivered much-needed improvements. Here, therefore, we turn from opinion to hard evidence, and we find it to be mixed. Within the limitations and variations of the methods used (which, especially before 2000, were considerable) and subject to the crucial proviso that Year 6 test scores constitute a very restricted concept of educational standards, we find claims about improvements in reading, numeracy and science which are, up to a point, reasonably secure. Alongside those, however, we are forced to rank evidence about the adverse side effects of testing, the limited impact of the literacy strategy, and the persistence of the 'long tail' of underachievement. We also note the testing system's lower level of dependability before 2000, which makes trends over time difficult to track, and a long list of assumptions and claims which are highly questionable yet have been prominent in the standards drive and its public justification.

147. This question takes us from the content and outcomes of policy to its processes. Despite the fact that from 2001 the government's first phase of public service reform was replaced by one which ostensibly balanced top-down pressures with pressures from below, the Review's 2007–9 data shows little evidence or perception of change in the way policies are evolved or in the way policy-makers behave. In this, education mirrors wider problems in Britain's political culture and decision-making, and a more fundamental malaise in the British version of democracy, for the formation and prosecution of policy relating to primary education does not stand apart from the trends characterised in the 2006 Power Report and by well-respected political commentators and historians.

148. The Review's evidence has highlighted variations on this larger theme of democratic deficit, many of them centering on the nature and quality of the information on which both sound decision-making and effective education depend in the primary sector: the unreliability of some official information, particularly in the crucial domain of standards; its lack of independence; the creating and nurturing of educational myths in order to underwrite an inflated account of political progress; the key role of the media in shaping the information that reaches government as well as the information that flows from it; the failure to give proper weight to ideas running on other than approved lines, and evidence from other than approved sources.

149. Alongside recent concerns about policy and the policy process there is the more traditional disquiet about funding. The edge of complaints about funding has been blunted by the considerable increase in support for primary education since 1997, but in relation to what schools now have to do this may not be enough. Further, the primary/secondary funding differential, first criticised in the 1931 Hadow Report and then in virtually every subsequent report on primary education, persists. Its effect is to make it difficult for schools to ensure that they have the expertise and flexibility they need for combination of entitlement and standards across the curriculum which the Review commends, together with all their other responsibilities.

150. **Assumptions and formulae for funding primary education should be reviewed. The primary/ secondary funding differential is based on long-outdated assumptions about curriculum, teaching, learning and the expertise these require at the primary stage, and should be eliminated. The staffing of primary schools should be curriculum, activity and needs led, and funding should be at a level to enable schools to meet the obligations of an entitlement curriculum taught to the highest possible standards, as discussed earlier, as well as the many other tasks which schools are now expected to undertake. There should be a new funding formula, and it should be preceded, as we have already argued, by a full staffing review. Excessive funding variation between local authorities and key stages should also be eliminated.**

151. Our proposals on reforming primary school staffing and supporting head teachers have financial implications and the various models suggested here will need to be properly costed. However, other proposals allow for considerable savings – for example the ending of the primary national strategy, a pattern of assessment reform which makes better use of teachers' professional judgement, more extensive use of school partnership and clustering, and the considerable reduction of the role and infrastructure of central government and its agencies. Bearing in mind that the literacy, numeracy and primary strategies alone have cost £2 billion to date,[5] considerable savings will accrue from the single act of terminating them and shifting the funding from government and local authorities (as the strategy's agents) to schools themselves. Longer term, the benefits of task-led staffing which delivers high standards, guarantees curriculum entitlement and reduces the attainment gap are incalculable.

152. The experiment in centralised reform has produced important and necessary changes in relation to children and children's services, but in relation to curriculum and pedagogy there is widespread agreement that it has gone too far. In light of the previous recommendation we must note that it has also been extremely expensive. The role of government should revert to providing the administrative and financial framework, setting out in clear and straightforward terms the goals and scope of the national curriculum and the standards which primary schools should be expected to achieve (defining standards broadly in relation to entitlement, rather than narrowly as hitherto), and in other areas providing frameworks to support the work of schools rather than detailed prescriptions of what teachers should do and how they should think.

153. The politicisation of primary education has also gone too far. Discussion has been blocked by derision, truth has been supplanted by myth and spin, and alternatives to current arrangements have been reduced to crude dichotomy. It is time to advance to a discourse which exemplifies rather than negates what education should be about.

THE RECOMMENDATIONS: SIGNPOSTS

The broad direction of the Review's 75 recommendations can be summarised as follows:

Respect and support childhood (4–21)
- respect children's experience, voices and rights, and accept the UN Convention on the Rights of the Child as the framework for policy
- build on new research on children's development, learning, needs and capabilities
- ensure that teacher education is fully informed by these perspectives.

Narrow the gap (6–8)
- maintain the focus of policy on reducing under-achievement
- intervene quickly and effectively to help disadvantaged and vulnerable children
- give the highest priority to eliminating child poverty.

Review special needs (18, 21)
- institute a full SEN review which re-assesses its definitions, structures, procedures and provision.

Start with aims (32–37)
- establish a new and coherent set of aims, values and principles for 21st century primary education, in addition to any wider aims for the schooling system as a whole
- make the aims drive rather than follow curriculum, teaching, assessment, schools and educational policy.

New structures for early years and primary education (22–31)
- strengthen and extend early learning provision
- extend the foundation stage to age six

- replace KS1/2 by a single primary phase from 6 to 11
- examine the feasibility of raising the school starting age to six.

A new curriculum (38–53)
- introduce a new primary curriculum which:
  - is firmly aligned with the aims, values and principles in 32–37
  - guarantees children's entitlement to breadth, depth and balance, and to high standards in all the proposed domains, not just some of them
  - ensures that language, literacy and oracy are paramount
  - combines a national framework with a locally-devised community curriculum
  - encourages greater professional flexibility and creativity
- wind up the primary national strategy and re-integrate literacy and numeracy with the rest of the curriculum.

A pedagogy of evidence and principle (54–61)
- work towards a pedagogy of repertoire rather than recipe, and of principle rather than prescription
- ensure that teaching and learning are properly informed by research
- uphold the principle that it is not for government, government agencies or local authorities to tell teachers how to teach.
- avoid pedagogical fads and fashions and act instead on those aspects of learning and teaching, notably spoken language, where research evidence strongly converges.

Reform assessment (62–74)
- retain summative pupil assessment at the end of the primary phase, but uncouple assessment for accountability from assessment for learning
- replace current KS2 literacy/numeracy SATs by a system which assesses and reports on children's achievement in all areas of their learning, with the minimum of disruption
- monitor school and system performance through sample testing
- make greater use of teacher assessment.

Strengthen accountability, redefine standards (40, 47, 53, 75–85, 150)
- move forward from debating whether schools and teachers should be accountable (they should) and concentrate instead on how
- redefine primary education standards as the quality of learning in all curriculum domains, knowledge and skills to which children are entitled, not just some of them.
- develop a model of school inspection which is in line with the aims and principles proposed in Chapter 12.

Review primary school staffing (118–19, 124–28, 132–33)
- undertake a full review of current and projected primary school staffing
- ensure that schools have the teacher numbers, expertise and flexibility to deliver high standards across the full curriculum
- develop and deploy alternative primary teaching roles to the generalist class teacher without losing its benefits
- clarify and properly support the role of teaching assistant.

Leadership for learning (134–42)
- share leadership in order to nurture the capacities of teachers and emphasise schools' core tasks and relationship with their local communities
- provide time and support for heads to do the job for which they are most needed – leading learning.

Reform teacher education (119–23, 128–31)
- align teacher education with new aims, curriculum, and approaches to pedagogy
- refocus initial training on childhood, learning, teaching, curriculum and subject knowledge
- examine alternative ITT routes for different primary teaching roles
- replace the current TDA professional standards by a framework validated by professional development research and pupil learning outcomes
- balance support for inexperienced and less able teachers with freedom and respect for the experienced and talented.

Schools for the community (110–17)
- build on recent initiatives encouraging multi-agency working, and increase support for schools to help them ensure that the growing range of children's services professionals work in partnership with each other and with parents
- strengthen mutual professional support through clustering, federation, all-through schools and the pooling of expertise.

Schools for the future (86–109)
- take an innovative approach to school design and timetabling which marries design and function and properly reflects the proposed aims for primary education.

Reform school funding (149–51)
- eliminate the primary/secondary funding differential
- ensure that primary school funding is determined by educational and curricular needs
- devise and cost alternative models of curriculum/needs led primary school staffing
- set increased costs against savings from terminating the primary national strategy (PNS), transferring its budget to schools, and otherwise reducing government control and infrastructure.

Reform the policy process (50–53, 143–53)
- re-balance the responsibilities of the DCSF, local authorities and schools
- replace top-down control and prescription by professional empowerment, mutual accountability and respect for research evidence and professional experience
- make good the wider democratic deficit.

A new educational discourse (147–48, 153)
- abandon the discourses of derision, false dichotomy and myth and strive to ensure that the education debate at last exemplifies rather than negates what education should be about.

NOTES

1 CACE (1967): recommendations 44 and 195.
2 Rose (2009): 33.
3 http://www.dcsf.gov.uk/primarycurriculumreview/. Accessed on 29 April 2009.
4 *Hansard*, 14 October 2008.
5 £1.93 billion between 1998 and 2008 (*Hansard*, 14 October 2008). Recently, annual expenditure on the PNS has averaged about £200 million, so the total will exceed £2 billion in 2009.

EDITOR'S POSTSCRIPT (AUGUST 2009)

This report went to press in spring 2009. By then it was evident that the Review's 31 interim reports were influencing both policy and the wider debate. Of developments between then and the report's publication, three merit comment in light of the conclusions and recommendations above.

On 30 April 2009, the government accepted the proposals of the Rose review of the primary curriculum. Since this nominally independent review adhered to a narrow government remit, refrained from questioning existing policy and for good measure was managed by DCSF, its adoption was a foregone conclusion.

While there is much to commend in Rose, the reservations recorded in this report must stand. Rose is a tidying-up operation rather than the promised 'root and branch' reform. Its off-the-shelf aims for primary education, like its references to the Cambridge Review's own proposals, are cosmetic. Its seductive promises of professional freedom are nullified by continuing central control. Its insistence that the main problem is 'quarts into pint pots', or curriculum overload, deflects attention from the real challenge: matching vision and task with appropriate expertise and resources. That challenge is exacerbated by a reluctance to ask how far the generalist classteacher system remains fit for contemporary purpose, given the evidence that what distinguishes expert teachers from the rest is the depth of their engagement with what is to be taught. So the debate about the quality of the primary curriculum, as well as its purposes and content, remains wide open.

Next, government modified the line on assessment and testing to which it had held for over a decade. In May 2009 its 'expert group' proposed that science should no longer be tested at the end of KS2 – though the literacy and numeracy SATs were to remain intact – and report cards were offered to broaden the scope of the pupil outcomes for which schools are held to account. In June 2009, the Conservatives, hitherto strong supporters of national testing, upped the stakes by announcing that if elected in 2010 they would move the KS2 tests to the beginning of KS3 in order that primary schools might recover the curriculum freedoms the tests had denied them.

When the Review's research surveys on these matters were published in November 2007, ministers dismissed them out of hand. By 2009 the tide of concern about the post-1997 testing regime, swelled by a highly critical report from the cross-party House of Commons select committee, had become irresistible. It would be good to think that the policy realignments of 2009 grasped the constructive potential of critiques of the kind offered by the Cambridge Review. However, though the implacable earlier line may have wavered there is as yet little evidence of properly considered alternatives, so the debate on assessment and standards also remains open.

Third, in June 2009 a government white paper announced that the primary national strategy, successor to the flagship literacy and numeracy strategies, would be wound down from 2011 and replaced by a 'much more tailored approach'. Until then, government had rejected all criticism of the strategies, including, again, that presented by the Cambridge Review. But professionals, the Select Committee and the media had given strong support to the Review's proposal, in its February 2009 report on the primary curriculum, that the strategies should be abandoned and their substantial budget redistributed to schools. The announcement in the June white paper, four months later, closely mirrored the Cambridge proposal, though the cited reasons were very different.

The apparent demise of the national strategies, and the government's promise to replace centrally-directed reform by school self-determination, might seem to make redundant some of this report's recommendations. However, though several newspapers and many teachers applauded 'the end of centralisation', history renders their applause premature. The end of centralisation was promised when phase 2 of the government's programme of public service reform was launched in 2001, yet the Review's evidence shows that by 2008–9 little had changed. The 2009 white paper offers autonomy yet warns that government 'will still expect every primary school to be teaching daily literacy hours and daily mathematics lessons' in accordance with what it defines as best practice – a familiar requirement which will no doubt be enforced in the familiar way: for when in 1998–99 the supposedly non-statutory literacy and numeracy strategies were introduced, Ofsted said that it would expect to see them taught in every school.

A process which has concentrated so much power at the centre, and over the course of two decades has so decisively re-configured the relationship between government and teachers, cannot be instantly unpicked. In 2009, the national strategies and their attendant assumptions are firmly embedded in the TDA professional standards and teacher training requirements. They dictate Ofsted inspection criteria, procedures and judgements. They provide the 'school improvement' script for local authority advisers and inspectors, and indeed it is national strategy funding which keeps many such people in employment. Centrally-determined versions of teaching, flawed though the research evidence shows some of them to be, are all that many teachers know. The hegemony of a state theory of learning will not vanish overnight.

Nor can public accountability for the strategies and their impact be evaded by saying, as of other political controversies since 1997, that it is time to 'draw a line and move on.' For what does the sudden jettisoning of the strategies really mean? That they were a success? That they were a failure? That they were too expensive? That they became an electoral liability? It is vitally important that the benefits and costs of this vast and intrusive educational experiment are examined and that the lessons are learned. The evidence summarised in this report points the way.

In matters such as these, the Cambridge Review takes the longer perspective. The centralising trend goes back to the 1980s and arises from a political process which retains all the defects of which the 2006 Power Report on the condition of Britain's democracy was so critical. Meanwhile, some of the more intractable problems of English primary education escape attention because their longevity makes them invisible to a policy mindset in which there is a present and short-term future but no past outside the realm of political myth.

No assurance, U-turn or pre-emptive strike in the months before what looks likely to be a bitterly-contested general election can invalidate the wealth of evidence with which this enquiry was provided by its thousands of research sources and contributors, or the conclusions and recommendations to which that evidence inexorably leads. In fact, these conclusions are vindicated rather than undermined by the policy shifts exemplified here. So there's a simple test of the changes announced in the June 2009 white paper, and of the wider democratic reforms promised in the wake of the May 2009 parliamentary expenses scandal: will this final report from the Cambridge Review be dismissed in the same summary fashion as its 31 interim predecessors, and indeed those many other contributions to the educational debate which were constructive and authoritative but 'off message' or 'not invented here'?

For now though, the politics of the moment are abjured. The Cambridge Primary Review is for the longer term, not the next election; and as an exercise in democratic engagement as well as empirical enquiry and visionary effort its final report is not just for transient architects and agents of policy. It is for all who invest daily, deeply and for life in this vital phase of education, especially children, parents and teachers.

Appendix 1
The Cambridge Primary Review
Remit, process and personnel

The Cambridge Primary Review is a wide-ranging independent enquiry into the condition and future of primary education in England. It was supported from 2006–10 by Esmée Fairbairn Foundation and based at the University of Cambridge. The Review was launched in October 2006. Between October 2007 and May 2008 it published as interim reports 28 research surveys and an account of the 2007 regional Community Soundings. In February 2009 it published a two-volume special report on the primary curriculum. Its final report was published in autumn 2009.

The launch of the Review was preceded by nearly three years of planning and by consultation with government, opposition parties, DfES/DCSF officials, the all-party Commons Education and Skills (now Children, Schools and Families) Committee, public bodies involved in the primary phase of education, the teaching unions and a range of other interested organisations.

The Review was initiated and directed by Professor Robin Alexander, Fellow of Wolfson College at the University of Cambridge and Professor of Education Emeritus at the University of Warwick. Its Advisory Committee was chaired by Dame Gillian Pugh, Visiting Professor at the University of London Institute of Education, Chair of the National Children's Bureau and formerly Chief Executive of Coram Family.

REMIT

The remit for the Cambridge Primary Review, as agreed between Esmée Fairbairn Foundation and the University of Cambridge in 2005–6, is as follows:

1. With respect to public provision in England, the Review will seek to identify the purposes which the primary phase of education should serve, the values which it should espouse, the curriculum and learning environment which it should provide, and the conditions which are necessary in order to ensure both that these are of the highest and most consistent quality possible, and that they address the needs of children and society over the coming decades.
2. The Review will pay close regard to national and international evidence from research, inspection and other sources on the character and adequacy of current provision in respect of the above, on the prospects for recent initiatives, and on other available options. It will seek the advice of expert advisers and witnesses, and it will invite submissions and take soundings from a wide range of interested agencies and individuals, both statutory and non-statutory.
3. The Review will publish both interim findings and a final report. The latter will combine evidence, analysis and conclusions together with recommendations for both national policy and the work of schools and other relevant agencies.

ESSENTIAL FEATURES

The Cambridge Primary Review:

- is financially and politically independent;
- focuses on the statutory primary phase, 4/5–11;

- is grounded in national and international evidence;
- has sought views across a wide range of professional, political and public constituencies;
- combines assessment of current provision with the development of a vision for the future;
- has produced interim reports and briefings, and a final report containing findings, conclusions and recommendations for future policy and practice.

PERSPECTIVES AND THEMES

The Cambridge Primary Review is conceived as a matrix of ten themes and four strands of evidence, overarched by three perspectives:

- The lives and needs of children and the condition of childhood today
- The condition of the society and world in which today's children are growing up
- The present condition and future prospects of England's system of primary education.

The ten themes addressed by the Review are:

1. Purposes and values
2. Learning and teaching
3. Curriculum and assessment
4. Quality and standards
5. Diversity and inclusion
6. Settings and professionals
7. Parenting, caring and educating
8. Children's lives beyond the school
9. Structures and phases
10. Funding and governance.

In respect of these themes, each of which is elaborated as the sub-themes and contributory questions listed in Appendix 2, the Review aims to address two fundamental questions:

- *Evidence:* how well is England's system of primary education doing?
- *Vision:* how can it best meet the needs of children and society over the coming decades?

EVIDENCE

The Cambridge Primary Review has four main strands of evidence:

Submissions. Following the convention in enquiries of this kind, written submissions were invited from all who wished to contribute. By March 2009, 1052 submissions had been received. They ranged from brief single-issue expressions of opinion to substantial documents of up to 300 pages covering several or all of the themes and comprising both detailed evidence and recommendations for the future. The majority of the submissions were from national organisations, but a significant number came from individuals.

Soundings. This strand had two parts. The community soundings were a series of nine regionally-based one to two day events, each comprising a sequence of meetings with representatives from schools and the communities they serve. They took place between January and March 2007, and entailed 87 witness sessions with groups of pupils, parents, governors, teachers, teaching assistants and heads, and with educational and community representatives from the areas in which the soundings took place. The national soundings were a programme of more formal meetings with national organisations both inside and outside education. Some of these, with government, statutory agencies, public bodies and unions, took the form of regular consultations throughout the Review's duration. Others, which included three seminars with specially-convened groups of teachers and two sessions with representatives of major non-statutory organisations, took place between January and March 2008 and explored issues arising from the Review's by then considerable body of evidence. The National Soundings helped the team to clarify matters which were particularly problematic or contested, in preparation for the writing of the final report.

Surveys. Several months before the launch of the Review, 28 surveys of published research relating to the Review's ten themes were commissioned, on the basis of competitive bidding and peer review, from 66 academic consultants in leading university departments of education and allied fields. The resulting research reports and their accompanying briefings and media releases were published in cross-thematic groups over several months, starting in autumn 2007. They provoked considerable media, public and political interest, and provided the top UK news story on several occasions.

Searches and policy mapping. With the co-operation of DfES/DCSF, QCA, Ofsted and TDA, the Review tracked recent policy and examined official data bearing on the primary phase. This provided the necessary legal, demographic, financial and statistical background to the Review and an important resource for its consideration of policy options.

The balance of evidence. The four evidential strands sought to balance opinion-seeking with empirical data; non-interactive expressions of opinion with face-to-face discussion; official data with independent research; and material from England with that from other parts of the UK and from international sources. This enquiry, unlike some of its predecessors, looked outwards from primary schools to the wider society, and made full but judicious use of international data and ideas from other countries.

Other meetings. In addition to the formal evidence-gathering procedures, the Review's director and other team members met national and regional bodies for the exchange of information and ideas. At the time of going to press (April 2009) 146 such meetings had taken place or were scheduled, in addition to the 92 community and national soundings, making a total of 238 sessions.

REPORTS

The Cambridge Primary Review has published both interim and final reports. The main series of 29 interim reports, which included 28 of the commissioned research surveys and the report on the community soundings, served a formative function, seeking to provoke further debate which then fed back into the Review. The interim reports were published on the Cambridge Primary Review's website (www.primaryreview.org.uk) together with a record of their extensive media coverage. Electronic and print versions of the reports and briefings were widely circulated.

Two special reports on the primary curriculum were published in February 2009. Written as part of the Review's final report, they were brought forward and adapted as contributions to the formal consultation on the interim report of the government's Rose Review of the primary curriculum.

The Cambridge Primary Review final report draws on the various strands of evidence outlined above to address the ten listed themes and attendant questions. It combines findings, analysis, reflection and conclusions, together with recommendations for policy and practice. Its companion volume includes the commissioned surveys of published research, updated in light of recent research and policy.

OUTLINE TIMETABLE

Phase 1: *Preparation* (January 2004 – October 2006)

Phase 2: *Implementation*
- Submissions (core submissions October 2006 – April 2007, additional submissions to April 2009)
- Community Soundings (January – March 2007)
- Research Surveys (July 2006 – January 2008)
- Policy searches (November 2006 – April 2009)
- National Soundings (January – March 2008)
- Other consultations (October 2006 – April 2009)

Phase 3: *Dissemination*
- Interim reports and briefings (October 2007 – May 2008)
- Special report on the primary curriculum (February 2009)
- Final report (autumn 2009)
- Other dissemination events and activities (from autumn 2009)

Phase 4: *Longer term evaluation and follow-up* (from late 2009)
- Programme to be agreed.

FUNDING

The Review was undertaken with the support of Esmée Fairbairn Foundation. To date (2009), the Foundation's Trustees have awarded the Review four grants: (i) the main Review implementation grant (Phase 2 and the first part of Phase 3 above), from 1 October 2006 to 30 September 2008; (ii) a supplementary implementation grant, from 1 October 2007 to 30 September 2008; (iii) a grant for dissemination (the second part of Phase 3), from 1 October 2008 to 30 September 2009; (iv) a further dissemination grant, from 1 October 2009 to 30 June 2010.

PERSONNEL

Director of the Cambridge Primary Review: Professor Robin Alexander (2006–10)
Chair of the Cambridge Primary Review Advisory Committee: Dame Gillian Pugh (2006–9)
Chair of the Cambridge Primary Review Management Group: Hilary Hodgson, Esmée Fairbairn
     Foundation (2006–9)
Director of Communications: Dr Richard Margrave (2006–10)
Dissemination Co-ordinator: Julia Flutter (2007–10)
Administrator: Catrin Darsley (2006–9)

The Cambridge Primary Review Cambridge team: core members
Professor Robin Alexander (2004–10)
Catrin Darsley (2006–9)
Christine Doddington (2006–8)
Julia Flutter (2007–10)
Dr Linda Hargreaves (2006–8)
Dr David Harrison (2006–8)
Ruth Kershner (2006–8)

The Cambridge Primary Review Cambridge team: occasional members, 2007 and 2008
Qais Almeqdad
Dr Yan-Shing Chang

Calvin Dorion
Chloe Gayer-Anderson
Professor John Gray
Alex James
Boris Jokić
Catherine Kitsis
Dr Hsing-Chiung Lin
Katherine Shaw
Dr Sharlene Swartz

The Cambridge Primary Review research consultants (2006–8)
Professor Mel Ainscow, University of Manchester.
Dr Maria Balarin, University of Bath.
Dr Ian Barron, Manchester Metropolitan University.
Professor Peter Blatchford, Institute of Education, University of London.
Professor Mark Brundrett, University of Manchester (now at Liverpool John Moores University).
Professor Peter Bryant, University of Oxford.
Dr Hilary Burgess, Open University.
Dr Rita Chawla-Duggan, University of Bath.
Professor James Conroy, University of Glasgow.
Dr Jean Conteh, University of Leeds.
Dr Andrea Creech, Institute of Education, University of London.
Dr Peter Cunningham, University of Cambridge.
Professor Harry Daniels, University of Bath.
Professor Julie Dockrell, Institute of Education, University of London.
Professor Alan Dyson, University of Manchester.
Professor Michael Fielding, University of Sussex (now at Institute of Education, University of London).
Dr Frances Gallannaugh, University of Manchester.
Professor Usha Goswami, University of Cambridge.
Professor Kathy Hall, Open University (now at National University of Ireland, Cork).
Professor Susan Hallam, Institute of Education, University of London.
Professor Wynne Harlen, University of Bristol.
Dr Rachel Holmes, Manchester Metropolitan University.
Professor Christine Howe, University of Cambridge.
Dr Moira Hulme, University of Glasgow.
Professor Judith Ireson, Institute of Education, University of London.
Professor Mary James, Institute of Education, University of London (now at the University of Cambridge).
Professor Liz Jones, Manchester Metropolitan University.
Professor Peter Kutnick, King's College London.
Professor Hugh Lauder, University of Bath.
Dr John Lowe, University of Bath.
Professor Stephen Machin, University College, London.
Professor Maggie MacLure, Manchester Metropolitan University.
Professor Berry Mayall, Institute of Education, University of London.
Dr Elaine McCreery, Manchester Metropolitan University.
Dr Sandra McNally, London School of Economics and Political Science.
Professor Olwen McNamara, University of Manchester.
Professor Ian Menter, University of Glasgow.
Professor Neil Mercer, University of Cambridge.
Dr Christine Merrell, University of Durham.
Dr Yolande Muschamp, University of Bath.

Sharon O'Donnell, National Foundation for Educational Research.
Dr Philip Noden, London School of Economics and Political Science.
Professor Kamil Øzerk, University of Oslo.
Nick Peacey, Institute of Education, University of London.
Dr Andy Pickard, Manchester Metropolitan University.
Professor Andrew Pollard, Institute of Education, University of London.
Dr Jill Porter, University of Bath.
Dr Philip Raymont, University of Cambridge.
Dr Tess Ridge, University of Bath.
Anna Riggall, National Foundation for Educational Research.
Dr Carol Robinson, University of Sussex (now at University of Brighton).
Dr Graham Ruddock, National Foundation for Educational Research.
Dr Katherine Runswick-Cole, Sheffield Hallam University (now at Manchester
    Metropolitan University).
Dr Maha Shuayb, National Foundation for Educational Research.
Caroline Sharp, National Foundation for Educational Research.
Professor Ian Stronach, Manchester Metropolitan University (now at Liverpool John
    Moores University).
Professor Harry Torrance, Manchester Metropolitan University.
Liz Twist, National Foundation for Educational Research.
Professor Peter Tymms, University of Durham.
Dr Karl Wall, Institute of Education, University of London.
Professor Rosemary Webb, University of Manchester.
Professor Anne West, London School of Economics and Political Science.
Chris Whetton, National Foundation for Educational Research.
Professor John White, Institute of Education, University of London.
Dr Felicity Wikeley, University of Bath.
Dr Dominic Wyse, University of Cambridge.

The Cambridge Primary Review Advisory Committee (2006–9 unless otherwise indicated)

Appointed by Esmée Fairbairn Foundation

Dame Gillian Pugh (Chair) Visiting Professor, Institute of Education, University of London;
    Chair of the National Children's Bureau; former Chief Executive, Coram Family.
Patricia Clark, Senior Consultant, London Centre for Leadership in Learning.
Christina Coker, Chief Executive, Youth Music.
Kevan Collins, Director of Children's Services, Tower Hamlets Borough Council (2006–8).
Sheila Dainton, formerly Education Policy Adviser at the Association of Teachers and Lecturers
    and Advocate for Human Scale Education.
Bernadette Duffy, Head, Thomas Coram Early Childhood Centre, London Borough of
    Camden.
Adwoa-Buahema Fadahunsi, parent-governor (2006–7).
Kate Frood, Head Teacher, Eleanor Palmer Primary School, London Borough of Camden
    (2008–9).
Professor David Hargreaves, Fellow of Wolfson College, University of Cambridge; Associate
    Director (Development and Research) Specialist Schools and Academies Trust; Senior
    Associate, DEMOS.
Elizabeth Hartley-Brewer, author, journalist, parenting and family policy consultant.
Diane Hofkins, former primary editor of The Times Educational Supplement.
Anna House, former Head Teacher, Ridgeway Primary School, London Borough of Croydon.
James Hughes-Hallett, Trustee, Esmée Fairbairn Foundation.
Pat Jefferson, former Executive Director for Children and Young People, Lancashire County
    Council.

Melody Moran, Head Teacher, Brentside Primary School, London Borough of Ealing.
Stephen Pisano, Education Consultant for Coram.
Professor Andrew Pollard, Professor of Education in the Institute of Education, University of London, and Director of the ESRC Teaching and Learning Research Programme.
Usha Sahni, Her Majesty's Inspector, Ofsted.
Sue Tite, primary school adviser for East Riding Local Authority; former Head Teacher, Selby Abbey Primary School, Selby, North Yorkshire.

Ex officio

Robin Alexander (Director of the Cambridge Primary Review)
Dawn Austwick (Chief Executive, Esmée Fairbairn Foundation)
Catrin Darsley (Cambridge Primary Review Administrator and Committee Secretary)
Hilary Hodgson (Esmée Fairbairn Foundation)
Richard Margrave (Director of Communications, Cambridge Primary Review)
Jo Rideal (Esmée Fairbairn Foundation)
James Wragg (Esmée Fairbairn Foundation)

The Cambridge Primary Review Management Group (2006–9)

Hilary Hodgson (chair)
Robin Alexander
Dawn Austwick
Richard Margrave
Gillian Pugh
James Wragg

The Cambridge Primary Review Policy Group (2006–9)

Gillian Pugh (chair)
Robin Alexander
Dawn Austwick
Sheila Dainton
David Hargreaves
Elizabeth Hartley-Brewer
Hilary Hodgson
Pat Jefferson
Richard Margrave

Appendix 2
Perspectives, themes and questions

The coverage of the Cambridge Primary Review is expressed as a hierarchy of perspectives, themes and questions. We start with three broad *perspectives*: children, the world in which they are growing up, and the education which mediates that world and prepares them for it. These are the Review's core concerns and recurrent points of reference. Next, ten *themes* and 23 *sub-themes* unpack the education perspective in greater detail while remaining permeated by the other two. Finally, for every theme there is a set of *questions*.

PERSPECTIVES

P1   Children and childhood
P2   Culture, society and the global context
P3   Primary education

THEMES AND SUB-THEMES

T1   *Purposes and values*
      T1a   Values, beliefs and principles
      T1b   Aims
T2   *Learning and teaching*
      T2a   Children's development and learning
      T2b   Teaching
T3   *Curriculum and assessment*
      T3a   Curriculum
      T3b   Assessment
T4   *Quality and standards*
      T4a   Standards
      T4b   Quality assurance and inspection
T5   *Diversity and inclusion*
      T5a   Culture, gender, race, faith
      T5b   Special educational needs
T6   *Settings and professionals*
      T6a   Buildings and resources
      T6b   Teacher supply, training, deployment & development
      T6c   Other professionals
      T6d   School organisation, management & leadership
      T6e   School culture and ethos
T7   *Parenting and caring*
      T7a   Parents and carers
      T7b   Home and school
T8   *Beyond the school*
      T8a   Children's lives beyond the school
      T8b   Schools and other agencies

T9   *Structures and phases*
    T9a   Within-school structures, stages, classes & groups
    T9b   System-level structures, phases & transitions
T10   *Funding and governance*
    T10a Funding
    T10b Governance

Perspective 1: Children and childhood
- What do we know about young children's lives in and out of school, and about the nature of childhood, at the start of the 21st century?
- How do children of primary school age develop, think, feel, act and learn?
- To which of the myriad individual and collective differences between children should educators and related professionals particularly respond?
- What do children most fundamentally need from those charged with providing their primary education?

Perspective 2: Culture, society and the global context
- In what kind of society and world are today's children growing up and being educated?
- In what do England's (and Britain's) cultural differences and commonalities reside?
- What is the country's likely economic, social and political future?
- Is there a consensus about the 'good society' and education's role in helping to shape and secure it?
- What can we predict about the future – social, economic, environmental, moral, political – of the wider world with which Britain is interdependent?
- What, too, does this imply for children and primary education?
- What must be done in order that today's children, and their children, have a future worth looking forward to?

Perspective 3: Primary education
- Taking the system as a whole, from national policy and overall structure to the fine detail of school and classroom practice, what are the current characteristics, strengths and weaknesses of the English state system of primary education?
- To what needs and purposes should it be chiefly directed over the coming decades?
- What values should it espouse?
- What learning experiences should it provide?
- By what means can its quality be secured and sustained?

Theme 1: Purposes and values
- What is primary education for?
- Taking account of the country and the world in which our children are growing up, to what individual, social, cultural, economic and other circumstances and needs should this phase of education principally attend?
- What core values and principles should it uphold and advance?
- How far can a national system reflect and respect the values and aspirations of the many different communities – cultural, ethnic, religious, political, economic, regional, local – for which it purportedly caters?
- In envisaging the future purposes and shape of this phase of education how far ahead is it possible or sensible to look?

Theme 2: Learning and teaching
- What do we know about the way young children develop, act and learn – cognitively, emotionally, socially, morally, physically and across the full spectrum of their development?
- What are the pedagogical implications of recent research in, for example, neuroscience, cognition, intelligence, language and human interaction?

- What is the relationship between children's physical health, emotional wellbeing and learning?
- What is the impact of gender on learning?
- What are the personal and situational circumstances for effective learning and what conditions are likely to impede it?
- As children move developmentally through the primary phase how do they learn best and how are they most effectively taught?
- Judged against all this evidence, how do current teaching approaches fare?
- How well do they capitalise on the findings of research?
- What is the proper place of ICT and other new technologies in teaching and learning?
- How can teaching, and the system as a whole, most appropriately respond to differences in children's development, ways of learning and apparent capacities and needs?
- In what ways might teaching, and the organisation of classrooms and schools, change in order to enhance young children's engagement and learning and maximise their educational prospects?

Theme 3: Curriculum and assessment
- What do children currently learn during the primary phase?
- What should they learn?
- What constitutes a meaningful, balanced and relevant primary curriculum?
- What kinds of curriculum experience will best serve children's varying needs during the next few decades?
- Do notions like 'basics' and 'core curriculum' have continuing validity, and if so of what should 21st-century basics and cores for the primary phase be constituted?
- Do the current national curriculum and attendant foundation, literacy, numeracy and primary strategies provide the range and approach which children of this age really need?
- How are the different needs of children, including those with specific learning difficulties, currently diagnosed?
- How should their progress and attainment be assessed?
- What is the proper relationship and balance of assessment for learning and assessment for accountability?
- What are the strengths and weaknesses of current approaches to assessment, both national and local?
- What assessment information should be reported, and to whom?
- What is the most helpful balance of national and local in curriculum and assessment?

Theme 4: Quality and standards
- How good is English primary education?
- How consistent is it across the country as a whole?
- Have standards risen or fallen?
- How do they compare with those of other countries?
- How should 'standards' and 'quality' in primary education be defined?
- How should quality and standards be assessed?
- What is the available range of national and international evidence on these matters?
- How reliable is it?
- How well, and how appropriately, is it used?
- What are the most effective contributions to assessing and assuring standards and quality of, for example, research, inspection, government initiatives, school and teacher self-evaluation, performance management, pre-service training and in-service training?
- What are the proper roles in the processes of systemic review and quality assurance of DfES, Ofsted, the other national agencies and Parliament?

Theme 5: Diversity and inclusion
- Do our primary schools attend effectively and equitably to the different learning needs and cultural backgrounds of their pupils?

- Do all children have equal access to high quality primary education?
- If not, how can this access be improved?
- How can a national system best respond to the wide diversity of cultures, faiths, languages and aspirations which is now a fact of British life?
- Of what is identity constituted in a highly plural culture, and what should be the role of primary education in fostering it?
- How can primary schools best meet the needs of children of widely-varying attainments and interests, including children with special educational needs and those who display or may have exceptional talents?
- How can schools secure the engagement of those children and families which are hardest to reach?

Theme 6: Settings and professionals

- What are the physical and organisational characteristics of our best primary schools?
- How are they resourced and equipped?
- How are they organised and led?
- What are the lessons for school design and organisation of recent national initiatives?
- What balance of expertise, and of teachers, assistants and other para-professionals, should schools contain and how should they be used?
- What are the conditions for their success?
- What are the future workforce needs of the phase as a whole?
- How can these be met?
- How well are teachers and other professionals involved in this age-range trained?
- How effectively are they deployed?
- How well is their development supported at school, local and national levels?
- How can the nation secure and retain the best professionals for this phase of education?

Theme 7: Parenting, caring and educating

- What are the parenting and caring conditions on which children's welfare and their successful primary education depend?
- But what, too, should educational and other services do to support parents and carers in their work?
- How are the challenges of home-school relationships most effectively met?
- By what means can parents/carers, teachers and other professionals operate as far as possible in harmony and pursue goals which, while not identical, are not in such conflict that they damage the child's educational prospects?

Theme 8: Beyond the school

- What do we know about children's lives beyond school and the impact of those groups and influences – family, peers, community, media and so on – to which they are subject?
- What kinds of learning take place outside school?
- What is the current division of responsibilities between the people, institutions and agencies who are principally concerned with young children's education and those who are concerned with their upbringing and welfare – parents and carers especially, but also health services, social services and other statutory and voluntary agencies?
- How successfully does their work articulate and cohere?
- In the context of changing familial demographics and growing concern about young children's wellbeing, might these relationships, and the attendant responsibilities, be differently conceived?

Theme 9: Structures and phases

- How well do existing structures and phases – 'educare' and schooling, pre-school in its various forms, infant/junior/primary, first/middle, foundation/KS1/KS2 – work?

- What are the salient characteristics, strengths and weaknesses of the various institutions and settings in which primary education takes place?
- Are there problems of coherence, transition and continuity within and between phases?
- How can these be overcome?
- What can the primary phase profitably learn from developments in the phases which precede and follow it?
- How are children grouped within the primary phase and what are the advantages and disadvantages of the different grouping arrangements?
- When should formal schooling start, bearing in mind that many other countries start later than we do and conceive of the relationship of pre-school and formal schooling somewhat differently?
- Are there more effective alternatives to current structures?

Theme 10: Funding and governance
- How adequately is the system of primary education in England funded and how efficiently is it controlled and administered?
- Does it have the right balance of control and responsibility between national government, local government, local communities and schools?
- What has been the impact of the post-1988 drive to a more centralised system?
- What should be the position of faith schools?
- Through what system of school governance are the interests of children, teachers, parents and local communities most effectively and equitably addressed?
- How might matters be differently ordered?

Appendix 3
Submissions

The initial call for written submissions, in October 2006, produced a wide range of individual and organisational responses. Those submitting evidence were invited to look first at the Review perspectives, themes and questions. Many evidently did so, but because the invitation was open the submissions touched on almost every conceivable aspect of children's lives in and out of school.

Analysis of the submissions data was done in two stages. Submissions were first classified according to length, format, source, constituency and theme. They were then coded under the Review's themes and sub-themes using NVIVO qualitative data analysis software. This facilitated a fine-grained analysis of the entire dataset, allowing us to combine and compare responses relating to specific themes and questions, to identify meta-themes, and to examine response tendencies within and between constituencies.

Over the three years of the Review, 1052 submissions were received, many of them with extensive supporting material. 'Core' submissions below are those received in response to the initial call. The others arrived mainly in response to the interim reports.

SUBMISSIONS RECEIVED, OVERALL TOTALS

Core (in response to the initial call)	822
Other	230
Total	1052

SUBMISSIONS RECEIVED FROM INDIVIDUALS, BY CONSTITUENCY (394)

Children	161
Consultants	32
Governors of schools	6
Head teachers	43
Local authority advisers	20
Parents	20
Academics and teacher trainers	60
Teachers and teaching assistants	72
Others	41

Note: Because many individual submissions were from children, and many others requested anonymity, we decided to withhold the names of all those who made individual sunmissions.

SUBMISSIONS RECEIVED FROM ORGANISATIONS (658)

Note:

- An asterisk indicates that it is unclear whether the submission is on behalf of the organisation as a whole.

- Many organisations sent more than one submission, often at different stages of the Review's progress.
- The list excludes those organisations which asked to remain anonymous.

4Children
Achievement and Inclusion Group, London Borough of Harrow
Aspect
Association for Citizenship Teaching
Association for Language Learning
Association for Science Education
Association for the Study of Primary Education
Association of Professionals in Education and Children's Trusts
Association of Religious Education Inspectors, Advisers and Consultants
Association of School and College Leaders
Association of Teachers and Lecturers
Association of Teachers of Mathematics
Barnardos
Basic Skills Agency
Bath Spa University*
Bath Spa University, Department of Primary Education
BBC Radio 4: *Analysis – Miserable Children* (submitted as evidence)
Beaconhouse Schools, Pakistan*
Beechfield School*
Behavioural Optometrists Association
Billinghay Church of England Primary School
Birkdale Primary School*
Birmingham City Council, Directorate of Children, Young People and Families
Bishop Grosseteste University College
The Book Foundation
Bradford Standing Advisory Council for Religious Education
Brentside Primary School
Brighton and Hove Children and Young People's Trust*
British Association of Teachers of the Deaf
British Council for School Environments
British Educational Research Association*
British Humanist Association
Burntwood Infant and Junior School
Catch Up
Catholic Education Service
Cawood Church of England Primary School*
Centre for Policy Studies
Changing Faces
Childhood Bereavement Network
Church of England Education Division and The National Society
The Churchill School*
CiLT, the National Centre for Language Teaching
The Citizenship Foundation
Commission for Racial Equality
Comprehensive Future
ContinYou
Coram Family

Council for Education in World Citizenship*
Coventry City Council, Children, Learning and Young People's Directorate
Creative Partnerships
Derby Diocesan Board of Education
Design and Technology Association
Development Education Association
Devon Association of Head Teachers
Devon County Council, Primary Consultants
Dorset County Council, Pupil and School Improvement
Early Childhood Forum
Early Education
Early Years Curriculum Group
East Grinstead Pupils' Forum
Eastfeast
Edenthorpe Hall Primary School*
Edexcel*
Elloughton Primary School*
English Association
EPPE 3–11 Project
Essex School Improvement and Advisory Service
Free Church Education Committee
Futurelab
Gateshead Council
General Teaching Council for England (GTCE)
Geoffrey Field Infant School*
Geographical Association
Grange Primary School*
Hackney Music Service
Hamilton Trust
Hampshire County Council, Hampshire Nurture Group Project
Heading for Inclusion
Herefordshire Council School Improvement Service
Herefordshire Heads
Hillstone Primary School*
Human Scale Education
Humanities Education Centre
Independent Association of Prep Schools (IAPS)
I CAN
International Learning and Research Centre (ILRC)
Ireland in Schools
Isle of Man Government, Department of Education
John Keble Church of England Primary School*
Kids, the Disabled Children's Charity
Knowsley Council
Learning Spaces
Learning without Limits
Lincolnshire Group of Head Teachers
Link Community Development
London Borough of Barking and Dagenham, Primary Phase Team, Quality and School
    Improvement Division
London Borough of Barnet, Schools and Learning Group
London Borough of Enfield School Improvement Service
London Borough of Hounslow, Primary Advisors

London Borough of Lambeth, Children and Young People's Service
London Borough of Newham, Primary Consultants and School Development Officers
London Borough of Wandsworth
London Play
London Symphony Orchestra
Longwell Green Primary School
Loughborough Primary Development Group
Lyminge School*
Lyndhurst First School
Manchester Metropolitan University, Centre for Mathematics Education*
Mayflower Primary School
Media Association
Medway Council, Primary Consultants and Advisors
Michael Hall School*
Museums, Libraries and Archives Council
Music Education Council*
The Muslim Council of Britain
National Advisers and Inspectors Group for Science
National Association for Language Development in the Curriculum
National Association for Primary Education
National Association for Small Schools
National Association for the Teaching of English*
National Association of Advisers for Computers in Education
National Association of Head Teachers
National Association of Parent Teacher Associations
National Association of Teachers of Religious Education
National Association of Teachers of Travellers
National Centre for Language and Literacy
National Education Business Partnership Network
National Education Trust
National Literacy Trust
National Middle Schools Forum
National Network of Science Learning Centres
National Primary Head Teachers Association
National Union of Teachers
Newcastle City Council
No Outsiders Project
Northumberland County Council, Nurture Group Network School Improvement Service
Northumberland Head Teachers Forum
Nottingham City Council, Children's Services Directorate
Nurture Group Network
Petersfield Church of England Primary School*
Office of the Chief Rabbi
The Open University*
Open Eye
Optimum Education
Oundle CE Primary School
Oxfordshire County Council, Primary Strategy Team
Parentline Plus
Parish Church of England Primary School*
Peafield Lane Primary School*
Play England
Plover Primary School*

Promethean
Qualifications and Curriculum Authority*
Rotherham Council
Royal Borough of Kingston upon Thames
Royal Geographical Society
Royal Society for the Prevention of Cruelty to Animals
St Hugh of Lincoln Catholic Primary School
St Martin's College, Lancaster*
Sancton Wood School
SAPERE
Save the Children
School Councils UK
Shelter
Skills Active
Somerset Association of Primary Head Teachers and Officers
Somerset SCITT Consortium
Specialist Schools and Academies Trust
Sri Sathya Sai Education
Staffordshire County Council
Suffolk County Council, Suffolk Advisory Service
Suffolk County Council, Suffolk Inclusive School Improvement Service
Swim 2000 UK
Tamworth Business Link Partnership
Teacher Status Project
Training and Development Agency for Schools
Teacher Artist Partnership Programme
Teachers' TV: *The Big Debate – Too Much Too Young?* (submitted as evidence)
Terry Freedman Limited
Thomas Coram Research Unit
Trade Unions Congress
Universities' Council for the Education of Teachers
United Kingdom Literacy Association
United Kingdom One World Linking Association
United Synagogue Agency for Jewish Education
University of Birmingham, School of Education*
University of Cambridge, Faculty of Education *
University of Cambridge Faculty of Education, the Teacher Status Project
University of Exeter*
University of Liverpool*
University of London Institute of Education*
University of London Institute of Education, School of Curriculum, Pedagogy and Assessment*
University of Sunderland, No Outsiders Project
University of Warwick Institute of Education*
University of the West of England, Faculty of Education
University of Winchester*
Voices Foundation
Wednesbury Learning Community
Wellcome Trust
West Hertfordshire Primary Care Trust, children's occupational therapists
West London Partnership, Kingston University
West Sussex County Council, Children and Young People's Service
Wiltshire County Council, Primary Advisors
York City Council, Learning, Culture and Children's Services

Appendix 4
Community and national soundings

THE COMMUNITY SOUNDINGS

The community soundings took place between January and March 2007. Each was based in a primary school, though some also moved on to other local venues. Each sounding included separate sessions with children, parents, teachers, heads, teaching assistants, school governors, heads from other schools and a variety of community representatives. The sessions were led by the Cambridge team, supported by members of the Advisory Committee.

The programme was as follows:

1 February 2007: London (Ealing)
8 February 2007: London (Croydon)
14 and 15 February: North East (Northumberland)
1 and 2 March 2007: Yorkshire (North Yorkshire)
5 March 2007: Midlands (Birmingham)
14 March 2007: London (Wembley)
21 and 22 March 2007: South West (Cornwall and Devon)
26 March 2007: South East (Kent)
29 and 30 March 2007: North West (Lancashire)

The venues were chosen with the aim of capturing something of England's cultural, economic, environmental and educational diversity. One part of each sounding followed a programme of discussion common to all nine soundings, structured by the Review's perspectives, themes and questions. The other pursued matters of specific local interest and concern. The report on the Community Soundings was published in October 2007 (Alexander and Hargreaves 2007).

Community soundings	9
Regions	London (3), North East (1), North West (1), Midlands (1), Yorkshire (1), South East (1), South West (1)
Witness sessions held	87
Witnesses	757
By constituency	*Within the sounding base schools*
	Pupils (197)
	Teaching assistants and non-teaching staff (64)
	Teachers and heads (106)
	From the wider communities
	School governors (34)
	Parents (74)
	Head teachers from other local schools (60)
	Other community representatives (from other education sectors, local authorities, voluntary agencies, faiths, arts, police, magistrates, hard-to-reach groups etc) (222)

THE NATIONAL SOUNDINGS

The national soundings considered issues arising from the evidence collected by the Review, structured according to the Review's themes, in order to assist the team in its analysis of that evidence and in its preparation for the writing of the final report. There were two sets of national soundings: for organisations (two full-day seminars, held in London in February 2008); and for practitioners (three full-day seminars, held in Cambridge between January and March 2008).

The national soundings for organisations: themes and discussion groups

Education, community, society and polity: the context of primary education

1. The changing national and international context
2. Diversity, cohesion, equality and equity
3. Children and childhood
4. Parenting, caring and educating
5. The national primary education system: structure, governance, finance
6. The national primary education system: policy, politics and reform

Schools, learning and teaching: the nature of primary education

1. What is primary education for? Aims and values
2. The primary curriculum
3. Learning and teaching
4. Standards, quality and assessment
5. Inclusion, minorities, special needs, the hard-to-reach
6. Teachers and other professionals
7. Schools: structures, ages, stages, transitions and leadership

The national soundings for organisations: participating organisations

Amnesty International
Association for Science Education
Association of Directors of Children's Services
Association of Educational Psychologists
Association of Teachers and Lecturers
British Association of Social Workers
British Association for Early Childhood Education
British Educational Research Association
British Humanist Association
Catholic Education Service
Confederation of British Industry
Church of England Education Division
Centre for Studies in Inclusive Education
Early Childhood Forum
Equality and Human Rights Commission
Family and Parenting Institute
Geographical Association
Historical Association
International Learning and Research Centre
National Association of Head Teachers
National Association of Standing Advisory Councils for Religious Education

National Association for Small Schools
National Association of Schoolmasters Union of Women Teachers
National Association of Teachers of Religious Education
National Association of Teachers of Travellers
National Confederation of Parent Teachers Associations
National Union of Teachers
Oxfam UK
Save the Children
School Councils UK
Suffolk County Council
Training, Advancement and Co-operation in Teaching Young Children
UNICEF UK
United Kingdom Literacy Association
Universities Council for the Education of Teachers
Youth Music

The national soundings for practitioners: themes and discussion groups

Children: their development, learning and needs

1. Appreciating difference and achieving inclusive education
2. Increasing interaction in the classroom
3. The importance of consulting pupils about their learning and their schools
4. Pressure on children within and outside their schools

Children: their world beyond the school

1. Parenting, caring and educating
2. Valuing children's lives and learning outside school
3. The impact of new technology and media on children's lives and education

Primary education: ages, stages and structures

1. The ages and stages of primary education
2. The primary curriculum
3. Assessment: its form and purposes

The national soundings for practitioners: participating schools and children's centres

Askwith Community Primary School, Askwith, West Yorkshire
The Batt Church of England Primary School, Witney, Oxfordshire
Brentside Primary School, London Borough of Ealing
Charles Dickens Primary School, London Borough of Southwark
Footprints Children's Centre, Knowle, Bristol
Great Torrington Junior School, Great Torrington, North Devon
Holy Trinity Primary School, Bradley Stoke, Bristol
Ilfracombe Infant School, Ilfracombe, Devon
Lauriston Primary School, London Borough of Hackney
Luckwell Primary School, Bedminster, Bristol
Millfields Community School, London Borough of Hackney
Northbury Infant School, London Borough of Barking and Dagenham
Oxley Park Primary School, Milton Keynes

Redlands County Primary School, Fareham, Hampshire
Ridgeway Primary School, London Borough of Croydon
Ripple Junior School, London Borough of Barking and Dagenham
Rookery Primary School, Handsworth, Birmingham
Selby Abbey Primary School, Selby, North Yorkshire
St John's College School, Cambridge
South Milford Community Primary School, South Milford, Leeds
The Westborough Primary School, Westcliff-on-Sea, Essex
Withycombe Raleigh Church of England Primary School, Exmouth, Devon
The Wroxham School, Potters Bar, Hertfordshire

Appendix 5
Other consultations, including sessions with Government, opposition and non departmental public bodies

In addition to the community and national soundings, Review personnel were involved in a large number of other consultations. Initially these had a formative purpose, helping to shape the Review's focus and programme. Next, like the community soundings, they responded to the Review's themes and questions. Later, they considered issues emerging from the interim reports. Most of the consultations were with representatives of organisations. Some, like those with DfES/DCSF, were regular meetings. Others were one-off events. At the time of going to press 146 such meetings have taken place or are scheduled, in addition to the 92 community and national soundings, making a total of 238 sessions. The format for the meetings ranges from informal gatherings of a few representatives from each side, to formal seminars and large-scale conferences.

ORGANISATIONS INVOLVED

Note: the difference between the number of organisations (55) and the number of sessions (146) reflects the fact that with several organisations there were repeated meetings.

10 Downing Street Policy Unit
All Souls Group
Association of Educational Psychologists
Association of Teachers and Lecturers
British Association for International and Comparative Education
Cambridge Assessment
Catholic Education Service
Children's Society
Children, Schools and Families Select Committee
Church of England Education Division
Conservative Party
Department for Education and Skills / Department for Children, Schools and Families
Development Education Association
Early Childhood Forum (representing 50 early childhood organisations)
Edexcel
Essex Primary Heads Association
Esmée Fairbairn Foundation
General Teaching Council for England
Good Childhood Enquiry
House of Commons Education and Skills / Children, Schools and Families Committee
Implementation Review Unit
Kettner's (education publishers group)
Labour Party
Learning Without Limits
Leadership for Learning

Liberal Democrat Party
National Association for Primary Education
National Association for Teachers of English
National Association of Head Teachers
National Association of Teachers of Travellers
National College for School Leadership
National Literacy Trust
National Institute of Adult and Continuing Education
National Union of Teachers
New Vision Group
Office of the Chief Rabbi
Ofsted
Oxfam
Paul Hamlyn Foundation
Primary Capital Programme
Primary Learning Group
Primary National Strategy
Primary Umbrella Group (representing 35 primary education organisations)
Prime Minister's Strategy Unit
Qualifications and Curriculum Authority
Royal Society of Arts, Manufacture and Commerce
School Councils Forum
Specialist Schools and Academies Trust
Sustainable Development Commission
Training and Development Agency for Schools
The Worshipful Company of Weavers
ESRC Teaching and Learning Research Programme
Universities' Council for the Education of Teachers
United Kingdom Literacy Association
Westminster Education Forum

MEETINGS WITH GOVERNMENT, OPPOSITION AND NON-DEPARTMENTAL PUBLIC BODIES, OCTOBER 2006–MARCH 2009

Meeting with	Sessions
Government	
Secretary of State	1
Secretary of State's senior policy adviser(s)	2
No 10 Policy Unit directorate member(s)	2
Prime Minister's Strategy Unit member(s)	1
DCSF senior officials, including members of Rose review	7
DCSF Primary National Strategy	1
DCSF Implementation Review Unit	1
Non-departmental public bodies	
Ofsted	3
QCA	3
TDA	1
NCSL	1
Implementation review Unit (IRU)	1

Linked to DCSF but not an NDPB
GTCE   3

Opposition
Conservative education shadow/advisers   4
Liberal Democrat education shadow/advisers/groups   8

All-party group
House of Commons CSF Committee and/or chair   4

Meetings with government/DCSF members and advisers   15
Meetings with members of NDPBs and other DCSF-linked bodies   12
Meetings with other political parties   12
Meetings with all-party CSF Committee   4

Total   43

ALL STAKEHOLDER MEETINGS (COMMUNITY SOUNDINGS, NATIONAL SOUNDINGS, OTHER MEETINGS): SUMMARY, BY CONSTITUENCY

Constituency	Number of sessions
Children	20
Teachers, teaching assistants and head teachers	45
School governing bodies	7
Parents	8
Community representatives	15
Government (DfES/DCSF, Downing Street)	15
Opposition parties (Conservatives, Liberal Democrats)	12
House of Commons Select Committee	4
Non-departmental public bodies and similar	12
Professional groups and associations, including teaching unions	35
Other groups and organisations	46
Advisory Committee and its sub groups	19
Total	**238**

Appendix 6
Searches of offical data

With the co-operation of DfES/DCSF, QCA, Ofsted, TDA and OECD, the Review searched a range of official data bearing on the primary phase. This included standard documentation from these organisations, much of it now available electronically, together with the following:

DFES/DCSF PUPIL DATA

- Pupil Achievement Tracker (PAT): pupil level data back to 1999.
- School Census/PLASC data, at pupil, staff, school and local authority levels (1997–2006).

DFES/DCSF SCHOOL DATA

- Edubase: includes current school level data on location, pupil numbers etc, and policy coverage.
- The DfES/DCSF School and College Achievement and Attainment Tables (formerly Performance Tables) giving school-level achievement data and attendance figures (2000–2006).
- Annual statistical releases covering schools, pupils and teacher workforce, attainment, funding and provision (1995–2006).
- Value for Money Unit data on school-level inputs and outcomes, efficiency and effectiveness, uses of Ofsted and DfES/DCSF data and research. Includes international comparisons (2000).

DFES/DCSF LOCAL AND NATIONAL DATA

- Local authority level data on staff, teacher numbers, teacher-pupil ratios, salaries, funding, initiatives, SEN figures (1997–2005).
- Government trends data relating to national targets and money and time investments in schools, workforce, pupil attainment, pupil numbers (1990s–2006).
- Additional data on attainment at pupil, school and local authority levels in relation to measures of deprivation including Free School Meals (FSM), the Income Deprivation Affecting Children Index (IDACI) and social class (1990s–2006).
- Comparative data from Northern Ireland, Scotland and Wales.

OECD INTERNATIONAL COMPARATIVE DATA

- Educational attainment of the adult population.
- Links between education, economic growth and social outcomes.
- Impact of demographic trends on education provision.
- Educational expenditure per student.
- Public and private investment in educational institutions.
- Total public expenditure on education.
- Enrolment in education from primary education to adult life.

- Participation in secondary and tertiary education.
- Education and work status of the youth population.
- Total intended instruction time for students in primary education.
- Class size and ratio of students to teaching staff.
- Teachers' salaries.
- Teaching time and teachers' working time.
- Access to and use of ICT.
- Age and gender distribution of teachers and staff employed in education.

OFSTED DATA AND REPORTS

- HMSCI annual reports, 1960s–1994 (HMI); HMCI annual reports 1994–present (Ofsted).
- Inspection reports and school self-evaluations.
- School-level data: 1994–2005 covering school performance, social and economic measures, leadership, management and pupil achievement based on inspection judgements; lesson/ subject area data (1994–2005), covering pupil achievement and teaching quality.
- Inspection Judgement Recording Statements (1994–2005) at national, school and (some) lesson/subject levels.
- HMI and Ofsted surveys and special reports.

OTHER OFFICIAL DATABASES

PICSI, PANDA and now RAISEOnline databases comparing school data to the national picture. The most recent data (2004+) allow more regional, local and pupil-level and value-added comparisons.

Appendix 7
The research surveys and other interim reports

The 31 interim reports, 28 of them specially-commissioned surveys of published research, were released in nine groups between October 2007 and May 2008, with two further reports published in February 2009. On each occasion, several types of document were issued: (i) the reports in full; (ii) 3–4 page briefings on each report; (iii) 3–4 page overview briefings on each group of reports published together; (iv) a press release. These gave readers the choice of accessing the reports at any level from the short summary to the full report, with a fuller summary in between. The reports are listed below in order of publication.

12 October 2007   The community soundings

Community Soundings: the Primary Review regional witness sessions, Robin Alexander and Linda Hargreaves. ISBN 978-1-906478-00-1.

2 November 2007   How well are we doing? Research on standards, quality and assessment in English primary education

Standards and quality in English primary schools over time: the national evidence (Research Survey 4/1) Peter Tymms and Christine Merrell. ISBN 978-1-906478-01-8.

Standards in English primary education: the international evidence (Research Survey 4/2) Chris Whetton, Graham Ruddock and Liz Twist. ISBN 978-1-906478-02-5.

The quality of learning: assessment alternatives for primary education (Research Survey 3/4) Wynne Harlen. ISBN 978-1-906478-03-2.

23 November 2007   Children's lives and voices: research on children at home and school

Children's lives outside school and their educational impact (Research Survey 8/1) Berry Mayall. ISBN 978-1-906478-05-6.

Parenting, caring and educating (Research Survey 7/1) Yolande Muschamp, Felicity Wikeley, Tess Ridge and Maria Balarin. ISBN 978-1-906478-06-3.

Primary schools and other agencies (Research Survey 8/2) Ian Barron, Rachel Holmes, Maggie MacLure and Katherine Runswick-Cole. ISBN 978-1-906478-07-0.

Children and their primary schools: pupils' voices (Research Survey 5/3) Carol Robinson and Michael Fielding. ISBN 978-1-906478-04-9.

14 December 2007   Children in primary schools: research on development, learning, diversity and educational needs

Children's cognitive development and learning (Research Survey 2/1a) Usha Goswami and Peter Bryant. ISBN 978-1-906478-08-7.

Children's social development, peer interaction and classroom learning (Research Survey 2/1b) Christine Howe and Neil Mercer. ISBN 978-1-906478-09-4.

Children in primary education: demography, culture, diversity and inclusion (Research Survey 5/1) Mel Ainscow, Jean Conteh, Alan Dyson, and Frances Gallannaugh. ISBN 978-1-906478-10-0.

Learning needs and difficulties among children of primary school age: definition, identification, provision and issues (Research Survey 5/2) Harry Daniels and Jill Porter. ISBN 978-1-906478-11-7.

18 January 2008   Aims and values in primary education: national and international perspectives

Aims as policy in English primary education (Research Survey 1/1) John White. ISBN 978-1-906478-12-4.

Aims and values in primary education: England and other countries (Research Survey 1/2) Maha Shuayb and Sharon O'Donnell. ISBN 978-1-906478-13-1.

Aims for primary education: the changing national context (Research Survey 1/3) Stephen Machin and Sandra McNally. ISBN 978-1-906478-14-8.

Aims for primary education: changing global contexts (Research Survey 1/4) Rita Chawla-Duggan and John Lowe. ISBN 978-1-906478-15-5.

8 February 2008   The structure and content of English primary education: international perspectives

The structure of primary education: England and other countries (Research Survey 9/1) Anna Riggall and Caroline Sharp. ISBN 978-1-906478-17-9.

Curriculum and assessment policy: England and other countries (Research Survey 3/1) Kathy Hall and Kamil Øzerk. ISBN 978-1-906478-18-6.

Primary curriculum futures (Research Survey 3/3) James Conroy, Moira Hulme and Ian Menter. ISBN 978-1-906478-19-3.

29 February 2008   Governance, funding, reform and quality assurance: policy frameworks for English primary education

The governance and administration of English primary education (Research Survey 10/2) Maria Balarin and Hugh Lauder. ISBN 978-1-906478-20-9.

The funding of English primary education (Research Survey 10/1) Philip Noden and Anne West. ISBN 978-1-906478-21-6.

The trajectory and impact of national reform: curriculum and assessment in English primary schools (Research Survey 3/2) Dominic Wyse, Elaine McCreery and Harry Torrance. ISBN 978-1-906478-22-3.

Quality assurance in English primary education (Research Survey 4/3) Peter Cunningham and Philip Raymont. ISBN 978-1-906478-23-0.

18 April 2008   Primary teachers: training, development, leadership and workforce reform

Primary schools: the professional environment (Research Survey 6/2) Ian Stronach, Andy Pickard and Liz Jones. ISBN 978-1-906478-25-4.

Primary teachers: initial teacher education, continuing professional development and school leadership development (Research Survey 6/3) Olwen McNamara, Mark Brundrett and Rosemary Webb. ISBN 978-1-906478-26-1.

Primary workforce management and reform (Research Survey 6/4) Hilary Burgess. ISBN 978-1-906478-27-8.

16 May 2008   Learning and teaching in primary schools: processes and contexts

Learning and teaching in primary schools: insights from TLRP (Research Survey 2/4) Mary James and Andrew Pollard. ISBN 978-1-906478-30-8.

Classes, groups and transitions: structures for learning and teaching (Research Survey 9/2) Peter Blatchford, Susan Hallam and Peter Kutnick and Judith Ireson, with Andrea Creech. ISBN 978-1-906478-29-2.

Primary schools: the built environment (Research Survey 6/1) Karl Wall, Julie Dockrell and Nick Peacey. ISBN 978-1-906478-24-7.

20 February 2009   The primary curriculum: an alternative vision

Towards a New Primary Curriculum: a report from the Cambridge Primary Review. Part 1: Past and Present, Robin Alexander and Julia Flutter. ISBN 978-1-906478-31-5.

Towards a New Primary Curriculum: a report from the Cambridge Primary Review. Part 2: The Future, Robin Alexander. ISBN 978-1-906478-32-2.

References

Aaronovitch, D. (2008) 'Do old-style subjects deaden young minds?', *The Times*, 9 December.

Adams, D., Alexander, E., Drummond, M.J. and Moyles, J. (2004) *Inside the Foundation Stage: recreating the reception year*, London: Association of Teachers and Lecturers.

Adelman, C. and Alexander, R.J. (1982) *The Self-Evaluating Institution: practice and principles in the management of educational change*, London: Methuen.

Ainscow, M., Booth, T. and Dyson, A. with Farrell, P., Frankham, J., Gallannaugh, F., Howes, A. and Smith, R. (2006) *Improving Schools, Developing Inclusion*, Abingdon: Routledge.

Ainscow, M., Conteh, J., Dyson, A. and Gallannaugh, F. (2010) 'Children in primary education: demography, culture, diversity and inclusion' in R.J. Alexander, with C. Doddington, J. Gray, L. Hargreaves and R. Kershner (eds) *The Cambridge Primary Review Research Surveys*, London: Routledge, Chapter 8.

Ainscow, M., Dyson, A., Goldrick, S., Kerr, K. and Miles, S. (2008) *Equity in Education: responding to context. The third report of the Centre for Equity in Education*, Manchester: University of Manchester.

Alderson, P. (2003) *Institutional Rights and Rites: a century of childhood*, London: Institute of Education.

Alderson, P. (2008) *Young Children's Rights* (2nd edition), London: Jessica Kingsley.

Alexander, R.J. (1984) *Primary Teaching*, London: Cassell.

Alexander, R.J. (1991) *Primary Education in Leeds: twelfth and final report of the Primary Needs Independent Evaluation Project*, Leeds: University of Leeds with Leeds City Council.

Alexander, R.J. (1995) *Versions of Primary Education*, London: Routledge.

Alexander, R.J. (1997) *Policy and Practice in Primary Education: local initiative, national agenda*, London: Routledge.

Alexander, R.J. (2001a) 'Basics, cores and choices: prospects for curriculum reform' (paper commissioned for the 1997–8 National Curriculum review), in J. Soler, A. Craft and H. Burgess (eds) *Teacher Development: exploring our own practice*, London: Paul Chapman: 26–40.

Alexander, R.J. (2001b) *Culture and Pedagogy: international comparisons in primary education*, Oxford: Blackwell.

Alexander, R.J. (2004a) 'Still no pedagogy? Principle, pragmatism and compliance in primary education', *Cambridge Journal of Education* 34(1): 7–34.

Alexander, R.J. (2004b) *Talk for Learning Project: the second year*, Northallerton: North Yorkshire County Council.

Alexander, R.J. (2008a) *Essays on Pedagogy*, London: Routledge.

Alexander, R.J. (2008b) *Towards Dialogic Teaching: rethinking classroom talk* (4th edition), York: Dialogos.

Alexander, R.J. (2009) *Towards a New Primary Curriculum: a report from the Cambridge Primary Review. Part 2: The Future*, Cambridge: University of Cambridge Faculty of Education.

Alexander, R.J. and Flutter, J. (2009) *Towards a New Primary Curriculum: a report from the Cambridge Primary Review. Part 1: Past and Present*, Cambridge: University of Cambridge Faculty of Education.

Alexander, R.J. and Hargreaves, L. (2007) *Community Soundings: the Primary Review regional witness sessions*, Cambridge: University of Cambridge Faculty of Education.

Alexander, R.J., Rose, J. and Woodhead, C. (1992) *Curriculum Organisation and Classroom Practice in Primary Schools: a discussion paper*, London: DES.

Alexander, R.J., Willcocks, J. and Nelson, N. (1996) 'Discourse, pedagogy and the National Curriculum: change and continuity in primary schools', *Research Papers in Education* 11(1): 81–120.

Alldred, P., David, M. and Edwards, R. (2002) 'Minding the gap: children and young people negotiating relations between home and school', in R. Edwards (ed) *Children, Home and School: regulation, autonomy or connection*, London: RoutledgeFalmer.

Amabile, T. (1996) *Creativity in Context*, Oxford: Westview Press.

Annesley, B., Horne, M. and Cottam, H. (2002) *Learning Buildings*, London: Schoolworks.

Anning, A. and Edwards, A. (1999) *Promoting Children's Learning Birth to Five*, Buckingham: Open University Press.

Ansell, N., Barker, J. and Smith, F. (2007) 'UNICEF "Child Poverty in Perspective" Report: a view from the UK', *Children's Geographies* 5(3): 325–30.

Ariès, P. (1962) *Centuries of Childhood*, Harmondsworth: Penguin.

Armstrong, D. (2005) 'Reinventing "inclusion": New Labour and the cultural politics of special education', *Oxford Review of Education* 31(1): 135–151.

Armstrong, M. (1980) *Closely Observed Children: the diary of a primary classroom*, London: Writers and Readers in association with Chameleon.

Arnold, C., Merriman, H. and Watts, P. (2006) *Wraparound Services: the consumer's views*, Sandwell: Sandwell Metropolitan Borough Council.

Arnold, M. [1862] (1973) 'The Twice-Revised Code', in G. Sutherland (ed.) *Arnold on Education*, London: Penguin: 27–50.

Arnold, M. [1869] in S. Collini (1993) *Culture and Anarchy and Other Writings*, Cambridge: Cambridge University Press.

Arts Council (2006) *This Much We Know: research digest 2002-6*, London: Arts Council.

Ashby, P., Hobson, A., Tracey, L., Malderez, A., Tomlinson, P. *et al.* (2008) *Beginner Teachers' Experiences of Initial Teacher Preparation, Induction and Early Professional Development: a review of the literature.* London: DCSF.

Ashton, P., Kneen, P., Davies, F. and Holley, B. (1975) *The Aims of Primary Education: a study of teachers' opinions*, London: Macmillan.

Assessment Reform Group (2002) *Assessment for Learning: 10 principles*, London: Institute of Education.

Assessment Reform Group (2008) *Changing Assessment Practice: process, principles and standards*, Belfast: ARG.

Association of Teachers and Lecturers (2007) *Subject to Change: new thinking on the curriculum*, London: ATL.

ATL, DfES, GMB, NAHT, NASUWT *et al.* (2004) *Guidance for Schools on Higher Level Teaching Assistant Roles for School Support Staff*, online: http://www.tda.gov.uk/upload/resources/pdf/w/wamg_hlta_roles.pdf (accessed 21 January 2009).

Audit Commission (2002) *Special Educational Needs: a mainstream issue*, London: Audit Commission.

Audit Commission (2008) *National School Survey Results: the school survey, England*, London: Audit Commission.

Auld, R. (1976) *William Tyndale Junior and Infants Schools Public Inquiry*, London: Inner London Education Authority.

Baillargeon, R., Li, J., Ng, W. and Yuan, S. (2008) 'A new account of infants' physical reasoning,' in A. Woodward and A. Needham (eds) *Learning and the Infant Mind*, New York: Oxford University Press.

Baird, G. (2006) 'Prevalence of disorders of the autistic spectrum in a population cohort of children in South Thames', *The Lancet* 368(9531): 210–5.

Bakhtin, M. (1981) in M. Holquist (ed.), *The Dialogic Imagination*, Austin, TX: University of Texas Press.

Bakhtin, M. (1986) *Speech Genres and Other Essays*, Austin, TX: University of Texas Press.

Balarin, M. and Lauder, H. (2010) 'The governance, administration and control of primary education' in R.J. Alexander, with C. Doddington, J. Gray, L. Hargreaves and R. Kershner (eds) *The Cambridge Primary Review Research Surveys*, London: Routledge, Chapter 26.

Ball, S. (ed.) (1990) *Foucault and Education: disciplines and knowledge*, London: Routledge.

Balls, E. (2008) *Supporting the 21st Century School*, online: www.everychildmatters.gov.uk.

Barber, M. (2001a) *Large-Scale Education Reform in England: a work in progress*, paper for the Managing Education Reform Conference, Moscow, 29-30 October.

Barber, M. (2001b) 'High expectations and standards for all, no matter what: creating a world class education service in England', in M. Fielding (ed.) *Taking Education Really Seriously: four years' hard Labour*, London: Routledge.

Barber, M. (2007) *Instruction to Deliver: fighting to transform Britain's public services*, London: Politico's.

Barber, M. and Mourshed, M. (2007) *How the World's Best Performing School Systems Come Out on Top*, London: McKinsey and Co. Ltd.

Barker, I. (2007) 'Extended schools chip away at play', *Times Educational Supplement*, 23rd November.

Barnes, C. *et al.* (2000) *Lives of Disabled Children, Research Briefing 8*, Swindon: Economic and Social Research Council.

Barnes, D., Britton, J. and Rosen, H. (1969) *Language, the Learner and the School*, Harmondsworth: Penguin.

Barron, I., Holmes, R., MacLure, M. and Runswick-Cole, K. (2010) 'Primary schools and other agencies' in R.J. Alexander, with C. Doddington, J. Gray, L. Hargreaves and R. Kershner (eds) *The Cambridge Primary Review Research Surveys*, London: Routledge, Chapter 5.

Bayliss, V. (1999) *Opening Minds: education for the 21st century*, London: RSA.

Bazalgette, C. (ed.) (1994) *Balancing Literature, Language and the Media in the National Curriculum: report of the Commission of Inquiry into English*, London: BFI Publishing.

Bearne, E. (2002) 'A good listening to: Year 3 pupils talk about learning', *Support for Learning* 17(3): 122–127.

Bedford, H. and Elliman, D. (2000) 'Concerns about immunisation', *British Medical Journal* 320: 240–243.

Beck, U. (1992) *Risk Society*, London: Sage.

Becta (2007) *Harnessing Technology Schools Survey 2007*, Coventry: Becta.

Becta (2009) *Becta's contribution to the Rose Review*, Coventry: Becta.

Benavot, A. and Braslavsky, C. (eds) (2007) *School Knowledge in Comparative and Historical Perspective: changing curricula in primary and secondary education*, Dordrecht: Springer.

Benn, M. and Millar, F. (2006) *A Comprehensive Future: quality and equality for all our children*, London: Compass.

Bennett, N. (1976) *Teaching Styles and Pupil Progress*, London: Open Books.

Bennett, N., Andreae, J., Hegarty, P. and Wade, B. (1980) *Open Plan Schools: schools council project*, Windsor: NFER.

Bennett, N., Desforges, C., Cockburn, A. and Wilkinson, B. (1984) *The Quality of Pupil Learning Experiences*, London: Lawrence Erlbaum.

Bercow, J. (2008) *A Review of Services for Children and Young People with Speech, Language and Communication Needs*, London: DCSF.

Berliner, D.C. (1994) 'Expertise: the wonder of exemplary performance', in J.M.Mangieri and C.C. Block (ed.) *Creating Powerful Thinking in Teachers and Students*, Fort Worth, TX: Holt, Rinehart and Winston, pp. 141–186.

Berliner, D.C. (2004) 'Expert teachers: their characteristics, development and accomplishments', *Bulleting of Science, Technology and Society* 24(3), 200-212.

Berliner, D.C. and Biddle, B.J. (1995) *The Manufactured Crisis: myths, fraud and the attack on America's public schools*, New York: Perseus Books.

Berry, C. and Little, A. (2006) 'Multi-grade teaching in London', in A. Little (ed) *Education for All and Multi-Grade Teaching: challenges and opportunities*. Dordrecht, the Netherlands: Springer.

Black, P.J. (1997) 'Whatever happened to TGAT?', in C. Cullingford (ed.) *Assessment vs Evaluation*, London: Cassells.

Black, P.J. and Wiliam, D. (1998a) 'Assessment and classroom learning', *Assessment in Education* 5 (1): 7–74.

Black, P.J. and Wiliam, D. (1998b) *Inside the Black Box*, Slough: NFER-Nelson

Black, P.J. and Wiliam, D. (2002) *Standards in Public Examinations*, London: King's College School of Education.

Black, P., Harrison, C., Lee, C., Marshall, B. and Wiliam, D. (2002) *Working Inside the Black Box*, Slough: NFER-Nelson.

Black-Hawkins, K., Florian, L. and Rouse, M. (2007) *Achievement and Inclusion in Schools*, London: Routledge.

Blakemore, S. and Frith, U. (2005) *The Learning Brain*, Oxford: Blackwell Publishing.

Blatchford, P. and Baines, E. (2006) 'Grouping together: adopt strategies to keep your class work effectively in groups', *Junior Education* July: 12–13.

Blatchford, P., Bassett, P., Brown, P., Martin, C. and Russell, A. (2004) *The Effects of Class Size on Attainment and Classroom Practices in English Primary Schools (Years 4 to 6) 2000–2003, research briefing*. London: DfES.

Blatchford, P., Bassett, P., Brown, P., Martin, C. *et al.* (2008) *Deployment and Impact of Support Staff in Schools and the Impact of the National Agreement (Strand 2, Wave 1 - 2005/06)*, London: Institute for Education University of London.

Blatchford, P., Galton, M., Kutnick, P. and Baines, E. (2005) *Improving the Effectiveness of Pupil Groups in Classrooms*, Final Report to ESRC, London: ESRC.

Blatchford, P., Hallam, S., Ireson, J. and Kutnick, P., with Creech, A. (2010) 'Classes, groups and transitions: structures for teaching and learning' in R.J. Alexander, with C. Doddington, J. Gray, L. Hargreaves and R. Kershner (eds) *The Cambridge Primary Review Research Surveys*, London: Routledge, Chapter 21.

Blatchford, P. and Kutnick, P. (2003) 'Developing group work in everyday classrooms', *International Journal of Educational Research* 39:1–8.

Blatchford, P., Kutnick, P., Baines, E. and Galton, M. (2003) 'Toward a social pedagogy of classroom group work', *International Journal of Educational Research* 39: 153–72.

Blatchford, P., Russell, A., Bassett, P., Brown, P. and Martin, C. (2007) 'The effect of class size on pupils aged 7 to 11 years', *School Effectiveness and Improvement* 18(2): 147–172.

Blyth, W.A.L. (1965) *English Primary Education: a sociological description*, London: Routledge and Kegan Paul.

Blyth, W.A.L., Cooper, K.R., Derricott, R., Elliott, G., Sumner, H. and Waplington, A. (1976) *Place, Time and Society 8–13: curriculum planning in history, geography and social science*, Glasgow: Collins.

Board of Education (1905) *Reports on Children under Five Years of Age in Public Elementary Schools, by Women Inspectors*, London: HMSO.

Board of Education (1931) *Report of the Consultative Committee on the Primary School* (the Hadow Report), London: HSMO.

Boddy, J., Cameron, C., Mooney, A., Moss, P., Petrie, P. and Statham, J. (2005) *Introducing Pedagogy into the Children's Workforce: Children's Workforce Strategy: A response to the consultation document*, London: Thomas Coram Research Unit, Institute of Education, University of London.

Bond, L., Smith, T., Baker, W.K. and Hattie, J.A. (2000) *The Certification System for the National Board for Professional Teaching Standards: a construct and consequential validity study*, Greensborough: University of Greensborough.

Boydell, D. (1974) 'Teacher-pupil contact in junior classrooms', *British Journal of Educational Psychology*, 44: 313–18.

Boyden, J. and Ennew, J. (1997) *Children in Focus: a manual for participatory research with children*, Stockholm: Rädda Barnen.

Boyle, W. and Bragg, J. (2008) 'Making primary connections: the cross-curriculum story', *The Curriculum Journal* 19(1): 5–21.

Bradshaw, J. (2005) 'Conclusions', in J. Bradshaw and E. Mayhew (eds) *The Well-being of Children in the UK* (2nd edition), London: Save the Children.

Bradshaw, J., Middleton, S., Davis, A., Oldfield, N. *et al.* (2008) *A Minimum Income Standard for Britain: what people think*, York: Joseph Rowntree Foundation.

Brehony, K. (2005) 'The changing role of teachers: a historical account', paper presented at the ESRC Teaching and Learning Research Programme Seminar Series *Changing Teacher Roles, Identities and Professionalism*, King's College London, 20 January.

Brettingham, M. (2007) 'Teachers told "boycott interviews by pupils"', *The Times Educational Supplement*, 25 May: 10.

Bristol City Council (2005) *Supplementary Schools in Bristol: their contribution to raising achievement*, Bristol: Bristol City Council.

British Educational Suppliers Association (2007) *Information and Computer Technology in UK State Schools*. BESA summary report, London: BESA.

British Medical Association (2006) *Child and Adolescent Mental Health – a guide for healthcare professionals*, London: BMA.

Bronfenbrenner, U. (ed) (2005) *Making Human Beings Human: bioecological perspectives on human development*, Thousand Oaks, CA: SAGE.

Brooker, E. (2002) *Starting School: young children learning cultures*, Buckingham: Open University Press.

Brooker, E. and Siraj-Blatchford, I. (2002) '"Click on Miaow!" How children aged 3 and 4 experience the nursery computer', *Contemporary Issues in Early Childhood* 3(2): 251–72.

Brookes, M. (2008) *General Secretary's Address to the National Association of Head Teachers Annual Conference*, May 4.

Brooks, G., Schagen, I. and Nastat, P. (1997) *Trends in Reading at Eight*, Slough: NFER.

Brooks, R. and Tough, S. (2006) *Assessment and Testing: making space for teaching and learning*, London: IPPR.

Brown, G. and Desforges, C. (1977) 'Piagetian psychology and education: time for revision', *British Journal of Educational Psychology* 47: 7–17.

Brown, P. and Lauder, H. (1997) 'Education, globalisation and econmic development', in A.H. Halsey, H. Lauder, P. Brown and A.S. Wells (eds) *Education, Culture, Ecomomy, Society*, Oxford: Oxford University Press: 172–192.

Brown, R., Rutland, A. and Watters, C. (2008) *Identities in Transition: a longitudinal study of immigrant children*, Swindon: ESRC.

Brugel, I. and Weller, S. (2007) *Locality, School and Social Capital*, Final report to the Economic and Social Research Council, Swindon: ESRC.

Bruner, J.S. (1963) *The Process of Education*, New York: Random House.

Bruner, J.S. (1983) *Child's Talk: learning to use language*, Oxford: Oxford University Press.

Bruner, J.S. (1996) *The Culture of Education*, Cambridge MA: Harvard University Press.

Bruner, J. and Haste, H. (eds) (1987) *Making Sense: the child's construction of the world*, London, New York: Methuen.

Bryant, P. and Trabasso, T. (1971) 'Transitive inferences and memory in young children', *Nature* 232: 456–8.

Bryant, P.E. (1974) *Perception and Understanding in Young Children*, Methuen, London.

Buckingham, D. (2003) *Media Education: literacy, learning and contemporary culture*, Cambridge: Polity Press.

Buckingham, D. (2005) *Schooling the Digital Generation: popular culture, the new media and the future of education*, London: Institute of Education.

Bulmer, M. (1986) *Neighbourhoods: the work of Philip Abrams*, Cambridge: Cambridge University Press.

Bunn, R. (2006) *Sustainable Schools: getting it right*, London: BCSE.

Burgess, H. (2010) 'Primary workforce management and reform' in R.J. Alexander, with C. Doddington, J. Gray, L. Hargreaves and R. Kershner (eds) *The Cambridge Primary Review Research Surveys*, London: Routledge, Chapter 25.

Burke, C. and Grosvenor, I. (2003) *The School I'd Like*, London: RoutledgeFalmer.

Burn, A. and Leach, J. (2004) *A systematic review of the impact of ICT in the learning of literacies associated with moving image texts in English, 5–16*, in Research Evidence in Education Library, London: EPPI-Centre, Social Science Research Unit, Institute of Education, University of London.

Butt, G. and Gunter, H. (2005) 'Challenging modernisation: remodelling the education workforce', *Educational Review* 57(2): 131–137.

Cabinet Office (2007) *Reaching Out: think family*, London: Cabinet Office Social Exclusion Task Force.

Cabinet Office (2008) *Excellence and Fairness: achieving world class public services*, Norwich: HMSO.

Central Advisory Council for Education (England) (1967) *Children and Their Primary Schools: a report of the Central Advisory Council for Education (England)* (the Plowden Report), London: HMSO.

Campbell, R.J. (1985) *Developing the Primary School Curriculum*, London: Cassell.

Campbell, R.J. (1993) 'The National Curriculum in primary schools: a dream at conception, a nightmare at delivery', in C. Chitty and B. Simon (ed.) *Education Answers Back: critical responses to government policy*, London: Lawrence and Wishart.

Campbell, R.J. (1994) *Primary Teachers at Work*, London: Routledge.

Campbell, R.J. (2001) 'The colonisation of the primary curriculum', in R. Phillips and J. Furlong (eds) *Education, Reform and the State: twenty-five years of politics, policy and practice*, London: Routledge: 31–44.

Campbell, R.J. and Neil, S. (1994) *Curriculum Reform at Key Stage 1: teacher commitment and policy failure*, London: Longman.

Cardini, A. (2006) 'An analysis of the rhetoric and practice of educational partnerships in the UK: an area of complexities, tensions and power', *Journal of Education Policy* 21(4).

Carrington, B. and McPhee, A. (2007) 'Boys' "under-achievement" and the feminization of teaching', *Journal of Education for Teaching* 2: 109–120.

Carrington, B., Tymms, P. and Merrell, C. (2008) 'Role models, school improvement and the "gender gap" – do men bring out the best in boys and women the best in girls?', *British Educational Research Journal* 34(3): 315–327.

Cassen, R. and Kingdon, G. (2007) *Tackling Low Educational Achievement*, York: Joseph Rowntree Foundation. Online: www.jrf.org.uk/bookshop/eBooks/2063-education-schools-achievement.pdf .

Cazden, C.B. (2001) *Classroom Discourse: the language of teaching and learning*, Portsmouth, NH: Heinemann.

Chamberlain, T., Lewis, K., Teeman, T. and Kendall, L. (2006) *Schools' Concerns and their Implications for Local Authorities: annual survey of trends in education 2006: research summary*, Slough: NFER.

Chawla-Duggan, R. and Lowe, J. (2010) 'Aims for primary education: changing global contexts', in R.J. Alexander, with C. Doddington, J. Gray, L. Hargreaves and R. Kershner (eds) *The Cambridge Primary Review Research Surveys*, London: Routledge, Chapter 11.

Cheminais, R. (2008) *Engaging Pupil Voice to Ensure that Every Child Matters*, London: David Fulton/Routledge.

Child Poverty Action Group (2007) Written evidence to Commons Select Committee on Work and Pensions. Memorandum submitted by CPAG Session 2007–08.

CPAG (2008) *Child Poverty: the stats: analysis of the latest poverty statistics*, London: Child Poverty Action Group.

Children and Young People Now (2007) 'Study undermines Tory setting plans', 3 October. Online: http://www.cypnow.co.uk/Archive/login/741930/

Children' Rights Alliance for England (2008) 'Schools must consider the views of students', press release (13.11.08), online: http://www.crae.org.uk/news/press.html#Schools

Children's Society (2006) *Good Childhood? A question for our times: The Good Childhood Inquiry launch report*, London: The Children's Society.

Children's Society (2007) *The Good Childhood: a national inquiry Evidence summary two   family*, London: Children's Society.

Children's Society (2008a) *The Good Childhood: a national inquiry. Evidence summary three – health*, London: Children's Society.

Children's Society (2008b) *Reflections on Childhood – Family*. GfK NOP survey results, online:www.childrenssociety.org.uk/resources/documents/good%20childhood/Reflections%20on%20Childhood%20Family_3191_full.pdf

Children's Society (2008c) *Reflections on Childhood – Friendship*. GfK NOP survey results, online: www.childrenssociety.org.uk/resources/documents/good%20childhood/Reflections%20on%20Childhood%20Friendship_3189_full.pdf

Children's Society (2008d) *Reflections on Childhood – Health*. GfK NOP survey results, online: www.childrenssociety.org.uk/resources/documents/good%20childhood/7082_full.pdf).

Children's Society (2008e) *Reflections on Childhood – Learning*. GfK NOP survey results, online: www.childrenssociety.org.uk/resources/documents/good%20childhood/Reflections%20on%20Childhood%20Learning_3193_full.pdf

Children's Society (2008f) *Reflections on Childhood – Lifestyle*. GfK NOP survey results, online: www.childrenssociety.org.uk/resources/documents/good%20childhood/6293_full.pdf

Chitty, C. (2008) 'The UK National Curriculum: an historical perspective', *Forum* 50(3): 343–347.

Christian Research (2005) *English Church Census*, Swindon: Christian Research Ltd.

Civitas (2009) 'Misdiagnosing the cause of present-day educational failure', online: http://www.civitas.org.uk/wordpress/?p=705

Clark, A. and Moss, P. (2001) *Listening to Young Children: the Mosaic approach*, London: National Children's Bureau.

Clark, A. and Moss, P. (2005) *Spaces to Play: more listening to young children using the Mosaic approach*, London: National Children's Bureau.

Clark, A., Kjørholt, A.T. and Moss, P. (2005) *Beyond Listening: children's perspectives on early childhood services*, Bristol: Policy Press.

Clark, L. (2007) 'Children being robbed of their innocence by "guns, gangs and celebrities"' *Daily Mail*, 11 October.

Claxton, G. (2006) 'Mindfulness, learning and the brain', *Journal of Rational-Emotive & Cognitive-Behavior Therapy* 23(4): 301–14.

Claxton, G. (2008) *What's the Point of School? Rediscovering the heart of education*, Oxford: Oneworld Publications.

Close, R. (2004) *Television and Language Development in the Early Years: a review of the literature*, National Literacy Trust, online: http://www.literacytrust.org.uk/research/TV.html.

Cockburn, T. (1998) 'Children and citizenship in Britain', *Childhood* 5(1): 99–117.

Coffield, F. (2005) 'Learning Styles: help or hindrance?' *NSIN Research matters No 26*, London: Institute of Education, University of London.

Coffield, F., Edward, S., Finlay, I., Hodgson, A., Spours, K. and Steer, R. (2008) *Improving Learning, Skills, and Inclusion: the impact of policy on post-compulsory education*, Abingdon: Routledge.

Coffield, F., Steer, R., Allen, R., Vignoles, A., Moss, G. and Vincent, C. (2007) *Public Sector Reform: principles for improving the education system*, London: IoE Publications.

Cohen, J. (1977) *Statistical Power Analysis for the Behavioural Sciences*, New York: Academic Press.

Cole, M. (1996) *Cultural Psychology: a once and future discipline*, Cambridge, MA: The Belknap Press.

Cole, M. (ed.) (2006) *Education, Equality and Human Rights: issues of gender, 'race', sexuality, disability and social class* (2nd edition), Abingdon: Routledge.

Cole, M. and Blair, M. (2006) 'Racism and education: from Empire to New Labour', in M. Cole (ed.) *Education, Equality and Human Rights: issues of gender, 'race', sexuality, disability and social class* (2nd edition), Abingdon: Routledge: 70–88.

Cole, M. and Cole, S.R. (1996) *The Development of Children* (3rd edition), New York: W.H. Freeman.

Coleman, L. and Coleman, J. (2002) 'The measurement of puberty: a review', *Journal of Adolescence* 25: 535–550.

Collishaw, S., Maughan, B., Goodman, R. and Pickles, A. (2004) 'Time trends in adolescent mental health', *Journal of Child Psychology and Psychiatry* 45(8): 1350–1362.

Commission for the Built Environment (2008) *Threshold Needed to Halt Poor School Design*, online: http://www.cabe.org.uk/default.aspx?contentitemid=2643.

Commission for Racial Equality (2006) *Annual Report of the Commission for Racial Equality, 1 January–31 December 2005*, London: TSO.

Commission for Racial Equality (2007) *A Lot Done, A Lot to Do: our vision for an integrated Britain*, London: Belmont Press.

Commission for Rural Communities (2007) *State of the Countryside: tackling rural disadvantage*, Gloucestershire: Commission for Rural Communities. Online: http://www.ruralcommunities.gov.uk/files/socr2007-fullreport.pdf.

Commission for Social Care Inspection (2004) *The Commission for Social Care Inspection (Children's Rights Director) Regulations 2004*, Statutory Instrument 2004 No. 615, London: TSO.

Connolly, H. and White, A. (2006) 'The different experiences of the United Kingdom's ethnic and religious populations', *Social Trends* 36: 2006 edition. Office for National Statistics, online: http://www.statistics.gov.uk/CCI/article.asp?ID=1408&Pos=6&ColRank=1&Rank=224

Conroy, J., Hulme, M. and Menter, I. (2010) 'Primary curriculum futures' in R.J. Alexander, with C. Doddington, J. Gray, L. Hargreaves and R. Kershner (eds) *The Cambridge Primary Review Research Surveys*, London: Routledge, Chapter 16.

Conservative Party (2009) *Raising the Bar, Closing the Gap*, Policy Green Paper No 1, London: The Conservative Party.

Cooper, P. (2005) 'AD/HD', in A. Lewis and B. Norwich (eds) (2005) *Special Teaching for Special Children? Pedagogies for inclusion*, Maidenhead: Open University Press.

Cordingley, P., Bell, M., Evans, D. and Firth, A. (2003) *What do Teacher Impact Data Tell Us about Collaborative CPD?* London: DfES/EPPI/CUREE.

Cox, B. and Boyson, R. (1975) *The Fight for Education: Black Paper 1975*, London: J.M.Dent.

Cox, B. and Dyson, A.E. (1971) *The Black Papers on Education*, London: Davis-Poynter.

Cox, B. and Boyson, R. (1975) *The Fight for Education: Black Paper 1975*, London: J.M.Dent.

Craig, G., Adamson, S., Ali, N., Ali, S. *et al.* (2007) *Sure Start and Black and Minority Ethnic Populations*, London: DfES.

Creative Partnerships (2007) *This Much We Know: whole school case studies*, London: Creative Partnerships.

Creemers, B. (1994) 'Effective instruction: an empirical basis for a theory of educational effectiveness', in D. Reynolds, B. Creemers, P. Nesselrodt, E. Schaffer *et al.* (eds) *Advances in School Effectiveness Research and Practice*, Oxford: Pergamon.

Csikszentmihalyi, M. (1996) *Creativity: flow and the psychology of discovery and invention*, New York: Harper Collins.

Cuban, L. and Tyack, D. (1995) *Tinkering Towards Utopia: a century of public school reform*, Cambridge MA: Harvard University Press.

Cullingford, C. (1986) '"I suppose learning your tables could help you get a job": children's views on the purpose of schools', *Education 3–13* 14: 41–46.

Cummings, C., Dyson, A., Muijs, D., Papps, I *et al.* (2007) *Evaluation of the Full Service Extended Schools Initiative: final report,* London: DfES.

Cummings, C., Dyson, A., Papps, I., Pearson, D. *et al.* (2006) *Evaluation of the Full Service Extended Schools Initiative, Second Year: thematic papers*, London: DCSF.

Cunningham, M. and Hargreaves, L. (2007) *Minority Ethnic Teachers' Professional Experiences: evidence from the Teacher Status Project*, London: DfES.

Cunningham, P. (1988) *Curriculum Change and the Primary School Since 1945: dissemination of the progressive ideal*, Lewes: Falmer Press.

Cunningham, P. and Raymont, P. (2010) 'Quality assurance in English primary education' in R.J. Alexander, with C. Doddington, J. Gray, L. Hargreaves and R. Kershner (eds) *The Cambridge Primary Review Research Surveys*, London: Routledge, Chapter 28.

Currie, C., Gabhainn, S.N., Godeau, E., Roberts, C. *et al.* (2008) *Inequalities in Young People's Health. HSBC international report from the 2005/2006 survey*, Copenhagen: World Health Organisation Regional Office for Europe.

Curtis, P. (2008a) 'SATs results delayed by newly hired company's "style of management"', *The Guardian*, 5 July.

Curtis, P. (2008b) 'Schools failing gifted pupils by not recording their talent, says minister', *The Guardian*, 20 September.

Dale, R. (1997) 'The state and the governance of education', in A.H. Halsey, H. Lauder, P. Brown and A.S. Wells (eds) *Education: culture, economy, society*, Oxford: Oxford University Press: 273–282.

Daniels, H. (2001) *Vygotsky and Pedagogy*, London: Routledge-Falmer.

Daniels, H. and Porter, J. (2010) 'Learning needs and difficulties among children of primary school age: definition, identification, provision and issues' in R.J. Alexander, with C. Doddington, J. Gray, L. Hargreaves and R. Kershner (eds) *The Cambridge Primary Review Research Surveys*, London: Routledge, Chapter 9.

Daugherty, R. and Ecclestone, K. (2007) 'Constructing assessment for learning in the UK policy environment', in J. Gardner (ed) *Assessment and Learning*, London: Sage.

David, T., Goouch, K., Powell, S. and Abbott, L. (2002) *Birth to Three Matters: a framework to support children in their earliest years*, Canterbury Christ Church University College: Sure Start.

Davie, R. and Galloway, D. (1996) (eds) *Listening to Children in Education*, London: David Fulton.

Davies, D. and Rudd, P. (2001) *Evaluating School Self-Evaluation*, Slough: National Foundation for Educational Research.

Davies, J. and Brember, I. (2001) 'A decade of change: monitoring reading and mathematical attainment in Year 6 over the first ten years of the Education Reform Act', *Research in Education* 65: 31–40.

Davies, L. and Kirkpatrick, G. (2000) *The Euridem Project: a review of pupil democracy in Europe*, London: The Children's Rights Alliance.

Davis, P. and Florian, L. (2004) *Teaching Strategies and Approaches for Pupils with Special Educational Needs: a scoping study*, Nottingham: DfES.

Dawes, L., Mercer, N. and Wegerif, R. (2003) *Thinking Together: a programme of activities for developing speaking, listening and thinking skills for children aged 8–11*, Birmingham: Imaginative Minds.

Dawson, P. (1994) 'Professional codes of practice and ethical conduct', *Journal of Applied Philosophy* 11(2): 169–183.

Day, C. (2002) 'School reform and transitions in teacher professionalism and identity', *International Journal of Educational Research,* 37: 677–692.

Day, C. and Saunders, L. (2006) 'What being a teacher (really) means', *Forum* 48(3): 265–271.

Daycare Trust and Esmée Fairbairn Foundation (2008) *Ensuring Equality in Childcare for BME Families*, London: Daycare Trust and Esmée Fairbairn Foundation.

Deakin-Crick, R., Taylor, M., Ritchie, S., Samuel, E. and Durant, K. (2005) *A Systematic Review of the Impact of Citizenship Education on Student Learning and Achievement*, London: EPPI-Centre, Social Science Research Unit, Institute of Education.

Deary, I., Thorpe, G., Wilson, V., Starr, J.H. and Whalley, L.J. (2003) 'Population sex differences in IQ at age 11: the Scottish mental survey 1932', *Intelligence* 31: 533–542.

Dearden, R. (1968) *The Philosophy of Primary Education*, London: Routledge and Kegan Paul.

Dearden, R. (1976) *Problems in Primary Education*, London: Routledge.

Dearing, R. (1993a) *The National Curriculum and its Assessment: interim report*, London: NCC/SEAC.

Dearing, R. (1993b) *The National Curriculum and its Assessment: final report*, London: SCAA.

Delors, J. (1996) *Learning: The Treasure Within*. Report to UNESCO of the International Commission on Education for the Twenty-first Century.

De Muinck Keizer-Schrama, S.M.P.F. and Mul, D. (2001) 'Trends in pubertal development in Europe', *Human Reproduction Update* 7(3): 287–291.

Department for Children, Schools and Families (DCSF) (2007a) *Children Looked After in England (Including Adoption and Care Leavers). Year ending 31 March 2007*, London: DCSF.

DCSF (2007b) *The Children's Plan: building brighter futures*, London: DCSF.

DCSF (2007c) *Elective home education: guidance for local authorities*, London: DCSF.

DCSF (2007d) *Gender and Education: the evidence on pupils in England*, online: http://www.dcsf.gov.uk/ rsgateway/DB/RRP/u015238/index.shtml.

DCSF (2007e) *Narrowing the Gap*, London: DCSF.

DCSF (2007f) *Pedagogy and Personalisation*, London: DCSF.

DCSF (2007g) *Primary Framework for Literacy and Mathematics*, London: DCSF. Online: http:// nationalstrategies.standards.dcsf.gov.uk/primary/primaryframework.

DCSF (2007h) *Pupil Characteristics and Class Sizes in Maintained Schools in England: January 2007*, London: DCSF.

DCSF (2007i) *Statistics of Education (January 2007)*, London: DCSF.

DCSF (2008a) *2020 Children and Young People's Workforce Strategy: the evidence base*, London: DCSF.

DCSF (2008b) *21st Century Schools: a world-class education for every child*, London: DCSF.

DCSF (2008c) *The Assessment for Learning Strategy*, Nottingham: DCSF.

DCSF (2008d) *Being the Best for our Children: Releasing Talent for Teaching and Learning*, London: DCSF.

DCSF (2008e) *Byron Review: children and new technology. Executive summary*, London: DCSF.

DCSF (2008f) *The Children's Plan: one year on*, Nottingham: DCSF.

DCSF (2008g) *Children's Trusts: statutory guidance on inter-agency co-operation to improve well-being of children, young people and their families*, London: DCSF.

DCSF (2008h) *Departmental Report 2008*, London: DCSF.

DCSF (2008i) *The Early Years Foundation Stage: about the EFS Framework*, online: http://www. standards.dfes.gov.uk/eyfs/site/help/about.htm#faq18.

DCSF (2008j) *Education and Training Statistics for the UK: 2008*, London: DCSF.

DCSF (2008k) *Every Child Matters Outcomes Framework*, online: http://publications.everychildmatters. gov.uk/eOrderingDownload/DCSF-00331-2008.pdf.

DCSF (2008l) *Guidance for Local Authorities on Setting Education Performance Targets, Part 1: LA statutory targets for Key Stages 2, 4, early years outcomes, children in care, Black and minority ethnic groups, attendance*, London: DCSF.

DCSF (2008m) *The Independent Review of the Primary Curriculum: responses to the call for evidence*, London: DCSF.

DCSF (2008n) 'New law to strengthen Children's Trust Boards – improved accountability for child safety plans', Press notice (18 November 2008).

DCSF (2008o) *Permanent and Fixed Period Exclusions from Schools and Exclusion Appeals in England 2006–7*, London: DSCF.

DCSF (2008p) *Power to Innovate Guidance*, London: DCSF.

DCSF (2008q) Primary Curriculum Review questionnaire to schools, February.

DCSF (2008r) Primary Curriculum Review remit letter from Secretary of State Ed Balls to Sir Jim Rose, 9 January.

DCSF (2008s) *Primary Framework for Literacy and Mathematics*, online:http://www.standards.dfes. gov.uk/primaryframework/

DCSF (2008t) *Provision for Children Under Five Years of Age in England: January 2008*, Statistical First Release, Nottingham: DCSF.

DCSF (2008u) *Pupil Characteristics and Class Sizes in Maintained Schools in England*. SFR 09/2008, London: DCSF.

DCSF (2008v) *A School Report Card: consultation document*, London: DCSF.

DCSF (2008w) *School Workforce in England*, London: DCSF.

DCSF (2008x) *Special Educational Needs Coordinators (SENCO) Regulations 2008*, London: DCSF.

DCSF (2008y) *Special Educational Needs in England, January 2008*, London: DCSF.

DCSF (2008z) *Statistical First Release: outcome indicators for children looked after: twelve months to 30 September 2007, England*, London: DCSF.

DCSF (2008aa) *Statutory Guidance: the roles and responsibilities of the lead member for children's services and the director of children's services*, London: DCSF.

DCSF (2008ab) *Personalised Learning: a practical guide*, London: DCSF.

DCSF (2008ac) *The Primary Capital Plan*, London: DCSF.

DCSF (2009) 'Ed Balls tells school heads that report cards will herald a revolution in how schools are measured.' Press release 13 March 2009, online: http://www.dcsf.gov.uk/pns/DisplayPN.cgi? pn_id=2009_0057.

DCSF/Department for Culture, Media and Sport (DCMS) (2007) *National PE, School Sport and Club Links Strategy*, London: DCSF/DCMS.

DCSF/DCMS (2008) *Fair Play: a consultation on the play strategy*, London: DCSF/DCMS.

DSCF and Department for Innovation, Universities and Skills (DIUS) (2008) 'Spending per pupil in real terms', *Time Series*, online: http://www.dcsf.gov.uk/rsgateway/DB/TIM/m002001/index.shtml.

DCSF/Ministry of Justice (2007) *Children of Offenders Review*, London: DCSF / Ministry of Justice.

Department of Education and Science (DES) (1965) *The School Building Survey 1962*, London: HMSO.

DES (1972) *Teacher Education and Training* (the James Report), London: HMSO.

DES (1975) *A Language for Life* (the Bullock Report), London: HMSO.

DES (1977a) *Local Authority Arrangements for the Curriculum* (Circular 14/77), London: DES.

DES (1977b) *Ten Good Schools*, London: DES.

DES (1978a) *Primary Education in England: a survey by HM Inspectors of Schools*, London: HMSO.

DES (1978b) *Special Educational Needs: report of the Committee of Enquiry into the education of handicapped children and young people* (Warnock report), London: HMSO.

DES (1979) *Aspects of Secondary Education in England: a survey by HM Inspectors of Schools*, London: HMSO.

DES (1980a) *A Framework for the School Curriculum*, London: DES.

DES (1980b) *A View of the Curriculum*, London: HMSO.

DES (1981) *The School Curriculum*, London: DES.

DES (1982a) *Education 5 to 9: an illustrative survey of 80 first schools in England*, London: HMSO.

DES (1982b) *Mathematics Counts* (the Cockcroft Report), London: HMSO.

DES (1983a) *9-13 Middle Schools: an illustrative survey*, London: HMSO.

DES (1983b) *Teaching in Schools: the content of initial training*, London: DES.

DES (1984) *Initial Teacher Training: approval of courses* (Circular 3/84), London: DES.

DES (1985a) *Better Schools*, London: HMSO.

DES (1985b) *The Curriculum from 5 to 16*, Curriculum Matters 2, London: HMSO.

DES (1985c) *Education 8 to 12 in Combined and Middle Schools: an HMI survey*, London: HMSO.

DES (1986) *Local Authority Policies for the School Curriculum* (final report on responses to Circulars 14/77 and 6/81), London: DES.

DES (1989) *The Enquiry into Discipline in Schools* (the Elton Report), London: DES.

DES (1990) *Management of the School Day* (Circular 7/90), London: DES.

DES (1993) *The Initial Training of Primary Teachers: criteria for courses* (Circular 14/93), London: HMSO.

DES/Welsh Office (WO) (1988) *Task Group on Assessment and Testing: a report*, London: DES/WO.

DES, WO and Department of Education Northern Ireland (DENI) (1988) *Assessment of Performance Unit Science at Age 11*, London: HMSO.

Department for Education (DfE) (1993) *The Initial Training of Primary School Teachers: criteria for courses*, London: DfE.

Department for Education and Employment (DfEE) (1994) *Code of Practice on the Identification and Assessment of Children with Special Educational Needs*, London: Central Office of Information.

DfEE (1997) *Excellence in Schools*, London: HMSO.

DfEE (1998a) *The Learning Age: a renaissance for a new Britain*, London: TSO.

DfEE (1998b) *The National Literacy Strategy: framework for teaching*, London: DfEE.

DfEE (1998c) *Teachers: meeting the challenge of change. Green paper. Executive summary*, London: DfEE.

DfEE (1999a) *The Education (School Day and School Year) (England) Regulations* (Statutory Instrument No 3181), London: DfEE.

DfEE (1999b) *The National Numeracy Strategy: framework for teaching mathematics from Reception to Year 6*, London: DfEE.

DfEE(1999c) *The Induction Period for Newly Qualified Teachers*. Circular 5/99, London: DfEE.

DfEE/QCA (1999a) *The National Curriculum: handbook for primary teachers in England*, London: DfEE/QCA.

DfEE/QCA (1999b) *The National Curriculum: handbook for secondary teachers in England*, London: DfEE/QCA.

Department for Education and Skills (DfES) (2001a) *Inclusive Schooling: children with special educational needs*, Nottingham: DfES.

DfES (2001b) *Professionalism and Trust: the future of the teaching profession. Secretary of State's speech to the Social Market Foundation: November 2001*, London: DfES.

DfES (2001c) *Special Educational Needs Code of Practice*, Nottingham: DfES.

DfES (2002a) *Assessing the Net Capacity of Schools*, Nottingham: DfES.

DfES (2002b) *Time for Standards: reforming the school workforce*, London: DfES.

DfES (2003a) *Every Child Matters* (Green Paper), Norwich: TSO.

DfES (2003b) *Excellence and Enjoyment: a strategy for primary schools*, London: HMSO.

DfES (2004a) *Every Child Matters: change for children*, Nottingham: DfES.

DfES (2004b) *Every Child Matters: change for children in schools*, Nottingham: DfES.

DfES (2004c) *Five Year Strategy for Children and Learners: putting people at the heart of public services*, London: DfES.

DfES (2004d) *Raising Standards and Tackling Workloads: implementing the National Agreement. The National Agreement one year on*, London: DfES.

DfES (2004e) *Removing Barriers to Achievement: the government's strategy for SEN*, London: DfES.

DfES (2005a) *Children's Workforce Strategy: a strategy to build a world-class workforce for children and young people. Consultation paper*, Nottingham: DfES.

DfES (2005b) *Higher Standards, Better Schools* (White Paper), London: DfES.

DfES (2005c) *Learning Behaviour: the report of the practitioners' group on school behaviour and discipline*, London: DfES.

DfES (2005d) *Supporting the New Agenda for Children's Services and Schools: the role of learning mentors and co-ordinators*, London: DfES.

DfES (2006a) *Ethnicity and Education: the evidence on minority ethnic pupils*, London: DfES.

DfES (2006b) *Learning Outside the Classroom Manifesto*, London: DfES.

DfES (2006c) 'Adonis praises success of supplementary schools and looks to support them in future', press release (21 April 2006), online: http://www.dcsf.gov.uk/pns/DisplayPN.cgi?pn_id=2006_0059 (accessed 2 December 2008)

DfES (2006d) *School Based Expenditure Per Pupil in Real Terms Since 1992–93 in England*, London: DfES.

DfES (2006e) *Strong and Prosperous Communities* (White Paper), London: DfES.

DfES (2007a) *Better Buildings, Better Design, Better Education*, Nottingham: DfES.

DfES (2007b) *Every Parent Matters* (White Paper), London: DfES.

DfES (2007c) *Gender and Education: the evidence on pupils in England*, London: DfES.

DfES (2007d) *Making Good Progress*, consultation, London: DfES.

DfES (2007e) *The Early Years Foundation Stage: setting the standards for learning, development and care for children from birth to five*, Nottingham: DfES.

DfES/National Statistics (2006) *Provision for Children Under Five Years of Age in England*: January 2006, online: http://www.dcsf.gov.uk/rsgateway/DB/SFR/s000674/SFR32-2006.pdf.

DfES/ Ofsted (2004) *A New Relationship with Schools*, London: DfES and Ofsted.

Department of Health (DH) (2007) *Dental Screening (Inspection) in Schools and Consent for Undertaking Screening and Epidemiological Surveys*, London: Dept of Health.

DH (2008a) 'Parents will be told if their children are overweight', online: https://nds.coi.gov.uk/content/detail.asp?ReleaseID=375803&NewsAreaID=2&HUserID=878,793,889,851,776,865,866,845,786,674,677,767,684,762,718,674,708,683,706,718,674

DH (2008b) *Tackling Health Inequalities: 2007 status report on the programme for action*, London: Health Inequalities Unit, Department of Health.

DH and DCSF (2008) *Healthy Weight, Healthy Lives: a cross-government strategy*, London: DH/DCSF.

Department of Health and Social Security (1980) *Inequalities in Health* (The Black Report), London: DHSS.

Department for Work and Pensions (2008) *Households Below Average Income. An analysis of the income distribution 1994/5–2006/7*, online: www.dwp.gov.uk/asd/hbai.asp

Desforges, C. and Abouchaar, A. (2003) *The Impact of Parental Involvement, Parental Support and Family Education on Pupil Achievement and Adjustment: a review of the literature*. DfES Paper RR433, London: DfES.

Devine, D. (1993) 'A study of reading ability groups: primary school children's experiences and views', *Irish Educational Studies* 12: 134–42.

De Zulueta, F. (2006) *From Pain to Violence: the traumatic roots of destructiveness*, Oxford: John Wiley and Sons Ltd.

Dixon, P. (2007) 'We paint modern art', *Primary First* 2: 15.

Doddington, C. and Flutter, J., with Bearne, E. and Demetriou, H. (2002) *Sustaining Pupils' Progress in Learning at Year 3*, Cambridge: University of Cambridge Faculty of Education.

Doherty, P., Stott, A. and Kinder, K. (2004) *Delivering Services to Hard to Reach Families in On Track Areas (Home Office Development and Practice Report 15)*, London: The Home Office.

Donaldson, M. (1978) *Children's Minds*, London: Fontana.

Douglas, J. (1967) *The Home and the School*, London: Panther Books.

Disability Rights Commission (2006) *Equal Treatment: closing the gap*, Stratford upon Avon: DRC.

Dreyfus, H.L. and Dreyfus, S.E. (1986) *Mind Over Machine*, New York: Free Press.

Duckworth, K. (2008) *Influences on Attainment in Primary School Interactions between Child, Family and School Contexts*, London: DCSF.

Dudek, M. (ed.) (2006) *Children's Space*, London: Architectural Press.

Dunford, J. (1998) *Her Majesty's Inspectorate of Schools Since 1944: standard bearers or turbulent priests?* London: Woburn Press.

Dunn, J. (2004) *Children's Friendships: the beginnings of intimacy*, Oxford: Blackwell Publishing.

Dunn, J., Brown, J. and Beardsall, L. (1991) 'Family talk about feeling states and children's later understanding of others' emotions', *Developmental Psychology* 27: 448–55.

Dweck, C.S. (1999) *Self-Theories: their role in motivation, personality, and development*, Philadelphia, PA: The Psychology Press.

Dweck, C. (2006) *Mindset: the new psychology of success*, New York: Random House.

Dyson, C. (2008) *Poverty and Child Maltreatment*, London: NSPCC, online: http://www.nspcc.org.uk/Inform/research/Briefings/poverty_wda56897.html.

Earl, L., Watson, N., Levin, B, Leithwood, K. *et al.* (2003a) *Watching and Learning: OISE/UT evaluation of the implementation of the national literacy and numeracy strategies*, Nottingham: DfES.

Earl, L., Watson, N., Levin, B., Leithwood, K. *et al.* (2003b) *Watching and Learning 3: final report of the external evaluation of England's National Literacy and Numeracy* Strategies, Toronto: Ontario Institute for Studies in Education.

Early Childhood Forum (2007) *Championing Young Children's Rights and Entitlements*, London: Early Childhood Forum.

Early Education Advisory Group (2009) *The Independent Review of the Primary Curriculum Initial Response: a note from the Early Education Advisory Group.* Unpublished.

Easton, C., Eames, A., Wilson, R., Walker, M. and Sharp, C. (2006) *Evaluation of the National Remodelling Team: year 3*, online: http://www.nfer.ac.uk/publications/pdfs/downloadable/RMQ.pdf.

Eccles, J. (2006) 'Motivation and family influences', Presentation to the Centre for the Wider Benefits of Learning, University of Michigan.

Education Otherwise (2009) *Home educators' petition rejecting the state as parent of first resort strikes a chord*, press release 9 March 2009. Online: http://www.freedomforchildrentogrow.org/pr090309.pdf

Edwards, A., Barnes, M., Plewis, I. and Morris, K., *et al.* (2006) *Working to Prevent the Social Exclusion of Children and Young People: final lessons from the National Evaluation of the Children's Fund*. Briefing No. RB734, Nottingham: DfES.

Edwards, A.D. and Westgate, D.P.G. (1994) *Investigating Classroom Talk*, 2nd edition, London: Falmer Press.

Edwards, R. and Alldred, P. (2000) 'A typology of parental involvement in education centring on children and young people: negotiating familialisation, institutionalisation and individualisation', *British Journal of the Sociology of Education* 21: 435–455.

Eke, R. and Lee, J. (2004) 'Pace and differentiation in the Literacy Hour: some outcomes of an analysis of transcripts', *Curriculum Journal* 15(3): 219–232.

Elias, N. (1978) *The Civilising Process*, Oxford: Blackwell.

Ellis, S., Tod, J. and Graham-Matheson, L. (2008) *Special Educational Needs and Inclusion: reflection and renewal*, Rednal: NASUWT.

Elliott, J. (1996) 'School effectiveness research and its critics: alternative visions of schooling', *Cambridge Journal of Education* 26(2): 199–224.

Emerson, E. and Hatton, C. (2007) *The Mental Health of Children and Adolescents with Learning Disabilities in Britain*, Lancaster: Institute for Health Research, Lancaster University.

Engeström, Y. (1996) *Perspectives on Activity Theory*, Cambridge: Cambridge University Press.

Epstein, D., Elwood, J., Hey, V. and Maw, J. (eds) (1998) *Failing Boys? Issues in gender and achievement*, Buckingham: Open University Press.

The Equalities Review (2007) *Fairness and Freedom: final report of the Equalities Review*, London: The Cabinet Office. Online: http://archive.cabinetoffice.gov.uk/equalitiesreview.

Equality and Human Rights Commission (2008) *Sex and Power 2008*, Manchester: Equality and Human Rights Commission.

Ereaut, G. and Whiting, R. (2008) *The Alternative Discourse of Education*, London: Oxfam.

Ermisch, J. (2007) *Changing Patterns of Family Formation*, Essex: Institute for Economic and Social Research, ESRC.

European Commission (2001) *European Commission White Paper: A New Impetus for European Youth*, Brussels, Belgium: European Commission.

Evangelou, M., Sylva, K., Edwards, A. and Smith, T. (2008) *Supporting Parents in Promoting Early Learning: the evaluation of the Early Learning Partnership Project*, Nottingham: DCSF.

Eysenck, H.J. (1973) *The Inequality of Man*, London: Temple Smith.

Faupel, A. (ed.) (2003) *Emotional Literacy: assessment and intervention ages 7–11*, London: NfER Nelson.

Fenson, L., Dale, P.S., Reznick, J.S., Bates, E. *et al.* (1994) 'Variability in early communicative development', *Monographs of the Society for Research in Child Development* 59(5, Serial No. 242).

Feinstein, F. (2003) 'Inequality in the early cognitive development of British children in the 1970 cohort', *Economica* 70: 73–97.

Finn, J.D., Pannozzo, G.M. and Achilles, C.M. (2003) 'The "whys" of class size: student behaviour in small classes', *Review of Educational Research* 73(3): 321–368.

Fitzherbert, K. (1980) 'Strategies for prevention', in M. Craft, J. Raynor and L. Cohen (eds) *Linking Home and School – new review* (3rd edition), London: Harper and Row.

Fletcher-Campbell, F. and Lee, B. (2000) *A Study of the Changing Role of Local Education Authorities in Raising Standards of Achievement in Schools*, London: DfES.

Florian, L. (ed.) (2007) *The SAGE Handbook of Special Education*, London: SAGE

Flutter, J. and Rudduck, J. (2004) *Consulting Pupils: what's in it for schools?* London: RoutledgeFalmer.

Foster, P., Gomm, R. and Hammersley, M. (1996) *Constructing Educational Inequality: an assessment of research on school processes*, London: Falmer Press.

Fox, K. and Riddoch, C. (2000) 'Charting the physical activity patterns of contemporary children and adolescents', *Proceedings of the Nutrition Society* 59: 497–504.

Foxman, D., Hutchinson, D. and Bloomfield, B. (1991) *The APU Experience, 1977-1990*, London: Schools Examination and Assessment Council.

Franklin, B. (2002) 'Children's rights and media wrongs: changing representations of children and the developing rights agenda', in B. Franklin (ed.) *The New Handbook of Children's Rights*, London: Routledge.

Frederickson, N. and Cline, T. (2002) *Special Educational Needs, Inclusion and Diversity: a textbook*, Buckingham: Open University Press.

Freedman, T. (2009) 'Should ICT be taught as a discrete subject?' *Computers in Classrooms 3*, April 2009. Online: http://www.ymlp155.com/pubarchive_show_message_iframe.php?terryfreedman+263.

Furlong, J. (2009) 'Initial teacher education: ten questions', unpublished paper given at a seminar for the House of Commons Children, Schools and Families Committee, 10 February, Oxford: University of Oxford Department of Educational Studies.

Futurelab (2006) *Learner Voice: a handbook from Futurelab*, London: Futurelab.

Futurelab (2008) 'It's all about vision: building primary schools for the future', *Vision*, July–December 2008: 2–4.

Gage, N. (ed) (1963) *Handbook of Research on Teaching*, Washington, DC: American Educational Research Association.

Gage, N. (1978) *The Scientific Basis of the Art of Teaching*, New York: Teachers College Press.

Gaine, C. and Weiner, G. (eds) (2005) *Kids in Cyberspace: teaching anti-racism using the internet in Britain, Spain and Sweden*, Oxford: Symposium Books.

Galton, M. (1987) 'Change and continuity in the primary school: the research evidence', *Oxford Review of Education* 13(1), 81–93.

Galton, M. (2007) *Learning and Teaching in the Primary Classroom*, London: Sage.

Galton, M. and Fogelman, K. (1998) 'The use of discretionary time in the primary school', *Research Papers in Education* 13: 119–30.

Galton, M., Gray, J. and Rudduck, J. (1999) 'The impact of school transitions and transfers on pupil progress and attainment', London: DfES.

Galton, M., Gray, J., Rudduck, J., Berry, M. *et al.* (2003) *Transfer and Transition in the Middle Years of Schooling (7–14): continuities and discontinuities in learning*, London: DfES.

Galton, M., Hargreaves, L., Comber, C., Wall, D. *et al.* (1999) *Inside the Primary Classroom – 20 years on*, London: Routledge.

Galton, M., Hargreaves, L. and Pell, A. (2003) 'Progress in the middle years of schooling: continuities and discontinuities at transfer', *Education 3–13* 31(2): 9–18.

Galton, M. and MacBeath, J., with Page, C. and Steward, S. (2002) *A Life in Teaching? The impact of change on primary teachers' working lives*, London: University of Cambridge / National Union of Teachers.

Galton, M. and MacBeath, J. (2008) *Teachers Under Pressure*, London: SAGE.

Galton, M., Rudduck, J. and Gray, J., *et al.* (2003) *Progress in the Middle Years of Schooling (7–14): continuities and discontinuities in learning*, London: TSO.

Galton, M. and Simon, B. (eds) (1980) *Progress and Performance in the Primary Classroom*, London: Routledge.

Galton, M., Simon, B. and Croll, P. (1980) *Inside the Primary Classroom*, London: Routledge and Kegan Paul.

Gardner, H. (1983) *Frames of Mind: the theory of multiple intelligences*, New York: Basic Books.

Gardner, H. (1987) 'Beyond the IQ Education and human development', *Harvard Educational Review* 57: 187–93. Reprinted in H. Gardner (2006) *The Development and Education of the Mind: the selected works of Howard Gardner*, London: Routledge.

Gardner, H. (1995) 'Reflections on MI Myths and message', *Phi Delta Kappan* 7(3): 200–209. Reprinted in H. Gardner (2006) *The Development and Education of the Mind: the selected works of Howard Gardner*, London: Routledge.

Gardner, H. (1999) *Intelligence Reframed: multiple intelligences for the 21st century*, New York: Basic Books.

Gillard, D. (2007) *Education in England: a brief history*, online: www.dg.dial.pipex.com/history/.

Garner, R. (2007) 'The pain of a generation forced to grow up before their time', *The Independent*, 12 October.

Garner, R. (2008) 'The anxiety epidemic: why are children so unhappy?' *The Independent*, 11 March.

Gershon, P. (2004) *Releasing Resources to the Front Line: a review of public sector efficiency*, Norwich: HMSO.

Gibbs, C. (2004) *Transfer and Transition Project: key stage 1 to 2*, Business Administration Unit, West Sussex County Council.

Gilbert, C. (2008) Ofsted Press Briefing, 23 January.

Gladwell, M. (2002) 'The talent myth: Are smart people overrated?' *New Yorker*, 22 July: 28–33.

Glaser, D. (2000) 'Child abuse and neglect and the brain – a review', *Journal of Psychiatry and Psychology* 41(1): 97.

Glaser, R. (1996) 'Changing the agency for learning: acquiring expert performance', in K.A. Ericsson (ed) *The Road to Excellence: the acquisition of expert performance in the arts and sciences, sports and games,* Lawrence Erlbaum.

Glennerster, H., Hills, J., Piachaud, D. and Webb, J. (2004) *One Hundred Years of Poverty and Policy*, York: Joseph Rowntree Foundation.

Goldstein, H. and Blatchford, P. (1998) 'Class size and educational achievement: a review of methodology with particular reference to study design', *British Journal of Educational Research* 24(3): 255–268.

Goleman, D. (1996) *Emotional Intelligence: why it can matter more than IQ*, London: Bloomsbury.

Good, T. and Brophy, J. (2002) *Looking in Classrooms*, 9th edition, Boston, MA: Allyn and Bacon.

Goodman, R. and Scott, S. (2005) *Child Psychiatry*, 2nd edition, Oxford: Blackwell.

Gopnik, A., Meltzoff, A. and Kuhl, P.K. (1999) *Scientist and the Crib: what early learning tells us about the mind*, New York: William Morrow.

Gorard, S. (2006) 'Value-added is of little value', *Journal of Educational Policy* 15(5): 559–573.

Gorard, S. (2008) 'The value-added of primary schools: what is it really measuring?' *Educational Review* 60(2): 179–185.

Gorman, T. and Fernandes, C. (1992) *Reading in Recession: a report on the 'Comparative Reading Survey' from the National Foundation for Educational Research*, Slough: NFER.

Goswami, U. (2001) 'Cognitive development – no stages please – we're British', *British Journal of Psychology*, reprinted in H. Daniels and A. Edwards (eds) (2004) *The RoutledgeFalmer Reader in Psychology of Education*, London: RoutledgeFalmer.

Goswami, U. and Bryant, P. (2010) 'Children's cognitive development and learning', in R.J. Alexander, with C. Doddington, J. Gray, L. Hargreaves and R. Kershner (eds) *The Cambridge Primary Review Research Surveys*, London: Routledge, Chapter 6.

Gove, M. (2008) 'Why Conservative social policy delivers progressive ends', speech delivered at IPPR, 4 August.

Gray, J. (1990) 'The quality of schooling: frameworks for judgements', *British Journal of Educational Studies* 38(3): 204–223.

Gray, J. and McLellan, R. (2006) 'A Matter of Attitude? Developing a typology of boys' and girls' responses to primary schooling', *Gender and Education* 18(6): 651–672.

Great Britain (1988) *Education Reform Act 1988*, London: TSO.

Great Britain (1996) *Education Act 1996*, London: TSO.

Great Britain (1999) *The Changing of School Session Times (England) Regulations 1999. Statutory instrument 1999 no. 2733*, London: TSO.

Great Britain (2003) *The Education School Governance (Constitution)(England) Regulations 2003 (SI 2003/348)*, London: TSO.

Great Britain (2005) *Higher Standards, Better Schools for All*, London: TSO.

Great Britain (2006) *Education and Inspections Act 2006*, London: TSO.

Green, H., McGinnity, A., Meltzer, H., Ford, T. and Goodman, R. (2005) *Mental Health of Children and Young People in Great Britain*, London: Office for National Statistics.

Green, S., Bell, J., Oates, T. and Bramley, T. (2007) 'Alternative approaches to national assessment (KS1, KS2, KS3)', unpublished paper.

Gregg, P., Harkness, S. and Machin, S. (1999) *Child Development and Family Income*, York: Joseph Rowntree Foundation/YPS.

Grimmett, P.P. and McKinnon, A.M. (1992), 'Craft knowledge and the education of teachers' *Review of Research in Education,* 18, 385-456.

GTCE (2008a) *Code of Conduct and Practice: draft for consultation*, London: General Teaching Council for England

GTCE (2008b) *Annual Digest of Statistics, 2007–8*, online: http://www.gtce.org.uk/shared/contentlibs/gtc/141488/201080/stat_digest_08.

Grossman, P. (1995) 'Teachers' knowledge', in L.W. Anderson (ed.) *International Encyclopaedia of Teaching and Teacher Education*, Oxford: Elsevier.

Gulbenkian Foundation (1982) *The Arts in Schools: principles, practice and provision*, London: Gulbenkian Foundation.

Gulland, D. and Phillips, J. (2008) 'New directions in learning', in R. Lueder and V. Berg Rice (eds) (2008) *Ergonomics for Children: designing products and places for toddlers to teens*, New York and London: Taylor and Francis.

Hall, K. and Harding, A. (2002) 'Level descriptions and teacher assessment in England: towards a community of assessment practice', *Educational Research* 44: 1–15.

Hall, K. and Øzerk, K. (2010) 'Primary curriculum and assessment: England and other countries' in R.J. Alexander, with C. Doddington, J. Gray, L. Hargreaves and R. Kershner (eds) *The Cambridge Primary Review Research Surveys*, London: Routledge, Chapter 15.

Hallgarten, J. (2000) *Parents Exist, OK? Issues and visions for parent–school relationships*, London: IPPR.

Halliday, M. (1989) *Spoken and Written Language*, Oxford: Oxford University Press.

Halsey, K., Gulliver, C., Johnson, A., Martin, K. and Kinder, K. (2006) *Evaluation of Behaviour and Education Support Teams*, Nottingham: DfES.

Hamilton D. (1996) 'Peddling feel good fictions', *Forum* 38: 54–56.

Hamilton, D. (1999) 'The pedagogic paradox (or Why No Didactics in England?)' *Pedagogy, Culture and Society* 7(1), 135-152.

Hanvey, C. (2003) 'The lessons we never learn', *The Observer*, 26 January.

Hardman, F.G., Smith, F. and Wall, K. (2003) ' "Interactive whole class teaching" in the National Literacy Strategy', *Cambridge Journal of Education* 33(2): 197–215.

Hargreaves, A. and Goodson, I. (1996) *Teachers' Professional Lives: aspirations and actualities*, London: Routledge.

Hargreaves, D.H. (1978) 'Power and the paracurriculum', in C. Richards (ed.) *Power and the Curriculum: issues in curriculum studies*, Driffield: Nafferton Books.

Hargreaves, D.H. (2004a) *Learning for Life: the foundations for lifelong learning*, Bristol: Policy Press.

Hargreaves, D.H. (2004b) *Personalising Learning 1: next steps in working laterally*, London: Specialist Schools and Academies Trust.

Hargreaves, D.H. (2004c) *Personalising Learning – 2: student voice and assessment for learning*, London: Specialist Schools and Academies Trust.

Hargreaves, D.H. (2006a) *A New Shape for Schooling?* London: Specialist Schools and Academies Trust.

Hargreaves, D.H. (2006b) *Personalising Learning 6: school design and organisation*, London: Specialist Schools and Academies Trust.

Hargreaves, D.H. (2008a) *Leading System Redesign – 1*, London: Specialist Schools and Academies Trust.

Hargreaves, D.H. (2008b) *Leading System Redesign – 4. Innovation networks in action*, London: Specialist Schools and Academies Trust.

Hargreaves, L., Cunningham, M., Hansen, A., McIntyre, D., Oliver, C. and Pell, T. (2007) *The Status of Teachers and the Teaching Profession in England: views from inside and outside the profession*, Cambridge: Faculty of Education University of Cambridge/DfES.

Harlen, W. (2005) 'Trusting teachers' judgment: research evidence of the reliability and validity of teachers' assessment used for summative purposes', *Research Papers in Education* 20(3): 245–270.

Harlen, W. (2007) *Assessment of Learning*, London: Sage.

Harlen, W. (2008) 'Science as a key component of the primary curriculum: a rationale with policy implications', *Perspectives on Education* 1: 4–18, London: The Wellcome Trust.

Harlen, W. (2010) 'The quality of learning: assessment alternatives for primary education' in R.J. Alexander, with C. Doddington, J. Gray, L. Hargreaves and R. Kershner (eds) *The Cambridge Primary Review Research Surveys*, London: Routledge, Chapter 19.

Harris, A. and Goodall, J. (2006) *Parental Involvement in Education: a review of the literature*, Warwick: Warwick University.

Harris, P.L. (1989) *Children and Emotion: the development of psychological understanding*, Oxford: Blackwell.

Hart, B. and Risley, T.R. (1995) *Meaningful Differences in the Everyday Experience of Young American Children*, Baltimore, MD: Brookes Publishing Company.

Hart, S., Dixon, A., Drummond, M.J. and McIntyre, D. (2004) *Learning Without Limits*, Maidenhead: Open University Press.

Hartley-Brewer, E. (1999) 'Are home-school deals just pie in the sky?', *The Independent*, 28 July.

Hartley-Brewer, E. (2006) *Praising Boys Well: 100 tips for parents and teachers*, Cambridge, MA: Da Capo Lifelong Books.

Hartley-Brewer, E. (2009) *Making Sense of Your Child's Friendships*, London: Piccadilly Press.

Hatcher, R. (2006) 'Social class and schooling: differentiation or democracy?', in M. Cole (ed.) *Education, Equality and Human Rights: issues of gender, 'race', sexuality, disability and social class* (2nd edition), Abingdon: Routledge.

Health Protection Agency (2008) 'Measles figures soar', Press release, 28 November. Online: http://www.hpa.org.uk/webw/HPAweb&HPAwebStandard/HPAweb_C/1227774034336?p=1204186170287.

Helwig, C. and Turiel, E. (2002) 'Children's social and moral reasoning', in P.K. Smith and C.H. Hart (eds) *Blackwell Handbook of Childhood Social Development*, Oxford: Blackwell.

Herbert, M. (2005) *Developmental Problems of Childhood and Adolescence: prevention, treatment and training*, Oxford: BPS Blackwell.

Her Majesty's Inspectorate (HMI) (1978) *Primary Education in England: a survey by HM Inspectors of Schools*, London: HMSO.

HMI (1983) *9–13 Middle schools: an illustrative survey*, London: HMSO.

HMI (1985) *Education 8–12 in Combined and Middle Schools: an HMI survey*, London: HMSO.

HM Treasury (2004) *Choice for Parents, the Best Start for Children: a ten year strategy for child-care*, London: TSO.

HM Treasury (2006) *Prosperity For All in the Global Economy: world class skills* (the Leitch Report), London: TSO.

HM Treasury/DfES (2007) *Aiming High for Disabled Children: better support for families*, Norwich: Office of Public Sector Information.

Hirsch, D. (2006) *What Will It Take to End Child Poverty? Firing on all cylinders*, York: Joseph Rowntree Foundation.

Hirsch, D. (2007a) *Chicken and Egg: child poverty and educational inequalities. CPAG policy briefing*, London: Child Poverty Action Group.

Hirsch, D. (2007b) *Experiences of Poverty and Educational Disadvantage*, York: Joseph Rowntree Foundation.

Hobsbawm, E. (1994) *Age of Extremes: the short twentieth century 1914–1991*, London: Abacus.

Hobsbawm, E. (2007) *Globalisation, Democracy and Terrorism*, London: Little, Brown.

Hobson, A.J., Malderez, A., Tracey, L., Homer, M. *et al.* (2007) *Newly Qualified Teachers' experiences of their first year of teaching: Findings from Phase III of the 'Becoming a teacher' project*, London, Department for Education and Skills.

Hofkins, D. (2008a) 'A thorny transition', *Education Guardian*, 17 June.

Hofkins, D. (2008b) *Enriching the Experience of Schooling: a commentary by the Teaching and Learning Research Programme*, London: TLRP.

Hollingworth, S., Allen, K., Hutchings, M., Kuyok, K. and Williams, K. (2008) *Technology and School Improvement: reducing social inequity with technology?* London: BECTA.

Holmes, E. (1911) *What is and What Might Be: a study of education in general and elementary education in particular*, London: Constable.

Holmlund, H., McNally, S. and Viarengo, M. (2008) *Impact of School Resources on Attainment at Key Stage 2. Research Brief*, London: DCSF.

The Home Office (2002) *Building Cohesive Communities*, London: TSO.

Hoover-Dempsey, K.V., Battiato, A.C., Walker, J.M.T., Reed, R.P. *et al.* (2001) 'Parental involvement in homework', *Educational Psychologist* 36(3): 195–209.

House of Commons (1986) *Achievement in Primary Schools: third report from the Education, Science and Arts Committee*, London: HMSO.

House of Commons (1994) *The Disparity in Funding Between Primary and Secondary Schools: Education Committee second report*, London: HMSO.

House of Commons (1996) *House of Commons Committee of Public Accounts: improving poorly performing schools in England. Fifty-ninth report of session 2005–06*, London: HMSO.

House of Commons (1999a) *The Work of Ofsted: fourth report of the Education and Employment Committee*, London: HMSO.

House of Commons (1999b) *Government's and Ofsted's response to the Fourth Report from the Committee, Session 1998-9: the work of Ofsted*, London: HMSO.

House of Commons Committee on Education and Skills (2006) *Special Educational Needs: Third Report*, London: House of Commons.

House of Commons (2007) *Sustainable Schools: are we building schools for the future? Seventh Report of Session 2006–7, Volume 1*, London: House of Commons.

House of Commons (2008a) *Testing and Assessment: Fifth Special Report of the Children, Schools and Families Committee*, Session 2007–8. London: TSO.

House of Commons (2008b) *Testing and Assessment. Third Report of Session 2007–8*, Volume 1, London: HMSO.

House of Commons (2008c) *Testing and Assessment: government and Ofsted responses to the Committee's third report of session 2007–08. Fifth special report of session 2007–08*, London: TSO.

House of Commons Children, Schools and Families Committee (2009) *National Curriculum: fourth report of session 2008-9*, London: HMSO.

House of Lords Hansard reports (19 February 2007) *Schools: all-age institutions.* Comment by Lord Adonis, online: http://www.publications.parliament.uk/pa/ld200607/ldhansrd/text/70219w0006.htm#07021941000415.

House of Commons Hansard reports (14 October 2008) *National Curriculum Tests*, online: http://www.publications.parliament.uk/pa/cm200708/cmhansrd/cm081014/debtext/81014-0003.htm#08101459000003.

House of Lords Select Committee on Economic Affairs (2008) *The Economic Impact of Immigration. H L Paper 82-I*, online: http://www.publications.parliament.uk/pa/ld200708/ldselect/ldeconaf/82/82.pdf.

Howarth, C., Kenway, P., Palmer, G., and Miorellia, R. (1999) *Monitoring Poverty and Social Exclusion 1999*, London: Joseph Rowntree Foundation.

Howe, C. and Mercer, N. (2010) 'Children's social development, peer interaction and classroom learning' in R.J. Alexander, with C. Doddington, J. Gray, L. Hargreaves and R. Kershner (eds) *The Cambridge Primary Review Research Surveys*, London: Routledge, Chapter 7.

Howson, J. (2007) *23rd Annual Report of Senior Staff Appointments in Schools in England and Wales*, London: EDS Data Surveys Ltd.

Hoyle, E. (1969) *The Role of the Teacher*, London: Routledge Kegan Paul.

Hoyle, E. (2001) 'Teaching: prestige, status and esteem', *Educational Management Administration and Leadership* 29: 139–152.

Hughes, M. and Greenhough, P. (2006) 'Boxes, bags and videotape: enhancing home-school communication through knowledge exchange activities', *Educational Review* 58(4): 472–87.

Hughes, R. (2007) 'Changing but narrow', *Primary First* 2: 16–17.

Hurd, S., Dixon, M. and Oldham, J. (2006) 'Are low levels of book spending in primary schools jeopardising the National Literacy Strategy?' *The Curriculum Journal* 17(1): 73–88.

Hurt, J.S. (1979) *Elementary Schooling and the Working Classes 1860–1918*, London: Routledge and Kegan Paul.

Improvement and Development Agency (2009) 'What does the Education and Inspections Act 2006 mean for councils?', online: http://www.idea.gov.uk/idk/core/page.do?pageId=6013605.

The Independent (2006) 'Welcome to the green school', 29 June.

Ingvarson, L.C. and Hattie, J. (eds) (2008), *Assessing Teachers for Professional Certification: the first decade of the National Board for Professional Teaching Standards. Volume 11, Advances in Program Evaluation*, Amsterdam: Elsevier Press.

Invernizzi, A. and Williams, J. (eds) (2008) *Children and Citizenship*, London: Sage.

Ivins, C. (2008) *Survey of Parents in England, 2008*, London: DCSF.

James, M. and Pollard, A. (2010) 'Learning and teaching in primary schools: insights from TLRP' in R.J. Alexander, with C. Doddington, J. Gray, L. Hargreaves and R. Kershner (eds) *The Cambridge Primary Review Research Surveys*, London: Routledge, Chapter 20.

Jamieson, I. and Wikeley, F. (2000) 'School effectiveness and consistency', *School Effectiveness and School Improvement* 11(4): 435–452.

Jeffrey, B. and Woods, P. (1996) 'Feeling deprofessionalised: the social construction of of emotions during an Ofsted inspection', *Cambridge Journal of Education* 26(3): 325–44.

Jencks, C. and Smith, M., Acland, H., Bane, M.J., Cohen, D., Gintis, H., Heyns, B. and Michelson, S. (1972) *Inequality: a reassessment of the effect of family and schooling in America*, New York: Basic Books.

Johnson, M. (2007) *Subject to Change: new thinking on the curriculum*, London: ATL.

Jones, K. (2003) *Education in Britain: 1944 to the present*, Cambridge: Polity Press.

Joseph Rowntree Charitable Trust / Joseph Rowntree Reform Trust (2006) *Power to the People: the report of Power, an independent inquiry into Britain's democracy*, York: Joseph Rowntree Trusts.

Joseph Rowntree Foundation (2007a) 'Experiences of poverty and educational disadvantage', paper synthesising findings from eight reports from the Joseph Rowntree Foundation's Education and Poverty Programme. York: Joseph Rowntree Foundation.

Joseph Rowntree Foundation (2007b) 'Poverty twice as likely for minority ethnic groups: education fails to close the gap', press release, 30 April.

Joseph Rowntree Foundation (2007c) *Poverty, Wealth and Place in Britain 1968–2005*, Bristol: The Policy Press.

Joseph Rowntree Foundation (2008) *Poverty Updates*, online: www.jrf.org.uk/child-poverty/updates.asp.

Joubert, M. (2001) 'The art of creative teaching: NACCCE and beyond', in A. Craft, B. Jeffrey and M. Leibling (eds) *Creativity in Education*, London: Continuum.

Kamin, L.J. (1982) 'Mental testing and immigration', *American Psychologist* 37 (January 1982): 97–98.

Karlsen, G.E. (2000) 'Decentralised centralism: framework for a better understanding of governance in the field of education', *Journal of Education Policy* 15: 525–538.

Kazdin, A.E. (2005) *Parent Management Training*, Oxford: Oxford University Press.

Kelly, D. (1997) 'Education and difficult children: the teaching dilemma', in *Young Minds Magazine* 29.

Kendall, S. and Atkinson, M. (2006) *Some Perspectives on Home Education*, Slough: NFER.

Kendall, S., Lamont, E., Wilkin, A. and Kinder, K. (2007) *Every Child Matters: how school leaders in extended schools respond to local needs*, Nottingham: National College for School Leadership.

Kent, M. (2008) 'How about "teacher voice" for a change?' *Times Educational Supplement*, 11 April.

Kinder, K., Wakefield, A. and Wilkin, A. (1996) *Talking Back: pupils' views on disaffection*, Slough: NFER.

King, J. (2004) *Commissioning Children's Services and the Role of the Voluntary and Community Sector*, London: Local Government Association, the Improvement and Development Agency, the Connaught Group of Voluntary Organisations, NCH and the National Council of Voluntary Child Care Organisations.

King, R. (1978) *All Things Bright and Beautiful? A sociological study of infants' classrooms*, Chichester: Wiley.

Kishayama. M., Boyce, W., Jimenez, A., Perry, L. and Knight, R. (2008) 'Socio-economic disparities affect prefrontal function in children', *Journal of Cognitive Neuroscience*, posted online 27 August.

Kohlberg, L. (1981) *Essays on Moral Development: Vol 1. The philosophy of moral development*, San Francisco: Harper and Row.

Kramer, S.N. (1973) *History Begins at Sumer. Thirty-nine firsts in recorded history*, New York: Doubleday.

Kutnick, P., Hodgkinson, S., Sebba, J., Humphreys, S. *et al.* (2006) *Pupil Grouping Strategies and Practices at Key Stage 2 and 3: case studies of 24 schools in England*, London: DfES.

Kutnick, P., Sebba, J., Blatchford, P., Galton, M. *et al.* (2005) *The effects of pupil grouping: literature review*, Brighton: Brighton University.

Lansdown, G. (1995) *Taking Part: children's participation in decision-making*, London: Institute for Public Policy Research.

Lawton, D. (1983) *Curriculum Studies and Educational Planning*, London: Hodder and Stoughton.

Lawton, D. and Gordon, P. (1987) *HMI*, London: Routledge and Kegan Paul.

Layard, R. and Dunn, J. (2009) *A Good Childhood: searching for values in a competitive age*, London: Penguin Books.

Leaney, F. (2008) 'Ambassadors in a new school culture', *The Times Educational Supplement*, 9 May.

Learmonth, J. (2000) *Inspection: what's in it for schools*, London, Routledge.

Learning and Teaching Scotland, in association with the Department for International Development (2007) *The Global Dimension in the Curriculum: educating the global citizen*, Edinburgh: Learning and Teaching Scotland.

Lewis, A. (2006) *My School, My Family, My Life – telling it like it is*, London: Disability Rights Commission.

Lewis, A. and Norwich, B. (eds) (2005) *Special Teaching for Special Children? Pedagogies for inclusion*, Maidenhead: Open University Press.

Lewis, A., Parsons, S. and Robertson, C. (2007) *My School, My Family, My Life: telling it like it is*, Birmingham: School of Education, University of Birmingham.

Lewis, K., Chamberlain, T., Riggall, A., Gagg, K. and Rudd, P. (2007) *Annual Survey of Trends in Education 2007: schools' concerns and their implications for local authorities* (LGA Research Report 4/07), Slough: NFER.

Liberal Democrat Party (2009) *Equity and Excellence: policies for 5-19 education in England's schools and colleges*, Policy Paper 89, London: Liberal Democrats.

Lipman, M., Sharp, A.M. and Oscanyan, F.S. (1980) *Philosophy in the Classroom*, Philadelphia, PA: Temple University Press.

Lloyd, E. (2008) 'The interface between childcare, family support and child poverty strategies under New Labour: tensions and contradictions', *Social Policy and Society* 7(4): 479–494.

Local Government Association (2007) *Standard School Year*, online: http://www.lga.gov.uk/OurWork.asp?lsection=59&ccat=420.

Local Government Association, with the Department for Children, Schools and Families and the Improvement and Development Agency (2007) *Narrowing the Gap: an overview*, London, LGA

Local Government Association, with DCSF and the Improvement and Development Agency (2008a) *Narrowing the Gap*, London: DCSF.

Local Government Association, with DCSF and the Improvement and Development Agency (2008b) *Narrowing the Gap: final guidance Year 1*, London: LGA.

Locke, A., Ginsborg, J., and Peers, I. (2002) 'Development and disadvantage: implications for the early years', *International Journal of Language & Communication Disorders* 37(1): 3–15.

Lord, P., Kinder, K., Wilkin, A., Atkinson, M. and Harland, J. (2008) *Evaluating the Early Impact of Integrated Children's Services*, Slough: NFER/Local Authorities Research Consortium.

Lortie, D. (1975) *Schoolteacher: a sociological study*, Chicago: University of Chicago Press.

Lourenço, O. and Machado, A. (1996) 'In defense of Piaget's theory: a reply to 10 common criticisms', *Psychological Review* 103(1): 143–164.

Luke, A. and Carrington, V. (2002) 'Globalisation, literacy, curriculum practice', in R. Fisher, M. Lewis and G. Brooks (eds) *Language and Literacy in Action,* London: RoutledgeFalmer.

Luxton, R. and Last, G. (2000) *Interactive Whole Class Teaching: a briefing note*, London: London Borough of Barking and Dagenham.

MacBeath, J. (2006) *School Inspection and Self Evaluation*, London: Routledge.

MacBeath, J., Myers, K. and Demetriou, H. (2001) *Consulting Pupils: a toolkit for teachers*, Cambridge: Pearson Publishing.

MacBeath, J. and Oduro, G. (2005) *Self Evaluation and Inspection: a new relationship?* London: NUT.

MacBeath, J., Oduro, G. and Waterhouse, J. (2004) *Distributed Leadership in Action: a study of current practice in schools*, Nottingham: National College for School Leadership.

Machin, S. and McNally, S. (2010) 'Aims for primary education: the changing national context' in R.J. Alexander, with C. Doddington, J. Gray, L. Hargreaves and R. Kershner (eds) *The Cambridge Primary Review Research Surveys*, London: Routledge, Chapter 10.

Maclure, S. (1988) *Education Re-formed: a guide to the Education Reform Act 1988*, London: Hodder and Stoughton.

Maclure, S. (2000) *The Inspectors' Calling: HMI and the shaping of educational policy 1945-1992*, London: Hodder and Stoughton.

Madge, N. and Barker, J. (2007) *Risk and Childhood*, London: RSA.

Madge, N. and Wilmott, N. (2007) *Children's Views and Experiences of Parenting*, York: Joseph Rowntree Foundation.

Mahony, P. and Hextall, I. (2000) *Reconstructing Teaching: standards, performance and accountability*, London: Routledge Falmer.

Mansell, W. (2007) *Education by Numbers: the tyranny of testing*, London: Politico's.

Margo, J., Benton, M., Withers, K., Sodha, S. *et al.* (2008) *Those Who Can?* London: IPPR.

Marks, N., Shah, H. and Westall, A. (2004) *The Power and Potential of Wellbeing Indicators: measuring young people's well-being in Nottingham*, London: New Economics Foundation.

Marley, D. (2007) 'Deprived areas lose clubs, while the prosperous flourish', *Times Educational Supplement*, 9th November.

Marsh, J. and Millard, E. (2000) *Literacy and Popular Culture: using children's culture in the classroom*, London: Paul Chapman Publishing Ltd.

Mathers, S., Sylva, K. and Joshi, H. (2007) *Quality of Childcare Settings in the Millennium Cohort Study*, Nottingham: DfES.

Matthews, P. and Sammons, P. (2004) *Improvement Through Inspection: an evaluation of the impact of Ofsted's work*, London: Ofsted.

Mattock, C., Ness, A., Deere, K., Tilling, K. *et al.* (2007) 'Early life determinants of physical activity in 11 to 12 year olds: cohort study', *British Medical Journal* 336: 26–29.

Maughan, B. (2008) 'Mental health – trends', presentation to The Children's Society Good Childhood Forum: *Mental Health and Well-being*, 21 April 2008, London.

Maughan, B., Brock, A. and Ladva, G. (2004) 'Mental health', in *The Health of Children and Young People*, London: Office for National Statistics.

Maxwell, G.S. (2004) *Progressive Assessment for Learning and Certification: some lessons from school-based assessment in Queensland,* paper presented at the third conference of the Association of Commonwealth Examination and Assessment Boards, Nadi, Fiji (March).

Mayall, B. (2002) *Towards a Sociology for Childhood: thinking from children's lives*, Buckingham: Open University Press.

Mayall, B. (2010) 'Children's lives outside school and their educational impact' in R.J. Alexander, with C. Doddington, J. Gray, L. Hargreaves and R. Kershner (eds) *The Cambridge Primary Review Research Surveys*, London: Routledge, Chapter 3.

Mayall, B. and Storey, P. (1998) 'A school health service for children?', *Children and Society* 12: 86–97.

Mayer, J.D. and Salovey, P. (1997) 'What is emotional intelligence?', in P. Salovey and D. Sluyter (eds) *Emotional Development and Emotional Intelligence: implications for educators*, New York: Basic Books.

McGarrigle, J. and Donaldson, M. (1974) 'Conservation accidents', *Cognition* 3: 341–50.

McNamara, O., Webb, R. and Brundrett, M. (2010) 'Primary teachers: initial teacher education, continuing professional development and school leadership development' in R.J. Alexander, with C. Doddington, J. Gray, L. Hargreaves and R. Kershner (eds) *The Cambridge Primary Review Research Surveys*, London: Routledge, Chapter 24.

Meadows, S. (2006) *The Child as Thinker: the development and acquisition of cognition in childhood* (2nd edition), London: Routledge.

Measor, L. and Woods, P. (1984) *Changing Schools: pupil perspectives on transfer to a comprehensive*, Milton Keynes: Open University Press.

Meighan, R. (1977) 'The pupil as client: the learner's experience of schooling', *Educational Review* 29(2): 123–135.

Meighan, R. (1997) *The Next Learning System: and why some home-schoolers are trailblazers*. Nottingham: Educational Heretics Press.

Meltzoff, A.N. and Moore, M.K. (1983) 'Newborn infants imitate adult facial gestures', *Child Development* 54: 702–702.

Menesini, E. and Camodeca, M. (2008) 'Shame and guilt as behaviour regulators: relationships with bullying, victimisation, and prosocial behaviour', *British Journal of Developmental Psychology* 26 (2): 183–196.

Mercer, N. (2000) *Words and Minds: how we use language to think together*, London: Routledge.

Mercer, N. and Hodgkinson, S. (eds) (2008) *Exploring Talk in School*, London: Sage.

Mercer, N. and Littleton, K. (2007) *Dialogue and the Development of Children's Thinking: a socio-cultural approach*, London: Routledge.

Meyer, J., Kamens, D. and Benavot, A. (1992) *School Knowledge for the Masses: world models and national primary curricular categories in the twentieth century*, Philadelphia, PA: Falmer Press.

Michaels, E., Hartford-Jones, H. and Axelrod, B. (2001) *The War for Talent: how to battle for great people*, Boston, MA.: Harvard Business School Press.

Miliband, D. (2004a) 'Choice and voice in personalised learning', speech to the DfES/Dems/OECD conference *Personalising Education: the future of public sector reform*, London:

Miliband, D. (2004b) 'Personalised learning: building a new relationship with schools', speech to *North Of England Education Conference, Belfast* (8 January), online: http://www.dcsf.gov.uk/speeches/search_detail.cfm?ID=95,

Ministère de l'Éducation Nationale (2002) *Qu'apprend-on à l'École Élémentaire?* Paris: CNDP.

Ministère de l'Éducation Nationale (2008) *Horaires et Programmes d'Enseignement de l'École*, online: http://www.education.gouv.fr/bo/2002/hs1/som.htm.

Ministry of Education (1959) *Primary Education: suggestions for the consideration of teachers and others concerned with the work of primary schools*, London: HMSO.

Minty, S., Maylor, U., Issa, T., Kuyok, K. *et al.* (2008) *Our Languages: teachers in supplementary schools and their aspirations to teach community languages*, London: Institute for Policy Studies in Education, London Metropolitan University.

Monaghan, F. (2007) 'Gifted and talented statistics: PLASC data and EAL', *NALDIC Quarterly* 5 (Autumn).

Moon, B. (1998) *The English Exception: international perspectives on the initial education and training of teachers*, London: UCET.

Moore, M., Sixsmith, J. and Knowles, K. (1996) *Children's Reflections on Family Life*, London: Falmer Press.

Morris, E. (2001) *Professionalism and Trust: the future of teachers and teaching*, speech to the Social Market Foundation, November. Online: http://www.teachernet.gov.uk/_doc/1042/SMF_Report.pdf.

Morris, H. (1925) *The Village College. Being a Memorandum on the Provision of Educations and Social Facilities for the Countryside, with Special Reference to Cambridgeshire*, Cambridge: self-published text.

Morris, M., with Rutt, S., Kendall, L. and Mehta, P. (2008) *Narrowing the Gap in Outcomes for Vulnerable Groups: overview and analysis of available datasets on vulnerable groups and the five ECM outcomes*, Slough: NFER.

Morrow, V. (1998) *Understanding Families: children's perspectives*, London: National Children's Bureau.

Morrow, V. (2008) 'Dilemmas in children's participation in England', in A. Invernizzi and J. Williams (eds) *Children and Citizenship*, London: Sage.

Morrow, V. and Mayall, B. (2009) 'Measuring children's well-being: some problems and possibilities', in A. Morgan, E. Ziglio, M. Davies and R. Barker (eds) *International Health and Development: investing in assets of individuals, communities and organisations*, Amsterdam: Springer Publications.

Mortimer, E.F. and Scott, P.H. (2003) *Meaning Making in Science Classrooms*, Buckingham: Open University Press.

Mortimore, P., Sammons, P., Stoll, L., Lewis, D. and Ecob, R. (1988) *School Matters: the junior years*, London: Open Books.

Morton, J. (2004) *Understanding Developmental Disorders: a causal modelling approach*, Oxford: Blackwell.

Moss, G. (2007) 'Lessons from the National Literacy Strategy', paper presented at the annual conference of the British Educational Research Association, September.

Moss, P. and Haydon, G. (eds) (2008) *Every Child Matters and the Concept of Education*, London: Institute of Education University of London.

Moss, P.A., Pullin, D., Gee, J.P., Haertel, E.H. and Young, L.J. (eds) (2008) *Assessment, Equity and Opportunity to Learn*, Cambridge: Cambridge University Press.

Moyles, J., Hargreaves, L., Merry, R., Paterson, F. and Esarte-Sarries, V. (2003) *Interactive Teaching in the Primary School*, Maidenhead: Open University Press.

Mullis, I.V.S., Martin, M.O., Kennedy, A.M. and Foy, P. (2007) *PIRLS 2006 International Report: IEA's progress in international reading literacy study in primary school in 40 countries*, Chestnut Hill, MA: TIMSS and PIRLS International Study Center, Boston College.

Mumby, H., Russell, T. and Martin, A.K. (2001) 'Teachers' knowledge and how it develops', in V. Richardson (ed.) *Handbook of Research on Teaching (4th edition)*, Washington DC: AERA, 877–904.

Murrin, K. and Martin, P. (2004) *What Worries Parents: the most common concerns of parents explored and explained*, London: Vermillion.

Muschamp, Y., Wikeley, F., Ridge, T. and Balarin, M. (2010) 'Parenting, caring and educating' in R.J. Alexander, with C. Doddington, J. Gray, L. Hargreaves and R. Kershner (eds) *The Cambridge Primary Review Research Surveys*, London: Routledge, Chapter 4.

Myhill, D. (2005) 'Teaching and learning in whole class discourse', Exeter: University of Exeter School of Education.

Nair, P. (2005) *The Great Learning Street Debate. Fresh perspectives (February 2005)*. From the Designshare website, online: http://www.designshare.com/index.php/articles/great-learning-street-debate.

National Audit Office (2004) *Early Years: progress in developing high quality childcare and early education accessible to all*, London: TSO.

National Audit Office (2006) *Sure Start Children's Centres: National Audit Office value for money report*, London: National Audit Office.

National Advisory Committee on Creative and Cultural Education (NACCCE) (1999) *All our Futures: creativity, culture and education*, London: DfEE.

National Board for Professional Teaching Standards (NBPTS) (1998) *What Teachers Should Know and be Able to Do*, Detroit MI: NBPTS.

National College for School Leadership (NCSL) (2007a) *What are we Learning About the School Leadership Labour Market?* Nottingham: NCSL.

NCSL (2007b) *Primary Leadership: advice to the Secretary of State*, online: http://www.ncsl.org.uk/media-ad4-e3-advice-to-sos-primary-leadership-oct07.pdf.

NCSL (2008) *What We are Learning About: leadership of Every Child Matters*, Nottingham: NCSL.

National Commission on Education (1995) *Success Against the Odds: effective schools in disadvantaged areas*, London: Routledge.

National Curriculum Council (1993) *The National Curriculum at Key Stages 1 and 2: advice to the Secretary of State for Education*, York: National Curriculum Council.

National Education Research Panel/EPC (2007) 'The learning resource review: provision and use of educational learning resources in UK schools', online: www.publishers.org.uk/en/educational.

National Education Union (1870) Verbatim report of the debate in Parliament during the progress of the Elementary Education Bill, quoted in N. Whitbread (1972) *The Evolution of the Nursery-Infant School: a history of infant education in Britain, 1800–1970*, London: Routledge.

National Evaluation of Sure Start (2005) *Early Impacts of Sure Start Local Programmes on Children and Families.* Report 013, Nottingham: DfES.

National Evaluation of Sure Start (2008) *The Impact of Sure Start Local Programmes on Three-Year-Olds and their Families*, Annesley, Nottingham: DfES Publications.

National Forum for Values in Education and the Community (1999) 'Statement of Values', in DfEE/QCA *The National Curriculum: handbook for primary teachers in England*, London: DfEE/QCA: 147–9.

National Foundation for Educational Research (2007) *The support needs of home educators*, online http://www.nfer.ac.uk/latest-news/press-releases/the-support-needs-of-home-educators.cfm (accessed 16.03.09).

The National Health Service Information Centre (2008) *Health Survey for England 2006*, online: www.ic.nhs.uk/statistics-and-data-collections/health-and-lifestyles-related-surveys/health-survey-for-england

National Statistics (2006) *Family Spending: a report on the 2004-05 Expenditure and Food Survey*, London: HMSO.

National Statistics (2008a) *Life Expectancy at Birth by Health and Local Authorities in the United Kingdom (2004-2006)*, online: www.statistics.gov.uk/StatBase/Product.asp?vlnk=8841.

National Statistics (2008b) *Social Trends 38: 2008 edition*, online: www.statistics.gov.uk/socialtrends38/.

National Union of Teachers (NUT) (1979) *Primary Questions: the NUT response to the Primary Survey*, London: NUT.

NUT (2004) *Bringing Down the Barriers*, London: NUT.

NUT (2006) *The Impact of National Curriculum Tests on Pupils*, NUT Briefing (September).

NUT (2007) *The Roles and Responsibilities of Head Teachers*, London: NUT.

Neale, B. (ed) (2004) *Young Children's Ctizenship: ideas into practice*, York: Joseph Rowntree Foundation.

Nicholson, S., Jordan, E., Cooper, J. and Mason, J. (2008) *Childcare and Early Years Providers Survey 2007*, Nottingham: DCSF.

Nixon, J., Martin, J., McKeown, P. and Ranson, S. (1996) *Encouraging Learning: towards a theory of the learning school*, Buckingham: Open University Press.

Noden, P. and West, A. (2010) 'The funding of English primary education' in R.J. Alexander, with C. Doddington, J. Gray, L. Hargreaves and R. Kershner (eds) *The Cambridge Primary Review Research Surveys*, London: Routledge, Chapter 27.

Norman, K. (ed) (1992) *Thinking Voices: the work of the National Oracy Project*, London: Hodder and Stoughton.

Normington, J., and Kyriacou, C. (1994) 'Exclusion form high schools and the work of the outside agencies involved', *Pastoral Care* 12(4): 12–15.

North, A.C. and Hargreaves, D.J. (2008) *The Social and Applied Psychology of Music*, Oxford: Oxford University Press.

Norwich, B. (1990) *Reappraising Special Needs Education*, London: Cassell.

Nystrand, M. with Gamoran, A., Kachur, R. and Prendergast, C. (1997) *Opening Dialogue: understanding the dynamics of learning and teaching in the English classroom*, New York: Teachers College Press.

Oates, T. (2006) *Accumulating Problems in National Assessment – a vessel to bursting point?* Cambridge: Cambridge Assessment.

Ofcom (2006) *Media Literacy Audit*, online: www.ofcom.org.uk/advice/media_literacy/medlitpub/medlitpubrss/children/.

Ofsted (1993a) *Curriculum Organisation and Classroom Practice in Primary Schools: a follow-up report*, London: Ofsted.

Ofsted (1993b) *Well-Managed Classes in Primary Schools: case studies of six teachers*, London: Ofsted.

Ofsted (1994) *Primary Matters: a discussion on teaching and learning in primary schools*, London: Ofsted.

Ofsted (1995) *Teaching Quality: the primary debate*, London: Ofsted.

Ofsted (1996) *Subjects and Standards*, London: Ofsted.

Ofsted (1997a) *The Annual Report of Her Majesty's Chief Inspector of Schools: standards and quality in education 1996/7*, London: Ofsted.

Ofsted (1997b) *National Curriculum Assessment Results and the Wider Curriculum at Key Stage 2: some evidence from the Ofsted database*, London: Ofsted.

Ofsted (1997c) *Using Subject Specialists to Promote High Standards at Key Stage 2: an illustrative survey*, London: Ofsted.

Ofsted (1998) *Setting in Primary Schools: a report from the office of HM Chief Inspector of Schools*, London: Ofsted.

Ofsted (2000) *Small Schools: how well are they doing? A report by Ofsted based on the data from inspections and national test results*, London: Ofsted.

Ofsted (2002) *The Curriculum in Successful Primary Schools*, London: Ofsted.

Ofsted (2003a) *The Education of Six Year Olds in England, Denmark and Finland: an international comparative study*, London: Ofsted.

Ofsted (2003b) *Leadership and Management: managing the school workforce*, London: Ofsted.

Ofsted (2003c) *Transition from the Reception Year to Year 1: an evaluation by HMI*, London: Ofsted.

Ofsted (2004a) *ICT in Schools: the impact of government initiatives five years on*, London: Ofsted.

Ofsted (2004b) *Remodelling the School Workforce – Phase 1*, London: Ofsted.

Ofsted (2004c) *Standards and Quality 2002–3: the annual report of Her Majesty's Chief Inspector of Schools*, London: Ofsted.

Ofsted (2005a) *Inspection Framework*, London: Ofsted.

Ofsted (2005b) *Managing Challenging Behaviour*, London: Ofsted.

Ofsted (2005c) *Remodelling the School Workforce*, London: Ofsted.

Ofsted (2006a) *Creative Partnerships: initiative and impact*, London: Ofsted.

Ofsted (2006b) *Extended Services in Schools and Children's Centres*, London: Ofsted.

Ofsted (2006c) *Good School Libraries: making a difference to learning*, London: Ofsted.

Ofsted (2006d) *Inclusion: does it matter where pupils are taught? Provision and outcomes in different settings for pupils with learning difficulties and disabilities*, London: Ofsted.

Ofsted (2007a) *The Annual Report of Her Majesty's Chief Inspector of Schools*, London: Ofsted.

Ofsted (2007b) *The Foundation Stage: a survey of 144 settings*, London: Ofsted.

Ofsted (2007c) *Narrowing the Gap: the inspection of children's services*, London: Ofsted.

Ofsted (2007d) *Reforming and Developing the School Workforce*, London: Ofsted.

Ofsted (2007e) *TellUs2 Survey*, online: www.ofsted.gov.uk/portal/site/Internet/menuitem.75d4ee5e2788f064728a0d8308c08a0c/?vgnextoid=3d34f7a157346110VgnVCM1000003507640aRCRD.

Ofsted (2008a) *The Annual Report of Her Majesty's Chief Inspector of Education, Children's Services and Skills 2007/08*, London: Ofsted.

Ofsted (2008b) *The Annual Report of Her Majesty's Chief Inspector of Schools*, London: Ofsted.

Ofsted (2008c) *The Deployment, Training and Development of the Wider School Workforce*, London: Ofsted.

Ofsted (2008d) *Early Years: leading to excellence*, London: Ofsted.

Ofsted (2008e) *Framework for the Inspection of Schools in England*, revised version, London: Ofsted.

Ofsted (2008f) *How Well are they Doing: the impact of children's centres and extended schools*, London: Ofsted.

Ofsted (2008g) *Sustaining Improvement: the journey from special measures*, London: Ofsted.

Ofsted (2008h) *Using Data, Improving Schools*, London: Ofsted.

Ofsted (2009) *Twelve Outstanding Secondary Schools: excelling against the odds*, London: Ofsted.

Ofsted / DfES (1997) *National Curriculum Assessment Results and the Wider Curriculum at Key Stage 2: some evidence from the Ofsted database*, London: Ofsted.

Olthof, T., Rieffe, C., Terwogt, M.M., Lalay-Cederburg, C. *et al.* (2008) 'The assignment of moral status: age related differences in the use of the three mental capacity criteria', *British Journal of Developmental Psychology* 26(2): 233–247.

Office for National Statistics (ONS) (2004) *Mental Health of Children and Young People in Great Britain*, London: ONS.

ONS (2005) *Mental Health of Children and Young People*, London: HMSO.

ONS (2006a) *General Household Survey*, London: ONS/HMSO.

ONS (2006b) *Social Trends: 2006 edition*, online: http://www.statistics.gov.uk/StatBase/Product.asp?vlnk=13675.

ONS (2007) *Social Trends 37*, London: ONS/Palgrave Macmillan.

ONS (2008) *Social Trends 38*, London: ONS/Palgrave Macmillan.

Organisation for Economic Co-operation and Development (OECD) (1998) *Education at a Glance: OECD indicators 1998*, Paris: OECD.

OECD (2001a) *Knowledge and Skills for Life: first results from PISA 2000*, Paris: Organisation for Economic Co-operation and Development.

OECD (2001b) *Starting Strong 1. early childhood education and care*, Paris: OECD.

OECD (2004) *Equity in Education: students with disabilities, learning difficulties and disadvantages*, Paris: OECD.

OECD (2005) *Teachers Matter: attracting, developing, and retaining effective teachers*, Paris: OECD.

OECD (2006) *Starting Strong 11: early childhood education and care*, Paris: OECD.

OECD (2007) *Education at a Glance 2007: OECD indicators*, Paris: OECD. Online: http://www.oecd.org/dataoecd/36/4/40701218.pdf.

OECD (2008a) *Education at a Glance 2008: OECD briefing note for the United Kingdom*, Paris: OECD.

OECD (2008b) *Education at a Glance 2008: OECD indicators*, Paris: OECD.

OECD (2008c) *Growing Unequal? Income distribution and poverty in OECD countries*, Paris: OECD.

Osborn, M., McNess, E. and Broadfoot, P. (2000) *What Teachers Do: changing policy and practice in primary education*, London: Continuum.

Osborne, J., Simon, S. and Collins, S. (2003) 'Attitudes towards science: a review of the literature and its implications', *International Journal of Science Education* 25: 1049–1079.

Osgood, J. (2006a) 'De-constructing professionalism in early childhood education: resisting the regulatory gaze', *Contemporary Issues in Early Childhood* 7(1): 5–14.

Osgood, J. (2006b) 'Editorial: rethinking "professionalism" in the early years: English perspectives', *Contemporary Issues in Early Childhood* 7(1): 1–4.

Owen, R. (1816) *An Address to the Inhabitants of New Lanark*, London: Hatchard.

Oxfam (2008) *Getting Started With Global Citizenship: a guide for new teachers*, Oxford: Oxfam GB.

Palmer, S. (2006) *Toxic Childhood: how the modern world is damaging our children and what we can do about it*, London: Orion Books.

Paquette, J. (1998) 'Equity in educational policy: a priority in transformation or in trouble?', *Journal of Education Policy* 13(1): 41–61, reprinted in S.J. Ball, I.F. Goodson and M. Maguire (eds) *Education, Globalisation and New Times*, Abingdon, Oxon: Routledge: 335–359.

Partners of Prisoners and Families Support Group (2007) *Children of Offenders*, online: http://www.partnersofprisoners.org.uk/public/files/Children_of_Offenders_2007.pdf.

Peacey, V. and Hunt, J. (2008) *Problematic Contact after Separation and Divorce: a national survey of parents*, London: One Parent Families/Gingerbread.

Peach, E. and Henson, R. (2008) 'Key statistics in asylum seeker applications in the UK,' Information Centre about Asylum and Refugees, School of Social Sciences, City University, London.

Pedder, D., Storey, A. and Opfer, D. (2008) *Schools and Continuing Professional Development in England: state of the nation synthesis report*, Cambridge and Milton Keynes: University of Cambridge Faculty of Education and the Open University Department of Education.

Pell, T., Galton, M., Steward, S., Page, C. and Hargreaves, L. (2007) 'Promoting group work at Key Stage 3: solving an attitudinal crisis among adolescents', *Research Papers in Education* 22(3): 309–332.

Penn, H. (2007) 'Childcare market management: how the United Kingdom government has reshaped its role in developing early childhood education and care', *Contemporary Issues in Early Childhood* 8(3): 192–207.

Peters, R.S. (ed.) (1968) *Perspectives on Plowden*, London: Routledge and Kegan Paul.

Peters, R.S. (1978) *Ethics and Education*, London: George Allen and Unwin.

Petrides, K., Furnham, A. and Frederickson, N. (2004) 'Emotional intelligence', *The Psychologist* 17(10): 574–577.

Phillips, M. (1996) *All Must Have Prizes*, London: Little, Brown.

Phillips, M. (2008) 'Groundhog Day in primary school', *The Spectator*, 8 December.

Piachaud, D. (2007) *Freedom to be a Child: commercial pressures on children*, London: Centre for Analysis of Social Exclusion (CASE), London School of Economics.

Piaget, J. (1932) *The Moral Judgement of the Child*, London: Routledge and Kegan Paul.

Plomin, R. and Spinath, F.M. (2002) 'Genetics and general cognitive ability (g)', *Trends in Cognitive Sciences* 6: 169–176.

Pole, C., Mizen, P. and Bolton, A. (2001) 'Hidden hands: international perspectives on children's work and labour', in P. Mizen, C. Pole and A. Bolton (eds) *Hidden Hands: international perspectives on children's work and labour*, London: RoutledgeFalmer.

Pollard, A. (ed) (2002) *Readings for the Reflective Teacher*, London: Continuum.

Pollard, A. and Triggs, P. (2000) *Policy, Practice and Pupil Experience*, London: Continuum International Publishing Group.

Pollard, A. and Triggs, P., with Broadfoot, P., McNess, E. and Osborn, M. (2000) *What Pupils Say: changing policy and practice in primary education*, London and New York: Continuum.

Pollock, C. and Straker, L. (2008) 'Information and communication technology in schools', in R. Lueder and V. Berg Rice (eds) *Ergonomics for Children: designing products and places for toddlers to teens*, New York and London: Taylor and Francis.

Pons, F., Harris, P. and de Rosnay, M. (2004) 'Emotion comprehension between 3 and 11 years: developmental periods and hierarchical organization', *European Journal of Developmental Psychology* 1(2): 127–152.

Power (2006) *Power to the People: the report of Power, an independent inquiry into Britain's democracy*, York: Joseph Rowntree Charitable Trust.

Prais, S.J. (1997) *School Readiness, Whole Class Teaching and Pupils' Mathematical Attainment*, London: NIESR.

Pring, R. (1995) 'Educating persons: putting education back into educational research', *Scottish Educational Review* 27: 101–112.

Pring, R., Hayward, G., Hodgson, A., Johnson, J., Keep, E., Oancea, A., Rees, G., Spours, K. and Wilde, S. (2009) *Education for All: the future of education and training for 14–19 year olds* (the Nuffield 14–19 Review), London: Routledge

Pugh, G. (2007) *The Early Years: contribution to the New Vision Group Manifesto*, London: New Vision Group.

Pugh, G. (2008) Keynote speech to joint GTCE, Cambridge Primary Review and Children's Society conference on childhood, March 17.

Pugh, G. and Duffy, B. (eds) (2006) *Contemporary Issues in the Early Years* (4th edition), London: Sage.

PricewaterhouseCooper (2007) *Independent Study into School Leadership*, London: DfES/PwC.

Qualifications and Curriculum Authority (QCA) (2000) *Curriculum Guidance for the Foundation Stage*, London: QCA.

QCA (2003) *Marking: making a difference*, London: QCA

QCA (2006) *Primary Evidence Dossier: analysis of evidence from international studies into transfer from primary to secondary*, London: QCA.

QCA (2007a) *The Curriculum: taking stock of progress*, London: QCA.

QCA (2007b) *The National Curriculum at Key Stages 3 and 4*, London: QCA.

QCA (2008a) *About the Primary Curriculum*, online: http://curriculum.qca.org.uk.

QCA (2008b) 'Primary curriculum change: directions of travel in 10 countries since 2005', *Primary Evidence Dossier*, London: QCA.

QCA/DfEE (1999) *The National Curriculum: handbook for primary teachers in England*, London: TSO.

Quinton, D. (2004) *Supporting Parents: messages from research*, London: Jessica Kingsley Publishers.

Ramey, C.T. and Ramey, S.L. (1998) 'Early intervention and early experience', *American Psychologist* 53: 109–120.

Reay, D. (2006) '"I'm not seen as one of the clever children"; consulting primary school pupils about the social conditions of learning', *Educational Review (Special Edition: The potential of listening to pupils)* 58(2): 171–181.

Reay, D. and Wiliam, D. (1999) '"I'll be a nothing": structure, agency and the construction of identity through assessment', *British Educational Research Journal* 25: 343–345.

Reid, G. (2005) 'Dyslexia', in A. Lewis and B. Norwich (eds) *Special Teaching for Special Children? Pedagogies for inclusion*. Maidenhead: Open University Press.

Revell, P. (2005) *The Professionals: better teachers, better schools*, Stoke-on-Trent: Trentham Books.

Reynolds, D. (2007) 'Small school closures in Wales: new evidence', Institute of Welsh Affairs.

Reynolds, D., Creemers, B., Stringfield, S., Teddlie, C. and Schaffer, G. (eds) (2002) *World Class Schools: international perspectives on school effectiveness*, London: RoutledgeFalmer.

Reynolds, D. and Farrell, S. (1996) *Worlds Apart: a review of international surveys of educational achievement involving England*, London: Ofsted.

Richards, C. (1997) *Primary Education, Standards and Ofsted: towards a more authentic conversation*, Warwick: University of Warwick Centre for Research in Elementary and Primary Education.

Richards, C. (2001a) 'Entitlement or neo-elementary? The changing English primary curriculum', in C. Richards (ed) *Changing English Primary Education: retrospect and prospect*, Stoke on Trent: Trentham Books.

Richards, C. (2001b) *School Inspection in England: a re-appraisal*, Impact 9, London: Philosophy of Education Society of Great Britain.

Richards, C. (2005) *Standards in English Primary Schools: are they rising?* London: Association of Teachers and Lecturers.

Richards, C. (2006) 'The changing context of decision-making in English primary education: ages, myths and autonomy', Paper presented at the Children as Decision-Makers seminar series (No 1), at the University of East Anglia (November).

Richards, C. (2009) 'A Rose by any other name is still ... a government document', *Education Journal* 115: 11.

Richards, C. (in press) 'The changing context of decision-making in English primary education: ages, myths and autonomy', in S. Cox (in press) *Children as Decision-Makers*. London: Continuum Press.

Richardson, V. (ed) (2001) *Handbook of Research on Teaching* (4th edition), Washington, DC: American Educational Research Association.

Riggall, A. and Sharp, C. (2010) 'The structure of primary education: England and other countries' in R.J. Alexander, with C. Doddington, J. Gray, L. Hargreaves and R. Kershner (eds) *The Cambridge Primary Review Research Surveys*, London: Routledge, Chapter 14.

Rinaldi, C. (2001) *Making Learning Visible* (Reggio Children and Project Zero), Cambridge, MA: Harvard University Press.

Robinson, P. (1999) 'The tyranny of league tables: international comparisons of educational achievement and economic performance', in R.J. Alexander, P. Broadfoot and D. Phillips (ed) *Learning from Comparing: new directions in comparative educational research, Volume 1, Contexts Classrooms and Outcomes*, Oxford: Symposium Books.

Robinson, C. and Fielding, M. (2010) 'Children and their primary schools: pupils' voices' in R.J. Alexander, with C. Doddington, J. Gray, L. Hargreaves and R. Kershner (eds) *The Cambridge Primary Review Research Surveys*, London: Routledge, Chapter 2.

Roche, J. (1999) 'Children: rights, participation and citizenship', *Childhood* 6(4): 475–93.

Rose, J. (2006) *Independent Review of the Teaching of Early Reading: final report*, London: DfES.

Rose, J. (2008) *The Independent Review of the Primary Curriculum: interim report*, London: DCSF.

Rose, J. (2009) *The Independent Review of the Primary Curriculum: final report*, London: DCSF.

Rothermel, P. (2004) *Home-Education: comparison of home and school educated children on PIPS Baseline Assessments*. Paper presented at EECERA Conference 2004, Malta.

Ruddock, G. and Sainsbury, M. (2008) *A Comparison of the Core Primary Curriculum in England to Those of Other High Performing Countries*, London: DCSF.

Rudduck, J. (2006) 'The past, the papers and the project', *Educational Review* 58(2): 131–143.

Rudduck, J. and McIntyre, D. (2007) *Improving Learning Through Consulting Pupils*, London: Routledge.

Rudduck, J., Wallace, G. and Chaplain, R. (1996) *School Improvement: what can pupils tell us?* London: David Fulton.

Rudner, L.M. (1998) *Scholastic achievement and demographic characteristics of home school students in 1998*. ERIC Clearinghouse on Assessment and Evaluation, College of Library and Information Services University of Maryland, College Park

Russell, J. (2008) 'The NUT has cried wolf too often, but this time it's right', *The Guardian*, 26 March.

Rutter, M., Maughan, B., Mortimore, P. and Ouston, J. (1979) *Fifteen Thousand Hours*, London: Open Books.

Sachs, J. (2003) 'Learning to be a teacher: professionalism and activism', in F. Crowther (ed.) *Teachers as Leaders in a Knowledge Society*, College Year Book 2003, Australian College of Educators, ACT: Australia.

Sainsbury, M. and Clarkson, R. (2008) *Attitudes to Reading at Ages Nine and Eleven: full report*, Slough: NFER.

Sainsbury, M. and Schagen, I. (2004) 'Attitudes to reading at ages nine and eleven', *Journal of Research in Reading* 27(4): 373–386.

Salovey, P. and Mayer, J. (1990) 'Emotional intelligence', *Imagination, Cognition and Personality* 9: 185–211.

Sammons, P., Hillman, J. and Mortimore, P. (1995) *Key Characteristics of Effective Schools*, London: Institute of Education.

Sammons, P., Sylva, K., Melhuish, E., Siraj-Blatchford, I. *et al.* (2006) *Effective Pre-School and Primary Education 3-11 Project (EPPE 3-11): influences on children's attainment and progress in Key Stage 2: cognitive outcomes in Year 5*, Nottingham: DfES.

Sammons, P., Sylva, K., Melhuish, E., Siraj-Blatchford, I. *et al.* (2007a) *Influences on Children's Attainment and Progress in Key Stage 2: Cognitive Outcomes in Year 5 (EPPE 3-11 Project)*, DfES Research Brief no. RB828, London: DfES.

Sammons, P., Sylva, K., Melhuish, I., Taggart, B. *et al.* (2007b) *Effective Pre-School and Primary Education 3-11 Project (EPPE 3-11) Summary Report: influences on children's attainment and progress in key stage 2: cognitive outcomes in Year 5*, Nottingham: DfES Publications.

Sammons, P., Sylva, K., Melhuish, I., Siraj-Blatchford, I. *et al.* (2007c) *Effective Pre-School and Primary Education 3-11 Project (EPPE 3-11) Summary Report: influences on children's development and progress in key stage 2: social/behavioural outcomes in Year 5*, Nottingham: DfES Publications.

Sammons, P., Sylva K., Melhuish, E., Siraj-Blatchford, I. *et al.* (2008) *Influences on Children's Cognitive and Social Development in Year 6 (EPPE 3-11)*, Nottingham: DCSF.

Sampson, A. (2004) *Who Runs This Place? The anatomy of Britain in the 21st century*, London: John Murray.

Sanders, M.R., Cann, W. and Markie-Dadds, C. (2003) 'The triple P positive parenting programme: a universal population-level approach to the prevention of child abuse', *Child Abuse Review* 12(3): 155–171.

Sanders, D., White, G., Burge, B., Sharp, C., Eames, A., McEune, R., and Grayson, H. (2005) *A Study of the Transition from the Foundation Stage to Key Stage 1*, London: DfES.

Schön, D.A. (1983) *The Reflective Practitioner: how professionals think in action*, London: Temple Smith.

Schools Council (1983) *Primary Practice*, London: Methuen.

School Councils UK (2006) *School Councils and Every Child Matters. School Councils UK Briefing*, London: School Councils UK.

School Councils UK (2007) *Advanced School Councils: ideas for improvement*, London: School Councils UK.

Schoon, I. (2006) *Risk and Resilience: adaptations in changing times*, Cambridge: Cambridge University Press.

Scottish Government (2008a) *Curriculum for Excellence*, online: http://www.ltscotland.org.uk/curriculumforexcellence

Scottish Government (2008b) *Safeguarding our Rural Schools and Improving School Consultation Procedures: proposals for changes to legislation*, Edinburgh: Scottish Government.

Schweinhart, L.J., Barnes, H.V. and Weikart, D.P. (1993) *Significant Benefits: the High/Scope Perry Preschool study through age 27*. Monographs of the High/Scope Education Research Foundation 10, Ypsilanti: High/Scope Press.

Seaborne, M. (1971) *Primary School Design*, London: Routledge Kegan Paul.

Sebba, J., Brown, N., Steward, S., Galton, M. and James, M. (2007) *An Investigation of Personalised Learning Approaches Used by Schools*, London: DfES.

Seebohm, F. (1968) *Report of the Committee on Local Authority and Allied Personal Social Services* (the Seebohm Report), London: HMSO.

Sharp, C. (2000) *Review of Studies on Homework*, Ofsted / National Foundation of Educational Research.

Sharp, C., Keys, W. and Benefield, P. (2001) *Homework: a review of recent research*, Slough: NFER.

Sharp, C. and O'Donnell, S. (2007) 'Starting school at four: the English experience', CIDREE Yearbook 2007.

Sharp, P. (2001) *Nurturing Emotional Literacy: a practical guide for teachers, parents and those in the caring professions*, London: David Fulton.

Sharp, R. and Green, A. (1975) *Education and Social Control: a study in progressive primary education*, London: Routledge and Kegan Paul.

Silcock, P. and Wyness, M.G. (2000) 'Diligent and dedicated: primary school pupils talk about the reformed curricula', *Curriculum* 21(1): 14–25.

Shuayb, M. and O'Donnell, S. (2010) 'Aims and values in primary education: England and other countries' in R.J. Alexander, with C. Doddington, J. Gray, L. Hargreaves and R. Kershner (eds) *The Cambridge Primary Review Research Surveys*, London: Routledge, Chapter 13.

Shulman, L.S. (1987) 'Knowledge and teaching: foundations of the new reform', *Harvard Educational Review* 57(1): 1–22.

Shulman, L. (1987) 'Knowledge and teaching: foundations of the new reform', *Harvard Educational Review*, 57(1), 49-60.

Shulman, L.(2005) 'Signature pedagogies in the professions', *Daedalus* 134(3): 52–59.

Simon, B. (1964) *The Two Nations and the Educational Structure: 1780–1870*, London: Lawrence and Wishart.

Simon, B. (1981a) 'The primary school revolution: myth or reality?', in B. Simon and J. Willcocks (eds) *Research and Practice in the Primary Classroom*, London: Routledge.

Simon, B. (1981b) 'Why no pedagogy in England?', in B. Simon and W. Taylor (eds) *Education in the Eighties: the central issues*, London: Batsford.

Simon, B. (1992) 'Curriculum organisation and classroom practice: a discussion paper' (review article), *Curriculum Journal* 3(1).

Sinclair, J. McH. and Coulthard, R.M. (1975) *Towards an Analysis of Discourse*, Oxford: Oxford University Press.

Skelton, C. (2001) *Schooling the Boys: masculinities and primary education*, Buckingham, UK: Open University Press.

Skelton, C. and Francis, B. (eds) (2003) *Boys and Girls in the Primary Classroom*, Buckingham, UK: Open University Press.

Skidmore, D., Perez-Parent, M. and Arnfield, S. (2003) 'Teacher-pupil dialogue in the guided reading session', *Reading: Literacy and Language*, 37(2): 47–53.

Skinner, B.F. (1961) 'Why we need teaching machines', *Harvard Educational Review* 31: 377–98.

Smith, A. and Call, N. (1999) *The ALPS Approach: accelerated learning in primary schools: brain-based methods for accelerating motivation and achievement*, Stafford : Network Educational Press.

Smith, F. and Barker, J. (2002) 'School's out? Out of school clubs at the boundary between home and school', in R. Edwards (ed.) *Children, Home and School: regulation, autonomy or connection?* London: RoutledgeFalmer.

Smith, F., Hardman, F., Wall, K. and Mroz, M. (2004) 'Interactive whole class teaching in the National Literacy and Numeracy Strategies', *British Educational Research Journal* 30(3): 395–412.

Smith, G., Smith, T. and Smith, T. (2007) 'Whatever happened to EPAs? Part 2: Educational Priority Areas – 40 years on', *Forum* 49(1/2): 141–156.

Smith, L. (1996) 'The social construction of rational understanding', in A. Tryphon and J. Vonège (eds) *Piaget – Vygotsky: the social genesis of thought*, London: Psychology Press.

Smith, P., Cowie, H. and Blades, M. (2003) *Understanding Children's Development* (4th edition), Oxford: Blackwell.

Smith, R. (2000) 'The politics of homework', *Children and Society* 14(4): 316–25.

Smith, T., Smith, G., Coxon, K. and Sigala, M. (2007) *National Evaluation of the Neighbourhood Nurseries Initiative*, Nottingham: DfES.

Smithers, A. and Robinson, P. (2009) *The Good Teacher Training Guide 2008*, Buckingham: University of Buckingham.

Sodha, S. and Margo, J. (2008) *Thursday's Child. (Executive Summary)*, London: IPPR.

Somaiya, R. (2008) 'Make the grades or you're grounded', *Education Guardian* 1 July.

SooHoo, S. (1993) 'Students as partners in research and restructuring schools', *Educational Forum* 57: 386–392.

Sorrell, J. and Sorrell, F. (2005) *Joined Up Design For Schools*, London: Merrell.

Southworth, G. (2002) 'Instructional leadership in schools: reflections and empirical evidence', *School Leadership and Management* 22(1): 73–91.

Sport England (2003) *Young People and Sport: trends in participation*, London: Sport England.

Stannard, J. and Huxford, L. (2007) *The Literacy Game: the story of the National Literacy Strategy*, London: Routledge.

Statistical Commission (2005) *Measuring Standards in English Primary Schools: report by the Statistics Commission on an article by Peter Tymms*, London: Statistics Commission.

Steedman, H. (1999) *Looking into the Qualifications 'Black Box': what can international surveys tell us about basic competence?* Centre for Economic Performance: LSE.

Steer, A. (2009) *Learning Behaviour: lessons learned. A review of behaviour standards and practices in our schools*, London: DCSF Publications.

Steiner, C. (2003) *Emotional Literacy: intelligence with a heart*, Fawnskin, California: Personhood Press.

Stenhouse, L. (1975) *An Introduction to Curriculum Research and Development*, London: Heinemann.

Stern, N. (2007) *The Economics of Climate Change: the Stern review*, Cambridge: Cambridge University Press.

Sternberg, R.J. (1985) *Beyond IQ: a triarchic theory of human intelligence*, Cambridge: Cambridge University Press.

Sternberg, R.J. and Lubart, T.I. (1999) 'The concept of creativity: prospects and paradigms', in R.J. Sternberg (ed) *Handbook of Creativity*, Cambridge: Cambridge University Press.

Stiggins, R.J. (2001) *Student-Involved Classroom Assessment* (3rd Edition), Upper Saddle River, New Jersey: Merrill Prentice Hall.

Strand, S., Deary, I.J. and Smith, P. (2006) 'Sex differences in cognitive abilities test scores: a UK national picture', *British Journal of Educational Psychology* 76(3): 463–480.

Strand, S. (2008a) 'Educational aspirations in inner city schools', *Educational Studies* 34(4): 249–267.

Strand, S. (2008b) *Minority Ethnic Pupils in the Longitudinal Study of Young People in England: extension report on performance in public examinations at age 16*, Warwick: Institute of Education, University of Warwick.

Stronach, I., Corbin, B., McNamara, O., Stark, S. and Warne, T. (2002) 'Towards an uncertain politics of professionalism: teacher and nurse identities in flux', *Journal of Education Policy* 17(1): 109–138.

Stronach, I., Pickard, A. and Jones, L. (2010) 'Primary schools: the professional environment', in R.J. Alexander, with C. Doddington, J. Gray, L. Hargreaves and R. Kershner (eds) *The Cambridge Primary Review Research Surveys*, London: Routledge, Chapter 23 .

Such, E. and Walker, R. (2005) 'Young citizens or policy objects? Children in the "rights and responsibilities" debate', *Journal of Social Policy* 34(1): 39–57.

Suffolk County Council (2007) 'Guide to primary, infant, junior and middle-schools admissions 2008-9', online: http://www.suffolk.gov.uk/NR/rdonlyres/348FA608-9D16-4DD8-932D-E5D33BF 9540F/0/FinalSiSPrimary20082009.pdf.

Surgenor, A. and Butterss, I. (2008) *Putting a Price on Sustainable Schools*, Watford: Building Research Establishment Ltd.

Sustainable Development Commission (2007) *A Review of the Environmental Dimension of Children's and Young People's Education and Wellbeing*, London: SDC.

Sutherland, G. (2006) 'Voice of change: embedding student voice work', *Curriculum Briefing* 4(3): 8–11.

Swinson, J. and Harrop, A. (in press) 'Teacher talk directed towards boys and girls and its relationship to their behaviour', submitted to *British Journal of Educational Studies*, December 2008.

Sykes, E.D.A., Bell, J.F. and Rodeiro, C.V. (2009) *Birthdate Effects: a review of the literature from 1990 – on*, Cambridge: Cambridge Assessment.

Sylva, K., Melhuish, E., Sammons, P., Siraj-Blatchford, I. *et al.* (2008) *Final Report from the Primary Phase: pre-school, school and family influences on children's development during Key Stage 2 (Age 7-11)*, London: DCSF.

Sylva, K., Melhuish, E., Siraj-Blatchford, I. and Taggart, B. (2004) *The Effective Provision of Pre-School Education (EPPE) Project: final report*, London: DfES.

Sylva, K. and Pugh, G. (2005) 'Transforming the early years in England', *Oxford Review of Education* 31(1): 11–27.

Teacher Training Agency (1996) *Consultation Paper on Standards and a National Professional Qualification for Subject Leaders*, London: TTA.

Teachernet (2009) 'Local authority as commissioner', online: http://www.teachernet.gov.uk/management/ secondarytoolkit/objectives/diversity/lacomm/.

Teaching and Learning in 2020 Review Group (2006) *2020 Vision: report of the Teaching and Learning in 2020 Review Group*, Nottingham: DfES.

Teaching and Learning Research Programme (TLRP) (2006) *Neuroscience and Education: issues and opportunities*, London: TLRP/ESRC.

Tenenbaum, H.R., Alfieri, L., Brooks, P.J. and Dunne, G. (2008) 'The effects of explanatory conversations on children's emotion understanding', *British Journal of Developmental Psychology* 26 (2): 249–263.

Thomas, A. (1998) *Educating children at home*, London: Continuum.

Thomas, N. (1990) *Primary Education from Plowden to the 1990s*, London: Falmer Press.

Thomas, A. and Pattison, H. (2008) *How Children Learn at Home*. London: Continuum.

Thomson, P. (2007) *Whole School Change: a review of the literature*, London: Creative Partnerships.

The Times Online (20 Jan 2009) 'Home education "can be cover for abuse and forced marriage"'

The Times Educational Supplement (2008) 'Ofsted ratings to be based on exam results', 23 May.

Tizard, B., Blatchford, P., Burke, J., Farquahar, C. and Plewis, I. (1988) *Young Children at School in the Inner City*, London: Lawrence Erlbaum.

Tizard, B. and Hughes, M. (1984/2002) *Young Children Learning: talking and thinking at home and at school*, London: Fontana.

Tizard, B., Mortimore, J. and Burchell, B. (1981) *Involving Parents in Nursery and Infant Schools*, London: Grant McIntyre.

Tizard, J., Schofield, W.N. and Hewison, J. (1982) 'Collaboration between teachers and parents in assisting children's reading', *British Journal of Educational Psychology* 52: 1–15.

TNS Social Research (2007) *2006/7 School Sport Survey*, London: TNS.

Tomlinson, S. (2008) *Race and Education: policy and politics in Britain*, Maidenhead, Berks: Open University Press.

Training and Development Agency for Schools (TDA) (2004) 'HLTA professional standards', online: http://www.tda.gov.uk/support/hlta/professstandards/teachlearn.aspx.

TDA (2007a) *Professional Standards for Teachers: core*, London: TDA.

TDA (2007b) *Professional Standards for Teachers: post-threshold*, London: TDA.

TDA (2007c) *Professional Standards for Teachers: excellent teachers*, London: TDA.

TDA (2007d) *Professional Standards for Teachers: advanced skills teachers*, London: TDA.

TDA (2007e) *Professional Standards for Teachers in England from September 2007*, London: TDA.

TDA (2008a) *Induction Tutors*, online: http://www.tda.gov.uk/teachers/induction/rolesandresponsibilities/inductiontutors.aspx.

TDA (2008b) *Masters in Teaching and Learning*. ITT Providers Conference 7 May 2008.

TDA (2008c) *Masters in Teaching and Learning: summary of outcomes from regional consultation events*. Online: http://www.tda.gov.uk/upload/resources/pdf/m/mtl_consultation_report.pdf.

TDA (2008d) *The New Induction Regulations*, online: http://www.tda.gov.uk/teachers/induction/new_induction.aspx.

TDA (2008e) *Professional Standards for Qualified Teacher Status and Requirements for Initial Teacher Training (Revised 2008)*, London: TDA.

TDA (2008f) *Staff structure: primary school*, online: http://www.tda.gov.uk/teachers/overseas_trained_teachers/english_education_system/staff_structure_primary.aspx (accessed 17 December 2008).

TDA (2008g) 'What is an Extended School?', online: http://www.tda.gov.uk/remodelling/extendedschools/esresources/extendedschools.aspx.

TDA (2008g) *Strategic Plan 2008–2013*. London: TDA.

Turner, H., Mayall, B., Dickinson, R., Clark, A. *et al.* (2004) *Children Engaging with Drama: an evaluation of the National Theatre's drama work in primary schools 2002–4*, London: Institute of Education, University of London.

Turner-Cobb, J. (2007) *Children's Transition to School: learning and health outcomes*, Bath: ESRC.

Twist, L., Schagen, I. and Hodgson, C. (2007) *Readers and Reading: the national report for England 2006 (Progress in International Reading Literacy Study)*, Slough: NFER.

Tymms, P. (2004) 'Are standards rising in English primary schools?', *British Educational Research Journal* 30(4): 477–494.

Tymms, P. and Merrell, C. (2008) 'Science in primary schools: trends in attainment, attitudes and approaches', *Perspectives on Education: primary science* (Wellcome Trust) 1: 19–42.

Tymms, P. and Merrell, C. (2010) 'Standards and quality in English primary schools over time: the national evidence' in R.J. Alexander, with C. Doddington, J. Gray, L. Hargreaves and R. Kershner (eds) *The Cambridge Primary Review Research Surveys*, London: Routledge, Chapter 17.

UK Children's Commissioners' Report to the UN Committee on the Rights of the Child (2008) London: 11 Million, online : www.11million.org.uk/resource/31f7xsa2gjgfc3l9t808qfsi.pdf

UNESCO (1994) *Salamanca Statement and Framework for Action on Special Needs Education*, Paris: UNESCO.

UNESCO (2000) *The Dakar Framework for Action: education for all – meeting our collective commitments*, Paris: UNESCO.

UNICEF (2007) *Child Poverty in Perspective: an overview of child well-being in rich countries*. *Innocenti Report Card 7*, Florence: UNICEF Innocenti Research Centre.

UNICEF UK (2006) *Every Child Matters. The five outcomes and the UN Convention on the Rights of the Child (UNCRC)*, online: www.everychildmatters.gov.uk/_files/F1B3FBF728B196018E9616 C71D0BF592.pdf.

United Nations (1990) *Convention on the Rights of the Child*, Geneva: UN General Assembly Resolution 44/25, online: http://www2.ohchr.org/english/law/crc.htm.

United Nations (2005) *Millennium Development Goals Report 2005*, New York: United Nations.

United Nations Intergovernmental Panel on Climate Change (UNIPCC) (2007) *Climate Change 2007: synthesis report of the IPCC Fourth Assessment Report*, New York: United Nations.

Universities' Council for the Education of Teachers (1982) *Postgraduate Certificate in Education Courses for Teachers in Primary and Middle Schools: a further consultative report*, London: UCET.

University of East Anglia/National Children's Bureau (2007) *Children's Trust Pathfinders: innovative partnerships for improving the well-being of children and young people. National evaluation of children's trust pathfinders. Final report*, Norwich: UEA/NCB.

Urquhart, I. (2001) 'Walking on air? Pupil voice and school choice', *Forum* 43(2): 83–86.

Utting, D. (1998) 'Children's services: now and in the future', in D. Utting (ed.) *Children's Services: now and in the future*, London: National Children's Bureau.

Utting, D. (ed.) (2009) *Contemporary Social Evils*, York: Joseph Rowntree Foundation.

Valentine, G., Marsh, J., Pattie, C. and BRMB (2005) *Children and Young People's Home Use of ICT for Educational Purposes: the impact on attainment at Key Stages 1–4. Research Report no. 672*, Leeds: University of Leeds.

Volterra, V. and Erting, C.J. (eds) (1990) *From Gesture to Language in Hearing and Deaf Children*, Berlin/New York: Springer.

Vulliamy, G. (2006) 'Education policy under New Labour', in R. Webb (ed.) *Changing Teaching and Learning in the Primary School*, Buckingham: Open University Press.

Vygotsky, L.S. (1935, reprinted and translated 1978) (M. Cole, V. John-Steiner, S. Scribner and E. Souberman, eds and translators) *Mind in Society: the development of higher processes*, Cambridge, MA: Harvard University Press.

Vygotsky, L.S. and Kozulin, A. (1936, translated and revised 1986) *Thought and Language*, Cambridge, MA: MIT Press.

Vygotksy, L.S. (1962) *Thought and Language*, Cambridge: MIT Press.

Vygotsky, L.S. (1978) *Mind in Society: the development of higher psychological processes*, Cambridge, MA: Harvard University Press.

Wade, B. and Moore, M. (1993) *Experiencing Special Education: what young people with special educational needs can tell us*, Buckingham: Open University Press.

Walby, S., Armstrong, J. and Humphreys, L. (2008) *Review of Equality Statistics*, Manchester: Equality and Human Rights Commission.

Wall, K., Dockrell, J. and Peacey, N. (2010) 'Primary schools: the built environment' in R.J. Alexander, with C. Doddington, J. Gray, L. Hargreaves and R. Kershner (eds) *The Cambridge Primary Review Research Surveys*, London: Routledge, Chapter 22.

Waller, E. (2008) *Why is UNICEF's Rights Respecting Schools Having a Positive Impact on Young People and Adults Alike?* London: UNICEF UK.

Ward, H. and Milne, J. (2008) 'Climbie inquiry chairman slates "patchy" ECM drive', *Times Educational Supplement*, 4 April.

Warrington, M. and Younger, M., with Bearne, E. (2006) *Raising Boys' Achievement in Primary Schools: towards an holistic approach*, Maidenhead: Open University Press.

Watkins, C. and Wagner, P. (2000) *Improving School Behaviour*, London: Paul Chapman.

Webb, R. (ed.) (2006) *Changing Teaching and Learning in the Primary School*, Buckingham: Open University Press.

Webb, R. and Vulliamy, G. (1996) *Roles and Responsibilities in the Primary School: changing demands, changing practices*, Buckingham: Open University Press.

Webb, R. and Vulliamy, G. (2006) *Coming Full Circle? The impact of New Labour's education policies on primary school teachers' work*, London: Association of Teachers and Lecturers.

Webb, S. and Webb, B. (1936) *Soviet Communism – a new civilization?* New York: Scribner.

Wedell, K. (1988) 'Special educational needs and the Education Reform Act', *Forum* 31(1): 19–21.

Wedell, K. (2003) 'Concepts of special educational need', *Journal of Research in Special Educational Needs* 3(2): 104–108 (article first published in *Education Today*, 1981).

Weiner, G. (2002) 'School Effectiveness and the Audit Society: producing failure', in C. Reynold and A. Griffith (eds) *Equity and Globalization in Education*, Calgary, Canada: Detselig Enterprises: 119–134.

Weisberg, R.W. (1993) *Creativity: beyond the myth of genius*, New York: W.H. Freeman.

Wellcome Trust (2005) *Primary Horizons*, London: Wellcome Trust.

Wellcome Trust (2008) *Research into the Effects of Compulsory National Testing in Science on Teachers and Teaching at KS2*, London: Wellcome Trust.

Wells, G. (1999) *Dialogic Enquiry: towards a sociocultural practice and theory of education*, Cambridge: Cambridge University Press.

Wertsch, J.V. (1985) *Culture, Communication and Cognition: Vygotskian perspectives*, Cambridge: Cambridge University Press.

Wheeler, H. and Connor, J. (2006) *Parents, Early Years and Learning, Parents as Partners in the Early Years Foundation Stage – Principles into Practice*, London: National Children's Bureau.

Whetton, C., Ruddock, G. and Twist, L. (2010) 'Standards in English primary Education: the international evidence' in R.J. Alexander, with C. Doddington, J. Gray, L. Hargreaves and R. Kershner (eds) *The Cambridge Primary Review Research Surveys*, London: Routledge, Chapter 18.

Whitbread, N. (1972) *The Evolution of the Nursery-Infant School*, London: Routledge.

Whitburn, J. (2001) 'Effective classroom organisation in primary schools: mathematics', *Oxford Review of Education* 27(3): 411–428.

White, J. (1982) 'The primary teacher as servant of the state', in C. Richards (ed.) *New Directions in Primary Education*, Brighton: Falmer Press: 199–208.

White, J. (2010) 'Aims as policy in English primary education' in R.J. Alexander, with C. Doddington, J. Gray, L. Hargreaves and R. Kershner (eds) *The Cambridge Primary Review Research Surveys*, London: Routledge, Chapter 12.

Whitty, G. (2000) 'Teacher Professionalism in New Times', *Journal of In-service Education* 26(2): 281–295.

Whitty, G. and Wisby, E. (2007) *Real Decision-Making? School councils in action*. Research Report DCSF RR001, London: Institute of Education University of London.

Wikeley, F., Bullock, K., Muschamp, Y. and Ridge, T. (2007) *Educational Relationships Outside School*, York: Joseph Rowntree Foundation.

Wiliam, D. (2001a) *Level Best? Levels of attainment in National Curriculum assesssment*, London: ATL.

Wiliam, D. (2001b) 'Reliability, validity and all that jazz', *Education 3–13* 29(3): 17–21.

Williams, P. (2008) *Independent Review of Mathematics Teaching in Early Years Settings and Primary Schools: final report*, London: DCSF.

Williams, R.D. (2008) 'Faith, reason and quality assurance – having faith in academic life', lecture given at the University of Cambridge in the series *A World to Believe in – Cambridge Consultations on Faith, Humanity and the Future*, 21 February.

Williams, R.H. (1976) *Keywords: a vocabulary of culture and society*, London: Fontana.

Willow, C. (1998) 'Listening to children in local government', in D. Utting (ed.) *Children's Services: now and in the future*, London: National Children's Bureau.

Wilson, V. (2003) *All in Together? An overview of the literature on composite classes*, Glasgow: The SCRE Centre, Faculty of Education, Glasgow University.

Wilson, V. (2007) *Leadership in Small Scottish Primary Schools*, Edinburgh: Scottish Government Social Research.

Wood, D. (1997) *How Children Think and Learn: the social contexts of cognitive development* (2nd edition), Oxford: Blackwell.

Wood, E. (2000) *The Roots of Underachievement of Boys in the Early Years*, Exeter: University of Exeter School of Education.

Woodhead, C. (1998) 'Blood on the tracks: lessons from the history of educational reform', RSA Annual HMCI Lecture, 24 February.

Woodhead, M. (1989) 'School starts at five … or four years old?', *Journal of Educational Policy* 4(1): 1–21.

Woods, P.E. (1976) 'Pupils' views of schools', *Educational Review* 28(2): 126–137.

Woods, P. and Jeffrey, B. (2002) 'The reconstruction of primary teachers' identities', *British Journal of Sociology of Education* 23(1): 89–106.

Woods, P., Jeffrey, B., Troman, G. and Boyle, M. (1997) *Restructuring Schools, Reconstructing Teachers: responding to change in the primary school*, Milton Keynes: Open University Press.

Workforce Agreement Monitoring Group (2004) *Raising Standards and Tackling Workload: implementing the National Agreement*, online: http://www.tda.gov.uk/upload/resources/pdf/w/wamg_oneyearon.pdf.

World Health Organisation (2008a) *Closing the Gap in a Generation: health equity through action on the social determinants of health*, Geneva: WHO.

World Health Organisation (2008b) 'Inequities are killing people on grand scale, reports WHO's Commission', Media release, 28 August.

Wyse, D. and Jones, R. (2008) *Teaching English, Language and Literacy* (2nd edition), London: Routledge.

Wyse, D., McCreery, E. and Torrance, H. (2010) 'The trajectory and impact of national reform: curriculum and assessment in English primary schools' in R.J. Alexander, with C. Doddington, J. Gray, L. Hargreaves and R. Kershner (eds) *The Cambridge Primary Review Research Surveys*, London: Routledge, Chapter 29.

Yelland, N. and Masters, J. (2007) 'Rethinking scaffolding in the information age', *Computers and Education* 48: 362–82.

Zinn, H. (1996) *A People's History of the United States* (2nd edition), London: Pearson.

Index